SOVIET
FOREIGN POLICY
AFTER
STALIN

SOVIET FOREIGN POLICY AFTER STALIN

David J. Dallin

PROFESSOR OF POLITICAL SCIENCE
UNIVERSITY OF PENNSYLVANIA

GREENWOOD PRESS, PUBLISHERS
WESTPORT, CONNECTICUT

Library of Congress Cataloging in Publication Data

Dallin, David J., 1889-1962.
　Soviet foreign policy after Stalin.

　　Includes bibliographical references and index.
　　Reprint of the 1961 ed. published by Lippincott,
Philadelphia.
　　1. Russia--Foreign relations--1953-　　I. Title.
[DK274.D325　1975]　　　327.47　　　75-14596
ISBN 0-8371-8223-9

Copyright © 1960 by David J. Dallin.

Originally published in 1961 by J. B. Lippincott Company, Philadelphia

This edition published by arrangement with J. B. Lippincott Company, Philadelphia, New York.

Reprinted in 1975 by Greenwood Press,
a division of Williamhouse-Regency Inc.

Library of Congress Catalog Card Number 75-14596

ISBN 0-8371-8223-9

Printed in the United States of America

PREFACE

The Stalinist "cult of personality" was abundantly criticized by Stalin's successors, but mainly in connection with Soviet home affairs. Nikita Khrushchev has set forth how certain traits of the late ruler—his ambition, his self-confidence, his claim of superiority, his cruelty, his contempt for human life—affected the political system of the country and resulted in the assassination of leaders, massive purges, and a personal rule uninhibited by legal or moral considerations. Attributing the tragic events solely to Stalin's personal traits—which was wrong —neither Khrushchev, Mikoyan, nor any other of the prominent Soviet figures answered the questions how the peculiar traits of the late dictator were reflected in his foreign political course and whether a "thaw" was due in foreign policies as well as in home affairs.

Among Stalin's most phenomenal ventures was the building up of the huge Soviet empire and the addition of a hundred million non-Russians to the basically Russian realm, a venture that was all the more extravagant by reason of the fact that it was carried out in the most advanced and enlightened part of the world, in the most neuralgic areas of Europe. If Stalin's huge purges were the result of an aberration, his hope that the imperial Soviet structure, born in the mud and blood of a terrible war, was more than a passing phenomenon and an episode in world history arose from an even greater aberration. Stalin, in fact, expected that the empire would expand. But the new superstate formation, the emergence of which was made possible by the postwar paralysis of the free nations of the continent, met with obstacles and resistance. To maintain and develop the structure was a hard task, and all Soviet resources were devoted to it; concentration on this goal was the essence of Stalin's postwar foreign policies.

Discussing Hitler with Anthony Eden in Moscow in December, 1941, when German armies were forty miles from the Soviet capital,

Stalin made the comment that Hitler should not be underrated, that he was a very able man who had made one mistake—he had not known when to stop!

"I suppose I smiled," Eden says. "At any rate, Marshal Stalin turned to me and observed: 'You are smiling and I know why you are smiling. You think that if we are victorious I shall not know when to stop. You are wrong. I shall know!'"

Stalin considered himself, in this respect, different from and superior to Hitler. As soon, however, as circumstances changed in his favor, when he faced the great political vacuum in Europe at the end of the war, he felt the strange and mighty lure—and he succumbed. His *Weltanschauung* and his personal traits facilitated the development. His comrade and eventual opponent, Lev Kamenev, once called Stalin "a genius of dosage," a master of gradualness and circumspection. How wrong he was! As if in proof of his error, Kamenev lost his life in the avalanche of trials and assassinations that was the extreme opposite of gradualness.

The reason why the present Soviet leadership, in its condemnation of the "cult of personality," stopped short at the threshold of foreign affairs was that it had itself taken over Stalin's main ideas and goals in foreign affairs. Nikita Khrushchev in particular remained faithful to the magnificent imperial image of the growing and prospering "socialist camp" as it had emerged out of Stalin's phantasy and ambition. And because the cohesion and progress, against heavy odds, of the empire's components require, as before, the straining of all political, economic, and military forces, international tensions of great magnitude are the constant element of the post-Stalin era, as they were of the Stalin era.

This is not to say that in Soviet foreign affairs the period from 1953 on has been a period of Stalinism. Changes have taken place. A change of leader—from Malenkov to Khrushchev—brought certain changes in trends. The innovations in foreign policy were underpinned by modifications of established theory which, though remaining strictly within the framework of Communism, to a degree marked a deviation from old tenets and precepts.

A review of the constants and variables in the Soviet international course after Stalin is the purpose of this book. Part One deals with the legacy of the late dictator inherited by his successors along

Preface

with all its implications. Part Two reviews the Soviet course during the first period of transition, the Malenkov-Molotov-Khrushchev era. Part Three reviews the great rumblings in the empire, the uprisings in Europe, and the new Soviet course toward the "uncommitted nations." Parts Four and Five deal with Sino-Soviet relations, the emancipation of Chinese Communism, the new ascent of Khrushchev in 1957–58, and the resumption by Khrushchev of control in the European part of the "camp." The last chapter of Part Five reviews the stiffening of the Soviet course toward the West, the abortive "Summit" of 1960, the Cuba and Congo affairs. The author's general views and projections are briefly stated in the Conclusion.

One of the main tasks of the author was to unravel Soviet ideological innovations, slogans, and formulas and to translate them into realistic, distinctive actions and trends. The meaning of "zone of peace," the actual substance of "relaxation of tensions," the earthy essence of "national roads to Communism" and international Communism "under Soviet leadership," the prerequisites of "coexistence," and the Soviet aims in connection with the "summit conference" of the great powers are among the problems dealt with.

"Soviet empire" is used in this book as an historically objective description without moral or political overtones; it appears more exact than its synonyms "Soviet bloc," "socialist camp," etc., since the formidable supernational Soviet formation belongs in the category of the great empires from ancient times on. Almost all of these empires were unique, and the Soviet formation, too, is unmatched and inimitable. But the pattern of the rise and fall of empires—the facts of life of great powers—applies also to contemporary formations. While there is no doubt that the ideology that prevails in the Soviet bloc has a particularly formidable consolidating and cohesive power, it cannot bring about a departure from age-old historical patterns.

Russia was a multinational empire both before and after the revolution. We here use the term "Soviet empire" in a conditional sense, to indicate a new combination of Eurasian states with Russia as the leader. The designations "Soviet Russia," "Soviet Union," and "Russia" for the USSR are used interchangeably throughout the book to reduce repetitiousness. For the same reason and also with no political implications, Communist China is sometimes, when the meaning is clear, called "China."

The sources of information are cited throughout the book. As is so often the case with discussions of current material involving living persons in official positions, the identity of the sources of some of the information in this book cannot be disclosed at the present time. In these cases the source is indicated as a "D Paper." Anyone who can prove his legitimate interest may have access to the latter. Fifteen years after publication of this book the "D Papers" will be deposited with the New York Public Library.

Four years have been devoted to the preparation of this book, in connection with which a number of trips to Europe and the Far East had to be made. The work was made possible by the assistance of numerous persons and organizations, particularly the Relm Foundation of Ann Arbor, Michigan, the Foreign Policy Research Institute of Philadelphia, and Mr. David S. Collier and Mr. Eugene Davidson of the Foundation for Foreign Affairs, Chicago, to all of whom I hereby express my thanks. I am grateful to all of the scholars, authorities, and governmental agencies in this country and abroad who gave advice and made available important documents, and to Mrs. Tillie Klorman for editorial assistance.

DAVID J. DALLIN

CONTENTS

PART ONE: THE INTERNATIONAL SITUATION OF THE SOVIET
UNION AT THE END OF THE STALIN ERA   1

1. Stalin and His Lieutenants in Foreign Affairs . . .   3
2. Stalin's Empire Building 18
   1. No Second Communist Empire
   2. The Yugoslav Rebellion
   3. The "People's Democracies"
3. Germany: The Big Issue 45
4. The Far East 60
   1. The Korean War
   2. China
      Stalin's Course in China
      Who Is Leader in Asia?
   3. Japan
5. The Deadlock 101
   1. Stalin's Legacy in the Middle East
      The Balkans
      The Arab Nations
      The Mediterranean
      Eastern Turkey
      Iran
   2. Conflicts Everywhere

PART TWO: THE MALENKOV-MOLOTOV ERA 115

1. The Death of the Leader 117
2. Relaxation 125

3. The Course in Respect to the West 135
  4. Conferences and Crises 141
     1. The Berlin Conference
     2. The Geneva Conference
     3. Crisis in the Western Bloc
     4. The Anti-NATO Alignment
  5. The "People's Democracies" 166
     1. Rumblings in the East
     2. Conformity with Moscow
     3. Police and Internal Affairs
     4. The National Economies
     5. Abolition of Mixed Companies
  6. The Middle East 198
     1. The Balkan and the Baghdad Pacts
     2. Failure in Iran
  7. The Ascendancy of Nikita Khrushchev 218

PART THREE: THE FIRST KHRUSHCHEV ERA 225

  1. The Session of the Central Committee of July, 1955 . 227
  2. The Thaw and Its Limits 234
     1. No Success in London
     2. The French in Moscow
     3. The Western Socialists
  3. "Relaxation of Tensions" 247
     1. The Austrian State Treaty
     2. Relations with the Bonn Government
     3. Finland: Hesitation and Concessions
     4. The First Summit Conference
  4. The Uncommitted Nations 286
     1. No Neutrals?
     2. The Bandung Conference
     3. India and Burma
     4. Khrushchev and Bulganin in South Asia
     5. Afghanistan and the Drive to the Sea
     6. Indonesia and Pakistan

Contents

5. The Twentieth Party Congress and Foreign Affairs . 322
   1. Wars Are Not Inevitable
   2. Violent Revolutions Are Not Inevitable
   3. Overtures to the Socialist Parties of the West
   4. America Is the Enemy
   5. Partial Revision of Stalinism in Foreign Affairs
   6. The Communist Opposition

6. Ferment in Eastern Europe 335
   1. Away from Moscow!
   2. Tito's Short-lived Triumph
   3. The Polish Rebellion
   4. National Communism: Its Significance for the Soviet Union
   5. The Hungarian Uprising

PART FOUR: THE NEW COURSE IN THE MIDDLE AND FAR EAST . 383

1. The Middle East 385
   1. The Old Path
   2. A New Course and the Arms Deal
   3. Close Ties with Egypt
   4. The Suez Crisis

2. Moscow and Peking 422
   1. The Soviet Retreat
   2. China's Growing Aspirations
   3. Peking Support of Moscow against the Satellite Rebels

PART FIVE: KHRUSHCHEV IN COMMAND 443

1. The Year of Troubles 445
   1. Heavy Going
   2. The New Ascent
   3. The New Setup

2. The Crisis of Neutralism 464
   1. The Arab Nations

2. No Strings Attached
3. The Imperfect Monolith

3. New Impetus in China 489

4. Germany 501
    1. Unstable Stability
    2. Neutrality and Disengagement
    3. Berlin, the Abortive Summit, and New Militancy

CONCLUSION 521

INDEX 531

MAPS

MAP 1. The Soviet Bloc in Europe 35
MAP 2. Stalin's Designs for the Middle East 102
MAP 3. Postwar Designs for Iran (1946) 205
MAP 4. The Drive to the South, Asia 315
MAP 5. Kurdistan 475
MAP 6. The Geopolitical Significance of National Communism 482
MAP 7. Disengagement 505

PART ONE

The International Situation of the Soviet Union at the End of the Stalin Era

CHAPTER 1

STALIN AND HIS LIEUTENANTS IN FOREIGN AFFAIRS

The last few years of Stalin's life were years of triumph for him, his policies, and his movement. Never before in her history had Russia achieved as great a degree of influence in world affairs and as large an extension of her territory, alliances, and military might. Never before had Communism been able to speak in the name of a third of humanity, and never before had it been as certain of final victory. In his fight against his real, potential, or imaginary foes and disloyal friends, Stalin had won out. While a number of his enemies inside the country and abroad had met their end on the gallows or by murderers' bullets, Stalin was rising to unprecedented heights of power. He ignored the seeds of trouble, and he minimized the initial beginning signs of disintegration.

In the conduct of his postwar foreign policies Stalin had no use for the ordinary type of foreign minister. Trusting neither the intelligence nor the loyalty of his colleagues, he reserved all important decisions to himself. For a number of years the Politburo was practically eliminated; to "keep some members away from participation in the decisions," a "sextet" was appointed to deal with international as well as a number of other issues. Among the members of the small committee, in addition to Stalin, were Vyacheslav Molotov, Lavrenti Beria, Georgi Malenkov and, until his death in 1948, Andrei Zhdanov. Nikolai Voznesensky, added to the group on Stalin's suggestion, was arrested in 1949 and executed.[1] Soon afterward, Molotov's star began to fade. During the last year of Stalin's life even the "card-player com-

---

[1] *Bolshaya Sovetskaya Entsiklopediya* (Large Soviet Encyclopedia), 2d ed., Moscow, 1957, vol. 50, p. 739, gives the year of Voznesensky's death as 1950.

3

mittees," as Nikita Khrushchev later termed them, lost much of their importance. Stalin's personal rule in foreign affairs was absolute.

No less important than the "sextets" and "septets" was the large Foreign Department of the Central Committee of the Communist Party, the existence of which was not publicly acknowledged. Ostensibly concerned only with Communist movements abroad, it naturally dealt also with international affairs in general. It was divided into sections, by countries. The ties between these sections and the corresponding offices of the Ministry of Foreign Affairs were often very close. While the official Ministry of Foreign Affairs was not always headed by a member of the supreme Politburo-Presidium (for example, neither Maxim Litvinov nor Andrei Vyshinsky was a member of the Politburo), the Foreign Department of the Central Committee was the organ of the "general," or "first," secretary. This dual structure of the Foreign Department of the Soviet Union, which corresponded to the dual structure of the state-party machinery, left the ultimate power, even at times when a modicum of collective leadership existed, in the hands of the party's leader.

In the early 1940's the Foreign Department of the Central Committee was headed by Georgi Malenkov.[2] Malenkov was succeeded by Andrei Zhdanov, whose role was enhanced when the leadership of the dissolved Comintern was incorporated into one of the departments of the Central Committee.[3] In 1944–45, under Zhdanov's direction, the Foreign Section of the Central Committee carried out the remarkable operation of dispatching to the respective countries the leaders of the future governments of the satellites, selected from among *émigrés* in the Soviet Union.[4] The Foreign Section acquired growing importance in the postwar era as the channel for relations with the Communist parties of the satellites.[5]

[2] *The Report of the Royal Commission* (on the Igor Gouzenko Case), Ottawa, Canada, 1946, p. 27.

[3] Jesus Hernandez, *La Grande Trahison*, Paris, Fasquelle Editeurs, 1953, p. 249. After the dissolution of the Comintern, Dimitri Manuilsky told Hernandez: "You will keep in touch with Dimitrov, who will have his seat in the Foreign Section of the Bolshevik Party." (See also Enrique Castro Delgado, *J'ai perdu la foi à Moscow*, 6th ed., Paris, Gallimard, 1950, pp. 227–228.)

[4] Wolfgang Leonhard, *Child of the Revolution*, Chicago, Henry Regnery Company, 1958, chaps. 6 and 7.

[5] Soviet-Yugoslav diplomatic exchanges during 1948–1949, published in Belgrade, show that in Stalin's eyes the Soviet diplomats accredited to the satellites, although officially employees of the Foreign Office, were at the same time agents of the Central Committee. (*Soviet-Yugoslav Dispute*, London, Royal Institute of International Affairs, 1948, pp. 34 ff.)

Stalin in Foreign Affairs

In Stalin's later years his emotional attitude toward certain national groups began to affect his policies. His feelings toward members of some nationalities—among them the Chinese and the Jews—were often antagonistic. In personal contacts the nationality of the interlocutor was a conscious or unconscious element affecting Stalin's attitude. Vladimir Dedjer, the biographer of Tito, has mentioned a reception in 1946 at which Stalin invited him to join in a toast. Stalin did not call Dedjer by his name, nor did he address him as "Comrade." "Serb, come here!" he said. Recalling this incident later, Koča Popovič, the Yugoslav Minister of Foreign Affairs, observed: "There was a touch of chauvinism in it."[6] On another occasion Stalin made "un-Marxist" remarks about the Albanians ("primitive and loyal as dogs") and about the Chuvashes of the Soviet Union.[7]

Stalin's feelings toward the Chinese were somewhat the same. In old-time Russia, where thousands of Chinese had lived, there had been a widespread attitude toward them of a kind of racial superiority combined with contempt. Stalin's feeling about the Chinese was similarly nationalistic; ". . . all Chinese are boasters," he said to James Byrnes, the United States Secretary of State.[8] At receptions in the Kremlin, where rank was strictly observed, Chinese Communists were often seated in secondary places.

Stalin's anti-Jewish feelings, too, were plain, and the Soviet conflict with Israel during the last month of Stalin's life was due to a large extent to this cause.

Two of Stalin's lieutenants, Vyacheslav Molotov and Andrei Vyshinsky, who dealt with foreign affairs during the dictator's last years, must be mentioned.

Molotov, the "Soviet statesman of the Stalin era," as the press described him when he was at the peak of his career, though not a brilliant thinker was one of the small cohort initially assembled by Stalin as his field collaborators—men of energy and ability but without claim to ideological or political leadership. The prerevolutionary type of Bolshevik *Praktik* (as distinguished from the *Teoretik* and *Literator*) had become, since the 1950's, the standard type of Stalinist leader.

[6] Vladimir Dedjer, *Tito*, New York, Simon & Schuster, Inc., 1953, pp. 276, 374, 375.
[7] *Ibid.*, p. 303.
[8] James F. Byrnes, *Speaking Frankly*, New York, Harper & Brothers, 1947, p. 228.

Men of the Bukharin or Trotsky type of brilliant and original thinkers had been systematically exterminated. Molotov had served under Stalin since the early 1920's and, although aware of the future dictator's peculiar traits and methods, had maintained exemplary loyalty and devotion to him. A Party wheel horse before the revolution, he had suffered arrest, imprisonment, and exile; after each release from prison he had resumed his Bolshevik activity. During the Lenin era he had slowly climbed the ladder of the Soviet hierarchy, and in 1921 had been appointed a secretary of the Central Committee. For the rest of his life the distinction of having been one of Lenin's collaborators served him as a badge of honor and gave him a feeling of superiority over many others at the top levels of Party and government.

As a secretary of the Central Committee, Molotov worked under the "gensek" (general secretary). The pattern of their relationship during this early period—that of teacher and pupil, genius and mediocrity, general and major—continued for three decades. Molotov knew how to behave modestly in Stalin's presence, how never to contradict him, how not to talk unless asked to, how to let himself be guided, during long negotiations abroad, by instructions from the Kremlin. His experience provided him an unparalleled background, especially in foreign affairs. For eleven years he served as premier (chairman of the Council of People's Commissars), having succeeded Alexei Rykov in the post in December, 1930, when the rightist leader was dismissed. For another eight years, during the war and until 1949, he served as foreign minister. He was not liked by foreign diplomats; he could explain this dislike, not incorrectly, as due to his Communist intransigence rather than his personality. On occasions when foreign statesmen were seeking ways of conciliation and agreement with him, he appeared humane, even pleasant. "Once persuaded to make a concession," said a European diplomat who had had many dealings with Molotov, "he becomes friendly, and, being a well-educated person, casts off his obstinate mask and tries to meet you half way." [9] "I have seen in action all the great international statesmen of this century, beginning with those who met at the Hague Conference of 1907. I have never seen personal diplomatic skill at so high

[9] D Papers, July, 1957, XYZ, pp. 60–61.

Stalin in Foreign Affairs 7

a degree of perfection as Mr. Molotov's . . . ,"[10] wrote John Foster Dulles of the Soviet foreign minister.

Molotov's vast experience and his meticulous preparation of each international issue made his speeches at international conferences, while repetitious and sometimes dull, consistent and free of the factual errors that so often marked the pronouncements of his Western opponents. His collected speeches on foreign affairs remain an important document for students and writers.

Molotov's wife, Polina Zhemchuzhina, was active politically. She had been awarded the Order of Lenin and had advanced to the rank of minister (people's commissar); a Communist of Jewish origin, Mme. Molotov played a considerable role in the rise and fall of her husband's career. She was dismissed from her post in 1941, a few months before Russia entered the war; her origins, the fact that she had relatives in the United States, and her political temper may have contributed to the deterioration of her husband's relations with Stalin during the latter's last years. Later, her influence upon Molotov was bitterly resented by Nikita Khrushchev.[11]

Molotov, who had been awarded a number of orders, was often regarded as the highest Soviet dignitary after Stalin. The large province of Perm, where he was born, was renamed "Molotov" in his honor, and eleven cities and towns were named for him, as was a peak in the Pamirs only three miles from Stalin Peak. (Stalin Peak is 7,495 meters high, Lenin Peak 7,134, and Molotov Peak 6,852; Stalin Peak is the highest mountain peak in the Soviet Union.)

Homage during one's lifetime, in the Stalin era, was never secure or durable. In 1949 Molotov's prestige suffered severely when the Soviet blockade of Berlin ended in failure. Though the blockade had from beginning to end been Stalin's brainchild, the minister who was formally responsible for the operation was the scapegoat. Molotov, though given the title of vice-premier, was forced to cede the foreign ministry to his rising rival, Andrei Vyshinsky. During the remaining years of Stalin's life Molotov never resumed his prominent activity. In October, 1952, a short time before his death, Stalin, in an address before the plenum of the Central Committee, made "baseless

---
[10] John Foster Dulles, *War or Peace*, New York, The Macmillan Company, 1950, p. 29.
[11] See below, p. 232.

charges" against Molotov.[12] The situation was so dangerous that "had Stalin remained at the helm for another few months," Molotov might have been eliminated and liquidated. It is typical of Molotov that he nevertheless retained a warm loyalty to Stalin, grieved at the passing of the Leader, and remained one of the staunchest of the Stalinists among the Soviet leadership.

In many respects Andrei Vyshinsky was the opposite of Molotov. Seven years older than his rival, he had joined Lenin's party fourteen years later than Molotov. An active Menshevik in 1905–8 and again in the crucial years 1917–19, Vyshinsky, as a "rightist Menshevik," had opposed Bolshevism both before and after Lenin came to power. He slowly moved to the left, however, along with many other careerists, former enemies of Lenin, when they began to be convinced that the new regime would retain power for a long time. Toward newcomers of this kind, orthodox Bolshevism had mixed feelings of satisfaction and contempt. For many years after he joined the Communist Party Vyshinsky was closely watched by the GPU: was he an agent of the enemy assigned to penetrate the Communist ranks?[13]

Vyshinsky's Menshevik past haunted him to the end of his days. Aware of this stain on his biography, he tried to compensate for it by extreme devotion and loyalty, by engaging in risky operations, by servility toward the Great Teacher. Unlike Molotov, Vyshinsky was a prolific writer and speaker. A professor of law and later state prosecutor, he interpreted every Stalin zigzag in the legal field as the revelation of a genius. His role in the great purge trials of the late 1930's was further proof of the lengths to which he would go to gain favor with Stalin. He gained it, and not long after the conclusion of the trials he was elected to the Central Committee.

This recompense for his work did not mean much, however, for by that time (1939) the Central Committee, intentionally inflated in size to become a cumbersome body of 131 members and "candidates," diminished in significance. Only the Politburo was still more or less potent as a collective body of leaders, and Vyshinsky's ambition was to gain access to this body, a few of whose members had

---

[12] Khrushchev speech, February 24, 1956, at the closed session of the Twentieth Congress of the Communist Party of the Soviet Union.

[13] A report by a former agent of the GPU on the shadowing of Vyshinsky during his Communist years. D Papers, Y, p. 198.

been executed with his assistance. But a Menshevik was the worst type of criminal, and it was questioned whether Vyshinsky could ever be entirely reformed. Finally, in October, 1952, a few months before Stalin's death, Vyshinsky was elected a "candidate" to the Presidium (the former Politburo).

In 1940 Vyshinsky had been assigned to work in the People's Commissariat for Foreign Affairs, where he proved his special abilities. This was the time of the Stalin-Hitler pact, disagreements with the West, and conflicts with Poland. "In a way," a Polish representative in the Soviet capital stated, "Vyshinsky was the perfect diplomat. He was capable of telling an obvious untruth to your face; you knew it was a lie and he knew that you knew it was a lie, but he stubbornly adhered to it. No other diplomat was able to do this with such nonchalance." [14]

In the Commissariat of Foreign Affairs Vyshinsky worked at first under Molotov, the People's Commissar. The latent antagonism between the pure Bolshevik and the half-breed upstart apparently soon developed into conflict. Vyshinsky, humble and venerating, was gaining Stalin's personal confidence; he reported directly to Stalin over the head of his chief, and Stalin gave him assignments the performance of which at times called for extreme insolence: for example, the operation in Bucharest (the setting up of the Groza regime in March, 1945) and the negotiations at the Danube Conference in 1948, when he threw out the Western powers. Vyshinsky passed the tests and proved himself capable of maintaining Stalinist standards of "fighting" and "exposing" the archenemy, the United States.

Vyshinsky reached the peak of his career and saw his dream almost realized in 1949, when Molotov was apparently demoted and he himself was appointed foreign minister. Above him stood the Politburo, of which Molotov was a member; but the Politburo was becoming ineffective, and Vyshinsky was reporting to and dealing personally with Stalin. In 1952 Stalin openly turned against Molotov. Vyshinsky was elected a "candidate" of the Presidium. By that time, however, the Presidium, swollen in size (36 members), was obviously serving only as a face-saving device for Stalin. Vyshinsky's glory did not last long. Within a few days after Stalin's death, he lost both his position in the Presidium and his post as minister.

[14] D Papers, File No. 12, 1943.

The press in the West has sometimes compared Vyshinsky to Joseph Fouché, political turncoat of the French Revolution, first a leader of the terrorist Jacobins, then a minister under Napoleon, and finally chief of police in the restored monarchy. The analogy is correct in so far as in both cases political "convictions" were replaced by considerations of career, success, and the favor of the Leader. Vyshinsky, however, had no opportunities for repeating the performance of the French chief of police. Compared to the swift changes in France in Fouché's time, Russian Sovietism was a durable and stable structure, and its officials had little opportunity to turn their coats repeatedly. Besides, although as cynical as his French counterpart, Vyshinsky was less colorful and never attained the scope of power of Fouché.

Stalin's main ideas on postwar foreign policy, some of which have survived their creator, may be summarized as follows:

1. *The international crisis of capitalism and the process of transition to socialism was continuing;* the world-wide social revolution that had started in Russia in 1917 had made substantial progress since World War II. The capitalist system of economy, the reasoning went, was in a state of decay. Industrial prosperity in the capitalist world was either a false prosperity or one destined to be short-lived. Pauperization of the masses and unemployment were on the increase. Prices and taxes were rising, while wages were falling. A decrease in civilian consumption would lead to new depressions; the "capitalist market" was shrinking, while the "socialist market" was developing favorably from year to year.

The world was seen as divided in two groups only—into capitalist and socialist nations; a position between these two fronts—a no man's land—was not possible. He who is not with us is against us. Neutrality was a pretense. Social-Democrats and deviating Communists were part of the anti-Soviet coalition and must be fought.

The United States was seen as less affected than the other countries by the capitalist crisis and the social revolution. It aspired to world domination and subjugated its allies and was therefore antagonistic toward the Soviet Union. "Since the Soviet Union is the main opponent of war, the chieftains of the United States have arrived at the conclusion that war must be organized against the Soviet Union and the other partisans of peace." [15] The countries of Western Europe, on the other hand, were gradually renouncing their independence and following a line prescribed by the United States. "The rulers of Yugoslavia," too—"all those titos, kardeljs, rankoviches, djilases, pijades, etc."—are American agents, "complying with espionage and diversionist assignments of their American bosses."

2. *Whenever and wherever extension of the socialist realm was possible without armed conflict with a great power, such an extension was obligatory,* and in carrying it out, all diplomatic, legal, and propaganda obstacles must be disregarded.

The beginnings of this policy had been discernible since the early days of the Soviet era. During the first two decades, however, it could be applied only to territories distant from close international observation, such as Mongolia or Sinkiang. In Europe, in the Middle East, and in the Far East, on which international attention was focused, territorial progress was not possible until 1939.

The situation changed after the conclusion of the Soviet-German pact, and Stalin could extend his sphere without risking armed resistance. The Kremlin image of the Soviet Union as a superpower emerged in 1944–46. "Today," Molotov said in February, 1946, "no great issues of international relations can be solved without the Soviet Union or without listening to the voice of our Fatherland." [16] The Soviet Union, Stalin stated at the Potsdam Conference, like other nations, is interested in foreign territories. This statement, although it referred to the Italian colonies in Africa, epitomized the new departure in Soviet policy.

To move into a power vacuum, if one existed close to the Soviet borders, became a new feature of Stalin's course in international affairs. He embraced this maxim of empire-building, but he did not, of course, acknowledge the affinity of his mode of action to historical precedents; nor did his heirs.

3. *The new "socialist nations" must assume part of the burden of expansion* which the Soviet Union had up to now borne alone. This meant less direct fighting on the part of the Soviet Union and more on the part of its allies. In his last major speech, delivered on October

---

[15] Georgi Malenkov's report to the Nineteenth Congress of the Communist Party of the Soviet Union, October 5, 1952. (*Pravda*, October 6, 1952.)
[16] Speech of February 6, 1946.

14, 1952, before hundreds of guests and journalists, Stalin said that the Soviet and satellite governments were the "shock brigades" (*udarnaya brigada*) in the fight against capitalism. However, the obligations of the Soviet government and the obligations of the satellite governments were now reversed. The Soviet Union, Stalin said, had done much in her role of a "shock brigade" of socialism, but she had stood alone. "It was very hard to live up to this honorable role. But this time has passed. Now from China and Korea to Czechoslovakia and Hungary, new 'Shock Brigades' have appeared in the form of the people's democracies; it has become easier for our party to struggle, and the work has become merrier." [17]

To Stalin, the controversial problem of Soviet-satellite relations was part of this shock brigade theory: subordination of the people's democracies to Moscow was a prerequisite of continuing world-wide progress. With the shift in reciprocal roles as shock brigades, a less belligerent era would be inaugurated for the Soviet, while the people's democracies, in particular China and East Germany, would assume greater responsibilities.

4. *The Soviet Union must abstain from any move on the international scene that must lead to a war with the West in which it would be directly involved.* The reasons for this restraint were many: the American leading position in the field of nuclear arms, which would continue for a number of years; the warm feelings of the Russian people for their wartime allies; the general unpopularity of a war against the West. The main reason, however, was to avoid jeopardizing the Soviet system in Russia: defeat might mean the end of the Soviet system. Expansion was desirable; conservation of Soviet power was imperative. Only when expansionist moves involved no real danger could they be carried out as a course of policy. No chances must be taken that might imperil the existence of the "first socialist state."

Support of offensive moves by members of the Soviet bloc, if these did not directly involve the Soviet Union, was a matter of course, and the need to provide the satellites with diplomatic protection, defend them before world forums, and supply them with arms and expert personnel was only natural. China, Vietnam, Korea, and even Yugoslavia for a time enjoyed Soviet support in drives which, except

[17] *Pravda*, October 15, 1952.

Stalin in Foreign Affairs

for Stalin's aid, would certainly have failed. In situations in which Soviet military units (for example, the case of the Soviet radar experts in Korea) were indispensable, they were disguised in a way that would make it possible for Moscow to extricate itself in case of complications.

There were situations, however, in which it was not clear in advance how the West would react to a move on the part of the Soviet Union or her allies; in the cases of West Berlin and Korea, for example, Stalin's course was to take initial risks, advance to the brink, and then retreat if the threat of war became serious. Pursuing this path, Stalin sometimes succeeded and sometimes failed; but in all cases he could maintain that he had done his utmost for the advancement of Soviet Communism and that not a single opportunity for growth had been neglected.

Essentially this was "brink-of-war" policy. Somewhat later, after Stalin's death, United States Secretary of State John Foster Dulles explained that in his resistance to threatening moves by Moscow he had had "to walk to the brink of war." [18] For several years the Soviet press exploited the phrase as expressing America's warlike intentions. Actually, brinkmanship—not the term but the procedure—was introduced by Stalin long before the other powers adopted a similar course. Nor was it a product of Stalin's viciousness; it was indeed genuine "Leninism-Stalinism" applied to the international arena. It is both the privilege and the sacred duty of a leader of a great Communist government to advance and extend its own and its allies' power and influence to the limit. He would be an unworthy leader who failed in this obligation. Naturally such a course is fraught with dangerous situations, and these must be kept at a minimum. Here Stalin's personal ambitions, Russia's traditional imperial trends, and the requirements of global Communism coincided.

One of the outstanding examples of Stalin's brink-of-war policy was the Berlin operation of 1948–49. Stalin could have tried to put a stop to the American airlift, but this might have brought on a real war; he decided instead to withdraw, and early in 1949 he lifted the blockade. The Communist movement could not reproach Stalin with having neglected the duty of attempting to extend German Communist rule over the city of Berlin.

[18] *The New York Times*, January 12, 1956.

Another case in point was the Greek uprising of 1944–48. Defeated by loyalist forces and weakened by the Soviet-Yugoslav rift, the movement in Greece could be saved only by direct military intervention by Soviet forces. Stalin solved the dilemma whether to sacrifice his Greek supporters or risk a war against the British and Americans by retreating and leaving Greece to the Western alliances.

The war in Korea was another illustration of Stalin's war-and-peace tactics. In 1949–50 Stalin had every reason to believe that the United States government would refrain from sending its forces into a country which American military authorities viewed as strategically unimportant. The withdrawal of the United States army from South Korea in 1949 confirmed the Soviet conviction that the whole of Korea could be transformed into a people's democracy without a war. Had Stalin known how near the Soviet Union was to a great war, he would hardly have taken the chances that he did.

As a result of these retreats, the Soviet empire, at the time of Stalin's death, though vast and impressive, was less than what the Soviet postwar blueprints called for: West Austria, West Berlin, Greece, and Yugoslavia remained independent and outside the Soviet realm.

5. *War is inevitable as long as capitalism exists.* This concept was a constant element in the political philosophy inherited from Lenin, expanded by Stalin, adopted universally by Stalin's entourage, the Party, and Soviet social science, and embraced by the thousands of students from among whom would come the Soviet rulers of tomorrow.

The Communist concept of war as inevitable had undergone substantial changes since Lenin's party seized power in Russia. The earliest version of this concept was Lenin's denial of the possibility of "coexistence" between capitalist and socialist states; the Allied military intervention of 1918–19 was proof that the "terrible" and decisive war was imminent—had, in fact, started. "International imperialism, with its mighty capital, its highly organized military technique, which is a real fortress of international capital, could not under any circumstances, or any condition, live side by side with the Soviet Republic. . . ." [19] "One or the other must triumph in the end. And before

---

[19] V. I. Lenin, *Selected Works,* New York, International Publishers Co., Inc., 1943, vol. 7, p. 288. "War and Peace," Report to the Seventh Congress of the Russian Communist Party (Bolshevik), March 7, 1918.

that end supervenes, a series of frightful collisions between the Soviet Republic and the bourgeois states will be inevitable.[20]

In 1920–21, when the foreign military intervention in Russia ended and the regime was receiving diplomatic recognition, Lenin arrived at the conclusion that he had been wrong, and he admitted this more than once. Peaceful coexistence, he now believed, was possible, though only for a limited time. "Is such a thing possible that a Socialist republic could exist amid capitalist encirclement? This seemed unthinkable in both a political and a military sense. Now it is proved, it is a fact, that it is possible in both a political and a military sense." [21]

While a war between "capitalism" and the Soviet Union was now seen as not inevitable, or at least as not imminent, the old theory that "imperialist" states must inevitably clash with one another was still held. In the 1920's, when Stalin predicted an armed conflict between the United States and Britain, it was considered "inevitable" that the Soviet Union would be dragged into the fight. It was a sin to believe that war was not inevitable.[22] In December, 1927, in his report to the Fifteenth Congress, Stalin forcefully reiterated the thesis "that the *period of 'peaceful coexistence' is receding into the past*, giving place to a period of imperialist assaults and preparation for intervention against the USSR." [23] In making this statement Stalin had in mind Britain and France.

After the end of World War II Stalin introduced an innovation: peaceful coexistence, he maintained, could apply only to Soviet-imperialist relations; there was no compelling reason for an armed con-

[20] *Ibid.*, vol. 8, p. 33. "Report of the Central Committee of the Russian Communist Party (Bolshevik) at the Eighth Party Congress," March 18, 1919.

[21] V. I. Lenin, *Sochineniya* (Works; in Russian), 4th ed., Moscow, 1950, vol. 33, p. 126. Lenin's report to the Ninth All-Russian Congress of Soviets, December 23, 1921.

[22] Soviet leaders often accused one another, with or without justification, of this crucial deviation. At the Plenum of the Central Committee of July–August, 1927, Zinoviev reproached Bukharin for his statement on the "probability" (not "inevitability") of war. Stalin in turn quoted an article by Zinoviev attacking him: "In that article Zinoviev says that a new war is *possible*. A whole chapter in it is devoted to proving that war is *possible*. The chapter ends with the sentence: 'That is why it is legitimate and necessary for Bolshevik-Leninists to think now about the possibility of a new war.' Please note, comrades—'*to think*' about the *possibility* of a new war. In one passage in the article Zinoviev says that war 'is *becoming* inevitable,' but he does not say a single word, literally not a single word, about war already having become inevitable. . . ." (J. V. Stalin, *Works*, Moscow, Foreign Language Publishing House, 1955, vol. 10, pp. 49–50. Speech by J. V. Stalin delivered August 1, 1927, to the Joint Plenum of the Central Committee and Central Control Committee of the CPSU (B).)

[23] *Ibid.*, p. 294. Stalin's report of December 3, 1927 to the Fifteenth Congress of the Communist Party of the Soviet Union.

flict between the Soviet Union and the capitalist nations. The Soviet government, Moscow announced, would not attack its capitalist adversaries, and the Western powers, mindful of the German lesson of 1941–45, might abstain from attacking the Soviet Union. In the relations between capitalist powers, on the other hand, antagonism generated by the quest for markets and sites for investment of capital, according to Stalin, produces conflicts which "inevitably" develop into wars. At the root of this philosophy of Stalin's lay Lenin's theories of imperialism as a stage in economic evolution. Although the main antagonism at the present time, Stalin maintained, was between capitalism and socialism, the armed conflicts of tomorrow would develop within the capitalist family. Stalin reiterated this paradoxical view more than once, and he held to it until the end: a war between the United States and her European rivals, among whom Britain was the foremost, was inevitable; but in the relations of the Soviet Union with her former allies or enemies, war could be averted. These views were obligatory for all Communists; they were repeated by Malenkov in 1952, shortly before Stalin's death: peaceful coexistence among capitalist states over a long period is impossible, he told the Nineteenth Party Congress, but "co-existence of Socialist and capitalist nations is entirely possible."

The Soviet policy in war, carried out in the Fast East in 1941–45, had been laid down in the 1920's: the capitalist nations fight one another, while Russia remains neutral; as the conflict approaches an end and the outcome of the war becomes certain, the Soviet Union enters and reaps the harvest. This political strategy, a favorite idea of its creator, was first developed by Stalin in 1925; it was considered a strategic secret and was not made public until 1947: "If war breaks out we shall not be able to sit with folded arms. We shall have to take action, but we shall be the last to do so. And we shall do so in order to throw the decisive *weight* on the scales, the weight that can turn the scales." [24]

Stalin attempted to apply this policy to Nazi Germany when he signed the pact of 1939. His intention was to enter the war, when it was in its final stage, by joining the Allies, if they were winning, and advancing into Germany; or by allying himself with Germany and

[24] *Ibid.*, vol. 7, p. 14. Speech delivered at the Plenum of the Central Committee of the RCP (B), January 19, 1925.

Stalin in Foreign Affairs

moving into South Asia to occupy the post-British vacuum. When Germany invaded Russia in 1941, Stalin's miscalculation proved once more that it was not possible for Russia to play a balance-of-power role between contending power groups. Balance-of-power tactics, derived from the pattern of nineteenth century Britain, with her sea power, riches, and "splendid isolation," could not be applied to the political course of a strictly continental Eurasian power.

This and other blunders arising out of Stalin's theory of "inevitable wars" in conjunction with a more realistic evaluation of the consequences of war in our time later prompted his heirs to revise the theory. The revision did not commence, however, until several years after Stalin's death. Prior to that time it had been universally accepted in Russia and in the countries and parties allied to Russia that the series of great wars which would be the protracted "final crisis of capitalism" had not yet ended, that armed conflicts would soon break out between Western nations and the Soviet bloc, and that the Soviet Union must arm herself on a grand scale in order to enter the conflict when it reached an advanced stage, win the war, and, in doing so, abolish the remnants of the old social order.

CHAPTER 2

STALIN'S EMPIRE BUILDING

1. NO SECOND COMMUNIST EMPIRE

By the end of the Stalin era, in the early 1950's, the political organization of the Soviet sphere in Europe had attained only a modicum of stability and was far from complete. An uninterrupted land mass comprising six nations (Bulgaria, Czechoslovakia, East Germany, Hungary, Poland, and Rumania) and Albania, whose combined population of about 92,000,000 was equal to the combined populations of France and West Germany, was now a part of the Soviet sphere. The Eastern European territory of the sphere (without Yugoslavia), with an area of 392,000 square miles, exceeded the combined areas of France and West Germany (307,340 square miles).[1]

The western limits of the sphere ran from Lübeck in Germany to Petrich in Bulgaria, with paradoxical areas, such as multizonal Berlin and Austria, in between. The tentative "demarcation lines" of 1945 had hardened into fortified frontiers; temporary "frontier guards" had become armies with guns and an air force; new large armies were on the rise. The Soviet sphere (the "socialist camp") in Europe, which was expected gradually to coalesce with the Soviet Union, was still leading its own life, or rather as many lives as there were national units in the sphere.

[1] Breakdown:

Country	Population	Area, sq. miles
Albania	1,250,000	11,100
Bulgaria	7,450,000	42,741
Hungary	9,600,000	35,893
Poland	26,780,000	119,703
Rumania	16,500,000	91,654
Czechoslovakia	12,948,000	49,330
E. Germany	17,600,000	41,700
	92,128,000	392,121

No Second Communist Empire

The terms "empire" and "imperialism," so widely used in the last decades, can be misleading, since in the course of history there have developed a variety of empires and imperialisms, each with its distinct traits, aims, and methods. There have been land-bound and overseas empires, and empires with and without self-government for the local populations; there have been differences between what we now refer to as colonies and dominions. The far-flung British Empire comprised a multitude of political systems ranging from democratic self-government to strict autocratic colonial rule; the short-lived Japanese empire, the "Greater East Asia Co-Prosperity Sphere," with its appeal to the nationalism of the former Western possessions, differed from all other types of empires; etc.

Different also were the methods of aggrandizement which brought Russian rule from Moscow to Warsaw and Vladivostok. Each newly acquired territory, regardless of the nationality of its inhabitants, was eventually added to the old body of the empire. The new territory was partitioned into Russian-type *gubernias* (provinces) and administered by an appointed *gubernator* (governor); in some instances several *gubernias* were united under a *general-gubernator*. The newly acquired areas were brought into line with the others; as component parts of the great state, they rarely had any autonomy. At times the Tsar's government tried to conduct more liberal policies in the new territories, but each time it had to reverse these tactics in order to keep the territory within the empire. The most striking example of this method was the annexation to Russia, after the Napoleonic wars, of the part of Poland that then became the "Congress Kingdom" of Poland. In November, 1815, the Tsar granted Poland a liberal constitution providing for freedom of religion and press, elections, a parliament, and even a Polish army (foreign affairs, however, remained in the hands of the St. Petersburg regime). In the liberal climate, a strong national movement developed which aimed at the independence of Poland and culminated in the great uprising of 1831. The uprising was suppressed by Russian forces, and Poland was deprived of her autonomy and subjected to the general Russian system of administration.

In the last decades of old Russia, Finland was the only part of the empire that enjoyed real autonomy and political freedom. Conflicts between St. Petersburg and Finland broke out, however, early in the twentieth century. Encroachments on Finnish liberties multiplied, and had not World War I intervened, the political system of Finland would probably have been revamped according to the universal Russian pattern. From long experience, the Russian governments had drawn the conclusion that there were only two alternatives: complete homogeneity or separation.

In a way, the empire-building conducted by Stalin was a resumption of old Russian trends; in some important respects, however, it deviated from tradition and introduced new methods and new goals. Stalin adhered, for instance, to the old Russian conception of extending the realm to neighboring lands rather than to lands separated from Russia by other territories. Unlike the British, French, Spanish, Portuguese, Dutch, Italian, and Japanese, to name only the leading empires of the last centuries, Russia, in her thousand years of history, has, by expansion over the Eurasian continent and engulfment of one vacuum after another, grown into a single land mass. Rarely has she attempted to jump to a distant island or another continent. When she did so, she failed. In Napoleon's time, Tsar Paul tried to extend his influence to the island of Malta in the Mediterranean, but was forced to retreat before Britain. In the nineteenth century, the western lands of North America (California, the Hawaiian Islands) and even the East and West Indies were envisioned as future component parts of the Russian empire, while the northern Pacific was expected to become a Russian inland sea. But all thought of acquisitions in these parts of the world had to be given up.

The growth of Russia has been strictly on the continental pattern.

Stalin's experience in Spain in 1936–38 had again demonstrated that it was impossible for the Soviet Union to attain predominance in far-off lands and to make of such lands what later came to be called satellites. In 1945–46 Stalin tried to make a jump into North Africa and get a foothold in one of the Italian colonies. Meeting with determined resistance on the part of Britain, he had to give up. The empire remained a single land mass after the pattern of the Soviet Union itself and of the empire of old Russia.

In refraining from outright incorporating most of the new territories into the Soviet Union, formally partitioning them into Soviet "*oblasts*" or "Union Republics," and subordinating them to the laws and regulations of the Soviet state, Stalin deviated from the old Russian pattern.

In the initial postwar years, friends and foes of the Soviet Union alike expected an early attempt at incorporation of the "people's democracies," or at least some of them, into the Soviet state. Moscow had announced more than once that the Union of Soviet Socialist Republics was ready to incorporate any nation which would "fall off the imperialist system"; it went without saying that the "people's democracies" would go the way of the Baltic states, Eastern Poland, and Bessarabia. Since the early years the Bolshevik image of a multinational revolutionary state had been that of a strong, unified "socialist state" with a powerful executive. Now, it appeared, the time had arrived to bring such a state about. The international climate in 1945–48 seemed favorable for it. It was doubtful whether the West, demobilized and tired, would send its armies against Russia to preserve the fictitious remnants of independence of an East European country. Opposition of the Western powers, however, was not the main reason for Stalin's reluctance to incorporate one or more of the satellites into the Soviet Union. There were other reasons that prompted him to abstain from formal incorporation and vehemently insist on "full independence and sovereignty" for these countries.

In the early years of the Soviet regime, when from month to month it was expected that revolution would sweep over the continent, Stalin had already formed his ideas about the future relationship of Russia and her prospective Communist allies in Eastern and Central Europe. He did not agree with Lenin that a unitarian state ("federation") must be publicly proclaimed as the program of the Communist movement. When Lenin prepared his "Theses on the National and Colonial Question" for the Second Congress of the Communist International, in which "federation" was the basic idea, Stalin disagreed with his teacher and suggested "confederation." [2] "Unity" had to be

---
[2] Lenin's draft of his views on the question read as follows:
"The Federation is a transitional form of establishing a complete union of toilers of various nationalities. The practical application of the federative system has already proved its expedience, both in the relations between the Russian Socialist Federative Republic to other Soviet Republics (to Hungarian, Finnish, and Latvian—in the past, to Azerbaijan and to Ukraine at present), and within the Russian Socialist Federative Soviet Republic." (V. I. Lenin, *Sochineniya* (Works; in Russian), 4th ed., Moscow, 1950, vol. 31, p. 124.)

"as tight as possible," Lenin wrote; "we have to strive for a more and more close federation." [3]

Lenin did not discriminate between nations that had never belonged to the Russian empire and those that had formerly constituted Russian provinces. He believed that adherence to the new socialist state would be so beneficial and advantageous that all countries that were able to get rid of their "capitalists" would almost automatically join the Soviet republic.

Stalin opposed this view. To him, restoration of the territorial complex of prerevolutionary Russia marked the approximate limits of the growing Soviet state; as far as Eastern Europe was concerned, it would not be politic to incorporate it into a Soviet Russia. Speaking of a future Soviet Germany, Poland, Hungary, and Finland, Stalin answered Lenin on January 12, 1920:

"Such peoples, possessing their own state, their own army, their own finances, upon becoming Soviet nations, will not immediately agree to enter into a federative union with Soviet Russia, as did the Bashkir and the Ukrainian Republic: they will regard a federation of the Soviet type as a limitation of their self-determination, and as an attempt upon their independence.

"I have no doubt that to such nationalities the most acceptable form of drawing them together would be a Confederation (a union of independent states)." [4]

Lenin rejected Stalin's suggestion. The record of the controversy, including the letter from Stalin to Lenin quoted above, was therefore eliminated from the later editions of both Lenin's and Stalin's works.

Actually Stalin was no less a partisan of centralized "federation"

---

[3] *Ibid.*, p. 125.
[4] Stalin wrote further: "For nationalities which lived in old Russia, our Soviet type of Federation can and must be acknowledged as an expedient way toward international unity. The reasons are well known: in the past these nationalities either had no independent state of their own, or they lost this independence long ago. Therefore the [centralized] type of a Soviet Federation can be adapted to them without much friction.

"But this is not true in regard to nationalities which did not belong to old Russia, which had created their own states, and lived as independent nations; should they become Soviet nations, for instance, a future Soviet Germany, Poland, Hungary, Finland—they will be compelled by actual fact to establish some sort of inter-state relations with Soviet Russia. . . .

". . . And I leave out of consideration such backward nations as Persia and Turkey to which the Soviet type of Federation or any Federation at all is still less acceptable.

"Taking all this into account, I think that the idea of a Confederation has to be inserted in the paragraph of your theses dealing with the transitional form for bringing together the toiling people of the various nations." (V. I. Lenin, *Works* (in Russian), 3d ed., Moscow, 1937, vol. 25, pp. 615–618.)

than Lenin. He never intended to make "confederation," which implied the right of dissent for small nations, part of his pattern. But he maintained that it was strategically wrong to appear before the world as an old-fashioned "imperialist conqueror" and to grab territories and annex them to the empire. One or another satellite might perhaps be incorporated without complications, but annexation of Poland, Finland, and other nations would revive the image of old Russia and repel other countries whose adherence to the Soviet camp in one form or another appeared more important than that of the small countries. Such was Stalin's personal program.

In the 1948 correspondence between the Soviet government and Yugoslavia there was reference to a conversation between Edward Kardelj, the Yugoslav leader, and Soviet Ambassador Anatoli Lavrentiev. Yugoslavia "would like the Soviet Union," Kardelj said, "to regard them [the Yugoslavs] not as representatives of another country, capable of solving questions independently, but as representatives of one of the future Soviet Republics, and the Communist Party of Yugoslavia as a part of the All-Union Communist Party, that is, that our relations should be based on the prospect of Yugoslavia becoming in the future a constituent part of the U.S.S.R."

Without going into the crucial problem, Stalin deemed this view wrong: "We leave aside the primitive and fallacious reasoning of Comrade Kardelj about Yugoslavia as a future constituent part of the USSR and the CPY as a part of the CPSU."[5]

It was a tenet of Stalin's empire-building that no second socialist power of equal rank with the Soviet Union was to be tolerated. If the existence of a number of "sovereign socialist nations" was necessary, their "independence" must never permit the emergence of a second socialist empire. In the Soviet view, a multitude of great sovereign powers competing among themselves could and did exist among non-Soviet nations, but in the socialist world only one great power can lead the way to new successes and victories. If a satellite strides too far forward, as Yugoslavia did, for instance, it must be contained and cut down to size. One nation must lead, the others must follow.

[5] *The Soviet-Yugoslav Dispute. Text of the Published Correspondence,* London, Royal Institute of International Affairs, 1948. Letter from the Central Committee of the Communist Party of the Soviet Union to the Central Committee of the Communist Party of Yugoslavia, May 4, 1948.

Independence, permitted within certain limits, must never lead to coalitions of Soviet nations which would exclude Russia.

This attitude toward a second Communist bloc of nations had deep ideological roots in Leninist Communism, but it was motivated also by practical considerations of great importance.

The image of a single, well-knit, strong international Communist organization—a "monolith"—was and is still today a factor of emotional and propagandistic force in the world Communist movement. It has been inherent in Communism from its early days; it inspired future Communist leaders even before the Comintern was founded. The vision of a strong, centralized organization was juxtaposed with the "impotent," "ineffective" Socialist International, whose parties, scattered along various sides of the fronts, supported their governments in war. An international organization that has no power over its component parties, Lenin said contemptuously, is only a "letter box," not a fighting instrument in an era when civil wars and revolutions are about to transform the world and establish a new social and political order. The urge to create an International that would possess absolute power over its component parts and become a united army in the strict sense of the word was paramount when Lenin proceeded to organize the Comintern in 1918–19.

> There is everywhere a proletarian army [Lenin triumphantly told the Second Congress of the International], though it is sometimes poorly organized and requires reorganization; if our international comrades will help us to organize a unified army, no shortcomings whatsoever will prevent us from accomplishing our task. Our task is the cause of the international universal world revolution, the task of creating a universal Soviet republic. . . .[6]

Lenin enumerated the most important achievements of the Second Congress:

> The Congress has created a solidarity and discipline of Communist parties of the entire world such as has never existed before and which will permit the vanguard of the proletarian revolution to go forward rapidly to its great goal, the overthrow of the yoke of capital.[7]

[6] Lenin, *op. cit.*, 4th ed., vol. 31, p. 209.
[7] *Ibid.*, p. 246.

No Second Communist Empire

The term "army" as applied to the Communist International was more than a figure of speech. The Communist International was the "General Staff of the World Revolution." This phrase of Trotsky's, often repeated, was a precise description of the Communist notion of its international organization. Gregori Zinoviev, President of the Comintern, reported to the Petrograd soviet in August, 1920: "The Staff of the international revolution is organized; among its duties are the support of international proletarian discipline, since the experience of the Russian revolution has taught that without firm party discipline Soviet Russia would not withstand the onslaught of her numerous enemies from without as well as from within."[8] "Subordination" and "strict discipline" were primary characteristics of the new organization.

The general staff is, of course, subordinated to the commander in chief and his discretionary powers. No "autonomy" is possible. National Communist parties, which must comply with orders from above, can have no more "autonomy" than army divisions located at various sections of a war front. Tactics may differ, but the differences must be approved by the general staff of the world revolution.

The statutes of the Communist International embodied this notion of international intra-Communist relations. All Communist parties, like soldiers, must wear one uniform: the name of each party was to be "Communist Party of (name of country), Section of the Communist International." No second Communist party in the same country could be recognized. The Executive Committee of the Communist International was to "give directives" to and control the activities of all "sections"; decisions of the Executive Committee were obligatory and must be carried out forthwith. The Executive Committee had the right to cancel all decisions of the national Communist congresses and central committees; moreover, it was entitled to give orders contradictory to such decisions. It could expel members from Communist parties. The program of every Communist party must be approved by the Communist International and could be rejected. No congress of a national "section" could take place without the previous consent of the Communist International.

As if anticipating and attacking trends toward "national Com-

[8] *Petrogradskaya Pravda,* August 13, 1920.

munism," Lenin stated: "Bolshevism is valid as a pattern of tactics for all." [9]

In Lenin's prerevolutionary conception of the perfect socialist International there was no thought of Russian dominance over the other parties; Lenin rather expected that a Western party, most likely the German, would assume leadership. The situation changed when the ruling party of Russia emerged as the initiator and most dynamic element of the new Communist organization. For a long time, however, and probably until his death, Lenin was convinced that Russia's leading position was temporary and would have to be ceded to a Western party.

In this assumption Lenin was wrong. Russian leadership in the Communist movement proved durable. Over the years the factual control became institutional. The notion, however, of the Communist International as a monolith was maintained. In 1938 it was emphasized again that "the Communist International represents not a union of parties, but a unified world Communist party of the proletariat, a revolutionary organization bound by iron revolutionary discipline, built on the principles of democratic centralism and fearless Bolshevik self-criticism." [10]

When the Communist International was officially disbanded in 1943, everybody in the great family took it for granted that the Secretariat of the Central Committee of the Communist Party of the Soviet Union would assume responsibility for maintaining the Comintern's heritage, obligations, and aims. Between 1943 and 1947, when the Comintern was no longer in existence and the Cominform had not yet been born, Stalin's Secretariat practically assumed the privileges and duties of the old Executive Committee of the Comintern along with the responsibility for maintaining discipline among the Communist parties.

Since the last stages of World War II, Russian leadership in the international movement developed logically, according to the devious ways of history, into leadership of a new empire. Now the time-honored rules of Communist internationalism were to find application in new fields—the governments of the Eastern bloc. The Russian claim to leadership was strengthened by the role of Russian arms in

---

[9] Lenin, *op. cit.*, 4th ed., vol. 28, p. 270.
[10] *Large Soviet Encyclopedia*, 1st ed., Moscow, 1938, vol. 33, p. 717.

the defeat of Germany; it was enhanced by the growing East-West antagonism. "Iron discipline" was no less needed now than in the Comintern days.

To Communist ideology there were added the needs of practical policies when issues of Soviet empire-building began to come to the fore. Stalin rejected and violently fought against independence for individual Communist parties in the Soviet orbit not only because it was in contradiction to old tenets but also because the emergence of Communist governments, with their own particular trends in European and world affairs, would be tantamount to disintegration of the bloc. "Independence" would mean that a people's democracy could support or not support the Soviet course, obtain help, if necessary, from the West, join the Western course if it became dissatisfied with Soviet actions. Independence was tantamount to granting the right to the new "socialist nations" to confederate, federate between themselves, and perhaps even build a new "Socialist Federation" embracing most or all of the satellites—a federation that might rise to real power stature in Europe. Such a second empire would put a check on Soviet influence and place in question her claim to supremacy on the old continent. This could not be tolerated.

Stalin's rigid type of subordination and discipline was often explained by his morbid lust for power, his egotism, and his contempt for his co-workers. More to the point, however, was the fact that here again Stalin's personal inclinations coincided with the general Soviet image of its own greatness and destiny. Stalin's despotic rule was a part of Soviet dynamism.

Stalin's principles of empire-building were first applied in the case of Tito's Yugoslavia.

2. THE YUGOSLAV REBELLION

In 1945–47, Yugoslavia, under Tito, was well on her way to becoming a second great socialist power independent of and rivaling the Soviet Union. This situation constituted the main issue in the relations of Moscow and Belgrade when the break between them occurred in 1948. The other issues usually advanced as the cause of the deterioration in relations—Soviet advisers in Yugoslavia, the kolkhozes, espionage, etc.—were secondary.

Tito had been one of the most aggressive, dynamic, and rabid of anti-Western Communists; he had outdone Stalin in his head-on attacks on the "capitalist nations," especially England. During the war, when Russia was trying not to antagonize Churchill's England too much, Tito would not agree to a British landing in Yugoslavia. When Stalin tried to persuade Tito to work for a time with the Yugoslav king ("and then you can slip a knife into his back at a suitable moment"[11]), Tito rejected the suggestion. He shot down American planes; he proceeded to collectivize and industrialize Yugoslavia at an excessively fast tempo; he was the prime moving force behind the civil war in Greece. What appeared really ominous to Moscow, however, were Belgrade's ambitions in regard to the Soviet orbit. Tito and his party and army stood out as a force compared to the small forces of the other satellites and the "democratic coalitions" in Czechoslovakia and Hungary. At Moscow receptions of that period the Yugoslavs were treated as second only to the Russians. In the Cominform the Yugoslavs were the ones assigned to criticize the French and Italians.

In 1946 Tito, while on a triumphal trip through Warsaw and Prague, signed treaties of friendship with Poland and Czechoslovakia. After their experience with the Soviet armies, the civilian populations of these countries gave a warm greeting to this different type of Slav leader. In Warsaw the Polish president awarded Tito the highest military order.

> Wherever Tito went [wrote Fitzroy Maclean] he received an enthusiastic reception. In Prague, Warsaw and Sofia, in Budapest and Bucharest, enormous crowds turned out to see this legendary figure, each of whose uniforms was more magnificent than the last. Tito's fame had spread far beyond the frontiers of his own country. He was in a different class from any of the other rather drab satellite rulers. He was well on the way to becoming, in his own right, an international figure of the first magnitude.[12]

The Communist uprising in Greece, although greatly aided by Moscow, was in the main supported and controlled by Tito and Georgi

---

[11] Vladimir Dedjer, *Tito*, New York, Simon & Schuster, Inc., 1953, p. 233.
[12] Fitzroy Maclean, *The Heretic: The Life and Times of Josepi Broz-Tito*, New York, Harper & Brothers, 1957, p. 313.

The Yugoslav Rebellion

Dimitrov, with the design of annexing the southernmost Balkan country to the future "Balkan Federation" under Tito. In the north, Rumania, where Ana Pauker and a few others were highly sympathetic to Tito, was envisioned as another part of the federation. The ambitious projects went even farther: actually the whole belt from the Baltic to the Black Sea and the Adriatic, including Greece, and with Trieste annexed from Italy and Carinthia and Styria from Austria, was envisioned as the realm of a future huge alliance, confederation, or federation, with Tito, obviously, its prospective leader. While on a visit to Rumania (late January, 1948), Dimitrov told the press:

> When the question matures, as it must inevitably mature, then our peoples, the nations of the People's Democracy, Rumania, Bulgaria, Yugoslavia, Albania, and Greece!—will settle it. It is they who will decide what it shall be—a federation or confederation—and when and how it will be formed. I can say that what our peoples are already doing greatly facilitates the solution of this question in the future.[13]

In Moscow's eyes Tito was emerging as a prospective rival leader. To Stalin, the Titoist movement was a real and present danger. A second Communist empire in Europe would wipe out all the principles and strategy of three decades, destroy the "monolith," paralyze the world-wide attack on "imperialism," and stop progress toward global socialism; it would hurt Russian nationalist feelings and substantially curtail Stalin's stature.

In the beginning Stalin had agreed to a small South Slav Federation which would embrace Yugoslavia and Bulgaria (with tiny Albania a geographically logical addendum); Stalin believed that the Bulgarians and Albanians in the regime of the new federation could serve as a channel of infiltration by loyal pro-Russians and as a means of paralyzing any great-power moves on the part of the new regime and holding it to the status of an average satellite. Tito was not content with such a subordinate role. A series of treaties between Yugoslavia and her neighbors concluded during the last two months of 1947 marked the beginning of a new diplomatic offensive.[14] Stalin had not always been informed in advance. Moscow twice summoned the

---

[13] *Ibid.*, p. 321.
[14] A treaty with Bulgaria was signed on November 11, one with Hungary on December 8, and one with Rumania on December 19; these were followed by a Bulgarian-Rumanian treaty signed on January 16, 1948.

leaders of Yugoslavia and Bulgaria to Russia; Tito dispatched lieutenants, refusing himself to go. When the crucial discussions between Stalin and the Yugoslavs took place, in January and February, 1948, it was too late for Stalin's modest plan. Reconciliation proved impossible. On January 29, 1948, *Pravda* for the first time publicly attacked the federation idea. From then on everything went downhill. The Yugoslav Central Committee refused to bow. The subsequent well-known exchange of letters between Moscow and Belgrade, which began on March 20, culminated in a complete break. In the absence of the Yugoslavs, the Cominform, called upon by Stalin to try the dispute, took, of course, the Soviet side. A year later, as the Soviet-Yugoslav feud was reaching its peak, the Cominform expelled Tito's party from the official Cominform family.

In the following four years (1949–52) Stalin's fight against Yugoslavia continued intense and bitter; he expected an early downfall of Tito's regime. All treaties of alliance between Yugoslavia and the people's democracies were broken in September–October, 1949. Trade relations were practically broken off. The diplomatic exchanges that occurred were belligerent, recriminatory, and threatening. During the two years 1949–51 Yugoslavia addressed 128 diplomatic notes to the Eastern European governments protesting against discrimination and obstruction. During the same time, 145 Yugoslav diplomats and other officials were expelled from the Cominform countries, and 1,067 frontier incidents took place.[15] The publicized trials of Titoists in Eastern Europe included those involving the Rajk group in Hungary, the Kostov affair in Bulgaria, the Slansky affair in Czechoslovakia, and the Xoxe affair in Tirana. Actually, scores of trials of less well-known Communists took place throughout the Cominform countries; the official Yugoslav White Book indicated that there were "several dozen judicial farces." [16]

Anti-Tito propaganda was carried out on a grand scale by Moscow and the satellites. Special anti-Tito newspapers edited by "revolutionary exiles from Yugoslavia" appeared in Moscow *(For a Socialist Yugoslavia)*, in Prague *(New Struggle)*, in Warsaw *(For Victory)*, in

---

[15] *White Book on Aggressive Activities by the Governments of the USSR, Poland, Czechoslovakia, Hungary, Rumania, Bulgaria, and Albania towards Yugoslavia,* Belgrade, Ministry of Foreign Affairs of the Federal People's Republic of Yugoslavia, 1951, pp. 202, 447 ff.

[16] *Ibid.,* p. 139.

The Yugoslav Rebellion

Bucharest *(Under the Banner of Internationalism)*, in Tirana *(For Freedom)*, and in Sofia *(Forward)*.[17] Copies of these newspapers were smuggled into Yugoslavia. Radio broadcasts attacked the policy of the Yugoslav government.

The aggressiveness of the Soviet press toward Yugoslavia did not diminish with the passage of time. In the last years of Stalin's era Yugoslavia was pictured as a country where capitalism was being restored, land turned over to kulaks, true Communists cruelly persecuted, and old fascists restored to power.

> Hundreds of enterprises are already in the hands of Yugoslav and foreign capitalists, as the newspapers of the Yugoslav revolutionary émigrés report. . . .
>
> The Yugoslav capitalists who in the past received nearly full compensation for nationalized enterprises and thus are in possession of considerable funds, are also financing the enterprises which are near bankruptcy and are again becoming their full-fledged bosses. . . . 77,000 kulaks have seized 18 per cent of the land, whereas 629,000 poor peasants have only 7 per cent. The peasant cooperatives are in the hands of the kulaks, who are exploiting the peasants through these cooperatives. . . .[18]

In the Nationality Council in Belgrade, *Bolshevik* reported, 26 Serbian deputies out of a total of 30 were representatives of "the bourgeoisie"; of 60 Croatian and Slovenian deputies, it added, 33 had been

> . . . the leaders of ultra-revolutionary monarcho-fascist organizations, who took part in the most brutal suppression of Yugoslav Communists in the era of the most cruel monarcho-fascist dictatorship. The Tito-Rankovich clique has assigned about half of the ministerial seats in the federal government and in the governments of the republics to former ministers of royalist Yugoslavia.[19]

"Nothing can be bought, stores are empty, and market speculators get fantastic prices," reported *Under the Banner of Internationalism*, organ of Yugoslav *émigrés* in Rumania.[20] Consequently the people live in utter misery. "Malnutrition, horrible housing conditions, a work

---

[17] *Ibid.*, pp. 107–115; *Bolshevik*, Moscow, April, 1951, no. 7, p. 54.
[18] *Bolshevik*, Moscow, no. 7, April, 1951, p. 55. "The Tito-Rankovich Clique Is Turning Yugoslavia into a Base of Aggression."
[19] *Ibid.*
[20] *Ibid.*, no. 15, August, 1952, p. 43. "The Fascist Clique of Tito in the Service of American Imperialism."

day of 12 to 14 hours—all this has increased the ratio of illness among workers. . . . The peasants are deserting their land and fleeing from the villages. In many provinces waste land is already noticeable." [21]

Never before in Yugoslavia have there been so many beggars, ragged, barefoot and homeless people. Unemployment is increasing steadily. The first to be thrown out are the physically weak, invalids, and women, especially pregnant women and those with many children. . . . Toiling people are deprived of medical care, since at the end of last year prices of medicines and medical treatment in the hospitals were increased several times.[22]

Toward the end of the propaganda offensive it was reported that

The Belgrade butchers have turned Yugoslavia into a concentration camp. By means of brutal terror and slanderous anti-Soviet propaganda, they are trying to crush the will of the peoples of Yugoslavia and convert them into cannon fodder for the American aggressors.[23]

Great indignation was aroused in Moscow by Yugoslavia's *rapprochement* with the West. Quoting from an Austrian Communist newspaper *(Österreichische Volksstimme),* the *New Times* asserted that the real author of the new constitution which made Tito a dictator was United States Ambassador George Allen, and that this was well-known in Belgrade diplomatic circles.[24] Soviet anger was also aroused by the fact that Tito assumed the Western title of "President," rejecting the Stalinist title of "Chairman."

The magazine *Bolshevik* said:

Traitors to the fatherland, headed by the dyed-in-the-wool spy Tito, pledged to their bosses—the American cannibals—to drag the Yugoslav peoples into a war carnage.[25]

Statements made by Moscow at this late hour of Stalin's rule were an answer to Tito's reorientation. This time Tito's evaluation of the West was no shrewd tactic or maneuver but a genuine revision of tenets, a groping effort to probe new roads toward Communism. The failure of Tito's ambitious foreign-political course reduced the aggres-

---

[21] *Ibid.,* no. 7, April, 1951, p. 59.
[22] *Ibid.,* no. 15, August, 1952, p. 47.
[23] *New Times,* Moscow, no. 7, February 11, 1953, p. 31.
[24] *Ibid.,* no. 3, January 14, 1953, p. 15.
[25] *Bolshevik,* Moscow, no. 15, August, 1952, p. 42.

The Yugoslav Rebellion

siveness of his dictatorship to comparative reasonableness: Belgrade denounced the Korean war as Soviet and Chinese aggression. "No aggressor can count on the sympathy of the Yugoslav people irrespective of who he is." [26] When the Chinese "volunteers" joined the North Koreans, Tito's *Vjesnik* maintained that "China is serving the Soviet Union and its imperialist plans. This is a crime." [27]

A five-year Balkan pact, uniting Yugoslavia with the "capitalist nations" of Greece and Turkey (against the Soviet Union or its satellites) was signed on February 28, 1953. The pact was an important supplement to the military and economic ties between Yugoslavia and the United States. In September, 1952, Anthony Eden, the British Foreign Secretary, visited Tito in Belgrade; Tito returned the visit in March, 1953. In London, Tito was received by the Queen and conversed with Winston Churchill and numerous other "reactionaries" of old Britain.

Following a number of contacts during those years between Tito Communists and Western socialists, socialist delegations came to Belgrade as guests of the Yugoslav "Fourth Congress of the People's Front" in late February, 1953. At this gathering, which was boycotted by all pro-Soviet Communist parties, there were present non-Communist and anti-Communist leaders of British labor, the French Socialists, German Social-Democrats, and socialists of Norway, Sweden, Burma, and other countries. In his speech Tito attacked the "dark forces of reaction in East and West," and Yugoslav Vice-President Edward Kardelj defied the "state-capitalistic, terroristic, imperialistic" policies of Moscow. The People's Front was renamed the "Socialist Alliance of the Working People of Yugoslavia."

With these new trends in theory and practice, Tito's Yugoslavia reached the limit of her liberalization. The Yugoslav leaders did not intend to go any farther along this path; the one-party system remained unaltered, and the economic system remained what it was, although forcible collectivization was abolished. On April 12, 1953, Alexander Rankovich disclosed that a total of about 7,000 political prisoners were being held in Yugoslavia, of whom 4,500 were of the Cominform type. Among the others were many who had been jailed

[26] *The New York Times,* August 15, 1950.
[27] New York *Herald Tribune,* December 15, 1950.

during the postwar period for war offenses, etc. Of the 4,500 Stalinist Communists, 1,500 were in jail and 3,000 in labor camps.[28]

This was the state of Soviet-Yugoslav relations in March, 1953, when a new era dawned for the Soviet Union. The results of the five-year Stalin-Tito duel were often viewed as a victory of David over Goliath, but this is only half true. Certainly Yugoslavia remained intact after her courageous defiance of Moscow; she attained independence and obtained assistance from abroad. But Stalin did achieve one of his aims. The Titoist fever, which for a time seemed contagious, did not spread to the "people's democracies." Little Yugoslavia, though lost to the empire, was isolated by a tight *cordon sanitaire* from the rest of the Eastern bloc, which remained firmly within the Soviet fold. Or so, at least, it seemed in March, 1953.

3. THE "PEOPLE'S DEMOCRACIES"

Relations between the Soviet Union and the satellites developed on two levels: the official governmental level, with ties between central agencies; and the level of the Communist parties, with ties between the Central Committees, Politburo, and local units. Much of this system of relations is still in force.

On the official level the most important set of relations was that which usually exists between governments: exchange of ambassadors and embassies, attachés and consulates, trade and trade representatives. In addition there were "delegations" of various kinds, cultural exchanges, and connections with the press.

A network of widely publicized treaties tied the satellites and the Soviet Union into a single defense system. Most of these treaties, which were concluded during the last phase of the war or in the first postwar years, were called "treaties of friendship, mutual assistance and cooperation." They were directed (in Europe) against "aggression by Germany or any other state which may associate itself with Germany";[29] this formula was, at least since 1946, actually directed against Britain and the United States. In addition to the usual pledge of "noninterference in internal affairs" of the other government and

---

[28] *The New York Times*, April 13, 1953.
[29] Soviet alliances were concluded with: Czechoslovakia (December 12, 1943), Poland (April 21, 1945), Rumania (February 4, 1948), Hungary (February 18, 1948), Bulgaria (March 18, 1948). Although no identical mutual assistance treaty was concluded with the

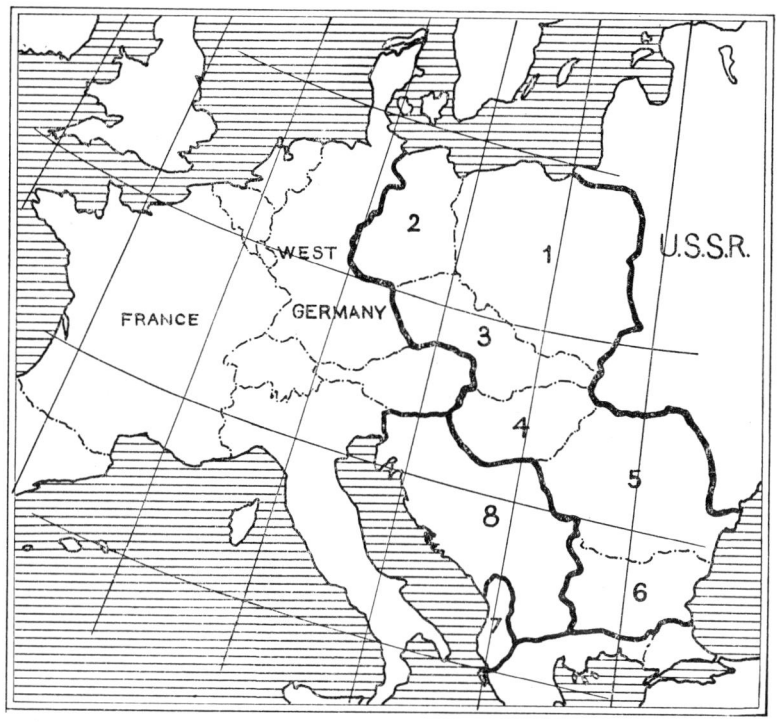

MAP 1. THE SOVIET BLOC IN EUROPE

1. Poland
2. The DDR (Soviet Zone of Germany)
3. Czechoslovakia
4. Hungary
5. Rumania
6. Bulgaria
7. Albania
8. Yugoslavia (in Soviet Bloc until 1948)

close political and economic cooperation, the treaties of alliance provided for "consultation" on all important international questions of mutual concern. Although, on paper, "consultation" was obligatory for both parties, Stalin never intended to submit his moves in foreign affairs to the scrutiny of the seven "people's democracies" of Europe or the four of Asia, and the "people's democracies" were wise enough not to make such a demand. On the other hand, for every move of a "people's democracy" in foreign affairs, "consultation" with Moscow

German Democratic Republic (DDR), such an agreement was implied in a number of bilateral agreements and statements, in particular the treaty of September 20, 1955, providing for "consultation" and "noninterference," and the statement of January 8, 1957, concerning "joint measures" against "imperialist reaction." In addition, a number of bilateral alliances between the "people's democracies" were concluded.

was a prerequisite.[30] By these means Stalin achieved an outwardly impressive unity of the "socialist bloc." In the United Nations, for example, the delegates of the satellites played roles no greater than those of the Ukraine and Byelorussia.

The Soviet ambassador in a satellite country had higher standing than a Soviet envoy in a Western capital. Both before and after Stalin's death, the Soviet ambassador, who derived his strength from the overriding powers of his government, often appeared superior to the government of the satellite; he "advised," gave orders, stopped actions or promoted them. In former enemy countries the Soviet ambassador created political parties and organized coalitions of these parties into "national fronts," "patriotic fronts," etc.[31]

In the satellite countries the Soviet ambassador maintained, as he did not in other countries, obvious and close ties with the leadership of the Communist Party. Although he met only rarely with the full Politburo, he cooperated with the first (general) secretary and the latter's closest lieutenants. In the eyes of the local Communist party he was the envoy of the "brotherly" Party, and the Soviet government has fought hard to have the dual capacity of its envoys recognized by the satellite parties and governments. Here again the Yugoslav experience revealed the Stalin pattern of the position and stature of the Soviet ambassador. When Tito and Kardelj complained about the too inquisitive behavior of the Soviet ambassador, Stalin explained the position of his envoys: Tito and Kardelj, he said, "identify the Soviet Ambassador, a responsible communist who represents the Communist Government of the USSR, with an ordinary bourgeois ambassador, a simple official of a bourgeois State, who is called upon to undermine the foundations of the Yugoslav State. . . . Do these comrades under-

---

[30] After the breach with Moscow, Yugoslavia revealed certain details of Stalin's system of "consultation": "The Government of the USSR endeavoured to have the Government of the FPRY take no step in foreign policy, even an unimportant one, without previous agreement from the Government of the USSR, whereas on the contrary, the Government of the USSR took steps in foreign policy regarding Yugoslavia and her immediate interests, not only without consultation with the Yugoslav Government, but even without informing the Government of the FPRY on the intention to take this or that step." (*White Book on Aggressive Activities by the Governments of the USSR, Poland, Czechoslovakia, Hungary, Rumania, Bulgaria, and Albania towards Yugoslavia, op. cit.*, p. 69.) (This procedure applied likewise to all the other people's democracies.)

[31] "On the direct inducement of the Soviet representatives, entirely new political parties were set up, as, for instance, the *National Demokratische Partei Deutschlands* (NDPD—National Democratic Party of Germany), the purpose of which was to organize the former Nazis. . . . Another party was the *Deutsche Bauernpartei* (German Peasant Party), which was supposed to attach the peasants to the Party." (D Papers, XYZ, July 1957, pp. 40, 41.)

stand that such an attitude towards the Soviet Ambassador means the negation of all friendly relations between the USSR and Yugoslavia? . . . How can they be suspicious of these simple elementary matters if they intend to remain in friendly relations with the Soviet Union?" [32]

The prerogatives and privileges of the Soviet ambassadors to satellite countries were far-reaching and extraordinary; they even embraced gathering of secret information by Soviet agents, including information about Communist leaders. This peculiar situation was revealed in 1955 at a plenary meeting of the Central Committee of the Communist Party of the Soviet Union, when Khrushchev and Mikoyan, attacking Molotov, told the story of Georgi Popov and Viktor Lebedev, Molotov's ambassadors to Poland, who tried to "assume leadership over the intellectual life of the country." [33] In East Germany the powers and privileges of the Soviet ambassadors were even more far-reaching. Walter Ulbricht, the general secretary of the Party, and Otto Grotewohl, the premier, "conferred" with Georgi Pushkin and Vladimir Semionov, the Soviet envoys; occasionally Pushkin met with larger groups of SED (*Sozialistische Einheitspartei Deutschlands*—Socialist Unity Party of Germany) leaders. It has been common among SED officials to take their problems to the Soviet ambassador: "*Wir wollen zu unseren russischen Freunden gehen*" (let us to go to our Russian friends) was a precept.[34]

Another network of above-ground Soviet-satellite relationships was the "Council for Economic Mutual Assistance" (CEMA) created in January, 1949, as a countermove to the American Marshall Plan. Its activities, although not entirely secret, were only rarely and scantily reported. The Mutual Assistance Organization was also intended to serve as a proof of the existence of normal relations between independent and sovereign nations.

Coordination of economic plans of the "people's democracies" and those of the Soviet Union had made little progress under Stalin. However since the combined Soviet-satellite military force depended on

---
[32] Letter of the Central Committee of the Communist Party of the Soviet Union, May 4, 1948, to the Central Committee of the Yugoslav Party (in *The Soviet-Yugoslav Dispute. Text of the Published Correspondence, op. cit.*, pp. 34–35).
[33] See below, p. 231.
[34] D Papers, July, 1957, XYZ, p. 44.

"heavy industry," and since the "people's democracies" had to become independent of "capitalist states," allotments of funds for "heavy industry" were repeatedly increased, especially after the start of the Korean War. The Secretariat of the Council for Economic Mutual Assistance, which had its seat in Moscow, was instructed to develop a general plan for its members; it was authorized to send advisers to member states, which were obligated to accept and follow their advice.

The two-year, three-year, and five-year plans that were initiated were for the purpose of accelerating the pace of industrial growth. This was by no means merely an economic issue. All elements of Communist thinking and action converged in the excitement over industrial growth: identification of military prowess with industrial capacity; the burning desire to catch up with and outdo the West in every aspect, economic and military; the belief that progress is identical with industrial progress; and the urge to impress the uncommitted nations by the prestige of economic progress in the Communist-controlled countries. Everything was to be super: superindustrialization by application of supertempos; supermilitarization by superweapons; superorder by superdiscipline; and superchallenge, superbellicosity in peacetime and superprestige for the Superleader.

A corollary to the "super" device was, of course, the "sub" factor on the other side of the social pyramid: substandard agriculture and housing, an undersupply of food, underpayment, economic privation—this was the price to be paid for "progress." The sub factors were rarely discussed and were glossed over in the press, but they were facts of common knowledge.[35]

[35] On January 7, 1933, during the early days of Soviet "industrialization" Stalin told the Central Committee of his Party: "We are told: This is all very well; many new factories have been built, and the foundations for industrialization have been laid; but it would have been far better to have renounced the policy of industrialization, the policy of expanding the production of means of production, or at least to have relegated it to the background, so as to produce more cotton fabrics, shoes, clothing and other goods for mass consumption.

"It is true that the output of goods for mass consumption was less than the amount required, and this creates certain difficulties. But, then, we must realise and take into account where such a policy of relegating the task of industrialization to the background would have led us. Of course, out of the 1,500 million rubles in foreign currency that we spent during this period on equipment for our heavy industries, we could have set aside a half for importing cotton, shoes and clothing. But we would not have a tractor industry or an automobile industry; we would not have anything like a big iron and steel industry; we would not have metal for the manufacture of machinery—and we would remain unarmed while encircled by capitalist countries armed with modern technique. . . .

"The Party, as it were, spurred the country on and hastened its progress. . . .

"Finally, the Party had to put an end, in the shortest possible space of time, to the weakness of the country in the sphere of defense." (Stalin, *Works, op. cit.,* 1956, vol. 13, pp. 184-87.)

The "People's Democracies"

During Stalin's last years the program of industrialization in the "people's democracies" called for an acceleration of pace. Hungary, Czechoslovakia, Poland, and Rumania increased their planned industrial output in 1950–51; in 1952 East Germany followed suit. Everywhere real wages remained low, industries manufacturing consumer goods were neglected, agriculture had a low priority, and tension was mounting.

Aside from the general pattern of government-to-government relations there were also the ties between three leading Soviet state agencies—the army, the police, and foreign affairs—and their counterparts in the satellites.

The armies of the satellites were an area of visible or invisible but direct Soviet control. In Poland, Soviet Marshal Konstantin Rokossovsky was the head of the military;[36] in Hungary the military chief was Moscow-born General Istvan Bata; in Czechoslovakia higher posts of command were given to Russians. For all practical purposes the armies of the "people's democracies" were, according to Stalin's great design, to act as parts of the Soviet army in both defense and offense. In this way, and long before the Warsaw Pact made it public, the Soviet government had a substantial auxiliary force outside the Soviet frontiers. The Yugoslavs, threatened by pro-Soviet neighbors, fearful of the menace of Stalin and therefore alert to any expansion of the forces of the satellites, estimated the strength of the satellite armies in 1951–52 at a little short of 2,000,000; other estimates put it at from 1,000,000 to 2,000,000, not counting East Germany.

The three former German allies, Hungary, Rumania, and Bulgaria, were encouraged to transgress the limits set to their military forces by the peace treaties. Hungary had over 200,000 in her army, which was limited by treaty to a maximum of 65,000; Rumania, limited to a maximum of 138,000, had 275,000; Bulgaria, limited to 65,000, had 200,000; East Germany had begun to build up her army in 1951. Poland and Czechoslovakia, former allies and therefore not restricted by treaties, had created large military forces—300,000 in the former and 220,000

---

[36] "Rokossowski does not mix in Warsaw Party policies. He rarely attends the sessions of the Politburo and at the same time he hardly ever informs [President] Bierut on military matters. He is in direct contact with the Soviet General Staff from which he gets instructions and to which he reports. He is Moscow's special envoy to Poland, and organizationally completely independent from the PZPR [Polish United Workers' Party]. ("The Swiatlo Story," in *News from behind the Iron Curtain,* New York, vol. 4, no. 3, March, 1955, p. 8.)

in the latter. The military equipment of the satellite armies was partly Russian, as were the army instructors, and some of the officers had come from Russia.

Close, though invisible, ties connected the police ministries of the Soviet Union and the satellites. In the latter, the new police agencies were organized with the help of Soviet advisers and on the Soviet pattern based on the huge Soviet experience in fighting the "internal enemy." A number of trials of "foreign agents" and "American spies" took place in the "people's democracies" during 1949–52, all of them carried out with the help and under the guidance of Soviet investigators and advisers; some were engineered on Soviet initiative. Imprisonment without trial was a widespread practice. Lavrenti Beria, Stalin's Chief of Internal Affairs, in his relations with the satellite police did not have to go through cumbersome Communist Party channels to give advice and orders; he was in direct contact with the equivalents of the MGB in the satellites. In Czechoslovakia "the Ministry of State Security is the only branch of State Administration which works directly with corresponding institutions in the satellite states." [37] In Poland "the squeeze is exerted by a group of Soviet advisers, so-called, headed by the chief adviser, General Lalin." [38] In East Germany "the Soviets have built up the State Security on their own pattern; they control it and lead it according to their own principles and there are no indications that they will give up their leading role." [39]

Beria's word was an order except in cases involving arrest and punishment of supreme local Communist leaders. In such cases the general secretary of the local party sometimes had a say.

On the whole, political repression in the satellites did not reach the high mark that it did in the Soviet Union; purges, though carried out, were far less sweeping and bloody than in Russia. Terrorism never approached the Yagoda-Yezhov peak. In the case, for example, of Wladyslaw Gomulka, the Polish leader was arrested and imprisoned, but he was still alive after Stalin's death, contrary to the advice of Moscow. Sympathetic feeling for the West, after five, six, or seven years of Soviet-satellite relations, was strong among the non-Com-

---

[37] Bedrich Brügel, former Czech diplomat, in *International Affairs*, London, January, 1951, p. 35.
[38] "The Swiatlo Story," *op. cit.*, p. 4.
[39] D Papers, File G, July, 1957.

The "People's Democracies"

munist strata of the populations; sympathy for Titoism, although suppressed and concealed, was widespread in Communist circles.

In foreign affairs, and especially in relations with the West and with Tito, there was direct Soviet guidance. In no other area of government activity was the guidance as thorough and consistent as in the relations of the satellites with the "capitalist" nations. In this area Russian predominance was absolute, and no deviation was tolerated. As a result, the foreign ministers of the satellites rapidly lost their individuality and foreign affairs no longer occupied a prominent place in the deliberations of the satellite regimes. Discussion was futile. ". . . questions of the international situation and external policies," wrote Imre Nagy, former premier of Hungary, "played an insignificant role in the politics of the Party and the government. . . ."[40] In Poland, "the Ministry of Foreign Affairs did not play any role at all."[41] A minor exception was the relations between the satellites themselves; in this field there developed, behind the scenes, controversy, tension, and conflict, as for instance in the relations between Poland and East Germany[42] and Poland and Czechoslovakia.[43]

The party-to-party relations between the Soviet Union and the satellites have been less evident but more important than the official governmental ties, since the Communist Party is superior to the government in a Communist-ruled nation. The most important avenue of communication in this system of party relations was the summit meetings, generally held in Moscow, of the leadership of the Communist Party of the Soviet Union with the leadership of the "people's democracies." In the order of business of these summit conferences first place was accorded to the nomination and selection of Communist Party leaders (secretaries) for the satellites, and sometimes also of prime ministers, when these were not identical with the Party secretaries. Because the political course in the people's democracies was determined by one, two, or perhaps three persons, the selection of such persons was tantamount to entrusting the affairs of the country to their care; the selection was tantamount to the appointment of a viceroy.

---

[40] *Imre Nagy on Communism: In Defense of the New Course*, New York, Frederick A. Praeger, 1957, p. 38.
[41] D Papers, File P, June 13, 1957.
[42] *Ibid.*, November 2, 1957.
[43] *Imre Nagy on Communism*, op. cit., p. 240.

Whether and how a people's democracy would continue normal collaboration with and adherence to the Soviet-guided bloc of nations, whether it would follow Soviet instructions and advice, support the Soviet foreign-political course, and move toward "Communism" in the Stalinist sense, depended on the personal qualities and political inclinations, loyalty, and experience of the future satellite leader. Leadership of the Soviet sphere in Europe lay in the hands of a group of some ten or fifteen men, Russians and non-Russians, who were controlled by Stalin. This body of leaders had to be reliable, able, and totally pro-Stalin. Stalin was fortunate in the selection and formation of this cohort out of the stock of East European Communist activists who had, over the decades, proved their ability and their loyalty: Rakoszi, Bierut, Gheorghiu-Dej, Gottwald, Ulbricht, Chervenkov, all of whom remained loyal after Tito defected. Kostov, Rajk, Slansky, and a few others were weeded out.

Every journey to Moscow of the leaders of the satellite parties and their collaborators, both during the Stalin era and after Stalin's death, represented a page out of unofficial Soviet foreign policy and at the same time a page out of the history of Soviet control over Eastern Europe. In the case of Poland, for example, it was ". . . Bierut who goes to Moscow to get the instructions; often he is accompanied by Berman and Minc. This does not mean that he does not from time to time take along other members of the Warsaw Politburo, particularly when matters to be passed on fall within the competence of Ochab, Mazur or one of the others. However, Bierut is the only recipient of the fundamental political decisions."[44] Rakoszi of Hungary and Gottwald of Czechoslovakia were also regular visitors of Stalin; contrary to Rakoszi's advice, Moscow appointed Imre Nagy premier of Hungary shortly after Stalin's death.[45] Meetings of Ulbricht, Gottwald, and other leaders with Stalin were likewise frequent. "Ulbricht was very often in Moscow, conferred with Stalin, Suslov and others. Also elaborated in Moscow was the political course of the West German Communist Party, the so-called KPD *(Kommunistische Partei Deutschlands).*"[46]

Regular liaison between the Soviet and satellite parties was cen-

---

[44] "The Swiatlo Story," *loc. cit.*
[45] *Imre Nagy on Communism, op. cit.*, p. 250.
[46] D Papers, XYZ, July, 1957, p. 30.

The "People's Democracies"

tered in the Foreign Departments of the Central Committees which were mentioned before; this network may be viewed as the successor to the Comintern. Even before the dissolution of the Comintern, the Soviet Foreign Department of the Central Committee was the guiding force in the international organization. After the dissolution, and with the emergence of the people's democracies, these Foreign Departments acquired greater importance. As the Communist parties of the satellites established their large party offices, the Foreign Departments served as the direct link to Moscow's Central Committee and to its general secretary.

In Moscow the Foreign Department of the Central Committee was organized on the model of a large foreign office. Its supreme chief was Stalin; Malenkov and Zhdanov, as Stalin's deputies, served successively as heads of the department. The functions performed by the OMS (*Otdel Mezhdunarodnykh Svyazei*—Department of International Liaison) in the Comintern era—providing couriers, issuing orders, money, and arms, and making appointments—were now performed by the Foreign Department of the Central Committee.

The regular daily work of the Foreign Departments of the satellite countries was routine: correspondence with the "brotherly parties," scheduling of meetings, gathering of information and literature, dispatching of delegations to one another. Dispatching of secret agents was also the responsibility of the Foreign Departments. In East Berlin, for example, "this department directs the collaboration of the SED with the Communist parties abroad, especially with the CPSU and the Communist parties of the satellites." The department publishes a bulletin, *Aus der Internationalen Arbeiterbewegung* (The International Labor Movement).[47] In Poland, "the Department of Foreign Relations of the Central Committee was primarily occupied with espionage abroad and with supplying of financial means to parties abroad (for instance to the Italian Communists, and also to the Nenni group)."[48]

The technical equipment for maintaining the liaison between the Soviet and satellite Foreign Departments of the Central Committees included:

---

[47] Carola Stern, *Porträt einer bolschewistischen Partei: Entwicklung, Funktion und Situation des SED* (Portrait of a Bolshevik Party: Development, Function and Situation of the SED), Köln, Verlag für Politik und Wirtschaft, 1957, p. 341.
[48] D Papers, File P, June 13, 1957, p. 2.

First, the special communication lines, the so-called V-Ch, which provide for complete secrecy. The V-Ch network extending to the capitals of all European and Far Eastern "people's democracies," in particular the costly equipment, is supervised and guarded by Soviet security officers.[49]

Second, the Party's own couriers (additional to those of the Foreign Office), who traveled between the satellites and the Soviet Central Committee, and vice versa. In urgent cases, the courier used aviation facilities; otherwise he traveled by train.

Third, visits to Moscow by officers of local Communist parties, and vice versa.

Fourth, *Pravda* of Moscow, in which the skillful reader could find important hints and advice. The text is teletyped to the satellites during the night and is in the hands of the local leaders even before it appears in Moscow.[50]

Foreign policy, on the other hand, is a function of the official Foreign Office; it is not among the main responsibilities of the Foreign Department of the Central Committee.

At the time of Stalin's death the Soviet bloc was far from being a complete success. This peculiar kind of a supernational organization, the members of which had only ostensible sovereignty and were actually in subordination to Moscow, and which was regarded as the prototype of a growing alliance, was the only international Communist state formation possible in the climate of the 1940's. It was the only possible Communist solution of the vexing problem of empire-building. It was not a happy solution, however, and subsequent years revealed the shortcomings. Dissatisfaction and instability pervaded East Europe. A mere breeze could open the gates to new political movements.

The breeze was soon felt.

[49] *Ibid.*, November 2, 1957.
[50] *Ibid.*

CHAPTER 3

GERMANY: THE BIG ISSUE

The background of the present stage in Soviet-German relations is a two-century history of alliances and wars between the two expanding nations. Russia, growing and moving consistently to the West, approached and then advanced into the crucial zone of Central Eastern Europe inhabited by Poles, Lithuanians, and other nationalities, while Prussia, bordering that area on the west, was likewise assuming great-power stature. These political and geographical realities, along with the power ambitions of both of them, lay at the root of the intermittent conflicts and efforts at cooperation. The conflicts resulted in human losses that exceeded those of any other series of wars in history; their alliances sometimes resulted in aggrandizement for both nations on the largest scale. The Russian-Prussian-Austrian triumvirate was for a long period the basis of European order. At the end of the nineteenth century, when Germany was growing more aggressive and belligerent and Russia had joined France in an anti-German alliance, close ties still bound the sovereigns of St. Petersburg and Berlin. The ties lasted until a war broke out in which Germany and Russia and the sovereigns of both were losers. The new weak Germany and Soviet Russia, now, as it seemed, secondary powers, tried to help each other out of their postwar misery. Their impotence and their common antagonism toward the West produced new ties and collaboration between them. The ties were again broken, this time by Hitler in 1934–39, but a new *rapprochement* was created when Hitler announced: "In historically long periods of the past it was proved that the peoples of these two biggest states of Europe were most happy when they lived in friendship." [1]

It would be an oversimplification to say that in regard to Ger-

[1] Speech of October 6, 1939.

many, or even in general, Soviet policy trod the prerevolutionary paths; on the contrary, the new era brought substantial changes, although the attraction to Germany remained. Birthplace of Marxism, fatherland of the orthodox and rapidly growing revolutionary (so it seemed) socialist movement, the most industrially advanced country of the continent, Germany appeared to Russian Marxists as the most likely initiator and leader of the imminent world revolution; England and France, monsters of colonialism and imperialism, were still, as in the old times, objects of Soviet hatred. Stalin had inherited and embraced Soviet pro-German trends as a component part of Leninism. His remarks to Emil Ludwig in an interview on December 13, 1931, were not the product of a momentary mood, but expressed deep conviction. Ludwig remarked that everywhere in Russia he had observed "an extraordinary respect for everything American, even a worship of everything American." "Is this correct?" Ludwig asked. "You exaggerate," Stalin replied, "we have no special respect for everything American. . . . If one is to speak about our sympathies for any nation or, to be more exact, for the majority of any nation, one would, of course, speak about our sympathies for the Germans. There can be no comparison between these sympathies and our feelings for the Americans."

At that time—the interwar era—Moscow was impressed by Germany's rapid industrial rehabilitation and newly acquired impact on world affairs. In her universities and research institutions Germany was devoting closer and more attentive study to Russia than to any other country. Even German criticism of Soviet affairs and German antagonism to Soviet theory and practices impressed Moscow more than did the compliments and often naïve enthusiasm of the Western world.

Stalin was convinced that Germany's defeat in World War II did not mean that she had been permanently reduced to a second-rank power, and he predicted her complete rehabilitation:

> To think that these countries [Germany and Japan] will not try to get on their feet again, will not try to smash the U.S. "regime," and force their way to independent development, is to believe in miracles. . . .
> After the First World War it was similarly believed that Germany had been definitely put out of action, just as certain comrades

Germany: The Big Issue

now believe that Japan and Germany have been definitely put out of action. Then, too, it was said and clamoured in the press that the United States had put Europe on rations; that Germany would never rise to her feet again, and that there would be no more wars between capitalist countries. . . .[2]

This attitude of Stalin's toward Germany contrasted with his negative view of the West, and especially America. In 1952, when Germany was in a low state and the United States was at the peak of world influence, Stalin had

> . . . a much higher estimate of the European nations and of the British than of the US: He found it difficult to take Americans seriously and seemed to derive a jovial pleasure from his teasing diplomacy.[3]

This attitude toward Germany and the United States was not only a constant element of Stalinism but continued after the dictator's death and greatly influenced Soviet policy in the 1950's. An eminent and intelligent European diplomat who spent some time in Moscow in the 1950's summarized his impressions, gained from conversations with Soviet leaders, in these words:

> Germany is the only nation which is both esteemed and feared in Moscow. As far as the Americans are concerned, the Soviet leaders somehow don't take them quite seriously. They are aware, of course, of the high American standard of living and of their technical achievements, but in political affairs they consider the Americans lax and loose. Mikoyan talked much about American shortcomings. We asked him which of the nations he considers more important in international affairs. Without hesitation he answered: Germany.[4]

Since the start of the war in 1941, Stalin's designs for Germany were, like the plans of the Western powers, altered more than once.

The first Soviet blueprint of the future Germany, in effect from 1941 to 1945, envisaged dismemberment of the enemy country. Long before the United States and Britain had accepted the details of the future partition, Stalin had formed some basic ideas about postwar Germany. As early as December, 1941, when Anthony Eden, the Brit-

---
[2] *New Times,* Moscow, no. 44, October 29, 1952, Supplement, pp. 14–15.
[3] "Nenni and Stalin," Stalin interview with Pietro Nenni in *New Statesman and Nation,* September 20, 1952.
[4] D Papers, XYZ, July, 1957, pp. 62–63.

ish Foreign Secretary, visited Moscow (this was a week after the United States entered the war), Stalin came out with far-reaching plans for new frontiers in which partition of Germany was implied,[5] while Winston Churchill still viewed these issues as lying in "a future which is uncertain and probably remote."

"To raise such issues publicly now," Churchill said, "would only be to rally all Germans round Hitler." Stalin realized the force of this argument; he not only refrained from "raising publicly" the issue of Germany's dismemberment in wartime, but went much further. In his public statements he appealed to German national feelings and against Hitler: "History teaches that Hitlers come and go, but the German people and the German state remain."[6] At the same time that he was creating patriotic German societies (unions) among prisoners of war, Stalin continued to press for the territorial partitioning of the enemy nation. Stalin will insist that Germany be broken up into a number of states, Eden reported in March, 1943, following a recent contact with Moscow;[7] Maxim Litvinov and Ivan Maisky, the Soviet ambassadors in Washington and London, confirmed that Germany "must be broken up." At the Teheran Conference

> Stalin appeared to regard all measures proposed by either the President or Churchill for the subjugation and for the control of Germany as inadequate. He on various occasions sought to induce the President or the Prime Minister to go further in expressing their views as to the stringency of the measures which should be applied to Germany. He appeared to have no faith in the possibility of the reform of the German people and spoke bitterly of the attitude of the German workers in the war against the Soviet Union. . . .
>
> He said that there would always be a strong urge on the part of the Germans to unite and that the whole purpose of any international organization must be to neutralize their tendency by applying economic and other measures including, if necessary, force.[8]

In contrast to the attitude in Moscow, Britain and the United

[5] Winston S. Churchill, *The Grand Alliance*, Boston, Houghton Mifflin Company, 1950, pp. 628–30. A well-documented analysis of Stalin's attitude is given by Boris Meissner in his article "Stalin und die Oder-Neisse Linie," in *Osteuropa*, Stuttgart, no. 1, October, 1951, pp. 2–11.

[6] Stalin's Order of the Day to the Red Army, February 23, 1942.

[7] Robert E. Sherwood, *Roosevelt and Hopkins*, New York, Harper & Brothers, 1948, pp. 711–13.

[8] *Ibid.*, pp. 782, 798.

Germany: The Big Issue 49

States vacillated between various plans for postwar Germany. Churchill and Eden at first opposed partition; yielding to President Roosevelt, who was himself uncertain and hesitant, Churchill even signed the Quebec decision incorporating the severe Morgenthau Plan for the elimination of certain industries, wrecking of mines, and "converting Germany into a country primarily agricultural and pastoral in character." In Washington, Henry L. Stimson and Cordell Hull opposed Morgenthau, Harry Dexter White, and Harry Hopkins, while President Roosevelt vacillated between the proposals.[9]

At the Yalta Conference, Stalin, again the driving force, faced a hesitant Roosevelt and even more reluctant British leaders; nevertheless, the Yalta formula called for the dismemberment of Germany as a "requisite for future peace and security."[10] However, the dismemberment of the country as it actually developed bore only a faint resemblance to the wartime designs.

The main changes took place in Germany's eastern provinces, in which Russia, naturally, was most interested. Here cessions of territory occurred in accord with Soviet schemes. The Third Reich, of course, lost areas annexed in 1938–39 from Czechoslovakia and Poland; other territories, likewise claimed by Poland, were turned over to the new Polish authorities; and Austria regained independence. To this extent the dismemberment meant the restoration of the prewar status, with some modifications. In addition, however, the Soviet Union annexed a new territory in East Prussia (with a population of about 1,300,000 in 1939), while the rest of the province was turned over to Poland.

Most important, however, was the other part of the dismember-

[9] Henry L. Stimson and McGeorge Bundy, *On Active Service in Peace and War*, New York, Harper & Brothers, 1947, pp. 570–83; also *The Memoirs of Cordell Hull*, New York, The Macmillan Company, 1948, vol. 2, pp. 1233–4, 1265, 1604–8. Winston S. Churchill stated: "The so-called Morgenthau Plan, which I had not time to examine in detail, seems to have carried these ideas to an ultra-logical conclusion. Even if it had been practicable I do not think it would have been right to depress Germany's standard of life in such a way. . . . All this was of course subject to the full consideration of the War Cabinet, and in the event, with my full accord, the idea of 'pastoralizing' Germany did not survive." (*Triumph and Tragedy*, Boston, Houghton Mifflin Company, 1953, p. 157.)

[10] Edward R. Stettinius, *Roosevelt and the Russians*, New York, Doubleday & Company, Inc., 1949, pp. 122–4, 136–9, 162–3, 280, 344. In the end it was decided not to publish the program of dismemberment only because "it might increase enemy resistance." On Stalin's attitude see also Herbert Feis, *Churchill Roosevelt Stalin: The War They Waged and the Peace They Sought*, Princeton, Princeton University Press, 1957, pp. 124, 126, 619, and Winston S. Churchill, *The Hinge of Fate*, Boston, Houghton Mifflin Company, 1950, p. 803.

ment—the emergence of the Soviet occupation zone as a political unit and as the embryo of a state formation; the area of the zone was 41,645 square miles and its population, about a quarter of that of all Germany, amounted to 17,300,000. In addition, the eastern "sector" of Berlin (1,550 square miles and 1,588,000 population), too, came under Soviet occupation.

This was as far as military operations could extend Soviet rule; the demarcation line cutting Europe in two delineated the limits of Stalin's immediate successes. Further progress in the west and south of Allied-controlled Europe was possible only in the wake of Communist movements which Moscow expected would break out.

It appeared likely that in France and Italy, where the Communist leaders were members of the newly formed governments, "people's democracies" on the Eastern pattern might soon emerge; in West Germany, too, the revival of a Communist movement was expected. It seemed probable that the East-West frontier line would soon be removed and that the Soviet orbit would engulf more of the whole continent. If this should happen, the new leaders of East Germany would be called upon to carry the Communist banner to the West, and their partisans abroad would take over in the countries beyond the Rhine.

The program of a "dismemberment," which would antagonize all classes and all parties, was now obviously outdated. Germany was now a potential ally in the event the West should resist the expected social and political transformation of France and Italy. "Dismemberment" as a slogan had to be replaced by "reunification" as the first step toward a both new and very old Russian-German type of alliance against the West. Three months after the Yalta Conference Stalin announced that "the Soviet Union does not intend to dismember Germany." [11]

The United States, supported by Britain and France, more than once in 1945–47 suggested to Stalin a treaty calling for long-range demilitarization of Germany. A draft of the so-called "Byrnes Treaty" was submitted to the conference of the four foreign ministers in April 1946, but Molotov "had no idea of discussing the treaty in a serious manner, but was simply looking for excuses for delay." [12] A year later, at the Moscow Conference, George Marshall, the new United States

---

[11] Stalin's victory speech, May 9, 1945.
[12] James F. Byrnes, *Speaking Frankly*, New York, Harper & Brothers, 1947, p. 175.

Germany: The Big Issue 51

Secretary of State, again proposed a twenty-five- or forty-year treaty. Molotov's objections "were so irrelevant and absurd they indicated a deliberate intent to make certain they could not be accepted." [13]

The Soviet Union, according to the new contention, was Germany's friend. "Neutralization of Germany," a program that Moscow was emphatically to demand a few years later, was now rejected. While Stalin and Molotov were looking for a way to turn down the "neutralization" program, Walter Ulbricht was free to disclose the basic idea: Germany must march together with the Soviet Union; neutrality is unacceptable. "The slogan of neutrality comes from the offices of the American agency"; "those who want to maintain peace must join in the fight against the policy of neutrality." [14] Said Molotov:

> ... Remaining a united state, Germany will continue to be an important factor in world trade—which corresponds to the interests of other nations as well. On the other hand, a policy of annihilating Germany as a state, or of agrarianizing her and wiping out her principal industrial centers, would turn her into a breeding ground of dangerous sentiments of revenge, and would play into the hands of the German reactionaries and deprive Europe of tranquility and stable peace.[15]

An integrated "democratic nation," which was the Soviet program for Germany, was repeatedly advanced at international conferences, in the press, and on the radio. The most perfect form of democracy, in the Soviet view, was a "people's democracy," and the Soviet government did not conceal its intention to see such a "people's democracy" erected for the whole of Germany. On April 2, 1947, Molotov explained how the representative body of the German "people's democracy," a kind of parliament, was to be organized: like the representative body proposed for Korea, it would embrace "all democratic parties," trade unions, and other "anti-Nazi organizations." These "mass organizations" (of which, of course, any number could be created overnight) would ensure a majority for the pro-Soviet political programs. Reunification meant the merger of the Eastern with the Western zones under East German guidance. A new German state, Moscow-oriented and opposed to the West, was to emerge; but so

---
[13] *Ibid.*, p. 176.
[14] Quoted in Boris Meissner, *Russland, die Westmächte und Deutschland* (Russia, the Western Powers and Germany), Hamburg, H. H. Nölke Verlag, 1953, pp. 222–224.
[15] V. M. Molotov, *Problems of Foreign Policy: Speeches and Statements April 1945–November 1948*, Moscow, Foreign Languages Publishing House, 1949, pp. 64–65.

long as the international situation and popular attitudes in Germany would prevent such a formation, the East zone would have to be conserved as a state unit. This combination of actual adherence to Germany's partition with an extensive propaganda for reunification was the pattern for many years.

Stalin greeted the formation of the "German Democratic Republic" (DDR): "The formation of a German democratic and peace-loving republic is a turning point in the history of Europe. There can be no doubt that the existence of a peace-loving democratic Germany, side by side with the existence of the peace-loving Soviet Union, excludes the possibility of new wars in Europe.... If these two peoples resolve to fight for peace with the same concentration of their forces with which they waged the war, then peace in Europe can be considered sure." [16]

A shift from violent anti-Germanism, from "dismemberment," to "unification" and the prospect of an alliance was easier in Russia than in the West, where war wounds were still hurting; in particular, France, ruled and maltreated by Germany for four years, could not digest the idea of *rapprochement* with the wartime enemy; the inclusion of West Germany into a Western alliance proved more difficult than the signing of the Soviet-DDR agreements and the rebuilding of a German army in the Soviet zone. The Soviet government was in a position to make abundant use of this psychologically natural but politically unreasonable reluctance of the West.

On November 11, 1949, the three Allied high commissioners signed an agreement "to prevent with all possible means the formation of German military forces." Speaking for the West, Robert Schuman, the French foreign minister, protested in July, 1949:

"Germany in the Atlantic Pact? Never!" and exclaimed, "Germany has no army and shall have none. She has no arms and will not have them."

Jules Moch, French Socialist Minister of the Interior, "speaking for himself," told a public meeting on August 30, 1949:

"If it were proposed to integrate Germany in the European Council on an equal footing with other countries, and to allow her to arm and then betray her allies, we should be madmen if we agreed to it." [17]

---

[16] *Pravda*, October 14, 1949.
[17] *New Times*, Moscow, no. 51, December 19, 1951, p. 11.

Germany: The Big Issue

Addressing the Bundestag on December 3, 1949, newly elected Chancellor Konrad Adenauer "most emphatically" rejected German rearmament.

In the summer of 1948 there appeared the first formations of the Eastern zone's military force, the nucleus of the future *"Bereitschaften."* In 1950–51 the German military force of the Eastern zone numbered 50,000 to 60,000 men, in addition to about 17,000 in the frontier guards. Stalin and Molotov continued their demand for the "demilitarization" of the, in fact, demilitarized country; the essence of the Soviet demand was a four-power control agency for the Ruhr region "to prevent the repetition of a German aggression."

The establishment of the DDR did not imply, at least in the beginning, any important change in the situation in the Eastern zone. The policy of the DDR was dependent on instructions from Moscow, and its Ministry of State Security was under the control of Moscow's MGB. Large numbers of Eastern-zone industrial units were operated under Soviet management, and the emerging military force was Soviet-controlled. The SED (*Sozialistische Einheitspartei*—the Communist Party after its prescribed merger with the Social-Democratic Party of the Eastern zone), under Walter Ulbricht, became one of the loyal parties in the Communist family. More than any other Eastern government, at least in those formative years, the Pieck-Grotewohl regime deserved the name of satellite.

The Berlin blockade in the second half of 1948 was the culmination of the Soviet drive to the West. With the Soviet retreat in Berlin, which was followed by other failures in Europe (Greece, Yugoslavia), Soviet attention gradually turned toward the Far East, where China, an ally of enigmatic loyalty, was rising to new high stature.

The outbreak of the Korean War initiated the third phase of Soviet postwar policy with respect to Germany. This phase lasted until Stalin's death in March, 1953.

The events in the Far East had sounded an alarm in America and Europe; it appeared possible that Stalin would apply his Korean strategy to a divided Germany, and that the great war would start before the West, demobilized and occupied with other ventures, was ready effectively to resist. From that time on the issue of German rearmament dominated the international scene.

Since 1948–50, as the feeling grew that Germany's military contribution was badly needed, the approach to the solution of the problem appeared like an effort at squaring the circle: the task was to direct German strength against the East without at the same time making Germany strong in general. It was a paradoxical situation. The Western powers lost four years trying to solve the puzzle.

The French plan of rearming Germany, which was accepted by the other Western powers in 1950, called for the incorporation of the future German military force into a "European army" in which the French would have more troops than any other single nation. The plan, which was accepted in principle by NATO on December 19, 1950, was an intricate, almost impossible project. The structure of the multilingual armies and staffs and their relationship to the various sovereign governments, problems of supplies and armaments, relations with NATO, and scores of other issues were solved, on paper, with great ingenuity in the course of intensive study and discussions, but there was no conviction that the plan would work. In addition, Britain refused to have her armies included in the collective force, and France reserved the right to remove her divisions to points outside of Europe, for instance to Africa, should the military need arise. The plan was unpopular in France itself, was rejected by the strong German Social-Democratic Party, and in Britain was received, by British labor at least, without enthusiasm.

Because of a multitude of disagreements on partial issues, the preliminary negotiations on a plan of German rearmament dragged out over eighteen months, and it was not until May 26, 1952, that the Western powers signed, in Bonn, their *"General-Vertrag"* with the German Federal Republic as a substitute for a peace treaty. The following day the treaty of the European Defense Community was signed in Paris. German Minister Theodor Blank ("Adviser on Security Questions") announced two weeks later that within two years, that is, in 1954, a German "contingent" of 500,000 would become a part of the European army.

Before the European Defense Community Treaty had been ratified by all of the signers, Stalin died. In 1954, France refused to ratify, and EDC broke down.

Taking advantage of the delays in forming the European army, the Soviet government proceeded to carry out a consistent "campaign"

Germany: The Big Issue 55

against the rearming of Germany. The first official Soviet statement in this campaign was in the form of an ominous diplomatic note addressed to the three Western powers on October 19, 1950. The Soviet Union, the note stated, "will not tolerate" the recreation of a German army in West Germany because the formation of a West German army "stands in utter contradiction to the ruling of the Potsdam Conference on the demilitarization of Germany"; therefore

> The Soviet Government states that it will not tolerate such measures of the Governments of the United States, Great Britain and France aimed at reviving the German regular army in Western Germany.[18]

An exchange of notes followed in which the Soviet government charged its wartime allies with belligerent plans; in special notes to France and Britain, Moscow accused the two governments of violating the treaties of alliance. Both sides agreed to a conference; a preconference was held in the spring of 1951 for the purpose of preparing the agenda. After seventy-four meetings, the conference closed without having arrived at any agreements.

The Soviet press followed the developments closely and violently attacked the new "Hitlerite *Wehrmacht*." The German people, the Soviet press reported, refuse rearmament and resist; the French are indignant because they will have to stand under the command of Hitlerite generals; war criminals are being released from prisons to serve as generals in the new army and to command the military forces of the other nations.

Reunification of Germany was at the same time emphasized as one of the main points of the Soviet's positive program; the Soviet government was trying to create the impression that, in contrast to Russia and the DDR, the Western powers were not eager to see Germany united. But the Soviet program for German unity was actually conditioned on rule by a Communist government, at least in one part of Germany, and unification was considered possible by extension of the DDR over the whole of Germany or, if this was not feasible, by a confederation of the two Germanys on an equal footing, despite their unequal size, population, and importance. An all-German government with a guaranteed 50 per cent pro-Russian membership (and probably

[18] *The New York Times*, October 20, 1950.

a few vacillating members from West Germany) could serve to detach West Germany from the West. According to the Soviet scheme, a peace treaty would be signed with this all-German government.

Rejecting "confederation" in the Ulbricht sense and wanting a new German government to emerge out of a popular election, the three Western powers, with Bonn in accord, demanded free elections in both parts of the country as a prerequisite to the conclusion of a peace treaty. Moscow could not reject this demand outright, and in 1951–52 the issue of democratic elections throughout Germany became an item in diplomatic exchanges, in the press, and in political statements. During a United Nations session in January, 1952, an East German delegation brought to Paris a plan of German reunification based on free elections; Andrei Vyshinsky talked to Western visitors about the conditions under which a German election would be conducted.[19] Finally, Moscow, in diplomatic exchanges, came out officially though not sincerely for "free elections."

With the conclusion of a Western "Contractual Agreement" and the founding of the European Defense Community near, after years of debate and procrastination, the Soviet government increased its efforts to have the project rejected. The European Defense Community (EDC) provided not only for a European army but also for the rearming of Germany and the inclusion of her future twelve divisions in a total of forty-three European divisions. The disagreements which for almost two years had divided the Western powers now appeared to have been definitely settled, and the specter of a large, united, well-armed European-American anti-Soviet military force was becoming a reality. All of this took place in the "Korean climate" of 1952, when Soviet charges of "bacteriological war" and "American atrocities" were being disseminated and when the Soviet hate-America campaign was at one of its highest points.

Moscow initiated a new round of diplomatic notes to the West proposing the already well-known program of a peace treaty with a unified, or at least confederated, Germany. The March 10, 1952, Soviet draft of a peace treaty provided for the withdrawal of Allied forces from Germany one year after the signing of the treaty, for guarantees of "freedom of activity" of "democratic parties and organizations in Germany," prohibition of antidemocratic organizations, rehabilitation

[19] *Ibid.*, May 28, 1952.

Germany: The Big Issue

of former Nazis (except those convicted by courts), and limitation of new German military forces to the size of defense needs. Germany's territory, under the Soviet-proposed treaty, would remain as "determined by the Potsdam agreements" (meaning that those areas that had been annexed to Russia, Poland, and Czechoslovakia would not be returned). As to the foreign policy of the future Germany, the proposed treaty provided that "Germany shall pledge herself not to enter into any coalition or military alliance directed against any country whose armed forces took part in the war with Germany." The latter provision meant that Germany could not join NATO or any other Western political community, and amounted to a pledge of permanent neutrality—the embryo of the set of ideas which, some years later, developed into the program of "disengagement."

The three Western powers countered with a plan of German unification based on free elections followed by the convening of a German assembly to constitute the nation and organize the new government.[20]

At this juncture the Soviet government made its last effort to torpedo EDC: in the hope that the prospect of a peaceful unification of Germany would help to postpone or even defeat the separate Western solution of the German problem, it agreed to "free elections." But the three Western powers, aware of the character of "free elections" as conducted in the Soviet bloc, proposed, as a prerequisite, an investigation to determine whether political conditions in Germany made "honest elections" possible. This proposal was unacceptable to Moscow. Inspection by foreign governments, Moscow countered, would be humiliating to a free nation. The Soviet government, protector of all peoples against offense and degradation, would not agree to inspection even if it were to be carried out by small nations not involved in the dispute. On August 23 Moscow suggested the convening, in October, of a four-power conference on the Soviet-proposed "peace treaty." The suggestion was not accepted. Negotiations again reached an impasse.

The Soviet government had never, either before or after Stalin's death, agreed to what the West expected from a German election—a unified parliament, ruled by the majority of its members, and, con-

[20] The Western notes were dated March 25, May 5, and July 10; the Soviet notes, April 9, May 24, August 23, and September 23.

sequently, undoubtedly a pro-Western regime for the whole of Germany. In the Soviet view, the real result of such elections in Germany would be the loss to the "socialist camp" of its most important "people's democracy." Elections were a camouflage, a Western stratagem, a banana peel on which the Soviets might slip. To "expose" the enemy, in such a case, was the duty of a Soviet statesman. Whatever the plans that existed in Soviet minds at the time, the yielding of the Eastern zone was not among them.

Meanwhile the Contractual Agreement and the EDC Treaty had been signed, the first in Bonn on May 26, 1952, the second in Paris the following day. The signing of the treaties, however, did not mean that they would be implemented; ratification of them by the three governments proved a thorny, dangerous, and protracted process. At the time of the signing of the treaties the West greatly exaggerated its success, and Moscow exaggerated its failure.

The reaction of the Soviet government and press to the Western treaties was violent and acrimonious. *Izvestia* maintained that they were no more than a "conspiracy between Wall Street and the German magnates." Eugen Tarle, the Soviet historian, in an article in *New Times*,[21] May 21, said that West Germany was being degraded to a "protectorate," a permanently occupied nation. In another article, *New Times* maintained that "the terms of the Bonn treaty are much more onerous even than those of Versailles. . . . May 26, the day when the treaty was signed, is regarded by the German people as the Black Monday of their history, and they are determined to foil the plot of the Bonn compactors. . . . The fate the American imperialists are now preparing for the German people is even more terrible than what they suffered at the French invader's hands at the beginning of the last century.[22]

A number of "peace" groups and other international German organizations, sponsored by the Soviet government or the Communist parties, exerted great activity in support of the Soviet position; congresses published resolutions "for peace and conciliation"—interpreted in the Soviet way. It was claimed that 8.2 million West Germans had "voted" in favor of the Soviet-initiated "peace treaty," but no details of the "vote" were given.

[21] Moscow, no. 21, May 21, 1952.
[22] *New Times*, Moscow, no. 23, June 4, 1952, pp. 6–7, 9.

Germany: The Big Issue

Developments took an even more favorable turn for Moscow than Moscow had expected. Opposition to EDC, which appeared to have subsided, again became loud, especially in France, and also in Britain. By the end of 1952 the anti-EDC trends definitely prevailed. The French Communists were, of course, opposed to EDC, but so were the nationalist groups, the rightists, and General Charles de Gaulle himself. French Foreign Minister Schuman, a staunch defender of EDC, was forced to quit early in January, 1953. France demanded a revision of the already-signed treaty. The project, the result of years of effort, was again undone; everything would have to start again from the beginning. In the scuttling of the treaties the Soviet government played a prominent part. The result represented one of its most successful actions concerning Germany.

The deadlock on the German issue was complete.

CHAPTER 4

THE FAR EAST

At the time of Stalin's death the Asian section of the socialist bloc firmly embraced, in addition to Asiatic Russia, two countries, China and Outer Mongolia. North Korea and North Vietnam, although occupied by Communist forces, were not yet definitely established. Within the frontiers set up later, the territories and populations of the four allies of the Soviet Union in Asia were as follows:

	Population	Area, sq. miles
China	582,603,417	3,858,900
Outer Mongolia	1,010,000	606,000
North Vietnam	12,000,000	64,451
North Korea	8,300,000	46,814
Total	603,913,417	4,576,165

1. THE KOREAN WAR

The major international event of Stalin's last years was the Korean War; it was still being fought when the Soviet dictator died.

The conflict, which had been planned, prepared, and initiated by Stalin, was an example of the kind of a war that, in Stalin's view, could and must be supported by the Soviet Union without being directly involved in it. All the facets of Stalin's political personality—his aggressiveness and slyness, his caution and "brinkmanship"—were reflected in his guidance of the Far Eastern conflict. If successful, the conduct of the Korean War would serve as a model for policy in other divided nations: Indochina, Germany, Austria. In these latter countries the war could be clothed in nationalist garb and propagandized as a fight for national unification; it could be presented as a civil war, a revolutionary war between classes; at the same time, and in fact, it would serve as a multilateral offensive, in both the East and the West, against

The Korean War

the United States. If American military forces participated directly, this would, in contrast to Soviet nonparticipation, be proof of military intervention by the imperialists in a civil war similar to the unhappy pattern of the intervention in Russia in 1918–20. In the heated discussion that took place abroad in those days as to whether Stalin wanted war or peace, both sides were right: Stalin wanted Korean-type limited and protracted wars with the United States, with peace for the Soviet Union assured.

Moscow had to hold the reins in the Korean conflict; the war could not have been conducted in any other way. Half of a small former Japanese colony, backward in many respects, North Korea could challenge and fight the strongest power in the world only with the guidance and military supplies of the Soviet Union. Among the "socialist countries," North Korea stood near the bottom, the Soviet Union at the top; in a war situation the relationship could only be that of sun and satellite.

Even after the Chinese "volunteers" joined the North Koreans in the war, Moscow continued to minimize its own leading role. The Peking government was still young, and, for all its experience and self-confidence as the victor in a civil war, the Chinese military force was still, in some respects, no more than a huge mass of "cannon fodder," in need of Soviet supplies and Soviet strategic and political leadership.

A Korean Communist organization had existed in the Russian Far East, within the framework of Stalin's party, since the 1920's; hundreds of Russian Koreans and Korean *émigrés* had served in the Red Army and taken part in Soviet wars; others had served with Soviet intelligence agencies and the NKVD. After World War II a number of these Soviet citizens of Korean descent returned to Korea (they now had dual citizenship) and aided in the Stalin-type "liberation" of their country. It was these loyal Stalinists, who maintained close ties with Vladivostok and Moscow, who stood at the head of the North Korean government and its army during the war. The commander in chief was the Soviet-trained General Kim Il-sung; General Nam Il, Chief of Staff and Chief of the Security Agency, and a former Soviet officer, was second in political command and leader of the truce teams. His deputy, Lee Sang Jo, Chief of Military Intelligence, had arrived from Russia a few weeks after the outbreak of the war. Another important negotiator was General Kim Pa, former Soviet MVD agent. The head of the rebellious prisoner-of-war camps was Pak Sang Hyon (Ro Sung Saeng), who had been dispatched from Russia to Korea in 1945.[1]

The training of the Northern army was supervised by Russians and partially carried out on Soviet soil. In 1949 about 10,000 Koreans were shipped to Siberia, where they were trained and equipped and returned home, to be replaced by another division. The large North Korean army was assembled, trained, and tactically and strategically guided by Soviet instructors. Heavy equipment was supplied by the Soviet Union; large numbers of naval mines used during the war were of Soviet manufacture; all aircraft, including replacements for planes shot down, were of Soviet make, as were antiaircraft guns. In all, the Soviet supplied 4,400 aircraft to the North Koreans during the first two years of the war.[2] Groups of Soviet aviation technicians in specialties unknown to the Koreans and Chinese were included among the "People's Volunteers" of China and wore the latter's uniforms. Among the pilots, too, there were a number of Russians.[3]

Some of the best-known Russian generals were active at headquarters, mainly the headquarters in Manchuria; it was reported that Marshal Georgi K. Zhukov was at one time in Mukden and General Kuzma Derevyanko in Changchun. Marshal Rodion Malinovsky, General Ivan Kozhedub, and Lieutenant General Slussarov worked at headquarters.[4] Soviet military advisers were assigned to every Korean unit, up to Supreme Headquarters. The total number of such advisers was estimated at several thousand.

In the United Nations the Soviet government assumed the demeanor of a vigorous protector—not a war ally—of the North Korean and Chinese Communist side; it maintained the position of an outsider, and even claimed recognition of its formally neutral position. In order to perform its Far Eastern task, the Soviet delegation, which

---

[1] Headquarters United Nations and Far East Command, Military Intelligence Section, General Staff, *The Communist War in POW Camps: The Background of Incidents among Communist Prisoners in Korea,* January 28, 1953, pp. 8, 20.

[2] Henry Cabot Lodge, Jr., in the United Nations, February 26, 1953; Secretary of State Dean Acheson, in the United Nations, October 24, 1952.

[3] "We were permitted to fly only over North Korean territory [states a former Soviet specialist] to avoid landing or cruising on United Nations territory. Any plane that tried to cross the air line would be shot down by Chinese anti-aircraft guns." (D Papers, vol. 5, January, 1957, pp. 316–17.)

[4] D Papers, vol. 5, January, 1957, pp. 316–27. Also *The New York Times,* April 1, 1951.

The Korean War

had for several months boycotted the United Nations, resumed participation in July, 1950, after the start of the Korean War.

Unprecedented methods of anti-American propaganda were used by the Soviet during the Korean War. It is hard to discern the authorship of each individual accusation leveled at the United States, but Stalin's personal contribution is easily recognizable. When prisoners of war in the compounds of the United Nations refused repatriation to their Communist-ruled fatherland and, in protest, tattooed themselves and signed petitions in blood, the Soviet radio and press used the incident as the basis of accusations of heinous crimes perpetrated by the Americans. "Petrol is poured on the prisoners of war and then ignited. Bright electric light from powerful bulbs is directed on their eyes until they are blinded. Their fingernails are torn out. Their bodies are burned by red-hot irons. Many prisoners of war are taken out to the field and fired at as if they were targets. . . . In many cases women were first raped, then their breasts were chopped off, their arms and legs were torn off, and finally they were soaked with petrol and burned alive. . . . Thousands of prisoners of war were shipped by the Americans from Asia to the West on a British ship to be used in atomic bomb tests. . . ."[5]

In Russia this was the first stage of a systematic propaganda drive which lasted over a year and which in viciousness sometimes outdid Nazi propaganda.

In May 1951, 1,400 prisoners of war were secretly shipped to the United States for experiments with atomic weapons. The lists of these prisoners of war were destroyed. On July 15, 1951, a hundred prisoners were machine-gunned in POW Camp #62 "for the purpose"—as the document states—"of teaching the operators of machine-guns how to shoot at moving targets." On February 18, 1952, in the same group, 300 POWs were killed in the same way. . . .

A terrible crime was committed by the aggressors [the Americans] on May 27, 1952 in Camp #77 [this referred to the mutiny on Koje-do]. The documents state that on a big group of POWs who demanded that they be returned home, flame-throwers of new construction were tried out. On this day 800 POWs were burned alive. On May 20 and 30, in the same camp, a total of thirty-seven prisoners of war were killed or wounded.[6]

[5] *Pravda*, February 23, 1952.
[6] TASS telegram from Pyongyang, published under the headline "Monstrous Crimes of American Interventionists," in *Pravda*, November 29, 1952.

Yuri Rastvorov, a member of the Soviet mission in Tokyo who later defected, reported how Moscow collected information on American atrocities:

> Moscow ordered our mission in Tokyo to collect through the channels of the Japanese Communist party all possible evidence that the United States was planning to start a germ war offensive. The Japanese Communists came through with a "document" of some 20 pages. As I translated this paper into Russian for Moscow, I could not help laughing at some of it. Even my chiefs found various items impossible to swallow. One charge was that the U.S. Army had been purchasing Japanese corpses which were shipped to an American hospital in the center of Tokyo for experiments in extracting bacteria.[7]

The first official announcement by the North Korean Minister for Foreign Affairs, Pak Heung Yung (he was later arrested and, in 1955, executed), to the effect that "the aggressor" (meaning the United States) was making use of bacteriological warfare was made on February 22, 1952. Two days later Chinese Communist leader Chou En-lai joined the chorus, and now *Pravda* took over the propaganda offensive, which became a veritable campaign. Regularly and systematically, and with the use of much space in the press devoted to the "bacteriological war," people were aroused against the inhuman, barbaric, murderous war techniques of the Americans (other United Nations members were spared). Sometimes two and three reports of this nature appeared in a single issue of a newspaper. Prominent writers and scientists, among them Ilya Ehrenburg, Frederic Joliot-Curie, and Denis N. Pritt, joined in the attack. A huge meeting of the Soviet Academy of Sciences heard leaders of Russian science condemn the bestial Americans; meetings for the same purpose were held in industrial plants all over the country. The Russian-guided international "Association of Democratic Lawyers" published the results of its investigation: the Americans are guilty of waging a germ war. (The President of the Association, Professor Brandweiner, was dismissed from his post at Graz University in Austria a few days later.) Finally, lengthy confessions of six American officers were made public which puzzled even people of pro-American sentiments. On July 21, *Pravda* carried a false report to the effect that "General [James A.] Van Fleet [Commander of the United States Eighth Army] recognizes the fact

---

[7] *Life*, December 6, 1954.

The Korean War

of the bacteriological warfare." Soviet citizens were unaware that on March 4 the United States Secretary of State had issued a categorical denial of this charge; that a week later the United Nations secretary general had made a similar statement; that on May 16 the United States Secretary of Defense had scored the accusation as a "base lie." On May 22 the commander of the United Nations forces in Korea, General Mark Clark, issued a statement to the effect that in not a single case had bacteriological means been used by his troops.

In the United Nations the Soviet delegation and its allies rejected the suggestion of a neutral investigation. But it was not until after the end of the war, and when most of the American prisoners had returned home, that the "confessions" of the American officers were refuted by their signers; the methods used to extract the "confessions" became known in detail (though not in Russia), and the guiding role of Russian police officers was revealed. "Interrogations" of utmost cruelty, it was revealed at the end of 1953, had often been conducted under the guidance of Soviet specialists; a number of American fliers had been interrogated by Russians. A number of Chinese "interrogators" had undergone eighteen months of training in a Soviet-operated school in Peking.[8]

To those familiar with the Soviet purge trials of the 1930's, the authorship of the "bacteriological war" accusations was obvious. For almost three decades Stalin had manifested a peculiar interest in "bacteriology"; he was obviously intrigued by the potentiality of "bacteriology" in war, and the charge of using germs had figured in numerous Soviet criminal cases since the 1930's. In 1933 Stalin had accused Russian professors of "infecting cattle with plague germs and Siberian anthrax." A few years later his chief of police, Genrikh Yagoda, was accused of and condemned for preparing and using poison against Soviet leaders. At the trial in Khabarovsk in 1949, Japanese were falsely charged with having "cultivated in enormous quantities plague germs, cholera, typhus, Siberian anthrax" and having used them in the war. In 1950 the Moscow Academy of Sciences published a book entitled *The Bacteriological War—A Criminal Instrument of Imperialist Aggression*, in which the history of preparations for bacteriological war was described as having started with experiments during World

---
[8] Charles W. Mayo, report to the Political Committee of the United Nations (*The New York Times*), October 27, 1953. The Soviet press did not make any mention of the Mayo statement.

War I; Germany, Japan, and especially the United States were charged with having engaged in such preparations.

The initial Soviet expectation that the United States, which had withdrawn its army from Korea in 1949, would not fight "for Syngman Rhee" but would at most carry on only a mock war, had not materialized; the hope, widespread in the West, that the war would end in unification and independence for Korea also proved vain. After a year, with the war at a stalemate and the front back at the thirty-eighth parallel, the situation was ripe for truce or peace. A cease-fire was impossible, however, because of disagreements concerning the fate of prisoners of war; in this debate, the Soviet side, meaning Stalin, was again the guiding spirit.

In the truce conference which opened in the summer of 1951 all issues were settled except that of the fate of prisoners of war. Early in 1952, and quite unexpectedly, the prisoner-of-war issue developed into an almost world-shaking problem. When the Communist side requested repatriation of all Chinese and North Korean prisoners, "in accordance with the Geneva convention," the United Nations negotiators were at first inclined to consider this a logical and natural demand.

The prisoner-of-war camps, which had been established at the beginning of the Korean conflict to accommodate several thousand, were soon housing more than 100,000; the number continued to grow until there were over 150,000—130,000 Koreans and 20,000 Chinese—on Koje Island alone. The United Nations command was not in a position to control this human mass, idle behind barbed wire; it was not aware that Communist Party leaders among the prisoners were continuing their political activity in the camps, organizing cells and committees, lecturing on political questions, distributing literature, and exacting strict obedience to their orders. Nor did the United Nations command know that in a sharp division between devoted Communist leaders and bitter anti-Communists in the camps a fight was developing which would soon take the form of assassinations and bloody battles, that kangaroo courts would operate inside the camps, and that brutality, always characteristic of civil strife, would engulf the compounds. "Self-government" was prescribed for the prisoner-of-war camps by the Geneva convention; the United Nations command, unable to cope with the unexpectedly huge task, did not realize its

The Korean War

importance. The Korean-Chinese negotiators at Panmunjom, General Nam Il and his deputies, found ways to maintain contact with the Communist leadership in the prisoner-of-war camps on Koje Island. Agents dispatched from Panmunjom transmitted information and orders of the High Command to the Communist leaders in the camps; in order to carry out their assignments, Nam Il's agents deliberately gave themselves up to become prisoners. In other cases Communist guerrillas roaming South Korea carried the messages. These excellent techniques were proof that experienced Soviet MVD officers were serving as instructors.

Early in 1952 prisoners of war were informed through secret channels from Panmunjom that a truce agreement would soon be signed and that all prisoners would be repatriated to their homelands. Of 16,978 Chinese prisoners confined on Koje in Camp No. 1, 12,440 signed, in blood, petitions declaring that they would rather kill themselves than return to Red China. More than 3,000 prisoners tattooed on their bodies anti-Communist slogans that would mean death if they were returned: "Oppose Communism—Resist Russia!" This was a challenge and an appeal to the humanitarian feelings of the Western nations.

The United Nations negotiators were no less surprised by these developments than were the Communist leaders. Both sides tried to determine whether the anti-repatriation sentiments were as strong as the petitions and mass tattooing would seem to indicate. The United Nations side ordered a screening of prisoners of war. The questions asked were: "'Do you want to go home to North Korea or China?' If a prisoner answered 'yes,' the interview ended. If he said 'no,' he was asked . . . 'Would you resist repatriation?' 'Do you know what this means to your family at home, and that you may never see them again?' 'Have you considered that you may never go home again?' 'Do you understand that you are being promised nothing if you remain?' 'Do you still say you won't go back to Communist control?' 'What would you do if we took you back by force?'" To influence the prisoners, the Communist side, on the suggestion of the Americans, made amnesty broadcasts; the messages were rebroadcast by the United Nations to the prison camps two days before the screening started.[9]

[9] *The New York Times,* April 26, 1952; New York *Herald Tribune,* May 7, 1952.

The results of this combined American-Communist effort were poor. Although only those were viewed as opposed to repatriation who were prepared to "resist by force," only 70,000 out of 170,000 prisoners agreed to be repatriated.

The result of the ballot was played down by the Allies in order not to aggravate the truce negotiations. Peking and Moscow refused to acknowledge the facts. The fury of the anti-American propaganda now assumed hysterical proportions. To Moscow, the fact that members of Communist nations preferred death to living under a Communist regime was intolerable; it was treason *en masse;* it was likely to place in doubt or destroy the "popular" essence of the Communist system.

The governments of both the Soviet Union and the United States remembered well the post–World War II prisoner-of-war issue: thousands of Russian prisoners of war in Allied hands, mainly in Germany and Austria, had resisted repatriation and been taken by force, and many had committed suicide. At that time Soviet authorities in East Germany were holding about 60,000 liberated Americans whom they were using for purposes of pressure: unless the Allies agreed to repatriate all of the 2,000,000 Soviet citizens found in Germany, Austria, France, and Italy after the war, Moscow would stall on the return of the American soldiers. The Soviet government asked the Western powers not to publicize the repatriation issue; news of the resistance to repatriation of Russian prisoners of war would have been too damaging to Soviet prestige.

The situation in Korea was similar: by refusing to sign the truce, the Communist side could continue to hold United Nations prisoners in the camps of North Korea and China; this was a strong—a "Stalinist"—means of pressure.

In the fall session (October–November, 1952) of the General Assembly of the United Nations, Andrei Vyshinsky spoke at length in support of what he termed the position of China and Korea on the issue of prisoners of war and truce negotiations; it became known, however, that the uncompromising position was that of Stalin rather than the real attitude of China and North Korea. Stalin's envoy was hard. The new purge in Russia, which was just starting, had as its corollary on the international scene a severe anti-Western course. Vyshinsky reiterated all the horrors of American brutality, bacteriological warfare, and executions of prisoners of war, the "millionaires' interest" in armaments, the "American policy" of conquering and grabbing independent nations—and demanded unconditional repatriation of prisoners of war. Not the slightest concession was made to the opposing point of view. The Soviet foreign minister was not concerned that, in the voting, not a single nation except the two satellites, Poland and Czechoslovakia, supported him. This attitude was symptomatic of Stalin's new mood.

The Indian government offered to attempt to arrange a compromise between the parties. On November 11, 1952, it introduced a plan on the prisoner-of-war issue which it communicated to Peking and Pyongyang. "China's reaction," Prime Minister Nehru later told the House of People, "was not disapproval"; adhering to the principle of general repatriation of prisoners of war, the Chinese government "gave to understand that it appreciates our attempts," Nehru said. Peking was obviously prepared to discuss the Indian proposal; so was North Korea. Without waiting, however, for the reaction of China and North Korea, Vyshinsky, presuming to speak for both, rejected the plan outright. Four days later, Chou En-lai announced that he would accept only the Soviet truce plan. The incident illuminated the essence of Soviet-Chinese relations of the time.[10]

The stalemate continued until Stalin's death. On February 17, 1953, India's Krishna Menon visited Stalin to discuss the Korean situation, but no agreement was reached. The old despot was already unconscious when Vyshinsky, on March 2, 1953, resumed his violent attack on the United States, refusing to accept voluntary repatriation and rejecting all compromises. On the same day *Pravda* reverted to charges of "bacteriological warfare" by the Americans. On March 4, V. Zorin and Polish Representative Skrzyzewski addressed the United Nations on the subject of "bacteriology."

Stalin died the next day. The Korean deadlock was complete, and the outlook was gloomy.

2. CHINA

As Moscow saw it, in 1949–50, Asia was aflame: the Chinese Communists had just overwhelmed and driven out the old regime; in

[10] Sir Francis Low, *Struggle for Asia*, London, Frederick Mueller, Ltd., 1955, p. 192.

Vietnam the war was taking a favorable turn; there was fighting in Laos; Malaya and Indonesia were on their way to "real" liberation; North Korea would soon be united with South Korea; and in India the rule of the "British lackey" Nehru was only a passing thing. The successes in the Orient dwarfed the achievements in Europe. Now the majority of the human race had been won over. Lenin's prediction that "Russia, India, China" will determine the outcome of the struggle because they embrace the majority of the world's population seemed to have materialized.

The balance of power in the world, Georgi Dimitrov announced, had now shifted in favor of socialism, the final victory of which was assured. The vista was more radiant than ever.

China's role was eulogized in Soviet comments:

> The gold stars gleaming on the red flag of the Chinese People's Republic symbolize a new phase in the development for victory of the national-liberation movements of Asia—and not only of Asia, but of the whole colonial world. The victory of the Chinese people is bound to have reverberations in the countries fighting for their independence, for deliverance from their imperialist enslavers. This inevitably presages a further contraction of the sphere of imperialist domination.[11]

Elaboration of strategy for Communist movements in the East was the task of a "Trade Union Conference" in Peking convened by the Soviet-controlled World Federation of Trade Unions a few weeks after Mao Tse-tung established his government in the old capital. In the expectation that the revolutionary movements would spread rapidly, the most important committees of the conference dealt not only with political but also with military issues of the future Far Eastern upheaval: creation of guerrilla units, arms supplies, sabotage, dislocation of shipping in the Pacific, and "illegal" methods of operation. Three Russian delegates, Soloviev, Yakovlev, and Rostovsky played the leading roles in the conference; among the Chinese were Liu Shao-chi (now President of Communist China) and Li Li-san, Communist trade-union leader.

One of the purposes of the conference was to elaborate blueprints for Southeast Asia, Australia, and especially India, and to arrange "contacts" in the United States. Soviet delegate Rostovsky expected

---

[11] *New Times,* Moscow, no. 3, January 18, 1950, p. 7. E. Zhukov, "Historic Significance of the Victory of the Chinese People."

China

the "war" to break out in the summer of 1950. The plans apparently contemplated a grand-scale Far Eastern revolution to break out simultaneously with the Korean War.[12] The leading body of the new Far Eastern organization included a Russian, a Chinese (Liu Shao-chi), an Indian, and an Australian. This division of command was indicative of Soviet-Chinese relations of the time. Peking was to serve as a geographical base, the site of headquarters (the "Asian-Australian Bureau of the World Federation of Trade Unions"), while real leadership was to remain in Soviet hands. Thus Mao's earlier suggestion of a special Far Eastern section of the Cominform (to work under his control) was altered in favor of a bureau in which the top role went to a Russian. "The Russians dominate all the conclaves," the reports emphasized, and Russian suggestions were tantamount to orders. The Soviet Union was superior to Communist China.

Stalin's attitude toward China and the Asian revolution had undergone considerable change, as he himself later acknowledged. During the last phases of the Communist offensive against the Nationalist forces, Stalin had tried to slow down the pace of the attack but had failed. Edward Kardelj, the Yugoslav leader, later reported Stalin's statement, made in 1948, concerning his (Stalin's) advice to the Chinese Communist leaders to discontinue the war against the Nationalists and join the Chiang Kai-shek regime as a partner in a coalition.

> After the war [Stalin had said] we invited the Chinese comrades to come to Moscow and we discussed the situation in China. We told them bluntly that we considered the development of the uprising in China had no prospects, and that the Chinese comrades should seek a *modus vivendi* with Chiang Kai-shek, that they should join the Chiang Kai-shek government and dissolve their army. The Chinese comrades agreed here with the view of the Soviet comrades, but went back to China and acted quite otherwise. They mustered their forces, organized their armies and now, as we see, they are beating the Chiang Kai-shek army. Now in the case of China, we admit we were wrong.[13]

Somewhat later (early 1949), on a similar occasion, Stalin was again reported instructing his Chinese comrades to go slowly.

[12] On the Peking Conference. D Papers, vol. 8, July, 1953, pp. 668–69; vol. 3, December 10, 1956, pp. 184–86; and *Daily Telegraph and Morning Post*, London, March 24, 1950.

[13] Vladimir Dedjer, *Tito*, New York, Simon & Schuster, Inc., 1951, p. 322.

There were various reasons for Stalin's reluctance and hesitation. The first was his desire to make the utmost use of the alliance with the West, which he did not want to see broken up until the last drop had been squeezed out of the "unity" of the "great alliance." His attitude toward the Yugoslav monarchy, the Greek rebellion, and the Chiang regime were to a large extent dictated by this strategy. During the early years of the war he accused the Tito group of exaggerated antagonism toward Britain; in his view, the Titoists were animated by local considerations and lacked the global view, which called for an alliance with London. He was similarly dissatisfied with the impetuousness of his Chinese friends. Not until he had exhausted all other means did he assume a more aggressive posture. Stalin's personal antipathy toward the Chinese [14] may also have played a role in this situation.

The third reason for Stalin's reluctant attitude toward the new Chinese regime was more important and more lasting: the need to manipulate the future China into her proper place in the empire. There was too much risk involved in permitting the emergence overnight of a Communist-led nation of tremendous size and possible far-reaching expansionist ambitions. In China's Communist movement the nationalist element (against foreign interference) was as strong as the social element (against the rich). The rise of a huge unified Communist China might mean not only abolition of "feudalism" and "capitalism" but also a drive toward reacquisition of former Chinese possessions—a drive that might be directed against Russia—and a drive toward autonomy if not total independence from Moscow.

Stalin had underrated Mao's chances of total victory, but this had not been a mere mistake in strategic calculation. As is so often the case in political strategy, desires pointed in the same direction as "objective" facts; in this case they pointed to gradualness in the solution of the Chinese problem. The golden rules of Soviet empire-building were now to be applied in the East, for another experiment with "independence" on the Belgrade pattern must be avoided. China's accession to the socialist camp had to proceed at a pace and in stages that would fit into the basic Soviet principle that Russia must play the guiding role.

When Communist forces "liberated" Manchuria and North China in 1947–48 these operations still fitted into the Soviet scheme. From

[14] See p. 5.

China

the Himalayas to Korea, the whole north of China, which neighbors on Russia, was in a sense a Soviet sphere of interest; here the new Chinese Communist authorities would have to reckon with the established system and somehow accommodate things into the Soviet scheme. A powerful Soviet army was stationed in Manchuria; the railways in the area were under Soviet control; the industry that had been revived in the region was under Soviet supervision; Soviet instructors were engaged in training and teaching; whatever trade there was was moving in the direction of Russia. What was more, a Communist government was set up for the new "Northeast liberated area" under Kao Kang, a member of the Central Committee of the Chinese Communist Party and a man of outstanding ability, whose regime was oriented toward the Soviet Union. When Mao Tse-tung was already driving to the south and the reunification of the country under Communist leadership appeared near, Stalin was giving his blessings and *de facto* recognition to the separate regime of Manchuria, accepting its agencies as the "people's democratic authorities" of Manchuria, and even as the "government" of the province.[15] A one-year truce agreement with the "delegation of the authorities," headed by Kao Kang, was signed in July, 1949. Moscow made an effort to resurrect Manchuria as a semistate under a new name and with other foreign ties, but with the modicum of independence it had had in the 1920's and '30's.

A similar situation prevailed in another province of China, Sinkiang. Although in no way a rival to rich and populous Manchuria, Sinkiang was even more "autonomous" under strong Soviet influence. Its geographical location in the far northwest and its lack of railways leading to China's main areas made it more dependent on adjacent Soviet Central Asia than on Peking or Nanking; the fact that the overwhelming majority of the population was non-Chinese (it is Uighur, akin to the nationalities of Soviet Central Asia) made Sinkiang a source of contention between the Soviet Union and China. As in Manchuria, Russian encroachment into this area had started long before the revolution and had continued after 1917. For a long time Sinkiang had been under the rule of Sheng Shih-ts'ai, who was often considered a Soviet puppet. During the latter part of the war and after the war, when Moscow's relations with the Nationalist government had improved, Sinkiang was for a time in Chinese hands. In 1947,

[15] *Pravda*, July 31, 1949, and February 15, 1950.

however, Stalin resumed his offensive and easily took over almost complete control. In the late 1940's, Russian advisers, teachers, doctors, engineers, and politicians were in control of the machinery of the government, both civil and military. All key posts were held by Soviet citizens from Central Asia who often passed as members of the tribes of Sinkiang.[16]

In this case again, "local authorities," recognized by Moscow, served as the channel and instrument of Soviet policy. Late in the day (May, 1949), when the victory of Chinese Communism was imminent (three months later most of the members of the old provincial government had left Sinkiang), the Soviet government hastily renewed its air pact with the local representative of the Nationalist government; other Soviet proposals—for example, to grant Moscow a fifty-year monopoly in Sinkiang's mineral resources, to permit full freedom of export for Soviet agencies in Sinkiang, and others—could not be accepted. This was another of Stalin's attempts to place before the emerging Communist regime the accomplished fact of Soviet privileges and prevailing influence.

The last Soviet move was made at the moment when the Communist forces had advanced to nearby Kansu. In his revealing book on Sinkiang, Allen S. Whiting quotes "a firsthand source" (the report, he says, "is difficult to corroborate") to the effect that the Soviet consul general approached the Chinese authorities in Sinkiang, namely, General T'ao Shih-yeath, with the proposal to declare Sinkiang independent, like Outer Mongolia, and after the Communist victory in China to incorporate Sinkiang "into a federal Republic" (obviously the Kazakh Soviet Republic). The Nationalist government, then in Canton, rejected this proposal.[17] Whatever the details of Stalin's drive into Sinkiang, the province became one of the first points of dispute between Moscow and Peking when the Communist government was set up in the latter capital.

Another issue between China and the Soviet Union was Outer Mongolia, which, like Manchuria, had been a province of the Chinese empire. Detached from China by the prerevolutionary Russian regime and in the 1920's constituted by Moscow a "sovereign" Mongolian

---

[16] *The New York Times,* March 23, 1951.

[17] Allen S. Whiting and General Sheng Shih-tsai, *Sinkiang: Pawn or Pivot?* East Lansing, Michigan, Michigan State University Press, 1958, pp. 118 ff.

People's Republic, Outer Mongolia had always been a sore point for the Nationalist Chinese as well as the Communists. It was the Mongolian issue that had made Moscow's negotiations with China so difficult in the early 1920's. These negotiations had ended with Soviet recognition of Outer Mongolia as a "component of the Chinese Republic" and the undertaking that the USSR "will respect China's sovereignty." Gregori Zinoviev gave to understand that the Soviet Union would return Mongolia to China as soon as the Communists achieved power—"when the Chinese will liberate themselves from their aggressors." [18]

The Chinese Communists had taken the promise—so logical and so consistent with the early tenets of Leninism—seriously and literally. It appeared sensible that the great socialist neighbor, the liberator and savior of humanity, should refuse to return to the "reactionary" regime of China former Chinese territories which could serve to increase the ability of the "reactionary" regime to fight the "popular" movements in the country. Things would change, of course, if and when China herself became a liberator and savior, at which time everything would be restored to her. In his elaborate program, Mao Tse-tung appeared as a unifier of China, a kind of Chinese Ivan III, a "gatherer of lands" who assembled the dismembered nation after ages of disasters. Mao was about to inherit a China disfigured and dismembered by her own autonomous war lords as well as by the British, French, Japanese, and Russians—with the Russians in a very prominent place among the "pirates" as far as the extent of her encroachments was concerned. And among the Russian encroachments, Soviet operations in the north, from the Himalayas to the Pacific, were at least on a par with those of prerevolutionary Russia.

As a matter of fact, the territory and concessions extracted from China by St. Petersburg and Moscow before and during the revolution far exceeded the gains that had resulted from British and French imperialist efforts. China had been subjected to Russian penetration along the whole Russo-Chinese frontier: in Sinkiang, Outer Mongolia, Tannu-Tuva, and North Manchuria, Russia had been the attacking and annexing power. The city of Vladivostok was built by Russia on former Chinese territory; the very name of the city proclaimed a program: Vladivostok means "rule the East."

[18] *Novyi Vostok,* Moscow, 1925, vol. 8-9, pp. 218–19.

The program of the Chinese Communists was the liberation of all detached areas, with priority accorded to those that had fallen to Japan, Britain, and France. Russia was not completely forgotten, however. In an elaborate statement, Mao outlined his program to Edgar Snow in 1930:

> It is the immediate task of China to regain all our lost territories, not merely to defend our sovereignty below the Great Wall. This means that Manchuria must be regained. . . . If the Koreans wish to break away from the chains of Japanese imperialism, we will extend them our enthusiastic help in their struggle for independence. The same thing applies for Formosa. As for Inner Mongolia, which is populated by both Chinese and Mongolians, we will struggle to drive Japan from there and help Inner Mongolia to establish an autonomous State. . . . When the people's revolution has been victorious in China *the Outer Mongolian Republic will automatically become a part of the Chinese federation*, at their own will. *The Mohammedan and Tibetan peoples* likewise will form autonomous republics attached to the China federation.[19]

Later, in 1945, during the last stage of the war, Mao made it clear that his plans and ambitions went far beyond the confines of China. He had a program for Asia that implied "help" to Korea, emancipation of South Asian nations, and an upheaval in Thailand. Mao and his regime have consistently adhered to this program.

> The Chinese people [Mao told his party's Congress in 1945] must help the Korean people to achieve liberation.
> We would like India to become independent, because an independent, democratic India is important not only to the Indian people, but also to the cause of peace on the entire globe.
> In regard to the nations of the southern seas—Burma, Malaya, Indonesia, Vietnam, the Philippines—we would like that, upon the rout of the Japanese invaders, the people of these countries should achieve the right to build their independent democratic states. As to Thailand, it will have to be dealt with in the same manner as will the fascist satellites in Europe.[20]

His ideal, Mao told the Congress, was a China which would be not only free and united, but also tremendously strong: an "independent, free, democratic, united, rich and mighty country. . . ." "Our aim

---

[19] Edgar Snow, *Red Star Over China*, New York, Modern Library, Inc., 1944, p. 96. Italics ours.

[20] Mao Tse-tung, *Izbrannye Proizvedeniya* (Selected Works; in Russian), Moscow, Foreign Languages Publishing House, 1952, vol. 4, p. 554.

is to create [repeated] . . . an independent, democratic, united, rich and mighty new China." [21]

Stalin's Course in China. These were the roots from which grew the Soviet-Chinese relations of 1949–52, following Mao's victory. Chinese Communism did not forget or relinquish its far-reaching programs and ambitions; the Soviet course, based on Stalin's conceptions, was not always identical with that of the Chinese.

Although admitting his mistakes of the past, Stalin was not prepared to accord China an equal place with the Soviet Union in the "socialist camp"; Mao could join the family only as a satellite of Stalin. Stalin never reneged on this pattern of "internationalism." In the last four years of his life he consistently tried, first, to divert the attention and forces of his Chinese ally from the north (the Soviet sphere) to the south, where huge territories, formerly Chinese as well as non-Chinese, had been acquired over the years by the "imperialists" and their "agents"; second, not only to maintain the Soviet position in separated Manchuria, but to enlarge Soviet military facilities there (in addition, in view of the "imminent" great upheavals in the Pacific areas and South Asia, new military bases in North China were required); third, to conserve Soviet political and economic privileges in Sinkiang; fourth, to keep the Mongolian People's Republic, which was actually tied to the Soviet Union, definitely separated from China; fifth, to maintain his influence in the young Korean People's Democracy (which had emerged as a Soviet rather than a Chinese satellite) even after the entire country should be "liberated" from the Americans; and sixth, for the purpose of strengthening the anti-imperialist drives, to supply arms and certain economic aid to China, although, in view of Russia's own needs at the time, on only a modest scale (Soviet aid in the form of military, police, educational, and other advisers and facilities for Chinese students in Russia could be more substantial).

As far as the drive to the south was concerned, the program of Chinese Communism was identical with that of Moscow. In fact, Peking was already in close touch with the insurgents of Indochina and was helping, as much as it could, the Vietminh of Ho Chi-minh; it stretched its hand toward Tibet; it looked with interest to Nepal;

[21] *Ibid.*, p. 454. "The Two Fates of China," speech, April 23, 1945.

it promised to regain Formosa; and it hinted that the British were only tolerated in Hong Kong.

Beyond this, however, China's ambition was to lead the drive for the "liberation" of other Asian nations. Chinese Communism advanced the theory that the stages and methods of the revolution in most of the Asian countries could not follow the Soviet pattern; the Communist parties of these countries rather would have to take a leaf from China; China, not Russia, was the logical leader of the Asian (and African) world. Mao's right-hand man, Liu Shao-chi, announced at the Trade Union Conference in Peking in November, 1949:

> The path taken by the Chinese people to defeat imperialism and its lackeys and to establish the People's Republic of China is the path that should be taken by the people of the various colonial and semicolonial countries in their fight for national independence and people's democracy. . . .
>
> Its distinct strategy is: coalition with other parties, a national front under the leadership of the Communist party, a "liberation army." "Armed struggle is the main form of struggle."
>
> The national liberation movement in the colonies and semicolonies can be led only by the proletariat and its party, the Communist Party.[22]

Basically, Mao's government could not agree to Stalin's desires in regard to the northern regions: no, the Soviet Union, too, must retreat, and this was imperative. Certain territorial concessions, especially in the Sinkiang-Mongolia area, were made to Stalin; these were inevitable if an agreement was to be reached. On the whole, however, neither the personal convictions of China's new leaders, the standing of these leaders in the country, nor their prestige among other subjugated nations would permit their acquiescing to the granting of privileges to a foreign power on Chinese soil. Although the Soviet Union was of course not ranked among the "imperialists," the Nationalists as well as the West would continue to stress the similarity of Soviet encroachments to those of old Russia, and China's own intelligentsia was extremely sensitive on this point. Mao's government had to move forward in the north as well as the south, though the policy was different in each case. Russia was its most valuable ally and protector, and Stalin was the infallible prophet. Whatever issues

[22] *For a Lasting Peace, for a People's Democracy,* December 12, 1949.

Stalin's Course in China

existed between Peking and Moscow, they must be settled behind the scenes in a spirit of compromise; officially, and before the public, the complete solidarity of the two nations must be stressed.

Chinese military and economic dependence on Russia precluded even a shred of overt feuding. The Yugoslav path was taboo for China: the entire region from Sinkiang to Manchuria could easily be cut off from the rest of China, and with Soviet armed forces on the spot and Chinese puppets in leading places the region could be constituted one satellite state or several separate ones. The remnants of Mao's forces, declared Titoist by Moscow and lacking arms and supplies, would fall to the Kuomintang. No Yugoslav path was open to the Chinese. Agreement was imperative. Besides, every Communist party and every Chinese general was aware of the measures that the Soviet government might take if China were to act without previous agreement with Moscow or contrary to Moscow's desires.

According to both Chinese and Russian official statements, Stalin and Mao met for the first and last time at the Moscow Conference, which opened in December, 1949, a few weeks after the establishment of the Chinese Communist regime, and lasted, contrary to all schedules, for two months. Congratulations were mixed with painful queries, and happiness, undoubtedly sincere, was intermingled with disagreement. Each party had brought its programs and demands; at one stage, when the going became rough, Mao's chief lieutenants were summoned from China. The final result was a balanced but temporary compromise.

Mao viewed himself and his regime as the sole representatives of the whole of China, just as Stalin was the representative of the whole of Russia. For Mao this was certainly a political achievement. The official Soviet announcement of the conference listed the heads of the local governments, represented by "Vice-Chairman Li Fu-chun of the North-East Government," and the "Vice-Chairman of the People's Provincial Sinkiang Government, comrade C. Azizov." [23] Representing Manchuria was the less important Li Fu-chun rather than Kao Kang, the head of the "local authorities." According to an un-

---

[23] *Pravda*, February 15, 1950. The "provincial governments" were already subordinates of the Central Government in Peking.

published report on the Moscow Conference, Mao had asked Stalin "to help him control Kao Kang." [24]

In the negotiations relating to the Northwest, Mao was less successful. Sinkiang's location thousands of miles from the main areas of China, the deserts separating the province, and the ethnic affinity of its population to certain tribes in Russia had made its ties with the Soviet Union stronger than its ties with China. In particular, the Communist Party in Sinkiang had been part of the Soviet rather than the Chinese Party. At the end of January a special delegation from Urumchi arrived to join the Soviet and Chinese leaders in their talks; among its leading members was the vice-chairman of the provincial government, the Russianized Uighur Seyfuddin, a graduate of Soviet schools, a member of the Communist Party of the Soviet Union, and the man who had served as a leader of the pro-Soviet "Eastern Turkestan People's Republic" as well as of other Soviet ventures in Sinkiang.[25] When Mao's sovereignty over the province was acknowledged in Moscow, the local Communist organization was turned over to the Chinese Communist Party, and the "Russian Communist" Seyfuddin became a "Chinese Communist" of considerable rank. The special position of the Soviet in Sinkiang's economic affairs, however, was recognized unreservedly. A Soviet-Sinkiang agreement was signed on March 27. A number of Soviet enterprises, among them two "joint stock companies," were to be established; airlines were to continue communication ties of Sinkiang with Russia; Soviet technical experts were to locate and develop Sinkiang's natural resources. The solution of the Sinkiang problem was the establishment of a practical condominium. Like most condominiums, it was imperfect and subsequently led to various disagreements.

Outer Mongolia was also discussed at the Moscow Conference, although no details of the discussion are available. In this area the Chinese faced accomplished facts of a quarter of a century's duration and a hard stand on the part of Russia. There was no possibility of bringing about a change in the status of Mongolia. The same applied to another former Chinese area, Tannu-Tuva, which had been officially incorporated into the Russian SFSR during the last stage of World War II. The official Soviet *New Times* stressed the finality of the

[24] D Papers, File CH, p. 4.
[25] Union Research Service, *Biographical Series 120*, Hong Kong, August 23, 1957.

arrangements when it said, somewhat later, that the "liberation of China, except for Tibet, is completed." [26]

In an exchange of letters signed by Vyshinsky and Chou on February 14, 1950, the two governments confirmed that "the independent status of the Mongolian People's Republic has already been fully secured as a result of the referendum conducted in Outer Mongolia in 1945, which confirmed the aspiration for independence of that country, and as a result of its establishment of diplomatic relations with the Chinese People's Republic." [27]

The concessions made by Stalin at the Moscow Conference, it appeared, were, in the first place, in connection with the migration of Chinese into Outer Mongolia. Though apprehensive of Chinese immigrants (large migrations had often been precursors of Chinese territorial expansion), the Soviet government had to concede to a small degree, and Peking quickly took advantage of the new privilege. Some trade between China and the Mongol People's Republic was encouraged.

The basic treaty signed at the end of the Moscow Conference, on February 14, 1950, was of the standard Soviet "mutual assistance" type; it was pointed at Japan or "any other state which should unite in any form with Japan in acts of aggression."

> Both High Contracting Parties undertake jointly to take all the necessary measures at their disposal for the purpose of preventing a repetition of aggression and violation of peace on the part of Japan or any other state which should unite with Japan, directly or indirectly, in acts of aggression. In the event of one of the High Contracting Parties being attacked by Japan or States allied with it, and thus being involved in a state of war, the other High Contracting Party will immediately render military and other assistance with all the means at its disposal.

The crucial questions in this and similar treaties were who was to decide that "military and other assistance" must be rendered and at what moment. From the time of the conclusion of the "mutual assistance treaties" between Moscow and the three Baltic states in 1939, it had always been Moscow that had the privilege of deciding and that had then dispatched its armies. This was obviously what the

[26] Moscow, no. 30, July 26, 1950.
[27] *Vedomosti Verkhovnogo Soveta SSSR* (Proceedings of the USSR Supreme Soviet), November 16, 1950, p. 4.

Soviet intended when Vyshinsky signed the treaty with Chou En-lai; it was strictly in the Stalin spirit.[28]

Another regular element of a treaty with a satellite was the "consultation" clause citing the obligation of each of the parties to consult with the other on all pertinent international issues. The Stalin interpretation of "consultation" has already been mentioned (page 35). The new Sino-Soviet treaty prescribed:

> Both High Contracting Parties will consult each other in regard to all important international problems affecting the common interests of the Soviet Union and China, being guided by the interests of the consolidation of peace and universal security.

Another part of the treaty dealt with Manchuria. China's achievement on this issue was the Soviet promise to turn over the Chinese Changchun Railway to the Communist government "not later than the end of 1952" and "without compensation." (According to the Soviet-Chinese treaty of 1945 the railway was not to be turned over to China until 1975.) Somewhat later the Soviet government agreed to transfer to China, without compensation, all property acquired during the war from Japanese owners in Manchuria by Soviet economic agencies. More symptomatic was Moscow's stipulation that it would in the meantime introduce a better system of administering the "mixed" railway. Certain paragraphs of the agreement, however, revealed the bitterness of the Chinese over their treatment by the Soviet; for example, the "existing administration" of the railway was to "remain unchanged" until the "completion of the transfer," with one exception: the humiliating Soviet system of "filling posts" with Russians was to be changed forthwith, and "alternation is laid down for filling of positions" in the administration of the railway, presidency of the management, and other departments.

A Soviet-Chinese Military Commission was created to succeed the all-Russian command at Port Arthur, which was likewise scheduled to be returned to China not later than the end of 1952. But China had to pay an unspecified sum for Soviet "installations" (this became part of the growing debt of China). The fate of Port Dairen (Dalni)

---

[28] A number of unpublished agreements were reported to have been signed on the same occasion, and one of these may have prescribed the form of Soviet assistance in case of war. In diplomatic circles it was affirmed that, for such an eventuality, the Soviet government had requested seven "treaty ports" in North China and other military-political privileges.

Stalin's Course in China

was left open, but the civil administration of the port was turned over to China, and property in Soviet hands acquired from Japan at the end of the war was to be transferred to the new authorities.

A Soviet loan of $300,000,000 at 1 per cent interest annually was granted to China, to be used at the rate of $60,000,000 a year over a period of five years for payments for Soviet imports; the import goods enumerated in the agreement were exclusively in the "heavy industry" category. The size of the loan was far below Chinese expectations (reports mentioned a request by Mao for a loan of $2,800,000,000). At that moment, however (this was only five years after the war), Soviet modesty was only natural.

In addition to the loan, the setting up of a number of "mixed" Soviet-Chinese companies was projected.

A few weeks after the end of the Moscow Conference the Sino-Soviet "mixed companies" were organized: two for oil and metals in Sinkiang, one for civil aviation between the two countries, and one for shipbuilding in Dairen. In addition, some industrial privileges in Manchuria were apparently reserved to the Soviet Union, although exact reports on this have never been published. The Soviet government, with the use of some former Japanese property which it had taken over at the end of the war, continued to operate certain enterprises. This is seen from the fact that the list of property returned to China in 1950 was incomplete.

On the whole the Moscow Conference did not signify an about-face in Sino-Soviet relations. Some leeway had to be granted to Mao's policies, and Stalin had to accede to a number of Chinese demands. But Moscow succeeded in temporizing and in delaying and conditioning the rise of China. Stalin had no reason to revise his basic views about his allies, about the structure of the Soviet bloc, or about his own role as the leader of that bloc.

Of the Sino-Soviet agreements of 1950, that on Soviet "advisers" in China was not discussed in the Soviet press; not even the numbers of Soviet technicians and officers assigned to China were revealed.

Soviet advisers were not a novelty in Communist China, but after 1950 they moved in in a broad stream. Urgently needed by Peking, they at the same time served Moscow as a means of checking and control. Along with engineers, technicians, professors, and economists, several thousand military men were rushed to China to help raise her armies from the guerrilla level to the status of a modern military force. "Within four weeks after the signing of the Sino-Soviet pact, on 14 February 1950, over 3,000 Russian officers and advisors were unpacking their cheap suitcases in the hotels of Mukden, Peking, Shanghai and other Chinese cities." [29] A "Soviet influx into Red China," reported Christopher Rand in May, 1950. The Soviet goal is "to raise the Chinese effectiveness." The number of military personnel sent to Red China was said to total 23,000.

> An overwhelming proportion of Russians now reaching China—perhaps 90 per cent—are reported to be military personnel (though they often appear in civilian clothes or Chinese army uniform). . . . The Chinese Communist Air Force is a Russian air force, one trained observer said. . . . Russians manage its flying, servicing and anti-aircraft protection of the planes.[30]

Soviet military advisers were reported training Chinese units for an invasion of Taiwan; training of aviators was another important Soviet task. Scores of Soviet professors arrived in the fall of 1950 to

[29] Peter S. H. Tang, referring to Appendix III of the 1950 Treaty, gives the following numbers of prospective Soviet advisers: ". . . ammunition production (1,500–5,000), . . . steel (500–1,000), textiles (500–1,000), machine production (1,000–3,000), mining (3,000–5,000), oil refining (300–1,000), electricity (500–1,000), aeronautics (100–1,000), shipbuilding (100–1,000), and automobile (100–1,200). Agriculture was to have 1,000–5,000 specialists, forestry 1,000–2,000, and water conservation projects 500–2,000. Other assignments included education and culture, 2,000–3,000 each; railways, 2,000–3,000; highways, 500–1,000; trade and medicine, 1,000–2,000 each; and financial and cooperative management, 500–1,000. Among many others, the printing, paper-making, rubber-making and cinema industries were to have 100 to 500 advisers each." (Peter S. H. Tang, *Communist China Today: Domestic and Foreign Policies*, New York, Frederick A. Praeger, 1957, p. 392.) The numbers of advisers were no doubt substantially increased as Soviet aid to China's economy grew.

As to military advisers, W. W. Rostow (W. W. Rostow and others, *The Prospects for Communist China*; published jointly by The Technology Press of Massachusetts Institute of Technology and John Wiley and Sons, Inc., New York, 1954, p. 208) has given the following figures:

	Advisers from the Spring of 1950 to the Summer of 1952	Number to Be Increased in the Future to
Army	5,000	10,000
Navy	1,000	2,500
Air force	1,000	2,500

This "future" estimate, Rostow states, may be approximately correct for mid-1954.

Richard Walker (*China Under Communism: The First Five Years*, New Haven, Yale University Press, 1955, p. 159) mentions an estimate of 150.000 Soviet advisers in China, but considers this figure to be exaggerated. From 6,000 to 7,000 Chinese students were in Russia between 1950 and 1956.

[30] New York *Herald Tribune*, May 7, 1950.

teach at the University of Peking. Among Soviet military leaders in China were Marshal Kiril Meretskov, Military Adviser to the Chinese Government, and the ambassador, Nikolai Roshchin. Information on the number of Soviet advisers and their organization was kept secret; cautious estimates put the number at from 15,000 to 25,000. There was a "General Adviser to the Chinese Cabinet," from whom other Russian experts took orders.[31]

The initial influx of Soviet advisers marked the beginning of disputes that lasted for a number of years and eventually led to a reduction of the number of advisers and strict instructions concerning their behavior. The Soviet side maintained an optimistic and confident view: the Soviet specialists in China "are working under the guidance of the Chinese comrades, their salaries are on a par with those of Chinese specialists of the same grade. . . . Soviet specialists are teaching Chinese industrial managers in seminars . . . SKOGA (aviation) is training Chinese pilots. . . ."[32]

On the other hand, reports from China indicated the existence of tension between the Chinese and the Soviet advisers:

> The present Soviet colony in China—in contrast with the émigrés who had lived for years in Harbin—are described as conceited "swollen heads" and "impossible." The Chinese are said to resent their boasts that all is wonderful in the Soviet Union and simultaneously watch them buy up all available watches, shoes, furs and clothing. . . .[33]

Stalin succeeded also in directing China's dynamism toward the south. Having left many issues concerning the north unsettled (for example, defining the border [34]), Mao's regime hastened to round up its possessions in regions distant from the Soviet borders. The drive into Tibet, which had started in 1949, ended in the agreement of May, 1951, under which Tibet acknowledged her adherence to China and, for the first time since the war, opened her gates to Chinese military forces. In Nepal, the road to India, political crises developed along

[31] *China News Analysis*, weekly newsletter, Hong Kong, no. 179, May 3, 1957.
[32] Yu. V. Arutyunyan, *Nerushimaya Druzhba Narodov Sovetskogo Soyuza i Kitaiskoi Narodnoi Respubliki* (Inviolable Friendship of the Peoples of the Soviet Union and the Chinese People's Republic), Moscow, 1954, pp. 19 and 20.
[33] *The New York Times*, July 9, 1951.
[34] In a revealing analysis of Chinese geographical maps, *China News Analysis*, no. 129, April 27, 1956, arrives at the conclusion that the changes in the boundaries on the official maps follow, "in large lines, the general trend of Peking's international policies—briefly: subservient friendship with the Soviet Union, and expansionist tendencies in South-Asia."

with increased activity of the Nepalese Communist Party; in India anxiety was mounting. The development which had started in Tibet, Prime Minister Nehru said, "was not a thing that they [the Indians] liked—the way it was taking place—because it did bring in certain rather new factors which might cause trouble." [35]

In the south, too, China started construction of the 250-mile railway line to Yunnan, leading to Indochina, where the long and bloody Communist uprising was going on. In their efforts to help Ho Chi-minh, the Chinese, it was reported, made use of old Soviet and Soviet-captured arms; later China sent a number of tanks to Indochina. This Soviet-Chinese assistance enabled Ho Chi-minh to hold out and in the end achieve a more than honorable peace. Also in the south, disputes with Burma flared up; Chinese Communist units which invaded the eastern areas of Burma remained there for years. There was intensive preparation for an invasion of Taiwan, and in Malaya aid was given to insurgents.

In the north, on the other hand, there was no military action. North Korea, which had been created by Soviet instructors and generals, remained Moscow's responsibility. The Soviet-Korean agreement on economic and cultural assistance, signed in March, 1949, was the only part of their relationship to be publicized. More important were other, unpublished components of an alliance.[36]

By that time American troops had been almost completely withdrawn from South Korea, and Washington had confirmed that it was not strategically interested in Korea. The South Korean army was poorly trained and equipped. There was every reason to assume that the conflict between the north and the south would remain an internal affair, a civil war of Koreans against Koreans. And civil war, akin to revolution, was close in spirit to Soviet philosophy and propaganda. The Soviet ambassador in Pyongyang, General Terenti Shtykov, was assuring Moscow that the United States would not send its forces to take part in the fighting. The situation seemed favorable for an attack from the north and victory.

[35] *The Times*, London, January 17, 1951.
[36] On October, 1949, the South Korean defense minister, Sin Seong No, and the foreign minister, Lin Byong Jik, disclosed in a joint statement that Soviet Russia and North Korea had reached a military alliance which provided that Soviet Russia was to equip five divisions, all the police units, three armored divisions, and provide 20 patrol craft, 100 fighters, 20 bombers, 100 reconnaissance planes for North Korea. (D Papers, File CH, p. 34.)

Stalin's Course in China

There are no reliable reports of the discussion concerning Korean affairs that took place at the Stalin-Mao conference in December–January 1950–51. Subsequent developments, however, made it appear certain not only that the forthcoming effort in Korea was discussed, but also that it was expected that the fighting would be neither long nor hard and that neither China nor the Soviet Union would have to intervene directly. Apparently Mao Tse-tung took upon himself the obligation to turn over to North Korea thousands of Korean soldiers and officers and scores of units that had been incorporated into his armies. He carried out this obligation. Soon after the Moscow Conference the movement of Koreans from China to Korea started; in April, 1950, the "Fifteenth Independent Division" moved into Korea, where it was designated the "Seventh North Korean Division" (later "Twelfth Division"). This phase of Chinese activity was completed before the attack of June 25. The then Thirty-Eighth, Thirty-Ninth, and Fortieth Divisions were moved from South China to the Korean border; the Forty-Second Army, already in Manchuria, was added. By the time the hostilities in Korea started, a probable aggregate of 40,000 to 60,000 Chinese-trained Koreans had been released from China and integrated into the North Korean army.[37]

"Peking and Moscow had agreed," says a knowledgeable United States diplomat who spent those years in the Far East, "that the North Koreans would start the war. They counted on the North Koreans to win without outside military assistance. Only when the Americans started to win did the Chinese have to enter the war. . . ."[38]

That Mao was not girding himself for a long campaign was seen from the course he took in Chinese internal affairs:

> Mao did not seem to believe that participation in the Korean war was inevitable, as is evidenced by the adoption of a set of resolutions on demobilization, stabilization of finances, and prevention of inflation by the National Convention of the Chinese Communists before the Korean war.[39]

[37] *Fourth Report of the United Nations Command in Korea*, September 18, 1950.
[38] D Papers, vol. 2, November 26, 1956, pp. 128–29. A Communist-led conference in Chibu, a province in Japan, in April, 1950, was reported to have adopted a resolution which read: "The North Korean armies will carry out the southern campaign for the unification of the country at the beginning of the rainy season. They will be assisted by the Chinese Communist forces. To facilitate the achievement of this objective, we will engage in guerrilla activities directed at the destruction of imperialist industry. Our operations are scheduled, until further notice, for August." (Swearingen and Langer, *Red Flag in Japan*, Cambridge, Mass., Harvard University Press, 1952, p. 240.)
[39] D Papers, File CH, p. 35.

Not until the war started to take a catastrophic turn, that is, after the operation at Inchon, where the North Korean army was decimated, did Moscow request that China join in the venture. Various sources report that Mao's first reaction was negative, but that he agreed in principle and then began to present demands and advance conditions. Yuri Rastvorov, a member of the Soviet Mission in Tokyo, related how Stalin pressed the Chinese leaders, while "Mao kept on insisting that the Chinese lacked gasoline, planes, artillery and what not. The two of them [Stalin and Mao] were firing stiffer and stiffer messages back and forth between Peking and Moscow. Finally after long argument they reached an agreement but only after Stalin promised China all kinds of aid." [40]

Judging from official United States information and on the basis of research, it appears certain that the Chinese decision actively to intervene was made about two months after the start of the war, that is, in mid-August, 1950. Later, in September, Chinese communication and supply forces began crossing the Yalu, and in October combat forces started moving into Korea at the rate of one to two army corps per week. Troop movements occurred chiefly at night and involved a relatively short march of twenty to forty miles to the rear of the North Korean Communist forces being pushed back by the advancing United Nations armies. The first combat between United Nations and Chinese Communist forces took place on October 12. By December 15 the Chinese had moved approximately ten army corps, comprising thirty divisions, into Korea, and had thus made certain that there would be no early collapse of the Communist effort to occupy all of Korea by force.[41]

China's active participation in the Korean War was the first phase of China's rise in prestige, as compared with the other "socialist countries," in her relations with Moscow: the mere fact that China could make demands and set conditions, and that Moscow accepted them, augured badly for unrestricted Soviet leadership. This was the beginning of a series of developments over the next few years that ended

[40] Yuri A. Rastvorov, "Red Fraud and Intrigue in Far East," *Life,* December 6, 1954, p. 175. In Belgrade it was likewise known how hard it had been to induce Peking to enter the war (*The New York Times,* December 27, 1950).

[41] *Department of Defense Office of Public Information Release 465–54,* May 15, 1954, "Chinese Communist Aggression and Barbarism in Korea," p. 3; *The New York Times,* September 29, 1950.

Who Is Leader in Asia? 89

in a new type of relationship between China and the Soviet Union.

The Soviet part in the newly emerging war coalition was threefold: first, global propaganda and protection in the United Nations; second, advice on strategy, training of Chinese and Korean forces, and supplying of military matériel; and third, direct, although cautious and limited, participation in military operations. The latter refers to those special technical jobs that the Chinese and Koreans had not yet mastered (in the fields of radar, aviation, etc.). The total number of Soviet troops that participated directly in the war has been estimated at from 10,000 to 12,000.[42] The first Soviet jets appeared over Korea about the end of 1950.

Who Is Leader in Asia? For another two years and four months Stalin was able, as China's ally, to inspire the Korean War. Every war alliance, this closest form of international collaboration, increases the cohesion between its members. The principle of solidarity is emphasized, even exaggerated, for the benefit of the morale of the army and public opinion, and to impress the enemy. Behind the scenes, however, tension is inevitable, and there has hardly ever been a war coalition in which the allied governments did not reach a point of weariness and discouragement; but however weary and discouraged the parties, the ties of a war coalition have rarely been broken.

This applies to the course of Soviet-Chinese relations in 1951–52. An incessant stream of declarations of loyalty and devotion poured on Peking from Moscow and on Moscow from Peking. Mao regularly congratulated Stalin, and Stalin responded in kind. Leaders on both sides praised the other's virtues, achievements, and loyalty. At the famous banquet in the Kremlin, toasts were drunk to the health of the "great Stalin," "Chairman Mao," and the "inviolable friendship" of the two nations. More than once Mao Tse-tung stressed that without the help of the Soviet Union Communism in China could not win.[43] The Sino-Soviet Friendship Association, which in 1949 had 700,000 members, announced a membership of 17,000,000 in December, 1951, and 34,000,000 in November, 1952. A telephone line linking Moscow and Peking was installed in December, 1950; through railway traffic

[42] *Department of Defense Office of Public Information Release 465–54, op. cit.,* "Truth about Soviet Involvement in the Korean War," p. 5.
[43] *Large Soviet Encyclopedia,* 2d ed., vol. 21, pp. 243–244.

between Moscow and Peking was started in March, 1951; new trade agreements were signed on June 15, 1951, and April 12, 1952. On January 1, 1953, in accord with the Moscow agreements of 1950, the joint Soviet-Chinese administration of the Chinese Changchun Railway ended, and the Soviet section was turned over to the Chinese; ceremonies took place in Peking and Harbin, and Mao sent a congratulatory telegram to Stalin.

Never, it was claimed, had there been a firmer, more honest, or more self-sacrificing relationship and alliance.

Behind the scenes and behind the high paper walls of the press, however, divergencies developed, some of them of major importance. China's position in the Soviet bloc was again at stake.

That the Chinese government, only recently persuaded to turn southward, was called upon to apply its force also in the north, in the Soviet-organized and Soviet-sponsored Korean War, was tantamount to admission of a Soviet failure. Chinese ambitions, far-reaching before the Korean War, were receiving added nourishment from the encounter with the greatest of the world powers. There was nothing extraordinary in the fact that Mao, the orthodox Communist, decided to send the armies of his ruined, impoverished, long-suffering nation to Korea; this was in conformity with the old tenet that "liberation" has priority over the well-being of the population. But to Moscow, the turn of events in Korea represented a defeat. Stalin, in his usual way, punished a few scapegoats (he not only removed Shtykov, the ambassador to Korea, but stripped him of his titles and medals),[44] but the failure was a hard fact.

Hundreds of thousands of Chinese—soldiers, officers, and Party men—invaded North Korea. The pro-Chinese elements in Korea, which had been neglected or pushed aside under the strictly pro-Soviet regime, now raised their heads and grew in influence. Remnants of the Korean Emancipation League, which in the late 1930's and '40's had collaborated with the Chinese Communist leadership in Yenan, reappeared. Soon the role of the Soviet military advisers was reduced.[45]

Behind the scenes disagreements were mounting with respect to all phases of the war—supplies, training, prestige:

[44] Rastvorov, *op. cit.*, p. 175.
[45] *The New York Times*, December 25, 1950. Previously eight Soviet advisers had been attached to each Korean regiment. They were removed after China joined the war; only at the divisional command level were Soviet advisers retained.

Who Is Leader in Asia? 91

If one digs down below the level of the half dozen top Chinese generals, one is not likely to find men formally educated in the scope of modern warfare. China has many generals but few really good ones for the size of her forces. Are any of these many generals doing anything to raise their professional talents? Yes, they are being helped by the Soviets, but the Russians are not giving away all their top secrets on strategy, army groups, and high logistics and staff planning. The Soviets are feeding the Chinese on a diet of old manuals and texts, dating in concept from World War I. . . . the Soviets are giving the Chinese a firm military foundation, adding a few up-to-date frills like armor and airborne [troops], but in the main treating them for what they are—amateurs in modern war and modern logistics. . . . The Soviets may bend them partially to Russian will and design—but in the end these Chinese militarists will prove to be Communists first, Chinese second, and Soviet puppets last.[46]

Who would be the leader in Asia? A few months before, the issue seemed to have been definitely resolved, but developments during the Korean War raised some doubts. A growing new force was menacing old Russian theories. In Indochina, Chinese Communist elements were achieving successes. Chinese Communist ties with Japanese Communists, reminiscent of the Yenan era, were enlarged; a "Free Japan" radio in China initiated broadcasts in Japanese.[47] Chinese Communism began to view itself as *the* great power of Asia. Before Korea, in the elation over the victory of Communism in China, Moscow had more or less acquiesced in the thesis that China's specific road to victory (via a large insurrectional army plus cooperation with "capitalist" elements) would be the general path of revolution in underdeveloped colonial and semicolonial countries. But if China established the pattern for Asia, it was logical that she should lead the way. In that case Chinese Communism would be the leader of the rising movements, and Peking, not Moscow, would be the center of the Eastern Communist world. The momentous successes of the Chinese drives, and now the thrusts to the north into Korea and Japan, were obviously the embryo of a new Communist commonwealth that would be not inferior in importance and superior in size to the Soviet Union.

Moscow began to revise the thesis. It was Moscow, after all, and not Peking that was the capital of the new world—Stalin would be the

[46] Rigg, *Red China's Fighting Hordes*, op. cit., pp. 55–56.
[47] In May, 1952. D Papers, vol. 1, pp. 64–67.

last to budge from this point. Behind-the-scene rumbling found almost outspoken expression in discussions at the Academy of Sciences, in November, 1951, when Yevgeni Zhukov, mouthpiece of the Central Committee, read a paper on the people's democracy in the East:

> It would be risky to view the Chinese revolution as a kind of pattern for the popular-democratic revolution in other Asian countries. In particular, it is doubtful whether other countries of the East which take the road toward a people's democracy could expect to be able to get the most important advantage of the Chinese revolution, namely, a revolutionary army.[48]

And Stalin, not Mao, was the supreme leader of the peoples of the East:

> The broadest masses of the peoples of the non-Soviet Orient, on their road to people's democracy, and fighting for national liberation, for peace, nourish the greatest confidence in and love for the Soviet Union, for Comrade Stalin.[49]

In a comparatively free discussion, Zhukov was supported by the experts on India Balabushevich and Nesenko (the Indian Communist Party had been told by Moscow earlier that "Chinese methods" were not appropriate for the Indian party):

> It is risky [Balabushevich said] to view the Chinese revolution and the ways of her development as an obligatory pattern for people's democratic revolutions in other countries of Asia.

Zhukov summarized his views:

> To belittle the Chinese experience would be ridiculous; its significance is very great. But it should not be generalized, it cannot be considered as a universal rule for all situations which might arise in different Asian countries.

On the eve of the Nineteenth Congress of the Communist Party there arrived in Moscow, among others, Chou En-lai and the new premier of Mongolia, Yu Tsedenbal, successor to Choibalsan. In conferences with Stalin and Vyshinsky there was discussion of a number

---

[48] *Izvestia Akademii Nauk SSSR, Seriya Istorii i Filosofii* (News of the Academy of Sciences of the USSR, Series on History and Philosophy), Moscow, Izdat. Akad. Nauk, January–February, 1952, vol. 9, no. 1, p. 81.
[49] *Ibid.*

of Far Eastern issues the decisions on which were not made public until two years later. The most important issue was the Chinese-Mongolian project of a railway linking China with Ulan Bator, the capital of Mongolia. The Soviet side made no pledge of direct help (they later built a section in Mongolia). It was odd that Premiers Chou and Tsedenbal departed from Moscow before the Party Congress opened, leaving persons of lesser rank to greet the Communist leadership assembled from all over the world. Chou and Tsedenbal went to Peking, where, on October 4, they signed the first Sino-Mongol agreement (on "economic and cultural collaboration"). The Chinese started construction on the railway on May 1, 1953.[50] Years later the Chinese-Mongol segment of the railway became part of the Peking-Moscow trunk.

On the other hand, the Changchun railway and Port Arthur were to be restored by the Soviet Union to China not later than the end of December, 1952. Stalin refused, however, to hand over Port Arthur while the war in Korea was still on. On September 15, 1952, in a note polite to the point of hypocrisy, Chou En-lai "requested" the Soviet government to prolong the term until the conclusion of peace with Japan, and Vyshinsky replied in the affirmative.[51]

However, a break between China and Russia, which many Western observers predicted in those days, did not and could not materialize; to have expected it was wishful thinking. What did occur at that time was a shake-up and disruption of the orthodox notion of a "socialist bloc" and the placing of China in a secondary place within the framework of the bloc. If Stalin's pattern for other Communist nations was to convert them into satellites, the pattern—though Stalin never admitted this—was inappropriate in the case of China. Even before Stalin died, the orthodox view on China as a full-fledged satellite went up in the smoke of Korean cities and was buried in the ashes along with thousands of Chinese corpses.

[50] *Osteuropa*, Stuttgart, no. 12, December, 1957, p. 874.
[51] The real attitude of Stalin and his lieutenants toward China became evident at a reception held at about that time, to which Chou and the Chinese trade delegation were invited: ". . . the Chinese had been excluded from the inner dining room where Chou was being feted and relegated to an outside room where a very junior Russian diplomat greeted them and then vanished even before the toasts began. (Another fact which had long made me suspicious about the true state of Sino-Russian relations was the persistent and long-continued absence of the Chinese Ambassador from Moscow. With such protocol-conscious people as the Chinese and the Russians this could only be a sign of coolness.)" (Harrison E. Salisbury, *American in Russia*, New York, Harper & Brothers, 1955, p. 307.)

For Communist China, the Korean War was a phase of her ascendance to power. For Stalin's foreign policy, the Korean War was a failure.

3. JAPAN

The significance of the war in Korea went far beyond the limits of the Asian peninsula. The war was rather a new attempt on the part of the Soviet Union to solve the Japanese puzzle in the Soviet way. As long as the Korean War continued, therefore, there could be no peace treaty or "regularization of relations" between Japan and the Soviet Union.

It would be difficult to say which of the two issues, China or Japan, has been and is of greater importance to the Soviet Union. China weighs heavily by virtue of the size of her population, the solidity of her Communism, her place in the largest of the continents, and her contiguousness to Russia's frontiers. By her uncompromising attitude toward the "imperialists," the rapid transformation of her economy, and her attacks on Taiwan, China has achieved a prominent place in the "socialist camp"; today she is recognized as first in that camp after the Soviet Union. It was China's "transition to socialism" that convinced the international Communist leadership that the balance of power had shifted to its side.

But the official exaltation over China in the Soviet and pro-Soviet world could not counterbalance the gloomy aspects of the unsolved problem of Japan. True, Japan had been defeated and was disarmed and impotent, and in the today-and-tomorrow Soviet-Chinese plans and schedules Japan was a negligible quantity. But Moscow could not forget that Japan, alone among the nations of Asia, had been able to rise to the stature of a world power, control the Far East, and wage a four-year war on the West. That Japan would eventually be revived was never doubted; Stalin himself predicted—and more than once—that Japan would rise again. So long as this potentially strong nation continued to oppose the Soviet Union, China, and the Sino-Soviet alliance, no real peace was possible.

Disarmament of Japan was not, in Soviet eyes, a measure adequate to ensure her remaining impotent; the world had witnessed the revival of a defeated and disarmed Germany in the 1930's, and the

Japan

new trend of the American-Japanese alliance toward rearmament of Japan was apparent.

There could be only one real solution of the Japanese problem—to include her, directly or indirectly, in the Soviet orbit. Stalin had made one attempt after another to achieve this great goal, but each time he had failed. He tried to acquire territory in Japan (for example, the island of Hokkaido) for his occupation forces, but this had proved impossible because of the attitude of the United States. On the other hand, the Japanese Communist Party was preparing to assume the leadership of a satellite Japan, and its leaders viewed the victory of Communism in China as a stepping stone to their own rise to the high stature of Rakoszis, Ulbrichts, or Bieruts. In a statement published a year before the beginning of hostilities in Korea, Sanzo Nozaka, a high-ranking Communist leader, said:

> Should all of Korea follow the example of China, the influence on Japan would be extremely great. The islands of Japan instead of being surrounded on three sides by capitalism and reaction would be surrounded by people's democracies and socialism. The same waters which wash the docks of Shanghai, Pusan, and Vladivostok beat also against the shores of Japan. There is absolutely no barrier which can stem this tide.[52]

The Soviet hope of obtaining a foothold in Japan through the rising Communist movement there was also shattered despite all the efforts of the dynamic Soviet Mission in Tokyo. At the last Japanese elections before Stalin's death (October, 1952) the Communist Party lost all its twenty two seats in the Diet, and the number of votes cast for Communist candidates was less than 900,000 out of a total of 31,000,000.

Thus the Korean War was a Soviet attempt directed more against Japan than against Korea. Had the Soviet-Chinese side been the victors in the war, their guns would have been only a short distance from Japan's southern tip, and greatly increased pressure would have been exerted to oust the Americans from the Far East and obtain a Soviet foothold on Japanese soil. To the very end Stalin refused to acquiesce in the American-initiated plan for Japan. While he rejected the *status quo* for Korea, he could not agree to any peace treaty with Japan on

[52] Quoted in Swearingen and Langer, *op. cit.*, p. 241.

terms other than his own. His minister and his envoy participated in the discussions of the drafts of the peace treaty only to "reveal" their shortcomings and "expose" them to the Asian peoples. A peace treaty of the West with Japan was possible only if the Soviet Union and Communist China were not signatories. The deterioration in Soviet-American relations during the Korean War accelerated the conclusion of the treaty.

The United States government, which had previously been hesitant, in the fall of 1950 embarked firmly on negotiations for a peace treaty. The Moscow government was invited to attend the peace conference and did so. The personal negotiations between Jacob Malik, Soviet Deputy Minister of Foreign Affairs, and John Foster Dulles, the exchange of diplomatic notes, and the preparations of the draft took almost a year. The peace documents were finally signed at the San Francisco Conference on September 8, 1951.

In the Soviet scheme of peace treaties, demilitarization of Japan was one of the most important points. It was through sheer lack of understanding and shortsightedness that Japanese governments and American occupation authorities had introduced, between 1946 and 1948, a number of political directives and a constitution for Japan that called for the complete disarmament of that country. The experiment, which was hailed by the Soviet-Chinese coalition, was in obvious contradiction to Japan's real situation and defense needs. Taking advantage of these disarmament pledges, the Soviet representative in the Allied Council in Tokyo attacked the United States authorities for breaking promises and agreements, enlarging the "police forces" on land and sea, resurrecting Japanese military aviation, resuming production of arms, etc. Said General Andrei Kislenko:

> In his declaration [of December 31, 1950] General MacArthur proposes direct violation of Japan's Constitution of 1946. As is known, the Japanese Constitution states that Japan "renounces war forever," it also renounces "the threat of applying military force as a means of settling international disputes." Pretending that in this way he is approving the Japanese Constitution as a constitution that is expressing "one of the most lofty, if not the most lofty, ideal," General MacArthur states in his message of December 31 that "this ideal must give way to the higher tenet of self-preservation. . . ."
>
> . . . Article 9 of the Japanese Constitution states that "no land,

sea, aerial or other military forces will be maintained in Japan." This provision of the Japanese Constitution fully corresponds to the aim of barring the rebirth of Japanese militarism and securing the transformation of Japan into a peaceloving country. However, General MacArthur speaks in his declaration about the necessity for Japan "to accumulate strength"; in this way he calls upon the Japanese people to revive the Japanese armed forces. . . .[53]

Many of the points in the Soviet peace program for Japan were the same as those in her program for Germany. The situation in Japan, however, differed from that in Germany in two significant respects: first, in Japan there was continuity of government, and the Japanese government was recognized by Moscow; second, in Japan there was no separate Soviet zone, no nucleus of a rival regime. In the negotiations for a treaty for Japan, Moscow acted as the mouthpiece not only of the Soviet Union but also of China, Japan's long-time prime victim. Communist China, however, was not invited to negotiate, and India and Burma likewise stood aloof. The Soviet alliance with China, despite flaws and disagreements, was solidified by the common policy with regard to Japan. The Soviet claim that it spoke for other nations was supported by Peking and all the other Communist governments.

The main points of the Soviet peace program for Japan, which were restated at the San Francisco Conference, were part of the pattern of Soviet-Chinese predominance in the Far East: first, the return to China of former Chinese territories on the continent, as well as of Formosa, the Pescadores, and certain other islands, and the restoration to Russia of Southern Sakhalin and the Kurile Islands; second, limitation of Japan's future armed forces to a low level, coupled with a prohibition of an alliance directed against a power that had taken part in the war against her; third, democracy (in the Soviet interpretation, which meant prohibition of "fascist" and "militaristic" organizations—terms which could be made to embrace any group) and freedom of action for "progressive" organizations; fourth, complete withdrawal of American military forces and evacuation and return to Japan of American-occupied islands in the Pacific; and fifth, limitation of the use of the straits around Japan to the navies of nations adjacent to the

[53] *Pravda*, February 15, 1951.

Sea of Japan, that is the Soviet Union and China but not the United States or Britain.

The Soviet delegation at San Francisco did not sign the peace treaty; the treaty, Moscow continued to insist, was a "separate treaty," "illegal," a "document full of lies and hypocrisy," and the peace conference had been a "comedy"; the Japanese people live in "colonial slavery"; Japan is a nation conquered and ruled by the United States.[54]

If Japan had indeed been degraded to the level of a colony, then the well-known Soviet tactics of "national fronts"—meaning an appeal to all classes and political parties, including the "bourgeoisie," to join in an integrated effort to overthrow and drive the "exploiters" from Japanese soil—could be applied here. Still free from diplomatic inhibitions, Stalin, on December 31, 1951, in a rare gesture, addressed a "New Year's message" to the "people of Japan":

> It is not in the Soviet tradition for the Premier of one country to address messages of good will to the people of a foreign country. However, the deep sympathy the peoples of the Soviet Union entertain for the Japanese people in the distress that has befallen them owing to a foreign occupation . . . impels me to make an exception. . . .
>
> The people of the Soviet Union have themselves in the past experienced the horror of foreign occupation, in which the Japanese imperialists took part. They therefore fully appreciate the suffering of the Japanese people, deeply sympathize with them, and believe that they will achieve the regeneration and independence of their country, just as the peoples of the Soviet Union did.[55]

There was a certain advantage for the Soviet Union, although a minor one, in not signing the peace treaty with Japan. In 1945 Soviet forces had occupied certain Japanese territories, in particular South Sakhalin, the Kuriles, and a few small islands in the north. Restoration of Sakhalin to Russia had been promised by the Allies, but the southern islands of the Kuriles chain would have been in dispute, nor would the other powers have agreed to acquisition by the Soviet Union of other areas which it had occupied. The latter remained in Soviet possession only because of the absence of a peace treaty.

During the last stage of the negotiations on the peace treaty hints

---

[54] *Bolshevik,* Moscow, no. 17, September, 1951, and no. 13, July, 1952; *New Times,* Moscow, no. 32, August, 1951, and no. 17, April, 1952.

[55] *New Times,* Moscow, no. 2, January 9, 1952, p. 1.

Japan

and rumors emanating from Peking and Moscow pointed to a dangerous situation that might arise if China and Russia did not sign a treaty with Japan: for China and Russia the war situation would continue; moreover, they would be entitled to send occupation forces into Japan. These threats were not taken seriously, however, and they did not stop the negotiations.

In April, 1952, after the signing of the treaty, the Allied Council for Japan was dissolved, and the Soviet Mission in Tokyo—the large organization that was the substitute for a Soviet embassy—was invited to close. At the final meeting of the Allied Council, General Kislenko, the Soviet representative, strenuously criticized the dissolution of the Council as another "illegal" act since the Council had not yet "completed its tasks"; he was particularly critical of the fact that American troops were to remain, and said that this proved the "dependent position of Japan." On May 30 the Japanese Ministry of Foreign Affairs told the Soviet mission that, with the conclusion of the peace treaty "the Soviet part of the Allied Council for Japan [the Soviet Mission] has ceased to exist." The Soviet reply of June 11 made it clear that the Soviet Mission did not intend to comply with this decision and would continue as before:

> The Soviet Government considers that the coming into force of the separate peace treaty cannot be considered as a legal basis for the above statement to the Representation of the U.S.S.R. in Japan.[56]

As if to accentuate Soviet nonrecognition of the peace treaty, Soviet planes continued their regular flights over Japanese territory, specifically over Hokkaido Island. During the last six months of 1952 Soviet military planes making reconnaissance of United States and Japanese defense forces were spotted more than forty times. On January 13, 1953, Japan requested American help against "violation of Japan's territorial air" since Japan herself did not possess an air force. The American reply, three days later, stated that the United States Commander-in-Chief, Far East Command, will take the necessary measures to repel all such violators.[57]

On September 17, 1952, Jacob Malik, the Soviet United Nations representative, vetoed Japan's admission to the United Nations on the

[56] *Pravda,* June 12, 1952.
[57] *Department of State Bulletin,* January 26, 1953.

grounds that no peace treaty had been concluded between it and the Soviet Union and China. Although the vote was 10 to 1 for admission, the result nevertheless was a veto. Malik called Japan "an American colony" and an "American base for aggression in Korea and the Far East."

CHAPTER 5

THE DEADLOCK

1. STALIN'S LEGACY IN THE MIDDLE EAST

"Stalin had spoiled Soviet relations with Iran and Turkey," Premier Bulganin told the Iranians and Turks early in 1955; now the new Soviet leaders wanted to "return to Lenin's policy of respecting full sovereignty of other countries."[1] In December, 1955, Nikita Khrushchev told the Supreme Soviet that the deterioration of relations with Turkey was due, among other causes, to our "inappropriate statements": "We cannot say that this [deterioration] developed only because of Turkey's fault—we on our part also made inappropriate statements which clouded these relations."[2] Like Bulganin, Khrushchev was nostalgic for the Lenin days: "It is well known that when Kemal Ataturk and Ismet Inonu were Turkey's leaders our relations with her were very good, but later on they deteriorated."[3] But the Lenin days had gone forever. From a militarily impotent, isolated, and starving nation, Russia had become, under Stalin, a military power which was arousing worry and fear among its neighbors and keeping the world in a state of perpetual tension. A simple reversion to the type of Soviet-Turkish relations that had existed three decades before was not possible, and all Soviet efforts to achieve it were doomed.

The new Soviet policy in the Middle East can be understood only if viewed against the background of Stalin's efforts and achievements in this part of the world.

With the start of the European war in 1939 a substantial change occurred in Soviet policy in respect to the Middle East. During his

[1] George McTurman Kahin, *The Asian-African Conference, Bandung, Indonesia, 1955*, Ithaca, New York, Cornell University Press, 1956, p. 20.
[2] *Pravda*, December 20, 1955.
[3] *Ibid.*

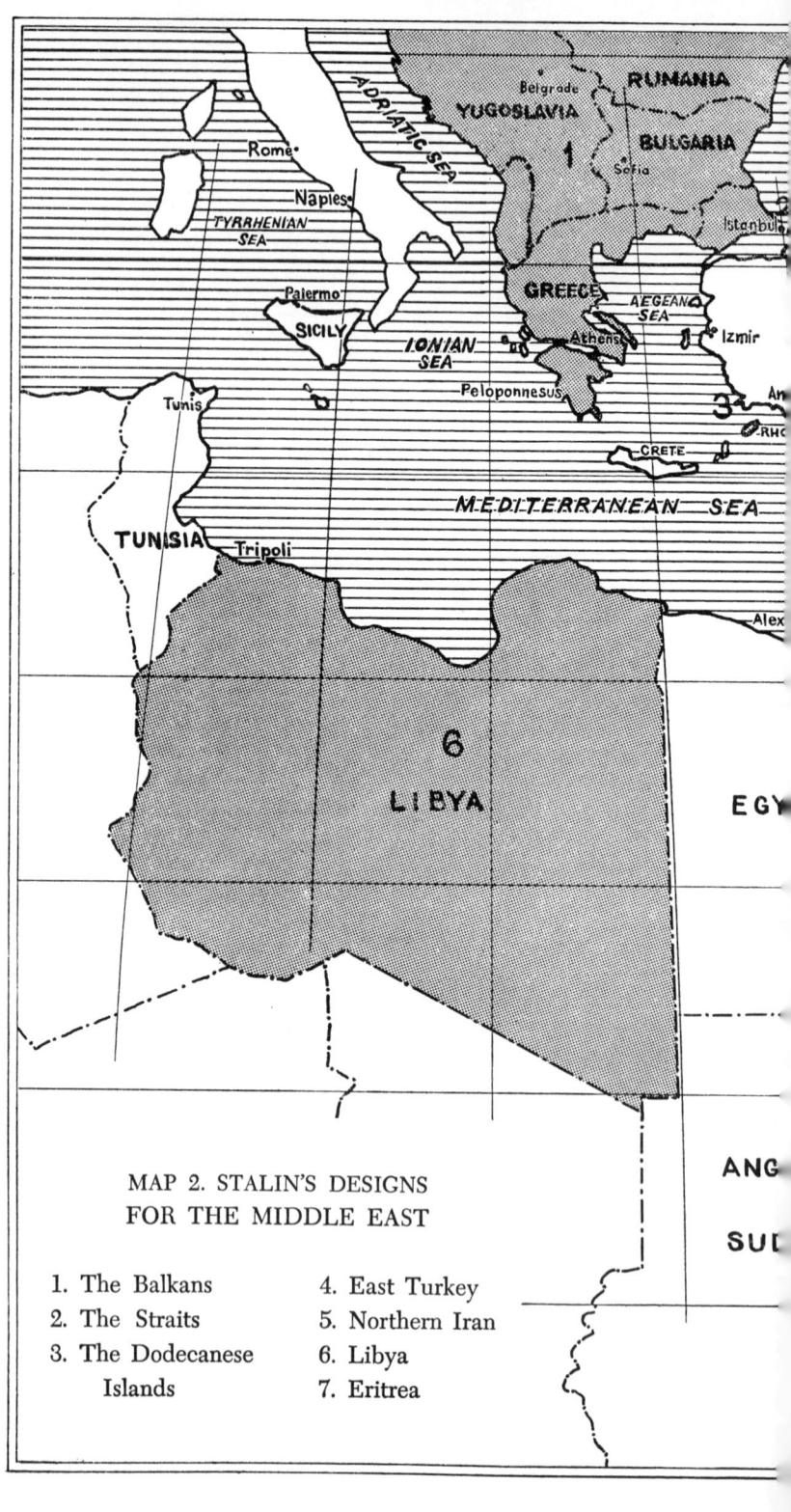

MAP 2. STALIN'S DESIGNS FOR THE MIDDLE EAST

1. The Balkans
2. The Straits
3. The Dodecanese Islands
4. East Turkey
5. Northern Iran
6. Libya
7. Eritrea

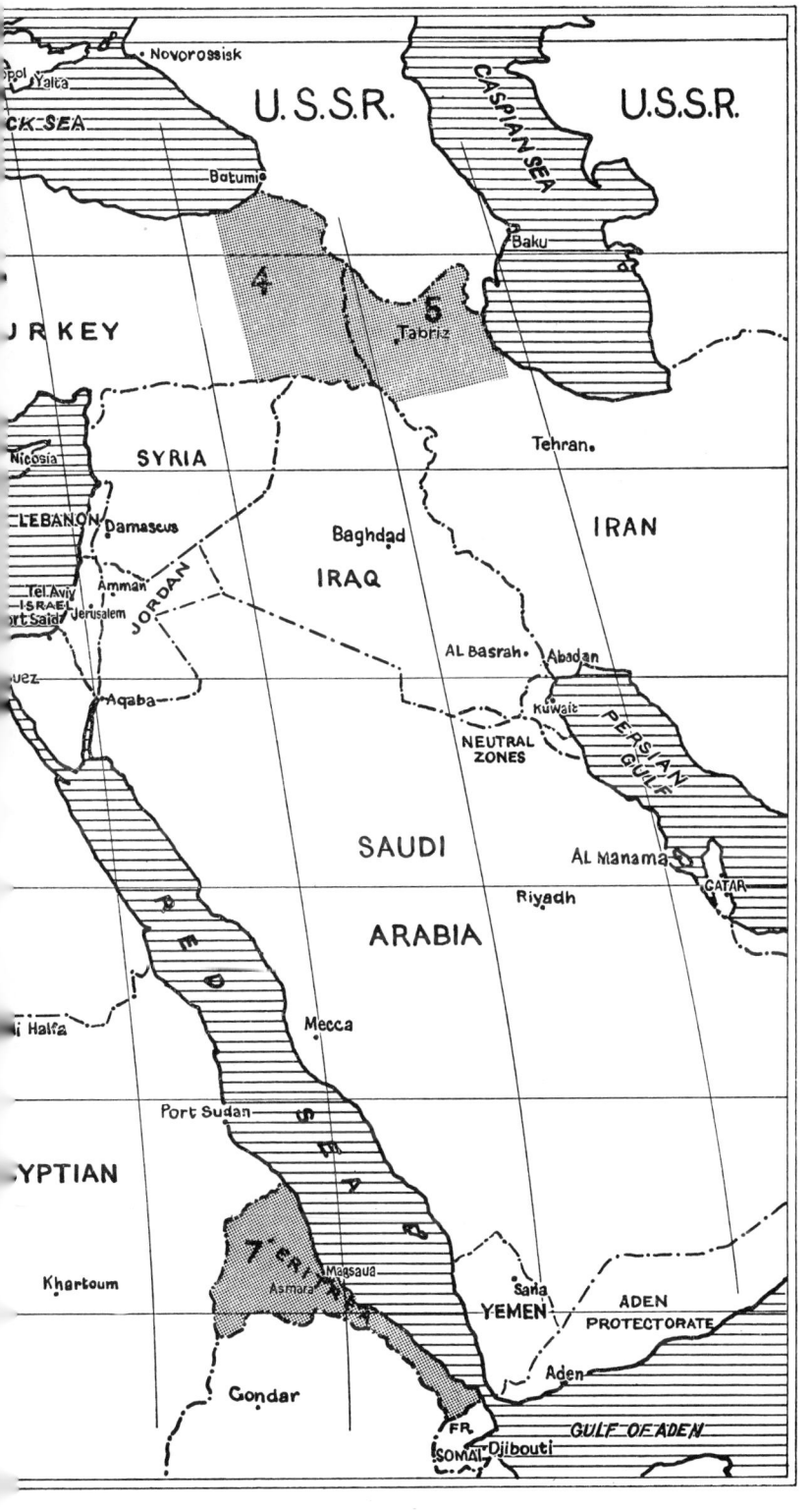

negotiations with Turkey and Germany in the summer of 1939 Stalin had demanded far-reaching rights and privileges in the straits leading from the Black Sea to the Mediterranean; the granting of such rights and privileges would have curtailed Turkey's sovereignty. Stalin was unsuccessful. In November, 1940, when Molotov came to Berlin, Hitler and von Ribbentrop proposed a set of treaties and protocols. In addition to a treaty which was to be made public, a secret agreement on the "delineation of their prospective spheres and interests" was to be concluded. According to the secret agreement Russia's sphere would stretch "in the direction of the Persian Gulf and the Arabian Sea." In addition, the Montreux Convention regulating traffic in the Turkish straits would be revised in a sense favorable to the Soviet Union. At the conclusion of the negotiations von Ribbentrop outlined the prospective Soviet spheres as the territories "south of the Soviet Union in the direction of the Indian Ocean." Molotov confirmed that his government was, in principle, prepared to accept the German suggestions; he took them along with him to Moscow for submission to Stalin.[4]

In Moscow the German proposals were discussed and revised. To Stalin they appeared not specific or far-reaching enough. Molotov handed the German ambassador the Soviet proposal in which, in a secret protocol, the prospective Soviet sphere was indicated as the areas stretching "south of Batum and Baku in the general direction of the Persian Gulf." The sphere would thus have included Iraq, Iran, part of Turkey, Syria, and possibly also Lebanon, Jordan, and Saudi Arabia. As far as the Straits were concerned, Stalin demanded military bases "on the Bosporus and the Dardanelles."

Facing new allies after the victory of 1945, and feeling stronger than ever, Stalin-Molotov came out with a far-reaching program of southward aggrandizement which in its general contours was only a new stage in what had been projected five years earlier. The new program was elaborated in greater detail than it had been in Hitler's time, if only because it now appeared more realistic and feasible.

The program called for the ceding to the Soviet Union (or Soviet

[4] *Nazi-Soviet Relations 1939–1941.* Documents from the archives of the German Foreign Office, ed. by Raymond James Sontag and James Stuart Beddie, U. S. Department of State, 1948, pp. 221–59.

sphere) of: the Balkans, etc. part of the Arab nations, military and commercial bases in the Mediterranean, the Turkish straits and Istanbul, northeastern Turkey, and northern Iran. The total population of these areas was about 45,000,000. (See Map 2, pp. 102–103.)

The Balkans. In 1945–47 it appeared certain that Bulgaria and Albania would come into the Soviet sphere; it appeared likely, too, that Yugoslavia would develop into a loyal ally of the Soviet Union. The uprising in Greece, supported by the Balkan satellites, would result in bringing that country also into the Soviet bloc. From 1945 to 1948 Moscow had reason to hope that she would gain predominance in all the lands and seas of the Balkans.[5] Tito's defection and the Truman Doctrine put an end to this grandiose hope.

The Arab Nations. Facing the Balkans on the other side of the Mediterranean was the Arab world, where the Soviet Union aspired to gain a foothold. The structure of the three Mediterranean empires— the Italian, the French, and the Spanish—was similar in that their metropolises, situated on the northern (European) shore of the sea, faced the underdeveloped African lands converted into colonies, which were a kind of projection beyond the sea of these metropolises. Stalin's drive to the Balkans implied the emergence of a new Mediterranean empire which, according to age-old tradition, would acquire its own possessions on the opposite shore; this would be the projected Soviet-dominated territory in North Africa.

The negotiations concerning the Italian colonies were seen as the appropriate avenue for achieving the Soviet goal.

At Potsdam, Stalin and Molotov requested Libya as a Soviet "trusteeship" (the term "trusteeship" was, in Soviet circles, often called a hypocritical euphemism for colonies that had already been abolished, but of course only when the Western nations were the trustees); they also indicated interest in Eritrea, on the Red Sea. In the subsequent conferences of foreign ministers the Soviet side continued to insist on its far-reaching demands.

The majority of Libya's population is Arab; in the cities of Eritrea the majority of the population is likewise Arab. With Libya, a member of the Arab League, in Soviet hands, the Soviet Union would be estab-

[5] The population of the Balkans was 35,000,000.

lished as a major colonial power in the Arab world. Situated between Tunis and Egypt, Libya would serve as a means of influencing and exerting pressure upon the eastern as well as the western Arabs. The Red Sea and the port of Massawa would open the way to Ethiopia, with its large Eastern Christian population. An interest in the Suez Canal, which would then appear legitimate, would make the Soviet government a major political power at Port Said.

In September, 1945, the Soviet government formally requested trusteeship over Tripolitania, which it correctly viewed as the most promising part of Libya.[6] The Soviet government insisted on "individual trusteeship," rejecting condominium with another power in the administration of the colony. In the conferences of foreign ministers Molotov made known the Soviet interest in the Mediterranean and Africa, in particular Tripolitania and Eritrea. The Soviet Union, he said, would like to assume the role of an individual trustee of this area and was fully qualified to perform the task. At the Conference of Foreign Ministers in Paris in April, 1946, Molotov formally requested control over the port of Massawa in Eritrea.

Not yet realizing the intent behind this Soviet program, United States Secretary of State Edward Stettinius, in a conversation with Molotov, confirmed that in his view the Soviet Union was "eligible" for trusteeship. Molotov then tried to base his demand on this "promise." When James Byrnes succeeded Stettinius in the State Department, he met with trouble when he tried to repudiate the half-pledge of his predecessor.

> He [Molotov] repeated this so often, I finally said "In the United States any citizen is eligible to become President, but that does not mean every citizen is going to be President. If you keep repeating that there is a commitment to support any request you make for a trusteeship, you will soon come to believe it yourself." I saw I had not convinced him, so I tried again. "If I tell a man I think he is eligible to own a house, I do not mean that if he asks for the Soviet Embassy I must support his demand for the house." That did not help. He still professes to believe that because of Secretary Stettinius' statement it is our duty to find a satisfactory territory that the Soviet Union can administer as trustee. Those were the opening arguments. With variations

[6] *Large Soviet Encyclopedia*, 2d ed., vol. 25, p. 98, points out that this tier of Tripolitania's oases is the most populated province in Libya.

and embellishments they were repeated throughout the next sixteen months until it became clear the issue could not be settled at present.[7]

Molotov's basic argument was the Soviet's new stature in world affairs. He told Byrnes: "The Soviet Union should take the place that is due it, and therefore should have bases in the Mediterranean for its merchant fleet." [8]

While the Soviet program had the support of the French, it met with stubborn opposition on the part of Britain, which was at the time master in this part of Africa. Had it not been for Ernest Bevin's consistent rejection of the program, the Soviet Union might today possess substantial territory in North and East Africa.

When Molotov became convinced that Britain's opposition could not be overcome, he shifted to a proposal for "collective rule" with Italy in Tripolitania; this proposal, too, was rejected. In the end none of Molotov's proposals were accepted. Discussion of the issue, which was also carried on in the United Nations, lasted for several years. The Soviet claim to a place in the collective administration of colonies contrasted sharply with its unilateral course in Eastern Europe; this was one of the factors in the rejection of the Soviet demands. The United States delegate to the United Nations, John Foster Dulles, gave a frank answer to Andrei Gromyko in April, 1949: "I wonder when the Soviet Union would submit for the judgment of the United Nations the matter of settlement for certain areas which the Soviet army had overrun during the war." [9]

The Mediterranean. The Soviet program for the Mediterranean had three parts: first, the old Montreux Convention of 1936, which regulated traffic in the Black Sea straits, must be abrogated and replaced by a more favorable agreement; second, the straits must become a "joint" Soviet-Turkish possession; third, the Italian Dodecanese Islands were to be developed as a Soviet naval base. The intent was that the Dodecanese were to be not only a commercial outpost but a strategic base in the vicinity of the Suez Canal.

The old Russian drive toward the Dardanelles, which had been repudiated by Lenin after the November Revolution, was resumed at the start of World War II. In 1939 Stalin discussed the issue with

---
[7] James F. Byrnes, *Speaking Frankly*, New York, Harper & Brothers, 1947, p. 96.
[8] *Ibid.*
[9] *Department of State Bulletin*, September 12, 1949, p. 373.

Germany and Turkey. In 1940 Molotov told Hitler and von Ribbentrop that the Soviet Union considered the Montreux Convention "worthless" and demanded "effective" guarantees—not guarantees on paper—concerning the straits as a precondition for a stable Soviet-German-Japanese alliance.[10] In June, 1945, after the defeat of Germany, Molotov presented a new set of demands to Turkey. Among them was a demand, similar to the earlier one, for revision of the Montreux Convention. Stalin referred to the matter at the Potsdam Conference. Soviet military bases in the Dardanelles, and the undertaking to defend the straits "jointly with Turkey," would have established the Soviet Union as the dominant power in those areas and made Istanbul a Soviet-dominated city.

Throughout 1946, in a long series of diplomatic exchanges with Turkey and Moscow's wartime allies, the Soviet government continued to insist on its demands relating to the Dardanelles—one of the most important component parts of its Middle Eastern program—but it met with consistent and growing opposition on the part of Britain and the United States. Molotov, for example, in his note to Turkey of August 8, 1946, said:

> Turkey and the Soviet Union, as the Powers most interested in and capable of ensuring the freedom of merchant shipping and security in the Straits, should jointly organize the defense of the Straits to prevent their use by other States for purposes hostile to the Black Sea Powers.

The Truman Doctrine, announced in March, 1947, was partially responsible for saving the independence of Turkey in the face of Stalin's political offensive.

The Soviet government did not consider the refusal final, but as only a "postponement." Stalin never retracted his demands on Turkey, and the result was a permanent state of tension between Moscow and Ankara during the postwar years.

Eastern Turkey. The Soviet program for the East related to Turkish territories bordering on the Caucasus. Since June, 1945, Molotov had been asking for the areas of Kars and Ardahan; they were formerly Russian territory, annexed by Turkey after World War I. (They had also belonged to Turkey before 1878.) In addition to this,

---

[10] *Nazi-Soviet Relations 1939–1941*, Department of State, Washington, D.C., 1948, pp. 244, 245, 252.

in December, 1945, two Georgian professors, obviously at the suggestion of Moscow, came out with a demand for an extensive Turkish territory of about 200 miles along the Black Sea coast and stretching down to the borders of Iraq and Iran, on the ground that centuries ago this area had belonged to ancient Georgia. The two Caucasian republics of Georgia and Armenia, as well as the Moscow press and radio, supported the demand. *Pravda* carried an article by the secretary of the Georgian Communist Party demanding the fulfillment of an "age-old dream of the Georgian people," namely, possession of eight Turkish provinces. The provinces in question constituted almost 20 per cent of Turkey's territory.[11] On the same day the Soviet radio broadcasted these "Georgian demands." In the United States a pro-Soviet "Armenian National Committee" distributed a map of Armenia prepared under the direction of President Wilson in 1920, showing a large East Turkish territory as part of the realm of independent Armenia.[12] In Syria and Lebanon, too, an "Armenian National Council," consisting of Armenian refugees, feverishly supported the Soviet program.

With Istanbul in the west practically in Soviet hands, the incorporation of these large Turkish territories in the east into the Soviet Union would have lost Turkey her significance and caused her to remain a small, impotent nation or become a member of the emerging Mid-Eastern empire of the Soviets. The Soviet Union would then have bordered on Iraq and Syria, where she could have counted on the support of a part of the Greek Orthodox clergy and community; her position in the Arab world would have become predominant.

Although never realized because of the deteriorating international climate, these demands of Stalin's were not withdrawn during his lifetime. They were the subsoil of the Soviet-Turkish animosity that lasted until the death of the Soviet ruler.

Iran. In the neighboring territory of Iran, a breakthrough to the south was planned in 1945–46, when Soviet troops were due to be withdrawn from Iran in accordance with the agreements of January 29, 1942. An "Azerbaijan Democratic Party" which emerged in northern Iran in 1945 under Soviet occupation, with the veteran Communist

---

[11] *Pravda*, February 25, 1946.
[12] *A Memorandum Relating to the Armenian Question*, issued by the Armenian National Committee, April, 1945; *The Frontier between Armenia and Turkey as decided by President Woodrow Wilson November 22, 1920*, Armenian National Committee (no place of publication or date given).

Jaafar Pishevari at its head, seized power and set up a pro-Soviet government in Tabriz. Soviet troops in Iran did not permit Iranian forces to enter the north, and Moscow refused to comply with her commitment to withdraw. About the same time a similar pro-Soviet regime was set up in Kurdistan, another area in northern Iran. The two territories, which lay between the Turkish-Iraqi border and the Caspian Sea, had evidently been groomed for incorporation into the adjoining Soviet republic.

Under strong political pressure on the part of the Western powers, Stalin finally agreed to withdraw his army from Iran, but not until Iran had consented in April, 1946 (she reneged later), to form a mixed Soviet-Iranian oil company in the northern provinces adjoining the Soviet Union.

In the end, and in striking contrast to his spectacular successes in the east and west, Stalin failed completely in his efforts to expand to the south. His heirs inherited a burdensome Middle Eastern legacy when they assumed power in March, 1953.

2. CONFLICTS EVERYWHERE

The situation in the Far East remained unsettled. Despite the fact that the Korean War was at a stalemate and there was no longer any prospect of a victory over the United Nations forces, despite the great human losses of the Chinese–North Korean side, despite the new situation in Japan and the weakening of pro-Communist trends in that country, and despite the finality of the peace treaty, Stalin refused to acknowledge the facts and accept the consequences. His well-known persistence was becoming sheer stubbornness; his earlier political flexibility was giving way to political sclerosis; he could not acknowledge even a local defeat, preferring to drag hopeless conflicts on and on.

The Far East was not the only part of the globe where these traits of Stalin's personality were giving events a somber and even tragic hue. In Europe, Austria was ripe for a settlement which would mean a Soviet retreat from the Eastern zone; scores of conferences were held and diplomatic notes exchanged in order to delay the day of the painful operation. Yugoslavia would not bow and could not be sub-

Conflicts Everywhere 111

dued by military means; Stalin took no action to "normalize" relations, and the deadlock was to continue.

During the last weeks before Stalin's death a new conflict broke out that was likewise a product of Stalin's unique combination of true Communist conviction and personal character traits. This was the conflict with Israel in February, 1953.

The deterioration of Soviet relations with Israel was in the main a result of the course of Soviet internal affairs. Soviet pro-Arab policy was at that time not yet pronounced, and Stalin's anti-Israeli trend had not yet developed into an effort to capture the favor of the Middle East. In Moscow, *New Times* [13] was stressing the role and influence of "Hitlerites" in Egypt and Syria, while a national roundup of Communists as "plotters" was carried out by General Mohammed Naguib, the new ruler of Egypt, and announced by his chief aide, Colonel Gamal Abdel Nasser.

Stalin's initial support of the creation of the State of Israel was motivated by his anti-British course rather than by pro-Israeli considerations. It was part of a consistent effort to oust Britain, the main power in that part of the world, from the Middle East. It was not so much sympathy for the small new nation as dislike of the great power of the West that moved Stalin in 1945–46. Subsequently the United States became, to a degree, a protector of Israel; this was not, of course, what Stalin had expected.

Since 1948 Stalin's anti-American orientation had been supplemented by the rising tide of anti-Semitism within the Soviet Union. The latter was a reaction to the pro-Western sentiments of a large majority of the Jewish population of Russia, their urge to emigrate from the "socialist state," their interest in Zionism, and their sporadic efforts to contact Jewish philanthropic organizations in the West. The years 1948–52 saw a rapidly mounting wave of Soviet anti-Semitism which, just before Stalin's death, was about to culminate in thousands of arrests; a number of executions had already been carried out. It was reported that wholesale deportations of Jews were envisaged and that "labor camps" were being erected in Eastern Siberia and elsewhere for the deportees.[14] In the satellite world Stalin's "anti-Zionist"

[13] January 7, 1953.
[14] *Sotsialisticheskii Vestnik*, December, 1957, p. 243; *Soviet Survey*, London, August, 1957, p. 2.

trends resulted in court proceedings of the Slansky trial type, the escape of groups of Jewish leaders (including Jewish Communists) from East Germany, arrests of Jewish leaders in Budapest, a purge of state officials in Hungary, initial steps toward a purge in Rumania and Poland, and, as usual, "confessions" from the arrested.[15]

When Moscow announced the arrest of a group of prominent Jewish doctors, violent anti-Soviet feeling was aroused among hundreds of thousands of Russian immigrants in Israel. Probably as an act of "retaliation," the Soviet bookshop in Jerusalem was set afire and a bomb was thrown at the Czech Legation. On February 9, 1953, a bomb exploded inside the Soviet Legation in Tel Aviv, injuring three members of the staff, among them the envoy's wife. The perpetrators were not apprehended.

The Israeli government expressed its "profound regrets" and promised to try to bring the culprits to justice. Thirty persons were arrested. Prime Minister Ben-Gurion pointed out, however, that the Soviet Legation had previously declined the services of a police guard in the courtyard from which the bomb was thrown. A Communist demonstration was held in Tel Aviv to express sympathy for the Soviet Union.

For a time the Soviet press and radio remained silent, obviously awaiting Stalin's reaction. This was not the first attack on Soviet diplomats, and the Soviet government might end the matter by accepting Israel's apology. For Stalin, however, in February, 1953, the bombing incident in Israel was an opportunity to take the offensive. On February 11, Andrei Vyshinsky handed a note to the Israeli envoy stating that the Israeli regime "is systematically fanning hatred toward the Soviet Union and inciting hostile actions."

> . . . the declarations and apologies of the Israeli Government, with regard to the terroristic act of February 9 on the premises of the Soviet Legation are a falsehood aimed at covering up the tracks of the crime committed against the Soviet Union and at evading the responsibility the Israeli Government bears for the crime. . . . The terroristic act which occurred February 9 proves the lack of elementary conditions in

---

[15] *The New York Times,* January 13, 18, and 19, and February 2 and 22, 1953; *Bulletin de l'Association d'Etudes et d'Information Politiques Internationales* (B.E.I.P.I.), Paris, no. 80, January 1–15, 1953, p. 16, and no. 81, January 16–31, 1953, p. 21.

Conflicts Everywhere

Israel for the normal diplomatic activities of representatives of the Soviet Union. . . .[16]

Consequently, the note stated, the Soviet government was breaking off diplomatic relations with Israel. *Pravda* described the Israeli leaders as "a pack of mad dogs" "loathsome and vile in their thirst for blood." *Izvestia* attacked the "scum of society" in Israel: "Trotskyites, bourgeois nationalists, cosmopolites," [17] and "men selling for dollars their honor, their people, and their country." [18]

With the severance of diplomatic relations the small-scale Soviet-Israeli trade stopped. At the time of Stalin's death no direct relations of any kind existed between the Soviet Union and Israel.

[16] *The New York Times*, February 12, 1953.
[17] *Pravda*, February 14, 1953.
[18] *Izvestia*, February 24, 1953.

PART TWO

The Malenkov-Molotov Era

CHAPTER 1

THE DEATH OF THE LEADER

Tension had been mounting in the first two months of 1953. A purge of the top leadership, including some of the oldest and most venerated, was in the offing. The first victims, among whom were Molotov, Voroshilov, and Mikoyan, had already been chosen.[1] Action against the "doctors' plot" was already in progress. In the highest echelons all men trembled for their lives, though they were innocent of misdeeds and loyal to the Leader. The year 1953 was to bring about the destruction of personalities, reputations, and organizations on a grand scale.

In foreign relations, the old course of belligerence and defiance continued. India's suggestion of a compromise in Korea, which was approved by the Chinese Communists, was rejected by Stalin. The political war on Tito, translated into trials and executions in the "people's democracies," was in full swing. With calculated insolence, the Moscow radio sent New Year's greetings to "the plain people of America." Vyshinsky, the Foreign Minister, was sending notes to small Western powers protesting their NATO commitments, and the possible appearance of foreign troops on their soil. Marshal Sokolovsky, Deputy Minister of Defense, publicly threatened England and France for permitting American bases in their countries.[2] Diplomatic relations with a number of small nations were broken off.

Among the foreign diplomats received by Stalin during the last months of his life there was not one representing a Western power. Stalin was obsessed by anti-Americanism, and only foreign personalities who could help in the fight against the archenemy enjoyed the privilege of an audience with him. Luis Bravo, the Argentine envoy, who came on February 7 to "express Juan Perón's desire for close

[1] Nikita Khrushchev's speech, February 24, 1956.
[2] *Pravda,* February 23, 1953.

economic relations," found Stalin "in the best of health" and "cordial"; the conversation was "pleasant and agreeable," and Stalin asked the envoy to give his greetings to Perón.[3] India's envoy, Krishna Menon, came to see Stalin on February 17. The last foreign guest, it appears, was the Indian Saiffudin Kitchlu, who had just been awarded the 100,000-ruble Stalin Peace Prize. In an hour-long interview with Kitchlu, Stalin predicted a rupture between the United States and her two European allies, Britain and France, and urged India to learn from Communist China. He was extremely aggressive toward the United States and bitterly attacked Winston Churchill.[4]

The issue of the highly official *New Times* that appeared when Stalin, paralyzed, lay on his deathbed, carried a large supplement containing "confessions" and "statements" by American prisoners of war on bacteriological warfare in Korea. The press carried appeals for "viligance" against the United States. In the United Nations, Vyshinsky, who was not always self-confident when he faced his boss, was aggressive and brazen when he confronted the world forum; here he reflected Stalin's offensive in world affairs. The slogan of "coexistence," though already in circulation, had a narrow meaning in the mouths of Stalin and Vyshinsky: it was limited to the effort to avoid a "hot" Soviet war with the United States; "cold" war was not incompatible with "coexistence."

The official version of Stalin's death was a plausible one, and it was widely accepted. On the night of March 1, the seventy-three-year-old leader suffered a stroke; he died three days later without having regained consciousness. From the daily medical bulletins it was clear that the illness would be fatal. The government's statement of March 3 said that "the severe illness of comrade Stalin will entail a more or less prolonged inability to participate in leading activities."[5] The statement reiterated the stereotyped phrases about redoubling efforts to "build socialism." *Pravda* and *Izvestia* referred to the "misfortune" that had befallen "our party and our people" and appealed to the nation to "show unity, firmness and watchfulness" and "redouble its energy in building Communism." Late in the evening of March 5 the

[3] *The New York Times*, February 9, 1953.
[4] *Ibid.*, February 25, 1953.
[5] *Pravda*, March 4, 1953.

The Death of the Leader

government and the Central Committee announced the death of the "wise leader and teacher" and appealed, in the Stalin vein, to "irreconcilability and firmness in the fight against internal and external enemies." The little-known Nikita Khrushchev was appointed chairman of the funeral commission.

Other versions of the circumstances surrounding Stalin's death circulated widely. One had it that at a meeting of the Party Presidium Stalin's colleagues, for the first time, revolted against his orders and threw their membership cards in his face; as Stalin reached out to ring for the guard, he suffered a stroke, brought on by the excitement. According to another story, one or two of the Kremlin doctors, themselves in mortal danger, with the aid of a few police officials, poisoned the leader, who was already dead when the first medical bulletin appeared.[6] All versions, except the official one, were variations on the theme of the Revolt of the Frightened. It may be many years before the truth becomes known.

The death of the Soviet leader was followed by both deep mourning and a deep sigh of relief. The combination was more than temporary; it determined the outward forms of the political course of the Soviet Union during the next few years.

The funeral was more spectacular than the funerals of Russian tsars. Delegations from governments and Communist parties from almost all of the countries of Europe, including Yugoslavia, attended. De Gaulle came from France. Mao Tse-tung sent Chou En-lai and ordered three days of mourning in China. Two hundred thousand messages of sympathy were received by the Central Committee.[7] Thousands upon thousands of people jammed the streets around the Kremlin, passing slowly before the bier with the yellowed corpse dressed in semimilitary jacket. The Soviet press overflowed with eulogies, while the press abroad rushed into print with conjectures about the consequences to the world of the death of the Soviet ruler.

The sounds of mourning were loud, the sighs of relief subdued. The swords of Damocles that had hung over the heads of the Soviet leaders, one of which had only a short time before fallen on Nikolai Vozensensky, vanished as if by a miracle. For thousands of persons

---
[6] *Est & Ouest,* Paris, no. 190, March, 1958, p. 2.
[7] *Pravda,* March 26, 1953.

who, with or without reason, had lived in mortal fear, the passing of Stalin had a direct effect on their personal fate.

The joint announcement of the supreme Soviet bodies—the Central Committee of the Party, the Council of Ministers, and the Supreme Soviet—pledged "uninterrupted and correct leadership" and prevention of "any kind of disarray and panic." The fear of panic was exaggerated; there was no panic. The unsophisticated millions paid their respects to the deceased, mourned or pretended to mourn, and went about their business as usual, just as millions of their counterparts in other countries had mourned every stern ruler at the moment of his death.

The disarray was great, but only at the summit of officialdom, not among the people. Stalin's lieutenants, proficient in their particular jobs, had no experience in either the methods or practice of large-scale decision-making, and least of all in issues of historical significance. Over long decades they had been accustomed to getting the last word from someone else; their own "collective" had been impotent. Now they were disoriented.

This combination of personal relief and political disorientation produced a state of continuing relaxation that gradually extended to the population. The severe tension that had prevailed on the eve of Stalin's death turned into its opposite. No new theories or ideas about the future Soviet political course emerged, and no program or slogans that deviated from Stalinism were put forth. A new policy without new ideas—this was the peculiarity of the situation. In Soviet internal affairs the first changes affected the police system and brought about the orientation toward "consumer goods"; in foreign affairs—the Korean War was to be ended rapidly. However, there was no new rounded-out doctrine; the alterations of and amendments to Stalinism —for example, the theories about the noninevitability of war, the role of parliaments, etc.—came later. After Stalin's death the emphasis was at first on the outward continuity of the political course. We shall see how great this emphasis was, particularly in foreign affairs. It was as if the new government sought to strengthen its unstable position by invoking Stalin's firmness; as if it were trying to create the image of constitutional succession where there was no constitutional succession.

The Death of the Leader

"Uninterrupted leadership" was the gist of the first post-Stalin announcement, which was made on March 6. The next day *Pravda* again stressed continuity. The naming of Malenkov as top leader, it said, "gives assurance that Stalin's policies will be continued." "The cause of Lenin and Stalin is in firm hands." On March 10 *Pravda* carried a photo which, it stated, had been taken three years before, in February, 1950. The photo showed three men, Stalin, Mao Tse-tung, and Malenkov. The purpose of publishing it was obvious—it gave more legitimacy to Malenkov and stressed the ties with Stalin as well as with the "great Chinese people."[8] Somewhat later it was reported that even before the Presidium was called together, Malenkov and Beria had jointly shuffled the main organs of control; the Central Committee was faced with a *fait accompli*.[9]

The organization of the government proceeded accordingly. Georgi Malenkov, the choice of Stalin, Stalin's loyal collaborator even during the last phase, and who had been let into most of the secrets of the regime, was the logical successor if Stalinism was to continue. Beria's former security and police departments, which had been split up by Stalin, were reunited and given back to him. Mikoyan was returned to his post as minister of trade. On March 14, Nikita Khrushchev replaced Malenkov as secretary[10] of the Central Committee. This was the beginning of a long, eventful fight, but for the moment Malenkov's supremacy was not disputed. Each leader was assuming what he considered his proper place. Only the foreign minister was a victim in the reorganization; Molotov took over Vyshinsky's post, and Vyshinsky was demoted to permanent representative to the United Nations and vice-minister of foreign affairs. On board ship from New York to Europe, correspondents noticed "tears in his eyes."

In foreign affairs, apparently only Molotov among the new members of the Presidium had experience and understanding. This was the reason why, at least for a time, Soviet foreign policy was Molotov policy—or, to be exact, Malenkov-Molotov policy. A staunch Stalinist,

---

[8] The three figures in the photo are behaving somewhat strangely—they are looking away from one another and appear bored. The fact is that the photo had been taken on the occasion of the signing of the Sino-Soviet treaty in 1950, at which nineteen persons were present. In the original photo Vyshinsky was in front and Malenkov in the rear, and all were obviously annoyed by the tedious proceedings. It was possible, in 1953, to eliminate sixteen figures from the original photo, but the expressions on the faces could not be changed.

[9] Giuseppe Boffa, *Inside the Khrushchev Era*, New York, Marzani & Munsell, Publishers, 1959, p. 27.

[10] Since September, 1953, "first secretary."

Molotov had not been inactive since his demotion in 1949. On his occasional assignments abroad he had made speeches in the most orthodox Stalinist vein. His attitude toward Titoism—he had taken an active part in the expulsion of Yugoslavia from the Cominform and the degradation of the country's leaders—was in line with Stalin's.[11] It is likely, however, that his attitude toward the Korean War, which had been launched by Stalin-Vyshinsky after his fall, was not entirely positive, which explains certain developments after his reappointment as foreign minister.

Back in his seat at the Foreign Office, Molotov recalled to Moscow the aides and personal assistants who had served under him during the decade of his ministership; now the *apparat* was firmly in his hands. He brought back Andrei Gromyko, his former secretary S. Kozyrev, the former general secretary of the Foreign Ministry A. Sobolev, the law expert F. Kozhevinikov, and K. Novikov, A. Alexandrov, and A. Pavlov. New ambassadors were appointed to the most important capitals—Peking, New Delhi, Warsaw, Prague, and Bucharest.[12]

Soon new, at times hypocritical, slogans were promulgated: praise of "collective leadership" and condemnation of the "cult of personality." For those on the inside, these slogans signified a departure from the autocratic system of Stalin, the emergence of a working Central Committee, a transition from one-man rule to rule by a group. But even these in fact anti-Stalinist moves were presented as a resumption of the Stalinist course. Abundant quotations from Stalin were used to prove the advantages of "collective leadership" and the shortcomings of the "cult of personality."[13] Officially, in the press and at Party meetings, continuity was stressed even in a field in which the break with the Stalin line was most pronounced.

[11] As late as July, 1951, Molotov spoke in Warsaw at the celebration of Poland's rehabilitation. "Everybody sees the fate of Yugoslavia, which through deceit has fallen into the hands of spies and provocateurs who have betrayed their people and sold themselves to the Anglo-American imperialists. Now everybody sees that the Tito-Kardelj-Rankovich gang has already reestablished the capitalist system in Yugoslavia, has deprived the people of all its revolutionary achievements, has turned the country into an instrument of the aggressive imperialist powers. Realizing it, the Yugoslav people hate this hired gang of criminals, who came to power stealthily and maintains its rule by bloody terror and fascist methods. This cannot go on for a long time. The people of Yugoslavia will find the path to liberty and to the liquidation of the fascist regime." (*Pravda*, July 22, 1951.)
[12] *Osteuropa*, Stuttgart, no. 2, 1954, pp. 113–14.
[13] For example, *Pravda*, April 16 and July 10, 13, and 26, 1953; *Kommunist*, no. 8, May, 1953, p. 15. Even the expulsion of Beria in July, 1953, was emphasized as necessary because Beria had violated Stalin's thesis of collective leadership.

The Death of the Leader

In home affairs there was both official and unofficial relaxation. Officially, Stalin's death was followed by an amnesty (an act which in Russia usually signified celebration of a joyful event), reduction in prices of consumer goods, the promise of an increase in the supplies of such goods, and the release from prisons of thousands, including "deviators" from Leninism-Stalinism. Officially, too, there was a promise of a reign of law—legality; though couched in Stalinist terms to stress continuity, and coupled with the usual threats against "spies and traitors" dispatched to the Soviet land by the "capitalist encirclement," [14] the antiterror trend was unmistakable. The most important act in this area was the dropping of the "doctors' case" and the release of the defendants. However, in the prevailing confusion this step was not taken until four weeks after Stalin's death.[15] (The press of the satellites continued the "anti-Zionist" campaign for another three weeks.)

The unofficial phase of the relaxation was at least as important as the official. Slowly, and at first timidly, the population began to grasp the meaning of the changes. The clouds of fear began to disperse. While there was no shred of political freedom, there had been some movement away from the dictatorial extreme. The expectations went much farther than the true situation warranted. Wherever suppression was most painfully felt—in the "labor camps," in certain of the satellites—hope coupled with impatience became a factor in the dramatic developments that followed.

The adulation of Stalin nevertheless continued for many months, although on a diminishing scale. In March, hardly an issue of a newspaper or speech omitted a memorial to the old leader. By April the memorials had diminished, but it was in that month that there appeared, in the issue of the Cominform's *For Lasting Peace, For a People's Democracy* (April 10, 1953), the most interesting example of enduring Stalinism: the issue carried Stalin's name 137 times on its first page.[16] At the May Day demonstrations, pictures of Stalin were displayed but, according to the press, "everybody was gay." [17] Subse-

---

[14] For example, *Pravda*, April 6 and 17, 1953. It was indicative of the prevailing chaos that along with steps toward relaxation, the press stressed the urgent need of "strengthening the state," especially its "punitive organs" (Beria's domain). (*Pravda*, March 19, 1953.)

[15] *The New York Times*, March 14, 1953. A week after Stalin's death a booklet which appeared on Moscow newsstands repeated the story of the "doctors" and attacked "Zionism."

[16] The count was made by the Paris office of *The New York Times*.

[17] *The New York Times*, May 2, 1953.

quently Stalin's name appeared only sporadically. Sometimes his name and his writings were mentioned only to show that in the hearts of his people he had not died.[18]

[18] For example, *Pravda*, June 28 and July 2, 4, and 7, 1953, and especially after the arrest of Beria.

CHAPTER 2

RELAXATION

This combination of actual anti-Stalinism and ostensible Stalinism, the confusion, and the ensuing relaxation form the background of the course of Soviet foreign policy in the initial era after Stalin's death.

The first statement on foreign affairs by the new head of the Soviet government was a short one made before the Supreme Soviet on March 15. Malenkov spoke, in the usual vein, of peace, security, defense, and "fraternal friendship and solidarity with the people's democracies," and added: "At the present time there is no disputed or unresolved question that cannot be settled peacefully by mutual agreement of the interested countries. This applies to our relations with all states, including the United States of America."[1] The statement was vague and, if taken literally, nonsensical: if it were true, why did so many issues remain unresolved? But Russia as well as the non-Soviet world sensed in Malenkov's brief words a hint of possible compromise. The statement, repeated frequently in subsequent days, signified the start of something new, though uncertain. In particular the reference to the United States indicated a tentative new approach to the Korean issue.

Otherwise the shift away from orthodox Stalinism caused confusion. Speaking before the General Assembly of the United Nations on March 11, 1953, Andrei Gromyko repeated the old intransigent arguments for the repatriation of prisoners of war as a precondition of an armistice. A kind of confusion unusual in the annals of Soviet-satellite diplomacy was caused by a strange action of the demoted Vyshinsky that indicated he was out of step with Moscow: on April 9, a week after Moscow announced its willingness to accept the Western principle of voluntary repatriation, Vyshinsky insisted in the United Nations that "the Geneva convention requires full repatriation

[1] *Pravda,* March 16, 1953.

of Prisoners of War." In defiance of the Soviet delegate, the Polish delegation, which had introduced a resolution in the Vyshinsky vein. withdrew the passage on "full repatriation." On April 7, Soviet delegate Valerian Zorin repeated the germ warfare charges. A few days later, and two weeks after the "doctors' affair" had been dropped in Moscow, Czech delegate Vaclav David told the General Assembly that Zionism is a "tool of American espionage";[2] Vyshinsky joined in the anti-Israeli move.

The Korean truce negotiations began to make progress almost immediately after Stalin's death. On March 28 China and North Korea accepted the United States suggestion of February 22 to exchange sick and wounded prisoners of war; in their statement of March 30, which had obviously been approved by Molotov, they went further and accepted the principle of voluntary repatriation. They proposed that "both sides pledge immediately upon the termination of hostilities to repatriate all those prisoners of war who are in their hands and who insist on repatriation, and to hand over the rest to a neutral state to secure a just solution of the issue of their repatriation."[3] Although the last part was somewhat evasive, the proposal represented a large step forward. Molotov issued a statement of solidarity with the new Korean-Chinese proposal, saying that the "Soviet government is prepared to assist in its realization."

A few days later negotiations began in Panmunjom, Korea, for the exchange of sick and wounded prisoners, and on April 6 an agreement was reached on the first part of the prisoner-of-war issue. The actual exchanges of sick and wounded, which began on April 20, was to involve 600 United Nations troops, 150 of them non-Koreans, and 5,600 Communist troops, only 700 of whom were Chinese.[4]

The Soviet press emphasized the Chinese-Korean "initiative"; when the exchange took place, TASS repeated the Chinese propaganda about the "difference in the state of health" of the two groups: "The prisoners of war handed over to the Korean-Chinese side looked

---

[2] The Czechoslovaks, fresh from the Slansky trial, were outdoing themselves in their anti-American and anti-Israeli moves. On March 23 and 24 the Czechs declared in the United Nations that the Prague trial had exposed Zionism and the American Joint Distribution Committee; the Poles said that "American dollars were paid to organize pogroms against the Jewish population." Consultations with the Soviet delegation must have preceded the Czech statements. (*The New York Times*, March 25, 1953.)

[3] *Pravda*, March 31, 1953. Statement by Chou En-lai.

[4] The actual number of sick and wounded prisoners exchanged was increased somewhat during the course of the operation.

awful. Almost all of them looked like walking skeletons with emaciated faces." [5] On the other hand, "Taking leave of our personnel, the sick and wounded of the American side expressed gratitude for good, humane treatment during the whole time of their captivity." [6]

Holding its protective hand over the Korean-Chinese negotiators, the Soviet government insisted on its status as a nonbelligerent.

The rapid settlement of this first Korean question and the generally improved prospects of peace in the Far East gave rise to a new assessment by the West of Soviet policy. Minor facts, hints, and rumors were often the basis for diplomatic reports from Western envoys to their governments at home and of statements to correspondents aimed at influencing the public. The widespread opinion was that the Malenkov-Molotov course would be more amenable to compromise than Stalin's had been.

A number of developments led to this new evaluation: in February, Anthony Eden had asked the help of the Soviet ambassador in London, Gromyko, to obtain the release of a number of British subjects being held in North Korea, and on March 18 a reply from Molotov promising "favorable consideration" was received. Civilians from other Western countries who were trapped in Korea and were being held by the Communist authorities were permitted to repatriate. In Germany, in March, several air incidents occurred in one of which seven British fliers lost their lives. Moscow claimed that the British bomber had violated the Soviet zone, but the Soviet commander in Germany, General Chuikov, although placing the blame for the incident on the British fliers, expressed a restrained regret and, in a departure from routine, proposed a Soviet-British conference to avoid "misunderstandings"; Churchill accepted the offer. On March 31, when the negotiations for the nomination of a new secretary general to the United Nations seemed almost hopeless, the Soviet delegation unexpectedly consented to the election of Dag Hammarskjöld. A group of American editors in Moscow were permitted to take pictures. For the first time since the early postwar years several Russians and their wives attended a reception at the American Embassy in Moscow. The Soviet request, made before Stalin's death, that the United States

[5] *Pravda*, April 26, 1953.
[6] *Ibid.*, April 25, 1953.

Embassy vacate its premises, which were located close to the Kremlin, was withdrawn. Traffic to and from Berlin was eased and obstacles removed.

What these minor concessions really indicated was not a comprehensive new program—Molotov would have been the last to conceive or propose such a program—but individual small moves necessary to create a climate of relaxation and coexistence. Molotov permitted himself to be pushed on minor matters, but he did not relinquish his general anti-Western attitudes. He maintained a long silence on long-range goals and attitudes, leaving the interpretation of his *démarches* to the foreign governments. A controversy soon developed in the West as to the meaning of these *démarches*. The optimistic British view was opposed to the more cautious and skeptical attitude of Washington. In Washington it was decided to sound out Moscow in an effort to gain some understanding of the new policy, and in particular the policy toward the crucial issues of the time—the Korean War, Austria, Germany, Eastern Europe, and disarmament. In a speech on April 16, President Eisenhower raised the questions publicly:

> What is the Soviet Union ready to do? . . . Is the new leadership of the Soviet Union prepared to use its decisive influence in the Communist world—including the control of the flow of arms—to bring not merely an expedient truce in Korea but genuine peace in Asia? Is it prepared to allow other nations, including those in Eastern Europe, the free choice of their own form of government? Is it prepared to act in concert with others upon serious disarmament proposals?

A few days later, on April 20, Churchill made a more optimistic statement in the House of Commons. His idea was a "summit conference" without a fixed agenda as a first effort toward reaching an understanding. Recent developments, he said, "may presently lead to conversations on the highest levels, even if informal and private between some of the principal powers concerned." [7]

The Soviet government finally responded to this expression of international perplexity. It came out with a more distinct program of Soviet foreign policy. An editorial in Moscow's leading newspapers of April 25, the first Soviet statement of its attitude toward international problems since Stalin's death seven weeks before, was obviously the outcome of deliberations at the very summit of the Soviet govern-

---

[7] *The New York Times*, April 21, 1953.

Relaxation

ment. Couched in the form of a polemic, it addressed itself to President Eisenhower and Secretary of State John Foster Dulles, criticized American policy, and stressed continuity and the correctness of Stalin's course in foreign affairs. President Eisenhower's idea that a new era in Soviet policy was beginning was wrong:

> We have no intention [*Pravda* stated] of entering into a discussion with the President on the rather strange statement of some "termination of a certain era in Soviet policy." But we cannot accept without surprise his conclusion that the Soviet Government must give up "succession" in foreign policy, the correctness of which has been proved by the entire course of international developments.[8]

President Eisenhower, now in the White House, Moscow noted, approves and continues the policies of his predecessor; why does he not, it asked, speak of a "new era" in America?

As to the Korean War, the editorial in the official Soviet press said, Moscow would assist in ending the conflict. On the subject of Austria it limited its answer to an elusive and guardedly optimistic statement:

> As regards the Austrian treaty, it can only be repeated that here, too, there are no issues that cannot be settled on the basis of the understandings already reached, provided the democratic rights of the Austrian people are really respected.[9]

These two issues, Korea and Austria, were the only ones on which the possibility of a compromise was vaguely indicated; on all other questions the government remained adamant. With regard to Germany, China, disarmament, and the North Atlantic Pact, it upheld the old Soviet course; it refused to discuss a change in Eastern European affairs; it accused the "Anglo-American bloc" of having caused deterioration in the relations between the former allies; it demanded expansion of international trade instead of financial assistance to underdeveloped countries.

Moscow was aware that the attitude of the United States toward the suggestion of an international summit conference was reserved and cautious, while the British wanted a conference without conditions. Moscow was therefore extremely favorable to Churchill's

[8] *Pravda*, April 25, 1953.
[9] *New Times*, Moscow, no. 18, April 29, 1953, "Concerning President Eisenhower's Speech," Supplement, p. 4.

speech in the House of Commons of May 11, which indicated disagreement with Washington. In his optimistic statement Churchill spoke of a possible "healthy evolution in Russia" and of a "change in Soviet attitude." It was wrong to assume, he said, that "nothing can be settled" with the Soviet government; the new proposals he said, on Korea, were serious and promising, and the Communist advance in Indochina (Laos) was not Soviet-inspired. The Labor Party supported Churchill and attacked the United States, thus creating the impression of a unanimous anti-American attitude on the part of the British people.

In the United States, the press, and even more so the members of Congress, were bitter about Churchill's "unwarranted optimism." The United States government was prepared not to retreat from its position. Secretary Dulles emphasized the preconditions demanded by the United States for a parley of the Four Powers:

> I doubt any very important results could come out of a high-level conference which included the leaders of Soviet Russia as long as the Soviet bloc of countries is promoting a war of aggression in Korea, a war of aggression in Indo-China against Laos, so long as in Europe they refuse to restore independence to Austria and to withdraw their occupation troops from that small and inoffensive country.[10]

The Soviet side, elated over the Washington-London controversy, came out in favor of Churchill. Without making any substantial new concessions, it supported the suggestion of a summit conference while strongly criticizing the plan of a preliminary conference of the Western powers (the United States, Britain, and France) which had been proposed to iron out the Anglo-American dispute. The plan to present to the Soviet Union, at the future conference, a united front of the West was, of course, contrary to Soviet interests. Moscow even hinted that the Soviet government might refuse to participate in the parley if it were to be preceded by a separate conference of the West.

> . . . such a conference, if the U.S.S.R. is to participate, could take place only if the parties come to it without any fixed preliminary demands. The purpose of the projected meeting of the heads of the Three Powers, however, is apparently to draw up such demands for presentation to the Soviet Union.[11]

[10] *The New York Times,* May 23, 1953.
[11] *Pravda,* May 24, 1953.

Relaxation 131

Despite the Soviet criticism, the Western governments decided to convene in Bermuda without Russia. At the end of June, however, Churchill, the driving force for *rapprochement,* fell seriously ill; Anthony Eden, it was announced, had to undergo another surgical operation. There was no meeting in Bermuda, but a conference was held in Washington on July 10–14. One of the decisions reached there was to invite the Soviet government to a four-power conference to be held in early autumn; the issue of Germany as a subject to be discussed was especially stressed.

The Molotov press, while it criticized the Western powers for their "separate meeting" and attacked them for the "resurrection of German militarism," indicated that the Soviet government would take part in the Four-power Conference; this was logical in view of the disagreements between London and Washington.[12]

There now began an exchange of diplomatic notes on international conferences which during the next few years became a kind of pattern. The Soviet government was usually ready and even eager to participate in a conference and often took the initiative in proposing one. Rarely did it break up a parley, even when agreement appeared impossible. But it always tried to make the best possible use of the discussions preceding a parley. In this instance it prepared a list of participants and an agenda which, Molotov was aware, were unacceptable to the West; for example, it included Communist China in the proposed list of participants, and it included in a proposed agenda the subject of prohibiting military bases in foreign countries or putting a stop to German rearmament. The Soviet government rightly counted on the support of a large segment of "unbiased," "objective," and "uncommitted" public opinion in the West which imagined that a conference necessarily meant a step forward, that the four contending powers once assembled at a "round table" would "compose" some of their differences, and that following the pattern of trade negotiations a compromise solution would be found. This segment of public opinion was unaware of the fact that the Soviet representatives arriving from Moscow brought with them a well-thought-through, meticulously prepared plan of action from which they could not deviate, and that a sudden retreat on their part was out of the question.

The first series of diplomatic notes on the subject of international

[12] *Pravda,* July 23 and 25, 1953.

conferences after Stalin's death extended from July to December, 1953. The notes exchanged were numerous because the two sides had different conceptions of the program of the conference; issues that were "urgent" for one side were secondary or unacceptable as items for discussion to the other. The Western notes were short and businesslike, the Soviet notes lengthy and explicit. Certain to be published in full abroad, the Soviet notes were obviously intended to engage the sympathies of political parties and leaders. In Russia, on the other hand, the dry and to-the-point Western notes were not published for several weeks, when they appeared in print along with the lengthy Soviet replies refuting the Western contentions and proving their bias or absurdity. During 1953 the following notes were exchanged:

	Authorship	Approximate Wordage
July 15	Western	500
August 4	Soviet	900
August 15	Soviet	2,200
September 2	Western	650
September 28	Soviet	2,000
October 18	Western	600
November 3	Soviet	2,700
November 16	Western	400
November 26	Soviet	1,300
December 8	Western	220
December 26	Soviet	230

This quantitative relationship between the Western and the Soviet notes remained typical of the diplomatic exchanges of subsequent years.

Once the principle of voluntary repatriation was accepted by the Communist side, the Korean War could be ended on the basis of the territorial *status quo*. On June 8 the agreement on prisoners of war was signed. A "Neutral Nations Repatriation Commission," under Indian chairmanship, was to handle the prisoners, that is, release those who wanted to be repatriated and detain the others for a period of not more than six months. The latter group were to receive "explanations" by representatives of their former governments. Those prisoners whom the "explainers" could not persuade to return would eventually be freed.

Relaxation

Syngman Rhee, the Korean President, and probably a large majority of the South Korean population, were violently opposed to the terms. In their view, India, as the agency that would decide the fate of the prisoners, was unobjective and suspect; besides, the imminent restoration of the line dividing Korea in two was contrary to their hopes and to promises given. On June 18, on orders of the President, Korean guards at certain of the prisoner-of-war camps released about 26,000 inmates. The prisoners made a fast escape with the aid of the civilian population, which hid and fed them.

While Washington and London energetically protested against Syngman Rhee's action, Moscow and Peking accused the Americans of having "silently approved" the release of the prisoners; *Pravda* held the United States responsible.[13] For a while it was feared in the West that the Communist side might interrupt the truce negotiations, especially when it demanded that the fugitives be apprehended and returned to the camps. However, the controversy soon ended, negotiations continued, and on July 27, 1953, the armistice was signed.

Premier Malenkov sent a message of congratulations. He hailed the armistice as "a great victory of the heroic Korean people, the valiant Chinese People's volunteers, and the entire camp of peace and democracy." In a conference with North Korean leaders, Malenkov attacked the "colonialism" of the United States, while Kim Il Sung praised the Soviet Union. The Soviet Union appropriated one billion rubles for assistance in the rehabilitation of North Korea; China followed suit and offered North Korea substantial help in the form of goods and otherwise during the period 1954–57.

The prisoners-of-war issue had a prominent place in the immediate postwar developments. Thirty-two teams of "explainers" arrived to persuade the prisoners to return to their homeland; the efforts had meager results. Only a small minority changed their minds and accepted repatriation; about 14,200 Chinese and 7,600 North Korean prisoners of war remained in India's custody at the end of the "explanations" period. They were released early in 1954. The failure of the Communist side was greater than anyone, including Moscow and Peking, had expected. It would certainly have been wiser not to have insisted on the procedure. To maintain its line, however, *Pravda* [14]

[13] *Pravda*, June 22, 1953.
[14] June 22, 1954.

still protested against the "illegal handing over of the Chinese and Korean prisoners of war to the American command."

When the hostilities ended and American prisoners of war returned home, the United States published shocking factual reports on the atrocities perpetrated by the Chinese-North Korean side. In the discussion of this matter in the United Nations, the Soviet and satellite delegates not only defended the Communist governments but resumed the charges of "bacteriological war" by the United States. It was Vyshinsky, the Stalinist master of insult and abuse, who distinguished himself in this debate. The American evidence, he said, was a forgery, a lie, and a slander; the atrocities of the Americans, he said, were comparable only to those of Hitler. The United States delegation offered to organize an impartial committee of inquiry; the suggestion was not accepted.

The most important legacy of the Korean War was again the divided country—one of the issues on which the war had actually been fought. A "political conference" to settle the problem of unifying Korea, which had been provided for in the truce, was discussed on all sides. Nobody seriously expected, however, that either side would budge from its position and sacrifice its part of Korea. In fact, the Geneva Conference, which was convened to discuss Korea, achieved nothing.[15]

The outcome of the war was symptomatic of Moscow's new course of foreign policy. Moscow was eager to stop the fighting, but concessions that would involve contraction of the socialist orbit were out of the question.

[15] See below, p. 148–150.

CHAPTER 3

THE COURSE IN RESPECT TO THE WEST

The new course of Soviet foreign policy, uncertain and vacillating at first, hardened and became more definite as time went on. In a way, the Berlin rising in June, 1953 (see pages 175 ff.)—this main event of the early post-Stalin period—served to point up the urgency to clarify and define the line.

In this early post-Stalin era Molotov's influence in foreign affairs was greater than at any other time before or after. Free of Stalin's rigid instructions and the eternal threat of repression, and having got rid of Vyshinsky, Molotov proved to be the most expert, consistent, and knowledgeable of all Soviet aspirants for his post. Although the dissension among the factions within the Central Committee had already started and Khrushchev's offensive against the Malenkov group was gaining momentum, foreign affairs remained terra incognita for the upstart miner from the Donbas. On the other hand, Molotov, after his decades-long training in the Stalin school of politics, was not inclined to try new roads, least of all in his relations with the West. London greatly exaggerated the novelty of post-Stalin Soviet foreign policy under the new leadership.

On minor issues the Malenkov-Molotov government maintained the changes initiated after Stalin's death. The restrictions that appeared to have been the result of Stalin's caprice or stubbornness could now be eliminated. Travel restrictions imposed on foreign embassies in Russia were eased in June, 1953; Russian wives of non-Russians and a number of children were permitted to leave the country. In Czechoslovakia, William Oatis, Associated Press chief in Prague, who had been sentenced in 1951 to ten years' imprisonment for "espionage," was released, obviously after consultation with the Soviet, in May,

1953, following President Eisenhower's letter to the president of Czechoslovakia.[1]

While the Malenkov government rejected the irritating and unreasonable ingredients of Stalin's course in international affairs, it continued in many respects along the old lines. Its interpretation of world events and its violent anti-Americanism were part of the old theories and the old course. Some of the old ideas, however absurd, were restated: the capitalist countries are at an impasse; "their economies are weakened, their financial and foreign exchange affairs are in a state of unparalleled chaos, their working masses are falling into deeper and deeper poverty and ruin is overtaking their middle class." [2] The old Leninist-Stalinist theory of the "impoverishment" of the working class was propagated in its crude and unrealistic form. The rise of a revolutionary situation was accepted as an axiom.

> The workers become impoverished not only relatively, but also absolutely. As a result of the intensified exploitation, the tremendous increase in unemployment, the rise in taxes and the uninterrupted rise in prices of consumer goods, the steady decrease in real wages continues. . . . Continuous deterioration of the economic conditions of the broad masses of the population leads to the steady accumulation of dissatisfaction. The contradictions between the bourgeoisie and the working class are becoming sharply aggravated.[3]

Huge unemployment in the West, it was said, was accompanied by starvation and suffering:

> According to even incomplete official information in the USA, England, Italy, West Germany and Japan, there are at present over 32 million totally or partially unemployed. The unemployed and their families are tormented by hunger, their children are doomed to suffering. . . [whereas] love and kindness surround the children in the Chinese People's Republic, in the countries of People's Democracy, where conditions are created to make motherhood and childhood happy and joyful.[4]

The orthodox theory of inevitable wars was maintained in its Stalinist form: wars between capitalist powers are inevitable, but not so wars between capitalist and socialist states:

---

[1] It was indicative of the still prevailing anti-Americanism that the Soviet press omitted mention of the intervention of President Eisenhower in this affair.
[2] *New Times*, Moscow, no. 26, June 24, 1953, editorial.
[3] *Pravda*, April 28, 1953, "Impoverishment of the Toilers in the Countries of Capitalism."
[4] *Ibid.*, June 1, 1953, editorial, "In Defense of Children."

The Course in Respect to the West

> Wars are a component part of imperialism. As long as imperialism remains in force, is maintained, the inevitability of war also remains in force. . . . The Soviet state has repeatedly exposed the criminal aims of all those who disseminate malicious inventions about the inevitability of war between the Soviet Union and the capitalist states, in particular between the U.S.S.R. and the U.S.A. A rebuff to these provocations of the enemies of peace was given by J. V. Stalin, who stated in his answer to James Reston, correspondent of the American newspaper New York Times: "I continue to believe that a war between the United States of America and the Soviet Union cannot be considered inevitable, that our countries can also live in peace in the future." [5]

And the reason why the Soviet Union may be spared is capitalism's fear that it will perish in a war:

> Historical experience has shown that a war against the U.S.S.R., as a country of Socialism, is more dangerous for capitalism than a war between capitalist countries. Whereas a war between capitalist countries poses only the question of the predominance of some of the capitalist nations over the others, a war with the U.S.S.R. must without fail pose the question of the very existence of capitalism.[6]

It might seem that these and a multitude of similar theories expanded in the Soviet press and taught in Soviet schools and universities had little to do with specific issues of foreign policy. In fact, however, they were part of the Soviet *Weltanschauung,* and they greatly influenced the Soviet course in international affairs. If the West was in the throes of crises due to unemployment and poverty, if revolutionary trends were on the rise, if a war between the United States and Britain was more than likely, then it was in the line of duty and in the self-interest of the Soviet government to stand firm, not to concede an inch of its political or territorial areas, and even, if this did not entail great risks, to forge ahead whenever possible.

In one important area, however, the transition from Stalin to Malenkov brought real progress. The small wars and local skirmishes —Korea, Greece, Indochina—sponsored or at least supported by Stalin were now found to be fraught with too great danger; in particular, America's direct participation in the Korean War and the American voices raised in favor of greater activity in Indochina contradicted the dubious theory that a war with the United States could be avoided

---
[5] *Kommunist,* Moscow, no. 7, May, 1953, pp. 25, 28, and 29.
[6] *Ibid.,* p. 29.

if the Soviet bloc refrained from more than local expansion. If the Soviet Union was to be spared a major war, then local operations, too, must be avoided, at least for the time being. Caution with regard to purely military activity and boldness where political and economic means could be effective were characteristic of the Malenkov-Molotov policy.

Malenkov expounded this policy in his first lengthy and comprehensive statement to the Supreme Soviet since Stalin's death. There were no problems, he reiterated, that could not be solved by negotiation; after a long period of tension, he said, a certain relaxation had set in in the field of international relations. Diplomatic relations, he pointed out, had been resumed with Greece, Yugoslavia, and Israel; the Soviet Union had made moves to accommodate Turkey's interests; and a number of trade agreements were being or would be concluded.

Despite these pacifying statements, Malenkov's attitude remained essentially unchanged. Germany was Point One in his program. "Militarization" of Germany, he said, was of the greatest danger to Europe and especially to Germany's neighbors to the east and west; he appealed to France in particular to desert the Western bloc and "resume an independent course" in foreign affairs; he attacked NATO and predicted its disintegration; he appealed to Japan to gain "independence" from the United States; he stressed "unity" among the Soviet bloc and demanded the admission of Communist China to the United Nations. In a somewhat obscure statement, the real meaning of which was not revealed until two years later, Malenkov referred to the connection between the Austrian and German questions. Finally, he announced, for the first time, that the United States was "not the only possessor of the hydrogen bomb." Malenkov's speech received a great ovation.

As usual, just prior to the anniversary of the November Revolution, the official slogans that were to adorn the banners in the processions were promulgated. The 1953 slogans differed from the old Stalinist ones. In those pertinent to foreign affairs, for example, the new formula was: "There are no controversial questions which could not be solved by agreement." One slogan advocated "lessening of international tension," and another, friendship with "the peoples of France and Italy." The terms "imperialist aggressors" and "warmongers" had disappeared, as had the appeal to overthrow Tito.

The Course in Respect to the West

In contrast to these holiday slogans was the more businesslike program announced by Molotov in a press conference about the same time (November 13, 1953). To the Western slogan of free elections in Germany he juxtaposed a program of immediate joining of the two parts of Germany, without preliminary voting, which was tantamount to at least international recognition of the DDR (*Deutsche Demokratische Republik*—German Democratic Republic), and perhaps even to the emergence of a Communist-influenced all-German government. Molotov viewed the recent Bonn and Paris agreements, which included Germany in the Western military alliance, as of the greatest danger to Europe, to peace, and to Soviet interests, and openly demanded nonratification of these agreements. He repeated that "unification of Germany" would become impossible once ratification was accomplished. In addition, he requested abolition of United States military bases in Europe and other areas neighboring on Russia.

The phrase "lessening of tension," which sounds even more awkward in Russian than in English (there is no word for "relaxation" in the Russian language), was put in circulation by Moscow, which even wanted it to appear as a specific item on the agendas of the international parleys. Molotov, a poor speaker and lacking both a sense of humor and literary style, reiterated the clumsy slogan twenty-four times in the course of the press conference. What Molotov understood by "lessening of tension" was:

Recognition of Eastern Europe as part of the Soviet sphere
Diplomatic recognition of the four Asian people's democracies (China, North Korea, Mongolia, North Vietnam)
A hands-off-the-"socialist-countries" policy
Withdrawal of the United States from Europe (which would leave Russia the dominant power on the old continent)
Abolition of NATO and the abolition of military bases abroad

The Molotov program for Germany implied recognition of two Germanys, establishment of a coalition government prior to the holding of any elections, the concluding of a peace treaty, and "neutralization" of Germany by limitation of her armed forces.

The exchange of notes between Moscow and the Western capitals continued throughout 1953. Attitudes on both sides stiffened. In his notes to Britain, France, and the United States of November 3, Molotov made nonratification of the agreements concerning the rearmament of Germany a precondition of Soviet participation in the proposed Four-power Conference. A bitter tone permeated the exchanges. The replies of the Western powers on November 16 were in a stern and irritable tone: The Soviet Government

> ... has made a meeting of the Foreign Ministers conditional upon the acceptance of a number of demands. Some of these have no relation to Europe, but must, in the Soviet view, be met before even the study of European problems be initiated. Others would entail the abandonment by the United Kingdom, France and the United States of all their plans to safeguard their own security. A defenceless Western Europe appears to be the price demanded by the Soviet Government for participation in a conference. The Soviet Government must be well aware that such demands are totally unacceptable.

Apparently, the notes concluded, "the Soviet Government does not wish at the present time to enter into new negotiations which might have positive results."

The conference was doomed before it started; even Winston Churchill, who had first proposed it, was now skeptical. Paradoxically, at this critical stage of the exchange the decision to hold the conference was reached quickly. So much hope had been aroused by the prospect of a conference, and so great was the fear of loss of popularity if there was a refusal to participate, that in the end both sides agreed to hold it.

CHAPTER 4

CONFERENCES AND CRISES

1. THE BERLIN CONFERENCE

Having decided to take part in the conference, the Soviet government proceeded, as usual, to prepare its moves at the future parley in the greatest possible detail, organize large-scale support abroad, and draft a number of "resolutions" which, although they were doomed in advance to be voted down, would constitute a basic document of Communist foreign policy, a document of "historical importance." The Soviet delegation, consisting of seventy-two persons, was much larger than that of any other government. Among its members, in addition to Molotov, were the best experts of the ministry—Andrei Gromyko, Jacob Malik, Georgi Pushkin, Vladimir Semionov—and the Soviet ambassadors summoned from Washington and Paris. The delegation also included specialists on the press and on propaganda.

A week before the opening of the conference a grand-scale campaign was initiated in East Germany which the Soviet press depicted as an overwhelming movement of the Germans in support of the Soviet program. The slogan was "Agreement between West and East Germany to collaborate." Workers, scientists, and writers of the Eastern zone adopted resolutions in this vein. President Wilhelm Pieck of the DDR attacked Konrad Adenauer for his refusal to join the "popular movement." "Peasants" of the Eastern zone came out for this type of reunification of their country; the city assembly of East Berlin supported it; even in West Germany, the Soviet press claimed, meetings were held to approve it.

Although fewer Soviet police and less police precautions were in evidence, Molotov rode about Berlin in a limousine with tinted bulletproof windows and brown curtains. He had reason to consider himself the chief actor in this beginning performance, the man on whose *da*'s and *nyet*'s developments in Europe in the coming years might depend. While he himself stressed his own outstanding role, his press emphasized the consistent Soviet initiative on all issues and the prominence of the Soviets among the great powers as a logical concomitant of her leading role in the international affairs of the times. It minimized the role of other delegates and delegations, often omitting publication of their statements and proposals.

The conference opened on January 25, 1954. To demonstrate his superior understanding of the urgent world needs, Molotov refused to accept the Western agenda, which included only the subjects of Germany and Austria. He proposed, as the first item of discussion—and his opposite numbers had to accept the proposal—an examination of "measures for lessening international tension." Four days were spent on disputes over Red China, disarmament, the European Defense Community (EDC), and the expansion of international trade. The Molotov proposals, which had been well-known for a long time, were stillborn; the remarks of the Western ministers were laborious and repetitious. The fight was, in the main, between the two men representing the extremes—Molotov and Dulles. As usual, there was some support for Molotov's ideas from several non-Communist press organs, for example, the London *Times* in connection with Communist China, and the Paris *Monde* in connection with EDC. The statements of these press organs, which were abundantly quoted in the Soviet press, appeared to support Molotov's claim to objectivity and reasonableness. In addition, headlines in the Soviet press proclaimed that "the German people" in general favored the Soviet program.

Before turning, on January 29, to the second item on the agenda, Germany, the conference discussed at length Molotov's suggestion to invite representatives of the German Federal Republic and the DDR to the conference. This proposal was also stillborn. It had been known in advance that the Western powers refused to deal with the DDR regime; besides, no real progress could be expected if to the Soviet Molotov there were added an East Berlin "Molotov" of smaller stature. Anthony Eden finally submitted the Western plan of free elections as a means of reunifying Germany: the future government of Germany would be created by a new German parliament which would emerge

The Berlin Conference 143

from the elections and which would represent the will of the nation. This plan was also not novel. Since there was no doubt about the outcome of such elections, Eden's plan could not be accepted by Molotov, in whose program preservation of the DDR was Point One. Consequently, Molotov reversed the sequence of future developments: the establishment of a new German government, which would be a combination of two equal elements, would be the initial step; Bonn and Pankow would try to form the governing body for the whole country, prepare an election law, and then conduct national elections. In Molotov's plan, elections were the final stage rather than the beginning, and were to take place only if the two German regimes were able to find a common language and introduce a voting system acceptable to both. In the event the two regimes could not agree on a political course (which was a foregone conclusion), each would continue to govern in its own territory. "The Provisional All-German Government may be set up in place of the existing Governments of Eastern and Western Germany or should this prove difficult at present, these Governments may be maintained for a certain period of time." [1]

The Soviet press and radio rapidly spread this set of Soviet proposals all over the world. "It can hardly be said . . . that 'two plans' [Eden's and Molotov's] for the settlement of the German question have been put forward in Berlin. There is only one plan, that proposed by the Soviet delegation. The position of the Western Powers has been one of pure negation and dissent." [2] In general, said the Soviet press, the significance of the Berlin Conference "is determined by the proposals of the Soviet Union." [3]

In addition to elections, the coalition government, according to Molotov's proposal, would have "to ensure freedom of activity for democratic parties and organizations, and prevent the existence of fascist, militarist and other organizations hostile to democracy and the maintenance of peace." [4] Since the Christian-Democrats, the ruling party of West Germany, were viewed by Moscow as antidemocratic, their legality could be put in question. Whether the Social-Democrats could exist openly as a party likewise appeared doubtful. The Communist Party, if Molotov's plan were accepted, would remain legal.

[1] *New Times*, Moscow, no. 7, February 13, 1954, Supplement, p. 9.
[2] *Ibid.*, p. 7, "The German People and the Berlin Conference," by L. Bezymensky.
[3] *Ibid.*, p. 3, lead article, "For an All-European System of Collective Security."
[4] *Ibid.*, Supplement, p. 9.

Another task of the coalition government prescribed by the Soviet scheme would be the signing of a peace treaty with the wartime enemies of Germany. The Soviet "Principles of a Peace Treaty with Germany" provided for the withdrawal of occupation forces within a year. However, another of Molotov's proposed resolutions, entitled "Safeguarding Security in Europe," provided for the right of the powers to return to Germany:

> The Powers which at present are exercising occupation functions in Germany shall [after the withdrawal] have the right to move in their forces in case the security of either part of Germany is threatened; the U.S.S.R. in regard to Eastern Germany, the U.S.A., the United Kingdom and France in regard to Western Germany.

This meant that in the event of popular movements arising in the Eastern zone which might again, as in 1953, endanger the pro-Soviet German regime, the Soviet army would have the right to return its forces to East Germany. In such a case the Western powers could do nothing in that part of the unified country nor could the Bonn government oppose the Soviet move since its military forces would have been limited by the peace treaty to the level of pure "defense."

Reunified Germany would have to break off military ties with the West, and German membership in NATO would not be tolerated: "Germany shall undertake not to enter into any coalition or military alliance directed against any power whose armed forces took part in the war with Germany." Under this provision, open adherence to an Eastern military bloc would likewise be prohibited. However—though this was never actually stated—control by the Soviet War Ministry of all satellite armies would continue.

Neutralization of Germany as a permanent element of the Eastern setup would be achieved.

The new political structure of Europe thus established would be crowned, according to Molotov's proposals, by a new treaty of "collective security in Europe" which would provide for assistance by the community of European states to any of its members that was attacked by another power; the members would also undertake not to join any coalition or alliance (for example, NATO) the aims of which "are contrary to the aims of the treaty of collective security in Europe." This kind of purely European United Nations could embrace every

The Berlin Conference

nation of the old continent, including the two Germanys, but of course not the United States; it would be an international formation in which Russian superiority would be acknowledged as a matter of fact. It would bring to realization the Soviet dream of leadership over the whole of Europe.

This Soviet proposal to bring France, Germany, and possibly Britain under Soviet control, and to achieve this with the consent of those nations, appeared "so preposterous that when Molotov read it, laughter rippled around the Western sides of the table to the dismay of the Communist delegation."[5] Molotov became angry. "When he called for the abandonment of a European Defense Community, the dismantling of the North Atlantic Treaty Organization, and the scrapping of United States bases, he spoke with no soft words. Gone was the post-Stalin 'new look.' Thus he made clear what, to some, had been in doubt."[6]

On February 13, after a fortnight of discussion, the German problem was tabled and the state treaty with Austria was, much to the dislike of Molotov, taken up. On the Austrian question, in connection with which there had been scores of international conferences and many concessions by the Western powers, Molotov could not, as on the German question, ride lofty principles and programs. The situation became even more difficult when the Western ministers indicated that on most of the disputed points they were ready to accept the Soviet demands.

Molotov remained adamant. His proposal was to tie the Austrian issue to the issue of a peace treaty with Germany and not to withdraw foreign troops from Austria until a German treaty was signed. This would mean a delay of years, perhaps decades, during which the Soviet government would remain in occupation of the eastern part of Austria. In addition, Molotov wanted to incorporate provisions guaranteeing Austrian neutrality and nonadherence to any power bloc.

In the discussion, Austrian Foreign Minister Leopold Figl, who had been invited to attend this part of the conference, indicated the willingness of his government to accept the neutrality provisions

---

[5] Report on Berlin by Secretary of State John Foster Dulles, February 24, 1954, in *Department of State Bulletin*, vol. 30, no. 767, March 8, 1954, p. 344.

[6] *Ibid.* Essentially the idea of "Europe for the Europeans" and the elimination of the United States had already been put forth in the last of the Soviet notes preceding the Berlin Conference.

(this was contrary to the advice of Secretary Dulles); the perpetuation of foreign occupation, however, was unacceptable to Austria, as it was to the three Western powers. Molotov would not yield his power position. The discussion produced no results.[7] "Figl," commented *Pravda*,[8] "acts against Austria's interests."

The conference was coming to an end. In private conversations among the ministers, Far Eastern issues, especially those of Korea and the Indochinese war, were touched upon. All of the delegates agreed, however, to convene a special conference on the two Far Eastern issues to be held in Geneva on April 26. Since Communist China was to participate in this conference, the question arose whether Peking should be among the inviting great powers, which was what Molotov wanted, or, as Dulles proposed, should be invited along with the two Koreas and others. The compromise arrived at was that the invitation to Communist China be sent by the Berlin Conference as a whole, "without the implication of diplomatic recognition."

On February 18 the Berlin Conference closed. The official statement said that "The four Ministers have had a full exchange of views on the German question, on the problems of European security and on the Austrian question, but they were unable to reach agreement upon these matters." [9]

In the view of polite diplomats the main achievement of the Berlin parley was that for the first time in five years the foreign ministers of the Big Four had assembled at one table. Other views were more candid: "It was all greatly disappointing," said Anthony Eden. The Soviet side claimed to see progress in the very fact that it had submitted schemes for the future of Europe, China, disarmament, and peace.

An aftermath of the Berlin Conference was the Soviet note of March 31, 1954, to the three Western powers which dealt again with Molotov's draft of a treaty on "European Collective Security" without the United States, and which was criticized not only abroad but obviously also in Moscow. In this new note the Foreign Minister agreed to include the United States in the treaty. Molotov, whose lack of a

---

[7] This attitude of Molotov's, later severely criticized by Khrushchev, was probably one of the reasons for his eventual dismissal.
[8] February 17, 1954.
[9] *New Times*, Moscow, no. 8, February 20, 1954, p. 3.

The Geneva Conference

sense of humor was proverbial, also expressed the willingness of the Soviet Union to join NATO.

2. THE GENEVA CONFERENCE

The Geneva Conference of April–June, 1954, was one of the peaks of postwar-era Communist successes. On all issues debated at Geneva everybody listened attentively to the Soviet foreign minister, whose position on war or peace was crucial. But it was Communist China that profited most from the Geneva climate. For Chou En-lai and Communist China and, along with them, all the "people's democracies," the conference was a triumph; in their eyes it marked a milestone on the "historical road" to power. The press attentively followed Chou's visit to Moscow on his way to the conference and the simultaneous arrival of the North Koreans, the two visits having obviously been synchronized. The Chinese delegation at Geneva, approximately two hundred strong, was the largest of all the delegations. Chou En-lai, evidently in accordance with the Oriental belief in splendor as a way to make friends and influence people, rented a villa for himself near Geneva.

The fact that the Chinese Communists were invited to a conference with the great powers, among them the United States, in itself represented a success; it was no secret that on this point disagreement had disrupted the unity of the Western governments and accounted for Secretary Dulles's appearing only briefly at the conference. Eden, more conciliatory toward the Chinese than Dulles, was the West's leading delegate.

The Geneva Conference actually consisted of two separate parleys, one on Korea, the other on Indochina. In the first, fifteen members of the United Nations, plus South Korea (South Africa had declined) and, from the other side, the Soviet Union, Communist China, and North Korea—a total of nineteen governments—participated. The Korean part of the Geneva Conference lasted from April 26 to June 15.

In the Indochina phase, which lasted from May 8 to June 21, nine governments were represented, namely, the four great powers, Communist China, Vietnam, Vietminh, Laos, and Cambodia. In both parts of the conference Molotov acted as the leader of the Communist delegations. For propaganda reasons the order of Communist speakers and resolutions emphasized the leading role of Nam Il, the North Korean foreign minister, in the discussion on Korea, and of Vice-President Pham Van Dong in the discussion on Indochina. The two native leaders were followed by Chou En-lai for Peking; only at the very end did orator Molotov enter the discussion.

The Communist proposals for the reunification of Korea, submitted by Nam Il, repeated in almost every detail Molotov's plan for Germany submitted only a short time before at the conference in Berlin. They provided for general elections in Korea to be held after "preparation" by a "commission" (a parallel to the German "confederation"). The Communist side proposed "to appoint an All-Korean Commission composed of representatives of North and South Korea, elected respectively by the Supreme People's Assembly of the Korean People's Democratic Republic and the National Assembly of the Republic of Korea. . . . The Commission should also include representatives of the major democratic public organizations of North and South Korea respectively." [10] According to the Communist proposals, all foreign troops were to be evacuated before any elections took place. Supporting Nam Il's proposal, Chou En-lai added a further point—repatriation of Korean and Chinese prisoners of war who were "forcibly" removed by the United States Command in June, 1953, and January, 1954, and were "impressed into military service." [11]

Molotov backed Chou and Nam Il and stressed Soviet support of the application to Asia of his anti-American "collective security." "The Soviet Union fully shares this desire to provide collective security for all the peoples of Asia, just as it desires to secure agreement on collective security for all of the peoples of Europe." [12] In a challenging statement the Communist side proposed that military alliances binding any part of Korea to a foreign power be voided.

This program for Korea, well thought through and prepared, was unrealistic for the same reason that its counterpart was unrealistic for Germany. Since free elections would be tantamount to the loss of North Korea to the Soviet side, the proposal for supervision of the elections by the United Nations or another objective agency was re-

[10] *New Times,* Moscow, no. 19, May 8, 1954, Supplement, p. 6. Statement by Nam Il, April 27, 1954.
[11] *Ibid.,* p. 23. Statement of Chou En-lai, May 3, 1954.
[12] *Ibid.,* no. 20, May 15, 1954, Supplement, p. 23.

The Geneva Conference

jected. The bilateral "commission" which was to prepare the elections was to consist of equal numbers of representatives from North Korea and South Korea, despite the fact that the population of South Korea was more than twice that of North Korea. The future "commission," with its built-in veto, was thus certain to end up in a stalemate; it could serve only as a means of propaganda. "Evacuation of foreign armies" would mean a withdrawal of American forces, while China would not only maintain her guard at the border but would also leave many thousands of her troops inside the North Korean army. Finally, the provision for the voiding of military ties of the two Koreas with their respective allies would be effective as between Seoul and Washington, while Moscow and Peking would certainly remain in control of North Korea through the firm but unpublicized ties between their Communist parties and the recognized supremacy of the Communist Party of the Soviet Union.

At certain points during the discussions it appeared that the Communist side might try to meet the West halfway, but the hope always vanished. The Soviet and Chinese delegates remained adamant to the end; they made no concessions. After several weeks of deliberations and speeches, Molotov returned to Moscow for two days (May 31 and June 1); from conferences with his colleagues there he returned in a bellicose mood to Geneva. His speech of June 8 confirmed the unfavorable expectations; it was the sharpest in tone and the most uncompromising of his speeches at Geneva. A few days later Chou En-lai made a similar speech.[13]

The futility of the conference became evident. On June 15 the delegations of the United States, Britain, France, and their allies, sixteen in all, signed a declaration in which they said:

> We believe . . . that it is better to face the fact of our disagreement than to raise false hopes and mislead the peoples of the world into believing that there is agreement where there is none.
> In the circumstances, we have been compelled reluctantly and regretfully to conclude that so long as the Communist delegations reject the two fundamental principles which we consider indispensable, further consideration and examination of the Korean question by the conference would serve no useful purpose.[14]

[13] *Osteuropa*, Stuttgart, no. 5, October, 1954, p. 372.
[14] *Department of State Bulletin*, vol. 30, no. 781, June 28, 1954, p. 974.

The Soviet side accused the signers of this statement of deliberate obstruction, citing as proof the fact that they refused to accept the Soviet proposals. Combining naïveté with impertinence, *New Times* commented:

> When the delegations which blindly followed the lead of the United States turned down the proposal made by the Soviet delegation on June 5 that the conference adopt basic principles for a Korean peace setlement, that was clear evidence that they had no desire to work for a peaceful solution of the Korean problem, nor to allow the establishment of an integral, democratic Korean state.[15]

Thus, on June 15, 1954, ended the Korean phase of the Geneva Conference. The result was not contrary to the aim of the Soviet bloc. Never intending to cede North Korea to the adversary, and realizing, on the other hand, the impossibility of acquiring the South, the Soviet side had taken part in the conference only in order to demonstrate its adherence to the lofty principle of unifying a divided country and its efforts to solve problems by negotiation. Probably exaggerating the propaganda value of such tactics, it had from the start viewed the conference as another way of appealing to the peoples of the East to support Moscow-Peking against the "imperialists."

In many respects the Soviet program for Indochina was analogous to that for Korea and Germany: it provided for the evacuation of all foreign troops from Indochina, for a prohibition against the supplying of arms, for the setting up of joint "conferences" of the two warring regimes, and, finally, for the holding of elections. Until unification of each of the three countries of Indochina (Vietnam, Laos, and Cambodia) was achieved, the governments of the two parts of each would continue to rule in their areas. This was tantamount to partition.

Following the pattern applied in building up Stalin's satellite empire in Europe, only on a smaller scale, Ho Chi-minh's forces had easily occupied adjoining areas in Laos and Cambodia and, once installed there, had proceeded to organize local governments. France denied the existence of these "movements"; the "governments," Bidault stated, were phantoms. But the Communists still pretended to take them seriously.

Military operations reached a catastrophic stage in the spring of

---

[15] *New Times*, Moscow, no. 25, June 19, 1954, p. 7.

The Geneva Conference

1954, and the question of British and United States military assistance to France was discussed in Paris, London, and Washington. Grave doubts prevailed in the latter two countries. Washington was the least willing to intervene in a colonial war; nor was London inclined to engage in the fight. The prospect of losing Indochina to the Communist bloc, however, made a decision difficult. After some vacillation, London decided against deeper involvement in the Indochinese war. The United States government assumed a position calculated to convince Moscow that full-fledged intervention was possible and that a large American military force might be dispatched. The French government was divided on all the issues. Thus the Western coalition was presenting a spectacle of internal disagreements, disorientation, and impotence.[16]

The French fortress of Dien Bien Phu in Vietnam fell to the Communist armies on May 7, 1954. For France and her allies this event represented the abyss. For the Soviet government, on the other hand, it was further proof of the correctness of its view of postwar France as a secondary power and the impotence of NATO if its main continental base was to be France. The situation seemed extremely favorable for Moscow. Under Stalin it might have developed into a grand-scale offensive; under his less bellicose successors all energies were being focused on the task of preventing another continental power from growing strong enough to replace France in the framework of the Western alliance.

Molotov told the conference on June 8 that "vast areas in the north, as well as in the center and the south of Vietnam, are administered by the government of the Democratic Republic of Vietnam. As to Laos, here, too, about half the country is not under the control of the official government authorities. In Cambodia, the area not under the control of the official authorities is less than in the other parts of Indo-China; but here, too, the struggle for national liberation is developing. . . ."[17]

There were, however, points of substantial difference between the situation in Indochina and that in Korea. In Vietnam, which was the main problem and the great issue, Ho Chi-minh's Communist regime enjoyed greater popularity and prestige than did the satellite

[16] *Life*, January 16, 1958.
[17] *New Times*, Moscow, no. 24, June 12, 1954, Supplement, p. 17.

government of Kim Il-sung in Korea; this was in turn the result of the shortsighted postwar policy of France in Indochina. When the Communist leader of the anti-Japanese resistance, Nguyen, proclaimed the independence of his country in 1945 and, assuming the name of Ho Chi-minh ("the wise," or, more accurately, "made wise by experience"), entered into negotiations with Paris, he at first reached agreements and won recognition. Later, however, the French government turned to Bao Dai, son of Khai Din, former Emperor of Annam, a playboy living on the Riviera who had collaborated during the war with Japan and had ignominiously abdicated in 1945. In 1949 France made him the ruler of the new allegedly independent country. The French troops assigned to defend the Bao Dai regime were too little and too late; the *Légion Française,* fighting for French Vietnam, consisted to a considerable extent of German fugitives from justice. Molotov hinted at this situation in his speech at Geneva on June 8:

> The defence of Dien Bien Phu was chiefly maintained not by the French, nor by the Vietnamese, but by all sorts of foreigners who had been gathered there. The Dien Bien Phu garrison consisted overwhelmingly of men who had no relation either to France or to Viet-Nam.[18]

Faced with the alternative of Bao Dai or Ho Chi-minh, the majority of the Vietnamese obviously would choose the latter. It was the judgment of Western observers that, given a free election in Vietnam at the time, Ho Chi-minh would have won. This was the reason why in this instance the Communist side, which usually tried to postpone elections as long as possible, first insisted on a vote after six months, while its opponents tried to delay it; and it was the reason why, finally, the elections, scheduled to take place within two years, were called off when South Vietnam refused to participate in them.

The prestige of France in Indochina was greatly diminished after the military reverses of the last few months before and during the Geneva Conference. Ho Chi-minh was rising. The disagreements between the Western powers about Indochina (their "contradictions," as *Pravda* referred to them with obvious delight) augured badly for the anti-Communist cause; a complete victory of Vietminh in Indochina was believed possible, even probable. Ho Chi-minh pledged at Geneva that he would unify his country by means of elections.

[18] *Ibid.,* Supplement, p. 19.

The Geneva Conference

The Western front presented a pitiful picture. A few weeks before the Geneva Conference Secretary Dulles had predicted that the Peking government would come to Geneva as a defendant, "to account before the bar of world opinion" for its role in Korea and Indochina. How wrong he was! Having proposed to England and France concerted action on Indochina, he met with a refusal on the part of London and only reluctant, partial agreement in Paris. A small group of American Air Force technicians was dispatched to Indochina, and even this tiny and entirely inadequate operation aroused protests in the United States.

For several weeks the outcome of the Geneva Conference on Indochina hung in the balance; it appeared likely that the conference would break down just as the Korean phase was also coming to an end, and that Ho Chi-minh would resume his offensive. The decision as to whether there would be war or peace in Indochina hung on the only power in a position to supply arms in quantity, and in 1954 this power was Russia. After Molotov's trip to Moscow the Indochina negotiations began to appear futile. If the war continued, the situation of France was almost hopeless. The government of Laniel-Bidault fell, and a new government headed by Pierre Mendès-France took over.

The new premier was known as an uncompromising opponent of the European Defense Community, which was much hated also by Moscow; he promised to resign if he did not achieve a truce in Indochina within five weeks (by July 20). This program was so attractive to Moscow that it changed its strategy almost overnight.

It was possible that by continuing the Indochinese war a larger territory would fall to the Communist side and that Laos and Cambodia might be overrun. To Moscow, however, to whom Europe was still the most important issue, the rejection of EDC by France outweighed many other considerations. To keep Mendès-France in power, at least until EDC was destroyed, was imperative, and if to accomplish this a quick truce in Indochina was required, then Ho Chi-minh must compromise. The French conditions had to be met. Moreover, prolongation of the war, though opening attractive vistas, was fraught with the danger of military intervention by the United States, as a result of which South Indochina might become an American military base. It did not appear logical to demand the abolition of American bases all around the world while at the same time making it possible for the United States to set up a new base in Indochina. A compromise settlement was preferable.

Immediately following the election of Mendès-France, Chou En-lai, with Soviet consent and on Soviet advice, sent word to Mendès-France suggesting a meeting. Mendès-France accepted. A few days later Chou, accompanied by aides and bodyguards, arrived in Bern in grand style, in a special railway car. The meeting was held at the French Embassy.[19]

Negotiations at Geneva took a turn for the better. The complicated questions of a truce in a foreign war and a truce in a civil war in which three separate countries were involved, the withdrawal of troops, the setting up of special agencies, etc., were discussed and settled before the crucial July 20 deadline; now it was the Communist delegations that were the most eager to reach a solution that would be acceptable to the other side.

The truce agreements signed on July 20 and 21 provided for the drawing of a demarcation line below the seventeenth parallel and withdrawal of troops to their zones in the north and south. Importation of new arms was prohibited. An "International Commission," consisting of Indian, Canadian, and Polish representatives, was to be set up to supervise the compliance of both sides with the truce conditions. Elections in both parts of Vietnam were to take place by July, 1956. France recognized the sovereignty of Vietnam, Laos, and Cambodia and pledged to evacuate her troops. No foreign military bases (meaning Chinese or American) were to be established in Vietnam; military alliances of Vietnam with foreign powers were likewise prohibited. The neutrality imposed on both parts of Vietnam precluded open adherence of North Vietnam to the Soviet bloc and the joining of SEATO by South Vietnam.

The outcome of the Indochinese war was a significant success for the Soviet-Chinese-Vietminh side; it provided for the legal and open emergence in Asia of a new "people's democracy" with a population of over 12,000,000. The new state greatly enhanced China's prestige in Asia. No treaty of alliance between them was necessary to establish a military force and provide for the supply of arms from the north.

[19] *The New York Times*, June 27, 1954.

Crisis in the Western Bloc 155

Guerrilla forces were now in a position to leave the jungle and develop into a regular army.

The United States did not sign the joint declaration of the other members of the conference; in President Eisenhower's words, "the United States has not bound itself by the decision taken." The United States, however, had no intention of disturbing the settlement. It rather turned to other non-Communist countries of Southeast Asia to help in establishing and strengthening SEATO, the counterpart of the emerging Asian bloc of Communist nations.

Although to the Soviet side the attitude of the United States, which Moscow presented as proof of its isolation, was a source of satisfaction, Moscow began vehemently to fight the emerging anti-Communist Asian-Pacific organization. America's disagreements with Britain and France proved, Moscow believed, that her leadership of the West was over and that, in consequence, a significant weakening, perhaps the onset of the disintegration, of the Western alliance was beginning.

In Soviet eyes the defeat of France confirmed the dim view of that nation that had prevailed in Moscow since the early 1930's. France was viewed as nearly impotent and artificially maintained as a power by her stronger allies. Consequently she was not as formidable an enemy in Europe as she had once appeared.

The leading role of the Soviet Union in the "socialist camp" was enhanced as a result of the Geneva Conference. The "camp" had proved its firmness and unity in the face of its bitterest enemies. And Communist China had won new prestige as a dynamic, fighting government, disinclined to retreat or to bow to powerful adversaries. To the Soviet Union and Communist China the conference signified progress.

3. CRISIS IN THE WESTERN BLOC

The firmness of Molotov's course at the Berlin Conference and the Soviet-Chinese achievements at Geneva were made possible by the deterioration within the Western coalition. The internal crisis of the Western bloc in 1954 and the prospect of its disintegration formed the background of the hard line taken by Moscow.

The European Defense Community, which had been initiated by France and accepted by her Western allies in 1952 as a means of integrating German power with their own, was rejected by the French National Assembly on August 30, 1954. Strong pro-Soviet tones sounded in the French Assembly when outstanding leaders took the floor, and the Moscow press, elated over the developments, reported them in great detail. "We want to have," said the aged Edouard Herriot, recalling the French-Soviet *rapprochement* of the 1930's, "a peaceful Europe in which Germany and the Soviet Union will find their place." [20] This was the essence of the debate and of the decision: to maintain ties with Moscow and to look for "European security" along lines similar to those proposed by Molotov.

The rejection by France of the European Defense Community, which was based on the overoptimistic evaluation of post-Stalin Soviet policies, resulted in Soviet defiance of Britain and the United States and a profound rift in the Western coalition. The Soviet government not only warmly approved the French action but even promised support to France. Events apparently confirmed the Soviet view that France was losing influence and that some years would pass before her place could be taken by West Germany. An official Soviet statement offered encouragement to France:

> It [the collapse of EDC] has proved that the patriotic forces of France were equal to the situation and rightly perceived in EDC a mortal threat to the security and independence of the French State.[21]

"France is not alone," exclaimed *New Times*,[22] "in her fight to prevent a German militarist comeback. France has the support of all the peace-loving peoples of Europe. Indeed, what talk can there be of French isolation when there is the Soviet proposal for a General European Treaty of Collective Security?"

Molotov's proposal at the Berlin Conference to eliminate the United States from European affairs had been greeted with laughter. But the ridicule did not kill it. Having been rejected without serious discussion in Berlin, the proposal soon reappeared as the content of a slogan intended to spread to Asia and Africa. This was the first stage of an operation which, within a year, resulted in the formal setting up

---

[20] *Pravda*, August 31, 1954.
[21] *Pravda*, September 10, 1954.
[22] Moscow, no. 37, September 11, 1954, p. 11.

Crisis in the Western Bloc

of an anti-NATO organization of the Soviet bloc embodied in the Warsaw Pact of May, 1955.

Elimination of the United States from European affairs, rejection of American aid to Western Europe, and withdrawal of American forces from the continent were the major consistent goals of Soviet foreign policy. Of the three power elements—America, Western Europe, and the Soviet bloc—the Western camp, embodied in NATO, constituted a bloc of the first two against the third, whereas Moscow aimed at a combination of the latter two against the first. Moscow's eventual agreement—a verbal concession—to include the United States and Communist China in certain parts of the projected European security scheme did not alter the essential anti-American aim and meaning of the project. In those years the term "collective" was sometimes used to serve peculiar semantic needs. "Collective leadership" meant a period of transition from one personal leadership to another; "collective security" meant elimination of the most prominent member of the collective.

"Europe for the Europeans" seemed so peaceful and democratic a slogan that it soon appeared in other parts of the world, though in other forms. Chinese Communism gladly adopted it to demand the expulsion of America from Asia, which implied Chinese domination over the Far East. Molotov's collective security, translated into Asian terms, was proclaimed by Chou En-lai a few weeks later at Geneva, and his words were repeatedly quoted with approval in the Soviet and satellite press:

> The government of the People's Republic of China believes that the nations of Asia should consult among themselves with a view to assuming mutual obligations providing for joint measures to safeguard peace and security in Asia.[23]

It was not long before the same set of ideas was adopted by the new neutralist movements. After Chou En-lai's meeting with India's Premier Nehru on June 25, 1954, Chou's statements were to serve as a program of the forthcoming Bandung Conference of the peoples of Asia and Africa.

"Collective security" in Europe and a peace treaty with the two Germanys formed the content of the diplomatic exchanges of the year

---

[23] *New Times,* Moscow, no. 19, May 8, 1954, Supplement, p. 11. Statement by Chou En-lai of April 28, 1954.

1954; the notes on both sides were repetitious and futile. Molotov's note of March 31 dealt in the main with the admission of the United States to "European Collective Security" and the inclusion of the Soviet Union in NATO. In the following days the three Western governments rejected the suggestion; Secretary Dulles called it "a maneuver" to break "the very precious asset," the North Atlantic Pact. In the May 7 diplomatic notes of the Western powers, the proposal of Soviet membership in NATO was rejected as "unreal." At the same time, the three Western powers requested the Soviet government to help solve the problems of Germany and the Far East and to take a different course in the United Nations.

In the Soviet reply of July 24, supplemented by the note of August 4, Molotov, while repeating his previous proposals, suggested the convening of a conference of all European nations on the problems of collective security, with the United States and China, the outsiders, to be invited; the conference was to take place "in the next few months," and a preparatory conference of the foreign ministers of the Big Four was to be held in August or September.

The Western replies, which were dispatched on September 10, expressed willingness to take part in a conference of the Big Four on the conditions that, first, Moscow sign the state treaty with Austria, and second, Moscow agree to the unification of Germany on the basis of free elections.

Molotov countered by presenting conditions of his own. In his note of October 23 he proposed: withdrawal of foreign troops from West and East Germany; agreement on limitation of German military forces in East and West and free elections on "peaceful and democratic" bases; and a conference on collective security. The Austrian issue was passed over in silence. In a public speech in Berlin on October 10, Molotov demanded, as Point One in his program, the withdrawal of all foreign troops from Germany.

Meantime, after the collapse of the European Defense Community the United States and Britain were taking other paths on the issue of European defense: if a combined army of the European powers proved unattainable, then an autonomous German military force must be brought about. A new series of conferences, negotiations between

Crisis in the Western Bloc

the European powers, and new plans and agreements [24] became necessary to set up the new Western European Union and to admit West Germany to NATO. West Germany was empowered to create an army of half a million, while Britain and the United States promised to maintain certain military forces on the continent. Germany agreed not to manufacture atomic and certain other weapons or build large warships and bombers.

By the end of 1954 the widely held Soviet expectation that France would break with the West and choose a "neutral" path appeared to have been frustrated. In October, 1954, West Germany was admitted to NATO. Moscow's anger was rising; insisting that his "collective security" was the only possible alternative to German rearmament, Molotov threatened France and England with renunciation of the wartime treaties of alliance of 1941 and 1942. On November 11 he proceeded unilaterally to invite all the governments of Europe to a conference on European security to be held in Moscow not later than November 29.

Molotov's haste in convening the conference was due to the vain hope that such a parley might prevent ratification of the Paris agreements and the rearming of Germany:

> To postpone the Conference to a later date would be inadvisable, inasmuch as examination of the question of ratifying the Paris agreements will begin in some European countries in December. Their ratification would greatly complicate the general situation in Europe and would jeopardize the possibility of settling outstanding European questions, primarily the German question.[25]

On December 16, in a threatening note to the French government, Molotov stated that the "ratification of the [new] Paris agreements will put the cross through the Franco-Soviet Treaty of Alliance and Mutual Assistance, will render it null and void." [26] A similar note was dispatched to London on December 20.

Nevertheless, the Paris agreements were ratified by the other nations during the early months of 1955. On May 7, 1955, the French and British alliances with Russia, which had lost their significance, were annulled by a decision of the Presidium of the Supreme Soviet.

---
[24] Of the new agreements the most important were the London Protocol of October 3, 1954, and the Paris agreements of October 23, 1954.
[25] *New Times*, Moscow, no. 46, November 13, 1954, Supplement, p. 4.
[26] *Ibid.*, no. 51, December 18, 1954, Supplement, p. 4.

Molotov had been right when he stated that the rearmament of Germany was incompatible with the letter of the wartime treaties and that the new international groupings were aligned against the Soviet Union. However, the emergence of the Soviet Union after the war as a new expanding power prevailed, of course, over the dead letter of the late treaties.

On November 29, and prior to the ratification of the new Western agreements, a "Conference of European Countries on Safeguarding European Peace and Security" opened in Moscow; the participants were the Soviet Union and the people's democracies (Yugoslavia refused to take part in a one-sided conference). In the course of the three-day parley the heads and delegates of nine governments, including the Chinese, made speeches, all in the same vein, attacking the United States, imperialism, and German militarism. The lengthy "declaration" adopted at the end of the conference reiterated the same ideas and provided for a further parley in the event the new Paris agreements were ratified. "The parties to the Conference have agreed, if the Paris agreements are ratified, to reexamine the situation with a view to taking reliable measures for the safeguarding of their security and for the maintenance of peace in Europe." [27] The presence of Soviet Marshals Georgi Zhukov, Nikolai Bulganin, and Klimenti Voroshilov at the signing of the declaration emphasized the military threat contained in it.

By the fall of 1954 the wind had shifted. The hope of eliminating the United States and finding avenues of *rapprochement* with France proved vain. NATO was not disrupted and the Western alliance was firmer; the Soviet rift with Paris and London, on the other hand, had widened. Germany was to receive new arms for a large army. Not a single non-Communist European country had joined Moscow in the international combination.

During this period Soviet diplomacy was proving more successful in Asia, where the new flower of "neutralism" was beginning to bloom.

4. THE ANTI-NATO ALIGNMENT

At the "Conference of European Countries on Safeguarding European Peace and Security," in which only members of the Soviet bloc

---

[27] *Ibid.*, no. 49, December 4, 1954, Supplement, p. 72.

The Anti-NATO Alignment

participated, attendance was complete and included China as an "observer." Yugoslavia, as noted, had declined to participate since participation would be tantamount to joining the Moscow coalition against the West. In a speech in Kopar on November 21, Tito had stated: "We cannot improve our relations [with the Soviet Union and other European countries] at the expense of our relations with the Western countries. We will not permit relations which were established with the Western countries to deteriorate simply for the sake of improving our relations with the East." [28] Consolidation of the military forces of the Soviet bloc as a countermove against the new consolidation of the West and the rearmament of Germany was the aim of the conference.

Actually the conference could not increase the force of the "socialist camp," if only because the military power of the "socialist camp" was already well-knit and controlled by Moscow. Whatever the degree of independence of an individual "people's democracy" in other fields, subordination of its military forces to the Soviet command in both peace and war was a matter of course; in this respect the shifts of leadership in Moscow had changed nothing. The two wartime allies Poland and Czechoslovakia had rebuilt their armies with Soviet help and guidance; the former enemies, Hungary, Rumania, and Bulgaria, with Soviet connivance and protection, had transgressed the limitations imposed by the peace treaties. The army of the DDR had emerged under strict Soviet control. All had obtained instructors and arms from Moscow. Strategy was uniform, as if all were one army. Besides, there existed (and certainly continues to exist) in the framework of the Soviet Defense Ministry a department for the satellites' armed forces; each satellite is represented there by a liaison officer and his staff.[29]

In the West, where the three great powers were beset by divergent views and political trends, and where France was devoting her forces to a war in Africa, unification of military effort, if achieved, could have meant progress. In the East, on the other hand, the official consolidation of what had unofficially existed for years was merely a demonstration, a way of reacting to the course of the Western powers.

The demonstration, however, was well arranged. In their speeches

[28] *Yugoslav Review*, New York, vol. 3, no. 9–10, November–December, 1954, p. 5.
[29] D Papers, February 18, 1960, File no. 10.

at the Moscow Conference of November 29 all of the participating leaders of the Communist governments stressed the great danger of "reviving German militarism," their solidarity with the Soviet Union, and the need for a united front against the United States and her allies. Molotov, symbolizing Soviet leadership, presided. Speeches followed a well-arranged order: first were the three governments directly interested in the German problem: Poland, Czechoslovakia, and the DDR; last was the Chinese envoy. Speaking for Czechoslovakia, Villiam Siroky suggested close collaboration with the two neighbors, Poland and East Germany. Otto Grotewohl of the DDR accepted the suggestion: "We also agree with the proposal of Prime Minister Siroky of Czechoslovakia that, if the Paris agreements are ratified, the Republic of Czechoslovakia, the Polish People's Republic and the German Democratic Republic, which will be specially endangered by this, should agree to joint measures." [30] This special position of the three northern people's democracies, which had been emphasized since early 1954, became of greater significance in the following years.[31]

The participation of China was highlighted, obviously to impress the West with this additional power. It might well be that this presentation of China as an ally in Europe was a major aim of the conference. As far as published treaties are concerned Communist China had up to then been tied to the Soviet Union as an ally, but only against Japan; besides, under Stalin the relations between Moscow and Peking had not been of the best. In October, 1954, however, Khrushchev, Bulganin, and Mikoyan visited China and, while making certain concessions to the Chinese, succeeded also in mending rifts and improving the political climate.[32] Among their achievements, apparently, was the obtaining from Mao of a pledge of military help to the Soviet bloc in case of a conflict in Europe. The Chinese envoy at the Moscow Conference promised support in general terms, but, as Grotewohl soon afterward disclosed, this commitment was far more explicit than had been reported: the Soviet-Chinese treaty, Grotewohl revealed, was to be applicable even in case of a purely European war.[33]

Marshal Bulganin, too, found an opportunity to point to China's potential contribution. At a reception for the conference delegates on

[30] *New Times*, Moscow, no. 49, December 4, 1954, Documents (Supplement), p. 41.
[31] See p. 154.
[32] See pp. 427–428.
[33] *The New York Times*, November 5, 1954.

The Anti-NATO Alignment

November 30 he proposed a toast to the military strength of the eight European allies, then apologized for having overlooked the "'great army of China, 20 million strong.' Turning to the Chinese Ambassador he said: 'I hope that is not a military secret.' The Ambassador indicated with a smile that it was not." [34]

The lengthy Declaration adopted by the conference said in part: "The parties to this Conference declare that they have decided, should the Paris agreements be ratified, to adopt joint measures in the sphere of organization of their armed forces and their command, as well as other measures required for strengthening their defensive power."

The second full-scale conference of the Soviet bloc took place in Warsaw on May 11–14, 1955, after the ratification of the Paris agreements. At this conference the "Pact of Mutual Assistance and Unified Command" was adopted. Represented were the same governments that had participated in the Moscow Conference, with Communist China again an "observer." All but one of the sessions, that of May 12, at which General A. I. Antonov discussed the military questions of the new organization, were public, and the press published the well-prepared speeches. Peng Teh-huai, the renowned Chinese general, again threatened Chinese intervention in the event of a European war: "If the peace of Europe is disturbed, if the imperialist aggressors launch war against the peaceable European states, our government and our heroic 600 million people will, shoulder to shoulder with the governments and peoples of our fraternal countries, fight the aggressors until final victory is won." [35]

Article 5 of the Pact signed by the eight European governments read: "The Contracting Parties have agreed to establish a Joint Command of the armed forces that by agreement among the Parties shall be assigned to the Command, which shall function on the basis of jointly established principles. They shall likewise adopt other agreed measures necessary to strengthen their decisive power. . . ." To stress another, nonmilitary purpose of the Pact (which was analogous to NATO), Article 6 provided for the organization of a Political Committee: ". . . a Political Consultative Committee shall be set up, in which each of the Parties to the Treaty shall be represented by a

[34] *Ibid.*, December 1, 1954.
[35] *New Times*, Moscow, no. 21, May 21, 1955, Documents (Supplement), p. 60.

member of its government or by another specifically appointed representative." It also declared that command of the unified military forces had been assigned to Soviet Marshal Ivan Konev, the counterpart of the American generals in command of NATO forces.

The Pact, which was signed in Warsaw at about the same time as the agreement on withdrawal of foreign troops from Austria was signed in Vienna, served the Soviet Union as a legal substitute for the latter. The peace treaties of 1947 with Hungary and Rumania had granted to the Soviet Union the privilege of stationing its troops in those two countries in order to safeguard "communication lines" with the occupied zones in Austria. With the signing of the new Austrian treaty, however, and the withdrawal of all foreign troops, this privilege expired. Now the Warsaw Pact, though not specific on these special rights, was to serve the Soviet Union as a legal basis for the presence of Soviet troops in the satellite countries. This issue became important the forthcoming year, in the course of the uprising in Hungary.[36]

Another major reason for the Warsaw Pact was to juxtapose the Soviet bloc with NATO and create the symbol of the claimed equality of the two organizations. In political propaganda as well as in diplomatic correspondence the Soviet government sometimes proposed the liquidation of "both NATO and the Warsaw Pact," pointing to the similarity in status and significance of the two organizations. The proposal was never accepted by the West.

The Warsaw Pact did not play a significant role in the international developments of the following years.

The special position of the three northern satellites—Poland, Czechoslovakia, and the German Democratic Republic—which was emphasized at the Moscow Conference, was repeatedly stressed in the following weeks. The intention was to prove that the alliance with the Soviet Union was dictated by the anti-German sentiments and interests of the "people's democracies" and not by Moscow, nor by Communist ideology, and that the Western nations which had likewise suffered from German aggression should understand and approve that course of policy and refrain from an alliance with Bonn.

In late December, 1954, a conference in Prague of members of the

---

[36] See pp. 368 ff.

The Anti-NATO Alignment

three parliaments (Warsaw, Prague, and East Berlin) issued a declaration against the "rebirth of German militarism" and appealed to France to oppose it. The Prague Conference was followed by public statements and a press campaign in the three "people's democracies." Johannes Dieckmann, Chairman of the parliament of the DDR, even announced that the three governments would have to agree on a common course.

The latter promise did not materialize, however. A united front of the northern satellites was all right for political propaganda, but a real confederation of a part of the satellite family was too dangerous. In the subsequent years the common anti-German interests of the northern sector were mentioned more than once, but no steps were taken and no new organization was created.

CHAPTER 5

THE "PEOPLE'S DEMOCRACIES"

For a time after Stalin's death there was little change in Moscow's relations with the "people's democracies" despite the measure of relaxation in Soviet internal affairs. The Soviet Union and the satellites claimed "gigantic" successes, especially in economic matters, heavy industry, and collectivization: the "people's democratic system" had brought freedom and happiness to millions of people and put an end to hunger, misery, and unemployment; the "people's democracies" continued on the road to prosperity, while the capitalist nations were passing from crisis to crisis to enter an era of decay; the individual peasantry of the "people's democracies," now aware of the shortcomings of private agriculture, were beginning to emulate the Soviet pattern; prices were being reduced, food was becoming plentiful and cheap, new housing was available to the workers; the foreign trade of the people's democracies was growing, and instead of raw materials they were now beginning to export industrial products:

> Thousands of guests from capitalist countries have visited, for example, people's democratic Poland in recent years and have been amazed at the epoch-making changes in that once backward country, where millions of the common people were the bonded or wage slaves of the landlords and capitalists. Today Poland is a mighty, truly independent, industrially developed country. Industrial output per capita in People's Poland has outstripped the level of Italy and is drawing close to that of Britain and France.[1]

The Soviet attitude toward the satellites was still pictured as "brotherly, broadminded, and disinterested"; Soviet economic assistance was "unprecedented in human history"; "what was impossible in the capitalist world is possible and being realized in the world of

[1] *New Times*, Moscow, no. 45, November 7, 1953, pp. 9–10. J. Medvedev, "Fraternal Cooperation of Free Nations."

The "People's Democracies"

democracy and socialism." Yugoslavia was still a thorn; Tito "the fascist" was being duly punished for his defection by economic reverses in Yugoslavia:

> When the treachery of the Tito clique was exposed, the Soviet Union naturally discontinued its assistance to that country. Instead, fascist Yugoslavia began to receive so-called "aid" from the United States, aid which was actually a disguise for robbing the Yugoslav people and pilfering their natural resources. The results of this soon became evident. In the People's Democracies, which enjoy the disinterested aid of the U.S.S.R., the iron and steel industry, for instance, is rapidly expanding; in Yugoslavia it is either making no progress or actually retrogressing.[2]

Conformity of the "people's democracies" to the Moscow line remained Point One in the unwritten covenant of the members of the "socialist camp." Since, however, a kind of evolution was taking place in the Soviet Union's methods of government, in its police system, and in its economic policy, it was expected that similar changes would occur in the satellite countries. Within the Soviet regime a number of important post-Stalin innovations had been introduced:

1. In the relations between the state and the Communist Party more autonomy was given to the state; the posts of first secretary of the Party and premier were separated; "collective leadership," meaning rule by the Politburo-Presidium, was established; the Presidium tolerated factions in its midst; it remained the supreme power.

2. There was less police and political repression; the secret police agency was purged and reorganized; an amnesty was declared, and there was partial rehabilitation of victims of Stalin.

3. Fewer sacrifices on the altar of industrialization were demanded; there was a slowing down of the growth of heavy industry; more attention was given to consumer goods and the standard of living of the people and to agriculture and husbandry.

The internal affairs of a Soviet satellite were part of the foreign affairs of the Soviet Union. In the Soviet Union the political course, including the accession to power of the new leadership in 1953, evolved out of internal developments. In the "people's democracies" evolution within their own countries was secondary to the ideas and

[2] For eloquent statements on this subject, see *New Times*, Moscow, no. 16, April 15, no. 18, April 29, no. 45, November 7, 1953, and *Kommunist*, Moscow, no. 7, May, 1953.

slogans produced in the Soviet Union. Reforms comparable to those in Russia were urgently needed in the satellites, if only to prevent rumblings and revolutionary movements. For a few years, under Stalin, the prevailing discontent could be held down by specific Stalinist methods, but now it might burst into the open.

A search was begun for satellite leaders who would fit into the new scheme of things. Just as Stalin had looked about for lesser, obedient Stalins in the satellite Kremlins, the post-Stalin Soviet leadership was now on the lookout for lesser Malenkovs and Khrushchevs able and willing to transplant the new course onto the soil of Eastern Europe.

The changes that began in the satellites in the spring of 1953 proved, however, how difficult the undertaking was. The achievement of conformity, which had appeared so logical under Stalin, now proved unexpectedly troublesome. Outside of Russia there were hardly any serious Communist groups that could serve as counterparts of the new Soviet leadership. The courses followed by Malenkov, Khrushchev, Molotov, and Mikoyan were peculiarly Russian; they could not be imitated. On the other hand, there existed in the satellites old and honored Stalinists, such as Mathias Rakoszi in Hungary, who were filling the posts of general secretaries; the others were Walter Ulbricht, Boleslaw Bierut, and Vulko Chervenkov. Most of these men were incapable of following any other course than a Stalinist one. But 100 per cent Stalinists were not exactly what Moscow now wanted to see at the head of the people's democracies.

There existed also in the satellites, unofficially, groups of different trend; sometimes called "rightist" or "nationalist," their programs included almost all the points of the post-Stalin program enumerated above, namely, opposition to an extreme pace of industrialization, to the neglect of the standard of living of the people and the disregard of peasant agriculture. The leaders of these groups, many of whom had been victims of purges, wanted less police oppression. They also wanted more freedom—though hardly democracy in the Western style. The crux of the difficulty, however, was that their programs went much further than these partial reforms: they wanted more independence from Moscow. Their programs called also for cessation of economic exploitation of the satellites by the Soviet Union, better relations with the West, and an autonomous foreign policy. More

Rumblings in the East

pro-Western than any group within the Soviet Union, they represented the other Communist extreme: their anti-Stalinism was actual or potential Titoism. With leaders of such orientation in control of the satellites the Soviet empire might disintegrate. They too were unsuitable.

This dilemma—a choice between blood-and-iron Stalinism and disintegration—haunted the Soviet government from then on. It lay at the roots of the Soviet-satellite crisis that started in 1953 and crescendoed through the years until it reached its peak in the outbursts of October–November, 1956.

1. RUMBLINGS IN THE EAST

The ferment in the satellites, which set in almost immediately after Stalin's death and within four months assumed large proportions, was an outstanding event of both Soviet internal policy and international affairs.

The first post-Stalin popular movement inside a people's democracy was the disturbance, which culminated in the strike of June, 1953, in Czechoslovakia. The second was the general strike and uprising in the Eastern zone of Germany, which also occurred in June, 1953. The third was the Poznan uprising in Poland in June, 1956. The fourth was the popular movement in Poland in October, 1956. The fifth was the uprising in Hungary in October–November, 1956.

One official explanation of the crises was the time-honored "foreign agents" abundantly "dispatched" by the imperialists to the socialist lands to subvert them back to the path of capitalism. Less awkward than the "foreign agents" explanation was the purely economic interpretation of the events which also came out of post-Stalin Moscow: the low wages, the poverty of the people, too much pressure in the name of industrialization. From this explanation it followed that the problem could be solved by economic reforms of limited scope. But this theory, too, was faulty.

The feature common to all the popular movements in the satellites was the interweaving of economic, political, and international issues into a single emotion, a fighting spirit, rather than a program. The banner bearers everywhere were the workers—the "ruling class" in a "people's democracy"—who were joined by students and intellectuals—the "socialist intelligentsia"; these groups were supported by a large majority of the population. Wage demands were only the starting point. Slogans voicing opposition to police oppression and dictatorship were added almost immediately. Expanding and reaching into the international field, the movements proclaimed their negative attitude toward Russian control and revealed a strong trend in favor of the West.

All of these elements were present in the first of the series of disturbances, that in Czechoslovakia. The currency reform announced there on May 30, 1953, wiped out most of the workers' savings and substantially reduced their wages; state loans and bonds were depreciated. On June 1, unrest developed in Pilsen at the former Skoda Works. The official radio announced that "rioters tore down pictures of Czech state leaders and hung up pictures of the imperialist agent Benes. The American gangsters stepped on pictures of Stalin and Gottwald and violated the Soviet flag. The archives in the town hall were burned." The American flag was hoisted in many places; posters proclaimed: "U.S., come back!" "Robbery is the Russian Paradise." [3] American and Czech flags were placed around the Masaryk bust.

Riots occurred also in the industrial area of Moravia-Ostrava, Grossnessedorf, and elsewhere. In the end, the government, trade union officials, and police were able to stop the riots. The ability of the police to quell the movement was peculiar to this first post-Stalin anti-Communist rising in the areas of the Soviet bloc. The developments in Czechoslovakia did not become a direct issue for the Soviet government, although they were an ominous foreboding.

Such was not the case, however, in the subsequent revolutionary uprisings in the Soviet bloc countries, all of which, although they differed in character, were suppressed by either direct foreign military power or the rattling of the foreign sword.

It was accidental that the first disturbance should have broken out in a Czechoslovak province; it might easily have broken out elsewhere in Eastern Europe. After Stalin's death the feeling prevailed everywhere that there would be substantial changes in the system, although no one, even the leadership, had any clear notion about the nature of the changes. There was expectation and hope rather than knowledge; there was no certainty, only burning desire. The promise

[3] *Time,* June 22, 1953, p. 33; *Look,* August 11, 1953, p. 26.

Rumblings in the East

of "amnesty" emanating from Moscow hung in the air. Among leading political circles it was already rumored that the days of individual dictators were numbered, that there would be an end to the cold war, that food and "consumer goods" would have higher priority. Popular emotion, which often runs ahead of reality, generated the hope that a new relationship between East and West would come into being.

The strikes and unrest in East Germany, which followed the Pilsen episode by only a fortnight, were of larger dimensions in terms of the number of casualties, the challenge presented, and the degree of Soviet involvement.

Less than a year had passed since the Socialist Unity Party (SED) at its conference in July, 1952, had approved Walter Ulbricht's far-reaching, aggressive program of "building socialism" in the German Democratic Republic; the intervening period had seen a great upsurge in "heavy industry," combined with claims of a "lowering of cost of production" and of an "increase in the productivity of labor," all of which was accompanied by low wages and supported by a stern police system; there was also implied an offensive against the "well-to-do" peasantry. Since Ulbricht had met the test of a loyal interpreter of socialist strategy and tactics, there was no doubt that the new offensive in East Germany was being continued in accord with the Kremlin.

About a month after Stalin's death the subject of East Germany, which had a high priority on the agenda, came up for discussion in the Soviet Presidium. In accordance with the new trends, the Soviet leadership addressed a letter to the Central Committee of the SED on April 16, 1953, suggesting a "turning away from the rigorous policy." The text of this letter, and of a subsequent note of June 3, have not been revealed.[4] In Berlin there was surprise and consternation; the instructions were contrary to what the leadership and the official press had been propagating daily. Disobedience, however, was out of the question; Ulbricht's Central Committee decided to make changes in its policy, but to proceed slowly.

[4] *SBZ-Archiv: Dokumente-Berichte-Kommentare zu Gesamtdeutschen Fragen* (Soviet Occupation Zone Archives: Documents, Reports, Commentaries on All-German Questions), Köln, Verlag des SBZ Archiv, no. 13, July 5, 1953, p. 200; *Europa-Archiv*, Frankfurt, Germany, no. 14/15, July 20–August 5, 1953, p. 5831; *SBZ von 1945 bis 1954: Die Sowjetische Besatzungszone Deutschlands in den Jahren 1945 bis 1954* (The Soviet Occupation Zone of Germany in the Years 1945–1954), Bonn, Germany, Bundesministerium für Gesamtdeutsche Fragen (Federal Ministry for All-German Problems), 1956.

In the following two months the Soviet government tried to steer the course in Germany to a less rigid, less Stalinist path; in this effort it was hampered by Ulbricht's time-honored, successful orthodoxy. It was reported that Molotov, the old Stalinist, tried to support Ulbricht in his daring offensive, while the more powerful Malenkov-Beria duo was inclined to extend the Soviet measure of relaxation to Germany. On April 22, Vladimir Semionov, the Soviet "political adviser" in East Germany, was recalled from his high post and replaced by Pavel Yudin. Later developments confirmed the German impression of disorientation in Moscow in regard to East German affairs.

A month later, in a rather unusual departure from the pretense of infallibility, the Soviet Control Commission in Berlin (General Chuikov) was publicly charged with responsibility for the blunders committed in East Germany. Chuikov and Semionov had never, of course, acted on their own initiative and without strict instructions from the Soviet government; their blunders were Stalin's blunders. Since it was impossible, however (this was still 1953), to put any blame on the defunct leader, Chuikov's office was made the scapegoat. Semionov returned to Berlin on May 28 with new instructions. The next day, at a meeting of the Central Committee of the SED, Premier Otto Grotewohl stated: "We are not alone responsible for the mistakes committed lately. We were wrongly informed and must reproach the Soviet Control Commission."[5] This statement could not have been made, of course, without Soviet consent. Moreover, the official Soviet *Tägliche Rundschau* stated on June 13: "The Politburo of the Central Committee of the Socialist Unity Party and the government of the German Democratic Republic are openly and honestly admitting to the whole population of the DDR that they have committed mistakes in the past." However, "the former Soviet Control Commission is also, to a certain degree, responsible for the blunders committed."

While the German Communists were free to blame the Soviet side, the Soviet press reported only mistakes "made in various fields" by the "governmental and administrative agencies" of the DDR.[6]

On May 28 the Soviet government abolished the Soviet Control Commission in Berlin and set up in its place the post of High Commissioner. While the removal of a formal "control" agency was a

[5] *SBZ-Archiv*, loc. cit.
[6] *Pravda*, June 12, 1953.

friendly gesture toward the DDR, the measure was, in the main, an effort to draw a line under the rigid Stalinist past. General Chuikov was replaced by General Andrei A. Grechko as supreme commander of Soviet military forces in East Germany, while Semionov returned triumphantly to Berlin as the Soviet high commissioner; Pavel Yudin became his assistant.

This succession of moves and countermoves, admitted blunders, anti-Stalinist gestures, resignations, and appointments produced utter disorientation among the SED leadership.

The Ulbricht regime, obviously misapprehending the developments in Germany, and without complete Soviet support, at first tried to salvage as much as possible of its former course. It clung to the policy of low wages (in the case of the building workers it even increased work "norms"); it decided to carry out a purge among the leadership. As late as May 14, Ulbricht's orthodox-Stalinist Central Committee adopted a resolution which maintained "the lessons of the Slansky trial" and quoted Stalin's well-known (and eventually repudiated) theory about the growing resistance of the capitalist classes as they go down.[7]

There was mounting unrest, but the Ulbricht group lacked the power to suppress it by police methods. Strikes and passive resistance multiplied all over the zone.

Moscow took the initiative. Early in June, High Commissioner Semionov forwarded to Ulbricht's office a Soviet resolution on the political and economic changes required in the DDR. To the East German leadership the demands appeared too far-reaching. "The members of the Politburo were startled when the paper was read. It was, of course, approved in its entirety; only linguistic changes were made (so that it should not sound like a translation from Russian). It became the 'platform' of the new course in East Germany which was inaugurated in the following days." [8]

Ulbricht, in accepting a set of orders contrary to his own line, proved once again his ability as a satellite leader. On June 9 the Politburo and on June 11 the government of the DDR adopted a series of important reforms: an amnesty, an end of the antichurch drive, no

[7] *SBZ-Archiv, op. cit.*, 1953, p. 169.
[8] Report of a former leading German Communist. D Papers, February, 1957, vol. 5, pp. 338–39.

forced collectivization of farming, concessions to well-to-do peasants, easing of traffic between the zones, and even a slowing down of militarization. Sentences of prisoners were to be reviewed and unjust verdicts voided; refugees to the West were invited to return.

On June 12 the press of the Soviet zone announced the reforms. The announcement produced confusion but also the expectation of new developments and liberal reforms. The next day, Semionov, in obvious compliance with Soviet designs, received the leaders of the loyal Liberal-Democratic Party of the zone. On June 14 the government announced that over 4,000 prisoners had been set free and 1,500 more would be released soon.

On the other hand, Ulbricht still insisted on increased "norms" for the building workers, and the official *Tribüne* of June 16 even criticized the relatively high standard of living of these workers. The same day, eighty building workers, whose wages had actually been cut because of the increased "norms," went out on a strike which, in the heated climate of those days, spread like wildfire and developed into a political event of the first magnitude. A workers' procession moved to the government section and demanded to see Ulbricht and Grotewohl. Refusing to face the crowd, the leaders sent Minister Fritz Selbmann to talk to the workers. The minister's explanations were of little satisfaction. Even the government's sudden abolition of the "norms" did not help. The German police did not interfere, and there were few arrests.

The movement had already grown into more than an economic strike. The general impression in Berlin was that the government would not dare to use force against the people, that the *Vopo* (*Volkspolizei*—People's Police) itself was vacillating, and that the Russians would not rush to the support of Ulbricht's regime. While Ulbricht assumed that the "working class" would never start a revolution against the "proletarian dictatorship," the population indulged in an illusion of its own, namely, that the Soviets would not use arms against a workers' uprising and, if faced with a choice, would choose to return the sympathies of the "proletariat" rather than support Ulbricht.

The strike in Berlin developed into an uprising. No sooner had the Western radio stations (especially well-informed RIAS in West Berlin) broadcast the news than strikes and demonstrations broke out

Rumblings in the East

all over the zone. This was June 17. In Berlin huge masses of demonstrators marched through the city, about 50,000 of them to the traditional Lustgarten. At the Potsdamer Platz the crowd burned official banners, removed and destroyed signs marking the frontier between the sectors, tore down signboards of the ministries and pictures of Stalin and Ulbricht, destroyed newspaper offices, rushed to the local jails to liberate political prisoners, and beat up security agents and Party functionaries. The *Vopo* made sporadic arrests, but the crowds attacked its precincts and menaced the buildings of the security agency. One hundred and fifty *Vopo* men defected to the West.[9]

Uprisings occurred in 60 cities all over the zone; in 19 places the crowds attempted to release political prisoners. In 129 places Soviet military forces paraded in the streets.

To the Soviet government the events in East Germany represented a showdown. Since the local police were either unable or unwilling to quell the movement, East Germany could be kept in line only by means of the armed might of the Soviet Union. The situation was an embarrassing one for a government that had just embarked on a program of "relaxation of tension" and promised "peaceful coexistence." But a fateful choice faced the Soviet leadership: military force and terror, or retreat and loss of East Germany and possibly other people's democracies in the wake of similar movements. Moscow was to face this dilemma again in the following years.

At first the Soviet troops were deployed with caution. Soviet tanks that tried to disperse the large crowds did not open fire. Hundreds of well disciplined Soviet soldiers watched a huge German crowd loudly cheer a group of young men who climbed the Brandenburger Tor and tore down the Soviet flag that had flown there since the Soviet capture of Berlin. Newspaper correspondents claimed knowledge of constant telephone consultation between Moscow and East Berlin. For a considerable time the Soviet instructions were: "Don't lose your nerve, don't let them provoke you." Eventually, however, the fateful decision was taken.[10]

At 12:40 p.m. Soviet General P. T. Dibrova was appointed commandant of the city; at 1 p.m. martial law was declared. The *Vopo*

[9] *The New York Times*, June 23, 1953.
[10] Curt Riess, *Der 17 Juni* (The 17th of June), Berlin, Verlag Ullstein, 1954, pp. 95 and 124.

were ordered to shoot into the crowds; Soviet tanks then joined the battle.

This was the end. The Soviet army could not be fought with bare hands. In some places strikes continued for several days, but these were also broken. Arrests increased. A week after the events, an announcement by the government indicated that the number of casualties had been small: 4 *Vopo* men and 21 civilians dead; 191 *Vopo* men and 187 civilians wounded. Three weeks later, however, *Welt* of Hamburg printed an unpublished report which had been prepared for the Soviet chief of police in Berlin and which stated that 267 demonstrators were killed and 1,071 wounded; 116 employees of the security forces, government officials, and members of political parties of the Soviet zone were killed and 645 injured, some seriously. To these figures there must also be added the 141 executed after sentencing by Soviet courts-martial, and 14 executed after sentencing by German courts. Among the 141 sentenced by courts-martial were 52 *Vopo* men and members of the SSD (security organs) sentenced for refusing to obey orders. During the curfew, 31 persons were killed and 28 injured. According to the report, Soviet losses amounted to 18 dead and 126 wounded.[11] The same report indicated that 5,143 persons had been arrested, of whom only 2,917 were released.

In the course of investigation some of the arrested made the desired confessions: that they had been dispatched from West Berlin to instigate a revolt, that the revolt was supported by the Americans and by German "fascists," that provocateurs had invited the Soviet troops to cross to the Western sector, etc. The Soviet press minimized the extent of the movement, and the role of Soviet troops in quelling it was described in such a way that the average reader would get no clear idea of the significance and extent of the operation and could assume that Soviet arms were used only against individuals ("provocateurs") and not against the crowds.

The Western press lied, *Pravda* said, when it talked of the antigovernment attitude of the population of East Berlin:

> In their endeavor to obscure the traces of their crimes the organizers of the Berlin provocation are trying to represent the unrest in Berlin on June 17 as an "expression of the feelings of the Germans." These gentlemen must, however, permit the question: how could these

[11] *Die Neue Zeitung*, Berlin, July 16, 1953.

Rumblings in the East

"feelings of the Germans" be compatible with the facts that at the start of the unrest American trucks appeared, loaded with bottles of gasoline, for setting buildings on fire at the border of the Soviet sector of Berlin? Were there not American loudspeakers set up to instigate the riots? Were not American officers dispatched for the same purpose into the midst of the fascist gangs? . . . Did not American planes drop leaflets, which were prepared in advance, over the democratic sector? [12]

The three Western commandants sent notes of protest to the Soviet side; these were not printed in the Soviet press, and only Dibrova's reply was mentioned.

> The Commandants of the three Western powers in Berlin expressed hypocritical discontent about the use of military force by the Soviet military authorities in Berlin. This they did to cover up their tracks and to relieve themselves of responsibility for those provocateurs who were lately dispatched from West Berlin to organize street disorders and arson in the democratic sector of Berlin and in regard to whom the Soviet military authorities were compelled to use arms on June 17th.[13]

A few days later the Soviet press reported that the workers of East Berlin were fully satisfied with the suppression of the revolt, that they supported the DDR regime, and that their standard of living was rising due to the measures recently taken.

Early in July the United States State Department offered to send 15 million dollars worth of food to East Berlin. The United States chargé d'affaires in Moscow, Elim O'Shaughnessy, told Molotov that his government had decided

> . . . to offer to the Soviet Union as the occupying power for distribution to the population of Eastern Germany shipments of food amounting in value to approximately $15 million and consisting of grain, sugar, lard, soy bean oil and some other commodities.[14]

The American offer, which was made widely known in the Eastern zone, provoked irritation on the part of the Soviet government. In a lengthy reply, Molotov told the United States to keep away from Eastern Germany:

> . . . Such manners at the present time would insult even the population of a colony, to say nothing of the German people and its legal demo-

[12] *Pravda*, June 23, 1953.
[13] *Ibid.*, June 20, 1953.
[14] *Department of State Bulletin*, July 20, 1953, vol. 29, no. 734, p. 69.

cratic government . . . the U.S.A. Government has not shown any sort of solicitude as to the food supply of the German people, but has decided to resort to a propaganda maneuver having nothing in common with concern for the real interests of the German population.[15]

Pravda seconded Molotov: "The working people of the German Democratic Republic know well the price of American 'aid.' To the importunities of the imperialist 'philanthropists' they reply: 'Take care, rather, gentlemen, that the unemployed of Western Germany are well fed. But let us live without your aid.' "[16]

The government of the DDR replied in a similar vein. Nevertheless, distribution of American shipments of food took place at the borders of the sectors, and nearly 70 per cent of the population of the Eastern part of the city availed themselves of it. On July 22 Soviet High Commissioner Semionov sent a challenging note to United States High Commissioner James B. Conant:

> Lately in Western Berlin, near the border of the Eastern Sector, American occupation forces, under the guise of selling food, are organizing special posts where fascist agents are active. Because of the mass protests of the unemployed of the Western sectors, as well as of the population of East Berlin, this sale had to be stopped. However, it became known from the communications of the press that preparations are at present being made in West Berlin to organize such posts at other points. Such action by the American authorities cannot be described otherwise than as a continued effort to use, with provocative aims, the fascist hirelings and criminal elements who took an active part in arson, robbery and other outrages on June 17th in East Berlin.[17]

The long-range implications of the Berlin uprising were gradually drawn. The German population had followed the developments with tension and vague hope; everybody expected the Western powers to act in one way or another. Their passivity, while a lesson in *Realpolitik*, was a source of great disappointment. To Moscow, of course, the impotence of the West was a source of great satisfaction.

The Malenkov-Molotov government, by its action in East Germany, was making it plain that the borders of the "socialist camp," as well as its political setup, would be maintained by the Soviet power at any cost; that, as far as the extent of the empire was concerned, the

---

[15] *Ibid.*, p. 68.
[16] *Pravda*, July 15, 1953.
[17] *Ibid.*, July 23, 1953.

Soviet regime would make no concessions to the other great powers; that whatever differences might exist between persons and factions in the Kremlin and in Pankow, rule by a Soviet-controlled regime would be perpetuated.

The United States, the leading Western power, which had fought an invasion of its zone in Korea, had set up an airlift when its sector in Berlin was endangered, and had insisted on the independence of Austria, could do little to help the insurgents in a Soviet-occupied territory. It appeared that the Soviet threat of war in case of action against one of its satellites had been effective. On the other hand, the events in Berlin revealed for the first time the weakness of a people's democracy in the face of internal opposition: the unreliability of its police force, the dubious loyalty of its army, and consequently the imperative need of Russian force to maintain its regime in power.

As a consequence of the unrest in the Eastern zone and in an effort to improve the internal situation by economic concessions, a widely publicized conference between Soviet and DDR leaders was convened in Moscow August 20–22, 1953. The Soviet concessions included cessation of reparations payments as of January 1, 1954, the transfer of Soviet enterprises in Germany to the DDR without indemnity, a ceiling of 5 per cent of the DDR budget on payments for maintenance of the Soviet army, cancellation of existing debts. In addition, the Soviet Union would supply the DDR, in 1953, with a substantially increased quantity of foodstuffs, coal, metals, and other goods, and grant credits of 485 million rubles at 2 per cent interest annually. German war prisoners sentenced for crimes (except major crimes) committed during the war would be released.[18]

2. CONFORMITY WITH MOSCOW

The spelled-out principles guiding the relationship between the Soviet Union and the "people's democracies" changed little in the first post-Stalin years under Malenkov-Khrushchev; if there was any movement away from these principles, this was not because new theories had been adopted. The Soviet leadership had not yet recognized that in this particular field its policies would have to be revised; as yet it

[18] *Ibid.*, August 23, 1953.

was still treading a path from issue to issue: from Beria as a leader to Beria as a criminal, from Tito as a fascist to Tito as a Communist, from emphasis on "continuity" to a "new course." The satellites, too, were confused and disoriented.

"National Communism" was still prohibited and the fight against Titoism and suppression of "Titoists" in the satellites continued. In the summer of 1953, however, the Soviet Union, and soon afterward the satellites, resumed conventional, although cold, diplomatic relations with Belgrade; at the same time the Soviet press continued to attack Yugoslavia in sharp terms. Bulgaria, Hungary, and Albania protested to Belgrade about "border incidents." As late as the fall of 1953, when the Trieste conflict flared up again and the Soviet government, inimical to Western-oriented Italy, had to take a pro-Yugoslav position, the Soviet press reflected this attitude in a guarded and reluctant manner.

Soviet control of the satellites was at first maintained by the customary means: the main lever, as before, was nomination of satellite party and government leaders by the heads of the Soviet party, and discussion with these leaders in Moscow of the course to be taken by the satellites. It did not occur to either side that, with Stalin's death, the mold had been broken, that a new era had begun, and that the very fundamentals of Soviet relationships would have to be scrutinized and possibly revised.

Separation of the posts of general (first) secretary of the Central Committee and premier, which had been the first Soviet step toward "collective leadership," was also effected among those "people's democracies" in which it did not already exist. In Czechoslovakia, Antonin Novotny became first secretary and Villiam Siroky premier; in Poland, somewhat later, Joseph Cyrankiewicz became premier, while Boleslaw Bierut remained as secretary; in Hungary, Mathias Rakoszi had to give up the premiership to Imre Nagy; in Bulgaria, Vulko Chervenkov had to relinquish the secretaryship to Todor Zhivkov; in the German Democratic Republic, Walter Ulbricht and Otto Grotewohl shared the two posts between them; in Rumania, Gheorghe Gheorghiu-Dej resigned as general secretary and Gheorghe Apostol was elected first secretary. In the people's democracies, however, even more so than in the Soviet Union, the premier actually served as deputy to the first secretary of the Party; the supremacy of the Communist Party and its head was not disputed.

In May–June, 1953, with that frankness that was peculiar to Soviet-satellite relations, the Malenkov-Khrushchev group requested the Hungarian leaders to come to Moscow for a conference at which nominations for the highest party and government posts in Hungary would be made. An important meeting of the Central Committee of the Hungarian Workers (Communist) Party was scheduled to convene in June, but Moscow wanted to talk with Rakoszi and his group in advance of the Hungarian conference; both the Russians and the Hungarians viewed such a procedure as natural. At the conference in Moscow, Malenkov asked Rakoszi whom he would recommend as his deputy. Rakoszi could name no one; he had objections to every nominee suggested. "Everyone was suspect except him alone." "This appalled us very much," Malenkov later stated. Rakoszi "wanted a premier who would have no voice in the making of decisions." "The matter involved," Khrushchev stated, "was that the leadership of the Party and the state should not be concentrated in the hands of one man or a few men; this is not desirable." [19] In the course of the discussion, the Russians—Malenkov, Molotov, and Khrushchev—"recommended" Nagy as premier. The Hungarians returned to Budapest, where the Central Committee of their party accepted the decisions made in Moscow. Rakoszi remained as first secretary and Nagy became premier.

The "collective leadership" that thus emerged in Hungary was not, in Moscow's view, the ideal solution. Rakoszi, the staunch Stalinist, would be counterbalanced by the "rightist" Nagy. Was collaboration between them possible? Would not each try to eliminate his opponent? There was, however, no faction in Hungary more acceptable to Moscow.

The developments in Hungary in 1953–54 proved that Moscow had not yet found the way to square the circle. Tension between the Rakoszi and Nagy factions was mounting, with Moscow trying to oppose Rakoszi's dynamism and intransigence.

Early in 1954 Malenkov remarked: " 'The faults we noted in June

[19] *Imre Nagy on Communism: In Defense of the New Course*, New York, Frederick A. Praeger, 1957, pp. 250–51.

[1953] are being remedied very slowly. Rakosi has not taken the lead in remedying the faults.'" [20] In May, 1954, at a conference in Moscow, Khrushchev said that "'in Hungary a true collective leadership failed to develop because Rakosi is incapable of working collectively.'" [21] Malenkov found that "Rakosi, as Party First Secretary, was not doing the job well." [22] Khrushchev criticized Rakoszi's hesitation in rehabilitating Communists who had been purged on his orders:

> "Rakosi is responsible for the arrests. Therefore he does not want to release these people. He knows that he is guilty and will compromise himself . . . rehabilitations should be carried out so as not to destroy Rakosi's authority. . . . We will protect Rakosi's authority only in so far as it is not prejudicial to Party authority. It may happen that on the pretext of protecting Rakosi's authority, the old policy will be reinstated and the freeing of the prisoners will not proceed. Of course, it is difficult for Rakosi to free the prisoners," Khrushchev said, "because he ordered the arrests." [23]

In Hungary this transition from Stalinism to "collective leadership" occurred behind a curtain and was accompanied by no immediate political earthquake.

While in the other satellites the circumstances surrounding the succession of top Communist leaders were not as dramatic as in Hungary, or so fraught with potential conflict, the issues were essentially the same; tensions continued and the situation remained unsettled and out of balance. In East Germany, for example, Ulbricht and Grotewohl, who had been chosen by Stalin years before and who had been checked and rechecked in meetings with the Soviet leadership in Moscow and Berlin, proved both reliable and flexible—so flexible, in fact, that the switch from one policy to its opposite in 1953 could be made in accordance with Moscow's ideas without a change in the personnel of the East German leadership. We have seen how Moscow acted against Ulbricht in May–June, 1953, and how Ulbricht submitted; he was certainly not an ideal viceroy for East Germany, but there was no one else.

[20] *Ibid.*, p. 271.
[21] *Ibid.*, p. 280.
[22] *Ibid.*
[23] *Ibid.*, p. 296.

3. POLICE AND INTERNAL AFFAIRS

Conformity in the systems of internal policy (civil rights, the press, the police, and the courts), this most important pillar of Soviet-satellite collaboration during Stalin's time, did not last long after his death.

The Soviet amnesty announced at the end of March, 1953, three weeks after the dictator's death, was promptly followed by amnesties in the people's democracies: on April 4 in Rumania, on May 3 in Czechoslovakia, between June 1 and 13 in East Germany, and on July 25 in Hungary. In the countries concerned—Russia as well as the satellites—the official amnesty did not rehabilitate innocent victims of former police operations, nor was it viewed as the inauguration of a new era without purges, show trials, or executions. It was considered at first an action of limited scope and significance.

The arrest and execution of Beria in December, 1953, was the beginning of an extensive purge of the Soviet police that lasted into 1955–56. The powers of the revamped *apparat* of terrorism were curtailed, and only a few new trials, most of them involving persons of lesser importance, were taking place. In the deluge, however, the strong reins of the Soviet MGB (now KGB) guiding the satellite agencies were loosened; in some political cases Soviet guidance was now lacking. Although scores of Soviet police advisers assigned to the people's democracies were still at their posts, there was no longer a strong hand to direct them from Moscow.

In Poland, for example, *Bezpieka*, the security agency built up under Stalin, served as both the Polish police and the means of Soviet rule over Poland. The heads of the seventeen departments of *Bezpieka* were Poles, but their Russian assistants and advisers made the decisions. Soviet General Lalin, and not the Pole, Radkiewicz, was the real head of the Polish police.

> In a crowd surrounding Bierut like an unsurmountable wall we can easily distinguish such representatives of the Polish community as a Soviet Colonel, F. Grzybowski, Director of the Department of Government Officials' Protection, his deputies, Soviet officers, Colonels Lebowski and Klaroff, and an adviser in the same department, Colonel Lozovoj. Next to them are several dozen men dressed in dark suits with their hands on the revolvers in their pockets. These are other

Russians, Ukrainians and Byelorussians from Bierut's private bodyguard unit. . . . The *Bezpieka* constitutes the spearhead of Soviet aggression by means of which Bierut, and through him Moscow, rules Poland. . . .[24]

The Beria crisis in Russia led toward stricter control by the Party of the revamped police and increased the power of the Party's central and local secretaries. In the people's democracies the consequences were even more far-reaching:

> . . . the Security apparatus has operationally been subordinated to the Party leadership. These changes occurred simultaneously with the process that took place in Moscow, where the Party gradually took over the MVD and MGB. . . . Bringing charges against Party members or a Government member, must previously be approved by the Politburo.[25]

Curtailment of the powers of a police system dominated by Russians increased the influence of the local Communist leadership, gave more power to the local Communist parties, and decreased the direct control of Moscow. Paradoxically, this development did not necessarily mean liberalization and a rule of law. The satellite leadership, which now frequently acted on its own initiative, saw no reason for promptly following Moscow in rehabilitating "purged" persons, liberating prisoners from jails, etc. In general, the satellite governments did not all move in the same direction. In Hungary, for example, it was announced that the number of arrests in the first six months of 1954 was 45 per cent less than in the same period of the preceding year; on the other hand, 57 proceedings were started during the first half of 1954 against officials who had violated legality, compared with 31 in the last six months of 1953. Internment camps had been closed.[26] Gabor Peter, former chief of the political police, was sentenced to life imprisonment, and his aide, Guyla Decsi, organizer of the Mindszenti affair, was sentenced to nine years.

In other people's democracies political trials of the Stalinist type, with "amalgams" and "confessions," continued throughout the year, and sentences were severe. In Prague, 25 persons were tried in December, 1953, for "espionage" and for helping people to escape from the country; the trial resulted in 2 death sentences and long prison terms.

---

[24] *News from behind the Iron Curtain*, New York, March, 1955, vol. 4, no. 3, pp. 6 and 22.
[25] *Ibid.*, p. 22.
[26] *Szabad Nep*, Budapest, June 17, 1954.

Police and Internal Affairs 185

In the same month, 9 "workers" were tried in Usti, one of whom was sentenced to life imprisonment and others to long terms. In the summer and fall of 1954, when collectivization of farming was still at a halt in other people's democracies, over 30 trials of "kulaks" accused of collectively leaving kolkhozes were reported in the Czechoslovak press; the sentences were severe. A group of former Social-Democrats were tried for "treason" and "espionage" in October, 1954; the sentences included life imprisonment and terms of twenty-five years. In April, 1954, 5 Slovak "bourgeois nationalists," allegedly connected with Slansky and Clementis, were sentenced to long prison terms. In November, 10 "espionage agents" were tried in Prague and sentenced to terms up to twenty-five years.

How little expectation there was of the development of a new political climate in Poland is seen from statements of Boleslaw Bierut, who said in March, 1953, that the dissolution of the Polish Communist Party in 1938 by the Comintern (an act that was to be repudiated soon after) had been entirely correct. It was reported from Warsaw at that time that Wladyslaw Gomulka, who had been in jail since July, 1951, would soon be brought to trial.[27] In the fall of 1953, in Warsaw, a group of "kulak wreckers" were sentenced to from seven to twelve years.

The arrest of Cardinal Stefan Wyszinsky in September, 1953, precipitated a new church-state crisis. In Stettin, 3 "neo-Nazis" were condemned, 1 to death, 2 to long prison terms. In January, 1954, 5 persons were tried in Opole for "espionage" in favor of the United States and West Germany; 2 were sentenced to death. In 1954 Bierut assailed the "rightist elements" and the "Gomulka clique." The Polish leadership did not institute real police reforms until Josef Swiatlo, a ranking police officer, defected to the West in December, 1953, and started a series of shocking revelations. In December, 1954, Security Chief Stanislaw Radkiewicz was dismissed and a reorganization of the police agency was inaugurated. It was not until then that Gomulka was released, and it was not until January, 1955, that Bierut came out with a public condemnation of the methods of the security agency.[28]

In the German Democratic Republic a public trial of a group of

[27] *SBZ-Archiv, op. cit.*, 1953, p. 166.
[28] Bierut's report to the Third Plenum of the Central Committee, *Trybuna Ludu*, January 26, 1955.

"kulaks" in May ended in sentences up to life imprisonment. A number of "imperialist agents" were sentenced in connection with the June uprising. In Rumania, Lucretius Patrascanu, the veteran theoretician of Rumanian Communism, and 10 others were tried in April, 1954. Patrascanu was executed. A potential Titoist who had spent time in concentration camps during the war, and a member of postwar governments, Patrascanu had been purged years before. The execution of this former "deviationist" was entirely in the Stalinist tradition. In October, 1954, Vasile Luca, former secretary of the Central Committee, and 3 of his subordinates were tried for "undermining the national economy." Luca was sentenced to death (the sentence was later commuted) and the others to prisons terms. Antikulak pressure increased in the spring of 1956, when the course of the economic policy throughout the Soviet orbit changed.

In Korea a large group of outstanding leaders, arrested in February, 1953, for their adherence to a purely Korean, as distinguished from a pro-Soviet and pro-Chinese, nationalism, were tried in August. At the trial, however, the real crime of the defendants, "national Communism," was not stated in so many words; the defendants "confessed" to other misdeeds. Early in August, five months after Stalin's death and after the Korean War had ended, 8 of them were sentenced to death and executed.[29]

The disorientation and lack of uniformity were most evident in Bulgaria. If Hungary's course in the first post-Stalin era may be viewed as the most anti-Stalinist trend toward Communist legality and economic readjustment, Bulgaria's was at the other extreme. Vulko Chervenkov, the "strong man," the Soviet-Bulgarian mongrel, was not inclined to favor the new trends. Though he had had to relinquish the secretaryship of the Party to Todor Zhivkov in January, 1954, he continued essentially on the same path. Curbing of the powers of the police in order to satisfy the general trend was only given lip service in Bulgaria; the *détente* was minimal. Arrests and trials in the Stalinist pattern were taking place. In September, 1954, the trial of General Ivan Vulkov and 10 others for acts committed while they were serving as Bulgaria's government in 1923–26 ended in a number of death sentences (later commuted). "Wreckers" and "agents of imperialism" were uncovered in economic agencies. As late as October, 1955, the

---

[29] These developments are covered in greater detail in Part Five, Chap. 1, sec. 2.

highly official *Kommunist* [30] (Moscow) reprinted, without comment, a report from the Bulgarian *Novo Vreme* containing a long record of newly discovered "counterrevolutionary" organizations in the coal industry, in foreign and internal trade agencies, in the electrical trust, in the building trades, etc.; a quotation from Stalin served as an ideological explanation. As if nothing had changed since Stalin, the tone of the report indicated a climate by far more offensive and aggressive than that which now prevailed in Russia.

4. THE NATIONAL ECONOMIES

In the most important economic field, industrial planning, there was more conformity. The Soviet course toward increasing the quantity of "consumer goods" and raising living standards was to be followed strictly throughout the "socialist camp."

The new course was intended to provide a remedy against the centrifugal trends in the Soviet empire which had become obvious in the unrest in Pilsen, Berlin, and elsewhere. The official interpretation of the political crises in the satellites attributed their cause to economic shortcomings, first of all to the low living standards of the workers. Easing of living conditions, it was believed, would reconcile rebellious populations to the political system and was therefore more important for the satellites than for the Soviet Union itself.

Premier Malenkov announced the new economic course on August 8, 1953. *Pravda* supplied the theoretical justification for the slowing down of "heavy industry" in favor of "food and consumer goods":

> The level of heavy industry development now permits the rates of development for light and food industry and socialist agriculture to be speeded up considerably. . . .
> Under a socialist economy it is completely conceivable, theoretically and practically, for the production of consumers' goods to increase even more rapidly for a time than production of means of production. . . .
> Heavy industry, which is equipped with the latest machinery and even in the future will remain the absolute basis of socialist economy, can expand reproduction of its basic stocks while speeding up development of the production of machines and equipment for light and food industry and for socialist agriculture.[31]

[30] No. 7, October, 1955.
[31] *Pravda*, December 29, 1953.

A few weeks later the Central Committees of the satellites began to work on the same problems and in the same direction (up to then, except for Nagy in Hungary, they had not pledged an increase in "food and consumer goods"). By mid-September all the satellites were well on the new road. Committees and planning commissions began to revise economic plans, and by December the new direction had been established.

The Soviet press, with obvious approval and satisfaction, reported this trend toward a new course in the "people's democracies," [32] which in most phases corresponded to the Soviet course. All reforms were introduced in agreement with Moscow. The press and Soviet leaders refrained, however, from extensive comments and explanations. The pretense of a stable economic course and "continuity" were maintained.

To understand how painful this rerouting was for the orthodox leadership it is sufficient to point to the place of "heavy industry" in Communist philosophy. Under Stalin, progress in heavy industry was one of the highest precepts; it was the way to "catch up and overtake." Stalin's lieutenants and pupils had accepted these precepts in their entirety; whatever the criticism of Stalin, it never extended to these particular sociological and political theories.

Stalin's ideas about heavy industry had often been carried to absurd extremes in the satellites. Whether or not this was in accord with national resources and economic calculations, every people's democracy had to develop its own "heavy industry." The obvious result of such a program was low wages and high prices. If standards of living were now to be raised, the whole precept of "socialist growth" was in question. A setback was inevitable.

Less conformity and less uniformity prevailed in relation to the second of the major sociological and economic problems, that of collectivization of farming.

In the Soviet Union this issue was considered to have been definitely solved. No new pattern could emerge in Russia to serve as a model for the satellites, nor was there an urgent need to accelerate or slow down the pace of the farming programs in the satellites. Consequently, Moscow offered no real guidance to the satellites in the field

[32] *Ibid.*, November 6 and 11 and December 7, 8, 12, 21, and 30, 1953.

The National Economies

of collectivization. The general trend toward relaxation, however, called for easing the pressure on the peasants, refraining from compulsion, and, in certain places, even permitting peasants to quit already existing collectives. Beginning in the second half of 1953, concessions to individual farming became part of the programs of the satellites. Premier Bierut of Poland announced in July, 1953, that individual farming would remain "for a long time to come." President Zapotocky of Czechoslovakia stated that his regime would not restrain peasants, even those who wanted to leave the kolkhozes. In Hungary, Nagy, the new premier, announced a similar course.

Like "heavy industry," however, "collectivization" was of the essence of Communist theory. Socialism, the theory held, cannot be achieved until collectivized farming becomes the prevailing economic system in agriculture; in Russia, for example, "socialism" was established not in 1917–18, but in 1930–33. If the people's democracies put brakes on the process of collectivization, or permitted withdrawals from kolkhozes, were these countries on their way to socialism or capitalism? In Russia, the New Economic Policy (NEP), which had been introduced in "earnest and for a long time," had survived Lenin by only a few years and had given way to a sweeping kolkhoz operation. In the doubts, ideological confusion, and quarreling among the factions in the satellites on the issue of collectivization there were already present the seeds of a new crisis and a reversal. After less than a year of the new course in agriculture in the satellites, loud voices began to be raised against the betrayal of lofty principles; this coincided with the decline of Malenkov and the rise of Khrushchev in Russia.

In Hungary, among the defeated Rakoszi group, which had remained loyally silent for several months, criticism and opposition were mounting. Criticism and opposition were natural enough since the halfhearted reforms had not, in a short time and against great obstacles, yielded significant results. "Our economic leaders," wrote Istvan Kovacz, Communist Secretary of Budapest, "have shown themselves incapable, during 15 months, of organizing the switch-over of our well-developed industry to the mass production of consumer goods."

Everywhere the controversy took on similar lines. One Communist faction maintained that increasing food production was a task of primary importance which should not be hindered by collectivization; others countered with the argument that a small peasant economy would never be able substantially to increase agricultural production and that only a system of kolkhozes or state farms could accomplish the task.

In Czechoslovakia, controversies among the leadership were openly admitted by Premier Villiam Siroky in *Nova Mysl*.[33] He and his group, he said, supported continuation of the new program calling for a slowing down in the collectivization drive; a number of experts (it was reported that they were joined by President Zapotocky) wanted more far-reaching concessions to private peasant economy; a third group, however, rejected any concessions to "capitalism in agriculture" and demanded strict collectivization. The latter faction, headed by First Secretary of the Party Antonin Novotny, was a strong one. A slowing down in heavy industry, never popular among Czechoslovak Communists, was likewise opposed. The Tenth Congress of the Czech Communist Party in June, 1954, once again emphasized "heavy industry" and reprimanded those responsible for its insufficient growth.[34]

When Moscow finally spoke up, it was only on the "heavy industry" issue. Dimitri Shepilov, a follower of Khrushchev at the time and editor of *Pravda*, came out in favor of orthodoxy and against the "rightist deviation":

> Views utterly alien to Marxist-Leninist political economy and to the general line of the Communist Party on some fundamental questions of development of the Socialist economy have begun to take shape of late among some economists and teachers in our higher educational institutions. . . .
>
> Lenin and Stalin emphasized a thousand times that the decisive link in Socialist industrialization is development of *heavy* industry, production of the means of production. "The center of industrialization, its basis, lies in development of heavy industry (fuels, metals, etc.), in development, when you come down to it, of production of the means of production, in development of our own machine building" [Stalin, *Works*, in Russian, vol. VIII, p. 130]. . . .
>
> It is commonly known that throughout the entire history of the Soviet land's economic development the Communist Party, guided by the

[33] May, 1954.
[34] *Kommunist*, Moscow, no. 7, May, 1955, p. 101.

The National Economies

Marxist theory of reproduction, pursued a consistent policy of forced tempos of development of *heavy* industry, of machine building.[35]

Shepilov's article, which was followed by Malenkov's resignation, became the program for the satellites. In Poland, "Shepilov's article struck us like thunder from a blue sky," reported a former officer of Warsaw's Central Committee.[36] Warsaw, of course, complied with the new thesis. *Kommunist* of Moscow published an article on Hungary, where Nagy's premiership was coming to an end, which attacked the "petit-bourgeois theories" of private peasant economy. In East Germany, Walter Ulbricht told the Plenum of the SED in the summer of 1955 that granting of priority to consumer goods industries was wrong in theory, and he even asserted that he had never accepted the theory. Nagy's name was not mentioned, but the attack on the "rightists" was obviously pointed at him:

> The rightist conceptions are in favor of the kulaks as exploiters and contrary to the interests of the toiling peasants; they are slowing down the rise of agricultural production and the improvement of living conditions in the villages. The Central Committee has appealed to all party members to consolidate and develop the cooperative movement in the villages and to strengthen the alliance between the working class and the laboring peasant masses. The Plenum has stated that at present the rightist danger is the main threat to the cause of Socialism and therefore the ideological defeat of the harmful rightist conceptions is an urgent task.[37]

The Cominform likewise attacked the Hungarian "rightists."[38] Nagy, who had suffered a heart attack, was unable to attend the meeting of the Central Committee at which Rakoszi's resolution of March 4, 1955, which sharply condemned the "right deviation," was carried. Once again Rakoszi had won. His resolution marked a reversion from "rightist Communism" to orthodox Stalinism, to the extent that the latter was still possible. It eulogized "iron discipline" and promised a "merciless fight against deviations"; the Party, it said, would again become supreme in all walks of Hungarian life; the greatest danger in this situation was the rightist danger; the fight against kulaks must be resumed; the standstill in the growth of collectives must end; "na-

---
[35] "The Party General Line and Vulgarizers of Marxism," *Pravda*, January 24, 1955.
[36] D Papers, File P, June 13, 1957, pp. 2–3.
[37] *Kommunist*, Moscow, no. 5, March, 1955, p. 66.
[38] *For a Lasting Peace, for a People's Democracy*, Bucharest, February 25, 1955.

tionalism and chauvinism" (meaning anti-Russian trends) were among the most dangerous traits of the rightist deviation. On April 19 Nagy was replaced as premier by the Rakoszist Andreas Hegedüs.

In other satellites, collectivization was not pushed, however. The orders from Moscow had related mainly to "heavy industry," giving more leeway in other economic fields to the local leadership. In Poland the Central Committee, in August, 1955, made public its decision to put off collectivization for five years. Poland's two neighbors, Czechoslovakia and Hungary, were already on their way back from "rightism" to "leftism" in economic matters. These trends prevailed until 1958–59, when Moscow resumed its forceful prodding toward a rapid collectivization of farming all over its satellite world.

5. ABOLITION OF MIXED COMPANIES

The abolition of mixed companies was one of the initial events in the post-Stalin evolution of Soviet-satellite relations. The action, begun in the first year after Stalin's death and completed in 1955, was not part of a prepared plan or program. In its relations with the people's democracies, as in its foreign policy of that period in general, the Soviet government groped from one issue to another without, however, abandoning the old beaten tracks.

The mixed company was Stalin's favorite method of achieving economic control of foreign countries. Ostensibly, the Moscow-sponsored mixed companies, in which 50 per cent of the shares and profits were held by the Soviet Union and 50 per cent by the partner, and whose "governing" board was composed of equal numbers of representatives of both sides, were an embodiment of the principles of equality of large and small nations. In fact, however, because of the political relationship between the Soviet Union and the partners, Moscow enjoyed great privileges and complete domination. Stalin had experimented with the mixed company in connection with the Chinese-Eastern Railroad in the 1920's; vehement Chinese protests in that instance culminated in the armed conflict of 1929.[39]

After 1929 Stalin had experimented with mixed companies in another Far Eastern country, Outer Mongolia.[40] When he revived the

---

[39] David J. Dallin, *The Rise of Russia in Asia*, New Haven, Yale University Press, 1949, pp. 254–59.

[40] Erich Thiel, *Die Mongolei: Land, Volk und Wirtschaft der Mongolischen Volksrepublik* (Mongolia: Territory, People and Economy of the Mongolian People's Republic), Munich, Isar Verlag, 1958; also private information from Professor Thiel.

Abolition of Mixed Companies

system of mixed companies after World War II, Stalin obviously overlooked the fact that his device had become known as a peculiar system of Soviet domination, a shrewd, sometimes ruthless, method of exploiting the economy of other nations.

After the war mixed companies were organized, on Soviet initiative, in the European "people's democracies" and somewhat later in China. In Europe the Soviet Union invested in the mixed companies the assets of German industrial, financial, mining, and trade enterprises taken over by Soviet agencies in occupied Eastern Europe; the Potsdam agreements of 1945 confirmed the transfer of German and Italian rights to Russia. In this way the Soviet government got rid not only of German rights in its satellites but also claims of the Allies to property taken over by Germany during the war. To get rid of these potential Western economic (and possibly political) fortresses in Eastern Europe was one of Stalin's main goals.

In Rumania, a total of 16 *Sovroms* were set up in oil, shipbuilding, forestry, construction, civil aviation, banking, and other fields. In Yugoslavia, *Juspad* and *Justa* (Shipping and Air Transport) were established in 1946–47. Four mixed companies (shipbuilding, construction materials, civil aviation, mining) emerged in Bulgaria. In Hungary, 4 mixed companies were created (oil, bauxite and aluminum, shipping, and airlines); others emerged in North Korea. In China, 4 mixed companies (2 in Sinkiang, 1 for shipbuilding and 1 for civil aviation) were organized in 1950–51, after the Chinese Communist victory in the civil war. In two other countries, Germany and Austria (and to some extent also in Rumania), the Soviet agencies themselves took over large numbers of industrial and trade units without investing the newly acquired assets in mixed companies. The Soviet side was obligated under the provisions to supply equipment, some materials, and technical assistance, in addition to its investment, which was the industrial unit itself, acquired as "war booty." The local government supplied working capital, local currency, etc.

The mixed company was represented in Russia as a source of great benefit to the local economy rather than to the Soviet Union; this was in line with the general picture of Soviet-satellite relations. Gratitude for the economic help was the general official reaction, for example, of China: "The people of Sinkiang province have joyfully acclaimed the announcement of establishment of Soviet-Chinese joint-stock companies for oil and for nonferrous metals. They declared that without the assistance of the Soviet Union the work of developing the national wealth could not even begin. Representatives of business circles declared the agreement will strengthen the economic position of the province." [41]

The Soviet government gained substantial privileges through the device of mixed companies. Usually it was Soviet experts who evaluated the investments of both sides, which were to be equal; mixed companies were not required to pay taxes; extraterritorial rights were accorded the Soviet side; exported and imported goods were free of duty and often even of the requirement of registration. Employees of the mixed companies often received higher salaries than were usual in the partner countries, and their attitude toward the population was often overbearing. The Soviet and satellite press rarely mentioned the mixed companies, and some clauses of the company agreements remained secret. To the population, however, and in particular the Communist leadership, of the "people's democracies" the mixed companies soon became an irritant and a source of intense anti-Russian feeling. To demand their abolition, however, would have meant rebellion against Stalin.

When the Yugoslavs raised the banner of rebellion in 1948–49, one of Belgrade's demands was for liquidation of the mixed companies in Yugoslavia. In its notes to Moscow of March and April, 1949, Tito's government cited "acts in the affairs of JUSTA and JUSPAD that were contrary to the agreements upon which these companies were founded and which caused Yugoslavia economic damage. . . ." [42] In his correspondence with Moscow on this issue Tito accused the Soviet agencies of "violation of the sovereign rights and legal provisions by Soviet officials," using *Justa* "to put pressure on Yugoslavia," "failure to invest nominal capital," "discrimination against state river shipping craft," "damage to Yugoslav economy." In the spring of 1949 the Soviet government consented to the liquidation of the mixed companies in Yugoslavia.

With the exception of the Yugoslav component the Soviet eco-

[41] *Pravda*, April 5, 1950.
[42] *White Book on Aggressive Activities by the Governments of the USSR, Poland, Czechoslovakia, Hungary, Rumania, Bulgaria, and Albania towards Yugoslavia*, Belgrade, Ministry of Foreign Affairs of the Federal People's Republic of Yugoslavia, 1951, p. 322.

Abolition of Mixed Companies

nomic empire continued to develop along Stalinist lines. The mixed companies were maintained everywhere.

The days of the mixed companies began to come to an end after Stalin's death. It is not known which of the leaders of the satellites was the first to raise the issue; it is likely that Mao Tse-tung, in his post-Korea pride and defiance, preceded the more subservient Communist leaders in an offensive against the presence of Soviet economic bases in his country. In Germany, Soviet competition with Bonn and the wide publicity given to the working methods of Soviet industrial agencies in the Eastern zone made a rapid retreat imperative. Two months after the Berlin strikes the Soviet government agreed to turn over to East Germany 33 industrial units; the Soviet press stressed the fact that the transfer did not involve any payment by East Germany.[43] The West German press, however, called attention to profits of about 3.5 billion marks earned by the Soviet Union in the operation of these industrial units over a period of seven years.

The opposition to Soviet economic domination continued in the satellites. Soviet negotiations with the people's democracies on the issue began, apparently, early in 1954; the first decisions were announced in September–October. The Soviet-Rumanian agreement, signed on September 18, 1954, provided for the return to Rumania of the Soviet shares in 12 mixed companies. On October 9, under a similar agreement, Soviet shares in 3 mixed companies in Bulgaria were turned over to the Bulgarian government. During the visit of Khrushchev, Bulganin, and Mikoyan to Peking in September–October, 1954, the 4 Soviet-Chinese mixed companies were similarly reorganized. A year later, in November, 1955, Soviet shares of the Bulgarian *Garubso*, and on December 15, 1955, of the Rumanian *Sovprompetrol*, were turned over to the local governments; only the *Sovromoquarts* (mixed companies in uranium mining) continued as before. Austria reacquired all enterprises from Soviet agencies in May, 1955. The 4 Hungarian mixed companies were dissolved by an agreement signed in Moscow on November 6, 1954; the Soviet shares were sold to the Hungarian state. In August, 1955, the Soviet Union transferred its shares in the *Sokao* mixed company to North Korea, which paid for them in installments by deliveries of goods. In East Germany the largest Soviet-

---

[43] *New Times*, Moscow, no. 36, September 2, 1953. Sixty-six other industrial units had been turned over to East German authorities in 1952.

controlled mixed company, *Wismut A.G.* (uranium mining), remained in Soviet hands. In May, 1957, the Mongolian industrial oil enterprises were turned over by the Soviet Union to Mongolia, as was "Soviet-Mongol-Metall," founded in 1955; payment for the transferred shares was to be made in thirty yearly installments beginning in 1962.

The abolition of the mixed companies and the transfer of enterprises to the local governments was widely publicized in the usual way as a continuation of traditional Soviet policy rather than as a modification of policy and a backing down. It was claimed that the mixed companies and enterprises had been organized in order to put the "people's democracies" on a firm footing and to help them educate a generation of technicians and administrators.

> The decision of the Soviet government to turn over its shares in the mixed companies aims at the further strengthening of friendship and cooperation between the Soviet Union and the people's democracies. In this cooperation there is embodied the new type of international relations between the countries of the Socialist camp. The vital power of these relations is the product of the full and genuine equality of all nations—small or large—of mutual confidence and friendship, of observance of national independence and non-interference in the internal affairs of other states. . . .[44]

The people's democracies were required to pay for Soviet shares in the mixed companies "in yearly installments" in the form of exports to the Soviet Union. The amounts and the periods allowed for payment were not revealed, and not even approximate figures have ever leaked out. In the case of relatively small Eastern Austria, where the Soviet economic agencies were turned over to the Austrian government in 1955, the transfer agreement provided for payment of 150 million dollars plus 10 million tons of oil. If these figures are used as a basis for an estimate, the total payments by the people's democracies must have amounted to several billion dollars. Extended over years, these payments have been fertilizing the Soviet economy and have not been unimportant as a factor in Soviet industrial growth. In 1956 Soviet sources reported that Soviet credits to the people's democracies amounted to 21 billion rubles. A year later Moscow announced that

[44] *Pravda*, November 13, 1954, lead article, "Economic Cooperation and Mutual Assistance of Free Peoples."

Abolition of Mixed Companies

these credits had amounted to 28 billion rubles.[45] No breakdown of this figure has ever been given. It is generally assumed that the debt of the people's democracies to the Soviet Union in connection with mixed-company transfers amounted to at least 18 billion rubles ($4,500,000).

What the Soviet Union was collecting in this way during the second half of the 1950's was the price of German, Italian, Japanese, and Western property taken over by it under the label of "war booty"; the property had been used and improved between 1945 and 1954 and then sold to local governments. The sales were certainly a concession to "national Communism," but they were at the same time a highly profitable operation for the Soviet government.

Eventually, during a moment of Soviet-satellite tension, the Soviet government saw fit to cancel certain satellite debts that had resulted from the developments of 1945–56 described above. On March 28, 1957, in a joint Soviet-Hungarian declaration, the Soviet government canceled Hungarian debts in the amount of 90 million dollars. Soviet-Rumanian negotiations in 1956 ended in an agreement (December 1, 1956) canceling Rumania's debt of 700 million dollars.[46]

Closing the mixed-companies chapter in Soviet foreign affairs, Anastas Mikoyan told a July, 1955, session of the Central Committee:

> ... mixed companies have been the most conspicuous form of Russia's interference in economic domestic affairs of the people's democracies. They were a sign of Soviet economic nationalism. They were a form of exploitation of weaker countries by the Soviet Union. Mixed companies have become an example of economic exploitation of the people's democracies and that is why they had to be dissolved.[47]

[45] *Kommunist,* Moscow, no. 7, May, 1956, p. 62; *Pravda,* July 14, 1957. The difference remained unexplained.
[46] *The New York Times,* March 28, 1957; radio broadcast by Prime Minister Chivu Stoica of Rumania (December 8, 1956); and information obtained from the Department of Commerce, February 18, 1960. Also, Joseph S. Berliner, *Soviet Economic Aid: The New Aid and Trade Policy in Underdeveloped Countries,* New York, Frederick A. Praeger, 1958, p. 53.
[47] "People's Capitalism Number 6," sixth talk by Seweryn Bialer over Radio Free Europe (no date).

CHAPTER 6

THE MIDDLE EAST

1. THE BALKAN AND THE BAGHDAD PACTS

At the time that the first post-Stalin government took office, lively discussions and negotiations concerning new alliances were going on all along the perimeter of the Soviet and satellite frontiers, from Greece in the West to Pakistan in the East. Turkey and Greece had just joined the Atlantic Pact; the two Balkan nations, along with Communist Yugoslavia, were about to form their own alliance; in Asia, Iran, Iraq, and Pakistan were intensively deliberating their relationship in peace and war and planning two-nation alliances.

Turkey occupied a key position in almost all these combinations. Hereditary enemy of Russia and recently again menaced by total destruction, Turkey felt the Soviet breath on her neck at every step. Turkey was the easternmost pillar of NATO; her latest *rapprochement* with Belgrade was closing the Balkan gap; her *rapprochement* with Iraq and Iran was intended to close all gaps. Because Turkey was involved everywhere in the Middle East, Moscow's attention was centered particularly on her.

The first move of the new Soviet government in the Middle East was an unprecedented diplomatic note of withdrawal; long before open criticism of Stalin began to be heard in Russia, the note, sent by Molotov to Turkey on May 30, 1953, announced, in so many words, Soviet renunciation of Stalin's program of territorial expansion. The pretense of "continuity" in foreign affairs, which Molotov tried to maintain in other areas, was dropped in this case; on the contrary, the Molotov note informed Turkey that a line had been drawn under the old schemes and that better Soviet-Turkish relations would now become possible.

The Balkan and the Baghdad Pacts 199

"The Soviet Government," the note read, "which has recently been concerned with problems of the U.S.S.R.'s relations with neighboring states has, among other things, studied the state of Soviet-Turkish relations." After referring to the former Soviet demands, the note went on: "This was taken amiss by government and public circles in Turkey, which could not but be reflected to some extent in Soviet-Turkish relations." Therefore, Molotov said, Soviet Georgia and Armenia (in whose behalf the territorial program had been launched) "renounce their claim," and "the Soviet Government declares the Soviet Union does not have any territorial claims whatsoever against Turkey."

Molotov would not have been in character if he had retreated all the way and brought an end to all Soviet-Turkish disagreements. In regard to the Black Sea and the Dardanelles his note did not state that the *status quo* (that is, as laid down in the Montreux Convention of 1936), which would be tantamount to complete sovereignty for Turkey, would continue; he used the vague formula of "conditions equally acceptable both for the U.S.S.R. and for Turkey."

The proposed new setup was to be covered by a bilateral Soviet-Turkish agreement (the other cosignatories of the Montreux Convention would not be parties to the agreement). This was a veiled and naïve offer of a Soviet-Turkish alliance against the West. Turkey's reply of July 18 was understandably cool and restrained. She was satisfied with the cancellation of Soviet territorial claims, but, she pointed out, "the question of the Straits is regulated by the Montreux Convention."

The meaning of the new Soviet ideas in regard to Turkey was revealed two days later, when Molotov addressed a note to Ankara concerning the imminent visit of American warships to Istanbul; soon there followed a visit of British warships. Although the visits to Turkish waters of American and British warships could not serve as a reason for diplomatic *démarches* on the Soviet side, Molotov nevertheless lodged a protest. Contending that the naval visits were "a kind of a military demonstration," the Soviet government requested "additional information" on the subject; to this it was not entitled. The Soviet note was futile; it irritated Turkey and worsened relations still further. Turkey's reply to Moscow of July 21, which contained a hint of a challenge, stated that the frequency of the naval visits "can only be interpreted as happy evidence of the friendly ties binding Turkey to the countries to which the invited fleets belong." On July 31 a new Soviet note was dispatched to Turkey which was intended to refute the general impression that Russia was mingling in the sovereign affairs of Turkey.

In the end, no real *rapprochement* was achieved. Molotov's hopes were frustrated. It was not possible to undo, by diplomatic notes, the effects of fourteen years of active policies or to dispel the menace of Soviet expansionism or the new threat created by the emergence of Bulgaria and Rumania as Soviet satellites. For Turkey there was no other way than to continue to rely on the West even if this called for military cooperation, and permit the Western powers to establish military bases in Turkey.

Turkey was also the eastern support of the new Balkan alliance. The sensational element of this alliance was the adherence of Tito's Yugoslavia to an international bloc (with Greece and Turkey) which was directed at their Communist neighbors, Bulgaria, Rumania, Hungary, and of course the Soviet Union. The initial phase of the alliance was a "treaty," signed in February, 1953, which undoubtedly prompted the Soviet government to increase its efforts to reach an agreement with Turkey and thus destroy this nucleus of a new military alliance.

Molotov's efforts, however, as we have seen, were in vain. How little his *démarches* impressed the other governments, and how firm was the world-wide impression that Soviet foreign policy after Stalin's death would continue as before, is best seen from the developments in connection with the Balkan Pact.

In a speech on May 5, 1953, Tito noted that "there is no sign of a general improvement of relations with the Soviet Union." On May 21, 1953, he pointed to the "satellite forces at Yugoslavia's frontiers" which "continue to fire on, wound and kill Yugoslav frontier guards. . . ." In general, he said, "we shall not change our attitude toward America, Britain, France and other countries in the West, no matter what our relations might be with the Soviet Union." On June 14, in his speech at Pazin, Tito said: "I cannot believe that they [the Soviet Union] will renounce their aim. . . . A great country which since the Second World War has completely taken the path of imperialism will not easily renounce its aim, certainly not so long

The Balkan and the Baghdad Pacts

as it looks upon force as the decisive factor in the world." In July the members of the Balkan Pact decided not to reduce their common efforts until the Soviet Union gave real proof of a more peaceful policy.

The situation did not change for more than a year. In July–August, 1954, the Balkan "treaty" was consolidated and transformed into the "Balkan Alliance," the military power of which, in case of emergency, was estimated at seventy divisions. The "Treaty of Alliance, Political Cooperation and Mutual Assistance" was signed at Bled on August 9, 1954. Although Tito would certainly have preferred a middle-of-the-road position between East and West, Molotov's course left him no other choice than to reject "neutralism." In the course of the negotiations for the Balkan alliance Tito's Foreign Minister Koča Popovič stated: "Yugoslavia follows too realistic a policy to have any neutralistic illusions."

Another Mid-Eastern alliance that matured during those years was that uniting Turkey, Iran, Iraq, Pakistan, and Britain and which eventuated in the Baghdad Pact in 1955. In November, 1951, and January, 1952, the Stalin government made several diplomatic *démarches* toward Mid-Eastern governments as well as the three Western capitals against the plans of a "Mid-Eastern Command," and the Soviet press devoted much space to attacks on these "aggressive" plans. In 1953–54, when soundings were being taken among Eastern governments, Molotov's efforts to prevent the birth of a Middle East alliance were energetic and consistent. He contended that the members of the prospective alliance would become dependencies of the United States and Britain, lose their sovereignty, and, by offering military bases to the West, become targets of Soviet military operations in case of war. A threat of an economic as well as a military nature was implied in the strongly worded Soviet notes.

In the preliminary vague discussions of a Mid-Eastern alliance a substantial difference appeared between nations situated near the Soviet borders and those at a distance from these borders. The former, the "northern tier," had more cause for concern about their independence and defense than the latter and were rather inclined to an alliance with the West; the latter would be satisfied with "neutrality." Molotov's protests were supported, for example, by India (which was mainly disturbed by Pakistan's joining a pro-Western bloc), but also by Afghanistan and, except for Iraq, by the Arab countries. In the Asian-African corner, conditions were more promising for Soviet policy than in most other places. Situated at a considerable distance from the Soviet border and concerned mainly with their own emancipation from Britain, France, Italy, and Spain, these governments saw no danger in the Moscow course. Although the time for close ties with Russia had not yet come, these governments preferred to remain aloof from pro-Western pacts. Molotov's *démarches* in 1953–54 tended to make the Arab world suspicious even of the United States, and this was the main, if not the only, success of Soviet policy in the Middle East in the Malenkov-Molotov era. The United States was the big culprit, and its actions were sometimes depicted in horrifying detail.[1]

On November 11, 1953, the Soviet government officially requested from Karachi "clarification" of the Pakistani-American negotiations concerning military cooperation and United States air bases in Pakistan. Next day, Pakistani Premier Mohammed Ali stated that "Pakistan will tolerate no interference in her domestic or foreign policy from any quarter"; but no military bases, he said, were being offered to foreign countries. A Pakistani note to this effect was dispatched to Moscow on December 12. Between March and May, 1954, there was another exchange of Soviet-Pakistani notes.

In disregard of Soviet protests, an agreement of "friendly cooperation" between Turkey and Pakistan was signed in Karachi on April 2, 1954. Before and immediately after the signing of this agreement the Soviet government sent diplomatic notes to the countries involved protesting the new alliance. In a note to Iraq, a prospective member of the alliance, Molotov remarked that adherence of Arab countries to the Mid-Eastern alliance would be viewed as "unfriendly and hostile." All of the governments concerned rejected the Soviet note. Turkey, in her reply of May 9, 1954, said: ". . . the Turkish Government regretted the Soviet Union's systematic remonstrations through diplomatic channels and every sort of propaganda whenever Turkey acted to strengthen peace." Iran, the other prospective mem-

[1] "The Arab press has pointed out that the murder of King Abdullah of Jordan, a faithful placeman of London, was the handiwork of American agents. The *Beirut*, a Lebanese paper, recently published evidence showing that the United States Consul-General at Tangier, Joseph Satterthwaite, was directly implicated in the overthrow of Sidi Mohammed ben Youssef, Sultan of Morocco." (*New Times*, Moscow, no. 2, January 9, 1954, p. 14.)

ber of the pact, received a Soviet memo on July 14, 1954, requesting an "explanation." The Iranian reply of July 18 stated that it was "entitled to take all measures that it judged desirable with a view of ensuring Iran's security and the defense of her independence and integrity."

The next phase in the emergence of the Baghdad Pact was the conclusion of a Turkish-Iraqi alliance on January 14, 1955.

The first full-fledged conference of the members of the Baghdad Pact took place in Baghdad on November 21–22, 1955. The reaction of the Soviet government was expressed in a number of critical statements; in its note to Iran of November 26, 1955, it said:

> As a connecting link between NATO and SEATO, the Baghdad bloc is a threat to peace not only in the Near and Middle East but also outside this area. In this connection the linking of the Baghdad bloc with the above-mentioned military groupings makes it possible for the Near and Middle Eastern countries to become involved in armed conflicts which may arise in other parts of the world.[2]

On the whole, the first post-Stalin Soviet government did not score great successes in the Middle East. No allies were found, no substantial trade developed, and the Mediterranean was as far away and unattainable as in Stalin's days. Under succeeding Soviet regimes new political methods were to be tried in the turbulent Middle East.

2. FAILURE IN IRAN

Among Iran's neighbors, the Soviet Union is the only great power. Russian power is felt everywhere and constantly in the offices, press organs, and trade organizations of Teheran, and, of course, in the Majilis. The Iranian capital, which somehow resembles a large Russian provincial city, has suffered Russian occupation more than once both before and since the revolution. A relatively large part of Teheran's population understands Russian; store signs are often in Russian; a huge Russian hospital is one of the capital's landmarks. The Soviet Embassy, situated in a walled area of gardens and houses, employs more people than any other embassy in Iran. A number of Soviet consulates over the country support the embassy in its various endeavors, except during times when the consulates have been

[2] *Pravda,* November 27, 1955.

closed down by the Iranian authorities. For Iran, Russia is Problem Number One. On the Russian issue hinges independence or subjugation, integrity or partition, and peace or war—and frequently also bread or starvation and trade or idleness, at least for some segment of the country.

This specific situation has placed Soviet representatives in Iran in a peculiarly prominent position. A mixture of fear and awe is induced by this group of men who can convert a storm into sunshine, and vice versa. Soviet representatives in Iran, while insisting that the Soviet policy was one of "noninterference," had greater liberties than elsewhere. Their intelligence activities, which sometimes became known to the Iranian authorities, went unpunished. Their ties with the Communist Party were accepted as a matter of fact. In the turbulent era of 1945–47 a Soviet official in Iran, Aliov, was the Soviet contact for the Tudeh Party. Later a Soviet consul, Agayan, a sociable man who spoke several languages, approached various persons with suggestions of cooperation of a special kind. Military attaché Rodionov, whose ties with the Tudeh Party were widely known, was very active; during his nine years in Teheran he advanced from the rank of colonel to that of general. Another Soviet official, Olifirenko, was assigned to gather information from Iranians. The Soviet trade delegation, with its large personnel, was viewed by the Iranians as a medium of intelligence operations.[3]

The Iranian national leader in the early 1950's was old Mohammed Mossadegh, a colorful and controversial personality of dynamic character and an excellent demagogue. A member of the Iranian aristocracy and a wealthy landowner, Mossadegh had no Communist sympathies. In 1944 he had taken a strict anti-Soviet position when Moscow tried to arrange for a concession as a means of gaining a foothold in the north of Iran. As premier since April, 1951, Mossadegh led the anti-British drive; he often had the support of the Soviet side as well as of Iranian Communism. His right-hand man in the crucial months of 1953, Foreign Minister Hussein Fatemi, was closer to the Tudeh and more accessible to Soviet suggestions than he was himself; Fatemi's obvious hope was eventually to succeed the old premier. A number of Tudeh sympathizers were appointed to ranking posts in the ministries, the army, and the police of the Mossadegh regime.

[3] D Papers, January, 1957, vol. 5, pp. 293, 301–2 and 307.

MAP 3. POSTWAR DESIGNS FOR IRAN (1946)

That Moscow did not and could not unreservedly support Mossadegh's government was due in the first place to Stalin's attitude toward "bourgeois nationalism" in general. Although Stalin's policy on this issue underwent several changes during the three decades of his rule, he in the end adhered to the orthodox tenets: the capitalist classes and their parties in the underdeveloped countries were unreliable as allies in the fight against imperialism; they were potential traitors. Only the working class—meaning the Communist Party—was a consistent leader in this fight. Iran's Mossadegh, the millionaire landlord, was the embodiment of this type of unreliable nationalism; he was to be supported only so long as he opposed the West, but essentially his government must serve as a bridge to a definitely Communist-led regime. Stalin's ideas still prevailed in the first year after his death.

The other reason for Moscow's suspicion was a reflection of the different attitudes of Moscow and Teheran toward the United States. To Moscow, the United States, leader of the capitalist world, main fighting element in Korea, first-rank atomic power, and ubiquitous opponent of Soviet expansionist drives, was the great enemy; compared to the United States, Britain was weak, accessible, and ready to compromise. Thus, any anti-British alliance that would leave the United States out as a target was unsatisfactory; popular movements with anti-British but not anti-American slogans were worth only tepid sympathy. The widening of every movement into an "anti-imperialist" drive aimed in the first place against the United States was a precept of both Soviet propaganda and Soviet diplomacy.

To orthodox Communists the identification of poverty and oppression with American influence was an axiom; not so to the nationalist, non-Communist movement in the Middle East. The United States had not acquired colonies in these lands, nor did she have a history of oppressing weak nations. On the contrary, American financial help, although it had been inadequate, was appreciated. In Iran, the United States had helped to train a new army and a new police force; unlike British officials, who were often viewed with suspicion and hatred, American advisers were invited by the nationalist regime to continue and expand their assistance. Moscow considered Mossadegh a weak leader because of his inconsistent attitude toward the Americans; Mossadegh's hope of a settlement of the oil conflict with American

Failure in Iran

assistance irritated Moscow. Why give aid to Iran if she was to settle definitely in the American camp?

In 1950 a Communist-sponsored Iranian "Society to Fight the Anglo-Iranian Oil Company" emerged. Twice renamed, it became, in 1952, the "National Union to Fight Imperialism": its attention had shifted from Britain to the United States.[4] In street demonstrations staged by the Tudeh, anti-American slogans were prominent. The American adviser to the Iranian government, Colonel H. Norman Schwarzkopf, was hated by the Tudeh. Colonel Schwarzkopf, the able and efficient former police chief of the State of New Jersey, quit Iran in 1948 after effecting a thorough reorganization of the police system, but years after his departure his name was regularly brought up in connection with all kinds of adverse developments.[5] The Soviet press likewise attacked him.

The reorientation of the Iranian government from anti-Britishism to anti-Americanism was never unequivocal and definite. As anti-British anger mounted, the moderate, pro-American voices were heard less and less, while the passionate anti-American outbursts of the Tudeh became more and more dominant. The slogan "away with the American advisers"—which if acted upon would have meant a weakening of the Iranian army and police in the face of the threat from the north—became heard even in the non-Communist Majilis.

At the center of Iran's internal and international crises was the large British oil concession which the nationalists considered as the embodiment of exploitation by foreign capital, the cause of the country's poverty, the symbol of Iran's dependence on British imperialism. There also existed in Iran, however, a rich Soviet fishing concession, Iranryba, the propriety of which began to be questioned by non-Communist elements: if national independence meant termination of sweeping economic privileges for foreigners, was it not time to turn also against Moscow and abolish Iranryba?

The Soviet fishing concession, negotiated in October, 1927, gave the Soviet Union a monopoly in fishing in the southern Caspian; the enterprise, which involved lucrative sales abroad of one of the best kinds of caviar, was rarely mentioned in the Soviet press or textbooks.

[4] *Large Soviet Encyclopedia*, 2d ed., Moscow, 1953, vol. 18, p. 423.
[5] George Lenczowski, *Russia and the West in Iran, 1918–1948: A Study in Big Power Rivalry*, Ithaca, New York, Cornell University Press, 1949, p. 272.

The fishery contract was to expire on January 31, 1953. On December 14, 1952, in the Majilis, Deputy Naser Solfagari voiced criticism of the Soviet concession and called for its termination. *Pravda* reacted with a violent attack on this "provocateur in the Iranian Parliament." How could one compare the beneficial Soviet-Iranian enterprise with the infamous British oil concession? "The imperialists," *Pravda* [6] said, are indignant that "another type of economic relationship is possible than imperialist enslavement and colonial exploitation."

Relying on the support of pro-Soviet groups in Iran, the Soviet government officially proposed an extension of the concession. A short time before the expiration date, however, Mossadegh informed the Soviet Embassy that the concession would not be renewed; in accordance with the Soviet-Iranian agreement of 1927, Iran would not grant the fishery concession to any foreign government or citizen for twenty-five years. The Soviet government acquiesced in Iran's demand.

These developments occurred on the eve of Stalin's death. The new Soviet government apparently had an easier position in Iran than in many other countries. With its stress on Soviet adherence to its obligations and its policy of noninterference in Iranian affairs, it could hope for some success and closer collaboration. It could also rely on the rapidly growing influence of the dynamic and bellicose Tudeh Party, which actually reached for power and almost grasped it in the hot August days of crucial 1953.

The Tudeh Party, which was the only well-organized group in Iran in spite of the fact that it operated underground, was similar in structure to other Communist parties, with "cells" as the basic units, local committees, a Central Committee, and a Politburo. It published a large number of newspapers; a number of "front" organizations (Democratic Youth, Democratic Women, and others) as well as the trade unions were affiliated with it. Financial help from Moscow (allegedly a percentage of the Soviet caviar concession and trade operations) is believed to have amounted to around 8 million rial (about $100,000) a month.[7] The membership of the Tudeh was estimated in 1953 at 15,000 to 20,000, of which about one-half was in the capital.[8]

---

[6] January 14, 1953.

[7] *Neue Zürcher Zeitung,* December 7, 1952, and *The New York Times,* January 23, 1953. The Teheran police reported on September 16, 1954, that 21,500,000 rial (about $300,000) was embezzled, on party orders, by Tudeh members employed by the National Bank and the Iranian State Railways.

[8] *The New York Times,* September 6, 1953.

Failure in Iran 209

Tudeh members successfully penetrated many governmental agencies. A Tudeh hand-grenade workshop was discovered by the police in 1953.[9] Arms were imported. The pride of the Tudeh was its excellent officers' organization, which comprised over 600 members, among them a number of army colonels. "Since the organization had its members in courts, prisons and the police, it was not hard to have a comrade's dossier 'cleaned' of most of its incriminating material, or else simply stolen. Warning members of impending arrest was a regular service. . . ."[10]

When the members of the officers' organization were arrested, in August, 1954, the investigating agencies arrived at the conclusion that "Their efforts have been to give the secrets of the army and security forces to the disbanded Tudeh Party and furnish that party with classified documents and material. The Tudeh Party placed the classified materials in their possession at the disposal of foreign groups."[11]

Of the eleven members of the Tudeh's Politburo, a few who had escaped arrest in 1949–50 lived in Moscow; others had escaped from jails and had likewise migrated abroad. Half a dozen or so *émigrés* in Moscow served as constant liaison with the Communist Party of the Soviet Union. On all important issues, all members of the Tudeh's Politburo, including those in Moscow, had to be consulted, which meant that the views of the Soviet party and government were practically decisive. Liaison with Moscow was regular and systematic. Close ties were maintained by means of couriers and ordinary mail. (The "Iran-Soviet Cultural Relations Society" was another channel of liaison.) For a time, Dr. Bahrami, Secretary of the Iranian Central Committee, stood at the Iranian end of the Moscow-Teheran line; later, Dr. Kia Nouri performed this function. In Moscow, the main figures among Iran's Communist leaders were Dr. Keshavrz and Dr. Rad Manesh.[12] An official of the Soviet Embassy was assigned to act as contact with the Iranian Politburo so that services could also be rendered via the diplomatic pouch.[13] These ties proved to be of con-

[9] D Papers, January, 1957, vol. 5, p. 305.
[10] Isaac Don Levine, "The Anatomy of a Red Spy Ring," *Life*, November 21, 1955, p. 182.
[11] *Black Book on Tudeh Officers Organization*, Teheran, Government Publication, 1956, p. viii.
[12] D Papers, File P, January 12, 1957, p. 3.
[13] D Papers, January, 1957, vol. 5, p. 312. In 1946, during the Jafaar Pishevari regime in Tabriz, instructions came from Baku. Subsequently Moscow took over direct guidance (*ibid.*, p. 314).

siderable significance in the anti-Shah uprising during the summer of 1953.

The Tudeh offered help and support to Mossadegh against the West and the Shah when it arranged mass demonstrations in the streets of Teheran on March 2, 1953. By that time the fronts had been drawn in Iran: on one stood the court and the Shah, the army, and the security forces with their obvious American contacts; on the other were the most extreme non-Communist nationalists and the Tudeh Party. The Mossadegh regime was driven more and more toward the Tudeh group. Anti-Shah slogans predominated in the demonstrations, and Mossadegh appeared as the most likely successor to the Shah if the monarchy fell.

Still refusing to identify himself with the Tudeh, Mossadegh sent groups of his supporters to fight the Tudeh crowds; the police succeeded in breaking up the demonstrations. But Mossadegh's forces were weakening, and Mossadegh, isolated from the most important non-Communist groups, was becoming a prisoner of the Tudeh: he could remain in power only with their support. Participation of the Tudeh in the regime would mean a political upheaval in Iran, military support by the Soviet Union, and almost inevitable conflict with the West.

The road seemed open toward the establishment of an "Iranian People's Democracy," which, it was assumed by the Tudeh leaders, could proceed without prolonged civil or foreign war. Mossadegh would become president of the new republic, to be replaced later by a Communist party secretary:

> It was discussed in the cell meeting [army captain Nezameddin Madani testified later] that in the beginning Dr. Mossadegh, who had supporters among the people, was to be elected as the President of the Republic and we would take part in his Government. We were to try to influence the government greatly and keep most of the posts in our hands. Later on if Dr. Mossadegh did agree with us, our eventual progress was ensured. Otherwise, because our forces, including our members and the number of workers who would follow the Tudeh party, would be superior, then we should be able to oust him from Presidency in the next elections ... we can then elect the Party's Secretary General, Dr. Radmanesh, as the President of the Republic.[14]

Thus Moscow had to decide the course of Iranian affairs. The

[14] *Black Book on Tudeh Officers Organization*, op. cit., p. 275.

Failure in Iran   211

Malenkov-Khrushchev regime, only a few months in office, was making efforts to ease relations with Britain and the United States. An end of the war in the Far East must not be a prelude to a war in the Middle East; friendly gestures toward Turkey (see above, p. 198) must not open the way to a war with Turkey's neighbor. Moscow would have been happy to see an anti-Western upheaval in Iran, but at the moment she could not provide armed help. American "containment" and the threat of "massive retaliation" were effective.

As the wave in Iran mounted in the summer months of 1953, a Tudeh victory seemed near; at the same time Soviet-Iranian relations were improving markedly. The Iranian regime, which had become more and more dependent on Tudeh support and, indirectly, on Moscow's benevolence, now opposed American efforts to settle the conflict with Britain by compromise. On June 26, President Eisenhower rejected Mossadegh's request for additional funds. On August 5, President Eisenhower expressed criticism of Mossadegh's collaboration with Communism. Anti-American demonstrations took place in Iran. Negotiations for a new Soviet-Iranian trade agreement were making good progress; a doubling of turnover was planned. In his review of world affairs on August 8, Premier Malenkov had only friendly words for Iran:

> The experience of thirty-five years has shown that the Soviet Union and Persia are interested in mutual friendship and collaboration. . . . At present, on the initiative of the Soviet Union, talks are being held concerning the settlement of a number of frontier problems and mutual financial claims. We hope that these talks will be successfully concluded.

Moscow's expectation that Iran would break off all ties with the West was the obvious motive of the conciliatory gestures. As for Iran, she was satisfied that her financial claims, going back to the war years, were to be settled.

In mid-July the Shah tried to dismiss Mossadegh, but the noisy riots that followed forced him to reappoint him. The final showdown took place between August 15 and 20. In a final conflict with Mossadegh on August 16, the Shah tried to oust the prime minister and appointed General Fazlollah Zahedi in his stead. Mossadegh did not submit; the Shah, defeated, flew to Iraq and from there to Italy. "The Shah has been a traitor," announced Foreign Minister Hussein Fatemi. Next day he wrote: "The Baghdad fugitive belongs on the scaffold." The Soviet press maintained that former American adviser General Schwarzkopf had conspired against Mossadegh in a conference with the Shah. The Tudeh, in its fiery appeal, demanded the expulsion of all Americans:

> ... the primary slogan of the Iranian people must be fulfilled: to chase from the country all American advisers; to liquidate throughout the country all institutions of the administration of Truman's Point Four program; to close the American consulates and other nests of American espionage; to annul all enslaving military and political agreements; to chase from the country politically active persons who intervene in the affairs of the country and deny them permission to return to Iran; to remove from all responsible positions in the state the exposed British and American hirelings, bring them to trial and punish them for their treacherous activities ... to secure freedom of action for the People's party, which is the only party representing the Iranian people and the most reliable bulwark in the fight against colonialism in the Middle East.[15]

A huge demonstration organized by the Union against Imperialism carried signs attacking both the Shah and the United States. This was apparently the first stage of an attempt at seizure of power by the Tudeh and transformation of Iran into a Soviet satellite. *Pravda* of Moscow reported on August 19:

> The former American adviser to the headquarters of the Iranian gendarmerie, General Schwarzkopf, has appeared in Iran. He was immediately received by the Shah. As was later learned, Schwarzkopf transmitted to the plotters direct instructions from their American bosses—to stage immediately a *coup d'etat*. ... The conspiracy was uncovered and suppressed at the most decisive moment. The Shah has fled Iran. ... The Iranian people have answered the machinations of the American agency by a huge demonstration under the slogans: "Death to the plotters!" "The Iranian people demand expulsion of American spies from their country!" Numerous inscriptions have appeared in the streets of Teheran: "Yankee go home!" and "Long live the people!"[16]

[15] *Pravda*, August 19, 1953.
[16] *Ibid.*

Failure in Iran 213

The Tudeh, at the peak of its successes, was still uncertain whether it could defeat the army and the non-Communist forces; at a decisive moment, it was felt, Soviet help would be needed. But the Malenkov-Molotov regime was not prepared to provide such help. Reflecting Soviet hesitation, a "rightist" faction in the Tudeh leadership began to vacillate, trying to avoid the crucial battle.

For a day or two the capital was in the hands of the insurgents:

> Teheran was for one day practically in the hands of the Tudeh. Neither the army nor the police were to be seen. Tudeh members were all over the city. It seemed strange: why don't they seize power? Obviously no instructions from Moscow to seize power had been received.[17]

> At a meeting of the Tudeh's Central Committee in the basement of a house behind the [Soviet agency] VOKS a fight was going on between the extremists and the moderates, led by Dr. Kia Nouri; the majority was on the latter's side. Instructions issued by the Central Committee often contradicted one another. Arms were distributed; then an order came to abstain from the revolt.[18]

Today Iranian authorities are convinced that the seizure of power by the Tudeh Party was checked by the reluctant attitude of Moscow.[19]

On August 19 the anti-Tudeh elements of the army, along with civilian groups under General Zahedi, defeated Mossadegh after a nine-hour battle. The following day Mossadegh was arrested. (He was later tried and sentenced to three years in prison.) The Shah returned from Rome on August 21. The uprising was crushed, its leaders were arrested, and Minister Fatemi, later discovered in a Tudeh hideout, was tried and executed. The new government, under General Zahedi, with American help found a way to compromise with Britain.

The British oil conflict was settled. Diplomatic relations were resumed early in December, 1953. For Communism in both Iran and Moscow the outcome of the struggle was a bitter defeat. Soviet prestige in Iran fell. The Soviet press, which had previously exaggerated

[17] D Papers, January, 1957, vol. 5, p. 292.
[18] *Ibid.*, pp. 311–12. On Mordad 29 (August 21) an order was sent to all members "to prepare for a revolt"; next day the order was canceled (*Black Book on Tudeh Officers Organization, op. cit.*, pp. 270–71).
[19] D Papers, January, 1957, vol. 5, p. 312.

the force of the pro-Communist revolutionary movement in Iran and had stressed Iran's sympathies for the Soviet Union, ran brief, unintelligible reports on the developments, in the main attacking the United States.

Despite the failure, the cautious Soviet course in those crucial August days made it possible for Moscow to continue relations with Iran. While the Soviet press violently attacked the Americans for their role in the Iranian developments, a new trade agreement was signed on September 3, a few days after the abortive uprising. The Soviet-Iranian "mixed commission" continued its work.

This pattern of Soviet policy toward Iran remained in force for a considerable time. Taking the August failure matter-of-factly, the Soviet government did not try, in the following years, to enlarge its sphere by the inclusion of Iran; it rather settled a number of outstanding issues, signed trade agreements with Teheran, and in general stressed its peaceful attitude. The Soviet press, on the other hand, attacked the Teheran regime for its *rapprochement* with the West, particularly its ties with the United States, and (in 1955) for joining the Baghdad Pact. A number of diplomatic *démarches* revealing displeasure on the part of Moscow led to no serious consequences.

Moscow had to remain silent when a number of its friends in Iran, among them some direct agents, were arrested and executed in the sensational affair involving Tudeh officers late in 1954. The revelations created an anti-Soviet stir in the Iranian press; the fact that Moscow had been in possession of Iran's most important political and military secrets aroused indignation and sharp attacks against the northern neighbor. The Soviet ambassador delivered a note to the Iranian government protesting the press campaign which, it was charged, was designed to "deal a blow to Soviet-Iranian good neighborly relations, for the benefit of third countries." [20]

To pass over the unhappy affair and reestablish relatively normal Soviet-Iranian relations, agreement was arrived at a few weeks later on the long-discussed question of the frontier line and financial claims. The agreement, signed on December 2, 1954, provided for an exchange of some border areas, the turning over to Iran by the Soviet Union

[20] Associated Press, September 23, 1954.

Failure in Iran

of 11,196,670 grams (12.34 U.S. tons) of gold, and payment in goods of the sum of $8,648,619 in settlement of war debts and the cost of billeting Soviet forces, food, etc.

Iran, however, also demanded the abolition of certain paragraphs in the Soviet-Iranian treaty of 1921. That treaty, concluded immediately after the Russian civil war, and having in view a military intervention against Soviet Russia or a new action by the White armies, gave Moscow the right, under certain conditions, to send its army into Iran:

> VI. The High Contracting Parties agree that in case any third countries intend to pursue a policy of transgression in Persian territory, or to make Persian territory a base for military attacks against Russia, and if thereby a danger threatens the frontier of Soviet Russia, or its federated associates, and if the Persian Government, after having been notified by the Soviet Government, is not able to remove this danger itself, the Soviet Government shall have the right to send the army into Persia in order to take the necessary military steps in its own defence.[21]

It had been recognized since the early 1920's that the foreign military intervention was definitely over and that the White armies no longer existed. The cited paragraph of the 1921 treaty remained in force, however, as a threat and a means of pressure on the part of Moscow. Iran's defensive alliances with other nations were presented as "granting of bases" to Russia's adversaries or as the creation of *"place d'armes"* in Iran, which could serve as a reason for Soviet military intervention. To Teheran it was irritating to live constantly under this Damocles' sword, and for this reason the Iranian government tried, in this new phase of Soviet-Iranian relations, to reach an agreement on this part of the old treaty; the Soviet side made vague promises but no hard-and-fast stipulation was ever given. Actually Moscow was holding fast to its contractual privilege. This became clear in 1959, when relations again began to deteriorate and *Pravda*[22] told the Iranians in so many words that the Soviet Union was not prepared to agree to the suggested alteration of the old treaty. In its regular diplomatic exchanges Moscow usually referred to the more equitable treaty of 1927.

---

[21] *Soviet Treaty Series: A Collection of Bilateral Treaties, Agreements and Conventions, Etc., Concluded between the Soviet Union and Foreign Powers*, vol. 1, 1917–1928, Washington, D.C., Georgetown University Press, 1950, p. 93.

[22] March 15, 1959.

On July 8, 1954, the Soviet government informed Iran, in an *aide-mémoire*, that

> ... a number of reports have lately appeared in the Iranian and foreign press concerning measures undertaken by the governments of the United States and certain other countries with the object of drawing Iran into the aggressive military bloc they are seeking to build in the Near and Middle East on the basis of the Turkish-Pakistan military alliance concluded in April of this year. . . . Accordingly, the Soviet Government draws the attention of the Government of Iran to the obligations assumed by Iran under the Soviet-Iranian Treaty of Guarantee and Neutrality of October 1, 1927. . . . In view of these obligations, the Soviet Government would like to receive the necessary elucidation from the Government of Iran on the subject of the question set forth herein.[23]

The reply of the Iranian government to this *aide-mémoire* was an emphatic denial and protest. Iran, it said, had never participated in alliances directed against the security and integrity of the Soviet Union and had always adhered to the treaty of 1927.

As the negotiations for the new treaty (the Baghdad Pact) were being concluded, the Soviet side came out with vague threats:

> Reports from Teheran indicate that certain circles which are striving to draw Iran into the aggressive bloc are cynically calculating that the Soviet Union, which has convincingly demonstrated its firm desire for peace by a number of concrete peace-loving actions, will reconcile itself to this violation of international agreements. Realistic Iranian politicians realize that such calculations are built on sand, for the Soviet Union cannot help but draw appropriate conclusions from the emerging situation.[24]

On October 7 the Shah told the Iranian Senate that "neutrality of Iran is futile and dangerous." On October 11 the Iranian government made the decision to join the Baghdad Pact. Molotov's vigorous protest in a note of October 12 was rejected. In the continuing exchange of notes, Molotov's obvious intention was to set forth the Soviet position in the most emphatic way.[25]

On this level of subdued hostility combined with outward polite-

---

[23] *New Times*, Moscow, no. 30, July 24, 1954, p. 7.
[24] *Pravda*, October 13, 1955.
[25] A Soviet note of November 26 was rejected by Iran on December 6.

ness the relations of the Soviet government with the small nations of the Middle East continued for a time. The great vision of an extension of the Soviet sphere to the south had not materialized for either Stalin or Malenkov. Other ways had to be found and a different foreign policy had to be inaugurated. This was the objective of the revised course of the second post-Stalin era.

CHAPTER 7

THE ASCENDANCY OF NIKITA KHRUSHCHEV

When the first post-Stalin regime emerged in the Soviet Union nobody in Russia or abroad would have believed it possible that, of all the heirs of the late leader, Nikita Khrushchev would ultimately take over the conduct of Soviet foreign affairs. Khrushchev's experience had covered all kinds of internal issues, but it had not included international relations. He had specialized in administration in the Communist Party machine, collective farms, and industry, but he had remained entirely removed from the practice of diplomacy and international affairs. Viewed as an able man, but only as a *praktik* (practician), he enjoyed neither high standing among his comrades nor prestige in foreign circles. His unattractive appearance and his drinking habits had barred him, apparently, from many posts, and his humble "worker and peasant" origins and lack of early education had left permanent scars of primitiveness. This was not 1918–20, but the 1950's, when the "new class" of Soviet society already valued good looks, good manners, and not so much expensive clothes as the ability to wear them with nonchalance—an ability, it should be said, that is inherited or takes long decades to acquire. Judged by these criteria, Khrushchev did not possess glamour.

But he possessed more important qualities: brains, dynamism, and a strong will. A first-rate actor, able to change in a moment from violent indignation to extreme amiability, he knew how to impress his co-leaders and his party, though he lacked the calculating shrewdness of the old dictator. His loyalty to Communism-Stalinism, like that of every other aspiring Soviet leader, could not be questioned. He had known since the time of the civil war, when he first entered the political field, that the Cause justified all means, that freedom and democ-

The Ascendancy of Khrushchev

racy are either a sham or an attribute of the police state, that sacrifices for the Cause are inevitable and necessary. He believed earnestly and firmly that there existed a "capitalist course" and a "Communist course" in foreign affairs, and that only fools, egoists, and charlatans did not believe that Communism would eventually triumph everywhere. He was self-confident and inaccessible to the arguments of opponents. He had taken an active part in the crusade against "left" and "right" Communism and had emerged an orthodox Leninist-Stalinist, immune to all deviations. Later, after his denunciation of Stalinism, he did not fit into the standard categories of "right" or "left" Communism. In internal affairs his course against police terrorism was close to the programs of the rightists, although the latter's antikolkhoz trend was alien to him; and some of his fantastic plans of economic reconstruction leaned toward the "leftist" side.

From the Stalin days there remained the memory of a public Malenkov-Khrushchev feud over the kolkhozes; whether the feud also extended to other issues was not known. The full-fledged fight between factions in the upper circles of the Communist Party which developed after Stalin's death was for a long time concealed under the formula of "collective leadership."

Ten days after Malenkov's ascendance to leadership Khrushchev registered his first victory—he was given the post of a Party secretary; it took him another six months to climb the ladder to the "first secretaryship," which made him a rival of the premier. The jurisdiction of the first secretary of the Central Committee has no definite limits, and within the framework of his own secretariat Khrushchev was the head of the ramified foreign department of the Central Committee. Even so, his activities at first were devoted mainly to economic, internal, and police issues rather than to foreign policy.

The first major international developments of this early post-Stalin period had not yet, as far as is known, provoked profound disagreements among the Party leaders. On the question of the urgent need to bring the Korean War to a close the government acted with a rapidity that would not have been possible otherwise. The advances made by Churchill and his suggestions of conferences were gladly, and probably unanimously, accepted in Moscow. The bitter opposition to West German rearmament would hardly have evoked dispute. It is probable, however, that only on the issues of Yugoslavia and Austria did serious differences arise.

Suddenly, in this first Malenkov-Molotov era, the Iranian problem emerged in all its ominous significance. As already described,[1] active Soviet intervention in Iranian affairs might have meant the difference between Iran as a "people's democracy" and Iran as an "American tool." Soviet policy in Iran was decided, of course, by the Presidium as a whole, although technically this was a problem for Khrushchev's Foreign Department, which was dealing with the leaders of the Tudeh Party. The Soviet government refrained from direct intervention; it did so out of an apprehension about a grand-scale conflict with the West. The Communist movement in Iran was suppressed, and the country, a Soviet neighbor, moved to join the Western coalition. The defeat in Iran was one of Khrushchev's first major experiences in international affairs.

The lessons of Iran had to be digested. The Iranian Communist movement only halfheartedly supported the "bourgeois nationalist" Mossadegh; was this correct? Was it necessary to try to overthrow Mossadegh immediately? Was cooperation with and participation in a Mossadegh-type regime really tabu for a Communist party? Mossadegh was one in a line of strictly "bourgeois" but anti-Western leaders; there were others in India, Indonesia, Egypt. Was the traditional Stalin-Molotov policy in regard to them correct? In the deliberation of these questions lay the seeds of Khrushchev's eventual orientation toward the "neutralists" in world affairs.

The fight among the factions, which was becoming more and more acrimonious in the winter months of 1953–54, culminated in Khrushchev's victory over Malenkov. The latter had actually been shelved as head of the government long before he formally resigned. Between April 26, 1954, and his resignation in February, 1955, Malenkov had made not a single substantial speech or important statement. Khrushchev's stature during the same period had been growing.

It was not until a year after Stalin's death that Khrushchev ventured into the foreign field: in March, 1954, he went to Poland to "bring Soviet greetings" to the Second Congress of the Polish Workers (Communist) Party. Visits to the congresses of the "brotherly parties" were among the duties of Party secretaries; while the Cominform was degen-

[1] P. 213.

erating into a lifeless *apparat,* these congresses were steadily growing in significance as the new framework of a Comintern.

This first sortie of Khrushchev's was anything but brilliant. In a long oration he repeated trite shibboleths: the "imperialist beasts of prey" view Poland as a "dainty morsel"; Lenin had recognized Poland's independence but the "Warsaw regime" refused to establish "friendly relations with Soviet Russia"; "the great successor of Lenin's work Joseph Stalin," hailed the postwar treaties with Poland as a "fundamental turn," etc.

Two months later, on June 15, 1954, Khrushchev appeared at a large meeting in Prague. On this occasion he impressed his listeners as an extremely aggressive leader. He emphasized his favorite idea of the time: the Soviet Union must increase her armaments and speak to the West from her own position of strength. The speech was such a belligerent one that in Moscow it was found impossible to publish it *in extenso*—Khrushchev was not yet the dictator. In the portions of the speech that were cut, Khrushchev said that "the Soviet Union has always been frantically engaged in building up its armed strength," and that the Soviet Union had invented the hydrogen bomb. "We always knew that to live with the enemy one must be strong. We have done everything possible. We have created atomic energy in our country; we created the atom bomb; we outstripped the capitalist class and created the hydrogen bomb before them." [2]

In the following months disagreements sharpened and the factions were now quarreling about every important issue. The rock on which the Malenkov ship went down was "heavy industry" versus "food and consumer goods." This was an issue in which, as has been shown earlier, a number of internal and external problems were involved. The consistent course of the West toward the rearming of Germany, the shattered hopes about France, Malenkov's failure to solve the food problem in "two or three years," and the growing protests of the "leftists" in the satellites against the curtailing of their industrial plans and prospects—all these helped Khrushchev's faction in its offensive. On February 8 Malenkov officially resigned and Khrushchev's partisan, Marshal Nikolai Bulganin, was elected premier.

Commenting on Malenkov's blunders, *Kommunist* urged a more bellicose attitude toward the West. Recalling the first meeting of the

[2] *The New York Times,* June 25, 1954.

Cominform in 1947, it quoted from the Manifesto: "The main danger for the working class at this moment lies in the underestimation of its own strength and overestimation of the force of the imperialist camp." *Kommunist* added: "This was correct for 1947. It is all the more correct for 1955." [3]

The climate of "collective leadership" that still prevailed made it possible not to extend the personal changes to foreign affairs. Despite his continuous disagreements with Molotov, Khrushchev did not try at that time to remove the venerated "statesman of the Stalin era"; it was also surmised that Molotov had supported Khrushchev against Malenkov on certain issues. Thus, during the next few months, Molotov's tested, though unimaginative and unsuccessful, course continued, provoking protests and conflicts in the Presidium. Sore points became more numerous; tempers erupted more frequently.

The Khrushchev course in international affairs was elaborated gradually and pragmatically. Crystallizing in internal fights, bitterly criticized by his opponents, it was never presented as a rounded-out complete set of ideas. It never achieved definite form because it continued to evolve and undergo substantial change. The essentials, however, of Khrushchev's foreign policy can be identified:

First, the situation in Europe had reached a modicum of stability, significant territorial changes were unlikely in the foreseeable future, and, consequently, the primary task of the Soviet government was to maintain the "socialist" realm by all possible means, including military means, but refraining from direct encroachments in other areas, for instance Finland or Austria.

Second, on the other continents the attitude toward the "neutrals" (the "uncommitted") had to be revised, *rapprochements* with their nationalist (though bourgeois) governments were imperative if the course pursued by these governments was directed against the West; abundant economic help, in addition to political *rapprochement,* must lead toward the emergence of a firm coalition of Communist-controlled nations with the "neutrals."

Third, the "socialist camp" can and must be rehabilitated to again embrace all Communist-controlled nations; the open conflict with Yugoslavia, and the hidden tensions over China, which, in Khru-

---

[3] *Kommunist*, Moscow, no. 4, March, 1955, p. 18.

shchev's view, were due to Stalin's personal policies, must be brought to an end; concessions necessary to effect this must be made, except that the guiding role of the Soviet Union must not be sacrificed.

In all these fields Khrushchev's course, while it adhered to Communist principles, represented a substantial deviation from Stalinism.

PART THREE

The First Khrushchev Era

CHAPTER 1

THE SESSION OF THE CENTRAL COMMITTEE OF JULY, 1955

Six months before the Twentieth Party Congress at which the first secretary made his "secret speech," a no less significant "Plenum" of the Central Committee took place. It was here that the first attempt was made to examine Stalin's course, and that the decision was taken to convene the Party Congress.[1] In contrast to the atmosphere at Party congresses, the discussion at this Plenum was heated and passionate. The issues of Yugoslavia and Austria brought the whole range of Soviet foreign affairs to the fore. At the close of the session Khrushchev made the statement that "since 1941 no such meeting of the Central Committee has taken place." In fact, during the last decade of Stalin's reign, serious discussion of foreign policy had been tabu at any gathering of Party leaders.

The contest at the Plenum was between Khrushchev-Mikoyan and Molotov. The first named duo were feeling their way to a new path in international relations; Molotov held to the conservative path. While he acknowledged that mistakes had been made, Stalin's number-one foreign policy operator adhered to, and on the whole justified, the old course. He apparently doubted that a non-Stalinist Communism was possible, and he questioned whether efforts to find a new road would not lead to deviation, revision, and heresy. Molotov was defeated, but from an orthodox Communist point of view there was much sense in what he defended.

At the Plenum, which opened on July 4, Khrushchev presented a report on his recent trip to Yugoslavia. This report served as the de-

---

[1] Giuseppe Boffa, *Inside the Khrushchev Era*, New York, Marzani & Munsell, Publishers, 1959, p. 29.

sign for a general review of the Soviet course in international affairs.

The Plenum closed on July 12. The proceedings were not published.[2]

In his initial report and remarks at the Plenum Khrushchev tried to present a new conception of Soviet foreign policy. His main theses were:

First, that a revolution in the Western countries was not imminent and any attempt of the Communist parties to precipitate an upheaval would end in defeat; second, that, on the contrary, the situation on the "periphery of capitalism" and in the uncommitted nations was favorable; the fate of Western capitalism would be sealed when India, following China, joined the socialist camp. The Soviet Union must therefore remain active in the West, without, however, precipitating conflicts; it must continue the offensive in the underdeveloped countries with the aim of detaching them from the capitalist fold and tightening their ties to the socialist camp.

Khrushchev told the Central Committee that in a series of earlier meetings of the Presidium many problems had aroused disputes, and that the proposed course was meeting with protests on the part of Molotov. These were therefore now being submitted to the plenary session.

As to Austria, Khrushchev explained and defended the concessions made by the Soviet government. The Soviet government, deviating from the Stalin-Molotov course, had agreed to the neutralization of Austria, the withdrawal of Soviet forces from that country, and the abolition of Soviet economic footholds there. It had been part of Lenin's strategy, Khrushchev pointed out, to take temporary losses entailed in a struggle for higher gains. In Austria the Soviet Union was losing certain bases, but in giving up these bases it was proving its peaceful orientation without at the same time increasing the military potential of its adversaries. Not even the Soviet zone of Austria, he noted, had been a socialist area, and the socialist camp was thus losing little by transforming Austria into a neutral.

[2] The report that follows is based on D Papers, File 1, June 18, 1959; D Papers, File P, June 11, 1957; U. S. Senate Committee on the Judiciary, Hearings June 8, 11, and 29, 1956, part 29 *(Scope of Soviet Activity in the United States)*, testimony of Seweryn Bialer; Senate Internal Security Subcommittee, *Scope of Soviet Activity in the United States*, release of July 11, 1957.

The Central Committee

The other and most controversial single issue discussed at the Plenum was Yugoslavia. Khrushchev charged that documents forged by Beria had been used to substantiate the accusations made against Tito in 1948-49. The behavior of Soviet specialists in Yugoslavia, about which Tito had complained, had, in fact, been outrageous, Khrushchev said. His and his colleagues' visit with Tito (which had taken place two months before, against Molotov's advice) had been highly useful. The Soviet visitors had convinced themselves that Yugoslavia was building socialism and that she was close to a solution of her complicated nationality problem. Finally, the loss of Yugoslavia, Khrushchev stressed, was the more painful because this country meant forty army divisions to the Soviet bloc.

Molotov was the next speaker after Khrushchev. In the tense atmosphere his speech was frequently interrupted by Khrushchev, Bulganin, and Mikoyan. He tried to stand on loyal ground: he talked with respect of the Presidium, acknowledged some mistakes of his own, condemned Beria and his forged documents, etc.; in the main, however, he defended the old course. Was Tito's party a real Communist party? he asked. No. It was rather of the type of French or German socialism. In justification of his argument Molotov quoted from the Yugoslav press and from pro-Tito statements made by Western socialists, and he stressed the gap between Soviet and Yugoslav Communism. Quoting from John Foster Dulles's *War or Peace,* he noted the solidarity of Tito and Dulles: both accused the Soviet of being imperialistic. The United States, Molotov pointed out, does not give millions of dollars to Tito for nothing; as a member of the Balkan Pact, Yugoslavia is tied up with NATO. To blame Beria and only Beria for the Soviet break with Yugoslavia would be a great error; Marshal Tito must bear a large share of the guilt. Tito's behavior in 1947-48 was anti-Soviet and provocative. If the Soviet Union had not adopted the strong and definite stand it did at that time, Molotov continued, it would have been confronted with grave complications in the other people's democracies.

Molotov's criticism was at its most severe when he asked what would happen if Moscow had been lenient on the Tito issue. Trends toward complete independence, he pointed out, were obvious in the Communist parties of the other people's democracies. Taking Poland as an example, he asked: which is more important to the Soviet Union, Poland or Yugoslavia? Poland's population is greater by 10 million than Yugoslavia's; and it was only too well known that all was not right with the Polish army at the time of the Soviet conflict with Tito. There was, too, Gomulka in Poland. If a strong stand had not been taken in the case of Yugoslavia, who knows what might have happened in Poland? Poland would have wavered and gone the way of Yugoslavia. Thus, Molotov emphasized, the sharp and definite reaction in the Yugoslav affair was justified; it had prevented an even greater disaster. He proposed the reestablishment of normal relations with the Yugoslav government, by which he meant diplomatic, economic, and other ties; he opposed any ideological *rapprochement* or the reestablishment of relations between the Communist Party of the Soviet Union and the Communists of Yugoslavia.

As to Austria, Molotov doubted whether the agreement on "neutrality" was a sensible one in the prevailing situation. It would be a great blunder, he said, if the German issue were to be solved on a similar basis.

Molotov concluded his speech with the proud statement that of all the members of the Presidium he was the last of the active and close collaborators with Lenin. Obviously refuting Khrushchev's appeal to Leninism (as against Stalinism), he called on the Central Committee to abstain from revising Leninism-Stalinism.

Eighteen speakers took part in the discussions, among them Mikoyan, Kaganovich, Bulganin, Shepilov, and Suslov. All sided with Khrushchev, and all were outspoken and eloquent in their attacks on Molotov and his Foreign Ministry. There had probably never been another Communist gathering at which so much unvarnished truth was spoken about Soviet behavior abroad.

Mikoyan maintained that it was the Soviet side that had forced Tito to take the path that he had. Soviet "specialists" in Yugoslavia had engaged in espionage and had interfered in Yugoslavia's internal affairs; Moscow had organized an anti-Yugoslav economic bloc; Soviet policy toward Yugoslavia was "imperialist." On the subject of "mixed companies," which had been represented as a pattern of brotherly collaboration of the Soviet Union with the "people's democracies," Mikoyan said, No, the mixed companies were the most conspicuous form of Soviet exploitation and interference in the domestic economic affairs of the people's democracies; they were an expression of Soviet nationalism, and for this reason they had to be dissolved. "Did we

The Central Committee 231

need these mixed companies?" Mikoyan asked. "Were we very happy when Comrade Mao Tse-tung put our nose out of joint by refusing to allow similar companies to be established in China? Should we not draw a lesson from past mistakes?" Mikoyan explained what he had in mind: after Stalin's death the Soviet government proposed to Mao the setting up of mixed companies in China for the production of tropical fruits to be exported to Russia. Mao not only rejected the idea but did so in aggressive words: if you want pineapples, he said, we are in the fortunate position of being able to sell them to you. No more mixed companies!

Mikoyan also touched upon the behavior of Soviet experts and delegates in the people's democracies. The work of Soviet experts abroad, he said, called for tact and modesty. Under no circumstances should the feelings of the local populations be offended. In practice, however, Soviet experts had constantly violated this rule. They had been patronizing and arrogant; they had assumed that everybody could learn from them but that they had nothing to learn from others. The excessively high salaries of Soviet specialists were a source of discontent, too, to local workers and employees.

Mikoyan admitted, in his discussion of Soviet-Yugoslav economic relations, that the breaking of the trade agreement with Yugoslavia in 1949 had been a violation of international law and that there had been many other instances, on a larger or smaller scale, of the breaking of trade agreements with Belgrade. These, Mikoyan said, were "imperialistic" moves.

Even Kaganovich joined in the attack. He criticized Molotov's ambassadors in Poland, one of whom, Georgi M. Popov, who had been stationed in Warsaw from June, 1953, to March, 1954, believed himself entitled to issue orders to the comrades in the leadership of the Polish party. He had grossly interfered in Polish internal affairs, stimulated intrigue among the Polish leaders, and incited them against one another; moreover, in the presence of Polish comrades, he had spoken disparagingly of the Polish party leadership. Such behavior on the part of a Soviet ambassador to Poland, Kaganovich said, was impermissible.

Kaganovich's report on Popov was supplemented by Khrushchev, who dealt with another ambassador to Warsaw, Viktor Lebedev (transferred to Finland in 1951). Lebedev had taken it upon himself,

Khrushchev said, to be a leader of political life in Poland; he would summon the highest Party dignitaries to the Soviet Embassy and tell them what to do; he had written a book on Poland which had already been sent to the printer, but publication was halted at the last moment. Had the book been published, it would have done irreparable damage to Polish-Soviet relations. Lebedev had stated in the book, among other things, that the bulk of the Polish intelligentsia was fascist. He said also that the Polish Workers Party had emerged as a result of the great Russian war victories.

At the end of the debate, Molotov "admitted" his errors and promised to act in accordance with the directives of the Central Committee. This kind of retraction—a standard procedure at the conclusion of Central Committee discussions on the part of a man who wants to retain his position—did not deceive the Committee.

In his closing speech, Khrushchev recommended flexibility: more understanding of the Soviet allies, but *rapprochement* with governments that were prepared to oppose the United States. "Dogmatism," he kept repeating, is an evil. Irritated by Molotov's claim to Lenin's mantle, he insisted that Vyacheslav Mikhailovich did not occupy a special place in the Presidium and that his ambitions were unfounded. Losing his temper for a moment, he turned to Molotov; "Your wife is your doom, she is bossing you, she is spurring your ambition. If this doesn't stop, you are in for big trouble."[3] Molotov sat silent. Khrushchev regained his composure and reverted to his main subjects.

The resolutions submitted by Khrushchev were carried, and this meant the practical defeat of Molotov. For about a year, however, Molotov remained at the head of the Foreign Ministry and only rare outward signs of his eclipse were visible; his diplomatic moves were the official acts of the Soviet government, and in his public speeches he remained loyal, never giving so much as a hint on what issues and why he diverted from the official course. Actually he had lost the high position that had come to him rightfully after Stalin's death; under Soviet conditions this meant that on all questions of major importance he had to seek the approval of Khrushchev, his actual superior in the hierarchy of the Communist Party.

It was in a seemingly minor incident that attentive Soviet readers

---

[3] Molotov's wife, Polina Zhemchuzhina, an active Communist and a former people's commissar, had been "repressed" by the NKVD during Stalin's time. See p. 7.

The Central Committee

and analysts saw a sign of Molotov's decline. Soon after the Plenum of July, 1955, Molotov published a letter in *Kommunist* in which he admitted an error in a speech he had made eight months before in which he said that in the Soviet Union "the foundations of Socialism" had been built, "while actually," he emended, "the building of Socialism has reached a degree of near completion." [4] His earlier remarks had been "theoretically wrong and politically harmful." The very fact of such an apology proved that Molotov was wounded and lame. He was on his way out.

Still a member of the Presidium, however, Molotov must have participated in the preparation of the agenda, theses, and resolutions for the forthcoming Twentieth Congress of the Communist Party, the first since Stalin's death, and which was to become a major landmark in Soviet history.

[4] *Kommunist*, Moscow, no. 14, September, 1955, p. 127.

CHAPTER 2

THE THAW AND ITS LIMITS

1. NO SUCCESS IN LONDON

As we have seen, the Soviet course toward the dislodging of the United States from Europe implied an attempt at *rapprochement* with the governments of England and France and collaboration with the socialist parties of the West. When the Twentieth Congress, held in February, 1956 (see Chapter 5, pp. 322–334), was over, the government began to concentrate on efforts in these directions.

Although an invitation to the Soviet leaders to visit Britain had been tendered at the Geneva Conference in the summer of 1955, Khrushchev and Bulganin did not make their visit to London until the spring of 1956. Their extended visits to the former "colonial and semicolonial countries" of Asia had stressed the priority accorded the East over the West, the "neutrals" over the "imperialists," members of the "peace zone" over the allies of bellicose America. In the East the task had been simpler. Political support of the Asian countries by the Soviet Union against the colonies' masters of yesterday, combined with loans and assistance in industrial projects, had been sufficient to ensure the success of the visits; the backing of the Soviet visits by the local governments was enough to call out huge, enthusiastic crowds and produce the impression that "the people" were on the Soviet side on the great issues of world affairs. According to the Soviet conception, "the people"—not to be identified with voters and electors or governments—were everywhere on the side of the Soviet. Would the visit to England prove this conception right?

Khrushchev and Bulganin arrived in England on April 18, 1956, on the cruiser *Ordzhonikidze,* accompanied by a group of fifteen advisers and experts and a large number of Soviet bodyguards; fifty

No Success in London

rooms were reserved for them at the Claridge Hotel. Their schedule included, among other functions, an audience with the Queen, visits with the mayor of London and the lords of the Admiralty, visits to the Harwell atomic laboratory, Oxford, Edinburgh, Chequers, the Birmingham Fair, and the House of Lords, and the placing of a wreath on the tomb of Karl Marx. Fifteen MVD men, a number of Scotland Yard agents, and twenty British motorcycle policemen guarded them on their movements through the capital. The fact that the Soviet leaders were again accompanied by General Ivan Serov, Soviet Chief of Security, did not make a favorable impression, since Serov's name had been associated since the 1940's with mass deportations of Soviet populations to exile and "labor camps."

The popular reception in London was unenthusiastic, and remained so throughout the visit; it was somewhat warmer in Oxford and Birmingham. There were some calls of greeting as the Soviet leaders passed by; there were also hostile demonstrations, mainly by refugees from Eastern Europe. But the average "man in the street" remained unimpressed. From the very beginning the theme of political prisoners in Communist-controlled countries hounded "K and B" wherever they went, on the streets, at dinners, in the press, and even in the reception rooms of the prime minister. A memo was delivered at the prime minister's office suggesting that the Soviet leaders be asked to account for the eleven thousand Polish officers executed in Russia in 1940.

The Soviet leaders tried to be polite and to show their eagerness for cooperation. In their speeches they stressed peace, coexistence, trade, cultural relations; they recalled the wartime alliance and the victory. But, irked by the chilly atmosphere, Khrushchev frequently discarded the tones of diplomatic politeness and reverted to somewhat earthy language. Unaware of the effect that military threats might produce in England, he spoke of Soviet hydrogen bombs and Soviet perfection of armaments: "'It remains a fact that we were the first to explode the hydrogen bomb from an airplane. Americans are only intending to do so. Their previous explosion was not that of a hydrogen bomb but of a hydrogen installation.'" In guided missiles, he said, "'We can compete . . . too. I am certain that we shall quite soon have a ballistic missile with a hydrogen bomb that can fall anywhere in the world.'"[1] He even hinted at a possible new Soviet-German alliance in the future. At a dinner with Labor leaders he insisted that the Soviet-German pact of 1939 had been correct; he opposed Eisenhower's "open skies" plans because nobody has the right to be admitted to the other's bedroom, "not even into the yard." Khrushchev apparently could not find the proper language for addressing the British.

The official negotiations with Anthony Eden and his ministers produced little result, mainly because Khrushchev's aim—to detach Britain from the United States—was too obvious. Bulganin and Khrushchev had brought with them a long list of Soviet orders for British machines, equipment, ships, etc., which would have increased Soviet purchases in Britain by £800,000,000 or even £1,000,000,000; however, large portions of the order consisted of goods embargoed in Britain by agreement with the United States. Khrushchev and Bulganin urged the British prime minister to abandon the embargo, but Eden refused. The embargo on strategic goods, he informed Khrushchev, was implicit in the Western alliance, and the Soviet leaders should understand that any unilateral abolition of the embargo by Britain would damage relations between Britain and the United States.

Nor was progress achieved when the discussion touched upon Germany, disarmament, and Soviet projects of collective security. The positions of both parties had been clearly defined in advance; neither would budge. The final communiqué on the visit bluntly noted that "an understanding on the means to achieve that end [peace in the world] was not reached." The British government made a special statement to point out the differences: "The achievement of German reunification in peace and freedom is a fundamental principle in the foreign policy of Her Majesty's Government. In our view, it is the most important means for the attainment of European security."

Discussion of the Middle East, one of the burning issues of those days, did not lead to a *rapprochement* of viewpoints. As later became known, Khrushchev bluntly warned the British that in the event the West indulged in military action in the Middle East, the Soviet Union too would use force. Eden responded to the threat in a similar, uncompromising vein. Recalling the London negotiations later, Khrushchev told a meeting in Germany on July 9, 1958:

[1] *Time*, May 7, 1956, p. 38.

No Success in London

At that time we frankly warned Sir Anthony and Mr. Lloyd: If you start a war in that area, we shall not be able to remain as onlookers. We have no special interests in the Middle East. But the Middle East is not so far away from the Soviet Union and a war there would threaten the security of our country. However, the British Government of that day did not heed our advice.[2]

The very fact, however, that the two heads of government had discussed together the problems of that traditionally British "sphere" was a sign of growing Soviet influence. The Soviet Union emerged from these talks a recognized Middle Eastern power.

One matter discussed between the British prime minister and his Russian visitors constituted a courageous transgression by Eden of the conventional "noninterference" in the internal affairs of the Soviet Union and the satellites. In a discreet way, and without informing the press (even after the departure of the Soviet leaders), Eden brought up the matter of the fate of two hundred political prisoners in the East European countries. The list of the prisoners contained the names of a number of clergymen who had been arrested years before and political leaders of various non-Communist parties. Eden was successful to the degree that he persuaded Bulganin and Khrushchev to listen and to agree to consider the request;[3] this was in contrast to another conversation on the same subject had at the dinner given by the Labor Party for the Soviet guests.

Contacts with the leadership of the Labor Party, one of the guiding forces of the Socialist International, were among Khrushchev's principal objectives in coming to Britain. He could hardly expect to achieve far-reaching agreements with the conservative Eden regime, but the Labor Party was worth a try. In the three decades since Ramsay Macdonald had recognized the Soviet government the British Labor Party had been systematically working for the improvement of relations with Moscow and had opposed the Tory policy of aloofness and intransigence. A left wing of the Labor Party went farther, demanding closer ties with the Soviet government even at the price of British estrangement from the United States. From statements in the

[2] Nikita S. Khrushchev, *For Victory in Peaceful Competition with Capitalism*, New York, E. P. Dutton & Co., Inc., 1960, p. 538.
[3] *Manchester Guardian*, May 3, 1956.

Soviet press it was apparent that the Labor Party was considered a field in which the new Khrushchev course of encouraging neutralism and anti-Americanism could reap a rich harvest.

The dinner given by the Labor leaders on April 23 in the House of Commons became a major political event, although things did not go the way either side wanted. A few nice words were first spoken by the Party chairman, E. G. Gouch, and by Bulganin. When Khrushchev rose, he spoke for an hour, becoming gradually more frank and blunt. He again stressed Russia's hydrogen might. He attacked British prewar policies, which, he said, had prompted the Soviet Union to sign the pact with Hitler. He criticized the rearmament of West Germany and talked scornfully of the control of disarmament. He threatened to make a deal with Bonn behind the back of NATO. His speech, which provoked interjections and protests, was hardly the proper way to *rapprochement*. Hugh Gaitskell, the leader of the Labor Party, rose to speak on the subject of the socialists jailed in Russia and the satellites. He presented a list, signed by American socialists and trade unionists, of about two hundred names of Russian Social-Revolutionaries, Social-Democrats, trade unionists, and labor leaders imprisoned in five "people's democracies."[4] Khrushchev reacted violently and offensively; he refused even to receive the paper. The dinner broke up in an atmosphere of ill feeling. When someone proposed a toast to "our next meeting," Khrushchev gave him a cold stare: " 'It is far more difficult,' he said, 'to discuss things with you Labor leaders than with the Conservative government of this country.' " Next day, Khrushchev remarked that if this was British socialism, he preferred to be a Tory.[5] *Rapprochement* with Labor was spoiled, although a small group of Labor leftists tried to mend the gap.

At the airport, on his return to Moscow, Khrushchev told the welcoming crowd about his main impressions of England. He spoke in officially polite and vaguely optimistic terms of his dealings with the British government. About his conversations with the Labor Party, however, Khrushchev spoke in angry and aggressive tones:

> We were asked especially prepared questions about some Social Democrats who are allegedly imprisoned in our country and in the

[4] *Socialist International Information*, London, May 5, 1956.
[5] *Time*, May 7, 1956, p. 39.

The French in Moscow

people's democracies. We resolutely refused to answer these provocative questions.

If these Labor Party leaders had had friendly intentions toward the Soviet Union, they would have found other questions to ask. After all, they know perfectly well that we are doing all we can to correct the mistakes made in a number of cases in the past and that innocent people who were convicted are now being rehabilitated, and that not only in the U.S.S.R., but also in the people's democracies, legal proceedings of doubtful validity are now being re-examined.

The whole world knows about this and so do the Labor Party leaders. Then why did they bring up this and similarly infamous questions? In order to curry favor with the reactionaries. It is difficult to find any other explanation.[6]

2. THE FRENCH IN MOSCOW

A few days later France's turn came, but in this case the conference was held in Moscow and the French were the guests. A French Socialist delegation preceded the governmental mission; both groups, in contrast to the situation in London, were headed by leaders of the same party because Guy Mollet, the general secretary, came in his capacity of prime minister; his successor in the party secretaryship, Pierre Commin, acted as head of the Socialist delegation.

In their essence and results, however, the British and French negotiations were strikingly, almost disturbingly, similar. Not only were the same issues discussed on both levels, but the suggestions made were almost identical, and the difficulties presented in the attempt to solve the problems were the same. The results of the negotiations with the French delegations were hardly encouraging. Except on a few secondary points, the first communiqué on the French visit sounded like a repetition of the London statement.

The Socialist delegation, consisting of eleven persons, remained in Russia from April 28 to May 14. In their prolonged conversations with the Presidium of the Communist Party (May 5 and 12) a number of current Soviet problems were touched upon, including the matter of the controversial agronomist Trofim Lysenko, the fate of Soviet Jews, a "second party" in Russia, and the fate of political prisoners.[7] Khrushchev strongly attacked the Baghdad Pact and defended

[6] *Pravda*, May 1, 1956.
[7] This report is based on D Papers, France, M-M5.

the sale of arms by Czechoslovakia to Egypt "because they serve in a struggle against the Baghdad Pact." "We are interested in the Arabs' position against Baghdad"; to which Mikoyan added: "Everything will change once the Baghdad Pact is abandoned."

Both Shepilov and Khrushchev stated firmly that no "second political party" would be permitted to emerge in Russia. (This was intended to put an end to some French expectations that the process of de-Stalinization might gradually transform the Soviet Union into a Western-type democracy.) The dictatorship of Communism was to remain intact. In a second conversation, at which Malenkov and Kaganovich were present, the French raised the Jewish question, and Khrushchev, wrongly assuming that Professor André Philip was Jewish, bared his basic views on this issue:

> At the beginning of the revolution the Jews played a great role. This was natural. They were more numerous in the revolutionary movement because there were more literate elements among them than in the other nationalities. That was natural. But things have changed since then, as the other nationalities have raised the level of their culture. Of course, we have some Jews who would prefer the old situation. But it must be realized that this is no longer possible. What would the population of Uzbekistan, for instance, say if they would have to accept Jews as their chiefs? . . . And also the Russians? . . . They would say: are we imbeciles? Are we incapable of having leaders of our own nationality?[8]

On this occasion, Kaganovich, one of the last old-type Bolsheviks interested in Marxist orthodoxy, criticized French socialists (including the late Jean Jaurès) for their stand in 1898 in favor of Captain Alfred Dreyfus, a Jew falsely accused of espionage. "No," said Kaganovich, "this was not a matter for the working class, and there was no need to mingle in this affair."[9]

In a private conversation, Commin spoke to Khrushchev about the imprisoned socialists. The Soviet leader was calm and promised

[8] D Papers, France, M4-M5.
[9] D Papers, February, 1957, vol. 6, p. 353. In the course of the Dreyfus affair a characteristic controversy developed between two socialist factions. The extreme Marxists, under Jules Guesde, viewed the Dreyfus case as a fight between two "bourgeois groups"; they maintained that it should be of no interest to the "working class." The moderate socialists, among whom Jean Jaurès was outstanding, were (and still are) accused in the Soviet literature of fighting in the Dreyfus affair from "positions of bourgeois humanism." Kaganovich's attitude in 1956 was typically "dogmatist" and "sectarian."

to consider the request; he added: "I don't want to give the impression that we are giving in, that we are showing weakness by giving you satisfaction. To the *démarche* of the Laborites in London I reacted differently because they wanted to make a political scandal and achieve a victory over the U.S.S.R." [10]

Khrushchev did not deny that numbers of socialists were imprisoned in Russia, nor did he say that his government was unable to influence the policies of the satellites. He promised to check all petitions of socialist prisoners in Soviet jails and labor camps and also "to use his influence on the Communist parties" of the satellite countries and suggest to them a similar procedure.

The French Socialist delegation left Moscow on May 14. Farewell speeches were made in which each side addressed the other as "comrades." In the final communiqué the French and Russians pledged "objectivity" in describing the situation in the other country. The friendliness and "objectivity" (actually praise) were not to continue for long, however. When the reports of the French Socialists began to appear in the press after the return home of the delegation, Moscow's attitude began to change. "It is a kind of state capitalism, not socialism," the French Socialists stated; the standard of living in Russia is very low. Six social classes, wrote André Philip, constitute the pyramid of the allegedly classless society. The "November revolution," said Commin, "has not worked for the good of mankind." *Pravda* [11] now violently attacked the French Socialists. Their reports, it said, were neither objective nor honest; their sociology was wrong; they had borrowed their theories from the "reactionaries." *Pravda* recalled the fact that during their stay in Moscow the French Socialist delegation often refused to visit suggested sites, and preferred "trips to prisons and a corrective labor camp"; they went to see "markets and old small alleys." Relations deteriorated. The Khrushchev-planned "united front" with the socialists was nearly dead.

The French government delegation arrived on May 15. Of all the Western nations France was Moscow's greatest hope. The French Communist party, in contrast to the British Communist party, was

[10] D Papers, France, M3.
[11] July 28, 1956.

large and strong, and in non-Communist circles "neutralism," coupled with a vague sympathy for Russia, was widespread. To Moscow it appeared that the German issues, which had been at the root of Soviet-French alliances both before and during the two world wars, was the rock on which a new coalition could be based.

The negotiations with Premier Guy Mollet, Foreign Minister Christian Pineau, and their groups were conducted by Khrushchev, Bulganin, and Molotov between May 15 and 19. Khrushchev was blunt, especially at the informal sessions and receptions. His appeal to the French was to seize the present opportunity before it was too late. His government, he indicated, might again turn to Germany and repeat the maneuver of 1939:

> Listen attentively to what I am going to tell you [he said at the informal reception]. Make use of the opportunity: either you accept our friendship or you turn against us. If you won't accept our friendship—and I am warning you—we will reach an understanding with Germany. We are now in 1939. The decision must be reached quickly. If not, you will be isolated. . . . Actually there exist at the present time only a few armed nations: England, France, the Warsaw Pact countries, and in the middle stands Germany. It is Germany that is the decisive element. This Germany wants more space. If she is rearmed she will not turn against the East because we are strong now. She will turn against Belgium, Holland and France. This Germany will look for an alliance with us. You have the choice. Remember what I told you, think it over and calculate. Our friendship could be an element of peace in Europe. I drink to Franco-Soviet friendship.[12]

The threat of a new Soviet-German alliance was a reiteration of what Khrushchev had told Eden a month before, only now Khrushchev's words were very emphatic. "Germany," he said, "is problem No. 1 for France," and France should accept Germany's permanent partition. "You keep your Germans, and we shall keep ours," he added.[13] And, if Germany should be reunified (under non-Communist leadership), and the United States should supply atomic arms to her, France's alliance with America would become a source of great danger.

In general, Khrushchev said, a coalition of Britain, France, and

[12] D Papers, February, 1957, vol. 6, pp. 356–57.
[13] *The New York Times,* June 4, 1956.

the Soviet Union would be able to countervail anyone, "including the United States."[14]

Mollet countered with the generally accepted Western thesis that security could best be achieved in the framework of a six-power European agreement embracing a unified Germany;[15] partition of Germany, on the other hand, would serve as a constant source of friction and conflict. When Khrushchev toasted "Franco-Soviet friendship," Mollet, feeling the pique against his Western allies, offered another toast: "To the friendship of all peoples of the world." Quite understanding Mollet's attitude in favor of Britain and the United States, Khrushchev reacted ironically: "All peoples. Then, let us drink to San Marino." And Mikoyan added, "There is also Monaco." And Arutyunian: "Don't forget Andorra!" The Soviet representatives roared with laughter.[16]

Khrushchev proposed another toast: "To the peaceful coexistence with capitalist countries." To which Mollet retorted: "Why only capitalist countries? Peaceful coexistence must also be observed with the countries of democratic socialism."

The Soviet offensive against the United States became obvious when the conference turned its attention to Franco-Soviet trade. As in London a few weeks before, the Soviet government submitted an interesting list of goods it might purchase in France; at the end of a three-year period Franco-Soviet trade turnover could grow to three or four times that of 1955. This, however, would only be possible "in the absence of restrictions and discriminations." Mollet replied that he was bound by certain agreements with his allies and would have to discuss the matter with them. The great plan was buried in a new Franco-Soviet committee set up to prepare a three-year trade blueprint.

Again as in London, disarmament was discussed, and again without positive results. The Soviet leaders mentioned the fact that the

[14] D Papers, February, 1957, vol. 6, p. 361. A few weeks later, when Guy Mollet met Konrad Adenauer, the two leaders talked about their conversations with Khrushchev. While Mollet repeated Khrushchev's suggestion of an anti-German Soviet-French alliance, Adenauer was in a position to tell him how the Soviet leader had insisted that for Germany the proper road was cooperation with Russia because "no one will be in a position to menace Germany if she marches hand in hand with the Soviet Union." According to French witnesses to this conversation, "the two Western leaders were greatly amused."
[15] *Le Figaro*, Paris, June 18, 1956.
[16] D Papers, February, 1957, vol. 6, p. 357.

Soviet Union had recently demobilized 1,000,000 troops and retired 375 warships; the other nations, they suggested, should follow the Soviet example. In cordial tones, Mollet replied that public opinion in the West was in doubt as to the extent of the Soviet demobilization "inasmuch as no checking has been effected," [17] and quoted John Foster Dulles on the subject. "This is childish," Khrushchev exclaimed. No agreement on disarmament was reached.

One of the few issues, however, on which agreement proved possible, if only on paper, was, quite unexpectedly, the conflict in Algeria. Having reacted violently to all Soviet and Arab efforts to discuss Algeria at international forums, the French ministers found it possible not only to converse officially with the Soviet government on the problem of Algeria but to include the Soviet Union in the final communiqué. "The Soviet ministers," the communiqué said, "have expressed the hope that the French Government, acting in a liberal spirit, will succeed in finding an appropriate solution for this important problem in the spirit of our times and in the interests of the people." [18]

At a reception in the Kremlin on the eve of the French delegation's departure, when the negotiations, which had yielded no real results, were over, Khrushchev made an anti-French gesture; he walked over to the Egyptian and Syrian envoys (France was viewed by Egypt and the other Arab nations as one of their main enemies) and drank a toast to the "Arabs and to all others struggling for national independence." [19]

3. THE WESTERN SOCIALISTS

The negotiations with Britain and France, which ended in May, 1956, left the world-wide area of conflicts in the same unsettled state it had been in before. After three years, Soviet concessions to the West had proved to be inadequate. The basis for an agreement was still

[17] *Le Figaro*, Paris, May 17, 1956.
[18] *The New York Times*, May 21, 1956. It is odd that the official French text differs from the Russian in regard to the phrase "liberal spirit." The French text reads: "The Soviet Ministers have expressed the hope that the French Government, in the liberal spirit that guides it . . ." (that is, the "liberal spirit" was already "guiding" and would not have been the outcome of the Moscow conferences, as implied in the Russian text).
[19] *Ibid.*

The Western Socialists

lacking, and the international crisis—the "cold war"—which had supposedly been buried a year before in Geneva, blazed with undiminished force.

Khrushchev's feelers among the Western socialists and his attempts to achieve a new united front were rejected by other socialist parties in addition to the French Socialist Party and the British Laborites. Fifteen socialist parties took part in a session of the Council of the Socialist International on March 24, 1956, which discussed the Soviet proposals. In their resolution they stated that

> . . . the changes of Communist tactics which emerged at the recent Party Congress of the Communist Party of the Soviet Union are not adequate proof of a genuine change in the principles and policies of Communist dictatorship and therefore provide no grounds for departing from the position taken up by democratic Socialism, which firmly rejects any united front or any other form of political cooperation with the parties of dictatorship.[20]

A month later the Bureau of the Socialist International again stated:

> Socialism and Communism have nothing in common. The Communists have merely perverted the very idea of Socialism. Where they are in power they have distorted every freedom, every right of the workers, every political gain and every human value which Socialists have won in a struggle lasting several generations.[21]

Similar decisions were published by the individual socialist parties.[22] Except for Pietro Nenni's Italian Socialist Party, which had been allied with the Italian Communists for many years, the rejection was universal.

Khrushchev was not discouraged by this reaction to his proposals. The process of rehabilitation and liberalization in the Soviet Union and the satellites was still expected to impress the West. As late as July, Khrushchev, adhering to his schemes, stated: "We must look for contacts with Socialist parties and other workers' parties which are not adhering to Marxism-Leninism. We must coordinate our activities

---

[20] *Socialist International Information*, London, March 10, 1956, vol. 6, no. 10, p. 158.
[21] *Ibid.*, April 14, 1956, vol. 6, no. 15, p. 249.
[22] *Ibid.*, also *Free Labor World*, Brussels, March, 1956; *The Times*, London, April 26, 1956.

with those parties in the fight for peace, for the relaxation of international tensions, for the liquidation of the 'cold war.'" [23]

The end of Khrushchev's united-front drive came with the crisis that developed three months later in Hungary and Poland.

[23] *Pravda,* July 18, 1956.

CHAPTER 3

"RELAXATION OF TENSIONS"

The first months of the Khrushchev-Bulganin era were marked by several innovations intended to signify an effort at relaxation. Censorship of reports of foreign press correspondents was eased. Foreign diplomats were permitted to visit the Soviet atomic energy plant. The government embarked on a large-scale exchange of visitors with the West. In June, when two Soviet planes shot down an American patrol plane over the Bering Strait and seven crew members were injured, the Soviet government offered to compensate for 50 per cent of the damage.

The phrase "lessening of tensions," or "relaxation of tensions," began to dominate Soviet diplomatic language during these years. As is often the case when a newly conceived formula emerges in Moscow, it rapidly crept into diplomatic notes, newspaper articles, and political addresses, and began with annoying repetitiveness to dominate the political style; it sometimes recurred ten, twelve, and fifteen times in a single oratorical or literary creation. The unspoken meaning behind the phrase was that the Soviet empire could and must be consolidated, that its extent must be recognized by the West as definite, and that while the Soviet side abstained from warlike moves and actions, the West would acquiesce in the Soviet positions in Central Europe and Asia. Political realism, Moscow expected, would persuade the Western powers not to try to disturb the setup, if only to avoid military conflicts with the Soviet Union. To strengthen the political "realists," Moscow tried to maintain a military force far beyond momentary needs and publicize its "defense" obligations toward its satellites and allies. The Warsaw Pact, the announcement of which was intended as a threat to the West, was signed on the same day as the pact with Austria which restored the independence of and provided for the withdrawal of Soviet forces from that country.

Thus the initial Khrushchev-Bulganin policy combined a few cautious pro-Western moves with military gestures. The new Soviet course was to affect Austria, Japan, Yugoslavia, Finland, and the Bonn government. The first Geneva Summit Conference appeared the crowning achievement on the Soviet road toward relaxation.

On the other hand, the strength of the Soviet armed forces, which had numbered 2,874,000 men in 1948 and which had more than doubled during the Korean War, was not reduced after the war ended in 1955—the year of Khrushchev's "relaxation"; it remained at 5,763,000.[1] The subsequent reduction was coupled with Moscow's emphasis on the size of its atomic arsenal and its superiority in missile weapons.

Thus the Soviet efforts at "relaxation" during the mid-1950's were built on two erroneous assumptions: first, that the Western powers would be able and willing to recognize the Soviet-satellite empire as a definite and acceptable setup; second, that an overwhelming Soviet military force could coincide with a "relaxation of tensions."

1. THE AUSTRIAN STATE TREATY

Austria was still one of the most conspicuous political dead ends. The old Soviet course with respect to that country had been an obvious failure, and no new path had opened up.

Stalin had envisaged Austria as a Soviet satellite: as an advanced Soviet base, and transformed into a "people's democracy," Austria would extend the limits of the Soviet sphere to the borders of Switzerland and Italy, so that only 300 miles would separate it from Paris. With this prospect in view, groups of Austrian Communist *émigrés* had been dispatched from Moscow to Vienna in 1945 to head the party there. Two attempts at a "popular uprising" in Austria were made, one in May, 1947, the other in September–October, 1950. The embryo of a Communist armed force was created in the Soviet zone. To attract Austrian intellectuals to the cause, a "progressive" theater was established, pro-Soviet and pro-Communist books were published, and a luxurious building was started for the Communist newspaper *Volksstimme*.

The effort to win over a substantial segment of the population failed. In the postwar elections the Communist vote was disappoint-

---

[1] Khrushchev's statement to the Supreme Soviet. *Pravda*, January 15, 1960.

The Austrian State Treaty

ingly low, not over 5 per cent. The population viewed the Communist party as a well-paid representative of the Soviet occupation power. "Our aim is clear," wrote the Communist leader Johann Koplenig. "We want a free and independent Austria. . . . Only a people's democracy can be such an Austria." [2]

Nor was the popularity of the Soviet Union enhanced by the methods of the Soviet police, the many kidnapings, the economic system introduced in the Soviet zone, the control of industrial and banking enterprises, the oil monopoly, and the activities of the USIA, the huge Soviet trade organization for Austria.

Stalin's early, ostensibly pro-Austrian, course had actually been abandoned in 1946. But Stalin still clung to his zone in Eastern Austria with the idea that at some time in the future it would become a component part of a Soviet Germany (because *Anschluss*, which had been condemned by Stalin under the Nazi regime, was envisaged as inevitable in a socialist Europe). Although a Soviet offensive was no longer possible, Stalin was reluctant to withdraw, as he was reluctant to withdraw from anywhere, except under duress (as, for example, in Iran); to him the growth of socialism was measured, among other standards, by the number of people and the number of square miles under Communist control.

This is why negotiations for an Austrian peace treaty (referred to as "State Treaty" to stress the fact that Austria had not entered the war of her own free will), which had started in 1946, dragged endlessly. At the time of Stalin's death more than 250 conference sessions had been held. The Soviet side discussed, disputed, and advanced a large number of issues, some of them irrelevant to the Austrian case, only in order to prolong the negotiations: how to dispose of former German property in the Eastern zone (the "German assets"); compensation for Soviet supplies and services rendered to Austria after the end of the war; the "insufficient" de-Nazification in the country. In the early 1950's the farfetched Trieste question was dragged in by Vyshinsky as a new delaying factor; etc.; etc. Most of the fifty-nine paragraphs of the proposed State Treaty were agreed to by the Allies; the Soviet side procrastinated. On the mistaken assumption that the trouble lay in the numerousness of the paragraphs of the treaty rather

[2] *Volksstimme*, Vienna, October 21, 1948.

than with Moscow's ultimate aims, the three Western powers proposed a new, "abbreviated" treaty of eight paragraphs in the hope that it would make negotiations easier. Moscow not only rejected the abbreviated treaty but made its withdrawal a precondition of further talks. The stalemate continued.

The Eastern zone was not under the control of a satellite government; unlike East Germany, it had not been separated and converted into a state. The state machinery, centered in Vienna, served the whole of Austria; although limited by Soviet military, police, and economic privileges in the East, it was recognized as the only authority. No iron curtain divided the country.

This made the situation an unusual and paradoxical one, since in general a curtain was a necessary appurtenance of the Soviet occupation system. Concealed behind a veil, the Soviet occupation in a number of other countries had succeeded in revamping the political setup. In Austria, on the contrary, whatever happened in the East was seen by the West. Soviet prestige was sinking; Communist leaders were losing face; preference for the West was almost universal. In the West, the predicament of this small country, torn asunder and trampled by military boots, was a powerful anti-Soviet propaganda weapon.

In the mellowing climate of 1953 after Stalin's death, Moscow introduced a number of reforms and partial concessions for Austria: traffic between the Eastern and Western zones was substantially eased; an amnesty for Austrian prisoners of war in the Soviet Union was announced; mail, telephone, and radio censorship was abolished; beginning in September, 1953, costs of Soviet occupation were to be borne by the Soviet treasury; fraternization between Russians and Austrians was permitted; in general, the military phase of the Soviet occupation was curtailed in favor of a less obvious civilian control system.

All these were, however, strictly unilateral concessions by the Malenkov-Molotov regime to Austria's population; no international action was envisaged, nor was progress made in the negotiations for the State Treaty. When Moscow was invited by Britain to send a representative to an international conference on Austria (May, 1953), it declined. On August 17 the Western powers bowed to Molotov's demand by withdrawing the "abbreviated" treaty. The Western powers proposed a new conference on Austria, but again the Soviet government refused to participate. The Soviet attitude, while it had softened toward matters inside Austria, remained stiff toward the West on the Austrian issue because an international settlement implied far-reaching concessions which the Malenkov-Molotov regime was not prepared to make.

In November, 1953, the three Western governments again proposed to Moscow that discussions on Austria be resumed. This time it was finally agreed that the subject would be taken up at the Berlin Conference, which was to take place in January–February, 1954. Actually it was Germany and not Austria that Moscow wanted to discuss; Molotov consented to Austria as a topic only because it was impossible to refuse.

How disinclined Moscow was to settle the Austria issue the Austrian government learned when it tried to approach Molotov through other channels. Austrian Foreign Minister Karl Gruber met with Indian Premier Nehru and his envoy Krishna Menon in June, 1953, in Switzerland to discuss Soviet-Austrian relations. The Austrians offered a pledge of absolute neutrality between East and West as their contribution to the State Treaty. When Menon returned to his post in Moscow, he discussed the matter with Molotov. Molotov's reaction was that neutrality was "insufficient," and he rejected the Austrian offer. His goal was obviously something beyond mere neutrality.[3] Thus the negotiations to be conducted in Berlin were doomed to failure.

As we have seen, the Austrian issue came up for discussion on February 12, 1954, at the Berlin Conference. Molotov's main thesis was that a connection existed between the Austrian and the German problem and that therefore the occupation of Austria must continue until a peace treaty with Germany was concluded. This would mean a delay of many years:

> Pending the conclusion of the German peace treaty [Molotov insisted] the four powers should continue to maintain troops in their re-

---

[3] Adolf Schärf, *Österreichs Erneuerung 1945–1955: Das erste Jahrzehnt der zweiten Republik* (Austria's Revival 1945–1955. The First Ten Years of the Second Republic), Vienna, Wiener Volksbuchhandlung, 1955, p. 345; Karl Gruber, *Zwischen Befreiung und Freiheit* (Between Liberation and Freedom), Vienna, Ullstein Verlag, 1953, p. 309.

spective zones of Austria, in order to prevent any attempt at a new *Anschluss*. All foreign troops, however, should be withdrawn from Vienna simultaneously with the abolition of the Allied Control Council. The troops temporarily retained in Austria should not be regarded as occupation forces, should not interfere in any way with the social and political life of Austria. . . .

Molotov's actual goal was a Soviet mutual security treaty with Austria on the pattern of the mutual security arrangements concluded between the Soviet Union and its small neighbors in 1939.[4]

Rejecting Molotov's new conditions, the three Western foreign ministers made a startling move: they proposed the immediate signing of the text of the State Treaty proposed by the Soviet side, excluding Molotov's new conditions. Molotov, perplexed, refused to withdraw his demands.

The Austrians then rejected Molotov's plan; they had arrived at the conclusion that the conditions that would be created if Molotov's ideas were accepted might even worsen Austria's situation.[5] If foreign military footholds in Austria were necessary to prevent an *Anschluss*, "who will decide when such a danger arises? We don't believe that the decision will be left to us. It will rather be the commanding Russian General in Austria who will decide, and it will be *he* who will take the counter-measures as he deems them appropriate." [6]

Molotov's other seemingly attractive proposal, namely, for the immediate withdrawal of all foreign troops from the Austrian capital, actually meant that Vienna would remain surrounded by a Soviet-occupied area and would become even more dependent on Moscow than before.

The West refused to accept Molotov's terms, and the discussions ended on February 18.

Following the abortive conference, Soviet policy in Austria stiffened, mainly in reaction against the alignment of the Austrian government with the Western powers at Berlin. This alignment, a natural consequence of Soviet intransigence, produced anger and nervousness on both the Austrian and Soviet sides, and the Soviet representatives

[4] D Papers, July, 1957, XYZ, p. 64.
[5] Schärf, *op. cit.*, p. 348.
[6] *Observator*, "Die Wahrheit über die Berliner Konferenz" (The Truth about the Berlin Conference), published by the Socialist Party of Austria (n.d.), pp. 14–15.

The Austrian State Treaty

in Vienna resumed their bellicose posture. On April 30, for example, Major General Kraskevich even rejected Austria's request to resume helicopter service for Alpine rescue work. On May 17, contrary to custom, Soviet High Commissioner and Ambassador Ivan I. Ilyichev summoned to his office the Austrian chancellor and vice-chancellor and reprimanded them for anti-Soviet activities in the country; he enumerated "slanderous fabrications" in the press against the Soviet occupation forces, shipment of anti-Soviet literature over the "democratic" line, association with military people in "fascist organizations," etc. The reprimand, which had obviously been prepared in Moscow, ended on a threatening note: "If the Austrian government will not take the necessary measures, in particular in regard to the chiefs of the Ministry of Internal Affairs, the Soviet occupation power will be forced itself to take appropriate measures in accordance with the decisions of the four powers."[7] The Soviet press, which rarely reported on Soviet occupation activities anywhere, joined in the anti-Austrian campaign and carried a number of slanted news items and indignant articles.

Actually, the Soviet diplomatic offensive in Vienna was concerned with the painful Khokhlov incident. Nikolai Khokhlov, secret agent of the Soviet security police, who had been dispatched abroad to carry out terroristic assignments,[8] defected in February, 1954, revealed his story to the United States agency in Germany, and helped to seize a number of his former accomplices along with a number of ingenious murder weapons. Captain Khokhlov, it was revealed, had been traveling abroad on an Austrian passport in the name of "Josef Hofbauer." When the Austrian authorities made a check of its authenticity, they found it to be "genuine": it had been prepared by the Austrian police in the Soviet zone on Soviet orders. To avoid more trouble, the Soviet authorities in Vienna ordered the Austrian Ministry of the Interior not to investigate further; on the same day, May 17, in a typical counterblow, Ilyichev attacked the Austrian government for its anti-Soviet, profascist orientation.[9]

The decline of Malenkov and, specifically, the deterioration of Molotov's position, brought a substantial change in Soviet policies in

[7] *Pravda*, May 18, 1954.
[8] According to Khokhlov's own statement, one of his assignments was to "liquidate" an anti-Soviet émigré leader in Germany.
[9] *The New York Times*, April 23, 1954. Khokhlov's testimony before the Senate Internal Security Subcommittee, May 21, 1954.

Austria. As so often happens in international affairs, adherence to an old course, under new circumstances, becomes fraught with danger. By that time (early 1955) the stalemate over Austria had become a rather dangerous situation: German rearmament was becoming a reality.

If Germany were rearmed with the consent and assistance of the United States and Britain, German armies would be placed along the German-Austrian borders, along Austria's western zones. The western zones, still under Western occupation, would live in constant conflict with the Soviet; an extension of the NATO area to include West Austria would become possible, even likely. Soviet maintenance of its rule over the Eastern zone would not compensate for the advance of the potential enemy to the heart of Eastern Europe. The Soviet Union faced the prospect of NATO at the gates of Vienna.

Would it not be more sensible to discard the old Stalin strategy, acknowledge the European stalemate, and at least try to save the *whole* of Austria from falling into the realm of the enemy? Was not a neutral Austria preferable to the vulnerable partition? A withdrawal of Soviet troops from these parts, if accompanied by a similar move of the American and British (the French had quit long before) would also contribute to the appeasement of Tito and serve as proof of Soviet peaceful intentions in general; it could enhance Soviet prestige in Germany and emphasize the advantages of neutrality coupled with disarmament.

The Austrian issue was tied up with the issue of Yugoslavia because, according to wartime agreements, Soviet armies could be stationed in Hungary and Rumania to guard the lines of communication to Austria. Withdrawal from Austria, therefore, might also mean the evacuation of Soviet forces from these two satellites—precisely those satellites which, bordering on Yugoslavia, had assumed a threatening position toward Tito.

The consistent and conservative Molotov, who was opposed to complete reconciliation with Yugoslavia, also took a dim view of the withdrawal from Austria; [10] to him a retreat was a retreat, a loss, a defeat. To Khrushchev and his majority, on the other hand, Molotov's ideas appeared obsolete and unrealistic. The loss of Austria, a country

[10] See pp. 343–344.

The Austrian State Treaty

that had not reached the level of a "people's democracy," would not be a painful loss, especially since Austria would be obliged, under the provisions, to buy her emancipation with substantial payments. Molotov bowed to the majority and undertook to carry out the new policy.

These developments took place in January–February, 1955.

The crucial Plenum of the Central Committee which was then in session was followed, as usual, by regular meetings of the Presidium. On February 8 Malenkov resigned. On the same day Molotov delivered to the Supreme Soviet his report on the international situation, in which he dwelt at length on the Austrian issue. While repeating his well-known "connection [of the Austrian question] with the German question," and stressing the danger to Austria's independence that would result from the "rebirth of militarism in West Germany," he left the definite impression that a new course for Austria would be inaugurated.

The Austrian government instructed its envoy in Moscow to study the implications of Molotov's speech. Soviet-Austrian discussions both in Moscow and Vienna followed. On March 11, Molotov's Ministry, in a lengthy statement, announced the change in policy:

> At the Berlin Conference the Soviet delegation insisted on the postponement of the withdrawal of foreign military forces from Austria until the conclusion of a peace treaty with Germany. Now the Soviet side proposes to carry out the withdrawal of the armies of the four powers from Austria, without waiting for the conclusion of a peace treaty, if an agreement is concluded on measures to make impossible a new Austrian *Anschluss* with Germany. [Because now] the Soviet side does not condition the solution of the Austrian question on the solution of the German question; it only points out the connection which exists between these two questions. . . . Austria shall not be drawn into any coalitions or military pacts directed against the states mentioned in the Soviet propositions; the use of Austrian soil for foreign military bases shall not be tolerated.[11]

This statement marked the turn of the tide for Austria.

Four members of the Austrian government, headed by Chancellor Julius Raab, were invited to Moscow for a preliminary discussion of the settlement. There were a number of economic issues—Austrian payments to the Soviet Union for "assets," Soviet rights in Austria's

[11] *Pravda*, March 12, 1955.

oil industry, etc.—that it would be impolitic and embarrassing to discuss in the presence of representatives of Western governments; besides, it was in general intended to stress the decisive role of the Soviet Union in all Eastern European affairs, in particular the emancipation of Austria from foreign occupation.

The two-power conference in Moscow lasted from April 12 to April 15, 1955. Two political issues dominated the discussions: withdrawal of foreign military forces, and Austrian neutrality. While the Austrians wanted the foreign armies to quit within ninety days after ratification of the treaty, Molotov proposed six months, but he did not insist, and the three-month (and "not later than December 31, 1955") period was accepted. The principle of Austrian neutrality had been accepted a year before at the Berlin Conference; now the exact wording for it had to be found. There were again, as in Berlin, Soviet hints and feelers about a mutual assistance pact to supplement Austrian neutrality: if Germany should again attempt an *Anschluss,* Soviet troops might be available to save Austria's independence. Such a pact, however, would leave it to the Soviet Union to decide whether her troops were needed. Recalling the Soviet mutual assistance pact with the Baltic states, the Austrians refused to go beyond "neutrality as practiced by Switzerland," [12] and this formulation was included in the final agreement, which read as follows:

> 1. In the spirit of the statement made by Austria at the Berlin Conference in 1954 that she will not join any military alliances or permit any military bases on her territory, the Austrian Federal Government will make a Declaration, in a form imposing upon Austria an international obligation, that Austria will maintain permanent neutrality of the same type as that maintained in Switzerland. . . .
> 4. The Austrian Federal Government will welcome a guarantee by the Four Great Powers of the integrity and inviolability of the territory of the Austrian state.[13]

[12] D Papers, July, 1957, XYZ, pp. 58–59, 85–86.
[13] *New Times,* Moscow, no. 22, May 28, 1955, Supplement, p. 5, "Memorandum on the Results of the Negotiations between the Government Delegation of the Soviet Union and the Government Delegation of the Austrian Republic." In the paragraph of the Soviet-Austrian agreement quoted above the German text uses the term *"Stützpunkte"* not "bases." During the negotiations Molotov inquired why the Austrians avoided the usual "military bases." The answer was that in German *"Basen"* means female cousins, and "military bases" would sound like "military cousins." Molotov acquiesced. (Walter Kindermann, *Flug nach Moscow* [Flight to Moscow], Vienna, Ullstein Verlag, 1955, p. 34.)

The Austrian State Treaty

Permission for Austrian prisoners of war to be repatriated was granted by Kliment Voroshilov, as the head of state; 613 regular prisoners, 74 "war criminals," and 39 persons sentenced as spies were amnestied. The economic components of the agreements were settled, mainly in conferences with Anastas Mikoyan; [14] although the negotiations were difficult, it was agreed in the end that Austria would, in the course of six years, pay 150 million dollars to the Soviet Union for the Soviet enterprises that were to be turned over to Austria, payment to be made in the form of shipments of Austrian products to the Soviet Union. Over a period of not more than ten years Austria was to deliver 10 million tons of oil; 2 million dollars was to be paid for the assets of the Danubian Shipping Company in East Austria; a five-year trade agreement between the two countries was to be concluded.

Molotov requested, and the Austrians agreed, that industrial units to be turned over to Austria should remain Austrian property and not be alienated; Molotov had in mind not only Germany and an economic *Anschluss* but also American penetration. As for employees and workers of Soviet-controlled industry and trade, Molotov requested that no discrimination be applied against them. Agreeing to Molotov's request, Chancellor Raab pointed out that it was hardly necessary to make such a demand in connection with Austria, with her powerful trade unions: "There is plenty of work for everybody," Raab said.[15]

During the dinners and festive receptions that followed the sessions of the conference, the usual toasts were drunk and the usual complimentary speeches were made. Some frank remarks were heard. The Austrian question, said the new Soviet Premier Bulganin, could not be solved earlier because for the Russians it was closely tied up with the German issue: "It was only the newest development—West Germany's joining of NATO—that brought about a new situation." [16]

Khrushchev, speaking of the benefits of Communism, told his Austrian guests at a large Kremlin reception: "'Gentlemen, bear in mind, light comes from the East.' 'In Austria the sun is also rising,' Figl interrupted. 'Yes,' Khrushchev said, 'but two or three hours later. . . .' 'Mr. Raab,' Khrushchev said, turning to the Chancellor, 'in

[14] The Austrian chancellor told Mikoyan that in Vienna, Mikoyan, the Soviet-Armenian, was viewed as a great commercial talent: "Ten Jews equal one Greek, ten Greeks equal one Armenian." (Kindermann, *op. cit.*, p. 37.)
[15] *Ibid.*, p. 59.
[16] *Observator*, "Der Lange Weg zu Österreichs Freiheit" (The Long Road to Austrian Freedom), published by the Socialist Party of Austria (n.d.), p. 41.

these days we got to know you as an honest and upright man. I give you good advice: follow my example and become a Communist.' " [17]

With the conclusion of the Soviet-Austrian talks in Moscow on April 15, exactly ten years after the entry of Soviet armies into Vienna, the Austrian issue was actually, although not formally, settled; there were no longer any obstacles to the signing of the State Treaty by the powers. The Soviet government and its friends in Austria claimed that praise and gratitude were due the Soviet Union for the restoration of Austria's independence. The contention was that Austria was obtaining its new status from Soviet hands. The Soviet government preferred to disregard the efforts of the West—the hundreds of meetings, the futile negotiations, the multitude of diplomatic *démarches*—to break down Soviet resistance, the drafts of agreements submitted only to be canceled, the international discussions in which the Soviet side stubbornly opposed any agreement, the thousands of unnerving details of the Soviet occupation that had to be dealt with. The propaganda line was that "The Initiative of the Soviet Union Brought Austria the State Treaty." This was, in fact, the title of a booklet published by the Soviet Information Service in Vienna. *Pravda* [18] said: "The solution of the Austrian question is the success of the peace-loving policy of the Soviet Union." Lest it appear as a Soviet defeat and surrender, the Soviet-Austrian agreement was presented in Moscow as a kind of victory over the West; the West, it was maintained, was actually opposed to Austrian neutrality.[19] *Pravda* quoted the French newspaper *Aurore* to the effect that the agreement meant a "semi-defeat for the United States"; the government of the DDR (German Democratic Republic) stated that "these results were achieved thanks to the consistent peace policy of the Soviet Union."

After the closing of the Moscow sessions the Soviet government suggested to the three Western powers a conference of foreign ministers on the Austrian question. The United States agreed, but proposed to prepare for the parley by means of a conference of the four ambassadors. Moscow reluctantly consented, although it viewed the preliminary conference as superfluous; it implied that in view of the

---
[17] Kindermann, *op. cit.*, pp. 78, 79.
[18] May 16, 1955, lead article.
[19] Kindermann, *op. cit.*, p. 54.

The Austrian State Treaty

Soviet-Austrian agreement there was no need for further discussion.

The ambassadors' conference encountered some unexpected difficulties. In a final review of the provisions of the State Treaty as they had emerged from the long negotiations, the ambassadors found some controversial items. For example, Paragraph 5, which dealt with the fate of refugees on Austrian soil, though it had previously been accepted by the Western powers, was now found to be at best ambiguous. On the basis of this paragraph it appeared possible that thousands of refugees from the countries to the east could be forcibly repatriated; many were Russian refugees in West Austria. A long dispute on this issue began. The West, as a matter of principle, could not yield. In Paris it became known that Dulles and Macmillan would refuse to go to Vienna unless Ilyichev acquiesced in the Western approach. The threat was effective and Ilyichev yielded. He likewise dropped objections on another issue, namely, the size, nature, and equipment of the future Austrian army. On the other hand, the dispute over certain Austrian airfields that had belonged to Western companies before the war and were now being claimed by their former owners ended in a decision against the Western companies.

Molotov arrived in Vienna for the foreign ministers' conference on May 14 and, in his speech of greeting at the airport, again referred to the Moscow negotiations, which "had completed the preparation of the Treaty."

Molotov presided at the conference; it was he who proposed the draft of the provision on Austrian neutrality.

The conference of the foreign ministers, which had been carefully prepared for in advance, lasted one day. There were no important controversies to deal with, and agreements were reached easily. The main provision of the treaty, that on Austrian neutrality, stated that the four powers "will respect and observe a statement of Austria's permanent neutrality of the kind as observed by Switzerland in its relations with other states." [20]

When everything was settled, Secretary Dulles proposed that celebration speeches of the four ministers be limited to two minutes. Molotov disagreed; his speech, which was a long one, stressed the

---

[20] Actually, in one respect Austria deviated from the Swiss pattern: with the consent of the powers, she joined the United Nations.

leading role of the Soviet Union, mentioning Germany, rearmament, and the adherence of his government to peace.

The State Treaty was signed on May 15 in the Belvedere Palace. It was one of the few international agreements of the postwar era that proved to be wise and lasting and that bore the signs of understanding on the part of all the participants. It was actually a peace treaty. Unlike the peace treaties with the Eastern European countries signed in Paris in 1946, which were soon violated and which served only as a stage in the building of the Soviet satellite empire, the Vienna accord was based on a clear knowledge of realities and dangers. Austria was definitely exempt from incorporation into the "socialist camp."

The treaty became effective on July 27, after its ratification by France; the Allied Control Council was dissolved on the same day, the dissolution being followed by enthusiastic celebrations in Vienna. Withdrawal of Soviet troops was completed on September 19; all other military forces were withdrawn by October 24. Two days later, when the Law of Neutrality was being discussed in the *Nationalrat*, Chancellor Raab expressed gratitude to the powers in this order: first, the United States, then the Soviet Union (which, he said, by changing its position made the treaty possible), then Britain and France; next came the neighbors, Switzerland, West Germany, Czechoslovakia, Hungary, Italy, and Yugoslavia. Oskar Helmer, Minister of the Interior, said in a public speech: "No thank-you letter to the people's democracies."

Some 350 Soviet-controlled industrial units had been turned over to Austria by October, 1955: 319 USIA (trade) enterprises, 28 oil wells, ships, and installations of the Danubian Shipping Company; about 1,000 kilometers of railway tracks; and over 4,000 acres of land were also turned over. The total number of workers in these enterprises was about 50,000. Some of the returned plants were in good condition, others were run-down and needed costly repairs.

To the Communist Party of Austria the end of Soviet occupation meant a great loss. Buildings and printing facilities, put at its disposal under the Soviets, had to be vacated; financial help in the form of paid advertising was no longer available; the commercial organization that had conducted trade with the Soviet bloc and served as a financial base for the party lost its monopoly. Some Communist newspapers closed down; members quit the party. In the election of 1956 the Communist vote dropped from 5.3 to 4.4 per cent.

On the whole, Soviet-Austrian relations developed satisfactorily after the signing of the treaty. The Austrian side was prompt in fulfilling its economic obligations, nor did it complain about Soviet prices paid for its products or Soviet efforts to exploit the new independent country. For a time Moscow tried to continue to use Vienna as an important propaganda and reconnaissance center. For a time the headquarters of the World Federation of Trade Unions and the World Peace Council remained in Vienna. In February, 1956, however, the Austrian government ousted the trade union unit for its activities which, it said, were contrary to Austria's neutrality. *Pravda* violently attacked the Austrian government for its alleged "rapprochement with the military and economic bloc of the Western imperialist powers" and breach of neutrality.

During the Hungarian uprising, which occurred a year after the Soviet withdrawal from Austria, thousands of Hungarians escaped to the West by the only route open—through East Austria. Where only a short time before the Soviet army and police would have barred their way, they were now welcomed. In certain satellite capitals, for example, Prague, it was suggested in November, 1956, that Austria's eastern provinces should be reoccupied by Soviet forces;[21] with the final defeat of the Hungarian uprising this propaganda died down, but the magnanimity of 1955 was certainly regretted in Moscow.

2. RELATIONS WITH THE BONN GOVERNMENT

Unlike other Soviet actions of 1955—the withdrawal from Austria, Finland, Port Arthur, and a few other places—which were viewed by the West with satisfaction, the establishment of diplomatic relations with the Bonn government contained a definite anti-Western element. Moscow's intention was to announce the finality of its solution of the paramount question of Germany and to emphasize the "two Germanys" concept as a mode of settlement; "coexistence" in this corner of Europe was to imply the legal equality of the "progressive" German Democratic Republic with the "reactionary" German Federal Republic until new developments should occur which would alter the map in favor of the East.

Soviet efforts at *rapprochement* with the Bonn government began

[21] D Papers, July, 1956, XYZ, pp. 91–92.

at the unfruitful Berlin Conference of January–February, 1954, where Molotov spoke about "possible contacts and ties between the Soviet Union and the West German Republic." Since the press had paid little attention to these words of his, Molotov ordered his press chief, Leonid Ilyichev, to emphasize them for the benefit of the newspaper correspondents.[22] A few days later Molotov suggested, in another speech at the conference, an exchange of "cultural delegations." A few months later Premier Malenkov resumed the drive in a conversation with Otto Grotewohl.[23]

The last-minute declaration of the Soviet government (January 15, 1955) indicated "the possibility of agreements" on the issue of general elections in Germany with guaranteed "democratic rights" for citizens and even "international supervision" of the process of voting. The precondition, however, was nonratification of the Paris agreements. On January 25, 1955, the Soviet government announced the cessation of the state of war with Germany; the satellites followed suit. The new Soviet moves, part of the strenuous effort to prevent the ratification of the Paris agreements, were coupled with an offer to "normalize" relations with Bonn if the Paris agreements were rejected.

The Adenauer government was beset by many doubts. The establishment of West German embassies in capitals where East Germany was already represented might serve as proof that the concept of "two Germanys" had been accepted. But the spring and summer of 1955 were the period of the optimistic "Geneva spirit." It appeared that "relaxation of tensions" might be achieved and that the first steps toward a solution of the German question might even be taken. On June 7, 1955, almost on the eve of the Geneva Summit Conference, Moscow dispatched a lengthy note to Bonn in which it proposed the establishment of diplomatic relations without preconditions. Chancellor Adenauer was invited to come to Moscow. The note contained a few gibes at the Western powers; it hinted at Moscow's willingness to make concessions if West Germany would loosen her ties with her allies:

> The Soviet Government cannot refrain from drawing the attention of the Government of the German Federal Republic to the fact that

---

[22] Werner Erfurt, *Die sowjetrussische Deutschland-Politik: Eine Studie zur Zeitgeschichte* (Soviet-Russian German Policy: A Study of Contemporary History), 2d ed., Esslingen, Germany, Bechtle Verlag, 1956, p. 88.

[23] *New Times*, Moscow, no. 25, June 19, 1954, p. 7.

definite aggressive circles in certain countries are nurturing plans designed to pit the Soviet Union and Western Germany against each other and prevent improvement of relations between our countries.[24]

Bonn had two outstanding issues to present for Soviet-German discussion: reunification of Germany, and the fate of German prisoners of war in Soviet hands. Two kinds of relationships, Bonn noted, were possible: either a limited "normalization" involving mainly trade and travel facilities, or a complete "normalization" including exchange of ambassadors. No German preconditions would be set for the first; the second, however, could not be effected without the fulfillment of some preconditions.

Since there was neither a German embassy nor a German staff in Moscow, the train on which the large German delegation traveled to Moscow served as its office and headquarters in the Soviet capital. Confidential conferences were held either in the German railway cars, where the Adenauer group enjoyed complete privacy, including isolation from microphones,[25] or in the *dacha* put at its disposal by the Soviet authorities.

The conference took place on September 9–13 in the Spiridonovka Palace in Moscow. At moments of tension, the outbursts of anger surpassed anything seen at other postwar parleys; at moments of *rapprochement*, the courtesy and friendliness were extraordinary. In the end both Khrushchev and Adenauer had to concede much of the terrain they had come determined not to concede.

Bulganin and Molotov were the official spokesmen for the Soviet side; Malenkov, who had recently resigned as premier, was also present. The most interesting participant, however, was the not yet generally recognized leader, Nikita Khrushchev. His speeches were shrewd and consistent. On one occasion he addressed Adenauer in the familiar form—"*Du,* Konrad"; and Adenauer responded with "*Du,* Nikita." After a few drinks, Khrushchev was telling the Germans, with tears in his eyes, "I was a shepherd, later a miner. It was all extremely hard. . . ."[26]

[24] *New Times,* Moscow, no. 24, June 11, 1955, Supplement.
[25] Wilhelm Backhaus, *Begegnung im Kreml: So wurden die Gefangenen befreit* (Meeting at the Kremlin: Thus Were the Prisoners Liberated), Berlin, Ullstein Verlag, 1955, pp. 32–33).
[26] D Papers, February, 1957, vol. 6, p. 350.

The conference began with trivialities. Bulganin repeated the Soviet thesis about the necessity for *rapprochement* between the two German states, the evil of arming, etc. Adenauer discussed reunification and prisoners of war and emphasized the finality of West Germany's ties with NATO. The prisoners-of-war issue gave Bulganin the opportunity to launch the serious offensive. There are no longer any prisoners of war in the Soviet Union, he said; those remaining—a total of 9,626—are "war criminals" guilty of the most heinous deeds and sentenced by the courts. In answer to Adenauer's plea for the release of these prisoners, Bulganin recounted the tragedies suffered by Russians in the war; his eloquent attack, calculated to attract wide publicity, had certainly been prepared in advance:

> The Soviet people cannot forget the grave crimes committed by these criminal elements, such as the shooting of 70,000 people in Kiev and Babii Yar. We cannot forget the millions shot, strangled and burned alive in the German concentration camps. Is it possible to forget the tons of women's hair taken from tortured women and stored in Maidanek's warehouses? In the camps of Maidanek and Oswiecim over five and a half million innocent people were slaughtered. The Ukrainians will never forget the innocent people destroyed in Kharkov, where many thousands were shot and strangled. I could name the concentration camps of Smolensk, Krasnodar, Stavropol, Lvov, Poltava, Orel, Rovno, Kaunas, Riga, and many others, where the hitlerites massacred hundreds of thousands of Soviet citizens.

Adenauer countered with references to the behavior of the Soviet army in Germany at the end of the war: the Soviet soldiers' attitude toward alien property and especially their treatment of women. "It is true," Adenauer said, "that many bad things happened. But it is also true that the Russian armies later, in defense—I certainly recognize this—advanced into Germany and that then many terrible things happened in the course of the war."

Adenauer's words gave Khrushchev, in turn, an opportunity for a great oratorical attack: Adenauer had offended the Soviet Army!

At moments like these tension reached a peak. The German writer Klaus Mehnert has described the session in his *Osteuropa:*

> The main characters were not those present at the conference table in the Spiridonovka Palace, but the dead and wounded, the prisoners of war and those ravished in the years 1941–45. They caused a sudden darkening of the bright conference room and filled the hearts

Relations with the Bonn Government

and the lips of the men who were negotiating. In a German legend the ghosts of the men killed in the great battles of European history continued their fight for many years afterward; the contest on the battlefield was so violent that they could not find peace. Russian mythology contains similar legends. I was reminded of it again and again on that Saturday. The sufferings and emotions of the years 1941 through 1945 were still so much alive that even the wise, nearly eighty-year-old Chancellor, with his iron nerves, could not help being upset. It all probably had to be said once, because too much has been accumulated in the feelings of both peoples, and a valve had to be opened.[27]

The storm of emotion revealed also the deeper roots of the Soviet attitude. To the Soviet leaders West Germany was the successor and heir of the old powerful and warring Prussia-Germany. The anti-Nazi protestations of Adenauer ("I would have strangled Hitler with my own hands"), the democratic reforms, and the slogans of liberty were of no avail: even had they been accepted they would not have changed the Soviet image of the neighbor nation. In the Soviet view Germany remained independent, dynamic, and a potentially strong power. In Adenauer's conduct at the vehement session the Soviet leadership saw force and pride, the two attributes that most impressed them.

The storm ended, the tension was discharged. Let us be free, Khrushchev pleaded, of feelings of revenge. He no longer expected, he said, that West Germany would break with NATO; he wanted to establish full-fledged diplomatic relations, including exchange of ambassadors. That evening both parties attended the ballet "Romeo and Juliet," based on the story of the ancient feud of the Capulets and Montagues. During the last scene, when the two young offspring of the feuding families fall into each other's arms, Adenauer rose and extended both hands to Bulganin. The audience enthusiastically applauded this gesture of reconciliation.

Although personal relations had been "normalized," the conference remained deadlocked. The German delegation soon realized that in regard to unification no concession was to be expected and no progress would be achieved. More than once the Soviet leaders emphasized their support of the DDR in glowing words. "The DDR," said Khrushchev, "is the future." Bulganin added that the German people

[27] *Osteuropa*, Stuttgart, December, 1955, p. 451.

support the DDR regime: "We have seen the real attitude of the German population toward their government [during our visit]."[28]

On the prisoners-of-war issue, the Soviet leadership refused to give in. It would have been impossible for them to admit that Adenauer, and not Grotewohl or Ulbricht, had won this concession for Germany. The German delegation announced that under the circumstances only a limited "normalization" of relations, without exchange of ambassadors, could be agreed to. The conference had reached a dead end. Adenauer ordered his plane flown to Moscow to take him back to Bonn.

The most lavish reception the Kremlin had ever seen was arranged. About five hundred guests moved between tables that almost broke down under the weight of plates overfilled with fruit, meat, fish, poultry, bottles of vodka, Georgian and Crimean wines, beer, and lemonade. Every few feet there were little pots of caviar or plates of salad. "It was obvious that this was Moscow's upper strata."[29]

At one of the tables, Khrushchev, Bulganin, Adenauer, Brentano, and the German Socialist leader Carlo Schmidt were deep in conversation on the prisoners-of-war issue. When all the arguments had been exhausted, Schmidt appealed to the "magnanimity" of the Soviet leaders, to their understanding of the feelings of the mothers and children of the German prisoners. As if overcome by emotion, Khrushchev suddenly agreed: "This was a good word; now we can continue."

It was not, however, sentiment that had prompted Khrushchev's concession. To him the "concession"—a few thousand German prisoners—was a trifle; but a breakdown of the negotiations would mean a major failure. At this time relations with West Germany were to him an extremely important matter; even the German delegates did not realize the weight that the Soviet attached to the issue. However, in order to maintain the prestige of the East German satellite, the agreement with West Germany on the prisoners of war was not made official or public; Bulganin and Khrushchev gave their "word of honor" to the German chancellor that no later than a week after the agreement to resume diplomatic relations was reached the prisoners would be permitted to return. The "word of honor" was kept a secret; the Soviet

[28] Erfurt, *op. cit.*, p. 105.
[29] Backhaus, *op. cit.*, p. 77.

Relations with the Bonn Government

press did not mention it. The day after Adenauer's departure it was announced that a delegation of the government of the DDR was on its way to Moscow. When it left Moscow, on September 20, an official statement was released that mentioned "the appeal of the President and government of the DDR and also the request of the government of the Federal German Republic [for the release of the prisoners]."[30] The requests were granted by the Presidium of the Supreme Soviet.

Among the minor questions raised by the Soviet side at the conference was that of the "repatriation" of displaced Soviet persons who, according to the official Soviet version, were being forcibly detained in the West (Moscow could not admit that Soviet citizens were remaining abroad voluntarily). The German delegation stated that displaced Soviet citizens were free to leave Germany at any time. In an effort to encourage the repatriation, the Soviet government, on September 17, immediately after the conference, announced its far-reaching amnesty.

Another Soviet complaint had to do with the balloons sent from Germany to the East as part of the American-sponsored "Crusade for Freedom"; the balloons, Molotov told the Germans, carried loads of propaganda material and in addition endangered aviation.

A "cultural relations" program for the two countries was suggested; no objection was raised to this. Discussion of future trade relations between West Germany and the Soviet Union took a considerable place in the conversations; Khrushchev indicated that China in particular was greatly in need of imports and that Germany could gain a large market in the East.

At the conclusion of the negotiations Bulganin and Adenauer exchanged written statements on the establishment of diplomatic relations between the German Federal Republic and the Soviet Union and the setting up of embassies in Bonn and Moscow. In a special note Adenauer listed two reservations: the first was in regard to Germany's frontiers, which, Adenauer proposed, "be drawn in a peace treaty"; the second stressed the right of his government to represent the whole of Germany in international affairs. TASS reacted immediately with a statement insisting on the finality of the frontier lines and the powers of the DDR.

[30] The final communiqué stated that the DDR had raised the prisoners-of-war question in June, that is, prior to Adenauer's visit.

The Soviet leaders and the Soviet press expressed satisfaction with the outcome of the negotiations; it appeared that the agreements reached in Moscow represented a substantial step forward on the road to the Soviet-planned European setup. To the West, on the other hand, Adenauer's tactics in Moscow were a matter of controversy because in regard to his main goal, reunification, nothing had been achieved. The British and American press were loud in their criticism. In its effort to defend Adenauer, the United States State Department exaggerated his success; it stated that the agreement meant "abandonment by the Soviet Union of its bankrupt German policies," even a "victory for the West."

Subsequent developments proved that the "normalization of relations" achieved in Moscow was rather limited and after a short time relations deteriorated anew.

For a long time after the Moscow Conference the two phases of the repatriation operation were the cause of a series of diplomatic conflicts. The reluctance of displaced Soviet citizens in Germany (their number was estimated by the Soviet at as high as 100,000) to return to the Soviet Union irritated Moscow; even after the announcement of the amnesty only few took advantage of the offer, and these included convicted criminals, misfits, and desperate persons; the majority preferred to remain abroad. The Soviet side requested the Germans to supply complete lists of the displaced persons. This demand frightened the DPs because the memory of the early postwar kidnappings and forcible repatriation was still fresh. The Germans, however, refused to produce lists without the consent of the DPs. On the whole, this phase of the repatriation operations was unsuccessful.

As the German prisoners were gradually being returned home, another issue arose that soon became controversial: numbers of German civilians in Russia claimed the right of repatriation; these were mostly former citizens of the Baltic states or of German-occupied Soviet provinces who had acquired German citizenship during the war. The legal problem was an involved one. Moscow vigorously protested the attention paid by the new German Embassy to these persons and their claims.[31]

Other disagreements that might have been easily resolved were aggravating Soviet-German relations. They were a symptom of the

[31] *Izvestia,* May 30, 1956.

Finland: Hesitation and Concessions

presence of a deep-seated irritating factor. The main German problem persisted. The "normalization" achieved in Moscow in September was giving way to a new series of conflicts. Soon Soviet-German relations had again deteriorated to such an extent that in 1958–59 Konrad Adenauer was again Enemy Number One in the roster of Soviet "class enemies."

3. FINLAND: HESITATION AND CONCESSIONS

Since the end of World War II the Soviet course toward Finland had been a sequence of zigzags. The small nation ruled by non-Communist governments was tolerated as an independent neighbor despite the fact that its transformation into a satellite would at certain moments have been possible. There were times, for example in 1948, when such a transformation had already been scheduled and almost initiated; but then the course would change again to one of tolerance and "coexistence." There was the old official Soviet claim that Lenin and Stalin, having made possible Finland's secession from the Russian empire, had helped to maintain her independence. In a room of the Smolny in Leningrad there is a plaque that informs visitors that it was here, in December, 1917, that Lenin signed the declaration of Finland's independence. During the Stalin era it was likewise maintained that since the days of the revolution Stalin had opposed any kind of control by Russia over Finland.[32]

These factors alone were not decisive, of course, in determining Moscow's course. A more important factor was that from a strategic point of view, control of Finland was of less significance to the Soviet Union. Since 1945, Germany had ceased to be Russia's great rival in the Baltic, and the sea itself was now Soviet-dominated. Although Communist ideology and the expansionist urge favored the acquisition of a new member of the "socialist camp," strategic considerations were not as weighty in this case as they were in Poland, Czechoslovakia, or the Balkan satellites.

An even more important factor in the Soviet course toward Finland was the issue of Sweden and Scandinavia as a whole. Transformation of Finland into a "people's democracy" would be followed

[32] For example, *Pravda*, April 8, 1948, editorial.

almost immediately by Sweden's joining the Western alliance, the Marshall Plan, and later NATO, and by her rapid rearming. Of all the Scandinavian countries Sweden was the strongest industrially as well as militarily; though greatly inferior to the Soviet Union, her posture as an opponent or enemy could be a danger. In 1949–53 Sweden, unlike the other Scandinavian countries, was neutral. To the great satisfaction of Moscow, she did not join the Western alliance; her neutrality, however, was tacitly predicated on the independence of the buffer state of Finland. Scandinavia as a whole, under Social-Democratic governments, was never 100 per cent pro-American, and Moscow doubted that it was worthwhile to obtain a foothold in Helsinki at the price of antagonizing a large part of northern Europe.

Early in 1948, when the upheaval in Prague took place, everything seemed ready for a coup in Finland, too. The sizable Finnish Communist organization was alerted; Soviet arms arrived. A mutual assistance pact on the pattern of the Baltic pacts of 1939, giving the Soviet Union the privilege of stationing its army in Finland, was proposed by Stalin, but Finland rejected the proposal. Stores of Communist arms were confiscated and other military measures were taken by the Finnish government. The Finnish army remained loyal. At the last moment Stalin retreated and called off the offensive.

Instead, the Soviet government, on April 6, 1948, concluded a treaty of "Friendship, Cooperation and Mutual Assistance" with Finland. The treaty, to remain in force until 1975, was actually an agreement between a defeated country and its vanquisher; it not only obligated Finland to resist aggression on the part of Germany "or her allies," but provided for armed Soviet assistance and the ominous "consultation" (Paragraph 2) with Moscow, which to the Finns was tantamount to Soviet dictation. Both Finland and the Soviet Union were obliged to refrain from joining coalitions "aimed at the other contracting party"—a provision that not only prohibited Finland from adhering to NATO but prohibited her from joining local Scandinavian conferences if Moscow was opposed. And Moscow, under Stalin-Molotov, was opposed.

Finland's adherence to the Nordic Council, which had been conceived as a regional association of five smaller powers (Sweden, Norway, Denmark, Iceland, and Finland), was opposed by Moscow. True

Finland: Hesitation and Concessions

to his general view of all coalitions and international combinations in proximity to the Soviet borders as inimical and anti-Soviet, Stalin considered the emerging Nordic Council as a link in the NATO chain; since Sweden could not openly join the main Western alliance, the Nordic Council, Moscow maintained, would serve as a subsidiary embracing Sweden and Finland. Nor did the Soviet government believe the objectives of the Nordic Council to be purely economic, social, and cultural; it insisted, although it never offered proof of this, that the real aims were military. Consequently, while Sweden joined the Nordic Council, Finland abstained; a place in the Council was left vacant for her in the event the situation should one day change.

Molotov, a co-author of Soviet-Finnish treaties and agreements, saw no reason to deviate from the old course after Stalin's death. In 1953 and 1954 statements and articles in the Soviet press [33] continued to condemn the Nordic Council as a tool of the United States and a preparatory stage for aggression. Other phases of Soviet-Finnish relations likewise remained intact. The hope of the Finnish people that the Soviet government would some day return a part of the large Finnish territory that had been formally annexed to the Soviet Union in 1947 was a vain one. The only gestures of friendship made by the Soviet government were the insignificant ones of elevating the Soviet and Finnish legations to embassies and bestowing the Order of Lenin on Finnish President Paasikivi.

Molotov continued his efforts to bind Finland more tightly to Moscow. During the second half of 1954 Finnish leaders met three times with Soviet ministers, and at each encounter an attempt in this direction was made (in July, during Kekkonen's stay in Moscow for trade negotiations; in November, during Mikoyan's visit to Helsinki; and on December 6, at the reception in the Finnish Embassy in Moscow). Moscow repeatedly invited the Finnish government to send a military delegation of high rank to the Soviet Union, but the Finnish commander in chief, General Heiskanan ("Cold Charlie"), contrary to the desire of his government, refused to go.[34] In 1954 Finland refused to take part in the conferences which would have led her into

---
[33] For example, *Izvestia*, April 10, 1953; *Kommunist*, Moscow, no. 2, 1954, pp. 104–7; *Pravda*, August 17, 1954.
[34] "Is this an order?" he asked the Premier. "No, not an order." "Good," said the General; "otherwise I would have tendered my resignation." Not until 1956 did a Finnish military mission visit Moscow; General Heiskanan himself went there for the first time in April, 1959.

the Warsaw Pact, and Molotov's hope of having at least one non-Communist-controlled nation in the Pact was frustrated.

The next year, 1955, the year of Malenkov's decline and Khrushchev's rise, the year of Bandung, the "Summit," and "relaxation," brought changes in Soviet-Finnish relations and some Soviet concessions. A start was made in regard to restoring to the Finns the large (152 square miles) Soviet naval base at Porkkala which, under the postwar treaties, had been leased to the Soviet Union for fifty years. Situated only twelve miles from the capital, the base was a source of constant irritation to the Finns. On the twenty miles of railway track from Helsinki to Turku which ran through the Porkkala base, car windows were shuttered, although nothing but forest could be seen from them. A Soviet-manned locomotive took over the train for this run; at the end of the run, the locomotive was again changed. The operation meant the loss of an hour to travelers, and many Finns preferred to use buses which bypassed the area in a roundabout way. In a bitter joke, Porkkala was referred to as "the longest tunnel in the world." On June 27 the Soviet authorities announced that the metal shutters would be removed from the car windows and that locomotives would not be changed.

Early in August, in another gesture of friendship, twenty-seven Finns imprisoned in the Soviet Union after the war were repatriated. In the same month a Soviet-Finnish agreement on scientific and technical cooperation was signed.

In September, when the "relaxation of tensions" campaign had reached its apex, and anti-Stalinism was growing, leaders of the Finnish government were invited to Moscow.

On September 15, the day after Chancellor Adenauer and his large delegation had left Moscow, Juho K. Paasikivi, the Finnish President, and Urho Kekkonen, the Premier, arrived there.

In the course of the negotiations, the eight-year-old treaty of mutual assistance was extended for twenty years without change. The Soviet leaders then announced that the Porkkala naval base would be returned to Finland and that all Soviet forces would be withdrawn; all barracks, stores, railways, and installations would be turned over to Finland without compensation.

The restoration of Porkkala, a major step in Soviet policy, was presented, in exaggerated terms in the official pronouncements, as a

Finland: Hesitation and Concessions

symbol of the Soviet's peaceful course; it was pictured as another chapter in the Soviet campaign for the "abolition of military bases on foreign soil" (the withdrawal from Porkkala had been preceded by the Soviet withdrawal from Port Arthur in May, 1955, while the large Soviet military bases in the satellites were considered to be in another category). Now Moscow was appealing to the West to follow the Soviet example. Premier Bulganin praised the withdrawal from Porkkala as a move toward general disarmament; and *Pravda*[35] wrote: ". . . the example shown by the Soviet Union should be supported by other great powers."

In the ten years since the end of the war the Porkkala base had lost much of its military importance. The Soviet Union had rebuilt and fortified the opposite (Soviet-Estonian) coast of the Finnish Gulf; new artillery, long-range arms, and the absence of other strong navies in the Baltic had made the Finnish base not only unnecessary but too costly in both the monetary and the propaganda sense. Moreover, if strong Soviet bases were maintained in Finland for too long, Sweden might take this as a reason to rearm. Thus, the restoration of Porkkala to Finland was not an act of pure magnanimity; nevertheless, it did not fail to impress the northern countries, to whom it was proof that, at least for the time being, no military aggression threatened from the east.

This impression was strengthened by another Soviet concession—agreement to Finland's joining the Nordic Council. In unpublished conversations during the September visit of the Finnish leaders, the Soviet government announced its change in attitude toward the Council: since the Council consisted of delegates from parliaments, the Finnish Communist Party, too, would be represented. The Council would now consist of five elements—Norway, Denmark, and Iceland from among the NATO powers, and the two neutrals, Sweden and Finland.

The following month a bill was passed by the Finnish Diet enabling Finland to join the Council; out of regard for Moscow's sensibilities, however, the Finnish government announced on this occasion: "'Should the Council discuss questions of a military character or those which demand the statement of its [Finland's] attitude towards problems on which there are differences between the Great Powers, the

[35] September 20, 1955, editorial.

representatives of Finland shall not take part in the discussion of such questions.' " [36]

The ardent desire of the Finns to regain part of the territory ceded to Russia in 1940, however, remained unfulfilled. It was expected that some day, and without a serious conflict, certain areas in the region of the Saime Canal, or even Viipuri, would be returned to Finland. The issue was raised during the September conversations in Moscow; the Soviet refusal was definite and final. Reporting to the Finnish Parliament on October 4, Premier Kekkonen said, without going publicly into the matter, that the Soviet government had rejected certain Finnish suggestions, and that he had failed to win all the concessions he had hoped for.

This failure to make greater concessions to the Finns indicated the limitations of Khrushchev's new policy. Although unrealistic, the Finnish hopes of regaining the lost territory were so strong that Khrushchev found it necessary, several years later, to put an end to them by a violent attack on "certain newspapers in Finland," in which he insisted on the finality of the established *status quo* as the only alternative to war.[37]

Thus, the Stalin-Molotov treaty of 1948, with the privileges it bestowed on the Soviet Union as well as the frontier line established after Finland's defeat, remained in force. Finland's neutrality, which was proclaimed about the same time as Austria's, differed greatly, however, from the latter's, which was guaranteed by the powers, including the Soviet Union. Finland's neutrality, unlike that of Switzerland and Austria, countries which had complete independence, was coupled with a permanent obligatory tie to the Soviet Union and aloofness from the other powers.

4. THE FIRST SUMMIT CONFERENCE

We have seen how Winston Churchill, the most sensitive of all the leaders of his time to new political breezes, became attentive to the new Soviet developments and suggested a meeting with the Soviet leadership. His idea, however, of an "informal conference," a "conference without an agenda," did not materialize, partly because

---
[36] *International Affairs*, Moscow, no. 4, April, 1956, p. 34.
[37] *Pravda*, May 24, 1958.

The First Summit Conference

Churchill himself fell ill and for some months was out of action politically.[38] The Berlin Conference of the four foreign ministers, which followed the Bermuda Conference of the three Western powers, was formal and businesslike and not what Churchill had in mind, and except for the decision to convene the conference on Asia in Geneva it had been abortive.

From that time on, proposals for conferences with the supreme Soviet leadership developed in Europe and America from a diplomatic device into a popular slogan. Churchill's idea lost its ingredient of caution and began to be considered a cure-all. The conviction that a conference—the mere fact of government leaders sitting down together—means progress was sad proof of the still low level of popular understanding of international problems.

The following year Churchill resumed his efforts. On his visit to Washington in the summer of 1954 he became convinced that the United States was still reluctant about a conference with the Soviet leaders. The United States, however, had no objection to Churchill making a try himself. On his way back to England, on July 4, Churchill sent Molotov a "secret and personal" cable inquiring how the Soviet government would like the idea of an "informal" conference, to last several days, with "no agenda, no objective"—just the two governments, the British and the Soviet, meeting in some neutral capital, Stockholm, Bern, or Vienna, for example. Molotov replied affirmatively on July 6. Some time elapsed between the exchange of notes and the closing of the Geneva Conference, at which both Molotov and Eden were busy. Before the promising correspondence could be resumed, Moscow dispatched notes to the European powers and the United States inviting them to a general conference.[39] This move, Churchill wrote later, "came as a rude shock"; he told Molotov in a cable that it had made the two-nation unofficial parley superfluous. In a new exchange of messages, Churchill explained why it would not be possible to hold both of the two proposed conferences; Molotov disagreed.[40]

Molotov's diplomatic actions of that time were part of the consistent Soviet drive against the European Defense Community and

[38] See pp. 127–129.
[39] See p. 160.
[40] *Pravda*, March 18, 1955.

the rearming of Germany; the large conference urgently proposed by Moscow was part of this drive. In his attempt to arrange the smaller parley, Churchill, who in this respect differed from many other political leaders in the West, was not prepared to relinquish the arming of Germany as a *quid pro quo* for Soviet concessions. To him an armed German power was an issue of the very first importance; he left no doubt that in his proposed meetings with Molotov and Malenkov he would try to convince them to take this part of the West's program as a *fait accompli* and acquiesce in it.

This was the reason why the Soviet government was not enthusiastic about Churchill's suggestion. In its view, "the fight against the new German militarism" had not yet been resolved, and the outcome of this fight was uncertain. To Moscow, international meetings made sense only if they helped to abolish the new Paris agreements or prevent their ratification. Churchill was aware that this was Molotov's position, and he preferred to delay his conference until the agreements providing for the rearming of Germany were final.

"Peace through strength," Churchill said in the House of Commons on March 14, in one of his last speeches as prime minister:

> What is of major consequence to the cause we serve is to range the mighty German race and nation with the free world instead of allowing it by infiltration or territorial bribery, by actual force or by our own tragic memories, to be amalgamated with the satellite states to carry the doctrine and control of Moscow into world supremacy.

In January, 1955, French Premier Mendès-France wrote Churchill that, since France could not leave unanswered the Soviet denunciation of the Franco-Soviet alliance, it would be sensible to convene a four-power conference in May and to begin negotiations. Churchill feared another French delaying maneuver in regard to German rearmament. No, he answered; so long as the rearming of Germany was not definitely accepted, negotiations must be delayed:

> I cannot feel . . . that at this juncture any negotiations with the Soviets about a four-power meeting . . . would help our common cause. Weakness makes no appeal to the Soviets. To mix up the process of ratification with what might well follow soon afterwards would very likely dilute both firmness and conciliation. The sooner we can get our united ratification the sooner the top-level four-power conference may come.

Although we have every sympathy with you in your difficulties and admiration for your exertions, the fact should be accepted that I and my colleagues are wholeheartedly resolved that there shall be no meeting or invitation in any circumstances which we can foresee between the four powers, either on the Foreign Secretaries level or on that of the heads of governments, until the London-Paris agreement have been ratified by all the signatories. In this we are in the closest accord with the United States. I cannot believe there is the slightest chance of any change of attitudes on this point in either of our two countries. Indeed, I feel that an indefinite process of delay may well lead to the adoption of other solutions, which are certainly being studied on both sides of the Atlantic. (*Keesing's Contemporary Archives,* 1955–56, p. 14228.)

In March, France definitely joined her allies in subscribing to the Paris agreements. Now there appeared to be no obstacles to an international conference, which was being loudly and vehemently demanded by various groups in the West. At his press conference of March 23, President Eisenhower proposed that the conference be convened; three days later Premier Bulganin approved the idea. British Foreign Secretary Harold Macmillan frankly told the House of Commons that the call for a summit conference was tied up with the new agreements on Germany. The ratification documents, he said, would be deposited by May 5 and would become effective the same day; four days later the meeting of NATO would open at which Adenauer would take part in the negotiations.

The summit conference was set to convene in Geneva on July 18. However, Churchill, the most consistent partisan of a summit conference with the Soviet leaders, a man who may be viewed as the father of the conference of 1955, was unable to take part in it; he had retired, because of advanced age, only three months before his favorite idea materialized. On the other hand, he was spared the great disappointment that would have been his had he been one of the leaders of a parley which, viewed historically, was the product of a chain of misunderstandings and which bore no fruit whatsoever.

The misunderstandings in the West related to the Soviet motivations. Ranking officers of the United States State Department assumed that the Soviet eagerness to go to Geneva was due to Soviet economic weakness and its need to buy certain goods abroad, and that therefore it would be willing to make substantial concessions to the West. Testifying before a House subcommittee on June 10, Secretary of State Dulles said that "the economy of the Soviet Union is on the point of collapsing." [41] The West was free, therefore, to advance far-reaching demands—for example, the liberation of the satellites and the curbing of international Communist activities—which had good prospects of being met. It is difficult to understand from what kind of intelligence these conclusions were drawn, but they, too, foredoomed the forthcoming conference.

On the other hand, Moscow's understanding of the Western course was no better. It was assumed that France had accepted German rearmament *contre-coeur,* that she actually preferred a divided Germany, and that now the West, acquiescing in the partition of Europe, would settle with Moscow on the *status quo.* A number of designs for this *status quo,* elaborated, as always, in great detail in the Soviet Foreign Office, and titled "Collective Security in Europe," etc., had been prepared for the Summit Conference.

On the German issue Moscow was prepared to stop its futile "campaign" against the Paris agreements, reconcile itself to the fact that West Germany was an independent and sovereign state, and reconcile itself to Germany's membership in NATO and the West European Union. After six years of violent opposition and threats, the Soviet government recognized that a change in its course was imperative. The change was to coincide with the Summit Conference.

In April, *New Times* [42] had written, in the old style:

> Those who succumb to the illusion that the Soviet Union has reconciled itself to the Paris agreements are headed for disappointment. Neither the Soviet Union nor the other peaceable European states can reconcile themselves to the resurrection of German militarism, for it would enhance the danger of war. . . . Only if the idea of rearming Western Germany and making it a party to military blocs is renounced, can the conditions be created for an effective solution of the German problem.

Two months later, however, Bulganin announced:

> . . . in the present state of affairs the Soviet government must reckon with the fact that Western Germany has joined the North-Atlantic alliance and Western European Union and that the Paris agreements

---

[41] This statement was not revealed until a month later (*The New York Times,* July 8, 9, and 12, 1955).

[42] Moscow, no. 14, April 2, 1955, "Talks for Relaxation of Tensions."

The First Summit Conference

have been ratified. The Soviet government does not at this stage suggest renunciation of the Paris agreements or that Western Germany resign from these alignments, that would be absolutely unrealistic.[43]

This was the only concession on Germany envisaged by Moscow. On the other German issue the Soviet government remained firm at Geneva: the West must recognize two Germanys. The demand for "reunification," which under Stalin had been tantamount to extension of the Eastern satellite to Western Germany, was dropped altogether; the Eastern satellite, however, was to be maintained and defended, and no Soviet concession on this issue was envisaged. Possibly, the Khrushchev group still underestimated—this was 1955—the significance of Germany's reconstruction in the eyes of the West, but the stubborn rejection of this program by the Soviet leaders doomed the conference.

However, "relaxation of tensions" among the great powers was not the sum total of the Soviet foreign political course of the time. Behind the screen of "coexistence," "relaxation," and "no cold war" the Soviet government—and here Khrushchev was again the driving power—was pursuing a grand offensive in the underdeveloped countries of Asia and Africa. As the Geneva Conference was being prepared, the Soviet-protected Bandung Conference was declaring its offensive against the West; this was followed by secret Soviet-Egyptian negotiations concerning Soviet and satellite arms for Egypt. At the very time that Bulganin and Khrushchev were attending a summit conference to "lessen international tensions," Dimitri Shepilov was in Cairo for talks with Colonel Nasser.

From all four capitals the road to Geneva was strewn with roses. For so long had the Summit Conference been talked about, wished for, demanded, and postponed, that when it finally was set to convene, the event was hailed with great enthusiasm. The World Council of Churches called for prayers. Nehru of India, Tito of Yugoslavia, U Nu of Burma voiced their hopes. All kinds of conventions, societies, and circles adopted resolutions and sent greetings. Thirteen hundred representatives of the press—a record number—applied for press cards. The International Socialist Congress, convening in London in mid-July, unreservedly greeted the forthcoming Summit Conference.

[43] *New Times*, Moscow, no. 31, July 28, 1955, Supplement, p. 4.

At the reception in the United States Embassy in Moscow on the Fourth of July, Khrushchev, Bulganin, and five members of the Presidium made their first appearance at the United States Embassy. Khrushchev addressed the select audience to refute the idea that the Soviet economy was in bad shape and that he was going abroad to try to remedy the Soviet's economic ills. His speech was not printed in the Soviet press, obviously in order not to disturb the optimistic mood on the eve of the summit.

Nor was the controversy about the "iron-curtain countries" and the "activities of international Communism" permitted to mar the festive presummit mood. Moscow tried to leave no doubt about its attitude toward these issues. The official TASS statement of June 14 read:

> Arguments to the effect that the conference should discuss such questions as "the problem of the countries of Eastern Europe" or "the activities of international Communism" cannot have anything in common with the desire to reach constructive results at the conference. It should be clear to all that there is no "problem of the countries of Eastern Europe," for the peoples of these countries, having overthrown the rule of exploiters, have set up popular democratic governments in their countries and will not permit anyone to interfere in their domestic affairs.
>
> As for the question of "the activities of international Communism," one might well ask how Mr. Dulles would regard the raising of the question of "the activities of international capitalism," for example, at the four-power conference.[44]

Eastern Europe, in this context, included East Germany. Unification of Germany was relegated to the background; it was drowned in a vague Soviet formula of "European security" or "collective security" which from now on was to be juxtaposed with genuine unification. Not until "a democratic [meaning that a Communist party could exist legally] and peace-loving [meaning either neutral or ally of the Soviet Union] Germany is restored will she occupy a worthy place." [45]

The expectations of the conference were optimistic, but the omens were not favorable.

The Soviet delegation was officially led by Premier Nikolai Bulganin. The other four members were Vyacheslav Molotov and Andrei

[44] *Pravda*, June 14, 1955.
[45] TASS statement of July 13, 1955.

The First Summit Conference

Gromyko of the Foreign Ministry, Defense Minister Marshal Georgi Zhukov, and a man with the modest rank of "member of the Presidium of the Supreme Soviet," Nikita S. Khrushchev. The wheel horses were, of course, Molotov and Gromyko; the overriding chief was Khrushchev. Zhukov was brought along to spread good humor as the smiling wartime "pal" of President Eisenhower; both sides were of course aware of the primitive character of this method of *rapprochement*. The Soviet delegates outdid themselves in displaying their new non-Stalinist look, riding in open cars, talking freely and in a friendly fashion with all and sundry, and toasting everybody at dinners and receptions. Repeating the Russian phrase, Western newspapermen reported "Russia wants a *détente*."

The optimistic mood did not abate when the heads of the delegations began to make their statements; their differing programs were viewed as the first stage of bargaining. President Eisenhower spoke of three issues: Germany, Eastern Europe, and international Communism; Edgar Faure for France and Anthony Eden for Britain followed suit. Bulganin proposed the well-known Soviet plan of pacification of Europe—disarmament, prohibition of atomic weapons, a collective security pact, withdrawal of foreign troops. Reunification of Germany, he said, "is made difficult" by the rearming of her Western part. He praised neutrality, which, he said, had been adopted as a policy by some governments as a pattern for other nations. As to the two main controversial themes of Eisenhower's statement, Bulganin said:

> We all know that the system of people's democracy was established there by the peoples themselves, through free expression of their will. Apart from everything else, we are not empowered to examine the situation in these countries.
> Thus there is no warrant for this question being discussed at our conference.
> Mention was also made here of the question of so-called "international communism." But we know that this conference was convened to discuss inter-governmental relations, and not the activities of political parties in the various countries, or the relations between these parties. We therefore believe that raising this question in the Conference of Heads of Governments cannot be considered appropriate.[46]

[46] *New Times*, Moscow, no. 30, July 21, 1955, Supplement, p. 19.

The two issues vetoed by Bulganin remained undiscussed; three points proposed by Bulganin for inclusion in the agenda—cessation of the cold war, neutrality, and Asia and the Far East—were likewise rejected. The concentration was on the issue of Germany which, in the Soviet plans, had been included in "collective security." The somewhat vague idea behind the Soviet draft of a plan was that "the two Germanys," admitted into a newly created all-embracing European organization, would achieve *rapprochement* and eventually merge into a single state. How and why this would happen was not explained. The Soviet delegation made it clear that aside from this it would refuse to discuss reunification of Germany. The actual rejection of "reunification"—a program that Moscow had proclaimed for a number of years—was motivated by West Germany's recent joining of NATO and her rearming.

The Soviet plan revived a former Western disarmament plan that would have limited the regular armies of nations other than the big four and China to a maximum of 150,000 to 200,000, as compared to the limit of 1,000,000 to 1,500,000 proposed for the Soviet Union, China, and the United States. Under this plan West Germany would be barred from attaining a new stature in international affairs, and this would recompense the Soviet government for the Paris agreements.

Eisenhower's contribution to the disarmament discussion was the idea of mutual aerial photography, the so-called "open skies" plan; this was not accepted by the Soviet delegation. The "Collective Security Pact for Europe," which Bulganin submitted to the conference, provided for the inclusion of the United States, along with an "observer" from Communist China; it also provided for the abolition of both NATO and the Warsaw Pact.

In three days of sessions the parties did not budge from their positions; the Soviet group was least of all inclined to change its political itinerary, which had been well laid out in advance. Since no real agreements on the questions discussed were possible, it was decided, in order not to have to announce the failure of the parley, to throw all the issues of the summit into the lap of a one-step-below-the-summit conference of foreign ministers. A collective "directive of the heads" to their foreign ministers, agreed upon by the four leaders,

The First Summit Conference

was a complete catalogue of current problems, with no hint as to how they might be resolved.

The Summit Conference closed on July 23.

The Soviet public was spared the disappointment and disillusionment that permeated the Western press after the close of the Summit Conference. Nobody in Russia said that the conference had been futile. This was in line with the usual practice: since the government had long advocated the conference, and its delegates had voted for its final "directives," an air of optimism, and even a pretense of victory, had to be maintained. For several weeks the Soviet radio and press claimed that the "cold war" was over, the hated American "position of strength" had been abandoned, and a "relaxation of tensions" had been inaugurated. "The spirit of Geneva," a popular phrase in the West during the first stages of the fruitless parley, survived in Russia for much longer. On August 4, *New Times*, mouthpiece of the Foreign Office, headed its leading article "The Geneva Spirit," and said:

> It [the conference] has changed the climate of the world arena and marked the beginning of a turn from the "cold war" to an atmosphere of mutual trust between countries. . . . Less than two weeks have passed since the Conference ended, but its beneficent effect is already making itself felt in various spheres of international relations. Primarily this is evident in the altered nature and tone of the statements made by many political leaders and the press in the Western countries on basic issues of foreign policy.[47]

On his way back to Moscow, Khrushchev stopped in Berlin to address a large meeting in the Lustgarten at which he told the East Germans that under the prevailing conditions he did not intend to facilitate reunification: since a Communist government was a great boon for a country, and its economic measures meant great improvement for the "toilers," Soviet policy protected the "real interests" of the German people:

> Could the working class of the German Democratic Republic agree to the elimination of all their political and social achievements, to the elimination of all their democratic reforms? We are convinced that the working class of the German Democratic Republic will never agree to enter such a path.[48]

[47] *Ibid.*, no. 32, August 4, 1955, p. 1.
[48] *Neues Deutschland*, July 28, 1955. Quoted in *Osteuropa*, Stuttgart, October, 1955, p. 369.

The formula was: reunification of Germany, after *rapprochement* between its two parts, "with consideration of the security interests of the peoples of Europe, including those of the German people." In the Soviet view, the "security interests of the peoples of Europe"—for example, Poland, Czechoslovakia, France, Belgium—were opposed to the reemergence of a united Germany. Opposition to the reemergence of a united Germany was definitely indicated as the Soviet course for the foreseeable future.

The "directives" to the foreign ministers issued by the heads of government at the close of the Summit Conference had been prepared at Geneva by the ministers to whom they were addressed and were only signed by the "heads," and they served to conceal the inability of the "historic conference" to achieve substantial results; they postponed the acknowledgment of the failure for a few months. The ministers' conference opened in Geneva on October 27, 1955, and ended three weeks later on November 16.

The main subject of the discussions was, naturally, Directive Number One, entitled "European Security and Germany"; of the fifteen sessions, ten dealt with this issue. The first part of the title was of Soviet origin, the second of Western, and the artificial combination was possible only on paper. The ministers were "instructed to consider," on the one hand, the favorite Soviet proposals, such as non-aggression pacts, limitation of arms, a demilitarized zone, etc.; on the other hand, the directive stated that the settlement of the German question "and the re-unification of Germany by means of free elections shall be carried out in conformity with the national interests of the German people and the interests of European security." [49]

In the discussions, Molotov accentuated "European security," by-passing unification of Germany. Since, he insisted, the words "European security" precede "Germany" in the directive, the ministers must follow that order. The discussion, which lasted several days, revealed no new viewpoints. During a recess of a few days, Molotov flew back to Moscow, and it was the talk around the conference that he would bring back a new shipment of the "Geneva spirit." Any hope that this

---

[49] *The Geneva Conference of Heads of Government, July 18–23, 1955*, Washington, D.C., Department of State, 1955, p. 68.

The First Summit Conference

would be so was disappointed; Molotov returned as inflexible as he had been before.

After another speech by Molotov, Macmillan proposed that discussion of this subject—an essential part of the agenda—be cut short. Molotov, obviously taken by surprise, hastily submitted new "concrete proposals": a limitation on the military forces of each of the two German states to 150,000, a reduction of occupation forces in Germany by 50 per cent, and a nonaggression pact. These new suggestions—the "refrigerator proposals"—did not impress the conference, and discussions ended. No better results were achieved on most of the other issues. Molotov then invited Secretary Dulles and his advisers to a bilateral discussion of other issues, mainly admission of eighteen countries to the United Nations, among them four Soviet satellites. The two sides agreed, except as to Mongolia, which Dulles voted against.

In the conference halls pessimism was universal. All the talk was of "deadlock," "failure," and the waning "spirit." Correspondents began to depart before the conference ended. When everything was nearly over, Molotov made an attempt to save the face of the conference: he circulated a paper containing proposals which, he thought, might be acceptable to all the parties—nonaggression, the need of disarming, etc. The meaningless proposals were rejected.

The three-week parley of the ministers had been a complete failure, as had been the parent Summit Conference. The Soviet government placed the blame on the Western powers. It firmly adhered to its course and, since Germany had been the crucial issue, left no doubt that it would not budge from its concept of "two Germanys." The "Geneva spirit" had not waned, Moscow said; its purity was being sustained by Moscow:

> The Soviet Union had invariably displayed good will. Even a cursory perusal of the proposals it put forth in Geneva will show that all of them are based on a realistic understanding of the situation, and are motivated by a desire to cooperate and lay groundwork for practical agreement between the Four Powers.[50]

[50] *New Times*, Moscow, no. 48, November 24, 1955, p. 3.

CHAPTER 4

THE UNCOMMITTED NATIONS

At the end of the Korean War the structure of the Soviet bloc was as follows: the Soviet Union proper, the geographic kernel of the complex edifice, was surrounded by a belt of allies, the "people's democracies," stretching along almost the entire perimeter from the Baltic to the Black sea and thence to the Sea of Japan. At the outer edge of this belt of satellites, and surrounding them, was a belt of uncommitted "neutrals," [1] neither allies nor foes, a kind of no man's land between East and West.

The satellite and neutral belts were not unbroken, however, and this was a source of major Soviet policy problems. Attention was focused on the gaps.

1. On their outer edge, East Germany and Czechoslovakia were unprotected by a "neutral"; they bordered on a growing German Federal Republic, avowedly pro-Western and an overt ally of the United States. This situation was one of the main issues of Soviet foreign policy.

2. A gap existed in the south, in the Caspian region, at the Turkish and Iranian frontiers. This was the only point at which the Soviet Union itself bordered on territory of pro-Western powers. Despite the fact that these two neighbors were powers of secondary importance, their pro-Western course rendered the Soviet defense line imperfect. This situation was part of the Soviet problem in the Middle East.

3. North Korea did not border on a neutral country; its neighbor was the pro-American Republic of Korea.

As far as Soviet policy was concerned, what emerged in the early 1950's was two different groups of neutrals. One group was neutral by reason of force of circumstances, the other by reasons of ideology.

---

[1] The leadership of the uncommitted nations often reject the term "neutrals," preferring to stress their nonadherence to power blocs.

The Uncommitted Nations

The power radiated by a great nation, armed on a grand scale, dynamic and sometimes aggressive, able to help but also to retaliate, able to defend but also to browbeat, is sometimes decisive for the political course of that nation's small, weak neighbors. The latter are restricted in their political moves. They cannot defy the great neighbor; they must rather accommodate themselves, however painful such accommodation may be. The neutral countries of Finland, Austria, and Afghanistan were in this first group. On either the east or north they bordered on the Soviet Union; their other borders were a sea, a desert, and another small power. For these countries the radiated power came from the east or north, not from the south or west, although the populations of at least Finland and Austria were pro-Western. A fourth "neutral" in this first group was Tito's Yugoslavia. A peculiar plant in the international garden, Yugoslavia could prosper only as a kind of neutral between East and West, because a victory of either side over the other would be fatal to Yugoslavia's political system.

The second type of neutralism, which had been emerging slowly since the late 1940's in Asia and Africa, did not reach full bloom until the middle of the 1950's. This neutralism was based on principle and ideology; it was businesslike, but it had also an emotional perspective. Developing, as it did, into a major phenomenon on the international scene, it soon changed the Soviet outlook in both the Middle and Far East.

The process of emancipation of colonial and dependent countries that set in after World War II, and which occurred mostly without violent revolutions or real wars, was "liberation" to the nations concerned. It closed a long chapter in their history. They were now entering, they believed, an era of progress, greater well-being, and peace. Their past had been one of serfdom and slavery; their future would be one of self-rule and freedom. The hated past was embodied in "the West," represented by Britain, Holland, France, and other Western powers; the present was themselves.

The effects of decades of liberation movements, with their street fighting, persecution, underground activities, imprisonment, and violent death were still felt when the new era began. The generation that had come to power between 1945 and 1953 in India, Indonesia, Burma,

Egypt, and a number of other nations had grown up in a climate of antagonism toward the "imperialist" nations; now, moving into governmental offices and parliaments, it brought with it its traditions, its affections and hatreds, its sympathies and feelings of gratitude toward friends.

Among these friends was the Soviet Union, traditional partisan of "liberation of colonial peoples," mainstay of anti-Westernism, archenemy of Britain in the 1920's and '30's. When crises in the old empire had shaken the ancient structures, the Soviet leadership and the Soviet press had rushed to the support of the "subjugated and exploited"—at least in fiery propaganda. Publications in all languages, Comintern resolutions, broadcasts, and speeches before international forums had created the image of the Soviet state as the paramount anti-imperialist power. Little was known about the nationality issue inside Russia, and later in the satellites, and the leaders of the turbulent Orient cared little about these controversial developments in far-off lands. Paradoxically, the fact that the Soviet drive to the south in 1945–47 had been a failure and that Russia was unable to acquire territory from Iran, Turkey, or the Arab nations had helped to enhance the image of her as an unselfish, liberating power.

The most outstanding leader of these liberated nations *in statu nascendi* was Jawaharlal Nehru, India's prime minister since the beginning of the new era. Nehru had spent ten years in British prisons. In 1928, after a visit to Russia, the gifted leader, certainly a non-Communist, had published a book in which he took, however, an extreme pro-Soviet position. ". . . I had no doubt that the Soviet Revolution had advanced human society by a great leap and had lit a bright flame which could not be smothered, and that it had laid the foundations for that new civilization towards which the world could advance." [2] Nehru's description of the Soviet economy, Soviet constitutions, and Soviet courts was in accord with official Soviet versions. He did not explain the role of the Communist Party in government. Soviet criminal law he found humane; of Soviet prisons he had "a most favorable impression." "We have the general law of the land applied humanely to the great majority of the population, say 95 per cent, and 5 per cent or so being suspected and watched and treated badly." In

[2] Jawaharlal Nehru, *The Discovery of India*, 2d ed., London, Meridian Books, Ltd., 1947, p. 13.

The Uncommitted Nations 289

the last chapter of his book Nehru discussed Britain, India, and Russia. He believed, as did the 1927 Stalin, that the war danger was acute because Britain wanted a war and was preparing for it. "England is notoriously preparing for war"; she "refuses to agree to any effective scheme for disarmament." Her "policy is to encircle Russia by pacts and alliances and ultimately to crush her," yet "Russia eagerly desires to avoid war." Therefore, a close alliance of India with Russia is advisable:

> We must continually proclaim, with words of the Madras Congress resolution, that in the event of the British Government embarking on any warlike adventure and endeavouring to exploit India in it for the furtherance of their imperialist aims, it will be the duty of the people of India to refuse to take any part in such a war or to co-operate with them in any way whatsoever! And if this declaration is made repeatedly and emphatically it may be that England may hesitate to embark on this adventure and India and the world may be spared the horrors of another great war.[3]

Nehru retained his convictions, as well as some of his illusions, about the Soviet Union when he came to power.

Another leader of an emancipated nation, President Sukarno of Indonesia, had spent fourteen years in prisons and had suffered deportation and exile. In his speeches as a defendant at a trial in 1930 [4] the Indonesian leader addressed the public as "comrades," quoted from the outstanding Marxists of the time, and used all the Marxist terms—"capitalist exploitation," "investment of capital as a source of imperialism," etc.[5]

U Nu, the outstanding leader of Burma, had been tried and sentenced to imprisonment before the war. Even in Egypt, where Communism was illegal and the Naguib-Nasser leadership had *not* languished in British jails, pro-Soviet and pro-Communist intellectuals were serving the new government as mouthpieces, interpreters, and executors. ". . . It is probably no exaggeration," writes an outstanding authority, "to say that most of the writers in the influential Egyptian dailies and weeklies are Communists who were arrested and im-

---
[3] *Ibid.*, pp. 197–98.
[4] The speeches were published in Moscow in book form after the attitude toward Sukarno changed.
[5] Sukarno, *Indoneziya Obvinyaet: Sellornik Statei i Rechei* (Indonesia Accuses: Collection of Articles and Speeches), Moscow, 1956.

prisoned at one time or another between 1950 and 1955. They have to a large extent created today's political climate in Egypt." [6]

This combination of anti-Western non-Communist trends produced the brand of neutralism which after the war, with Moscow's support, grew and asserted itself. In India's dispute with Portugal over Goa, Moscow supported India; when Indonesia claimed West Irian (New Guinea) from Holland, Moscow was on the side of Indonesia; when Egypt claimed Suez and demanded that the British be driven from the Mediterranean, she was encouraging two of Moscow's cherished dreams. The Korean War helped the emerging trend toward neutralism to acquire shape. Among the twenty belligerents in Korea, the "emancipated" nations, with their half billion population, were conspicuous by their absence; no Indian, Pakistani, Indonesian, Burmese, or Arab troops were among the United Nations forces. India chose the role of mediator and peacemaker in the conflict. Thus, entering onto the stage of world affairs, these Asian and African nations assumed a position that made *rapprochement* with the Soviet Union possible.

1. NO NEUTRALS?

There was no place in Stalinism for neutral nations or parties. For Stalin, the world was divided into two "camps"—the capitalist and the socialist—and there was no room for anyone between the fronts. He who is not with us is against us; he who is not our ally is our enemy. "Neutrality is a term to deceive the people," Mao Tse-tung echoed. It was all very simple.

This view, applied to all nations everywhere, assumed particular importance with respect to former colonies and semicolonial countries, which, according to Stalin's teaching, were unable to achieve independence by means of their own nationalist forces. At the present stage of history, according to this teaching, all "bourgeois parties," including leftist groups, had lost the courage and capacity to fight the imperialist powers; only the working class, meaning the Communist Party, or a coalition of parties in which Communists prevail, had the will and the power necessary for this task.

[6] Walter Z. Laquer, "The Prospects of Communism in the Middle East," in *Ter the Middle East*, ed. by Philip W. Thayer, Baltimore, The Johns Hopkins Univers 1958, p. 301.

When the proletariat enters the fight [for national liberation] as an independent political force, the upper strata of the national bourgeoisie betrays its people, and goes over to the camp of the imperialists. . . . At present the proletariat is the hegemon in this fight.[7]

The best example of the validity of this view, according to the Soviet teaching, was China, which, for as long as she had been headed by "bourgeois" leaders and the Kuomintang, had not been able to throw off the imperialist yoke, but had won real sovereignty under the rule of a Communist regime.

These ideas had been incorporated in a resolution of the Sixth Congress of the Communist International: the bourgeoisie, the resolution stated, is unable to liberate a colonial or semicolonial nation; it betrays its people and allies itself with imperialism; therefore, liberation can be achieved only under the leadership of the working class, meaning the Communist Party, meaning in alliance with the Soviet Union.

> The national bourgeoisie's betrayal of the colonies and semicolonies and its rapprochement with the imperialist powers lead in the end to tightening of the imperialist yoke, to a decline in the influence of the national bourgeoisie over the masses of the people, to the sharpening of the revolutionary crisis, to the unleashing of the agrarian revolution of the widest masses of peasants and to the creation of favorable conditions for the hegemony of the proletariat in its struggle for full national liberation.[8]

Prevailing over all rival trends and ideas, these principles became dominant in international Communism; they were incorporated into the programs of the Asian and African Communist parties; they controlled the Communist attitude toward the "nationalist bourgeoisie" and socialist parties; they served as the rationale for political exclusivity, insurrections, upheavals. In Russia the principles were taught in schools and universities and determined the propaganda line and the attitude of the press; they were part of the iron fund of international Communism. Scores of books were published, some written by out-

---

[7] *Large Soviet Encyclopedia* (in Russian), 2d ed., Moscow, 1951, vol. 6, p. 316.
[8] *Sixth Congress of the Communist International,* August 9–14, 1928, *The Colonial Question,* vol. 3 (in Russian), p. 162. Subsequently the role of the national bourgeoisie in colonial revolutions was discussed more than once and the question was solved in different ways. (A review in *Problemy Vostokovedeniya* [Problems of Orientology], Moscow, no. 2, 1959, pp. 60–75.)

standing Soviet experts on the Orient, to illustrate the unreliability and treacherous role of the "bourgeoisie and its lackeys."

> ... the Indian big bourgeoisie has become a specially trusted gendarme at the service of the Anglo-American imperialist masters. The development of historical events in Indonesia after the Second World War shows that the Indonesian bourgeoisie is also taking to a similar path. Bourgeois leaders like Sukarno and Hatta who for the time being headed the Indonesian Republic, from the very beginning oriented themselves toward the attainment of a "decent compromise with imperialism." [9]

When a number of Asian countries achieved independence after the war by means of "non-Chinese" strategies, under non-Communist leadership, and without military conflicts with the mother countries, Moscow's reaction was one of profound disbelief. What these countries had achieved, the Soviet said, was a sham, and the countries were still dependencies of the former imperialists. And the national heroes— Gandhi, Nehru, Sukarno, U Nu—were agents and servants of the foreign bourgeoisie. "Gandhism was the most powerful weapon in the hands of the bourgeois-landlord leadership of the National Congress ... he [Gandhi] has always been the principal traitor of the mass national liberation movement." [10]

The same Soviet expert wrote, in 1950: "The political and military-strategic dependence of both dominions [India and Pakistan] on England and the United States had found its expression in agreements which were concluded between these two countries and England at the Imperial Conference in October, 1948, and in April, 1949. ... On January 26, 1950, to deceive the masses, India was proclaimed an independent republic." [11]

On the Philippines the view was similar: "The political and economic system which the United States imperialists thrust upon the Philippines after World War II gives every reason to consider the

---

[9] E. M. Zhukov, "Sharpening Crisis of the Colonial System after World War II" (p. 17), in *Crisis of the Colonial System: National Liberation Struggle of the Peoples of East Asia*, reports presented in 1949 to the Pacific Institute of the Academy of Sciences, USSR, Bombay, People's Publishing House.

[10] A. M. Dyakov, "Crisis of British Rule in India and the New Stage in the Liberation Struggle of Her Peoples" (pp. 3–4, 32), in *Crisis of the Colonial System, op. cit.*

[11] A. M. Dyakov, *Indiya i Pakistan* (India and Pakistan), Moscow, Pravda Publishing House, 1950, p. 8.

No Neutrals?

Philippines not a sovereign state but an indirectly ruled colony."[12]

Moscow believed that U Nu had become premier of Burma after a number of Burmese ministers had been assassinated "at the instigation of British military circles." He was "closely connected with the heads of the Buddhist clergy and was supported by the 'socialist party,' which represents the interests of the Burmese bourgeoisie. . . . Burma is a state of landowners and capitalists, dependent on British monopoly capital."[13]

"The National Congress in India, Quirino and Romulo in the Philippines, etc. are obedient executors of the will of the British-American imperialists, their mainstay in the colonies."[14]

In Egypt, "at the end of January 1952, the American-British imperialists staged a *coup d'état* and appointed their men. On the night of July 23, 1952, power in Cairo was seized by a group of reactionary officers connected with the United States, with General Naguib at the head."[15]

This attitude toward nations which had recently won their independence was contrary to evident facts; it soon became an obstacle in the course of Soviet foreign affairs. After Stalin's death, and particularly after the emergence of the Khrushchev-Bulganin government, Moscow made strenuous and successful efforts at *rapprochement* with the countries of Asia and Africa; the antagonism of these countries toward the West was the strand with which their ties to the Soviet Union could be woven. A revision of the old tenets was in order. The implications of such a revision were so far-reaching that about a year elapsed before the outline of a new course became discernible.

Soon after Stalin's death, as if to provide an object lesson, history turned the limelight on a country where nationalism was becoming rampant. The revolutionary rumblings in Iran (described above in Part Two, Chap. 6, sec. 2), where the Tudeh (Communist) Party played a significant role, were a kind of test: here the "bourgeois and

---

[12] O. I. Zabolzaeva, "Borba Filippinskogo Naroda za Svoyu Nezavisimost'" (The Struggle of the Philippine Nation for Independence), in *Krizis Kolonialnoi Sistemy: Natsionalno-Osvoboditelnaya Borba Narodov Vostochnoi Azii* (The Crisis of the Colonial System: The National-liberation Struggle of the Peoples of Eastern Asia), Moscow, Akademiya Nauk SSSR, 1949, p. 233.
[13] *Large Soviet Encyclopedia* (in Russian), 2d ed., vol. 5 (1950), pp. 245, 246.
[14] *Ibid.*, vol. 6 (1951), p. 316.
[15] *Ibid.*, vol. 15 (1952), p. 460.

feudal" millionaire leader of the nationalist movement, Mohammed Mossadegh, was following an essentially "neutralist," violently anti-British course. Should he be supported or should he be fought and replaced by a truly "democratic" government? The traditional 100 per cent Stalinist belligerency had been announced in Moscow at the Nineteenth Congress of the Communist Party (1952) by R. Radmanesh on behalf of the Iranians:

> The present political bosses in Iran [Mossadegh] do not display due and resolute resistance to the interference and instigations of the imperialists. Because of their class interests they are not representing the anti-imperialist and anti-feudal movements of the Iranian people. They invariably try to confine the struggle of the Iranian people to half-way actions against the former Anglo-Iranian Oil Company. Therefore the present political bosses are hindering the national-liberation movement of the Iranian people.
> The Iranian People's Party [the Communists] is leading a tenacious struggle for the liquidation of the position of imperialism and reaction in our country. It is unmasking the half-way policy and the hindering role of the present political bosses of Iran. Only the People's Party of the Iranian working class, of the entire toiling people, armed with the ideology of Marxism-Leninism, is the vanguard of the liberation movement of the Iranian people.[16]

At the peak of the revolutionary tension, the Iranian Communists split. About half of their ranking leaders went into exile in Moscow, where they tried to obtain advice from the Central Committee of the CPSU. Obviously—this was the first summer after Stalin's death—no deviation from the Stalinist course was suggested. Mossadegh was actually isolated. In the end he was overthrown by the monarchist group, and the revolutionary successes turned into a catastrophe for the Communist Party.

The following years witnessed the revision of Moscow's course toward nationalism in the underdeveloped countries. On the political level the revision started after the dismissal of Malenkov,[17] with the Bandung Conference and the *rapprochement* with Egypt.

---

[16] *Privetstviya XIX S'yezdu Kommunisticheskoi Partii Sovetskogo Soyuza ot Zarubezhnykh Kommunisticheskikh i Rabochikh Partii* (Greetings to the Nineteenth Congress of the Communist Party of the Soviet Union from Foreign Communist and Workers Parties), Moscow, Pravda Publishing House, 1952, pp. 115–16.
[17] See pp. 296 ff.

No Neutrals? 295

In August, 1955, *Kommunist* (Moscow) reported with satisfaction that the Central Committee of India's Communist Party had resolved to support Nehru's government in foreign affairs, and that the Communist Party of Indonesia had issued an appeal on May 23, 1955, approving the foreign-political course of the Indonesian government. The timing of these political statements—this was the spring and summer of 1955—indicated that the basic Soviet decisions on a *rapprochement* with the neutrals had been taken around the beginning of that year.

On the ideological level, the highest Soviet authorities and experts on Asia one after another began to apologize for their errors and assert the changed views. Referring to India, Dyakov confessed:

> the Soviet experts on India were of the opinion that the liberation of India could take place only under the leadership of the proletariat . . . the bourgeoisie and consequently the National Congress and Gandhi were viewed as forces which impeded the liberation movement. . . . Sometimes Gandhi was characterized in Soviet works as the ally, occasionally even as an agent, of British imperialism. Such an evaluation was based on statements of J. V. Stalin at the 16th Party Congress [1930]. This evaluation has never been correct.[18]

Yevgeni Zhukov, another authority, also confessed his errors and asserted: ". . . despite certain defects, the national-liberation movement was a genuinely popular anti-imperialist movement." [19]

Alexander Guber, Director of the Oriental Institute of the Soviet Academy of Sciences, attacked "wrong formulations" in works on the history of India. In particular, the previously despised Gandhi took on a new stature:

> . . . The role of Gandhi . . . is treated [in Soviet literature] in a one-sided way and incorrectly. . . . An ardent patriot, Gandhi invariably based his activity against British imperialism on his philosophical concepts and on his firm belief in the possibility of liberating India from the colonial yoke by propaganda and nonviolence.[20]

---

[18] A. M. Dyakov and I. M. Reisner, "Rol Gandi v Natsionalno-Osvoboditelnoi Borbe Narodov Indii" (The Role of Gandhi in the National-liberation Struggle of the Peoples of India), in *Sovetskoye Vostokovedenie* (Soviet Orientology), Moscow, no. 5, November, 1956, pp. 22, 24.
[19] *New Times*, Moscow, no. 6, February 2, 1956, pp. 15–16.
[20] *International Affairs*, Moscow, no. 3, March, 1956, p. 62.

2. THE BANDUNG CONFERENCE

The Khrushchev-Bulganin regime's first large-scale experiment with neutralism was the Bandung Conference of April, 1955. Although the Soviet government did not participate directly, the conference, convened with the assistance of and sponsored by the Soviet Union's Asian allies, was an effort to organize a world-wide bloc of both Communist-controlled and neutral nations.

Political cooperation between the nations of Asia and Africa had often been discussed, and a number of sporadic attempts had been made since 1949 to unite them in one organization. One of the first in the series of such attempts was the conference convened, on India's initiative, in 1949 in New Delhi, to support Indonesia in her fight against the Netherlands. "Never before in the history of mankind," President Sukarno of Indonesia later proclaimed, "has such a solidarity of Asian and African peoples been shown for the rescue of a fellow Asian nation in danger." [21]

In December, 1952, on the initiative of the Naguib government of Egypt, a conference in Cairo of twelve Asian and African countries, among them India, Pakistan, Iran, Indonesia, and Egypt, discussed and condemned French policy in Tunisia and Morocco. Other conferences under Communist sponsorship ("For the Defense of the People of the Near and Middle East," and other titles) [22] held over the years and generally viewed as Communist "front," were of lesser importance. No Asian-African meeting, however, attained the significance that did the Bandung Conference of 1955. When Ali Sastroamidjojo, premier of Indonesia, proposed, at a convention of the Colombo powers in January, 1954, the convening of the future Bandung Conference, the suggestion was received coolly. Premier Nehru was especially unenthusiastic because he saw no point in a conference that would not include Communist China. In the neutralist field Nehru's voice was the most authoritative.

Soviet sources have stated that the decisive contacts were made

---

[21] Speech by President Sukarno at the opening of the Asian-African Conference, April 18, 1955, in *Let a New Asia and a New Africa Be Born*, issued by the Ministry of Foreign Affairs, Republic of Indonesia, 1955.

[22] For example, a conference in Rome in September, 1951, and a conference in Beirut in 1953 (*Pravda*, December 23, 1953). See also A. Appadorai, *The Bandung Conference*, New Delhi, 1955.

at a Soviet-sponsored "conference to lessen tensions in international relations" held in Stockholm in June, 1954. The Stockholm Conference itself was of no importance, but the idea of a general anti-Western convention of Asian and African nations was unofficially discussed and approved there by both the Chinese Communist delegation and the Indian representatives.[23] Then, apparently, the Indian premier's attitude changed. Chou En-lai, the Chinese premier, was to visit Nehru in June, 1954. This meant new contacts and possibly closer cooperation of India with Communist China.

The Sino-Indian agreement of April 29, 1954, on Tibet represented the first announcement of the program known as Pancha Shilla (or Panch Sila, "Five Principles") [24] of the new combination of powers: mutual respect for each other's territorial integrity and sovereignty, nonaggression, noninterference in each other's internal affairs, equality and mutual benefit, peaceful coexistence. The principles were reiterated in the Nehru-Chou statement of June 28, 1954, and incorporated in the U Nu-Chou statement of June 30, 1954; Indonesia and North Vietnam accepted them in their declarations of July 1 and 6. In their statement of October 12, 1954, the Soviet and Chinese Communist governments said that they would base their relations with the countries of Asia and the Pacific area on Pancha Shilla.[25] The declaration of the Supreme Soviet of the USSR of February 9, 1955, announced support of the "Five Principles of Peaceful Coexistence."

In each of these instances one of the partners to a statement or declaration was a Communist country, the other a neutral. To the Soviet government the "Five Principles" were standard. Incorporated in one form or another in Stalin's various treaties as a tribute to democratic principles, they were violated when necessary, as, for instance, in 1939 in respect to the Baltic states. But, neophytes in international affairs, the Communist as well as the non-Communist groups of the East were inclined to exaggerate the significance of these declarations of programs. The neutrals believed that Pancha Shilla was the symbol

[23] The Indian group was headed by Mrs. Rameshwari Nehru, adviser to the New Delhi government (*New Times*, Moscow, no. 1, January 1, 1955, p. 14). Subsequently a group of Communist sympathizers worked in New Delhi on preparations for the Bandung Conference (*Economist*, London, April 30, 1955).

[24] From the Sanskrit, meaning "five foundations." Premier Nehru's letter to Professor Russel H. Fifield in the latter's *Diplomacy of Southeast Asia 1945–1958*, New York, Harper & Brothers, 1958.

[25] *International Affairs*, Moscow, no. 8, March, 1956, pp. 45 ff.

of the awakening of Asia and a landmark in the history of mankind.

Added prestige for Communist China and a general *rapprochement* between the neutralist and Communist powers marked the summer months of 1954. While the Moscow government, which was still viewed with suspicion by many neutralists, was not among the direct participants in the events, it hailed every step toward a Bandung-type of international combination. In December, 1954, at another conference of the Colombo powers in Bagor, it was finally decided to hold the Bandung Conference. The pro-American Chinese Nationalist government was not among the invited, nor were the South Korean, Israeli, or South African governments; the participation of these countries would have made participation of Communist China and the Arab countries doubtful. Outer Mongolia and North Korea could not be invited either.

While they agreed to participate, and even showed enthusiasm for the conference, the neutralist governments were not altogether blind to the political traits of the Communist regimes of Asia; they had already learned from experience. Thailand and Cambodia had noted China's operations in areas adjoining their territory; Indonesia had noted China's interference in her affairs, in particular the financial operations of the Chinese Embassy in their country; the Indians were worried about the growing Chinese Communist interference in Tibet, Sikkim, and Bhutan; the Burmese had not forgotten the words of Liu Shao-chi when he attacked U Nu and called Sukarno and Nehru "imperialist stooges." [26] However, the delusion, widespread also in the West, that China's nonaggressiveness could be bought by proclamations of anti-Americanism, that ceding Taiwan to Peking would satisfy the latter, and that United States recognition of Communist China would help to detach China from Russia, were even more prevalent in the East; they animated many leaders of the Bandung Conference. Skeptics doubted the value of pledges and promises made by the Chinese government, but Nehru believed that the more Peking pledged and promised the harder it would be for the Chinese leaders to resume their dangerous course.

Three hundred and forty delegates representing twenty-nine countries were present at Bandung; the twenty-nine countries represented a

---

[26] George McTurman Kahin, *The Asian-African Conference, Bandung, Indonesia, April, 1955*, Ithaca, N.Y., Cornell University Press, 1956, p. 7.

The Bandung Conference

population of over 1.3 billion, more than half the population of the world. The participants fell into three groups: two Communist countries (China and North Vietnam) with a population of about 600 million; nine neutralist countries with a total population of 500 million; and eighteen medium-size or small countries, anti-Communist, pro-Western, with about 200 million total population. Thus composed, the conference, it would appear, would make a vigorous East-West controversy inevitable and doom in advance all efforts to build a united front of Asian and African nations. In fact, however, an anti-Western and especially anti-American, tone was dominant in the Bandung symphony and made it a success for Moscow and Peking. In particular, Chou En-lai, who played well his role of a modest and humble "Asiatic," scored a significant success for his government and, by implication, also for the Soviet Union.

Marshal Voroshilov, the Soviet President, sent his greetings to the conference, as did the Presidiums of the five Soviet republics of Central Asia. Vasily V. Kuznetsov, Soviet deputy foreign minister, in a statement on the eve of the conference, said: "The peoples of the Soviet Union understand fully the struggle of the nations of Asia and Africa against any form of colonial domination and economic dependence." [27]

At the very start of the conference India's Krishna Menon—certainly with Nehru's consent—sounded a harsh challenge: "Anyone tied up with America must have a bad conscience in the face of the collective African-Asian sentiment." [28] In the discussion, Nehru himself made some pro-Soviet statements: for example, Poland, Rumania, and other East European nations, he said, are free and independent of Russia; the governments represented at the conference, he proposed, should be forbidden to enter into alliances with the United States.

Chou En-lai's courtesy and friendliness were profuse. Prepared to meet his opponents halfway, he was in favor of reconciliation with the United States and even with Chiang Kai-shek; he promised never to interfere in the internal affairs of other nations. He held himself aloof from the Soviet Union: "Are we a poor imitation of America, of the Soviet Union of Europe? Certainly not—we are Asians." [29] In direct

---

[27] *International Affairs*, Moscow, no. 5, May, 1955.
[28] *Osteuropa*, Stuttgart, no. 5, October, 155, pp. 331–32.
[29] *Ibid.*, p. 335.

negotiations with the leaders of the southeastern nations, Chou and Pham Van Dong of North Vietnam promised concessions to their non-Communist neighbors. However, when Sir John Kotelawala of Ceylon asked Chou to promise that no help would be given the Communist parties of non-Communist nations, Chou refused.[30]

The main discussion and political struggle at Bandung centered on two issues, both significant for relationships with the Soviet Union. "Colonialism" was the main theme and the target of all attacks. Anti-Communist delegates, however, among whom the Turkish, Iranian, and Philippine leaders were prominent, stressed the "new colonialism" of the Soviet Union. The criticism of Soviet policy, which was often combined with a defense of the Western orientation, was vigorous and consistent, although many speakers avoided reference to the Soviet Union by name. Fadhil Jamali of Iraq mentioned Latvia, Lithuania, Estonia, Poland, Rumania, and Czechoslovakia as victims of colonialism; Mohammed Ali of Pakistan warned against opening the door to "new and more insidious forms of imperialism." Sir John Kotelawala said:

> There is another form of colonialism, however, about which many of us represented here are perhaps less clear in our minds and to which some of us would perhaps not agree to apply the term "colonialism" at all. Think for example of those satellite states under Communist domination in Central and Eastern Europe—of Hungary, Rumania, Bulgaria, Albania, Czechoslovakia, Lithuania, Estonia, and Poland. And if we are united in our opposition to colonialism, should it not be our duty openly to declare our opposition to Soviet colonialism as much as to Western capitalism?[31]

Carlos Romulo of the Philippines stated:

> ... this white world which has fostered racism has done many other things ... just as Western political thought has given us all our basic ideas of political freedom, justice and equity, it is Western science which in this generation has explained the mythology of race....[32]

The second controversial issue was the proposal of the anti-Com-

[30] Kahin, *op. cit.* p. 18.
[31] Carlos P. Romulo, *The Meaning of Bandung*, Chapel Hill, N.C., University of North Carolina Press, 1956, p. 28.
[32] Richard Wright, *The Colour Curtain: A Report on the Bandung Conference*, London, Dennis Dobson, 1956, p. 185.

munist side to accept the "right of each nation to defend itself singly or collectively." This thesis was contrary to the basic views and programs of neutralism. The basis of NATO and the Baghdad and SEATO pacts was "collective self-defense" and close collaboration with the West in the face of the Russian and Chinese menace. It was a major principle of neutralism that pacts and alliances of the latter kind, which might increase the threat of war, must be rejected. (A short while before, a number of countries of Southeast Asia, including India, had rejected the SEATO agreement.)

On both controversial issues a compromise between the defenders of the Soviet Union and the neutralists was arrived at. The term "new colonialism" and the name of the Soviet Union were dropped, and the vague term "colonialism in all its manifestations" was introduced. The use of the term "right of self-defense exercised singly or collectively" was likewise objected to. After further modifications, the initial "Five Principles" became ten. Moscow was not happy about the alterations, some of which were directed against Soviet policy; nor was Peking satisfied.

Therefore in the Soviet and pro-Soviet world the ten principles of Bandung were practically passed over and soon forgotten. In their dealings with the Asian nations the two main Communist powers reverted to the original "Five Principles," as if no revisions had occurred. "The Five Principles," said *International Affairs* after the Bandung Conference, "have been recognized by more than 30 countries with a combined population of 1,500 million people." [33] When Nehru visited Moscow almost immediately after the conference, he signed a joint statement with the Soviet premier in which the reference was to Pancha Shilla rather than to the "ten principles" of Bandung. The Soviet and North Vietnamese governments likewise subscribed (July 18, 1955) to the original "Five Principles"; Nehru and Cyrankiewicz, the Polish premier, approved them in their statement of June 25, 1955, as did Nehru in the communiqué on the negotiations with Nepal (August 1, 1955).

While Western observers often viewed the Bandung Conference as a success for democracy,[34] the Soviet government also assessed its

[33] V. Durdenevsky, "The Five Principles," in *International Affairs*, Moscow, no. 3, March, 1956, p. 45.
[34] For instance, Carlos P. Romulo in *The Meaning of Bandung, op. cit.*

achievements highly. In this controversy the Soviet evaluation was closer to the reality. Despite criticism of its policies by numerous delegates, the conference represented the emerging alliance of the Communist with the neutralist powers against the West, and the Soviet term for this combination of powers of the Soviet and neutralist bloc was "zone of peace." Beside the West, the Soviet juxtaposed its numerical weight (two-thirds of the human race) and its moral superiority (the exploited against the exploiters). In Soviet eyes, China emerged as the prime power in Asia, and the Soviet Union itself as the supreme protector of the entire "zone."

In its treatment of the Bandung Conference the Soviet press was enthusiastic and eulogistic. Disregarding the anti-Soviet and anti-Communist trends among the delegates, or mentioning them casually as "absurd" and malicious statements of American stooges, it expressed satisfaction and pleasure. For Moscow, Bandung represented a great success, a landmark in post-Stalin foreign policy, a symbol of Communist-neutralist cooperation, and a step forward into the Asian and African world.

3. INDIA AND BURMA

China, not Russia, was the immediate problem of the three powers of the south—India, Indonesia, and Burma. China was both potential menace and possible partner; her strength had been confirmed by the fact of her presence at Geneva and by her role in the agreements on Korea and Indochina. After the Geneva Conference, where Chou En-lai had pledged to observe the independence of Laos and Cambodia, there had followed the Sino-Indian agreements on Tibet, the China-Burma Conference, and finally Nehru's visit to China in October, 1955. China's pledge of nonexpansion and noninterference was recompensed by India's support of China's claim to a seat in the United Nations, her claim to Taiwan, and her general rejection of anti-Communist blocs.

The Soviet Union was in an even better position than China. There were no territorial or nationality issues as between Russia and the new nations of South Asia that were crucial to their relations. Another incentive for *rapprochement* with Moscow was the ability of the Soviet to assist the South Asian countries in their industrialization efforts. Thus the stage was set for improvement in the relations of the Soviet Union with India and the other nations of South Asia.

The first try was a Soviet contract for the delivery of a complete plant to an affiliate of the Birla industrial concern in India. This was followed by a project for the construction, with Soviet aid, of a large metallurgical plant there.

The Soviet-projected metallurgical plant was one of three huge units of comparable capacity which were viewed as the basis of India's industrialization. One of the units was to be built by British firms, and the second by West German firms. The Soviet plant was to be erected at Bhilai, in the state of Madhya Pradesh in central India. It was to have a total capacity of 1,300,000 tons, and its total cost was to come to about 23 million dollars. Russia's contribution was estimated at about half of this amount; the Soviet loan was for twelve years at 2½ per cent interest, and the plant was to be completed by 1958–59. The main problem in connection with the Bhilai project was climatic conditions: in May the temperature in the shade reaches 108 degrees, with 90 per cent humidity. The softening of the soil by summer rains and monsoons posed other difficult problems.[35]

During the first year following the signing of the agreement for the construction of the plant, designs and plans were prepared. Work then started at Bhilai. Two years later 250 Soviet specialists and 40,000 Indian workers were employed on the project. Three hundred Indian technicians were sent to Russia to be trained for their future jobs in the Bhilai plant.[36]

In a way, India's decision to construct three expensive steel mills in itself represented a Soviet success. Involved in the operation was the impact on India and on the Orient in general of Soviet theories of industrialization, among them the delusionary one about the miraculous capacities of "heavy industry"; this delusion assumed the proportions of a myth. The "imperialists," according to the Soviet theory, intentionally begin the industrial development of a backward country with the "light" branches—textiles, leather, soap, etc.—in order to delay progress; a socialist country, on the other hand, knows and recommends to its friends and allies the correct road to industrialization.

[35] *New Times,* Moscow, no. 44, October 27, 1955, pp. 23–25, and no. 6, February 2, 1956, pp. 17–18.
[36] *Pravda,* August 26, 1956; December 3, 1957; May 25, 1958.

In Russia, faith in the magical power of "heavy industry" was part of Stalin's realistic effort to build up the military-industrial force of his country to the neglect of the people's need for agricultural and consumer goods. As thus applied the "heavy industry" philosophy proved to be correct and successful. In suggesting the same course to its potential allies, the Soviet government was making an effort to strengthen the military potential of the anti-Western front and, indirectly, its own power. There were admirers of the Soviet methods in the underdeveloped countries.

> . . . In each underdeveloped country, there are some enthusiasts of industrialization who despise such branches of production as soap, cement, glass and staple fabrics and insist that industrialization should begin with steel mills and automobile and aircraft factories. In most cases these planners learn, sooner or later, how childish their dreams were.[37]

On the other hand, such advanced countries as Canada, Australia, New Zealand, Denmark, Norway, Finland, and Switzerland do not follow the "heavy industry" pattern, which can often be harmful to the national economy.

Negotiations were begun to increase Soviet-Indian trade. A number of Indian "delegations" of technicians, artists, musicians, lawyers, journalists, and physicians visited the Soviet Union. An exposition of India's domestic crafts industry opened in Moscow. In May, 1955, a delegation of the Indian Parliament came to Moscow. "The friendship and cooperation of the great peoples of India and the Soviet Union become stronger every day," wrote *International Affairs*.[38]

A translation into Russian of Nehru's *Discovery of India,* published in Moscow, contained a new introduction, written by Nehru, which was highly favorable to the Soviet Union. The official *Kommunist* commended the book. It pointed out Nehru's initial hope of and subsequent disappointment in American help to India's industrialization. It quoted Nehru: "None of the countries of the globe is at present as politically stable and economically well-balanced as the Soviet Union." [39]

---

[37] W. S. Woytinsky, "India's Five Year Plan," in *The New Leader,* August 20, 1956, pp. 17, 19.
[38] Moscow, no. 11, November, 1955.
[39] *Kommunist,* Moscow, no. 9, June, 1955, p. 105.

India and Burma

A few days after publication of Nehru's book in Russia (June 7), Nehru himself arrived in Moscow at the head of a delegation for an official "visit of friendship." After a few days in the capital the Indian visitors made a tour of Stalingrad, the Caucasus, Siberia, and the Urals. They returned to Moscow after a fortnight of gala celebrations, sightseeing, and enthusiastic speeches, during which the Soviet press had extended greetings to the guests and stressed India's neutralism. In a joint political statement made by Nehru and the Soviet premier, certain points of the Soviet foreign-political program were emphasized and approved: Communist China's right to Taiwan and to a seat in the United Nations, and prohibition of atomic testing and production of atomic weapons.

There were limits, however, to the Soviet-Indian *rapprochement*. The Soviet government, in line with its new methods of dealing with neutralist countries, offered Nehru Soviet arms on easy terms. In particular it offered 60 to 100 Soviet jet fighters at a low price. This opportunity to become independent of the British arms industry and to save money was so attractive that many officers of the Indian air force were ready to sign up with Moscow. Nehru, however, rejected the offer.[40] The prospect of becoming dependent on Soviet arms appeared ominous to the leader of a neutralist movement.

Nehru stressed this cautious attitude when he visited Yugoslavia on his way home from Moscow. Tito's relations with Moscow had improved markedly after the Khrushchev-Bulganin visit to Belgrade. Yugoslavia was determined, however, to maintain full independence in military affairs. In their joint statement of July 6, 1955, Tito and Nehru emphasized not only the "close identity of views on all the problems considered" but also the "policy of full independence followed by both countries."

Following Nehru's visit, the turn came for U Nu, the Burmese premier. In the Moscow view, Burma was in the same class of neutrals as India.

The Soviet and Chinese efforts to achieve a *rapprochement* of the nations of South and Southeast Asia profited from the trade difficulties that had developed between Rangoon and Washington. Burma's only

[40] *The New York Times*, August 27, 1956; D Papers, June 17, 1956, India file.

substantial export item was rice, a grain of which the United States possessed a large surplus. For political reasons, Communist China signed a trade agreement with Burma (November 22, 1954) for the purchase of 150,000 tons of rice; other countries of the Soviet bloc followed suit and entered into similar agreements. Thus the Soviet bloc suddenly appeared in the role of savior of the poor small southeastern nation. A three-year Soviet-Burmese trade agreement concluded on July 1, 1955, provided for the Soviet purchase of from 150,000 to 200,000 tons of rice and Soviet deliveries to Burma of machinery, industrial equipment, and other goods. Soviet technical assistance to Burma's industry was contemplated. To a degree, the Soviet bloc supplanted the sterling bloc countries as the chief trade partners of Burma.

U Nu arrived in Moscow on October 20, 1955. He visited the same places that Nehru had visited, and his statements were similar to those of Nehru. In their final declaration, issued on November 3, 1955, U Nu and Bulganin unashamedly stated that the "relations between the Soviet Union and Burma have always been sincere and friendly"; both premiers condemned "the policy of organizing blocs" and commended "nonjoining of blocs." In addition to the usual demands—cessation of atomic- and hydrogen-bomb tests, admission of Communist China to the United Nations—the declaration also called for adherence to the "Five Principles of Coexistence." At a press conference in Moscow, U Nu emphasized that the Soviet Union had been the first country to offer technical assistance on terms suggested by Burma. "Clearly, this agreement is only a stage on the road to broader economic cooperation." [41]

As if repaying the compliments, and implicitly apologizing for the harsh attacks on U Nu of the Stalin days, *International Affairs* published a highly favorable review of U Nu's book, *Burma under the Japanese,* which had appeared in England a year before.[42] U Nu in turn thanked the Soviet government warmly for the vital rice deal; "your purchase of our rice has saved us," he exclaimed at the reception in the Great Kremlin Palace.[43]

[41] *New Times,* Moscow, no. 46, November 10, 1955, "The Soviet Union and Burma," pp. 3–5.
[42] The author's name was given as Thakin Nu, U Nu's original name.
[43] *The New York Times,* October 23, 1955.

4. KHRUSHCHEV AND BULGANIN IN SOUTH ASIA

Nineteen fifty-five, the year of *rapprochement* with the neutrals, was crowned by the long, spectacular, and successful visit of Khrushchev and Bulganin to three South Asian countries—India, Burma, and Afghanistan—in November–December. The purpose of the visit was to strengthen the newly formed bonds. Extensive preparatory work had been done in Moscow: technical and human resources of South Asia had been assessed, possible loans and investments had been calculated, arms offers had been projected, speeches and statements had been outlined. Other members of the Presidium were worried about the fact that the two supreme leaders would be absent from the country for over a month, and some, it was later confirmed, opposed the trip; apparently, however, Khrushchev's emphasis on the proneutralist course, and perhaps also his personal desire to see more of the non-Soviet world and address millions of non-Soviet people, overcame all doubts and opposition.

In mid-November Khrushchev and Bulganin flew to New Delhi. Accompanying them was a group of about fifty men and women, among them General Ivan Serov, head of the security police (traveling with the party as "chief administrative officer" for the press); Andrei Gromyko, First Deputy Minister of Foreign Affairs; P. N. Kumykin, Deputy Minister of Foreign Trade, and other high-ranking personalities, who together formed a Soviet government in miniature.

The group stayed in India from November 18 to December 1; from India they flew to Burma, where they remained from December 1 to 7, after which they returned to India for another week. They then went to Afghanistan, where they spent four days, from December 15 to 19.

The reception in India was grandiose. Wherever the Soviet leaders appeared huge crowds greeted them. Nehru himself had never attracted the crowds that Khrushchev and Bulganin did; the Indian press estimated the total number of people who turned out for the Russian leaders at over 10 million. The government encouraged the population to accord the Soviet leaders an enthusiastic welcome, and the press went along. Schools were closed, and school children were marched to the meetings; thousands of paper flags bearing the Soviet and Indian emblems were distributed; the visitors were pelted with flowers and garlands were placed around their necks by loving hands; gifts were presented; Khrushchev rode an elephant and wore an embroidered Indian cap; he waved jeweled scimitars, beat drums, embraced dancers, and had *kumkum* smeared on his forehead by young Hindu women.[44]

There was a great deal of sincerity in this enthusiasm. To India, yesterday a colony and today still a poverty-stricken country, Russia's rapid technical progress and her rise to great-power stature appeared miraculous. The unprecedented extended visit of the two most powerful men of Europe was an honor. Their outspoken criticism of the "imperialist West" touched the right chord. The peace slogans and opposition to atomic armaments were popular.

The Soviet guests addressed the Indian Parliament, scientific institutes, and various societies. "*Hindi-Rusi bhai bhai*" (Hindus and Russians are brothers), Khrushchev exclaimed repeatedly, and Bulganin exclaimed, "*Jai Hind!*" (Long live India!)

Carried away by enthusiasm, Khrushchev often transgressed the limits of officiality. "We shall feed you," he proclaimed at Nangal, "we shall share the last piece of bread with India." Winston Churchill, reading the reports from India, called the Russians' performance a "surprising spectacle"; "a circus," some correspondents called it. Khrushchev seemed to enjoy greatly both the popular and the political features of the reception.

The division of labor between the two Soviet leaders was in line with diplomatic unrealities. Bulganin, the premier, was the Number One man, while Khrushchev was a modest "member of the Presidium of the Supreme Soviet." Bulganin was first to take the rostrum, with Khrushchev following him. Bulganin entered the car first, ahead of Khrushchev. Bulganin addressed the Parliament and the meetings first, and Khrushchev followed. In his speeches, however, Bulganin limited himself to trivialities about friendship, progress, and peace; the politically significant statements, and the risky ones, were Khrushchev's province.

"Anticolonialism," the main theme of the statements of the Soviet guests, was intended to cement the bond between the two nations. Sometimes, in an overflow of enthusiasm, Khrushchev went farther

[44] *Economist*, London, December 17, 1955, p. 1038, "Red Roses across Asia."

than his hosts and even his own entourage expected. His attacks on the West became violent. He obviously overshot the mark when he told the Indians that the partition of their country into two sovereign nations, India and Pakistan (which was contrary to the initial British plans) had been carried out by a "third power" (meaning, obviously, Britain) in accordance with "the well-known principle of 'divide and rule,' and contrary to the interests of the Indian people." He went even further when he told a meeting that "the British, French, and Americans started the second World War, sent troops against our country and these troops were the troops of Hitler Germany." [45] Speaking of Goa, the Portuguese colony on the Indian peninsula, Khrushchev attacked "countries which like a mite stick to a healthy body"; however, he said, "sooner or later it [Goa] will liberate itself from alien domination." [46]

Khrushchev and Bulganin visited the Kashmir province, over which India and Pakistan were in dispute. Soviet support of India's position on Kashmir was due to Moscow's antagonism toward Pakistan's participation in the Baghdad Pact. Although they paid lip service to the principle of national self-determination, Khrushchev and Bulganin, in their statements, approved the incorporation of Kashmir into India, and assumed a pronounced anti-Pakistan position.

The Pakistan government, expecting that there would be anti-Soviet demonstrations, made a futile attempt to prevent the visit of the Russians to Kashmir; it was also worried about the projected Soviet trip to another antagonist, Afghanistan.

On their arrival in Srinigar, capital of Kashmir, Khrushchev made the controversy public:

> The Ministry of Foreign Affairs of Pakistan called in the Soviet Ambassador and advised him that I and my friend Nikolai Alexandrovich Bulganin should renounce our visit to Kashmir. We don't at all like the Baghdad Pact, in which Pakistan is one of the most active participants, although no benefit derives from it either to the government or to the people. But we have patience and we are sure that the Baghdad Pact will burst like a soap bubble, and the only thing that will remain of the Pact will be an unpleasant memory. . . . The representative of the Ministry of Foreign Affairs of Pakistan told our Ambas-

---
[45] *Economist*, London, December 3, 1955, pp. 819–20. After this speech, many Britons demanded that the invitation to the Soviet leaders to visit Britain be canceled.
[46] *Missiya Druzhby* (Mission of Friendship), Moscow, *Pravda* publication, 1956, vol. 1, p. 133.

sador in that country that the government of Pakistan would want us not to visit Afghanistan, a country adjacent to ours. But the suggestion goes too far and persons making this kind of proposition take too much upon themselves.[47]

The final Soviet-Indian statement, signed by Bulganin and Nehru on December 13, called for the same program that the other Soviet-neutralist statements of that year did—admission of Communist China to the United Nations, banning of atomic weapons, no "regional military pacts" or alliances, and a new summit conference. A special agreement, providing for substantial Soviet supplies of industrial equipment, metals, and other goods, for Soviet purchases of Indian goods, and for steamships to ply between Soviet and Indian ports, was signed on the same day. An Ilyushin plane was offered Nehru as a gift.

The reception in Burma was friendly, although less enthusiastic than in India; essentially it was a continuation of U Nu's visit to Moscow of a month before. The usual type of political statement, signed at the end of the conference in Rangoon, maintained the principles of neutralism; an economic agreement provided for Soviet technical assistance, especially aid in an agricultural program, irrigation projects, and industrial construction on credit terms. No figures were mentioned, nor was the extent of the assistance indicated. "As a gift to the people of Burma," the Soviet leaders offered to construct a technical institute in Rangoon. Accepting the gift, U Nu proudly reciprocated with a gift of a "quantity of rice" which was accepted "with thanks" by the Russians.

"Advisers" from the countries of the Soviet bloc had already begun to arrive in Burma; their number was soon to reach considerable proportions. The appearance in Rangoon of Bulgarians, Czechs, and Poles, in addition to the Russians, marked the change from the former era of prevailing British and American influence to one of Soviet and East European influence.

5. AFGHANISTAN AND THE DRIVE TO THE SEA

Afghanistan, the last stop in the itinerary of the Soviet leaders, was the smallest and most backward of the countries visited, but it

[47] *Ibid.*, p. 160.

Afghanistan and the Drive to the Sea

was at that moment attracting much attention. The visit proved to be of considerable importance. It was more than a new stage in Soviet relations with Afghanistan; it affected the entire power structure of the Near East.

Little explored, underdeveloped, mountainous Afghanistan was in the path of Russia's drive to the Indian Ocean through Central Asia. The main adversary of the Soviets in this drive was not the local population, the almost unarmed tribes of nationality splinters, but mighty Britain, entrenched in India and jealously watching the approach of the avalanche from the north. In 1837, when Russia had reached Afghanistan's northern borders, an agreement between the two powers declared Afghanistan to be "outside" the Russian sphere.

The Soviet Union, from its earliest days, had continued the traditional Russian move to the south, although under new slogans and with a new philosophy: it was now carrying the torch of liberation to dependent nations. Afghanistan was precisely where the holy war of the peoples of the Orient against British rule was expected to break out soon. On Afghanistan's northern borders was Bukhara, the semicolony of prewar Russia which after 1917 had expected to regain independence. In fact, the Soviet government signed a "Treaty of Friendship" with Afghanistan (February 28, 1921) providing for the "independence and freedom of the governments of Bukhara and Khiva." It was not long before the two countries were incorporated into the Soviet Union and Russian pressure on Afghanistan was resumed.

So long, however, as pressure by Britain from the south was able to counterbalance the Russian impact, Afghanistan continued to be a barrier in the path of the latter's great drive.

When Britain withdrew from India in 1947–48, Afghanistan found herself in a new political position. The direct impact of British power gave way at first to American influence. As Russia started to recover strength, however, her influence in Afghanistan began to grow. The Soviet government regarded Afghanistan as an area from which other foreign influence should be eliminated; it was itself prepared to help develop Afghanistan's north. More than once since 1947 it had raised objections to the plans of other nations concerning these areas. An Afghan contract with France for exploration for oil (August, 1952) could not be signed because of Moscow's protests.

In Soviet-Afghan relations the complex nationality problems of Central Asia proved to be of great significance. State borders in this part of the world rarely coincide with nationality areas, and this was especially so in Afghanistan. Large numbers of Uzbeks and Tadzhiks in Afghanistan's north are akin to their co-nationals in Soviet Central Asia and could serve as a link with and a tool of the northern neighbor. Other millions speak the same Pushtu (Afghan) language (also called Pakhtu, or Pashtu) as their neighbors in Pakistan. The total number of Pushtuns is estimated at from 10 to 12 million, of whom about 50 per cent live in Afghanistan, the other half inhabiting adjacent territory in the former North-West Frontier province in Pakistan, which in turn borders on Kashmir, the region in dispute between India and Pakistan. The king of Afghanistan and the premier, Mohammed Daud, are Pushtuns.

Since 1947 Afghanistan had been insisting on "self-determination" for the Pushtuns of Pakistan and the creation of an autonomous or independent new state, Pushtunistan, on Afghanistan's eastern border. The area of the projected state was never exactly defined; the Afghans wanted it to stretch as far south as the Arabian Sea so that Afghanistan would acquire an outlet to the oceans. (See Map 4, page 315, prepared by the Afghan Information Bureau, London.)

If this were achieved, the configuration of states in this part of Asia would change decisively. Afghanistan, a Soviet ally or prospective Soviet satellite, would serve as a bridge to Pushtunistan, and the two states, Afghanistan and Pushtunistan, would open the road to completion of Russia's drive to the Indian Ocean. West Pakistan would be reduced in population or partitioned, and the Soviet banner would fly at India's borders.[48] What had not been possible in olden times would now be achieved under the guidance of the Soviets. At the same time the Chinese drive from the northeast, through Tibet and Nepal, would culminate in the encircling of India by the two main powers of the Soviet bloc.

In these long-range Soviet projections, Pushtunistan was a cherished idea, and Afghanistan was a friend and protégé. These circumstances explain Moscow's cautious and attentive attitude toward Af-

[48] This may also explain why the Soviet attitude in regard to Pushtunistan and Kashmir sometimes appeared highly illogical. India's consistent refusal to permit a popular election in Kashmir was approved by Moscow, while in the Afghan-Pushtunistan case a popular election and the creation of a new state were warmly supported.

ghanistan. It would, for instance, be possible to stage a "movement" in Afghanistan in favor of close affiliation with the Soviet Union; armed resistance to such a movement would certainly be slight and ineffective. Such an action would, however, alienate the "neutrals" and throw them into the pro-Western bloc; it would create hostile alliances all around the Communist powers. Thus, since Stalin's death, Soviet strategy had stressed Afghanistan's independence and the necessity to give her abundant economic help and arms and, at any cost, to achieve more power and prestige than the West in Afghanistan.

The leader of the Pushtu movement in Pushtunistan, Mullah Mirza Ali Khan, Fakir of Ipr, was reported in the mountains commanding a force of about 2,000. His program was to assemble all Pushtuns "from Chitral to Baluchistan and from the Khyber Pass to the Indus." In April, 1954, the government of South Afghanistan gave Mirza a handout to replenish his ammunition. In July, Mirza's lieutenants conferred with three Russian agents who pledged support; in November, Soviet representatives Demrovich and Alexovich confirmed the pledge made to Mirza.[49]

Beginning in the fall of 1953, and especially after the close *rapprochement* of Pakistan, Turkey, and the West, Soviet relations with Afghanistan improved markedly. Small Afghanistan could not consider joining the alliance. In December, 1954, Premier Mohammed Daud described the proposed American military aid to Pakistan as "a grave danger to the security and peace of Afghanistan"; a one-year trade agreement with the Soviet Union was signed.[50] The trade agreement was followed, in January, 1954, by an agreement providing for a credit of 3.5 million dollars over a five-year period for the construction by the Soviet Union of a number of industrial projects in Afghanistan.[51] Afghanistan was becoming the first recipient of Soviet "aid to underdeveloped countries." A new Soviet-Afghan agreement provided for the construction of a number of other projects at a cost of 2.1 million dollars.[52]

American projects in Afghanistan, although economically im-

[49] *The New York Times*, February 9, 1955.
[50] *Pravda*, December 26, 1953.
[51] *Izvestia*, January 29, 1954.
[52] *Ibid.*, November 30, 1954, and *Vneshnyaya Torgovlya* (Foreign Trade), no. 12, 1954.

portant, were confined to a distant province in the southwest. The Soviet government knew how to combine political aims with economic aid; its projects, mainly in the capital, were conspicuous. Since 1954, oil storage tanks, two granaries, and a bakery with modern machinery had been built.

> The modern machines they [the Soviet specialists] were using had never been seen in Afghanistan before. The building site was always surrounded by a crowd of people, enthralled by the rapidity with which Afghanistan's first modern grain elevator was rising. . . . The huge silver-painted reservoirs are surrounded by asphalted spaces, with convenient approach roads. All operations of the depots are mechanized. Each depot has a power plant and repair shops. When the floodlights were first switched on at the Kabul depot, multitudes of people came from the city and its environs to admire the unusual spectacle, for Afghan towns are still poorly lighted.[53]

At the same time, Soviet technicians began the job of asphalting the streets of Kabul.

> Before 1953 there were only three asphalted streets in the capital. . . . The Soviet specialists began by creating a plant producing asphalt and concrete, which was started in May 1955. From the plant the surfacing materials were delivered to the street repair sites ready for laying. Tip trucks and rollers were also supplied by the Soviet Union. Jobs which formerly took several months could now be done in a day. By the end of 1955, nearly all the main streets, as well as the highroad to the airport had been asphalted.[54]

By the time the Afghan-Pakistan controversy over Pushtunistan reached its peak, Soviet prestige in Afghanistan was high. On March 28, 1955, Pakistan took measures to tighten its rule over its Pushtu areas; the next day the Afghan government protested publicly; riots in protest against Pakistan and its mission in Afghanistan took place in Kabul, and a military force was mobilized. Pakistan reacted by closing the Afghan frontiers, which meant a complete stoppage of Afghanistan's shipping. Subsequently the Soviet Union and Afghanistan signed an agreement for the transport of Afghan goods through Russia; Afghanistan was now completely dependent, in matters of trade, on her northern neighbor. On August 27 the general Soviet-

---

[53] *New Times*, Moscow, no. 9, February 23, 1956, p. 15, "Soviet-Afghan Cooperation," by V. Petukhov.
[54] *Ibid.*

MAP 4. THE DRIVE TO THE SOUTH, ASIA

Afghan trade agreement was renewed;[55] progress was being made toward economic *rapprochement* with other countries of the Soviet bloc. In October, Czechoslovakia started preparations for the building of a cement factory, a glass factory, and a cotton mill in Afghanistan; a credit of 5 million dollars was granted by Prague.[56] Czechoslovakia, obviously on Soviet suggestion, offered arms to Afghanistan.

The tension between Pakistan, backed by the Baghdad Pact and

[55] *Izvestia,* August 30, 1955.
[56] *The New York Times,* November 2, 1955.

the West, and Afghanistan, backed by the Soviet Union, had reached its peak when Bulganin and Khrushchev made known their plan to visit Kabul.[57]

Passing over Pakistan on their flight, the Soviet leaders arrived in Kabul on December 15 to "strengthen ties" with the southern neighbor in a series of far-reaching statements and pledges. Although the enthusiasm of the population was not great compared to the reception in India, the discussions with the Kabul government resulted in the establishment of closer Soviet relations with Afghanistan than with any other country of Central or Southeastern Asia. Sharp attacks on the "colonialists" in Bulganin's speeches were hardly surprising; but at a dinner party at which Premier Daud was present, he went further, stating:

> We view with sympathy the policy of Afghanistan on the Pushtunistan problem. The Soviet Union stands for a just solution of the Pushtunistan problem, which cannot be achieved without consideration of the vital interests of the people living in Pushtunistan.[58]

Before their departure from Afghanistan the Soviet leaders announced another spectacular gift to the country—a 100-bed hospital and fifteen autobuses. An airplane, an Il-14, was given as a gift to the king of Afghanistan.

Political statements signed by both parties provided for the extension of the neutrality treaty of 1931 for ten years. More important was the economic agreement of December 18, which provided for a new loan of 100 million dollars on easy terms: thirty years, 2 per cent interest, repayment to begin after eight years and to continue for twenty-two years. Of the large sum, 40 million dollars was appropriated for the purchase of arms,[59] and other amounts for the building of airports and roads. In further negotiations it was agreed that the

---

[57] *Pravda* printed the resolution of Afghanistan's Big Jirga (Council of Tribal Chieftains) concerning both Pushtunistan and rearmament. "1. Since the people of Pushtunistan, our brothers by religion and race, have turned to us with the request of support of their right to independence, this becomes the duty of the people and the government of Afghanistan. Therefore the Big Jirga recommends that the government, in accordance with the tenets of the *shariat*, support the demand of the Pushtunistan people and secure for them the right to independent decision on their fate. . . . The Big Jirga, taking into consideration the requirements of the times, recommends that the government strengthen and arm the country for defense by every possible means in any possible honest way." (*Pravda*, November 23, 1955.)

[58] *Missiya Druzhby* (Mission of Friendship), *op. cit.*, vol. 1, p. 267.

[59] According to Pakistani sources, part of the arms was to be turned over to the Pushtu tribes (*The New York Times*, March 11, 1956).

Afghanistan and the Drive to the Sea 317

Soviet Union would supply materials and equipment for two hydroelectric stations, three vehicle repair shops, irrigation works, a laboratory, an airfield, and a new road over the Hindu-Kush. With its 100-million-dollar loan the Soviet Union outstripped the United States and all other countries in aid to Afghanistan. Soviet physicians began to arrive in Afghanistan in April, 1956; 100 additional technicians arrived in July; in August an Afghan military mission departed for Moscow. At the Kabul exposition, held in the summer of 1956, the Soviet and Chinese pavilions were the largest. In December, Premier Daud of Afghanistan visited Moscow, where he reaffirmed the Soviet-Afghan declarations and pledges.

What had proved impossible in India and Burma—the sale of Soviet and Czechoslovak arms—was realized in Afghanistan. Massive Soviet arms aid was financed by means of new credits amounting to 25 million dollars.[60] In 1956 Czech technicians began to arrive in Afghanistan; their number soon reached about five hundred. Czechoslovakia, which had traded with Afghanistan in the past, opened a depot in Kabul for the sale of industrial products and arms.[61] Early in September, 1956, Kabul radio announced an arms deal with the Soviet Union and Czechoslovakia. The government stressed, however, that no "strings" were attached to this or to subsequent acquisitions of arms and that the government continued to maintain full political independence.[62]

On their return to Moscow the two roving Soviet leaders reported to the Supreme Soviet. They again stressed the issue of neutralism, on which, they said, there was unanimity between the Soviet Union and the three nations visited; they defended Soviet-Indian solidarity on the Kashmir and Goa issues, and called for Soviet support for Afghanistan's position on Pushtunistan.

The resolution adopted by the Supreme Soviet not only expressed "complete satisfaction with the results" of the visit, but stated:

> The Supreme Soviet considers that the visit of Comrades N. A. Bulganin and N. S. Khrushchev has demonstrated the great importance of personal contact between statesmen for the promotion of mutual

[60] *The New York Times*, September 5 and 28, 1956.
[61] *Ibid.*, November 2, 1955, and September 28, 1956.
[62] *Ibid.*, September 5, 1956; *Osteuropa*, Stuttgart, no. 2/3, February–March, 1960, pp. 86–87.

understanding, establishment of confidence between states, and development of international cooperation.

The high praise of "personal contacts" was apparently intended as a rebuff to the opposition, and Malenkov in particular, who had objected to a prolonged absence of the Party and government leaders.

Defying the fallen gods of yesterday, Khrushchev dispatched his right-hand man Anastas Mikoyan on a long tour of neutralist Asia to apply the finishing touches to the "very satisfactory" beginnings. A trade and aid specialist, Mikoyan was to translate the ovations and the perishable garlands into prosaic economic agreements. He was accompanied on his trip by Sharaf Rashidov, the rising Communist from Soviet Uzbekistan, an antireligionist groomed to impress the outside Moslem world.

Mikoyan's official assignment was to take part in celebrations in Karachi; the two men also visited Afghanistan, India, Burma, North Vietnam, China, and Outer Mongolia. In Karachi, Mikoyan, imitating Khrushchev in his speeches at large meetings, promised eternal friendship and, like Khrushchev, ended his speeches with the Pakistani phrase *"Khuda Khefiz"* (God be with you). In New Delhi, Mikoyan and Rashidov placed a wreath of red roses on the gravestone under which Gandhi's cremated remains were buried.[63]

In Burma, Mikoyan and U Nu signed a joint statement in which the Soviet Union offered and Burma accepted as a gift from the Soviet the construction of a technological school, a hospital, a theater, a stadium, and a hotel, and in which Burma presented as a gift a "corresponding quantity of rice." Trade agreements were signed.

6. INDONESIA AND PAKISTAN

For various reasons, Indonesia, although one of the most important and populous of the "newly liberated" Moslem countries, seemed to have been neglected by Moscow in the era of the rise of the neutrals. She was not diplomatically recognized by the Soviet Union until January, 1950, three years after India; her leaders were the last "neutralists" to visit Moscow and join the "peace zone."

After the visit of John Foster Dulles to Indonesia in March, 1956, the Soviet Union and China began to pay more attention to that

---

[63] *Pravda*, March 27, 1956.

Indonesia and Pakistan

country. To counteract pro-American trends there, Soviet and Chinese artists and writers were sent into the country; a Soviet economic mission discussed Soviet-Indonesian trade agreements, and Soviet trade representatives proposed to the Indonesians the construction, on the Indian pattern, of substantial industrial plants. Even Soviet arms were offered.[64] In accordance with the established pattern, *rapprochement* was to be crowned by a visit to Moscow. The first trade agreement with the Soviet Union was signed in Jakarta on August 8, 1956, and a fortnight later President Sukarno left on a grand tour of the Soviet Union, China, Czechoslovakia, Yugoslavia, and Austria.

Sukarno's first stop was the Soviet Union. During his stay, he lived at the Kremlin. He took part in meetings and receptions, where he repeated the usual pompous and empty slogans of brotherhood, peace, and freedom.

> "Indonesians greet one another with 'Merdeka,' meaning freedom. You love freedom; we love freedom, too. I invite all of you to exclaim together with me: 'Merdeka!' Let us all together . . . say it five times, 'Merdeka.' When we say this word in Indonesia, we raise our hand like this"—and President Sukarno raised his palm upward. Following his example, thousands of hands rose and the whole square rang with the calls: " 'Merdeka!' 'Freedom!' " [65]

In Soviet Central Asia Sukarno was taken on a tour of Moslem sites. He visited a mosque, conversed with a mufti, and spoke to the praying: " 'To the Moslems who are present here, I turn with the Moslem greeting—Assaliam Aleikum! . . . Merdeka, Merdeka, and again Merdeka, which means freedom!' " [66]

The Soviet press published enthusiastic stories about the "great fighter for Indonesia's independence"; omitting mention of his activities while his country was under Japanese occupation, which would hardly have fit into the eulogistic narrative, his biographers instead described his years in prison and exile and his antagonism toward the West. Sukarno in turn praised Soviet kolkhozes, extolled the Bolshevik revolution, and attacked "imperialism" and "colonialism"; ties between the "brothers," Russia and Indonesia, he said, were "indestructible." Voroshilov decorated Sukarno with the Order of Lenin and presented him with an Il-14 (Ilyushin) plane.

[64] *The New York Times*, August 21, 1956.
[65] *Izvestia*, September 4, 1956.
[66] *Ibid.*, September 6, 1956.

The Indonesians and the Russians signed the usual declaration stressing the main points of Soviet neutralist policy: antagonism toward colonialism and atomic arms; admission of Communist China to the United Nations; peaceful settlement of the Suez issue; cooperation of the two governments in economic affairs; etc. Another point in the joint program was the familiar rejection of "military pacts" and coalitions.

Four days later an agreement providing for a 100-million-dollar Soviet loan to Indonesia was signed in Jakarta. The substantial loan was for a twelve-year period at 2½ per cent interest and was to be used for industrial construction.

With the happy inclusion of Moslem Indonesia into the circle of neutral friends, there remained only one—but a very distressing—gap in the neutralist alignment of South Asia. The foremost Moslem nation, whose official name since 1956 was "Islamic Republic of Pakistan," had joined the Baghdad and SEATO pacts. Soviet-Pakistani relations were at their lowest point at the time Khrushchev and Bulganin returned home from their triumphal tour of Asia.

For Soviet Russia and China this situation was more than painful. Pakistan belonged to the group of nations that had just liberated themselves from "the clutches of British imperialism," which were in danger of falling prey to "American imperialism," and which were supposed to view Russia and China as the bearers of pure intentions in international affairs. In the Moscow and Peking view it was natural that old capitalist countries such as Belgium or Portugal, or even Sweden, should join the Western pacts, but it was perverse and contrary to historical laws that one of the nations of the southeast should join its "exploiters" in fighting the greatest liberating powers of the world. Moscow and Peking were at a loss to find the proper way of dealing with this strange anomaly.

In January, 1956, immediately after the Soviet-Indian and Soviet-Afghan anti-Pakistan demonstrations, Soong Ching-ling, widow of Sun Yat-sen and holding a high place herself in the National People's Congress, arrived in Karachi at the head of a Chinese delegation. Early in February Bulganin himself, in a press interview, stretched out a hand to Pakistan. The Soviet Union, Bulganin said, could give substantial aid to Pakistan "without any conditions attached"; however

Indonesia and Pakistan

—and these were his conditions—the relationship must be based on Pancha Shilla (the "Five Principles"); the Soviet Union cannot "be indifferent to the fact that some of her neighbor countries, in order to oblige alien interests, are joining aggressive military-political groupings, which are a menace to the security of the Soviet Union. We are against military-political aggressive groupings such as SEATO and the Baghdad Pact, to which Pakistan belongs." [67]

In March, Molotov told the Pakistanis in Moscow that the Soviet government might be willing to build a steel mill in Pakistan like the one it had built in India, send Soviet technicians to Karachi, and even share atomic knowledge. A general trade agreement with the Soviet Union was signed in Karachi in June, and Pakistan-Afghanistan tension subsided.

The Soviet courtship of Pakistan was in vain, however. On September 26, the Pakistan government officially notified its diplomatic missions that it would remain faithful to its commitments to the West. This was to remain its position for a long time.

[67] *Pravda*, February 7, 1956.

CHAPTER 5

THE TWENTIETH PARTY CONGRESS AND FOREIGN AFFAIRS

The Party Congress of February, 1956, marked the peak of the post-Stalin liberalization. The thaw reached its warmest point when Khrushchev announced to the Congress the modifications in Communist precepts and noted the shortcomings and negative traits of the late dictator. The disputes and the angry rejoinders that had been made in the heat of the debate at the 1955 Plenum had been resolved into smooth-sounding new theses and theories.

The months that had intervened between the Plenum and the Congress had been filled with developments that apparently tended to confirm the correctness of Khrushchev's "new deal." Ties with Yugoslavia and China were becoming firmer; soon, it appeared, all Communist-controlled nations would be reunited in one grand alliance. *Rapprochement* with the neutrals of Asia was making progress since the Khrushchev and Bulganin visits. Arab nations were about to ally themselves with the Soviet Union. The fact that the Geneva parleys had ended in failure proved again the intransigence of American capitalism, and this too was in accord with Khrushchev's new theses.

1. WARS ARE NOT INEVITABLE

The first of the new theses was that wars are no longer inevitable. Lenin and Stalin had maintained that there would be no end to wars so long as capitalism prevailed in the major countries of the world, and there had been no change in this belief since Stalin's death. A highly official textbook written and edited by a group of prominent Communist authorities and published in 1954 in an edition of 1,400,000 copies, said that "at the present period the Leninist thesis of the in-

Wars Are Not Inevitable

evitability of wars between capitalist countries remains in force."[1] The Soviet press reiterated this thesis.

But now Khrushchev told the Congress: "There is a Marxist-Leninist principle which says that while imperialism exists, wars are inevitable." This was true, Khrushchev said, before World War II. Now, however, "there is no fatal inevitability of war. Now there are powerful social and political forces commanding serious means capable of preventing the unleashing of war by the imperialists, and—should they try to start it—of delivering a smashing rebuff to the aggressors and thwarting their adventurous plans." Mikoyan joined Khrushchev in the denial of the "fatal" inevitability of war.

The new thesis signified a major departure from Leninism-Stalinism. Lenin had maintained that capitalism, by the very nature of its system *must* try to expand, conquer new territories, and acquire new colonies. Since the world was practically divided between the great powers, capitalism could satisfy its urge only by wars; thus, "imperialist wars" were inevitable. Military catastrophes, a result of capitalist development, produce, as a reaction, revolutionary movements which culminate in the socialist transformation of the world.

The thesis of "inevitable war" was not an accidental element in Leninism-Stalinism, not a part which could be removed and replaced by another; it was indeed a thesis that rested on the deepest roots of the political philosophy. Facts, however, tended to disprove the thesis. It was impossible to deny the new upsurge of capitalist economy, which had occurred without wars.

Khrushchev's protégé, Dimitri Shepilov, took the floor to attack the "oversimplified" views about the "continuous line" of capitalist decay. Molotov indulged in mild self-criticism, stating that he and his Ministry had often been "prisoners of old habits"; in the past, he confessed, he had committed mistakes, but these had been corrected by the Central Committee and the Presidium. Mikoyan attacked the Stalinist theory of the "decay of capitalism"—without mentioning that Stalin had inherited the theory from Lenin. "Stalin's well-known pronouncement concerning the U.S.A., Britain and France," Mikoyan said, "to the effect that after the world market had been split up 'the volume of production in these countries will contract,' can hardly

[1] *Politicheskaya Ekonomiya* (Political Economy; textbook), Moscow, 1954, p. 288. Among the authors were D. T. Shepilov, K. V. Ostrovityanov, P. F. Yudin, L. A. Leontiev, and others.

help us in our analysis of the conditions of the economy of contemporary capitalism and is hardly correct. This assertion does not explain the complex and contradictory phenomenon of contemporary capitalism and the fact that capitalist production has grown in many countries since the war." All these doubts and reservations marked the atmosphere of cautious self-criticism that prevailed in 1956.

The slogan of "peaceful coexistence" among countries with different social systems—a corollary of "no inevitable wars"—was proclaimed one of the pillars of Soviet foreign policy. The slogan was not new; it had been launched, though only for propaganda purposes, in Stalin's time. Now Khrushchev in his report and the Congress in its resolution, combining "peaceful coexistence" with repudiation of Stalinism, were announcing that "peaceful coexistence" would be the direction for the future and the path of *rapprochement* with other countries.

Though the term "national Communism" was never mentioned at the Congress, the idea of different "national roads to socialism" was accepted as an old Leninist tenet. Khrushchev proceeded to enumerate approvingly the "different roads": one was the system as established in the East European "people's democracies"; another was the special path of Chinese Communism; a third was the system in Yugoslavia, under which "specific forms of economic control and of the state machinery" emerge. At this summit of *rapprochement* with the dissidents, Khrushchev pushed aside the apprehension that "national roads" might signify a desire among the dissidents for independence and separation; nor did he claim a leading role for the Soviet Union in the "socialist camp."

2. VIOLENT REVOLUTIONS ARE NOT INEVITABLE

The new orientation toward neutral nations made it expedient to change a second maxim of Soviet ideology and policy. Moving away from the obligatory thesis that violent revolution and upheavals are the only road to socialism, Soviet Communism was now ready to accept parliamentary processes as a substitute for violence and to consider nonviolent forms of social revolution as possible. Entering this path of revision of Marxism, the Soviet leadership maintained, as always in similar cases, that the old views had been correct in their

Violent Revolutions Are Not Inevitable

time but that they must now be amended to accord with the overriding role of the Soviet Union in world affairs.

"Violence is the midwife of every old society pregnant with a new one"—this Marxian thesis was one of the basic and immutable ideas of Leninism. But now, Khrushchev said, in a carefully prepared part of his address:

> Our enemies like to picture us, Leninists, as advocates of violence always and under all circumstances. It is true that we recognize the necessity of a revolutionary transformation of the capitalist society into a socialist one. . . . But the forms of the social revolution vary. And it is not true that we regard violence and civil war as the only way to remake society. . . .
>
> The winning of a firm parliamentary majority based on the mass revolutionary movement of the proletariat and the working people would create conditions for the working class of many capitalist and formerly colonial countries to make fundamental social changes.

Of course, Khrushchev added, violent revolutions will have to occur if "reactionary forces" try to resist; and, of course, the leading role in the nonviolent transformation must go to the "proletariat." In the main, however, "many countries can and will attain Socialism by parliamentary means." ("In the present historical situation," commented *Kommunist,* "the solving of arising problems . . . by the violent overthrow of the ruling classes—if necessary, by the use of armed force —is not the most expedient for the majority of nations.") [2]

The emphasis on "peaceful transformation" had a double aim. The governments of the underdeveloped, former "colonial and semicolonial" countries, such as India, Burma, and Egypt, were being wooed by the Soviet. To these governments the local Communist parties, with their revolutionary tactics, their undergrounds, and their arms, were an internal enemy, a potential source of civil war. To Moscow the solution of the problem presented by this situation was as difficult as squaring the circle. Refusing to acknowledge the dilemma openly, Soviet Communism tried to steer a middle course; its emphasis on nonviolence and parliamentary processes was an attempt at collaboration with both the governments and the Communist parties of a number of nations.

To vindicate, in the eyes of international Communism, its newly

---

[2] *Kommunist,* Moscow, no. 14, September, 1956, p. 20.

developed preference for parliamentary processes, Moscow made references to the fact that a number of loyal satellite governments had achieved power without violent revolutions. In Czechoslovakia and Hungary, for example, parliaments had served, in 1945–48, as the fighting arenas, and parliamentary majorities, not street barricades had marked the road to a Communist regime. Such developments, Moscow noted, were possible only because these nations lived in friendship with and were protected by the mighty Soviet Union. Given Soviet friendship and protection, a more peaceful strategy was possible elsewhere too.

Khrushchev's denunciation of Stalin in his "secret speech" at the closed session of the Congress dealt almost entirely with Soviet internal affairs, Stalin's purges, and police methods. In the 24,000-word secret report less than 1,000 words were devoted to what might be viewed as criticism of Stalin's foreign-political actions; unlike his remarks directed against Stalin's home policy, Khrushchev's criticism here was superficial and casual. Khrushchev told the Congress that:

1. The "risky situation" that developed into the Korean War was due to Stalin's "unrealistic appreciation of the position of the Western nations," meaning his underestimation of the United States' resolve to defend Korea.

2. In China, Stalin's "lack of faith in the Chinese comrades" had retarded the establishment of the Mao Tse-tung regime.

3. In the conflict with Yugoslavia, "Stalin played a shameful role," because "it was completely possible to prevent the rupture of relations with that country."

4. In regard to India, Stalin had misunderstood the significance of the emancipation of that country.

5. As to Germany, Stalin had relied too firmly on his pact with Hitler and did not prepare for a German attack. "Everything was ignored" by Stalin, Khrushchev said, on the eve of the war: warnings from abroad, warnings by Soviet army commanders, by deserters, and others. Stalin had decided that

> no preparatory defensive work should be undertaken at the borders, that the Germans were not to be given any pretext for the initiation of military action against us. Thus, our borders were insufficiently prepared to repel the enemy.

When the fascist armies had actually invaded Soviet territory and military operation had begun, Moscow issued the order that the German fire was not to be returned. Why? It was because Stalin, despite evident facts, thought that the war had not yet started, that this was only a provocative action on the part of several undisciplined sections of the German Army, and that our reaction might serve as a reason for the Germans to begin the war.[3]

Khrushchev was not critical of the Soviet-Nazi pact of 1939; rather, as he explained soon afterward, he continued to approve it; nor did he criticize Stalin's general attitude toward the West. Khrushchev's innovations did not imply total rejection of Stalinism in foreign affairs.

3. OVERTURES TO THE SOCIALIST PARTIES OF THE WEST

The governments of underdeveloped countries, mainly those in Asia and Africa, were the first targets of Khrushchev's appeal to the neutrals. The second targets were the socialist parties, whose weight and influence lay mainly in Western Europe.

A tentative approach was made in 1955, when Khrushchev's Central Committee sent out vague feelers to the Austrian, British, Danish, and Finnish Socialist parties. In November, 1955, when the Socialist premier of Norway, Einar Gerhardsen, visited Moscow, Khrushchev handed him a memo proposing establishment of contact and cooperation in various forms.[4] The French Socialist leadership, too, accepted an invitation to visit Moscow. At the Twentieth Congress, Khrushchev took a further step, proposing to the socialist parties of the world a new kind of united front:

> In many countries the working class has been split for many years and its different groups do not present a united front. . . . Life has put on the agenda many questions which not only demand rapprochement and cooperation between all workers' parties but also create real possibilities for this cooperation. The most important of these problems is that of preventing a new war. [Therefore] cooperation with those circles of the socialist movement which have views on the forms of transition to socialism differing from ours is also possible and essential.

Accordingly, the Congress resolution on the question read:

[3] Khrushchev's speech of February 24, 1956, in Bertram D. Wolfe, *Khrushchev and Stalin's Ghost*, New York, Frederick A. Praeger, 1957, p. 172.
[4] *The New Leader*, April 16, 1956, p. 12.

> In the interest of strengthening peace it is very important that all forces which are against war should act in a united front and not weaken their efforts in the struggle for the preservation of peace. Of utmost importance in this case is the overcoming of the split in the labor movement and the establishment of businesslike contacts between the Communist and the Socialist parties.

This was another departure from Stalinism. To Stalin, even in his "united front" periods, the Social-Democrats were enemies. Now the highly official *Kommunist* refused to accept this part of the Stalin legacy:

> The thesis which followed from Stalin's works, that to achieve victory over the bourgeoisie the main blow must be directed against the petty-bourgeois democracy (social-reformism) in order to achieve its isolation, was for a long time considered as universally accepted by the labor movement. Of course, the struggle against conciliators with the capitalists is necessary for the victory of the working class. But the conception that to achieve victory the main blow must be concentrated against social-reformism is coming more and more in conflict with reality.[5]

If it were successful, a united front with the socialists could bear abundant fruit. Countries in which the socialist party was in power (in Scandinavia, for example) could be expected to move away from NATO, break off their close ties with the United States, and join the family of neutral nations. In Germany and Britain the socialist parties, which were in favor of certain Soviet ideas about disarmament in Central Europe, could become allies of Moscow. In France and Italy, where anti-Americanism was pronounced, a rupture between the socialists and the "aggressors" of the West might turn the course of European history. Or so it appeared, at least, in early 1956, when the Twentieth Congress was in session.

4. AMERICA IS THE ENEMY

In all these mutations of Soviet theory and policy, one feature of the old days remained constant: hostility to the United States. In Soviet eyes, America continued to be the bulwark of reaction, exploitation, belligerency; the shadow of America lay over Europe and the Far East; American pressure prevented a Communist transformation

---

[5] *Kommunist*, Moscow, no. 14, September, 1956, p. 26.

in the West; America's international networks were the greatest evil of the times.

The great Soviet hope was for a rupture between the United States and her Western allies. The expectation of such a rupture had survived the man who had first predicted it, Leon Trotsky, as well as Stalin, who had borrowed it from his hated enemy. Thirty years before the Twentieth Party Congress, Stalin had announced: "The principal among the conflicts of interests is that between the United States and England." "The star of England is setting," he told his Central Committee in July, 1928; "the star of America is rising. What is this basic conflict fraught with? It is fraught with war. When two giants collide with each other, when this globe is too small for them, they try to measure their strength, they try to solve the vexing questions of world hegemony by means of war." [6]

Stalin's lieutenant Dimitri Manuilsky told a conference of the Communist Party: "Two forces will meet each other face to face in the future world war. They are, on the one hand, the strongly developed American imperialism; on the other, the declining British imperialism. We can foresee that in such a conflict Great Britain will suffer the same fate that Germany did. . . . In that war the Pacific Ocean will be the battleground." [7]

Decades passed. A great Pacific war was fought by a British-American alliance. Stalin held to his prediction. "Would it not be truer to say," he wrote a few months before his death, "that capitalist Britain, and, after her, capitalist France, will be compelled in the end to break from the embrace of the U.S.A. and enter into conflict with it in order to secure an independent position, and, of course, high profits?" [8]

The tenacity of Soviet anti-Americanism became evident in Khrushchev's otherwise revisionist theories. In almost the same terms that Stalin had used, Khrushchev told the Twentieth Congress:

> The greatest of all contradictions is that between the United States and Britain. Anglo-American antagonism embraces a wide range of matters. Under the banner of the "Atlantic commonwealth" the transoceanic rival is laying his hands on the key strategic and economic

[6] Speech, July 13, 1928.
[7] Speech at the Fifteenth Congress of the Communist Party of the Soviet Union, December, 1927.
[8] *Pravda*, October 3, 1952.

positions of the British Empire, is trying to straddle imperial communications, shatter the system of preferred tariffs, and subjugate to itself the sterling area. No wonder a tendency is growing in Britain and France to put an end to a situation in which the "Atlantic commonwealth" is advantageous for one partner only.

As if nothing had changed, Khrushchev maintained that "the United States is disorganizing the world market by carrying on unilateral trade, fencing off its market from foreign exports, prohibiting trade with the East, dumping agricultural produce and resorting to other measures which seriously affect other countries. The economic struggle among the capitalist countries is gaining momentum all the time."

5. PARTIAL REVISION OF STALINISM IN FOREIGN AFFAIRS

To his successors in the 1950's, Stalin's division of the world into two "camps" appeared oversimplified; something more sophisticated and closer to reality was needed. The "two camps" were now replaced by five sectors into which the approximately one hundred nations of the world were grouped:

1	2	3	4	5
Soviet Union	Communist China Other "socialist countries"	India Indonesia Egypt Other uncommitted nations	Britain France West Germany Japan Other members of the Western alliances	United States

At the extreme right stood the United States, at the extreme left, the Soviet Union. Between these extremes the other powers were grouped as follows. Close to the United States: members of the Atlantic Treaty Organization, the Baghdad Pact, and the Southeast Asia Treaty Organization; close to the Soviet Union: the groups of her own allies and satellites in Europe and Asia; in the center: the group of "neutral" nations that did not belong to any of the combinations.

As before, the United States held the position of the greatest adversary of the Soviet Union, the instigator of anti-Soviet movements, the organizer of anti-Communist uprisings, the supplier of arms to "reactionary" forces, the bulwark of ideological and political reaction.

The Communist Opposition 331

Real improvement in the world situation was not possible so long as America maintained her present position. Her power must be broken, if possible without war.

The members of the second group were America's allies and associates. Moscow's antagonism toward these governments, although strong and consistent, was less intense than toward the United States. Soviet efforts were directed toward the separation of members of this group from the United States. Every crack in the alignment of the nations of this group must be widened.

The progress of humanity toward its great goal was being and would be gradually achieved by:

1. The transition of one nation after another from group 4 (the West) to group 3 (the neutrals). It was expected in particular that France, in Europe, and Iran, in the Middle East, would make the transition soon.

2. The transition of one nation after another from group 3 (the neutrals) to group 2 (the Soviet bloc).

The transition would be achieved in various ways—by revolutions, civil wars, or less violent means. The end result would be the accumulation of such overwhelming power in the hands of the coalition (group 1 plus group 2) that its control over the rest of the world would be decisive.

6. THE COMMUNIST OPPOSITION

The ideological innovations of 1955–56 entailed a fight of the majority group of the Presidium against a consistent and stubborn opposition headed by the three venerable leaders, Molotov, Malenkov, and Kaganovich. Because of their long service and high rank they carried considerable weight in the Party, and the fight was a tough one. At almost every meeting of the Presidium the opposition advanced "its own course, remarks, and 'amendments'; it sometimes caused a delay in the resolving of questions under discussion." [9]

The opposition was never permitted, however, to make a statement publicly or before the Party Congress and not even, as far as is known,

[9] Statement by M. Z. Saburov at the Twenty-first Party Congress, in *Vneocherednoi XXI Syezd Kommunistischeskoi Partii Sovetskogo Soyuza* (Extraordinary XXI Congress of the Communist Party of the Soviet Union), January 27–February 5, 1959, Stenographic Report, vol. 2, Moscow, 1959, p. 290.

to develop a comprehensive collective program in a closed session. Its leaders apparently differed on certain issues; Molotov, for example, opposed the wide range of "rehabilitations." They also, it appears, differed on the question of the "virgin lands." [10] Yet they were able, by their common opposition to Khrushchev, eventually to combine their forces into a single faction and later even to divide among themselves the leading posts in the expected post-Khrushchev regime. Though ultimately defeated, the opposition constituted an important and legitimate faction of Communism, with ideological roots in Leninism and Stalinism, a faction more orthodox on some issues than the Khrushchev majority.

What we know about the political face of the opposition is based mainly on official Soviet statements,[11] which cannot be viewed as objective. Often made in the heat of battle, and with refutation impossible, they distorted the views of the opposition. The Khrushchev group depicted the foreign-political course of the opposition (this was probably Molotov's course, not always approved by the others) as follows: (1) it questioned the new no-war outlook, that is, the possibility of progress toward Communism without armed conflicts; (2) it rejected the idea of "no violent" roads to Communism, of progress by parliamentary means; (3) it was opposed to the new emphasis on "national roads to Communism" and adhered to the old thesis of uniformity and conformity; (4) it was opposed to *rapprochement* with the Social-Democratic parties; (5) it was opposed to the new *rapprochement* with Yugoslav Communism, agreeing to the desirability of relations between the two governments but not between the Communist parties of the two countries; (6) on the issue of the satellites it was opposed to the prevailing trend toward liberalization; (7) it questioned the benefits of frequent visits abroad by the highest Soviet leaders; (8) it was opposed to Soviet withdrawal from the occupied zone of Austria and acquiescence in the establishment of an independent neutral Austria; (9) it was opposed to opening negotiations with Japan with a view to concluding a peace treaty; (10) it refused to accept Khrushchev's orientation toward and emphasis on neutrals and neutrality, considering it a deviation from classical communism;

---

[10] Giuseppe Boffa, *Inside the Khrushchev Era*, New York, Marzani & Munsell, Publishers, 1959, pp. 108–9.

[11] *Izvestia*, July 12, 1957; *Pravda*, July 4 and 7 and August 28, 1957; *Trud*, July 13, 1957.

The Communist Opposition

(11) it was opposed to the abundant economic and military help being extended to the underdeveloped non-Communist countries of Asia and the Middle East. On this issue it "acted as men blinded by nationalist narrow-mindedness." [12]

These points of disagreement between the two Communist factions proved again that it was impossible to label either of them "rightist" or "leftist"; traits of both rightism and leftism were combined in the theory, and even more in the practice, of each. The Khrushchev group was prepared to try to collaborate with Titoism, Social-Democratic "traitors," and "capitalist" neutrals, which, it would seem, was a trend toward "rightism" and moderation. By selling arms to Egypt and Syria, however, it challenged the West, thereby provoking conflicts and warlike attitudes, and this was a trait of "leftism," as was also the "anti-American" orientation.

The Malenkov-Molotov group, on the other hand, while it was not always homogeneous and while it often clung to theories and slogans of Stalinism, sometimes insisted on measures and policies of moderation and accommodation. It did not believe, for example, that the Soviet Union should supply arms to the regimes of backward countries; in this group's eyes it was not machine guns but the local Communist party that was the lever for creating a people's democracy. Applied in practice, this would mean rejection, for example, of Khrushchev's experiments with the Arab countries, and consequently easing of relations with the West.

Soviet industrialization efforts in and large loans to the underdeveloped countries likewise aroused protests on the part of the opposition, which rejected the plan of building power stations in Burma, metallurgical units in India, etc., at the expense of the Soviet people. Large investments abroad by the Soviet government were a phenomenon of the Khrushchev era, and here too the source of the Soviet funds that were fertilizing the economies of other countries was the labor of the same Soviet peasants, workers, and intelligentsia. The larger the Soviet investments abroad, the inevitably lower the standard of living of the Soviet population.

It is uncertain precisely who supported and who opposed Khrushchev on the question of the suppression of the Hungarian uprising in November, 1956. From Khrushchev's speech at the Hungarian

[12] Saburov, *op. cit.*, p. 290.

Party Congress in December, 1959, it is obvious that some of the opposition leaders, despite their orthodoxy, disapproved the fateful Soviet operation.

On the whole, the course of the Khrushchev group was toward more realism and less oppression and terror inside Russia, but it also called for an intense offensive against the West and a straining of all forces for the transformation of the Soviet Union into an imperial power greater, stronger, and more awe-inspiring than any other nation in the world.

CHAPTER 6

FERMENT IN EASTERN EUROPE

1. AWAY FROM MOSCOW!

Although never intended as a step toward the political emancipation of the satellites, the easing of Soviet pressure in the post-Stalin era in fact developed into the first phase of a growing movement for independence. In most, although not all, of the "people's democracies" the urge toward emancipation, which grew stronger and stronger in 1955–56, became almost irresistible; the fighting spirit produced violent commotions, split the ruling parties, and finally caused the earthquakes of October–November, 1956.

The eighteen months from the spring of 1955 to the fall of 1956 were an especially important period. In rising popular movements, everything—success as well as setback—contributes to its progress: police repression produces indignation and protest; concessions on the part of the regime increase the self-confidence of the rebels; curbing of the press evokes expressions of contempt, easing of the curb produces bold defiance. Contrary to the widespread notion, increased pressures do not always lead toward revolution; on the contrary, it is often hesitation and lack of self-assurance on the part of the authorities that open the door to revolt.

Three developments in particular contributed to the rise of the post-Stalin emancipation movements among the Soviet satellites: first, the Moscow-initiated rehabilitation and partial liberalization, and the curbing of police powers; second, the Soviet *rapprochement* with Tito; third, the Twentieth Congress and the repudiation of Stalinism.

In 1955 it still seemed as if little had changed in the satellites. The picture was a motley one: in the summer of 1955 trials were taking place and severe sentences were being meted out to "spies" and

"American agents." On the other hand, amnesties were declared in Hungary in April, in Czchoslovakia in May, in Rumania in June and September, and in Bulgaria in September. Changes in the forced labor system in Eastern Europe were being made, and forced labor was being at least partially abolished. In Hungary, Cardinal Mindszenty was pardoned in July, 1955, Archbishop Gross was freed in October of the same year, and nine Catholic priests were freed in February, 1956.

As the effects of the new Soviet course became more widespread, the influence of "deviationists" and victims of police terror increased. In Poland, former prisoners Wladyslaw Gomulka and Marion Spychalski acquired political stature. Not only were Police Chief Stanislaw Radkievicz and his superior Jakub Berman removed in April and May, 1956, but Jacek Tozanski, head of the Police Investigation Department, and five officers of the Department were sentenced in December, 1955, and January, 1956. The press criticized the harsh penalties levied against the kulaks. In Bucharest it was officially announced that the police force had been reduced by 30 per cent.[1] Numbers of socialists in the satellites were released from prison, and a group of Social-Democrats were liberated in April.[2] In Czechoslovakia a number of political prisoners were liberated without official announcement; some purged Communists were posthumously rehabilitated. The old Communist Party of Poland, too, was rehabilitated.

Although these developments were strictly part of the home affairs of the respective countries, a strong and growing international undertone was discernible in them. The main undertone was anti-Soviet and anti-Russian. The belief that Moscow had been the instigator, organizer, and guide of the terroristic ventures of the past was universal; the complete silence of the satellite leadership and press about the Soviet role in their own political misery tended only to strengthen the anti-Soviet sentiments. The lesson drawn from the history of a decade was: political freedom in Eastern Europe was possible only in the framework of the independence of the countries of Eastern Europe from Soviet rule. The desire for emancipation from Moscow, an end to satellite status, and independence from foreign powers—a

---

[1] *The New York Times,* June 16, 1956.
[2] *Ibid.,* April 21, 1956.

natural reaction of a civilized nation to foreign control in general, and to the oppressive system of Stalinism in particular—was at the core of the strongly emotional as well as ideological trends. For about ten years the culture of these countries had been undergoing remodeling after the Russian pattern: their schools and universities taught social science according to the Russian interpretation; study of the Russian language was prescribed for their youth; in foreign affairs their governments had to assume pronounced and bellicose anti-Western attitudes which were contrary to both their tradition and their present sympathies; their military and police affairs were controlled by foreign agencies or agents; their economy served foreign economic needs.

An unusual development in the satellites was that a large section of the Communist leadership—often the majority—were carried away by the new trends. For several decades Russian leadership in the Communist world had been undisputed: Russian ideology was believed all-wise and all-embracing, and the teachings of Lenin and Stalin infallible; Russian strategy and Russian tactics were a source of inspiration and a model for emulation; Russian Communism never committed a blunder. There was great force in this Leninist and Stalinist tradition. The idea that world Communism is a great fighting army led by an experienced and skillful political strategist had had a strong emotional appeal for hundreds of young adherents. But now, after Khrushchev had shown the terrible face of the late dictator, disappointment in Russia as a leader was felt by large sections of the Communist world.

Away from Russia!—this was now the prevailing sentiment. Away from a movement and a party that had adopted these inhuman methods to achieve their objectives! Away from a party that had organized one blood bath after another! Away from a government that after almost four decades had not entered the path of freedom and real peace! Away from Moscow! was behind the emphasis on the variety of national "roads to socialism." Away from Moscow! was the meaning of the strikes in Poland and Hungary. Away from Moscow! was becoming the official Communist line in the United States. "Away from Moscow!" prominent French Communist intellectuals shouted when they threw away their membership cards and publicly condemned Soviet policy in Europe. Away from Moscow! was the prevailing sentiment in the Italian and other Communist parties.

The first in the series of ensuing crises took place in Poland. The death in Moscow of Polish leader Boleslaw Bierut, Stalin's former viceroy, which occurred at the time of the Twentieth Party Congress, marked the beginning of an era of violent rumblings in the largest of the European "people's democracies."

Khrushchev, who had gone to Warsaw for Bierut's funeral, took part in the election of his successor, Edward Ochab, formerly a loyal Stalinist, who had been praised by Stalin as "a good Bolshevik with sharp teeth." [3] In the new climate, however, Ochab turned to reforms and a modicum of "democratization." He declared a broad amnesty, dismissed prosecutors, and purged the secret police; the press was given more leeway than it had had in the past decade. In relations with the Soviet Union, however, Ochab remained circumspect and hesitant. Soviet Marshal Rokossovsky, head of Poland's military forces and member of the Polish Politburo, not only remained at his post but continued to take orders from the Soviet General Staff; he rarely attended the sessions of the Politburo. The Polish press, in which criticism was widespread and sharp, did not, however, assail Moscow's supremacy. To Moscow, this system of relations was acceptable as a compromise.

In the climate of "liberalization" and "de-Stalinization," ferment was growing rapidly. The popular unrest found its first expression in the great strikes that broke out in Poznan in June, 1956. Starting with purely economic demands, the movement of the Poznan workers quickly assumed all the traits of a political revolt. In some of the shops of the huge ZISPO enterprise (manufacture of railway cars), the workers, discontented and restless because their demands and appeals had been ignored for over a year, took it upon themselves to elect a delegation to conduct direct negotiations with the minister. Such an act—a free election—had not occurred for a long time. On June 22, 1956, the delegation departed for Warsaw, and five days later the minister came in person to Poznan to address the workers and promise reforms. The delegates, however, did not appear, and rumors spread that they had been arrested. The next day a strike broke out at the ZISPO plant in which members of the Communist Party took part. Crowds poured into the streets, and the huge demonstration

---

[3] According to Josef Swiatlo, in *News from behind the Iron Curtain*, New York, March, 1955, vol. 4, no. 3, p. 10.

moved on to other industrial plants and called upon all workers to join the strike.

Within a few hours the strike had become general. Moving through the streets, the strikers carried posters on which economic slogans merged with purely political slogans: "We Want Freedom!" "Down with Phony Communism!" "Down with the Russkies!" "Down with the Soviet Occupation!" "We Demand Lower Prices and Higher Wages!" "Down with Dictatorship!"

One of the demonstrations moved to the Justice Department offices to inquire about the fate of the delegates; another set out to look for them in the city prison, which was opened by force and from which 200 prisoners were set free. At this point there occurred the first armed conflicts with the police and army groups. Fighting broke out in Kochanowski Street, where the *Bezpieka* (political police) had its headquarters. Gun fighting continued for three hours, until tanks appeared in the streets and put an end to the fighting. The number of dead was announced as 38, and the number of wounded, including soldiers and security policemen, as 270.

Although the government victory was in this case achieved without direct Soviet help, the anti-Russian ingredients of the movement could not be ignored. The official Soviet explanation was the standard one: "imperialists," namely, the Americans and the Bonn-Germans, were behind the Poznan revolt; although foreign agents had incited the workers, the local authorities were also to blame. Obviously deviating from the Soviet version, however, the Polish leadership blamed also "the bureaucratic distortions of the proletarian State." [4]

The first effect of the revolt in Poznan was that the general Soviet attitude toward the liberating trends in the satellites began to change markedly. Further concessions to "national Communism" appeared dangerous. Bulganin struck a new note when he came to Warsaw to attend the celebration of the Day of Poland's Resurrection:

> We cannot pass by the attempts to weaken the international ties of the Socialist camp under the banner of the so-called "national peculiarities," the attempts to undermine the might of the people's democratic state under the banner of so-called "widening of democracy." By whatever good intentions the people undertaking such ventures might

[4] Konrad Syrop, *Spring in October: The Story of the Polish Revolution 1956*, New York, Frederick A. Praeger, 1957, p. 53.

be guided, they are acting contrary to the interests of their nations, contrary to the great cause of Socialism and democracy.[5]

Bulganin also attacked the Polish press for its too liberal manner of discussing the "cult of personality." When he offered Poland 25 million dollars in consumer goods to alleviate shortages, this was in line with the changed Soviet course. Political discontent in the "socialist nations," Moscow was convinced, could be remedied by economic means, mainly through supplies of Soviet goods.

After more than a year of concessions to "different roads to socialism," after the relaxation and conciliation of the preceding months, Bulganin's stern tone indicated that Moscow was having some afterthoughts. The unity of the imperial structure seemed to be in danger. Were the proponents of orthodoxy right, after all, in their warning, at least in part? Was it not time to turn back and again assert power and leadership?

The "monolith"—Stalin's favorite term for and notion of a correct type of Communist movement—crept back into the language. *Kommunist* [6] emphasized it anew. Was a relapse to Stalinism imminent?

2. TITO'S SHORT-LIVED TRIUMPH

One of the most important components implied in "relaxation of tensions" was a settlement of the protracted conflict with Yugoslavia. After the years-long Soviet offensive against "Titoism," after the fury of repressions against Titoists and the trials and executions of Titoist "traitors" and "spies," the Tito issue had become a most painful one for international Communism. It was high on the Soviet agenda when Moscow proceeded to regularize foreign relations. It is no exaggeration to say that in the years 1955–58 the Yugoslav problem occupied a place no less important than that of Germany in the concerns and activities of the Soviet government.

For Yugoslavia signified much more than a small country in a corner of the Balkans; it signified the main problem of the Soviet empire, and, for every "people's democracy," it was both an internal and an external issue. The old Stalinism had stood for Soviet imperial unity; Titoism stood for emancipation, though within the framework

[5] *Pravda*, July 22, 1956.
[6] Moscow, no. 11, July, 1956, p. 9.

of Communism—by no stretch of the imagination "formal democracy." It had hundreds of avowed and thousands of silent adherents. It constituted an internal danger to the Stalinist governments. During Stalin's time, the Stalin-or-Tito dilemma had been resolved in favor of the former; now the dilemma was again posed. A new course was imperative.

The conviction that prevailed at first was that relations with Yugoslavia could "be normalized" easily and quickly. The deterioration in 1947–52 was viewed as the product of Stalin's willfulness, intolerance, and personal ambition—one of his "excesses." "Normalization" would involve resumption of usual diplomatic and trade relations, cessation of border conflicts, and shutting down of the anti-Tito Yugoslav *émigré* publications in the countries of the "socialist camp" and the smuggling of them into Yugoslavia. The "coexistence" proposed to the "capitalists" nations must prevail also in the relations of the Soviet Union and the "people's democracies" with Yugoslavia.

What Molotov and his colleagues in the Presidium had in view in that initial era of seeking a settlement with Yugoslavia was simply a resumption of state-to-state relations, the type of international relations that would in no way differ from Moscow's relations with any "capitalist" government. "Coexistence" implies a polite and correct, though cool, system of relations, without use of force, boycotts, or political or economic quarantines.

In the Soviet conception of things, state-to-state relations develop on one level, party-to-party relations on another. In the Soviet bloc the latter call for the closest possible international collaboration. Soviet guidance and control in matters of arms, police, foreign affairs, and ideology are feasible only on the party-to-party level. The "socialist camp," as it emerged in the 1940's and continued in the 1950's, was always predicated on a peculiar type of party-to-party collaboration, with the Party of the Soviet Union as the leader.

"Titoism," in the Soviet view, remained an adversary, "hostile to the interests of the working class," its power based on "bloody dictatorship and terror," its secret police "powerful"; people "with dollars," the Soviet charged, were more comfortable in Yugoslavia than the Yugoslavs themselves, while the "poverty-stricken population" observed the foreigners "with indignation." [7] On the ideological level, Moscow,

[7] *New Times*, Moscow, no. 17, April 22, 1953, and no. 37, September 12, 1953.

as late as January, 1955, still adhered to the classic Stalinist thesis that "the attitude toward the Soviet Union, toward the camp of Socialism, serves as the best criterion of genuine proletarian internationalism." [8] Party-to-party relations seemed out of the question at that time.

Nor was Tito inclined to return to the Soviet fold. It had not been an easy matter for him to escape subordination to Stalin's rule and to establish an entirely novel system of foreign politics. Without joining a Western bloc he had obtained American economic and military help to the extent of hundreds of millions of dollars; he had established close ties with other neutrals (India, Egypt), while his own Balkan alliance (Yugoslavia, Greece, and Turkey) had just emerged when Stalin died. In his dealings with Moscow in 1953–54 he repeatedly emphasized his resolve to continue on the same path. Yugoslavia could approve only state-to-state relations with Moscow and the "people's democracies."

Seven weeks after the death of Stalin, Molotov, for the first time since the break in 1949, talked to the Yugoslav envoy. On June 6, 1953, he proposed to Yugoslavia a resumption of normal diplomatic relations. Tito later revealed that in the course of these preliminary negotiations the Soviet side admitted that "in 1948 Yugoslavia was unjustly treated and condemned." "Such statements," Tito said, "and others which will be known to the world one day, have contributed towards our agreeing to establish normal relations. . . ." [9]

Following the Soviet example, Hungary, Bulgaria, and Albania proposed the reopening of their diplomatic missions in Belgrade, and this proposal was accepted by Yugoslavia. Other of the "people's democracies" took this step later. On Yugoslavia's initiative, agreements designed to prevent border incidents were signed with the satellites. In the matter of navigation on the Danube, the Soviet government made concessions to Yugoslavia, and new agreements were signed in May and December, 1953. Agreements were also reached on a resumption of railway traffic.[10] Yugoslav prisoners in the "Soviet bloc" countries were set free; Cominform prisoners in Yugoslavia were, in turn,

---

[8] *Kommunist*, Moscow, no. 1, January, 1955, p. 11.

[9] Tito's address to the Indian Parliament, December, 1954, *Yugoslav Review*, New York, vol. 4, no. 1, January, 1955, p. 12.

[10] "Report on Foreign Policy of the Federal Executive Council of the Federal Assembly, January, 1954," in *Yugoslav Review*, vol. 3, no. 3, March, 1954, pp. 12–15.

liberated. Relations with Communist China were resumed in January, 1955.

Despite the caution and coolness, something substantial had changed. "Titoism" was re-emerging as a power and a problem.

As already noted, the Yugoslav issue had been dividing the two factions in the Soviet Presidium since at least 1954. While Molotov, adhering to the orthodox Stalinist conception of a centralized empire, refused to go beyond official state-to-state relations with the Belgrade defectors, Khrushchev-Mikoyan advocated larger concessions and closer ties with Tito. Khrushchev's idea was the resurrection of an International, although on a new basis, in which Tito and Titoists could find a place. The new International, which would be less rigid than in Stalin's time, might lack the former high degree of subordination and discipline, but it would again embrace all Communist elements of the world. In the eyes of the Khrushchev group the issue of national autonomy could be solved within the framework of a new type of international organization.

The divergencies between Khrushchev and Molotov on the attitude to the other "people's democracies" burst into the open in the fall of 1954 when a high-ranking Soviet delegation was scheduled to go to China. Khrushchev, Mikoyan, and Bulganin were among the members of the delegation, but Molotov, the Foreign Minister, was not. A number of important concessions to the Chinese Communists were made during the visit of the Soviet delegation: the return to China of Port Arthur, abolition of the mixed companies, granting of Soviet loans.

In the celebration speeches at the 1954 anniversary of the November Revolution, Khrushchev spoke of Tito as a "comrade." When Molotov invited all European nations to the conference on collective security that was to lay the foundation for the Warsaw Pact, the Yugoslavs refused to participate because participation would be contrary to their strictly neutralist policy. About the same time, Edward Kardelj, the Yugoslav Vice-President, then on a tour of western and northern Europe, was stressing Yugoslavia's desire to maintain friendly relations with the socialist ("reformist") parties and making some ideological concessions to evolutionary socialism. "National roads to socialism"—a term which was to be much in the fore during the next two years—was the idea behind the Yugoslav campaign to gain friends.

The new Molotov-Tito conflict developed rapidly into a Molotov-Khrushchev conflict. In his report to the session of the Supreme Soviet at which Malenkov was forced to resign (February 8, 1955), Molotov said that the Yugoslav leadership had deviated from the postwar path of collaboration with the Soviet Union, thus, in the typical Stalinist way, laying all the blame for the deterioration on Tito. "Evidently," Molotov said, "in these past years Yugoslavia has to some extent departed from the position which she held in the early years following the second world war. That, of course, is exclusively her internal affair. The Soviet Union is desirous of developing economic, political and cultural relations with Yugoslavia." [11] Consequently, according to the Molotov thesis, improvement was possible only if Tito reverted to a pro-Soviet line.

Belgrade reacted violently. Not only was Tito resolved to pursue his independent course, but he could never forget or forgive the terroristic anti-Titoist course of the Cominform, Stalin's insults and threats, the satellite armies stationed at his frontiers, and the "fascist," "traitor," and "lackey of the capitalists" labels that had been applied to him. His own stature and his party's pride had grown in the two years since Stalin's death. History, Tito maintained, had proved him right; his independence had been recognized everywhere—and now he was asked to repent! Addressing the Yugoslav National Assembly (March 7), Tito severely criticized Molotov and other Stalinists:

> Attempts are being made to explain the normalization of relations with our country [by the] allegation that we had . . . realized our mistakes and are making attempts to correct ourselves—and similar nonsense. . . . Of course, Mr. Molotov's reference to Yugoslavia in his statement to the Supreme Soviet does not correspond to reality. . . . I believe this is an attempt to withhold the true facts from their own people with a view to harming us.

For Khrushchev, the Molotov-Tito controversy came at a most unsuitable moment, since, under these circumstances, *rapprochement* would obviously be out of the question. *Pravda* published a long report on Tito's speech and took a soft line toward Tito, only mildly defending Molotov; *Pravda* proposed to let bygones be bygones and

---

[11] *New Times*, Moscow, no. 7, February 12, 1955, Documents (Supplement), p. 23.

Tito's Short-lived Triumph

to start on a new path of *rapprochement*. This was a rebuke to Molotov.

Khrushchev continued to prod forcefully; his goal now was further *rapprochement* with Tito and resumption of party relations. He wanted to invite Tito to Moscow. The Yugoslav leader, however, insisted on Khrushchev's first coming to Belgrade and on a kind of public apology.

The Soviet leaders' trip to Belgrade was a landmark in the postwar annals of Eastern Europe. For the moment it signified a victory of Communist independence over satellite status, of a nation's emancipation over subordination, of Tito over Stalin. As if to stress Stalin's blunders, the Soviet press, on the eve of Khrushchev's departure, emphasized, in contrast to what Stalin had said,

> ... that in Yugoslavia there prevails the public ownership of the basic means of production; that the main classes there are the working class and working peasantry, which have militant revolutionary and patriotic traditions; that there exist between the people of the two countries a long-established and thoroughgoing community in the realm of culture and thought; and the fact that the working people of the USSR and Yugoslavia have the same basic interests, the interests of the international working class movement, and the same ultimate aim of the working class—all these show that there exists a solid foundation for broad, comprehensive cooperation between the Soviet and the Yugoslav people.[12]

The delegation to Yugoslavia consisted of Khrushchev, Bulganin, Mikoyan, and Shepilov, but not Molotov; the Foreign Ministry was represented by the lesser figure Andrei Gromyko. In his speech at the Belgrade airport, Khrushchev referred to the strained relations between the Soviet and Yugoslavia in the past, and he laid the blame for this on Beria and other police leaders; Stalin's name was not mentioned. Khrushchev, in his vigorous manner, then went over to the offensive and proposed the resumption of party relations:

> We would not be doing our duty to our peoples and to the working people of the whole world if we did not do everything possible to establish mutual understanding between the Communist Party of the Soviet Union and the Yugoslav Communist League, on the basis of the teachings of Marxism-Leninism.[13]

[12] *Pravda*, May 18, 1955.
[13] *Ibid.*, May 27, 1955.

Tito remained silent. His press countered with a repeated emphasis on "independence" and "no blocs."

The Soviet delegation remained in Yugoslavia from May 26 to June 2, 1955. The content of their discussions with the leaders of Yugoslav Communism has never been reported in detail, but from subsequent developments it became plain that on international issues the Yugoslavs were inclined to condemn all forms of blocs of great powers, while the Russians opposed "military blocs," terming their own bloc purely "ideological." Much of what the Yugoslavs, in their years of isolation, had learned from Western socialism (nonviolent evolution toward socialism, the non-"inevitability" of war) was apparently digested by Khrushchev, who incorporated these ideas—and the idea of collaboration with socialist parties—in his report to the next Party Congress. It is also likely that the Yugoslav industrial setup, with its decentralized management, inspired Khrushchev's own subsequent industrial reorganization which, however, differed in many respects from the Yugoslav pattern.

As far as *rapprochement* of the Communist parties was concerned, Tito was not prepared to go the entire length; he was not prepared to join existing setups, like the Warsaw Pact, but "contacts," he believed, could do no harm.[14] He made a few minor moves to meet Khrushchev's wishes. To Khrushchev, Tito probably appeared as a man reluctantly and slowly inclining toward the goal of international reunification of Communism. On the other hand, Tito insisted on the dissolution of the Cominform (although not immediately—not as a demonstration of his victory); this was promised him.[15] Finally, Tito made some complaints about leaders and governments of satellite countries (mainly Hungary and Czechoslovakia), where Stalinism was strong and "Titoism" was still fought by police methods. The most important outcome of conversations, however, was the legalization of "national roads to Communism." This was boldly announced by Tito:

[14] "It would be wrong," Tito said, "to ask us to cooperate with Socialist parties in Europe and throughout the world on certain questions, and then expect us to completely refrain from the possibility of cooperation with the Soviet Communist Party when the issues involved concern certain questions of common interest . . . we won't refuse to exchange experiences gained in our respective countries." (*Yugoslav Review*, New York, vol. 5, no. 7, September, 1955, p. 6.)

[15] On August 3, 1955, the Belgrade *Communist* openly discussed the forthcoming dissolution of the Cominform. On September 2 Tito told an American visitor: "The Cominform is on the way out." (New York *Herald Tribune*, September 21, 1955.) The official dissolution was announced on April 17, 1956.

After Stalin's death the new leaders of the Soviet Union have reached the conclusion that one type of social system, regardless of what it is, cannot reign in the world—that there are many nations in the world with different historical developments; that it is necessary for all nations to determine their own course, and that it is impossible to subject them to any single standard pattern . . . they agreed that Yugoslavia should build a social system in her own way, and they would build theirs in their own way.[16]

The official communiqué issued at the end of the Soviet visit stressed the points of foreign policy that the two parties had in common; it indicated that a new chapter was opening in Soviet-satellite relations. However, at this stage the Soviet-Yugoslav *rapprochement* was limited to state-to-state relations; neither Tito, nor Khrushchev's Stalinist allies in the satellites were prepared to make the next step toward Khrushchev's goal—toward a new international framework embracing all parties and working under Moscow's leadership.

On his way back to Moscow Khrushchev stopped at Sofia and Bucharest to hold a conference with, and explain the events to, the assembled leaders of almost all of the "people's democracies."

The Belgrade Conference marked the beginning of a new, unprecedented ascendancy of Tito in Eastern Europe. Never before, not even during his triumphal tours of 1945–46, had Tito enjoyed the influence and respect that he did in 1955–56. The victorious rebel who had defied, survived, and defeated Stalin was a hero, even if the defeat came to the Soviet dictator after his death. The Soviet bloc was now receiving Tito—in some cases sincerely and in some hypocritically—with open arms. Tito's adversaries either apologized or retreated.

On September 1, 1955, Soviet-Yugoslav trade agreements were concluded; two days later an agreement on Moscow-Belgrade air traffic was signed. On December 19, 1955, and January 28, 1956, "scientific-technical" cooperation was organized. On February 2, 1956, the Soviet Union granted Yugoslavia a loan totaling 84 million dollars (54 million in goods and 30 million in gold) at 2 per cent. On May 17, 1956, a "convention" on cultural cooperation was signed, and on May 22, citizenship questions were settled. A number of Soviet engineers and technicians were to come to Yugoslavia in connection with

---

[16] *Yugoslav Review*, New York, vol. 5, no. 7, September, 1955, p. 5.

industrial construction projects there. In January, 1956, agreement was reached between Belgrade and Moscow on Soviet aid in building certain industrial units in Yugoslavia, and a Soviet credit estimated at from 110 to 120 million dollars, at 2 per cent, was granted.[17] Soviet and Yugoslav writers began to exchange visits. For the first time, in October, 1955, Soviet tourists (200) came to Yugoslavia. In December, 1955, the highly official Moscow *Kommunist* published Tito's article on Yugoslav economy.

Tito's relations with the satellites also improved, although less rapidly than with Russia and with greater obstacles. Trade and border issues were being settled; "delegations" were coming and going. The hardest negotiations were those with Hungary, where Rakoszi still ruled almost autocratically. The resignation of Rakoszi ("for health reasons") in July, 1956, represented one of Tito's greatest triumphs.

In February, 1956, Tito sent his greetings to the Twentieth Congress of the CPSU, which were received with loud and prolonged applause.[18] In his "secret speech" Khrushchev told the Congress about Stalin's attitude toward Tito in words that sounded like an elaborate apology and compliment to Tito:

> Once, when I came from Kiev to Moscow, I was invited to visit Stalin who, pointing to the copy of a letter lately sent to Tito, asked me, "Have you read this?"
>
> Not waiting for my reply, he answered, "I will shake my little finger—and there will be no more Tito. He will fall."
>
> We have dearly paid for this "shaking of the little finger." This statement reflected Stalin's delusions of grandeur, but he acted just that way: "I will shake my little finger—and there will be no Kossior"; "I will shake my little finger once more and Postyshev and Chubar will be no more"; "I will shake my little finger again—and Voznesensky, Kuznetsov and many others will disappear."
>
> But this did not happen to Tito. No matter how much or how little Stalin shook, not only his little finger but everything else that he could shake, Tito did not fall. Why? The reason was that, in this case of disagreement with the Yugoslav comrades, Tito had behind him a state and a people who had gone through a severe school of fighting for liberty and independence, a people which gave support to its leaders.[19]

---

[17] *The New York Times,* January 4 and 14, 1956; *Pravda,* January 4, 1956.

[18] According to one report, Tito had been informed in advance about Khrushchev's speech degrading Stalin; not all satellite leaders had been informed.

[19] Khrushchev's speech of February 24, 1956, in Bertram D. Wolfe, *Khrushchev and Stalin's Ghost,* New York, Frederick A. Praeger, 1957, p. 200.

On March 20, long before the United States State Department released it (June 4), Tito's *Borba* published a part of Khrushchev's speech.

In those days, the spring of 1956, there prevailed the conviction, actually an illusion, that the Soviet Union and Yugoslavia were on their way to a firm and lasting alliance and that their relations would grow closer and closer. There appeared to be no cloud on the horizon. The Stalinists in Moscow were as if paralyzed; Stalinists in the satellites, Tito's hereditary enemies, were to be ousted. In March, 1956, only a few weeks before the dissolution of the Cominform, Rakoszi had said: "I don't see any need [to dissolve it] right now." At about the same time, Zapotocky, the Czech leader, talked in the same vein: "The Cominform continues to exist, there has been no change in its status." [20] These two leaders had not been informed of the imminent dissolution, but Tito had known of it in advance. When the announcement of the dissolution appeared, it proclaimed that now the Communist parties

> ... find new useful forms of establishing relations and contacts among themselves. Undoubtedly, the Communist and Workers' Parties will at their own discretion and taking into account the concrete conditions of their work, exchange views, in the future too, on the general problems relating to the struggle for peace, democracy and socialism, the defence of the interests of the working class and all working people, and the mobilisation of the masses for struggle against the war danger; and will at the same time examine the matter of cooperation with parties and trends oriented towards socialism, and also with other organisations striving for the consolidation of peace and democracy.[21]

The Cominform was dissolved, but no successor organization was announced. In the preceding months, one Communist party after another (Ulbricht's SEP, the Austrian, and others) had come out with suggestions for a new international setup. All such schemes, however, were discarded, mainly because of Tito.

For Tito, other triumphs were in store. In Bulgaria, Premier Vulko Chervenkov, another of Stalin's most durable lieutenants, was publicly accused, in the presence of Tito's envoy, of adhering to the "cult

[20] *The New York Times*, April 28, 1956.
[21] *For a Lasting Peace, for a People's Democracy*, Bucharest, April 17, 1956.

of personality" and was relegated to a less important post. Everywhere in East Europe the political temperature was rising. The disorientation was unprecedented. Communist parties that had never wavered in their loyalty to Moscow joined the ranks of doubters, and their leading press organs published resolutions criticizing Moscow. One of the most venerated Comintern and Cominform leaders, Palmiro Togliatti, presented a devastating report to the Central Committee of the Italian Party; he said:

> The experience gained in the building of a socialist society in the Soviet Union cannot contain instructions for resolving all the questions which may present themselves today to us and to the Communists of other countries, whether in power or not, and to all the vanguard parties of the working class and of the people.[22]

For the future, Togliatti advocated "full autonomy of the individual Communist parties"; "bilateral relations" between them, he said, must replace guidance from one center. There must exist, he maintained, not one Communist international organization, but "various points or centers of development and orientation." The Soviet press did not report Togliatti's speech.

Togliatti was in accord with Tito, the main bearer of the ideas of national Communism. In his interview with the French paper *Le Monde*, Tito said: ". . . today an International, consisting of Communist parties which are in power and those which are not, cannot exist." He stressed "the great difference between . . . groups of Communists—between those who are in power and those who live under another system, who must fight in a parliamentary way and use various other methods to achieve, if possible, a majority." "But contacts are necessary," Tito said, "particularly between Communist parties of the East, including Yugoslavia." [23]

Tito was invited to Moscow for a prolonged visit. With his group he traveled a roundabout way in order to avoid passing through Rakoszi's Hungary. "I would not go through Hungary," Tito said later, "even if it would have meant making the journey three times shorter."

The reception in Russia was extremely friendly. Tito was feted as one of the great heroes of Communism. At the Leningrad railway

[22] *L'Unità*, Rome, June 26, 1956.
[23] Quoted in *Pravda*, May 8, 1956.

station he reciprocated by telling a large meeting: "In conversations with your comrades we became convinced that there exist no essential disagreements between us." [24] On the other hand, the Soviet leadership, always sensitive in the matter of rank and title, and never forgetting its claim of superiority, could not refrain from putting Tito in his right place so that nobody would equate Belgrade with Moscow. At a meeting at the Moscow Dynamo Stadium in honor of Tito, two huge displays read:

> Brotherly Greetings to the People of Yugoslavia
> *Building Socialism*

and

> Long Live the Great Soviet People
> *Builder of Communism.*

In the discussions in Moscow between the leaders, the general issue of the "people's democracies" in the framework of Soviet policy occupied a prominent place. From statements made later by Tito himself and by his press, some notion can be formed of the viewpoints of the two sides.

The Yugoslav thesis of total independence of the "people's democracies" from Moscow—implementation of "national Communism"—was unacceptable not only to the conservative group of the Soviet leadership but to the Khrushchev group as well; on the other hand, outright rejection of "Titoism" and a return to Stalin's *cordon sanitaire* around Yugoslavia was contrary to the new trend. In the verbal fights for and against emancipation, the difference between the two groups of East European countries, and the significance of the groups for the Soviet Union, again became obvious.

The three northern satellites—East Germany, Czechoslovakia, and Poland—with an aggregate population of about 60 million, were industrially and strategically of far greater importance to Russia than the southern satellites. Poland and Czechoslovakia lay on the historical road between West and East along which, over the centuries, huge armies had moved and the greatest of wars had been fought. Arming, disarming, and disengagement were problems that were related primarily to these traditional gates of invasion. Poland, formerly a big power, still played an important role in world affairs, and East Ger-

[24] *Ibid.*, June 8, 1956.

many and Czechoslovakia were the most industrially advanced areas of the "socialist camp." Together the three countries were, in Moscow's eyes, a component of the paramount issue of Germany.

The southern group of satellites, Yugoslavia's neighbors, were Rumania, Hungary, and Bulgaria, with a total population of about 35 million. This group was less economically advanced and less important to Russia than to Yugoslavia. During the Cominform era, tension on these borders had been severe; some of the worst anti-Tito trials took place in Budapest and Sofia; the most prominent satellite anti-Titoists resided in Hungary. If the Soviet desire for reconciliation and *rapprochement* was sincere, Moscow would have to accede to Tito's first request—to remove the sword pointed at Belgrade, reduce the armies of the southern satellites, and, at least by implication, grant Yugoslavia, the main power in the Balkans, at least a modicum of influence in the regimes of these nations.

Khrushchev was inclined to grant Tito a role in the affairs of the southern tier without conceding much in relation to the northern group; in particular, he believed, Tito should have a certain influence in the selection of party and government leaders in the southern cluster, a privilege which had up to now been exclusively Russia's. Whether this new Yugoslav "sphere of influence" was actually granted in so many words is, of course, not known; if it was, this was part of a party-to-party arrangement, a link in the chain of concessions to national Communism which were made in Moscow. It is possible, however, that the matters of the agreement and the "sphere" were then still in a tentative stage.

In particular, Tito inisisted on the removal of Rakoszi. In defense of Rakoszi, however, Moscow pleaded that he was an old revolutionary and an honest and prudent man. Referring to this argument, Tito commented:

> That he [Rakoszi] is old, this is granted, but that is not enough. That he is honest—this I could not say, inasmuch as I know him, especially after the Rajk trial and other things. To me, these are the most dishonest people in the world. The Soviet comrades said he was prudent, that he was going to succeed, and that they knew of no one else whom they could rely upon in that country. Just because our policy, both state and Party policy, is opposed to interference in the internal affairs of others, and in order not again to come into conflict

Tito's Short-lived Triumph 353

with the Soviet comrades, we were not insistent enough with the Soviet leaders to have such a team as Rakoszi and Gerö eliminated.[25]

One reason why the Soviet Union was interested in an agreement of this kind with Tito had to do with Tito's relations with violently anti-Soviet Turkey, a member of NATO and ally of Yugoslavia since 1953. A Soviet-Yugoslav agreement on the Balkans would help to dissolve this pact and make Yugoslavia a buffer and possible shield against the dangers from the South. (See Map 1, page 35.) In fact, Tito, after his return from Moscow to Belgrade, announced that his Balkan Pact (with Turkey and Greece), which was directed against Bulgaria and Rumania, "had been discussed in Moscow; now it will conserve its peaceful phases only, while its military side belongs to the past." [26]

Thus the old specter of a Balkan federation, which in 1948 had prompted Stalin's break with Tito, was reappearing on the horizon. The years of isolation, and the cold wars and hot "incidents" between Yugoslavia and her neighbors had strengthened Belgrade's urge to detach the latter from mighty Russia, give them a modicum of independence, or even harness them to its own chariot. To Moscow, the achievement of a state of real peace with Tito represented a concession, a granting to him of part of the unilateral Soviet rule in the southeast.

In every respect, however—in a good as well as a bad sense—Yugoslavia was singled out as a different kind of state among the "people's democracies." Khrushchev did not even try to reduce Yugoslavia to the level of a satellite; he only took care that Yugoslavia should not become a pattern for other satellites. "It was thought as follows," Tito later said about Khrushchev: "good, since the Yugoslavs are so stubborn we will respect and implement these declarations, but they do not concern the others because the situation there is, nevertheless, a little different than in Yugoslavia." [27]

The general Declaration signed by the two Communist parties in Moscow contained, as an obvious concession to Tito, many ingredients

---

[25] Tito's speech in Pula, November 11, 1956. Translation in *National Communism and Popular Revolt in Eastern Europe: A Selection of Documents on Events in Poland and Hungary, February–November, 1956*, ed. by Paul E. Zinner, New York, Columbia University Press, 1956.
[26] *Pravda*, June 29, 1956.
[27] Tito's speech in Pula, November 11, 1956, *op. cit.*

of "national Communism" but also the reestablishment of party-to-party relations:

> Believing that the path of socialist development differs in various countries and under various conditions, that the multiplicity of forms of socialist development tends to strengthen socialism, and proceeding from the fact that any tendency to impose one's opinion on the ways and forms of socialist development is alien to both—the two parties have agreed that their cooperation shall be based on complete voluntariness and equality, friendly criticism, and comradely exchange of opinion on controversial questions.[28]

The idea of a single Communist International organization was rejected; instead,

> ... the delegations have agreed that it [cooperation between the two parties] will be carried out through personal contacts, written and oral communications and exchange of opinions, through exchange of delegations, informational material, and literature, as well as through personal meetings of party leaders, when necessary, to discuss pressing problems of common interest, and generally through all forms of constructive comradely discussion.... This presupposes freedom of action for each and every participant in this cooperation, in conformity with the conditions of their development and their general progressive aims.

In the matter of foreign policies Tito was prepared to subscribe to most of the points of the Soviet program, as he had a year earlier in Belgrade; however, despite Soviet pressure, he refused to recognize the German Democratic Republic, if only because of his close economic ties with Bonn. The issues of China, rearmament, atomic arms, easing of trade, and unification of Germany were treated in the final communiqué in the Soviet way. At a mass meeting in Moscow, however, Marshal Zhukov, in Tito's presence, made a statement which he was not authorized to make: "... should war be imposed upon us we will struggle shoulder to shoulder for the benefit of mankind." [29] When he returned to Belgrade, Tito made a protest about this incident to the Soviet ambassador and also informed the Western envoys of it.[30]

On his way back from Moscow Tito stopped for a few days in Bucharest, in his new sphere, to seal the new agreements and stir enthusiasm in Rumania. The Yugoslav leader addressed a mass meet-

---
[28] *Pravda*, June 21, 1956.
[29] *The New York Times*, June 21, 1956.
[30] New York *Herald Tribune*, July 13, 1956.

Tito's Short-lived Triumph

ing, and joint declarations were signed by the two governments as well as by the leaders of the Communist parties of both countries.[31]

Tito departed from Moscow on June 22. Six days later the strikes and street fighting broke out in Poznan. In Moscow many people blamed the outbreak on "Titoism." There was, in fact, much similarity between the political slogans of the Poznan workers and Tito's program of national Communism. These days marked the beginning of a new, though gradual, deterioration in Soviet-Yugoslav relations. Every anti-Russian move was charged to Tito. "When the Poznan affairs happened . . . there occurred among the Soviet people [meaning the leadership] a sudden change of attitude toward us. They started to grow colder. They thought that we, the Yugoslavs, were to blame." [32]

In their reaction to Poznan the Yugoslavs differed from the Russians, and the Yugoslav press, without attacking the Ochab regime, emphasized the popular character of the movement, the discontent caused by the social problems and unsatisfactory living conditions. "But this is not a complete explanation of the bloody clashes," said *Borba*, insisting on the political causes of the movement: ". . . a considerable majority of the workers are lending support to tendencies which aim at a democratization of public life. . . ." [33]

The revival of old tendencies in Moscow after the Poznan strike reflected the growing apprehension about satellite defection. Even Khrushchev, at the time the foremost appeaser of Tito among the Soviet leaders, was seized by these misgivings. His behavior during this period was nervous and erratic, his moves were shrouded in secrecy. In August the Soviet-dominated Council for Economic Mutual Assistance organized a new Danube Commission as a rival to the official Danube Commission, in which Yugoslavia exerted considerable influence.[34] *Pravda* reported severe sentences meted out in Yugoslavia to two former pro-Stalinist *émigrés*, Miliutin Raikovich and Iovan Prodanovich, who had served as editors of the anti-Titoist

[31] *Pravda*, June 27, 1956.
[32] Tito's speech in Pula, November 11, 1956, *op. cit.*
[33] *Borba*, Belgrade, July 1, 1956.
[34] ". . . Eastern European leaders," reported the Austrian press, "were now split into two groups. One is reported to favor unification of Danube countries under Yugoslav leadership while the other is said to support the Soviet-controlled Danube union." (*Salzburger Volksblatt*, Salzburg, Austria, as quoted by *The New York Times*, September 2, 1956.) See also Ernst Halperin, *The Triumphant Heretic: Tito's Struggle against Stalin*, London, William Heinemann Ltd., 1958, p. 307.

newspaper *Nova Borba* in Prague; the sentences were eight and five years.[35]

Early in September Khrushchev's Central Committee sent a circular letter to a number of Communist parties warning them against Tito's independence movements. The Yugoslav League of Communists, the letter said, was not a pure Marxist-Leninist organization but had certain social-democratic tendencies. The message was that Soviet Communism must remain the directing party in the international movement, while all others must maintain close ties with it.[36] Belgrade learned of the offensive letter, and *Borba* criticized it: the letter, the Tito mouthpiece said, violated the agreement signed by the two leaders in Moscow. Later the incident was a subject of discussion between Khrushchev and Tito.

In July, Anastas Mikoyan was dispatched to the three southern satellites, his first assignment being the ousting of Rakoszi. Rakoszi was then about to launch a new purge of opponents; a list of 400 persons to be arrested, with Imre Nagy at the head, had been compiled. Istvan Kovacz, a ranking Hungarian Communist, informed Soviet Ambassador Andropov about Rakoszi's plans, which, in that year of *détente,* sounded like a challenge to Moscow. Mikoyan rushed to Budapest armed with the power and authority of Moscow, and Rakoszi was promptly removed. The official version was that he had resigned for reasons of ill health; actually Mathias Rakoszi was forced to resign. The matter of a successor to Rakoszi, however, was a controversial one between Tito and Moscow. Tito had his own candidate, Imre Nagy, while Mikoyan supported Rakoszi's old co-leader, Erno Gerö, a former *émigré* in Moscow; moreover, because of the new clouds in the Soviet-Yugoslav sky, the Soviet leaders "made it a condition that Rakoszi would go only if Gerö remained."[37] Despite the "new course" and "independence," the selection of the new dictator proceeded in the old way: Moscow made the appointment. Only now Gerö was instructed to make a *rapprochement* with Tito his first assignment. As a concession to Tito, however, Imre Nagy was readmitted to the party.[38]

The growing Soviet-Yugoslav rift was not healed by Mikoyan's

[35] *Pravda,* August 31, 1956.
[36] *The New York Times,* September 30 and October 12 and 19, 1956.
[37] Tito's speech in Pula, November 11, 1956, *op. cit.*
[38] Richard Lowenthal, "Tito's Affair with Khrushchev," *The New Leader,* October 6, 1958.

Tito's Short-lived Triumph

trip, and Khrushchev decided to make a personal effort at high-level diplomacy. Soon after Mikoyan's return, Khrushchev unexpectedly arrived in Belgrade "for a rest." He remained in Yugoslavia for more than a week, from September 19 to 27. At a dinner given by him for President Tito, Khrushchev spoke of the dangers to Communism from movements and trends like those which were growing in Hungary and Poland; Tito did not retreat, however.[39] Apparently unable to find a compromise between emancipation and dependence, Khrushchev invited the Yugoslav leaders (Tito, Rankovich, and Pukar) to accompany him to Yalta, in the Crimea, where they took part in a conference with Bulganin, Voroshilov, Furtseva, Kirichenko, and others; neither Molotov, Malenkov, nor Kaganovich was present. The controversial new secretary, Erno Gerö, came from Budapest.

The debates at Yalta again revealed a profound divergency between the Yugoslav and the Soviet leadership. The controversy was complicated by the internal fights within the Soviet Presidium itself on the issue of the "people's democracies," mainly Hungary and Poland. The Soviet leaders rejected full independence for the "people's democracies"; their reason and excuse were that pro-Western "reactionary" elements might profit if those countries enjoyed "a status such as that enjoyed by Yugoslavia." They refused most emphatically to "permit too much liberalization" in the three northern "people's democracies"—this might "be dangerous for the security of the Soviet Union and the other Communist states." Tito had reluctantly agreed that he "would not try to influence Poland, Czechoslovakia, and East Germany to follow their own roads to socialism." The southern "people's democracies," however, were in another class; here more concessions were made to Yugoslavia, in particular the promise of Soviet leaders to withdraw part of the Soviet troops from these countries.[40]

Back again in Belgrade, Tito claimed to have been successful, and facts at first seemed to confirm him. The satellite leaders of the southeast would now come to Belgrade; Gerö, too, had to make his bow in the Yugoslav capital. Resumption of party-to-party relations with Bulgaria was announced, but Bulgaria's supreme leaders had to wait a fortnight in Belgrade for Tito to return from Russia. Gerö followed,

[39] *The New York Times*, October 16, 1956.
[40] *The Times*, London, October 4, 1956; *The New York Times*, October 25, 1956.

and after him came the Rumanians. For a while it seemed as if Tito had acquired real influence in southeast Europe.[41]

The situation began to change when the crisis in Soviet-satellite relations developed.

3. THE POLISH REBELLION

Tension between Moscow and the satellites was growing. For the Soviet Union the crisis inside the "socialist camp" was more ominous even than the Suez affair, which was developing at this time.

Alarming reports streamed into Moscow of growing ferment in Poland and Hungary. On a smaller scale, but nevertheless disturbing, was the news from East Germany and Rumania of similar ferment. Yugoslavia's suspected anti-Moscow moves increased the uneasiness. Furthermore, the disagreements among the Soviet "collective leadership" on every important issue were adding to the gravity of the situation. The Soviet government concealed its concern over the mounting troubles, and its press, presenting an undisturbed countenance, devoted almost no space to the main developments in the Soviet bloc countries.

Communist Poland marched at the head of the rebels, closely followed by Hungary. Jakub Berman, the leading Polish Stalinist, resigned in May, 1956; Hilary Minc, the pro-Soviet economic leader, resigned early in October. All over Poland a wave of popular movements was mounting under the slogan of independence from Russia. The presence of Soviet generals and Soviet troops in Poland had become a serious issue. Reports from China indicated that Edward Ochab, the new proliberal Polish first secretary, was receiving encouragement from Chou En-lai; the Poles, Chou said, should continue their efforts to achieve independence.[42] Other countries, too, especially Yugoslavia, stressed their sympathy for the Polish demands.

The ball started rolling when the Politburo of the Polish party, in its decision of October 15, openly defied Moscow by resolving to convene the Central Committee within four days (on the nineteenth) for the purpose of electing a new Politburo (in which Soviet Marshal

---

[41] In his substantial study of the developments in Yugoslavia (*The New Leader*, October 6, 1958), Richard Lowenthal considered Gerö's visit to Belgrade as a kind of compromise on the part of Tito.

[42] *The New York Times*, October 19, 1956.

The Polish Rebellion

Rokossovsky would not be included), and to elect Wladyslaw Gomulka first secretary. This was an overt challenge. The failure to consult Moscow on the eve of such a momentous decision was contrary to tradition and rule and tantamount to revolt. Only a few months earlier, on the occasion of Ochab's election as the party's leader, Khrushchev had been present. The Polish intentions became known in Moscow through a group of pro-Soviet members of the Politburo who were in close touch with the Soviet ambassador in Warsaw. Khrushchev requested that the leaders of Polish Communism come to Moscow for consultation. The Polish leaders refused. If the Soviet leadership wished to discuss the situation, Ochab replied, they were invited to come to Warsaw—but not until after the meeting of the Central Committee. For the Soviet Union this was the most serious challenge since Tito's insurrection eight years before.

The dilemma was a difficult one. To accede to the new Polish course might mean the immediate loss of at least two "people's democracies" and the eventual loss of several more; it might also mean the loss of East Germany and the retreat of the Soviet back into the confines of the Soviet Union. The alternative was recourse to military force to suppress the popular movements in the "people's democracies."

Soviet reports and the Soviet press have never indicated how the discussion of this crucial issue proceeded. As the Polish crisis was coming to a climax and the ferment in Hungary was growing, a meeting of the Presidium took place in Moscow, probably on October 18, following Ochab's refusal to go to Moscow. The decisions taken at this meeting went in two directions: first, to order Soviet military units stationed in Poland and Hungary to prepare to move closer to the cities, and other units stationed in East Germany and Rumania to move closer to the frontiers of Poland and Hungary (the moves and war games to be conducted would impress the population and the rebellious leaders); second, to dispatch prominent members of the Presidium to Warsaw and Budapest to try to discuss the situation with the new leaders. The elements in the Polish leadership loyal to Moscow, among them Rokossovsky, were known to be preparing a *coup d'état* in the event negotiations failed; a list of about seven hundred persons to be arrested had been drawn up, along with a plan for seizing key posts. Moscow set a limit to possible concessions to the

Poles: a modicum of autonomy for Poland might be acceptable, but Tito-type complete independence was out of the question.

At this point Khrushchev and his group in the Presidium relinquished their two-year-old efforts at reconciliation with national Communism: if harsh methods were necessary to salvage the Stalin edifice, Khrushchev was prepared to use them. For a time the factions in the Presidium moved closer together. Molotov, who had not accompanied Khrushchev on the trips to Peking and Belgrade, was now to go to Warsaw; the other members of the delegation were Mikoyan and Kaganovich. Thus the foursome was composed of an equal number from each of the factions.

The Russian guests arrived in Warsaw almost unexpectedly just as the session of the Polish Central Committee was about to start. The delegation had obviously intended to reach Warsaw in time to prevent the election of a new leader without "consultation" and the inauguration of a new course.

The negotiations, held in the Belvedere Palace, were violent and full of threats. Khrushchev, as the leading Soviet representative, spoke in bellicose and offensive language. He used the term "traitor" in referring to Gomulka; he demanded the restoration of the old Politburo, including Rokossovsky; as to the Soviet privilege of exerting influence on Poland, he bluntly said: "The [Soviet] soldiers shed their blood here and now you want to sell the country to the Americans and the Zionists." Rokossovsky, as a member of the Polish Politburo, was present at these sessions. As the negotiations in the palace proceeded, reports were coming in from various parts of the country of Soviet tanks and armed vehicles moving toward Warsaw and of Soviet warships in Poland's Baltic ports. These reports were obviously calculated to exert pressure on the Polish protagonists. Ochab, still first secretary, remained firm. "If you do not stop them [the troops] immediately," he told the Soviet group, "we will walk out of here and break off all contact." "Breaking off contact" implied real warfare; the Soviet leadership knew that a Polish Internal Security Corps, well armed and now under General Waclaw Komar, a friend of Gomulka, was to fight a real war against the Russians, while the rest of Poland's armed forces was at best unreliable. Khrushchev ordered a halt to the troop movement.

Despite the vehement exchange of accusations and threats, the Poles left no doubt as to their intentions in regard to the Warsaw Pact

The Polish Rebellion

and the "socialist camp": they did not intend to break away. The Soviet apprehension that Poland might declare herself neutral or even "sell out to the Americans" was exaggerated. Even Gomulka, the black sheep, wanted independence in internal affairs but also continuation of "Soviet-Polish friendship," meaning coordination and synchronization on international issues with limited party-to-party relations.

The Soviet delegates departed from the prolonged sessions in a better mood. Having indicated that Moscow was prepared to drop Rokossovsky and the other pro-Soviet elements in the Polish leadership, they were taking with them the Poles' offer to come to Moscow soon after the sessions of the Central Committee. No final decisions were reached in these negotiations.

A brief official report on the conversations in Warsaw—a masterpiece of concealment—appeared in the press of both countries. The Soviet press during this period had been skillfully avoiding any hint of the developing crisis; the Polish press had discussed it abundantly.

The session of the Polish Central Committee took the expected course. The new Politburo included no members of the pro-Soviet group. Rokossovsky, who received 26 out of 75 votes, was not re-elected; he remained as chief of Poland's armed forces, but his dismissal from this post was only a matter of a few days. Gomulka was elected first secretary of the Central Committee. In his address to the Committee, in which he presented a kind of program for the next years, Gomulka tried to combine consistent "national Communism" with "Polish-Soviet friendship." This was to become a new, non-Stalinist, type of relations between "socialist nations" on the basis of sovereignty and independence. Gomulka's settling of accounts with Stalin was decisive and impressive. "The cult of personality"—Gomulka adhered to the use of this Moscow-invented term to describe the Stalin system—". . . was grafted to probably all Communist Parties, as well as to a number of countries of the Socialist camp, including Poland." [43]

Gomulka described the inner workings of the Stalinist empire:

> In the bloc of Socialist states it was Stalin who stood at the top of this hierarchic ladder of cults. All those who stood on lower rungs of

[43] Gomulka's address before the Central Committee of the Polish United Workers Party, October 20, 1956, *Nove Drogi*, no. 10, 1956, pp. 21–46, translated in *National Communism and Popular Revolt in Eastern Europe, op. cit.*

the ladder bowed their heads before him. Those who bowed their heads were not only the other leaders of the Communist Party of the Soviet Union and the leaders of the Soviet Union, but also the leaders of Communist and Workers Parties of the countries of the Socialist camp. The latter, that is the First Secretaries of the Central Committees of the Parties of the various countries who sat on the second rung of the ladder of the cult of personality, in turn donned the robes of infallibility and wisdom. But their cult radiated only on the territory of the countries where they stood at the top of the national cult ladder. This cult could be called only a reflected brilliance, a borrowed light. It shone as the moon does. . . .

In Poland, too, tragic events occurred when innocent people were sent to their death. Many others were imprisoned often for many years, although innocent, including Communists. Many people were submitted to bestial tortures. Terror and demoralization were widespread. On the soil of the cult of personality phenomena arose which violated and even nullified the most profound meaning of the people's power.

Insisting that there exists a "national road to Communism" for each country, Gomulka held firm, however, to Poland's ties with Russia:

> . . . if there is anyone who thinks that it is possible to kindle anti-Soviet moods in Poland, then he is deeply mistaken. . . . Polish-Soviet relations based on the principles of equality and independence will create among the Polish people such a profound feeling of friendship for the Soviet Union that no attempts to show distrust of the Soviet Union will find a response among the people of Poland.

Gomulka informed the Soviet leadership of the decisions taken by the Central Committee; Khrushchev, in a telephoned reply, indicated that the Presidium of the CPSU accepted them. Khrushchev apologized for his recent outburst and promised to withdraw Soviet military units to their bases. For Gomulka this was a triumph. Now the Soviet press, heretofore almost completely silent, began to report abundantly on Poland; it quoted speeches, resolutions, and articles stressing the firmness of the Polish-Soviet tie; even Gomulka's emphasis on "national roads" was not challenged. The satisfaction in the Soviet leadership was obvious.

In the meantime popular meetings, demonstrations, and emotional outbursts against the government's "halfway" policy in its dealing with Russia continued in Poland. The movement for complete independence was receiving encouragement and nourishment from the revolt

The Polish Rebellion

in Hungary. In Warsaw, buses carried the Hungarian colors; near the university, students placed beside the banners of Hungary a huge reproduction of a picture showing robots shooting down men and children, with an exclamation mark drawn through the picture. However—and in this Poland and Hungary parted ways—the new Polish leadership succeeded in keeping down the anti-Soviet ferment.

Poland's protestations of "friendship with the Soviet Union" were put to a severe test during the Hungarian uprising. Before issuing the orders to the Soviet troops in Hungary to shoot, Khrushchev sought the approval of the satellites for this action, and Gomulka, deserting his friends in Budapest, apparently granted it for Poland. A few days later (November 5), in the United Nations, Poland voted with the Soviet Union on the Hungarian issue. Little Hungary was isolated and deserted; the front of rebelling satellites had been broken; Khrushchev had won.

The arrival of the Polish delegation in Moscow on November 15 and the conference held there were therefore an anticlimax. In their published resolution, the two parties promised support of the pro-Moscow regime in Hungary, prolonged the stay of Soviet troops in Poland, and settled the question of repatriation of Polish citizens from Russia. A month later a special Soviet-Polish agreement on the status of Soviet forces stationed in Poland was signed and published. Intended to serve as a pattern for other satellites and to stress the new spirit of equality, it accorded the Poles far-reaching jurisdiction in regard to the size, movements, and legal status of the Soviet troops. The agreement, however, contained no exact figures or dates; its vagueness was increased by repeated references to "special agreements," which remained unpublished. The duration of the general understanding was for "so long as the Soviet forces will be stationed on the territory of the Polish People's Republic." [44]

Marshal Rokossovsky resigned on November 29 and returned to Russia; with him went ranking Polish-Russian generals and officers, more than thirty in all. The inglorious end of their activity in a "people's democracy" after a decade of service was a hard blow to Soviet prestige; it was never mentioned in the Soviet press.

Entering on her new road after her "October Revolution," Poland tried to combine a nonterrorist course in internal policies with Com-

[44] *Pravda,* December 18, 1956.

munist dictatorship. It tried to combine "building of socialism" with concessions to the peasantry, and independence with absolute loyalty to the Soviet Union in foreign affairs. The program was a knot of compromises, a contradictory system, an experiment with incompatible elements. For several years it worked, but it was not really successful, and it did not produce the promised pattern of a free socialist society, a really democratic "people's democracy."

4. NATIONAL COMMUNISM: ITS SIGNIFICANCE FOR THE SOVIET UNION

October, 1956, was a crucial period during which fateful decisions were taken. So long as national Communism had been only a set of ideas it had been tolerable; when it was converted into political plans it had called for compromise; but now, having become a reality, it placed the entire Soviet structure in question. Should or should not the Soviet Union revise the structure of its empire?

The real significance of the developments in Poland and Hungary for the Soviet Union may be seen from Map 6, page 482. Yugoslavia, Hungary, and Poland, where the new trends were centered, constituted an almost uninterrupted belt of nations stretching from the Baltic to the Adriatic. Their aggregate population of about 62 million was more than half that of all Eastern Europe, and their significance in European affairs was far greater than that of the other satellites. It would be logical for this group of nations, once they achieved independence, to form some kind of defensive alliance or federation. Such an alliance would become a political and military wall between Russia and the rest of Europe.

The consequences of such a development were easy to foresee: the DDR would be cut off from Russia by an independent Poland and in one way or another would have to unite with West Germany; pro-Soviet Czechoslovakia, nearly isolated in the West, would have to join the Tito-led new Eastern "socialist bloc." Stalin's two lines of Soviet growth, leading to West Germany in the north and to Italy in the south, would thus be cut off. In terms of the safety and integrity of Russia's own territory these implications of "national Communism" were not ominous; they were, however, contrary to the course taken

National Communism

since 1944 by Stalin as well as by his successors toward the conservation and growth of the empire.

In the case of Hungary there was also a military-industrial reason for Moscow's wanting to retain influence there: the Hungarian uranium mines. Experimental mining, which was begun by the Russians in 1953, had proved highly successful, especially in the areas near Pécs and stretching in the direction of Beja, along the Yugoslav frontier.[45]

In the face of the dilemma, Khrushchev and his faction displayed uncertainty and vacillation. For more than a year they had been criticized in the Presidium for their concessions to "Titoism" and warned of the consequences; now the danger was becoming real. The Molotov group, the Yugoslavs learned, was finding new supporters among Soviet military leaders.[46]

Early in October Khrushchev's Presidium inquired of the party leaders of the "bloc" concerning the question of Soviet armed intervention if the movements in the satellites assumed threatening proportions. Requested to speak up, most of the leaders of the "socialist countries" apparently took Khrushchev's position; however, there was substantial opposition, and the discussion continued throughout the month. It was the Chinese leader, Mao Tse-tung, who, on the Polish issue, advised Moscow against the use of military force and thus, as he subsequently claimed, actually saved the Gomulka regime.[47] In Moscow, too, there remained a group of doubters and opponents. Khrushchev referred to these a few years later: "Among our comrades there was also such conversation as this: will the Hungarian comrades understand us correctly if we give them assistance, since some of the workers, misled by the counter-revolution, are siding with the fascist rebels?"[48] The Italian Communist correspondent in Moscow Giuseppe Boffa, though loyal to the Soviet leadership, noted the disagreements at the top level. One could see, he said, "perplexity" among Soviet leaders; the decisions "were not lightly taken"; some of the leaders—a

---

[45] Experts had concluded that the Hungarian mines were making Hungary the second richest country in the world. In 1955, under Rakoszi, a secret Soviet-Hungarian agreement gave the Soviet Union exclusive rights in regard to Hungary's uranium. In 1956 over 2,000 workers and employees were working in the uranium mine industry under Soviet general manager Bogomolov. (*Osteuropa*, Stuttgart, no. 3, March, 1957, pp. 203–6.)
[46] *The New York Times*, October 21 and 23, 1956; *The Times*, London, October 26, 1956.
[47] *The New York Times*, January 11, 1957.
[48] *Pravda*, December 3, 1959.

nucleus of liberals among Communists—wanted "to let the Hungarian people take care of the conflict." [49]

In Moscow the influence of the opposition was growing; in some instances a "united front" of both factions could be formed. The equal representation of Khrushchevites and Molotovites in the Soviet delegations to Poland (October 19) and probably to Hungary (October 23–31) was another indication of the latter's growing significance. The whole problem of Soviet-satellite relations, their theory and practice, was again discussed.

When the satellite issue emerged in all its magnitude, Khrushchev assumed the view that "peaceful coexistence" was a formula for relations between countries "with different social systems," not for members of a socialist bloc; "people's democracies" were obliged to follow other sets of rules: they could not "desert"; if they tried to adopt a formula valid only for outsiders, if they broke away from the Warsaw Pact and declared their neutrality, then the armed force of the "socialist camp" must be hurled against them.

The behind-the-scenes fights were reflected in the "Declaration of the Government of the USSR on the Principles of Development and Further Strengthening of Friendship and Cooperation between the Soviet Union and Other Socialist States" of October 30, 1956. Obviously the product of a compromise, the Declaration contained elements of both orthodox "internationalism" and the liberalizing trends of "national Communism"; it repeatedly emphasized "complete equality" of nations and noninterference in their internal affairs, but it stated also that "that does not exclude close fraternal cooperation and mutual aid among the countries of the socialist commonwealth in the economic, political, and cultural spheres." In the terminology of the Soviet bloc, "cooperation and mutual aid" implied the police and military measures necessary to consolidate the "rule of the proletariat" (Communist Party) and suppression of "counterrevolution."

Outlining "cooperation" in the military and economic fields, the Declaration pointed in the first place to the Warsaw Treaty, especially to the obligation to take "concerted measures necessary for strengthening the defense capacity." It then explained the legal status of Soviet troops in the "people's democracies": "Soviet units are in

[49] Giuseppe Boffa, *Inside the Khrushchev Era*, New York, Marzani & Munsell, Publishers, 1959, p. 105.

National Communism

the Polish Republic on the basis of the Potsdam four-power agreement and the Warsaw Treaty." As a concession to the satellites, the Declaration announced that the Soviet government was prepared "to review" with them "the question of Soviet troops" stationed in their countries, and enunciated the general principle that such "stationing" is conducted "only with the consent of the state on the territory of which and at the request of which these troops are stationed or it is planned to station them." From this it would follow that in the absence of such an agreement, Soviet troops must be withdrawn.[50]

On the sore issue of Soviet "advisers" in the "people's democracies" the Soviet government said in the Declaration that it considered it urgent to discuss and revise their status; even the possibility of the recall of all "advisers" to the Soviet Union was indicated.

There was another turn in the zigzag line when the Declaration proceeded to explain the Soviet position in regard to Hungary. The past actions of the Rakosziites (actually Stalinists) were of course condemned; likewise condemned were trends toward restoration of "old landowner-capitalist ways"; the Soviet government, the Declaration stated, "deeply regrets that the development of events in Hungary has led to bloodshed." The carefully worded, though somewhat illogical conclusion was: Soviet forces will be withdrawn from Budapest, but as far as the presence of troops in Hungary as a whole is concerned, the Soviet government is prepared only to "negotiate": ". . . the Soviet Government has given its military command instructions to withdraw the Soviet military units from the city of Budapest as soon as this is considered necessary by the Hungarian Government. At the same time, the Soviet Government is prepared to enter into appropriate negotiations with the Government of the Hungarian People's Republic and other members of the Warsaw Treaty on the question of the presence of Soviet troops on the territory of Hungary."

The Declaration did not state in so many words that the para-

[50] In accordance with this Declaration agreements on the stationing of Soviet troops were concluded with Poland on December 17, 1956; with the DDR on March 12, 1957; with Rumania on April 15, 1957; and with Hungary on May 27, 1957. The agreements made public in the satellite press were not identical. According to the Soviet-Polish agreement, for example, movements of Soviet troops in Poland were possible only with the consent of the Polish government; in the DDR, on the other hand, only "consultation" was provided for. (Helmut Bohn and others, *Bonner Berichte Aus Mittel- und Ostdeutschland: Die Aufrüstung in der Sowjetischen Besatzungszone Deutschlands* [Bonn Reports from Middle and East Germany: Rearmament of the Soviet Occupation Zone of Germany], Bonn, Bundesministerium für Gesamtdeutsche Fragen, 1958, pp. 129–130.)

graph of the Warsaw Treaty relating to "defense capacity" was intended to serve as a legal basis for foreign (meaning Soviet) military intervention. Since this was its meaning, however, only secession from the Warsaw Pact could ensure nonintervention.

The praise given by the satellites and their press to Khrushchev's leadership and to the ambiguous Declaration meant that Khrushchev was free to take action as he pleased.

5. THE HUNGARIAN UPRISING

The impact on Hungary of the events in Poland was strong. Street demonstrations cheered Polish General Josef Bem, the Hungarian liberty fighter of 1848. Demonstrators carried banners and posters bearing the inscriptions: "Long Live the Polish People," "The Cause of Poland Is Also Our Cause," "Long Live the Polish Working Class." The demonstrations, which in the beginning were peaceful, assumed a warlike character on the evening of October 23, when the security police stepped in and opened fire. Within a short time thousands of workers had joined in the fighting, and the movement assumed all the features of a violent revolution. Early on the twenty-fourth, Soviet tanks and armored cars joined the battle. The fight went on, with workers and students on one side and the Soviet army and the AVH (Hungarian Security Police) on the other. The Soviet tank operations against the crowds in front of the Parliament building on October 25 marked the first climax of the fighting. In the provinces, where there was less fighting, "Workers Councils" on the Russian pattern of 1917 emerged.

For more than one reason the conflict in Poland was more easily resolved than was the conflict in Hungary. In Poland the Communist party under Ochab had already started to move away from the satellite status, and Gomulka commanded a considerable popular following. In Hungary, on the contrary, Erno Gerö, the unreformed Rakoszi man, acting as a Russian puppet, had to stay close to the secret police in order to maintain his party in power. He considered the popular movements in Hungary reactionary, anti-Soviet and proimperialist. The strength of Soviet forces in Hungary was estimated at 20,000 men and 600 tanks, and additional Soviet troops started to cross the frontier and move along Hungary's highways about October 20.

At the time of the uprising there were four centers of Soviet- and Hungarian-Communist control in and around Budapest.

First, towering over the civilian and military Russians, were the two Presidium members, Anastas Mikoyan and Mikhail Suslov, who had been dispatched to Hungary and who on at least two occasions in the course of the revolt had been in Budapest.

Second there was the Soviet Embassy, under Yuri Andropov. The Embassy, well-informed on all Hungarian developments, was the main channel of regular Soviet-Hungarian exchanges. Andropov's predecessor in Budapest, Ambassador Yevgeni Kiselev, was an intelligent, courageous, and influential man; it was Kiselev who, after Stalin's death, submitted to Moscow a gloomy but honest report on the situation in Hungary.[51] Andropov, who succeeded Kiselev in 1954, did not possess the good judgment of his predecessor.

Third were the headquarters of the Soviet military forces in Hungary, under Major General K. Grebennik, which were located first in Tököl, near Budapest; on November 4 they established offices in the Parliament building.

Fourth was the office of the Communist Party in the Academy street where the Hungarian Politburo and Central Committee met. During the uprising and the chaos in the governmental agencies the party's supreme body maintained a modicum of influence by its close collaboration with the Russians.

There was passionate debate later between East and West over precisely who had invited the Soviet troops to Budapest on October 23. The Soviet and satellite side have maintained that Imre Nagy, who became premier during the night of October 23-24, sent a message to the Soviet side asking armed help to quell the uprising. Nagy denied this, and the United Nations report on Hungary refuted the Soviet contention, proving that even the time schedule of the Soviet troop movements contradicted the official Soviet version.[52] Research conducted in the West indicates that it is probable the request for Soviet aid was signed by either Premier Hegedüs, Nagy's predeces-

---

[51] According to Tibor Meray (D Papers, File H, December 14, 1959, p. 2), at the time all Soviet ambassadors in the satellites were requested to make reports on the respective countries.

[52] United Nations, *Report of the Special Committee on the Problem of Hungary*, General Assembly, Official Records: Eleventh Session, Supplement no. 18 (A/3592), New York, 1957, pp. 34–40.

sor, or Erno Gerö, the real power behind the Hungarian premier. However, the issue of who signed the call for Soviet forces is of secondary importance. It would be wrong to assume that the Soviet troops intervened only because of a demand for such intervention by a satellite government. Soviet intervention—an act of major significance—was decided upon in Moscow without regard to what Gerö, Hegedüs, or any other Hungarian leader desired. Moscow's decision was made on the basis of reports from its ambassador, its military command in Budapest, its informers among the Hungarians. Once the decision in the Kremlin was taken, the Budapest regime of course had to sanction it and sign a paper on the dotted line. Most probably, the text of the "invitation" to intervene was presented to one of the Hungarian leaders by either the Soviet ambassador or a Soviet general.

The "restoration of order" in the capital by Soviet troops and tanks on October 24 was, of course, accomplished quickly and successfully; the action, however, inflamed passions and inspired the popular movement with hatred for the AVH and the Gerö leadership. As a first concession to the movement, Premier Hegedüs was removed; with Mikoyan's consent, Imre Nagy was appointed his successor. On the twenty-fifth, however, Gerö's position in the party became untenable. Extremely unpopular, he could no longer appear before the crowds or speak over the radio, and he had reason to fear for his safety. "Death to Gerö" was one of the slogans heard in the streets.

Mikoyan and Suslov joined in the attacks on Gerö, holding him responsible for the revolt. "You have stampeded Moscow," they told him, "by exaggerated and distorted pictures." Gerö was dismissed from his post, and Janos Kadar, Nagy's supporter, was named first secretary of the party. It was agreed that Nagy would inaugurate a number of reforms, but not until the twenty-eighth was Nagy free to act. The six days between October 28 and November 3 were the only period during which the government in Budapest enjoyed a degree of independence; its power and activity, however, were limited, not so much by Russian orders as by the multitude of local committees, with their own programs and threats of action, which emerged all over the country.

On October 30 Mikoyan and Suslov met in Budapest with General Marian Nashkovski, the representative of Gomulka, whose position was distinctly pro-Nagy. (Gomulka had insisted on the withdrawal

The Hungarian Uprising

of Soviet troops from Hungary.) In Warsaw it was announced that "complete agreement" was reached between the two parties on the Hungarian issue.[53]

In the few days of Nagy's independent rule the government was reorganized as a coalition of political parties, including the Smallholders, the Peasant, and, ultimately, the Social-Democratic parties. Newspapers sponsored by these parties began to appear. The official Hungarian Communist press severely criticized *Pravda*'s attitude to the events in Hungary, and Janos Kadar, now the leader of the Communist Party, publicly agreed to "avoid bloodshed" by abolishing the one-party system. The security police (AVH) were disbanded. The evolution in Hungary had already gone beyond the Polish-Gomulka limits and had started to approach Western patterns.

In this climate of general change, the Hungarian Communist Party, which, having lost its prominent leaders, was disintegrating, decided to reorganize. It discarded its Rakosziite title ("Hungarian Workers' Party") and assumed the name "Hungarian Socialist Workers' Party." Janos Kadar, a former victim of the Rakoszi system, who had spent three years in a Communist prison, was elected secretary of the party. Imre Nagy was among the members of the nucleus of the new party. This reorganization of the party, a unique phenomenon in the history of Communism, could never have taken place in a small "people's democracy" if the ranking guests from Moscow had been opposed to it. The emergence of Kadar, the pro-Nagy and pro-Tito man, as the party's supreme leader, became both an important and a confusing factor in the subsequent developments.

Tito greeted the Hungarian upheaval with enthusiasm. Without assuming an active role, he hailed the Nagy government and its program, including its slogan of "equality and respect for sovereignty," and the "taking the initiative for negotiations on the withdrawal of Soviet troops." When the Security Council of the United Nations debated the use of Soviet troops in Hungary, and Soviet delegate Sobolev indicated a Soviet veto, the Yugoslavs abstained from voting on the question. Tito had every reason to hope that Nagy's Hungary would develop into a close ally of Yugoslavia.

It has often been asserted that in acquiescing to a Nagy government and its reforms, Moscow wanted only to deceive, gain time, and

[53] United Press, Warsaw, October 31, 1956.

strengthen its forces in Hungary; that it never intended to seek a compromise; that the decision to crush the rebellion had been made in the very beginning.

There is more than one indication that this theory is inaccurate; for one thing, the attitude of the Soviet press to the Hungarian developments appears convincing. The first Soviet explanation of the revolt in Hungary was the standard one of "foreign agents" (in the main American and West German). This was a banal and unconvincing interpretation, as was the interpretation that the Soviet intervention had been at the "request" of the Hungarian government:

> The Government of the Hungarian People's Republic has turned to the Government of the U.S.S.R. with a request for assistance. In accordance with this request Soviet military units which are situated in Hungary in accordance with the Warsaw Pact came to the assistance of the army of the Hungarian Republic in re-establishing order in Budapest. [Consequently] the forces of the revolutionary order have started to repulse the rebels.[54]

Once "order" was restored, an optimistic note began to prevail in the Soviet press. The successes of the new Nagy government were even exaggerated; the situation in Hungary was reported as better than it actually was; the anti-Communist excesses were ignored. Beginning on October 26, the day after the first Soviet intervention, the Soviet press was reporting that the counterrevolutionary insurrection had been "liquidated" and that things were returning to normal; in general, according to the reports, the Hungarian capital was quiet. The terse reports were obviously intended to minimize the events and to present the past Soviet intervention as an almost trivial affair.

On October 30 the Soviet press carried an extremely optimistic but somewhat unrealistic TASS report:

> Budapest is returning to normal living. Life in Budapest is gradually resuming its normal ways. The newspaper *Szabad Nep* appeared today in its usual size. Work has been resumed in the majority of the industrial enterprises. Many food stores have reopened. . . .
>
> According to the Budapest radio peace and order are also being restored in the provinces. The Hungarian toiling masses noted with satisfaction the statement made yesterday by the Chairman of the Hungarian Council of Ministers, Imre Nagy. This statement was ap-

---

[54] *Pravda,* October 25, 1956.

proved by the Central Committee of the Hungarian Party of Toilers; it presented the program of government activities for the immediate future.[55]

Optimism still prevailed on November 1: "By evening life in the city became more animated. Many pedestrians and cars appeared in the streets." [56] Even such a development as the emergence of a coalition government (which had not occurred in the case of Poland) was accepted quietly and reported almost approvingly by the Soviet press. Janos Kadar, the party leader, it was pointed out, would serve as a member of the government. Soviet troops were leaving the capital. On November 2, *Pravda* reported that a number of newspapers of other than Communist parties were appearing in Hungary. This statement was not accompanied by criticism or the usual attack on the "traitors." It was as though the Soviet leadership was considering collaboration with an independent regime of pro-Yugoslav orientation.

The picture changed almost overnight on November 2–3. The optimistic exaggerations turned into exaggerations of gloom. The situation in Hungary was represented as much worse than it actually was. The Soviet press now reported "roistering," "murders," "lynch-law mobbings," armed supplies from the West arriving in Hungary by air, and the menace of "black reaction." "Block the Way to Reaction in Hungary," a *Pravda* headline read.

> The last days in the capital and provinces have been marked by roistering and riots by counter-revolutionary gangs. Offices of different societies and party organizations have been demolished, and there have been mass-mobbings and killing of public figures.[57]

This change in tone reflected the Soviet government's decision, apparently taken on or about November 1, to crush the Hungarian movement by military force.

In this fateful decision of the Soviet government, Nagy's move to quit the Soviet bloc and declare Hungary neutral was the last determining factor.

[55] *Ibid.*, October 30, 1956.
[56] *Ibid.*, November 1, 1956, "The Situation in Hungary."
[57] *Izvestia*, November 3, 1956.

From the first day of his premiership Nagy insisted on the removal of Soviet forces from every part of Hungary. On October 25, after Gerö's dismissal, Nagy and Janos Kadar broadcasted their program: "The Hungarian government," Nagy said, "will begin talks with the Soviet Union concerning the relations between the Hungarian People's Republic and the Soviet Union, and, among other things, concerning the withdrawal of the Soviet forces stationed in Hungary." This statement by Nagy could not have been made without the consent of Mikoyan and Suslov.

The cease-fire announced on October 28 was coupled with a Soviet promise to withdraw Soviet forces, but only from the capital. As to total withdrawal of Soviet troops, Moscow agreed only to "negotiate."

From that date on everything hinged on the removal of Soviet troops. Hungary's insistence on this was producing disagreements and uncertainty among the Soviet leaders; Mikoyan, in Budapest and in close contact with the developments, was obviously inclined to give in in order to avoid an armed intervention. On October 31 he told Minister Zoltan Tildy that troops which are in Hungary on grounds other than the Warsaw Treaty will be withdrawn from the country.[58] Polish leader Wladyslaw Gomulka confirmed that Mikoyan had met in Budapest with two members of the Polish Central Committee; they, too, had demanded that Soviet troops be withdrawn from Hungary.[59]

It is likely that Mikoyan was one of the few Soviet leaders who to the end opposed the armed operations in Hungary, and that it was to him that Khrushchev later referred in his speech in Budapest.[60]

Between October 29 and 31 Soviet troops were almost entirely evacuated from Budapest; elsewhere in the country they remained. In the first days of November new troops arrived.[61]

[58] United Nations *Report, op. cit.*, p. 54.
[59] *Neue Zürcher Zeitung*, Zurich, Switzerland, October 31, 1956.
[60] *Pravda*, December 3, 1959.
[61] That there was an increase in Soviet forces in the first days of November is, although Moscow denied it, beyond doubt. "At Zahony, the frontier station on the Transcarpathian border, at least 100 tanks were located on Hungarian territory, while a considerable force of motorized infantry, with artillery vehicles and supporting tank units, was moving westwards towards Nyiregyhaza. The next day, 133 light tanks and 80 of the latest model heavy tanks crossed the frontier of Zahony, more than compensating for the few tanks and infantry vehicles which were moving eastwards from Nyiregyhaza, with the local inhabitants cheering them on their way. . . .

On November 1 Nagy summoned Soviet Ambassador Andropov to tell him that the entry of new Soviet military units into Hungary had not been agreed to by the Hungarian government, that ". . . it was a violation of the Warsaw Treaty, and, if the new reinforcements were not withdrawn to their former positions, the Hungarian Government would denounce the Treaty."

As if feeling that he was on his way out of the Soviet bloc, Nagy, bypassing party channels, sent a telegram to Voroshilov, as head of the Supreme Soviet, in which he confirmed Hungary's desire "to undertake immediate negotiations concerning the withdrawal of Soviet troops from the entire territory of Hungary." He referred to the Soviet government's Declaration of October 30 and requested that a delegation be named and a place and date set for the negotiations.

Moscow's answer was prompt but evasive. Although it spoke of a "partial" withdrawal of Soviet troops, it suggested negotiations on two levels—one for political, the other for military matters. As for the newly arriving Soviet forces, Ambassador Andropov told Nagy that they were sent to relieve other troops and to protect Russian citizens in Hungary. Nagy found this answer unsatisfactory; a few hours after receiving it he informed the ambassador by telephone that fresh Soviet troops were still crossing the border and that the Soviet government obviously was trying to reoccupy Hungary. Nagy then made the crucial announcement to the Soviet ambassador that Hungary would withdraw from the Warsaw Pact and assume a course of neutrality.

On the same day (November 1), in his cable to the United Nations, Nagy demanded the instant withdrawal of Soviet forces, stated Hungary's repudiation of the Warsaw Treaty, and declared her neutrality. The next day, in another cable, Nagy asked the secretary general of the United Nations "to call on the Great Powers to recognize Hungary's neutrality." At 4 P.M. the Council of Ministers adopted the Declaration of Neutrality of Hungary and approved Hungary's withdrawal from the Warsaw Treaty. At 5 P.M. the Soviet ambassador was asked to come to the Parliament building where, in the presence

---

". . . The Zahony sector was the principal venue, but from 31 October, most of the roads leading into Hungary were being used for the conveyance of Soviet troops. . . .

". . . Fresh units came to Szolnok and Kecskemét by 1 November, while another unit appears to have crossed the Danube and to have established itself by that date at Dombovar, 20 kilometres north of the city of Pécs. The Soviet Army used also the main railroad lines passing through Zahony for the transportation of troops." (United Nations *Report, op. cit.*, p. 27.)

of the Council of Ministers, he received the Declaration of Neutrality of Hungary. In the course of these conversations Andropov assured Nagy that the Soviet troops would leave; he wanted the Hungarian government to withdraw its complaint to the United Nations. Throughout his negotiations with the Soviet representatives Nagy had been seconded by Janos Kadar, who acted in the name of the rejuvenated Communist Party. Kadar apparently was also present at the critical negotiations between Nagy and Andropov.

On the evening of November 1 Nagy read the Declaration of neutrality over the radio. The opening words were: "People of Hungary! The Hungarian National Government, imbued with profound responsibility towards the Hungarian millions, declares the neutrality of the Hungarian People's Republic."

This defection of a "people's democracy" to the neutrals was a severe blow to Moscow. The Soviet press never informed its readers about it; to the Russian people Hungary's withdrawal from the Warsaw Treaty remained a secret. Hungary's declaration of neutrality appeared as a Soviet failure and a Tito victory.

On November 2 the Soviet Embassy received three notes from the Hungarian government containing protests against movements of Soviet troops. The notes suggested speedy negotiations (to be conducted in Warsaw) concerning Hungary's withdrawal from the Warsaw Treaty, and named the Hungarian delegates who would participate in the proposed negotiations. The next morning, when Budapest was already encircled, Ambassador Andropov informed Nagy that Moscow had accepted the proposals to negotiate on the military phase of the withdrawal. On the same day, as if no change had occurred in the Soviet course, the negotiations with the Soviet generals began. Three Soviet generals (Malinin, Cherbanin, and Stepanov) met with a Hungarian delegation headed by General Pal Maleter in Tököl near Budapest to discuss the details of the withdrawal; the Soviet proposals, reasonable and logical, were accepted in principle.

Around midnight on November 2 telephone contact with the Hungarian delegation at Tököl was suddenly broken off. Reconnaissance parties dispatched from Budapest to Tököl failed to return. The negotiations were interrupted by the entry of a personage "who bore no insignia of rank," General Serov, Chief of the Soviet security police. Accompanied by Soviet officers, he announced that he was arresting the Hungarian delegation. The head of the Soviet delegation, General Malinin, astonished by the interruption, made a gesture of indignation. General Serov thereupon whispered to him; as a result, General Malinin shrugged his shoulders and ordered the Soviet delegation to leave the room.[62]

This action marked the end of the negotiations and the start of a new Soviet intervention.

Once again a Hungarian "request for help" from Moscow, part of the ritual, was necessary; obviously only a government other than that of Nagy would be willing to dispatch such a request. For this task, Kadar proved accessible. Without resigning from the Nagy regime, but under the guidance of the Soviet ambassador, Kadar proceeded to organize a new government. He did not immediately announce his planned *coup d'état;* to be successful the *coup d'état* had to be coordinated with the new operations of the Soviet troops. Everything was scheduled to take place on November 4.

The initial group of Kadar's regime was set up in Szolnok on the Tisza River, near Soviet military headquarters. The place had served as a refuge for hundreds of Hungarian Rakosziites who had reason to fear for their lives, among them former Premier Hegedüs. Kadar arrived there with his group to organize his future government with the assistance of the Soviet leaders and the Soviet Embassy.

Kadar made his first moves in secret, but eventually he announced both the formation of a new government and its request for military assistance. "The Hungarian Revolutionary Workers-Peasant Government, in the interest of our people, working class and peasantry, requested the Command of the Soviet Army to help our nation in smashing the sinister forces of reaction and restoring order and calm

---

[62] United Nations *Report, op. cit.*, p. 45. The Hungarian "White Book" (vol. 5) maintains that Pal Maleter was arrested by Kadar's authorities, not by Soviet authorities. "His arrest was ordered by the Revolutionary Workers' and Peasants' Government. . . ." (*Die Konterrevolutionäre Verschwörung von Imre Nagy und Komplizen* [The Counterrevolutionary Conspiracy of Imre Nagy and His Accomplices], published by the Information Office of the Council of Ministers of Hungary, Budapest, n.d., vol. 5, p. 72.) The attempt to represent the developments in Hungary as a purely internal affair, and the claim that the arrest of members of the Nagy regime was carried out by a Hungarian government, is in line with the standard Soviet pattern. Actually, at the time of the arrests the Kadar government was still *in statu nascendi,* possessed no police force, and was unable to act, let alone make arrests of ranking leaders of the other side.

in the country." Some 2,500 Soviet tanks and 1,000 supporting Soviet vehicles were already available.

When the news of Kadar's formation of a new regime reached Nagy, during the night of November 3–4, the latter summoned a cabinet meeting. At 5:20 A.M., November 4, Nagy made his last address over the radio: " 'Today at daybreak Soviet troops attacked our capital with the obvious intention of overthrowing the legal Hungarian democratic Government. Our troops are in combat. . . .' " [63]

The unequal fight, conducted with severity and ruthlessness, ended, as was to be expected, in a Soviet victory. On the morning of November 5 the Soviet press carried a triumphant report from Budapest: ". . . the attack of the forces of the reactionary conspiracy against the people's-democratic regime of Hungary has been crushed. The government of Imre Nagy, which cleared the road for the reactionary forces of the counter-revolution, has disintegrated and ceased to exist." [64] General Grebennik, now in complete control of the country, appealed in vain to the Hungarian army to "fight on the side of Soviet troops."

Meanwhile Nagy had sought and found asylum at the Yugoslav Embassy. Two days before the second Soviet intervention, as the tension was growing, leading members of the Socialist Workers' Party (of the pro-Nagy wing) inquired of Yugoslav Ambassador Soldatič whether the Embassy would give refuge, if requested, to a group of Hungarian Communists and their wives and children. During the night of November 3–4 the ambassador urged Nagy and other members of his group to come to the Embassy.[65] Early in the morning of November 4 a group of Hungarian leaders and their wives and children, in all about forty persons, arrived at the Yugoslav Embassy. While Soviet military forces were taking over the capital, the Yugoslav Embassy was harboring the Hungarian government.[66]

Khrushchev's military suppression of the Hungarian uprising and

---

[63] United Nations *Report, op. cit.*, p. 45.

[64] *Pravda*, November 5, 1956.

[65] *Die Konterrevolutionäre Verschwörung von Imre Nagy und Komplizen, op. cit.*, vol. 5, p. 157; United Nations *Report, op. cit.*, p. 157.

[66] Nagy, it was reported, had brought with him to the Yugoslav Embassy tape recordings of his conversations with Mikoyan and Suslov. If this is so, Tito is today in possession of important information which he could use against Moscow if he wanted to. (D Papers, December 14, 1959, File H, pp. 2–3.)

The Hungarian Uprising

the abolition of the Nagy government implied a severe defeat for Tito and "Titoism." Aiming his guns against alleged "imperialist agents" in Hungary, Khrushchev hit also, as he intended to, the ubiquitous image of "Titoism," symbol of national Communist emancipation. Tito's imaginary alliance with his neighbors, their independence of Moscow, Yugoslav influence on their affairs, the new prospects of a Balkan federation—all were buried in the ruins of Budapest. Tito was again isolated and surrounded by adversaries.

Tito, however, would not acknowledge his defeat and return to his isolation. It was only a few weeks since he had arrived at a friendly compromise with Khrushchev and his group, since Gerö had been removed, since new honors had been reaped on him by the leadership of his Communist neighbor nations. His attitude and policy, therefore, remained inconsistent and ambiguous. Besides, the advent of Kadar as successor to Nagy obviously confused Tito. He had met Kadar a few weeks before when the latter was in Belgrade as a member of Gerö's delegation. Kadar, the only former "Titoist" among the Hungarian guests, was liked and approved by Tito and his entourage. Now Tito preferred to disregard the fact that Kadar's elevation had been achieved with the help of Soviet tanks; he clung to his illusion that Kadar was his man.

In Moscow, on the other hand, Tito was suspected of fostering anti-Soviet trends in Hungary; it was reported that the Yugoslav Embassy in Budapest was in close touch with the members of the Nagy group before and during the crucial developments. Moscow was inclined to exaggerate Tito's role in the events in Hungary; actually Tito had been cautious and more than prudent. Paralyzed by conflicting trends and plans, he did not take a clear position on the Hungarian issue.

During the night of November 3–4 Tito received word from Moscow that a new Soviet armed intervention was imminent; he neither protested nor approved; his ambassador in Budapest was only instructed to offer asylum to Nagy and the other Hungarian leaders. On November 4, Tito's *Borba* attacked the "reactionaries" and *émigrés*, praised Kadar's first announcements, expressed the hope that the necessary conditions would be created for the withdrawal of Soviet troops. "Of course," *Borba* said, "we regard in a negative way the fact that the Hungarian government had to turn to the Soviet army for aid." However, "we cannot pass over the fact" that developments in Hungary were influenced by "reactionary forces"; etc.

The next day *Tanyug*, Tito's press agency, repeated the same ideas, stressing, belatedly, Yugoslavia's continuing interest in the internal affairs of Hungary. A few days later Tito gave his account of the Hungarian developments in a speech at Pula which was full of "yes, buts," "on the one hands," and "on the other hands," of friendly gestures toward Moscow and Kadar, and of cautious reservations. The Hungarian uprising was justified, Tito said, but Kadar "represents that which is most honest in Hungary." The first Soviet intervention "was not necessary"; the second, an alternative to a world war, was necessary. However, "you can rest assured that we never advised them to go ahead and use the army. We never gave such advice and could not do so even in the present crisis."

Pravda attacked Tito for his inconsistencies but not before it had been decided to seize the Nagy group of refugees in the Yugoslav Embassy by ruse and force and remove them from Hungary to another "people's democracy." [67]

Negotiations between the Nagy government and the Yugoslav Embassy concerning the fate of the refugees went on for over two weeks; the Soviet authorities did not directly participate in the exchanges, although their hand was evident at all stages. Nagy and his group requested permission to return to their homes or go to Yugoslavia; Kadar agreed to the former, but only on the political conditions that Nagy and Losonozy resign their posts in the government, issue statements approving the fight of the Hungarian government against the counterrevolution, make a public self-criticism of their early activities, and give guarantees that they would not undertake any moves against the Hungarian government.

The Nagy group refused to accept these terms. An agreement was reached to permit the refugees to return home without conditions. Kadar signed a letter addressed to the Yugoslavs in which he confirmed that his government "has no intention of taking punitive action against Imre Nagy and members of his group because of their past convictions. We understand that this discontinues the asylum granted to the group concerned, that they themselves will leave the

---

[67] *Pravda*, November 23, 1956.

The Hungarian Uprising

Yugoslav Embassy, and that they will return freely to their homes." [68]

Hungarian Minister Ferenc Munnich placed a bus at the disposal of the Nagy group, and on November 22 the group left the Yugoslav Embassy. The bus, however, was stopped by a Soviet police officer and directed to the headquarters of the Soviet Army. All trace of the refugees was lost.

The Hungarian authorities offered no explanation; the Communist press in other countries carried reports of the arrival of the refugees in Rumania. The Yugoslav government, in a strong note to Budapest, protested the breach of the agreement. Well aware that the entire action had been guided and controlled by the Soviet authorities, Tito's Foreign Office sent a note to the Soviet expressing its "surprise" at the fact that "Soviet organs in Hungary prevented the carrying out of the above-mentioned agreement which should have settled, in a friendly way, the question at issue between the Governments of Yugoslavia and Hungary. Because of that, the Government of Yugoslavia refers to the Government of the Union of Soviet Socialist Republics hoping that it will do all that is necessary to enable the above-mentioned agreement to be carried out." [69]

No satisfactory answer, of course, was expected. The answer appeared in an article in *Pravda* (November 23) which resumed, after an interruption of more than a year, the series of bitter Soviet press attacks on Tito. *Borba*, in turn, revealed the story of Nagy's kidnaping.

Soviet-Yugoslav relations deteriorated markedly. Tito was now a defeated and impotent adversary of the Soviet Union.

The number of persons killed in the course of the Hungarian uprising, according to the Hungarian Statistical Department, amounted to from 2,700 to 2,900, and the number of wounded to about 13,000. (These figures do not include Soviet casualties.) Four thousand buildings were completely destroyed. The official Hungarian White Book contained short notices on 194 of a total of 234 of "our martyrs." Of them, 118 were members of the police, 5 were party officials, 36 were members of the armed forces, and 35 were civilians.[70] The defenders

---

[68] *Borba*, Belgrade, November 25, 1956.
[69] *Ibid.*
[70] *Kontrrevolyutsionnye Sily v Vengerskikh Oktyabrshikh Sobytiyakh* (Counterrevolutionary Forces in the Hungarian October Events), Moscow, Foreign Literature Publishing House, 1957, vol. 3, pp. 135-52; *Die Konterrevolutionäre Verschwörung von Imre Nagy und Komplizen, op. cit.*, vol. 5, p. 17.

of the Rakoszi-Gerö regime counted about 250 dead, almost all from Soviet bullets.

Although this was officially denied, there was a large-scale deportation of arrested Hungarians to the Soviet Union, the number of deported running into the thousands. The deported were kept for a time in Soviet prisons not far from the Hungarian border, but were later returned to Hungary.[71]

While the ending of the Hungarian conflict signified a Soviet victory, and the restoration of a loyal satellite regime in Budapest represented a success, the victory and success were bought at a heavy price. Thousands of Soviet sympathizers in Western Europe and America became Soviet enemies. Socialist parties which had sometimes tended toward "friendship with Russia" turned their backs on the Soviet. The Communist parties did not conceal the internal crises engendered by the Soviet action in Hungary. The image of an empire which conquers small nations by the sword was again rising and supplanting the belief in Soviet respect for the principles of equality and sovereignty of nations.

Soviet prestige in Europe and America fell. It took a year of humiliations, failures, and internal conflicts for the Soviet Union to recover from the wounds inflicted in Hungary.

[71] The United Nations Committee which investigated the history of the uprising states, however, that it has no proof that more than a part of the deportees have been returned to Hungary (*Report, op. cit.*, pp. 33, 123–26, and 130).

PART FOUR

The New Course in the Middle and Far East

CHAPTER 1

THE MIDDLE EAST

1. THE OLD PATH

One of the great issues before the Soviet government in the postwar era was British succession in the Middle East. The problem took on unexpected features and added importance in 1954–55, when the time for Britain's withdrawal from Egypt arrived. To Moscow it seemed that the issue was a dilemma: the United States or the Soviet Union.

Other nations of Asia, such as India, Burma, or Ceylon, did not have to choose between the two giants; their neutrality, although viewed by Stalin-Molotov with suspicion, was accepted as a matter of fact. Distant from Russia's borders, these countries, whose role in world affairs was a minor one, did not attract as much Soviet attention and effort and as much radiation of Soviet power as did the immediate neighbors of the Soviet Union in Europe and Asia.

The Middle East, close to Russia's borders, was a region of another kind. Various areas of it had been coveted by Russian and Soviet empire builders; its Communist groups had constant contact with the Gensek's office in Moscow. In the possession of the potential enemy, military bases in the Middle East might endanger the Soviet Union. Moscow therefore did its utmost to achieve two ends: (1) to get Britain out of its strongholds in this part of the world, and (2) to prevent the entry of a third power into it. Propaganda, diplomacy, even advocacy of the partition of Palestine, were directed to the purpose of getting rid of the British in and around the Mediterranean. The power vacuum thus created was to be filled by a "progressive" element before the United States could assemble its resources and step into Britain's shoes.

The fact that the United States had no intention of taking over the British heritage in the Middle East or, in general, acquiring territories in Asia and Africa, was vehemently denied in Soviet doctrine. On the theoretical level, the admission that the United States was not a "colonialist," and therefore not an "imperialist," power would contradict the basic tenet that capitalism in its "highest stage" develops into imperialism. On the level of practical policies, acceptance of the United States as a nonimperialist nation would contradict the consistent and relentless Soviet course in foreign affairs which was, par excellence, anti-American.

Antagonism toward America in fact was becoming the main feature of all Communist policies in the Middle East at the time. In the eyes of the non-Communist nationalism of the Middle East, Britain and France were the traditional colonial powers, while the United States had often helped to find a peaceful solution of the problems of their withdrawal from the area: this was, for example, the case in Iran and Egypt. In the version of the Soviet-Communist governments and parties, on the contrary, American effort was extended only in order that the United States might replace the British and French: therefore the United States, not Britain, was Enemy Number One. The distinction between the prominently anti-British and the prominently anti-American course often differentiated the non-Communist from the pro-Soviet trends in the framework of Asian and African nationalism. American imperialism, the Soviet-Communist theory held, was at least as vicious as that of the other empires, except that it used other, sometimes more subtle, methods. A party or government which was prepared to come to terms with America could not enjoy the support of the Soviet Union.

Soviet *rapprochement* with the main nations of the Arab world developed as a consequence of new trends on both the Soviet and the Arab side.

At the beginning of the era of *rapprochement* (1953–54), Stalinist tradition prevailed in Soviet attitudes toward the Middle East. "Independence" of former colonies was a sham if the new independent countries were not ruled by "workers' parties" and the "imperialist powers" used the allegedly nationalist regimes as their tools. In a

The Old Path

book entitled *Imperialist Struggle for Africa,* published by the Soviet Academy of Sciences after Stalin's death, it was stated that of Africa's 180 to 200 million inhabitants no less than 140 million lived in possessions of the "colonial powers," that Ethiopia was in bondage to "Anglo-American imperialism," that Libya was actually in British hands, and that in Egypt, even after the revolution there, the

> bourgeois-landlord system, with all its evils, was being preserved, and the abdication of Farouk did not bring about any essential changes in the situation. The reaction in Egypt has increased.[1]

According to the same source, the "ruling classes," in their actually antinationalist course, "are resorting to severe repressions against the working class and its Communist vanguard, because they want to behead the national liberation movement and delay its development."

This was a sterile policy; maintaining tradition, it opened no prospects. In Iran it led to the fall of Mossadegh and success for the pro-American groups after the Stalin methods of head-on attack had ended in total defeat. At the wheel of Soviet policy at the time were Molotov, Stalin's pupil, and Malenkov.

In the second half of 1954, when Khrushchev's influence was growing, a substantial change in Soviet policy in the Middle East became obvious. The Khrushchev policy now signified, on the one hand, a more moderate course in the "underdeveloped" countries, one of collaboration with "bourgeois nationalism" of the Nasser type, without regard for the fate of the local "working class and its party." The policy of "peaceful coexistence with capitalism" in the Arab nations was like a retreat from ultrarevolutionary positions.

On the other hand, the *rapprochement* with the Arab "capitalist classes" was intended to constitute a component part of an increasingly powerful offensive against American "capitalism"—an offensive to oust the United States from all its positions and bases in Europe, Asia, and Africa. In Marxist-Communist parlance, Khrushchev's course in the Middle East contemplated an alliance of the world proletariat with the bourgeoisie of certain countries in an offensive against the bourgeoisie of other (imperialist) countries. Such a coalition was a

---

[1] L. Vatolina, "Egipet i krizis britanskoi kolonialnoi politiki" (Egypt and the Crisis of British Colonial Policy), in *Imperialisticheskaya Borba za Afriku i osvoboditelnoye dvizhenie narodov* (Imperialist Struggle for Africa and the Liberation Movement of the Peoples), Moscow, Izdatelstvo Akademii Nauk SSSR, 1953, pp. 124, 127.

stage in an all-out fight against the presence of the United States in any part of the world, in the first place Europe.

The Baghdad Pact had been signed in February, 1955. The importance of the pact was somewhat exaggerated by the Soviet government, and its conclusion was seen as a failure of Molotov's policy in the Middle East. Among the reasons for Molotov's subsequent eclipse was the Middle Eastern situation; a few months after the signing of the Baghdad Pact the Khrushchev-Molotov duel in the Central Committee (see pages 227 ff.) proved that Molotov's position had been shattered long before he was formally ousted.

The Baghdad Pact created an alliance of four "underdeveloped" countries—Turkey, Iran, Iraq, and Pakistan—under British leadership; Turkey and Iran, Russia's southern neighbors, constituted the nucleus of the alliance. As we have seen, the long belt of satellites and friendly neutrals artfully built up by Stalin around the Soviet Union along her European and Asian frontiers, showed one gap—at the point where the Caucasus and Soviet Turkestan border on Turkey and Iran. Now the whole group of Baghdad nations moved away and into the Western camp (Turkey had been a member of NATO), actually became allies of the United States, and could serve in time of war as American and British air bases against Russia.

The Soviet-Arab *rapprochement* of 1955–56, like most other moves in Soviet foreign affairs, had two roots. One was the age-old, almost natural, desire of the government of one country to combine forces with the adversaries of its adversaries; geopolitically this meant *rapprochement* of two powers against a power situated between them. From 1890 to 1917 Russia was France's ally against Germany, who was situated between them; Germany was Spain's ally against France; later, Poland was France's ally against Nazi Germany. Nietzsche's philosophy of "love to the furthest" instead of "love to thy neighbor" ("Love the furthest and the future ones") often rules in international relations. In our case the Arab nations, which were separated from Russia by Turkey-Iran-Iraq, were her "furthest" friends in their common opposition to the neighbor in between. Egypt, the largest power in the Arab world, was the Soviet's potential ally.

The other element in the Soviet orientation toward the Arab nations was the Communist urge to expansion, transformation of other countries on the Soviet model, and the establishment of "proletarian rule," at least in neighboring areas. Such upheavals could take place only under extraordinary conditions, and preparations for them called for help to the Communist parties of the countries involved. In this respect, not Egypt, but the two northern Arab states, Iraq and Syria, were to play a primary role.

That a new Soviet policy for the Middle East was being elaborated became apparent in February, 1955, after Malenkov's dismissal. A resumption of the Soviet drive to the south became possible because a northward current to meet it was moving up from the Arab world. The general trend toward neutralism that existed in a number of nations in the 1950's took on some special characteristics when it spread to the Arab lands. The new orientation, which came to the Arab nations several years later than to South Asia, was rapidly taking hold; here neutralism went further than it did elsewhere. Among the "neutrals" of Europe, Asia, and Africa, from Finland to Indonesia, the Arab nations were to move the closest to the Soviet Union.

In the West a misconception similar to Stalin's prevailed until 1953–54. Self-assuring superficial theories which held that deeply religious Moslem nations were immune to Soviet-Communist influence, that pro-Western traditions were firmly entrenched in these regions, and that the poverty-stricken Arabs, in search of aid and loans, must turn to the West rather than to the East, were widespread at the time. When the first serious contacts between Moscow and Cairo occurred, they were often understood in the West as only a clever maneuver on the part of the Arabs in their bargaining with the West.

The first post-Stalin Soviet government did not react favorably to Egypt's soundings-out concerning the purchase by Egypt of Soviet arms. In the second half of 1953 an Egyptian trade mission was sent to various European countries, including Russia, to submit and discuss various Egyptian industrial projects (building of plants, irrigation, and others); under the heading of "agricultural machines" the Egyptians included arms.[2] In Moscow the Egyptian proposals were received coolly. No real *rapprochement* with Egypt was planned. In March, 1954, when Moscow elevated its Cairo legation to the rank of an embassy, this friendly move was counterbalanced by similar action taken in Israel.

[2] *The New York Times,* February 11 and 14, 1954. D Papers, December 15, 1958, File E.

Moscow, as a matter of course, supported Egypt's drive for the withdrawal of Britain from Suez, and Arab "noncooperation" with the West was warmly approved. But in this respect, again, the American issue divided Cairo and Moscow. In Soviet eyes it was inconsistent for Egypt's campaign to be pointed at Britain only, and for the Egyptian government to refuse to assume an outright anti-American position. No real Soviet-Egyptian *rapprochement* was possible.

A British-Egyptian agreement concluded in October, 1954, provided for the withdrawal of British troops within twenty months, but granted certain privileges to Britain in case of war. The United States took part in the discussions and in the preparation of the agreement; in Moscow, on the other hand, the agreement was seriously criticized.

During this period Egypt's attitude toward Communism and the Soviet Union remained strictly negative. Colonel Nasser approved the defense measures taken by the Middle Eastern nations against the Soviet Union. At that time he saw Russia as the potential "aggressor." "The objective of the aggressor? To reach the oil fields of Abadan, Mosul, and Dhahran, and to reach Egypt on account of her strategic position which is of capital importance for Africa and the Mediterranean." [3] In Nasser's eyes Egypt belonged to "the West." "There seems no doubt that Egypt today holds in all respects to the side of the West," said his Revolutionary Command Council. "Her culture, her commerce, and her economic life are bound to the West." [4] "Ideologically she is definitely opposed to Communism. Militarily she considers that the only danger capable of threatening the Middle East is a Soviet invasion. . . ." [5] Nasser defended Britain's right to reenter the Suez Canal bases in case of war. This was tantamount to a British-Egyptian *rapprochement* against the Soviet Union in defense of Turkey.

In regard to Egyptian Communism Nasser was even more outspoken. In a number of speeches and statements he accused the Egyptian Communists of getting help "from the outside." [6] Among

[3] *Bourse Egyptienne*, August 23, 1954. As quoted in *World Today*, Chatham House Review, London, November, 1956, p. 448.

[4] *The New York Times*, September 3, 1954.

[5] *L'Orient*, Beirut, September 3, 1954. As quoted in *World Today*, op. cit., November, 1956. These pro-Western statements were somewhat weakened by an official denial which, however, "was directed entirely to the Egyptian public."

[6] For example, *United States News and World Report*, Washington, D.C., September 3, 1954.

The Arms Deal

his four internal adversaries he listed Communism as Number One. His security police formed pseudo-Communist cells and infiltrated genuine Communist organizations. Communist leaders were kept in prison, although a Communist underground continued to exist.[7]

2. A NEW COURSE AND THE ARMS DEAL

There was no substantial change in Soviet-Egyptian relations until the end of 1954, when the Baghdad Pact negotiations were in their final phase. While Iraq joined the pro-Western alliance, the situation in general was marked by a new upsurge of Arab nationalism and renewed Arab-Israeli tension. After the bloody Ghaza raid, Egypt dispatched a mission, under Hassen Fahmi Ragab, Under-Secretary of War, to various countries of Western and Eastern Europe to sound them out about the sale of arms to Egypt. The mission, which included Prague among the capitals visited (but not Moscow), received little encouragement. Thus the stage was set for Egypt's orientation toward the East.

At the Cairo Conference of Arab prime ministers Nasser assumed the leadership in a move against Iraq, Turkey, and the West. In accepting the invitation to the Bandung Conference, the Nasser regime actually joined the neutralist camp.

The Soviet *New Times* hailed this attitude; it was happy about the failure of Turkey's attempt to win the Arab nations over to the Baghdad Pact.[8] In his report made in February, 1955, Molotov hinted at a substantial change in Soviet-Arab relations:

> Auspicious facts have lately marked the relations between the Soviet Union and the Arab countries with the exception of Iraq. . . . It is presumably known in the Arab countries that the peoples of the U.S.S.R. entertain friendly feelings for them, and that in the Soviet Union they had, and will have, a reliable support in the defense of their sovereignty and national independence.

Asserting that the independence of the Arab nations was threatened by the United States and Britain, Molotov promised them "reliable support" in their opposition to the West.

---

[7] *The Times*, London, Weekly Review, September 23, 1954.

[8] *New Times*, Moscow, no. 3, January 15, 1955, p. 20, and no. 4, January 22, 1955, pp. 17–18.

Two months later two official statements dealing with the neutralist governments were published in Moscow. Appearing, as they did, on the same day (April 16), two days before the Bandung Conference opened, and dealing with the situation in a tier of countries stretching from the Atlantic to the Pacific, they obviously reflected the new Khrushchev spirit in foreign affairs.

"Security in the Near and Middle East" was the title of one of the "Statements by the Ministry of Foreign Affairs" of April 16.[9] The ideas, slogans, and type of criticism of Western policy contained in the statement were familiar. The fact, however, that this highly official and widely publicized statement dealt with problems of this area marked a new phase in Soviet activity. "Military blocs" in the Near and Middle East, the statement said, are essential to "aggressive American circles" as well as to the British aggressors, but not to the peoples of these regions. The Soviet, the statement continued, presents no menace to their independence; the Soviet peace policy meets with their "profound sympathy and support." "It stands to reason that the Soviet Union cannot remain indifferent to the situation arising in the Near and Middle East, since the formation of blocs in Near and Middle East countries has a direct bearing on the security of the U.S.S.R."

The Soviet government called on all nations of the Middle East to quit the "aggressive military blocs," the destruction of which was becoming the primary objective of Soviet policy. "The Soviet government will regard with favor all steps taken by the governments of the Near and Middle East countries to apply the principles set forth in the Declaration" (meaning a turning away from pro-Western alliances and entering the path of pro-Soviet neutralism).

The full significance of these Soviet statements was not recognized abroad. As part of the abundant flow of Soviet statements of every kind, they were viewed as a matter of routine and propaganda and were almost disregarded. Actually there was already implicit in them the tensions and conflicts of the following years; made on the eve of the Summit Conference in Geneva, they would, had they been digested and understood, probably have added a drop of realistic tar to the honey of the "Geneva spirit."

Personal contacts established at Bandung between Nasser and other Arab leaders on the one hand and the "socialist camp" on the

---

[9] The other was a message of greeting to the Bandung Conference.

The Arms Deal

other were facilitated by the strict adherence of the Egyptian leader to an anti-Western course. Cotton was Egypt's main worry; [10] the "socialist camp" was glad to try to fill the gap created by a drop in exports of this commodity. "Chou En-lai observed at the Bandung Conference that if every inhabitant of China were to consume one additional centimetre of cotton cloth, China would buy up Egypt's entire annual cotton crop." [11]

China's offer to buy cotton from Egypt, followed by similar offers from the European satellites, facilitated the solution of two other Egyptian problems: acquisition of arms from non-Western markets and gaining of international stature. Between June and November, Egypt signed economic agreements with China, Hungary, Poland, East Germany, Czechoslovakia, and the Soviet Union; from the latter Egypt bought 500,000 tons of crude oil in September, 1955. The politically most important of these agreements, however, was the arms deal between Egypt and Czechoslovakia, which was more than backed by the Soviet Union.

Having failed in his efforts to buy substantial quantities of arms in the West, or finding himself unable to meet the terms of payment offered, Nasser turned to the Soviet ambassador. The first conversation, held on Egypt's initiative, took place late in May. About two weeks later the Soviet government made its offer. It offered at first surplus arms from older stocks, payment to be made in installments.[12] This step marked the start of important developments.

The Soviet-Egyptian negotiations were conducted in the main with Daniel E. Solod, the Soviet ambassador. While the negotiations were in progress, Nasser informed United States Ambassador Henry Byroade that unless Egypt could obtain American arms she would turn to Russia; reluctant, however, to take the plunge into Soviet waters, Nasser refrained from dispatching his military mission to Moscow. The United States government agreed to sell Egypt a quantity of arms and Egypt submitted its list of items before the end of June.[13]

[10] Egypt's export of cotton had dropped from 817,000 bales in 1953–54 to 53,900 in 1954–55.
[11] *New Times*, Moscow, no. 37, September 8, 1955, p. 7, "The New Phase in Egypt," by L. Vatolina. A Sino-Egyptian trade agreement was signed in August, 1955.
[12] D Papers, December 15, 1956, File E, pp. 1–4.
[13] *The New York Times*, November 14, 1955.

The Geneva Summit Conference opened on July 18. While Khrushchev and Bulganin were on their way there to "relax international tensions," a party of ranking Soviet officials was dispatched to Cairo, ostensibly to participate in the celebration, on July 23, of Egypt's Liberation Day. Dimitri Shepilov, editor of *Pravda*, member of the Central Committee, a specialist in foreign affairs, and a favorite of Khrushchev, had been selected to put the finishing touches to the deal with Egypt. With Shepilov rather than a representative of the Foreign Ministry conducting the negotiations, the proceedings would appear less official—in case the issue should come up at Geneva. (It did not, however.) For the same reason it was Czechoslovakia rather than the Soviet Union that would supply the arms.

The final details of the agreement were discussed and settled during Shepilov's visit to Cairo, but no agreement was signed. Nasser was still awaiting the American reply to his inquiry. Early in August Cairo was informed that it could buy 27 million dollars' worth of arms from the United States; the difficult question of payment, however, remained open. The Soviet offer was for a much larger quantity of arms and an easier mode of payment. The decision was made about September 20, when the first arms agreement between Egypt and Czechoslovakia was concluded.

The full contents of the agreement have never been made public. The deal provided for the delivery of substantial quantities of MIG jet fighters, Il-28 jet bombers, tanks, guns of various caliber, command cars, self-propelled antiaircraft guns, light antitank guns, machine guns, bazookas, and other weapons. The financial arrangements represented an exchange of goods: a list of arms against a quantity of cotton; unit prices were not indicated, only totals were given. Only a small amount of cash was to be paid, the balance of payments to be made in goods (mainly cotton) over a number of years; the amount of each installment was to be about 5 per cent of Egypt's cotton export. The total amount involved in this first deal has been estimated at about 80 million dollars. Since some of the arms items to go to Egypt were already out of date in 1955, it is not possible to state their value exactly, but they were sold at far below their original prices, even below the prices paid by Communist China for arms sold to her. For the Soviet government the Egyptian operation was a political

The Arms Deal

rather than an economic one. If it succeeded, it would be worth more than the sums involved.[14]

The arms deal, even prior to the official announcement of it, caused great excitement in the West. It appeared almost incomprehensible that by means of a simple and inexpensive commercial operation the Soviet government had at one stroke emerged as a first-rate power in the Middle East, and that the Western governments had overlooked the birth of a new "Axis." At this late hour their reproaches directed against the Soviet minister for inaugurating a new "arms race" in the Middle East were hollow and pointless. Russia's penetration of this region, as of many other regions, was an effort to fill a new power vacuum following a British withdrawal, and not to have foreseen it was a mistake, just as it had been a mistake not to have realized in advance that the Soviet Union would move into Eastern Europe and try to enlarge her footholds elsewhere. The British withdrawal from Suez in 1954–55 was unavoidable. The lack of foresight as to the consequences of this step, and the inability to take measures against a new penetration of the region, were due to the continuing underestimation of Soviet dynamism and expansionism.

On September 27, 1955, British Foreign Secretary Macmillan told Molotov that the Soviet action would "precipitate an arms race." Secretary of State Dulles twice (on September 20 and 27) discussed the matter with Molotov, emphasizing his view that the deal "will not contribute to relaxing tensions."[15] The British and American ambassadors in Cairo made similar statements to President Nasser; a spe-

[14] The Israeli Embassy in London stated on July 6, 1956, that Communist arms had begun to arrive in Egypt in December, 1955: Egypt had received from Czechoslovakia, since December, 1955, 200 T-34 tanks and over 100 artillery pieces of various types; as to aircraft, the Egyptian-Czechoslovak deal provided for 200 jet fighters of the MIG-15 type and 60 Ilyushin heavy bombers, of which 150 MIGs and about 45 Ilyushins had already been delivered; as to naval equipment, Egypt had purchased two British destroyers and two Soviet destroyers of the Skory type. Concerning Syria, the Israeli statement said that Syria had made a deal with Czechoslovakia in April, 1956, involving 50 light tanks, 50 heavy Stalin tanks, 25 MIG-15 fighters, 60 pieces of heavy artillery, and 100 armored vehicles.

In November, 1956, it was officially announced in London that in the preceding twelve months Egypt had received military shipments from the Soviet bloc estimated at £150,000,000. The major items were: 150 Ilyushin jet bombers, at least 100 MIG jet fighters, about 300 medium and heavy tanks (including T-34s), over 100 armored troop carriers, 400–500 guns, rocket launchers, and other equipment. The Egyptian Navy had received: 2 destroyers, 4 mine sweepers, 15–20 torpedo boats, mines, etc.

Shipments to Syria, of the value of £20,000,000, included at least 100 medium tanks, at least 100 armored troop carriers, 50–100 self-propelled guns, and 150 other guns.

[15] United States State Department, *Department of State Bulletin*, vol. 33, no. 851, October–December, 1955, Publication 6037, October 17, 1955.

cial United States envoy, Assistant Secretary of State George V. Allen, was dispatched to the Middle East.

All these acts were futile. To each protest Molotov had the unimpeachable answer that every nation is entitled to trade with every other nation, and that arms are appropriate items on commercial lists. As a general answer to critics, TASS made public a statement to the effect that

> the Soviet government believes that every state has the right to defend itself and to purchase weapons for its defense from other states on a normal commercial basis, and that no state has the right to interfere in this or to make any kind of unilateral demands violating the rights or interests of other states. Since it was reported that talks were held recently between Egypt and Czechoslovakia on the sale of arms in exchange for cotton and rice and that groundless complaints were made about this to the USSR, the Soviet government has informed the Egyptian and Czechoslovak governments—as well as the British and U.S. governments, which made special statements on this question—of its point of view, as described above.[16]

President Nasser, in turn, asserted that he had been unable to acquire arms from the West because Britain and the United States had made the sale of arms to Egypt conditional on her "membership in a security pact," whereas the Soviet Union had attached no such condition; he emphasized that Egypt would continue to fight Communism inside the country:

> We are strong enough to cope with all internal subversion, including Communism. Communism is banned in Egypt. We have five or six underground Communist organizations, but we know all about them. They have no able leadership. Many other Communists are in prison.[17]

Matters took a logical turn after the conclusion of the arms deal. The consolidation of anti-Western Arab nations, with the approval and aid of Moscow, made rapid progress. The emerging Egypt–Syria–Saudi Arabia–Yemen group, supported by the Soviet Union, appeared to counterbalance the Baghdad coalition of Turkey-Iran-Iraq-Pakistan with Britain. In October, 1955, and April, 1956, Egypt concluded treaties of alliance with Syria and Saudi Arabia, providing for a joint command over their forces. On October 31, 1955, a "friendship pact"

---

[16] *Pravda*, October 2, 1955.
[17] *The Times*, London, October, 1955. Taken from Keesing's vol. 1955–56, p. 14449, October 1–8, 1955.

The Arms Deal

between the Soviet Union and Yemen was signed in Cairo. "The Soviet Union," the Yemenite envoy stated, "is one of the closest friends of Yemen." Arab Communism was also taking a conciliatory line toward Nasser as the leader of the anticolonialist drive.[18]

The Soviet Union offered arms to Syria and Saudi Arabia as well as to Yemen and the Sudan. In Cairo the proposals of the Soviet ambassador (now *persona gratissima*) of economic and scientific aid were received with enthusiasm. On October 10 Soviet Ambassador Solod announced to the press: "We will send economic missions, scientific missions, agricultural missions, meteorological missions, and any other kind of mission you can imagine that will help these [Arab] countries." [19]

Along with arms, which began to reach Egypt late in 1955, came scores of technicians from Czechoslovakia and Russia; their numbers soon rose to the hundreds. In Egypt these Soviet specialists were transported under guard and kept isolated from the population; because of the bright prospects that had opened in the Middle East, the Soviet side silently acquiesced in this unusual treatment of its representatives. Numbers of Egyptian officers went to the Soviet military base in Gdynia, Poland, for training.

In November, 1955, Syria started negotiations for purchases of arms. In March, 1956, Czechoslovak arms began to arrive in Syria: tanks, antiaircraft guns, ammunition, MIG fighters, small arms, etc. Syrian pilots were trained in Egypt by Soviet instructors, and large groups of Soviet experts settled in Syria. Soon small Syria acquired relatively great importance for the Soviet Union as a reservoir of arms for the Middle East. Latakia developed into a first-rate port for shipment of arms, and a submarine base near the port was projected. The personnel of the Soviet Embassy in Syria was increased fivefold; three military attachés were at work there. Small Bulgaria set up a trade agency in Damascus with twelve employees. A number of Syrian Communists were employed in the offices of these agencies.[20]

There followed new agreements with Egypt on further shipments of arms and naval units: destroyers, mine sweepers, motor torpedo boats, and submarines. In April and June, 1956, it was announced in

---
[18] Walter Z. Laquer, *Communism and Nationalism in the Middle East*, New York, Frederick A. Praeger, 1956.
[19] *The New York Times*, October 11, 1955.
[20] H. Lehrman, in *Weltwoche*, Zurich, February 3, 1956.

Cairo that torpedo boats had arrived in Alexandria. Soviet naval units arrived to strengthen the Egyptian Navy. Czechoslovak negotiations with Yemen, which began late in 1956, were completed in January, 1957; antiaircraft guns and small arms were delivered after October, 1957.[21]

3. CLOSE TIES WITH EGYPT

The attitude of the Soviet press toward Egypt changed markedly after the conclusion of the first arms deal. Now the Egyptian government was no longer "reactionary" or "fascist"; the outlawing of Egyptian Communist organizations and police actions against the Egyptian Communist leadership were no longer mentioned. In sacrificing the Communists of the Middle East the Soviet press went farther than it had, for example, in the case of the German Communists during the Soviet-Hitler pact era, when Nazi internal policy was neither reported nor analyzed in Russia. Nasser was praised for his new system of government, his efforts to resolve economic problems, etc.[22] In reports on Egypt, both *International Affairs* and *Pravda* had only praise for Nasser's new constitution; they pretended to believe in the "guarantees of freedom of speech, press, and association," which were actually denied to the Communist Party in Egypt. The Soviet Academy of Sciences published a book, *Araby v Bor'be za Nezavisimost* (Arabs in the Fight for Independence), which similarly passed over in silence Nasser's course against Communists, although it praised him for his nationalism. During the early period of the Khrushchev era attention was concentrated on efforts to bring about the disintegration of the pro-Western coalitions, even if the price was the existence or well-being of Communist parties in certain other countries. This course, which was full of internal and external dangers, was successful, but only for a few years.

The Soviet triumph in Egypt appeared so great, and the despondency and confusion of the "imperialists" so deep that the Soviet-Egyptian deal seemed to the "socialist camp" a master stroke. The members of the Soviet bloc moved rapidly to set up diplomatic and trade missions in the Middle East. Within a period of a few months

---

[21] *The Times,* London, January 14, 1957.
[22] *International Affairs,* Moscow, no. 2, February, 1956, pp. 122–24; *Pravda,* January 18, 1956.

Close Ties with Egypt

the Soviet Union had missions in the Sudan, Libya, Liberia, and Ethiopia; Poland and Hungary set up missions in Egypt and the Sudan; Bulgaria and Rumania had missions in Cairo; Czechoslovakia had missions in Egypt and Ethiopia; the German Democratic Republic set up trade missions in Egypt and the Sudan. In the spring of 1956 Egypt gave diplomatic recognition to Communist China, and in the summer of that year Syria did likewise. In April, 1956, Poland elevated its diplomatic mission in Egypt to an embassy, and Egypt took the same action in regard to its diplomatic mission in Poland.

To Khrushchev the easy penetration of the Middle East was a new step in his ascendancy to personal rule; for Shepilov, the engineer of the *rapprochement*, it was a step in the direction of Molotov's chair in the Ministry of Foreign Affairs.

In its own eyes the Soviet Union was becoming a kind of Robin Hood of the Middle East—the unselfish, noble friend, ever ready to rush to the aid of the weak and the poor and protect them from brigands and pirates. The West was Evil, the East was Good—this was the tone of a flood of stories on the Middle East which began to appear in the Soviet press, and of broadcasts from Moscow and the satellites which were echoed by the radio of Cairo.

Visiting Soviet ballet groups were an outstanding success in the Arab countries; the services of Soviet technicians were offered and accepted; Soviet help in projects of atomic energy for peaceful use were proposed in the winter of 1955, and an agreement on the matter was concluded in June, 1956; trade missions were coming and going. Expanding on Soviet yeast, Nasser, in Moscow's view, was becoming the recognized leader of the Arabs in their fight for liberation.

Under the thin crust of the visible events, however, there were hidden Soviet-Egyptian divergencies which were to become more obvious in the years ahead. The real aims of Moscow and Cairo were not always identical. Arab nationalism's first enemy was Israel, and its first aim was integration of all or certain of the Arab lands; its adversary on this road was the international combination known as the Baghdad Pact. To Moscow, on the other hand, Israel was a minor issue, and although Israeli policy was criticized, total destruction of the small new state was not envisaged. The Baghdad Pact was a target for both Cairo and Moscow, and the two governments were in agreement also in regard to Western "imperialism," but they did not see eye to eye on other issues, the importance of which was not yet fully recognized at the time. In particular, a merger, federation, or integration of Arab states was not in Moscow's interests.

In Syria Soviet influence increased to such a degree that the country was considered more pro-Soviet than any other Arab country. Entertaining great hopes in regard to Syria, Moscow stocked her with arms which, if necessary, could be shipped from Syria to other pro-Soviet regimes or movements. The most outstanding and loyal Communist leader among the Arab nations was the Syrian Khaled Bagdash, and the strongest of all the Communist parties of the Middle Eastern countries was the "Communist Party in Syria and Lebanon," whose prospects of further rapid growth were excellent.[23] When Syrian President Shukry-al-Kuwatly visited Moscow in November, 1956, Marshal Voroshilov promised him Soviet help "to reinforce [Syria's] complete independence." "Complete" independence implied also independence from Egypt.

In Jordan, anti-British riots took place in the winter of 1955–56 which led to the expulsion of the British General John Glubb Pasha; this development was hailed by the Soviet press.

Having acquired a new foothold in the Middle East, Moscow intended, above all, to assert itself and gain recognition as a power in the region; territorial acquisitions were not among its immediate aims. More than by anything else, the Soviet government was irritated by the lack of recognition of its new significance in that part of the world. In a statement on the Middle East made in February, 1956, Britain and the United States mentioned the declaration of the Western powers of February, 1950, by which they had assumed responsibility for major developments in the area; there was no mention in the statement of the Soviet Union. The declaration of 1950, said the Soviet press now, was a "spurious document"; it was "colonialist," "imperialist," and obsolete. The hint that a Western military force might be sent into the area in connection with the Arab-Israeli conflict—with Moscow, of course, not being consulted—aroused vehement protests. In its statement of February 13, the Soviet Foreign Ministry said:

[23] Laquer, *Communism and Nationalism in the Middle East, op. cit.*, pp. 166–67.

The moving of troops into the territories of the countries of the Near and Middle East would represent an act clearly contrary to the interest of strengthening peace, which would create a seat of dangerous friction and tension in the aforementioned areas. . . .

The U.S.S.R. Ministry of Foreign Affairs deems it necessary to state again that any action leading to complications in the area of the Near and Middle East and to increase tension in that area is bound to be a subject of legitimate concern on the part of the Soviet Government.[24]

In the Soviet pronouncements of the time, France was spared. Moscow still hoped to gain French support against West Germany and against the West in general. The United States, which tried to put brakes on the bellicose dynamism of its Western allies, was the main culprit. In the Soviet view, it was as colonialist and imperialist as the others; moreover, because of its size and power, it was the leader of an anti-Arab coalition.

Arab-Israeli tension reached a high point early in 1956. Bloody incidents became frequent, and retaliatory actions were becoming a pattern. On both sides feeling ran high, and the outbreak of an Arab-Israeli war appeared likely. The fact that Egypt could count on further generous Soviet support was making the situation extremely dangerous.

The Soviet government was on the Arab side in the conflict, although it preferred a more peaceful settlement. The arms it had supplied the Arabs were not intended to solve the local issue of Arabs against Jews; they were meant to be pointed ultimately at the West, and Moscow was doing its utmost to turn the guns in the right direction. It accused the West of inciting Israel to start a war:

When the attempt to force the Arab countries into the Baghdad pact met with a stubborn resistance, certain Western Powers proceeded to fan the Arab-Israeli conflict which their own policy had originally provoked, encouraging Israel to violate the armistice agreement. . . . Irritated by their failure, the Western imperialist circles decided to resort to military intervention, using the artificially provoked Arab-Israeli conflict as a pretext. The hypocritical talk about "the necessity to stop the fighting" served merely to camouflage the intervention planned in the interests of the oil monopolies which reap fabulous profits by exploiting the resources of the Middle East.[25]

[24] *Pravda*, February 14, 1956.
[25] *International Affairs*, Moscow, no. 5, May, 1956, "Way to Relaxation of Middle East Tension."

Although diplomatic relations between the Soviet Union and Israel had been resumed after Stalin's death, the general anti-Israeli trend continued; anti-Jewish tendencies, consistently fostered under Khrushchev both inside and outside the Soviet Union (although in a vein milder than Stalin's), made the *rapprochement* with Egypt logical and easier. Israel was viewed as "a tool" of the imperialist West. In an interview with an Egyptian newspaper, Khrushchev said that Israel was trying to maintain "a state of tension" in the Middle East in order to continue receiving Western aid. "That is why the Israelis keep launching aggressive attacks on Arab borders, regardless of the United Nations or the armistice agreements." [26]

In the course of the American-British-French conferences of January and February, 1956, on the general Middle Eastern situation, a number of proposals were made, including proposals to dispatch combined military forces and arms to Israel and order naval units to the area; Moscow was not consulted, if only because its course doomed in advance any agreement that might be arrived at. In the Soviet view, the United Nations (where, in the Security Council, the Soviet representatives enjoyed the right of veto) was the appropriate arena for discussion of Middle Eastern affairs; as for the West, the Soviet veto privilege was making the United Nations impotent. In the end it was agreed to dispatch Dag Hammarskjöld, the United Nations secretary general, to the Middle East to try to pacify the Arabs and the Israelis. Hammarskjöld had some success—which the Soviet government claimed was due to its own actions.

On the eve of Khrushchev's and Bulganin's visit to London, in April, 1956, the Soviet Ministry of Foreign Affairs published a mild statement on the Arab-Israeli issue which was an obvious effort to pave the way for an agreement with Britain at the expense of the Baghdad Pact. In this statement the Soviet government made a number of remarks that displeased its Arab allies. The Soviet Union, the statement said, supported the strengthening of the statehood of the nations of the Middle East; among the nations mentioned by Moscow was Israel. The Soviet government, the statement continued, maintained that an armed conflict in the Middle East must be avoided,

---

[26] *The New York Times*, July 2, 1956. The outright anti-Israeli interview appeared in the Egyptian *Al-Ahram;* it did not appear in the Soviet press; nor was it ever denied.

Close Ties with Egypt

called upon "the interested parties to refrain from any kind of action which may lead to an exacerbation of the situation on the existing demarcation line set up by truce agreements between the Arab countries and Israel," and suggested a compromise solution of the Israeli question "on a mutually acceptable basis, taking due consideration of the just national interests of the interested parties." [27] This solution called for recognition of Israel by the Arab states and a peace treaty between them.

In the discussion of the Middle Eastern situation with Khrushchev and Bulganin, which was mentioned in another chapter,[28] Prime Minister Eden accused the Soviets of supplying arms to the Arab countries and thus increasing the danger of war. Khrushchev and Bulganin countered with attacks on the Baghdad Pact and on the arming of its member nations by the United States and Britain; the Soviet Union, they indicated, would be ready to abstain from shipments of arms to the Middle East if the West would pledge to act similarly; they would be in favor of a general embargo, under the United Nations, of arms shipments to that part of the world. The Soviet offer meant that there would be a cessation of shipments of Western supplies to Iraq, and possibly also to Iran, which in turn would mean the disintegration of the Baghdad Pact and the isolation of the neighbors of the Soviet Union. On the other hand, Communist China, which was not a member of the United Nations, could continue to ship arms to Egypt. The Soviet suggestion was rejected.

In their frank conversation, Eden told his Soviet visitors that Britain was even prepared to use military force if necessary. Khrushchev's reply was a similar threat. The discussion, which was actually a prelude to the Suez conflict of six months later, ended in a deadlock; the official communiqué consisted of a few empty sentences; the governments, it said, will "do everything in their power to facilitate the maintenance of peace and security in the Near and Middle East. . . . The governments of the two countries call on the states concerned to take measures to prevent the increase of tension"; etc.[29]

The Soviet attempt to do away with the hated Baghdad Pact was poorly conceived and unrealistic. At the same time, in the Arab lands,

[27] *Pravda*, April 18, 1956.
[28] See above, pp. 236–237.
[29] *New Times*, Moscow, no. 19, May 5, 1956, Supplement (Documents), p. 4.

the Soviet slogan of "peaceful coexistence," applied to Arab-Israeli relations, appeared as an unfriendly sentiment and a proof of how futile were the expectations of Soviet assistance in the destruction of Israel as a state. In addition, the fact that the Soviet Union, without previous agreement with Egypt, had discussed Arab affairs with Britain was not viewed with satisfaction by Cairo. Most threatening, in the Egyptian view, was the possibility of an arms embargo, which had been conditionally accepted by Khrushchev and Bulganin, and which would endanger Egypt's status as the emerging leader of the Arab countries.

These were considerations that lay behind the official recognition of Communist China by Nasser a few weeks after the visit of the two Soviet leaders to London. When Nasser's spokesman announced (May 27) that Egypt "could get all the arms [it] needed from Communist China even if the United Nations imposed an embargo on weapons to the Middle East," [30] this appeared as a rebuff to Moscow. In a semiofficial article which appeared about that time, *Al Gumhuria* said:

> Gamal Abdel Nasser has recognized China and dealt a blow to the projected western blockade of the Arab states. . . . People's China is the biggest producer of armament at present and can supply the Arabs all the war material they need. Thus Gamal Abdel Nasser put Eden's noose around Eden's own neck.

Soviet-Egyptian relations obviously needed repair; moreover, Nasser was close to signing an agreement with the United States for a huge loan for construction of the Aswan Dam. These reasons prompted the trip of Dimitri Shepilov, now Minister of Foreign Affairs, to the Middle East in June, 1956.

The projected Aswan High Dam on the Nile appeared to Egypt as the embodiment of industrialization, a corollary to the "five-year plans" of India and China; it represented the road from abject misery and oppression to well-being and strength, a Promised Land of a bright future for a country "liberated" from the "clutches" of colonialism. Of the total projected cost of 1.3 billion dollars, Egypt, under the agreement with the United States, would contribute 900 million over

---

[30] *The New York Times*, May 28, 1956. Recognition of Peking by Cairo probably occurred with the prior knowledge and assent of the Soviet ambassador. Nevertheless it was an evident effort to play China against Russia—one of the first moves in the gradually evolving rivalry of the two Communist powers.

a period of twelve to eighteen years; the United States and Britain were prepared to grant the remaining amount, 70 million of it immediately. Moscow was apprehensive of an Egyptian-American *rapprochement* should the huge financial operation (which would be followed by a decade of American construction activity in Egypt) be implemented. In his hours-long conferences with Nasser, Shepilov made various offers of financial and industrial assistance on a number of similar projects; the Aswan Dam was also discussed. Although the content of the conversations has remained a secret, Nasser referred to them later in a public speech:

> Shepilov announced the willingness of the U.S.S.R. to render economic assistance to Egypt, including long-term credits. He said that any kind of aid would be granted by the Soviet Union without conditions. Shepilov told me: We don't try to get raw materials, because we have our own raw materials.[31]

The Soviet press at the time did not mention a Soviet proposal to finance the Aswam Dam, a project which, it was generally assumed, was too big for Soviet resources; nor could Egypt repay the huge loan in the twelve- or even twenty-year period prescribed by Soviet principles of financing construction projects abroad.[32]

Meantime doubts were growing in Washington, too. Nasser's government was intensifying its anti-British and anti-French activity. It was stressing a pro-Soviet orientation. It had recognized Communist China. It was fostering trade with the "people's democracies," and much of its resources was designated to go to the Soviet Union and her allies in payment for imports. In addition, it was uncertain whether Egypt would be able to provide her 900-million-dollar share of the cost of the dam. Nasser's course appeared ambiguous. To what use he would put the newly imported Soviet arms was an open question. Finally, protests of American producers of rice against import of this commodity from Egypt became loud.

On July 19 the State Department turned down the Aswan project, and Britain followed suit.[33]

---

[31] *Pravda*, July 28, 1956.

[32] On this trip to Egypt, Syria, and Lebanon, Shepilov carefully avoided giving definite answers to the Arabs' questions concerning Israel; he did not budge from the formula of "safeguarding the interests of all parties." He advised the Syrians "not to lose their nerve," and refused to make promises concerning Israel except that the Soviet Union would support the Arab point of view in the United Nations.

[33] D Papers, December, 1958, File E.

4. THE SUEZ CRISIS

When a big power attempts to lay down roots in a new part of the world, the resulting commotion develops into a political earthquake. The Suez affair of the summer and fall of 1956 was such an earthquake: the Soviet Union forced the gates of the Mediterranean in an attempt to settle on its shores as an equal of the other powers.

In the preceding chapters we have traced the various stages of the development. The sale of Soviet and Czech arms to Egypt and Syria—a "mere trade transaction"—in the summer of 1955 was the beginning. The next development was the fruitless Khrushchev-Eden discussions, with their ominous overtones, in London in April, 1956. There followed Egypt's gradual reorientation toward and *rapprochement* with the Soviet bloc, which led to the withdrawal of the United States offer to finance the Egyptian Aswan Dam project. The last link in the chain of events was the declaration by Nasser's government of the nationalization of the Suez Canal. Now the "Suez problem" became the "Suez conflict," and the "Suez conflict" became the "Suez war."

The *rapprochement* of the Soviet Union with Egypt was not, at least in its initial phases, intended to become a hard and fast military alliance. Egypt, because of the nature of her politics and the religions and anti-Communist trends that prevailed in the country, could not become a Soviet satellite. "We don't look for a second front in this sector," Molotov told John Foster Dulles. "We have simply given Egypt the opportunity to make a small gesture of independence." This was almost true. Moscow's intention was to bolster Nasser in his dealings with the Western governments. Nor did Nasser have to consult Moscow about the nationalization of the Canal. "We learned about it," wrote Bulganin—and this was probably true—"from newspapers and broadcasts."

Nevertheless, it was Soviet actions that had started the ball rolling, and it was Moscow that now intended to profit most from the developments. After a year of close collaboration, Soviet and satellite embassy staffs in Cairo had grown to several times their original size; several hundred Egyptian military and technical experts were in Eastern Europe, and various satellite teams were in Egypt. Dimitri Shepi-

The Suez Crisis 407

lov, now Minister of Foreign Affairs, was assigned to conduct the operation.

A former professor of political economy, a major general at the end of the war, chief editor of *Pravda,* a member of the supreme Party bodies, and an alternate member of the Presidium, Shepilov had specialized in foreign affairs since Stalin's death. Among his assignments had been the highly important arms transaction with the Arabs. His success in the dealings with the Egyptians had increased his stature. A loyal executor of Khrushchev's orders, he may be viewed as the engineer of the Soviet-Egyptian *rapprochement,* with the Middle East his special domain. Shepilov had assumed his new duties as Minister of Foreign Affairs a few weeks before Nasser announced the nationalization of the Canal. During the hectic period of the Suez crisis, which coincided with the Polish-Hungarian uprisings, Shepilov enjoyed great independence in his special field; his performance, however, was anything but brilliant. Recognized as a specialist in Marxism and a teacher of Leninism in the Soviet hothouse of social sciences, he proved less than adequate in the rough arena of international moves, countermoves, and conflicts.

When, in the summer of 1956, the United States withdrew its offer to finance the construction of the Aswan Dam the Soviet Union was not yet prepared to take on the project; the Soviet reacted by merely expressing sympathy for Egypt and indignation toward the Americans. "Extortion," was the charge of the Soviet press: the United States State Department, it said, wanted Egypt to join a pro-Western coalition as a condition of the loan. A week after the United States had turned down the Aswan project, Nasser announced the nationalization of the property of the Universal Suez Company. He took over the Canal itself as well as the administration of shipping on the waterway; the income from the operation, Nasser declared, would help to finance the construction of the Aswan Dam.

The nationalization of the Suez Canal was one of those political actions that arouse the most violent nationalistic emotions; and it was calculated to produce such an effect. President Nasser announced:

> "The Suez Canal was built by Egyptians and 120,000 Egyptians died building it. . . . Thirty-five million Egyptian pounds has been taken from us every year by the Suez Canal Company. We shall use

that money for building the High Dam. We shall rely on our own strength, our own muscle, our own funds. . . . We don't have to seek American or British aid for building the High Dam. We will build it ourselves and with our own money.

"A new Suez Canal Company will be formed," he declared, and added with a shout: "And it will be run by Egyptians! Egyptians! Egyptians!" [34]

Nasser promised to compensate the shareholders of the Suez Company and guaranteed the continuation of normal shipping operations. His promise could not, of course, overcome the irritation and anger in Europe, particularly in Britain and France, who were the actual masters in the Suez Canal Company. Europe depended on the Canal for its trade with the East; even a partial disruption of shipping could cut off oil supplies and paralyze her economy. While in the Arab countries and in other neutralist countries Nasser's action was greeted warmly, Britain and France assumed a belligerent posture. The British Navy was dispatched to the Mediterranean, reservists of the two countries were recalled; within two months a military operation appeared imminent. At a later stage of the ensuing developments negotiations for a military alliance between France and Israel against Egypt were conducted.

Israel was greatly alarmed by the rapid rearming of Egypt. Nasser's designs in regard to Israel were well known. He could turn his growing military power against his northern neighbor before he undertook any action against the West. In these circumstances the alliance of France with Israel—which Britain joined—was logical. The common target of the allies was Nasser himself: the overthrow of Nasser and the replacement of his government by a more peaceable one appeared to them the only way to solve the crucial problem. The projected upheaval implied also a rupture of the close Soviet-Egyptian relations and the withdrawal of the Soviet Union from the region. Thus, the Suez conflict was directed not only at Cairo but at Moscow as well.

The American position differed essentially from that of Britain and France. Not only was the United States independent of Mid-Eastern oil, but its position in general toward dependent nations and colonies was traditionally negative. Itself a former colony, and proud of her "revolutionary war" against England, the United States had

[34] *The New York Times*, July 27, 1956.

The Suez Crisis   409

been less affected by the international expansionist enthusiasm of the latter part of the nineteenth century; its main colony acquired at that time—the Philippines—was promised independence, and this was granted, without opposition, after World War II. In the Suez crisis the United States refused to agree to military measures against Egypt, nor did it indulge in legalistic disputes about Egypt's right to nationalize alien property; concerned only with the maintenance of normal shipping through the Canal, it attempted to find a compromise between Egypt on the one hand and Britain and France on the other.

In a series of international conferences held in August, September, and October, 1956, the United States presented plans under which large international bodies, in which both Egypt and Russia would participate, would administer the Canal, or cooperate with Egypt in its administration. The American proposals, predicated on an agreement between Egypt and the community of the "users" of the Canal, were in principle accepted by Britain and France; they were rejected, however, by Egypt, as an infringement of her sovereignty. Egypt was supported by the Soviet government, which remained adamant. Three days after Nasser's first declaration, Khrushchev found it necessary to insert a paragraph on Suez into a prepared speech:

> We consider that, in fact, nothing illogical has occurred. What is the issue? The Suez Canal. Where is it? In Egypt. Through whose hands was the Canal built? It was built by the hands of Arabs, inhabitants of Egypt. But it does not belong to Egypt. . . .
> The Soviet Union, directly interested in the maintenance of freedom of shipping through the Suez Canal and taking note of the declaration of the Egyptian government that the Suez Canal will be open for all, considers that there are no grounds for showing nervousness and alarm on this account. We are convinced that the situation in the Suez Canal Zone will not become tense unless it is artificially aggravated from outside.[35]

A few days later the Soviet government issued a detailed statement on the Suez issue. It stressed Egypt's right to nationalize the property of the corporation; it protested against military preparations on the part of Britain and France; it noted Egypt's promise to recompense the shareholders of the Suez Company and to maintain normal shipping through the Canal; and it questioned the jurisdiction and

[35] *Pravda,* August 1, 1956.

scope of the forthcoming conference (in which Egypt did not intend to participate). ". . . The Soviet Government considers that the above-mentioned [planned] conference cannot in any way be regarded, either in its composition or in character and purpose, as an international meeting authorized to take any decisions whatever on the Suez Canal." [36]

The same ideas were expressed in Premier Bulganin's three letters to Prime Minister Eden and his letter to Premier Guy Mollet in September and October, 1956.[37] Bulganin predicted a complete failure of the threatened military operations against Egypt—"an adventure," he termed it. "Egypt cannot be defeated, nor can Algeria." "I must declare to you, Mr. Prime Minister, that the Soviet Union, as a great power which is interested in the maintenance of peace, cannot stand aside from this question." In his reply (September 16) Eden pointed to Egypt's violation of agreements and her endangering of traffic.

> In the first place the ruler of Egypt is a militarist who glories in the fact. In his book, for example, he says "throughout my life I have had faith in militarism." Secondly, Colonel Nasser not only preaches militarism but employs it. . . . I must remind you that in 1946 the Soviet Government proclaimed their support for the international control of the canal.

The correspondence extended into October and ended, without result, one week before the attack on Suez.

On the hotly debated question whether the nationalization of the Suez Canal was legal, Moscow supported Egypt. It opposed the creation of any international body to supervise the Canal operations; it believed in Egypt's ability to do this herself. Shepilov told the London Conference on Suez on August 21, 1956:

> The very setting-up, contrary to Egypt's desires, of an international body to administer Egyptian property would constitute a political act that would have serious political consequences. That act would not in any way settle the Suez problem, but it would, undoubtedly, turn the Suez Canal area into a zone of constant tension and into a source of international friction and conflict.[38]

[36] *Ibid.*, August 10, 1956.
[37] The letters to Eden were dated September 11 and 28 and October 23, 1956; the letter to Mollet was dated September 11, 1956; all were published in *Izvestia*, April 23, 1957, pp. 4–5.
[38] *The New York Times*, August 22, 1956.

The Suez Crisis

A particular trait of Soviet policy at this time was its emphasis on United States solidarity with the "colonialists," Britain and France. For doctrinal reasons as well as out of practical considerations, Moscow could not admit the existence of nonimperialist elements in United States policy. Anti-Americanism had, since 1946–47, been the main trend of Soviet foreign policy; opposition to the United States was a primary Soviet principle. Foreign Minister Shepilov and the Soviet press were "exposing" the United States at every turn of events:

> Incidentally, the London Conference dispelled the myth that America's position on the Suez issue differed from that of Britain and France. The three Atlantic allies acted unitedly to force international control of the Suez Canal upon Egypt, thus disclosing their colonialist designs.[39]

A month later, *New Times* reiterated that

> developments in these past weeks have exposed the ugly role U.S. diplomacy is playing in the Suez crisis. The American press is trying hard to create the impression that the State Department sympathizes with the national aspirations of the Arab countries and is in favour of a just settlement of the Suez question. This has turned out to be far from the case. Every plan of "internationalization," that is, of wresting the canal from Egypt, bears the sign manual of the United States.[40]

Shepilov's insistence on America's sinister plans and motives was, however, in contrast with what he was to say and do a few weeks later.

Tension mounted as all efforts to find a peaceful solution of the Suez problem proved inadequate. The first London Conference (August 16–23) delegated a committee, under the Australian Robert Menzies, to confer with the Egyptian government; the negotiations, conducted in Cairo September 3–9, proved futile. The second London Conference (September 19–21), in which the Soviet Union did not participate, created the stillborn "Association of Users." Early in October the Suez question was debated in the Security Council of the United Nations, but no decision could be reached because of a Soviet veto.

On September 11 the Suez Company, with the knowledge and

---
[39] *New Times*, Moscow, no. 36, August 30, 1956, p. 6.
[40] *Ibid.*, no. 39, September 20, 1956, p. 2.

consent of the French and British governments, recalled its pilots, of whom the majority were non-Egyptians. The remaining Egyptian pilots, who were soon joined by new arrivals, many of them Russians, succeeded in maintaining shipping through the Canal at a normal level. A number of companies sent their ships on the long route around Africa.

With the negotiations between the powers on Suez making no progress, with Egypt rejecting concessions, and with the Soviet government supporting Egypt, the situation was becoming alarming. Israeli Foreign Minister Moshe Sharett asked the Soviet ambassador to outline the Soviet policy in the Middle East, but he received no reply. In October, France and Britain proceeded to prepare for military operations from bases on the islands of Cyprus and Malta, where a considerable air force was gathering; ships of the British and French navies were present in the Eastern Mediterranean. The British-French negotiations were kept secret, as was the alliance, concluded about the same time, between France and Israel. The United States government was not informed of the plans, but the Soviet government learned about them before the attack started; apparently Soviet intelligence had been able to obtain abundant information about the forthcoming developments. Some of the information was published:

> On October 23rd a decision was taken in London by the ministers of foreign affairs of France, Pineau, and England, Lloyd, about the start of the military intervention in Egypt in the nearest future.[41]

The next day *Pravda* reported:

> The Israeli authorities are urgently conducting a wide mobilization of reservists. . . . Artillerists, tankists, mechanics are being mobilized. Motor transport—passenger cars, busses, vans, trucks and even taxis—are being mobilized in large quantities . . . police precincts are getting instructions on expansion of mobilization.[42]

The Suez conflict entered the warring phase on October 29–30, when Israel moved its army into Egypt and occupied the Sinai peninsula and the Ghaza Strip. The invading Israeli army was able to capture huge stocks of arms, most of which had come from Eastern Europe, along with other equipment. The next day France and Brit-

[41] *Pravda*, October 27, 1956.
[42] *Ibid.*, October 28, 1956.

ain presented an ultimatum to Egypt and Israel to remove their forces to a distance of ten miles from the Canal; Israel agreed, but Egypt, for whom this would have meant further withdrawal inside her own territory, refused. At this point the air forces of the two Western powers went into action. Human losses and destruction were heavy in Port Said, which was then occupied by the British and French forces. The military equipment captured by the allies included arms of Soviet and Czech, but also British, manufacture.[43]

The military action resulted in almost isolating France and Britain politically. In a broadcast on October 31, President Eisenhower indicated the negative attitude of the United States toward the military actions of its Western allies:

> We believe these actions to have been taken in error, for we do not accept the use of force as a wise or proper instrument for the settlement of international disputes. . . . In the circumstances I have described, there will be no United States involvement in these present hostilities.[44]

The Soviet government, in its declaration of the same date, stated that it "unreservedly condemns the aggressive actions of Britain, France and Israel against Egypt." The next day the governments of Soviet republics with considerable Moslem populations (Russian Federation, Kazakhstan, Uzbekistan, Azerbaijan) published "demands" that the aggression be stopped.[45] The satellite governments and Communist China published similar demands. *Pravda*, with obvious approval, reported President Eisenhower's broadcast in which he requested that the Israeli army withdraw to its own territory.

In the United Nations also the Soviet Union now had to support the United States. Its delegates voted for the American resolution to order the belligerents to cease fire and withdraw their armies; in the Security Council, however, the resolution was vetoed by Britain and France. In the subsequent discussion of the issue in the General As-

[43] In his book (*The Memoirs of Anthony Eden: Full Circle*, Boston, Houghton Mifflin Company, 1960, p. 627) Anthony Eden gives the following figures on casualties on the Egyptian side: 650 dead, 900 wounded. He maintains that Egypt was ready to surrender when, later in the day, "the Russians took their decision"; "their hat was now in the ring." Eden admits, however, that "we may never be able to prove it" (pp. 618–19). Eden's version is doubtful.

[44] *The New York Times*, November 1, 1956.

[45] The timing and the text of the demands prove that the action was taken on directives from Moscow.

sembly the Soviet Union voted with the United States in support of a Canadian resolution. This kind of an alignment of powers was contrary to all plans and predictions: the United States was marching at the head of nations in a fight against "colonialism," and the Soviet Union was reduced to the rank of a supporter of the United States!

It might appear that for the Soviet government the general situation was a perfect one; it was a situation that had been predicted, dreamt of, and longed for for many years. The two oldest colonialist powers versus their former poor colony—this was a page from the Soviet primer. The warm support of Egypt by a host of Asian and African neutral nations, with a combined population of a billion, was a perfect situation; the reaction of the "working class of the imperialist powers," in the first place the British Labor Party, to the British course in Egypt was precisely what was called for at the critical moment; a "united front" of Communists and socialists appeared close at hand. Now, according to the primer, the standard bearer, the anticapitalist and anticolonialist Soviet Union, with its prestige and formidable force, would assume leadership over the multitude of wavering and feeble nations in a grand-scale attack on and a victory over imperialism.

These Soviet expectations did not materialize. There were a number of reasons for this, among them the fatal coincidence of the Suez war with the Hungarian uprising. To "expose" the enemies of Egyptian independence while at the same time suppressing a popular movement for independence in the heart of Europe; to call for United Nations action against the "aggressors" in North Africa while barring the United Nations from Hungary; to advocate a "peaceful solution" of international conflicts while solving its own international problems by means of battalions and tanks—this was more than even the cynical climate of world politics could tolerate. Russia in Hungary paralyzed Russia in Egypt. Soviet leadership in world affairs, even for a time and even on a single issue, was impossible.

But to trail behind the United States was humiliating, degrading. In those critical days the world witnessed how the Moscow government, and Dimitri Shepilov in particular, tried to surmount the barriers. The nervous and contradictory moves and gestures of Shepilov's Foreign Ministry at that time were strenuous but unsuccessful.

The Suez Crisis

Among Shepilov's first moves was an attempt to mobilize the Bandung powers, of which Egypt was a member, in aid of a victim of aggression. On November 1 Premier Bulganin wrote to Premier Nehru of India proposing a new Bandung conference on the Egyptian issue. Simultaneously, President Voroshilov addressed a similar proposal to President Sukarno of Indonesia. India and Indonesia, the leading nations among the neutrals, rejected the proposal. In his reply to Bulganin, Nehru urged that Bulganin avoid "any step that could lead to a world war." [46]

A few days later Moscow proposed to the United States the inauguration of joint Soviet-American action on Egypt. President Eisenhower rejected the proposal.[47]

In twenty cities of Britain large demonstrations, organized by the Labor Party, called for the resignation of Eden; at one of these demonstrations—"the wildest political demonstration since the 1930's"—in Trafalgar Square in London, Hugh Gaitskell and Aneurin Bevan attacked the British government. "Britain is stronger than Egypt," Bevan told the meeting, "but there are other nations that are stronger still." It was obvious whom he had in mind when he said, "If nations more powerful than ourselves accept this anarchistic attitude and launch bombs on London what answer have we got?" [48]

In Moscow, too, mass demonstrations, well organized, were held outside the British, French, and Israeli embassies; the posters read "Shame to the Aggressors!" "Down with the War!" The demonstration at the Israeli Embassy ended with a procession of women silently carrying their babies over their heads. The British and French envoys protested to the Soviet Foreign Ministry; they were told that no further demonstrations would be permitted. A friendly crowd that gathered in front of the Egyptian Embassy carried banners reading "Hands off Egypt!"

The Peking leadership joined in the world-wide movement. In Chinese cities mass meetings "for Egypt" were held, and a "People's Committee to Support Egyptian Resistance" was created. In Peking a large crowd descended on the garden of the British Legation and plastered it with banners reading, "Get Out of Egypt!"

---
[46] *The New York Times,* November 2 and 3, 1956.
[47] See below, pp. 416–417.
[48] *The New York Times,* November 5, 1956.

On November 5 the Soviet Ministry of Foreign Affairs sent notes to the belligerents—Britain, France, and Israel—and to the United States. In an odd and dramatic gesture calculated to attract the widest attention, the Soviet premier, in a letter to Eden, took up the words and the threat of Aneurin Bevan:

> What kind of position would Britain be in [Bulganin wrote] if she had been attacked by stronger powers with all kinds of modern offensive weapons at their disopsal? Yet at the present time such countries would not even need to send their naval and air forces to British shores, but could use other means, such as rockets. If rocket weapons were used against Britain and France, you would doubtless call that a barbarous act. But how does this differ from the inhuman attack carried out by the armed forces of Britain and France against practically unarmed Egypt? . . . We are fully resolved to use force to crush the aggressors and to restore peace in the East.[49]

Bulganin's letter of the same date to French Premier Mollet was in the same vein: "What kind of position would France be in if she were subjected to an attack by other states possessing terrible modern devices of destruction?" (The official *France Press* stated that the Bulganin note, as given out the next morning, did not contain the sentence about what rockets could do to France; and instead of "stronger powers," the phrase "other states" was used.[50])

Bulganin's letter to David Ben-Gurion, the Israeli prime minister, was almost abusive: "Carrying out the wishes of others, acting on foreign instructions, the Israeli government is toying in a criminal and irresponsible fashion with the fate of peace and the fate of its own people." The Soviet envoy to Israel was recalled to Moscow.

Another blunder was made in the Soviet note to President Eisenhower, which proposed joint military operations of the Soviet Union and the United States against Britain and France:

> The United States has a strong fleet in the Mediterranean area. The Soviet Union also has a strong military fleet and a powerful air force. The joint, immediate use of these resources on the part of the United States of America and the Soviet Union, in accord with a United Nations decision, would reliably guarantee the end of aggression against the Egyptian people and against the countries of the Arab East.

[49] *Pravda,* November 6, 1956.
[50] *The New York Times,* November 8, 1956.

The Suez Crisis

The Soviet Government appeals to the Government of the United States of America to join with it in its efforts to have the United Nations take decisive measures to stop the aggression.[51]

The Soviet suggestion was coolly received in Washington; a Soviet-American alliance against France and Britain was out of the question. In its reply, the White House not only rejected the Soviet suggestion but appealed to Bulganin to withdraw from Hungary. Henry Cabot Lodge, the United States delegate to the United Nations, said on November 5 that

> the Soviet proposal sets a somber record of cynicism and indifference to the values of international morality.
> The Soviet draft resolution embodies an unthinkable suggestion—that Soviet military forces together with those of the United States, should be sent into the fighting in Egypt, unless the fighting stops within twelve hours. This would convert Egypt into a still larger battlefield.
> The fact is that the United States, through the General Assembly, has acted and is acting on the situation in Egypt. . . .

To this statement of the American position Shepilov replied with a statement that the suggestion to use force in Egypt did not imply unilateral action, but action through the United Nations; he did not mention the Hungarian issue.

Britain and France reacted strongly to the threatening notes from Moscow, and pointed to the Soviet policy in Hungary. "I doubt whether the Soviet government has the necessary authority to speak of the shedding of 'innocent blood' when it is itself shedding rivers of blood in Hungary," French Premier Mollet wrote Bulganin on November 6. On the same day Prime Minister Eden, in his reply to Bulganin, wrote:

> Some casualties there must have been [in Egypt]. We deeply regret them. When all fighting has ceased it will be possible to establish the true figures. We believe they will prove to be small. They will in any event be in no way comparable with the casualties which have been and are still being inflicted by the Soviet forces in Hungary. The whole world knows that in the past three days Soviet forces in Hungary have been ruthlessly crushing the heroic resistance of a truly national movement for independence—a movement which, by declaring

[51] *Pravda*, November 6, 1956.

its neutrality, proved that it offered no threat to the security of the Soviet Union. At such a time it ill becomes the Soviet Government to speak of the action of H.M. Government as "barbaric." [52]

The United States backed the Canadian proposal to create an international military force of the United Nations and to dispatch it to the fighting area to supervise the cessation of military operations. This proposal, which was approved by Egypt, was accepted in the United Nations on November 7. Soviet delegate V. V. Kuznetsov, however, abstained from voting because, in his view, the international force would serve to remove the Suez Canal from Egyptian sovereignty.

On November 6 the one-week-old war came to an end when a cease-fire was accepted by Britain and France. Although the Soviet threats had certainly contributed to this decision of the belligerents, a controversy arose as to the causes and motives of the new British-French attitude. The Soviet side maintained that the Soviet Union was the actual peacemaker in the Suez conflict. The Soviet Academy of Sciences, for example, in a collective work published in 1957, said:

> The clear and firm position of the Soviet Union in defense of Egypt, its determination to take an active part in the restraining of the aggressors, in the restoration of peace in the Near East, in averting a new world war, proved to have a sobering influence on the ruling circles of England and France and to have played a decisive role in the cessation of hostilities.[53]

In the West, however, other reasons that had prompted Britain and France to stop the war were stressed. French Minister of Foreign Affairs Christian Pineau told the National Assembly that the French decision to cease fire was due to four causes which he listed in the following order of importance: (1) the profound division of British opinion; (2) American pressure; (3) United Nations pressure; (4) Russian intervention. In a serious study of the Suez affair, the British writers Michael Foot and Mervyn Jones arrived at similar conclusions.[54]

---

[52] *Ibid.*, November 16, 1956.

[53] *Suetskyi Vopros i Imperialisticheskaya Agressiya Protiv Egipta* (The Suez Issue and the Imperialistic Aggression against Egypt), Moscow, The Academy of Sciences of the USSR, Institute of World Economics and International Relations, 1957, pp. 101–2.

[54] Michael Foot and Mervyn Jones, *Guilty Men, 1957: Suez & Cyprus*, New York, Rinehart & Company, Inc., 1957.

The Suez Crisis

The relaxation which set in after the cease-fire was proclaimed was, however, only gradual. In particular, the three allies were reluctant to withdraw their forces from Egypt. In a new bellicose gesture, the Soviet government came out with a threat of "volunteers" for Egypt who would fight against "the aggressors" in case the latter did not withdraw forthwith. According to the Soviet press, Egypt had asked for volunteers, and the Egyptian Embassy in Moscow was receiving "large numbers of applications" from Soviet citizens. Although sympathy for Egypt among the Soviet population was genuine and widespread, voluntary enlistments were possible only upon suggestion or on orders of state or party agencies. That the "volunteer" movement was a well-organized one initiated from above was seen in the fact that among the applicants were the entire personnel of organizations and collective groups; the fact that there were numerous reserve officers among the applicants also testified to its official character.

> A clear expression of the warm sympathy of the Soviet people for the Egyptian people [read the Soviet statement on Egypt of November 10, 1956] as well as for the other peoples of the East fighting for their national independence and freedom are the numerous applications of Soviet citizens among whom are a great number of pilots, tank men, artillery men and officers who took part in the great war of the fatherland and are now in reserve, asking to be allowed to go to Egypt as volunteers to fight together with the Egyptian people to drive the aggressors from the Egyptian land.[55]

The press stressed especially the numerous applications from the Moslem republics of the Soviet Union, from universities, from farms and factories. TASS anounced that if Britain, France, and Israel did not withdraw their forces, "the appropriate agencies in the Soviet Union will not prevent the departure of Soviet citizens—volunteers—who wish to take part in the struggle of the Egyptian people for their independence."

In the United States, on the other hand, President Eisenhower stated that he would oppose the sending of any forces to the Middle East and would turn the issue over to the United Nations. "Volunteers" were remembered from the Korean War days as a device to combine actual belligerence with a pretense of neutrality and adher-

[55] *Pravda,* November 11, 1956.

ence to "peace." "It would be the duty of the United Nations, including the United States, to oppose such an effort," Eisenhower said at his press conference on November 4, 1956.

The United States opposition was heightened when reports about "volunteers" began to arrive from other countries. Peking announced that 250,000 men had applied to go to Egypt. The Egyptian ambassador in Peking stated that he had received over 2 million letters from the inhabitants of the city (its total population was 2,700,000) in support of the holy war.[56] In the case of China, however, the driving force behind the obviously exaggerated picture of volunteering was the ardent desire of its government to equal Russia or even put itself in the lead of the "anticolonialist movement."

In the end no volunteers from any country were dispatched to Egypt. The British and French forces were withdrawn when the United Nations proceeded to ship its newly organized military units into the fighting area; Israeli troops were withdrawn somewhat later.

The acute phase of the Suez conflict came to a close before the end of the year. The Soviet Union emerged from it as a firmly entrenched Mid-Eastern power, the protector of the Arabs; Egypt became, like India, a favored nation, worthy of protection and economic help. Despite the propitious situation, however, despite the fiasco of London and Paris, and despite the trend in Asia and Africa to minimize the issue of Hungary as compared with the issue of Suez, the Soviet Union did not derive as much influence and prestige from the conflict as it might have. Its political strategy, its threats, and its contradictory course offset the positive effects of its policy and reduced its gains to a minimum.

On January 15, 1957, soon after the end of the Suez affair, Shepilov was dismissed as Minister of Foreign Affairs. Up to then loyal and even devoted to Khrushchev, he soon joined the "anti-Party group" of Molotov, Malenkov, and Kaganovich to take part in the June "palace" conspiracy. When the abortive attempt was over, Shepilov was forced to quit political activity; he was sent to Central Asia to work in a scientific institute of the Kirghiz Academy of Sciences.

The new foreign minister was Andrei Gromyko, a Soviet "old

[56] *China News Analysis,* Hong Kong, November 23, 1956.

hand" in international affairs. Not a member of the Presidium, and less independent in his actions than his predecessor had been, he was expected to serve strictly as a subordinate of the supreme chief, who was now concentrating all foreign affairs in his own hands—Nikita Khrushchev.

CHAPTER 2

MOSCOW AND PEKING

1. THE SOVIET RETREAT

In his message on the occasion of Stalin's death, Mao Tse-tung stated that Stalin had felt a "great and profound friendship" for the Chinese:

> The great and profound friendship which Comrade Stalin felt for the Chinese people will forever be remembered with gratitude by the Chinese people. The undying light of Comrade Stalin will forever illuminate the road along which the Chinese people march forward.[1]

It was widely known, wrote Mao,

> that Comrade Stalin ardently loved the Chinese people and considered the forces of the Chinese revolution to be tremendous. He manifested extreme wisdom on the problems of the Chinese revolution. Following the teachings of Lenin-Stalin, relying on the support of the great Soviet State and of the revolutionary forces of all states, the Chinese Communist Party and the Chinese people a few years ago achieved historical victories.[2]

Chou En-lai was in the first row of personages in the Stalin funeral procession. The press of both countries stressed the "warm feelings" of the deceased leader for the Chinese people. Although a measure of cant is called for on such an occasion, and although the real feelings of the mourners were mixed, in no case was the exaltation of Stalin as hypocritical as it was in the case of China, and the leadership of both governments was well aware of this.

Three years, however, were to pass before the truth about Stalin's attitude toward Chinese Communism was revealed by Nikita Khru-

---

[1] *New Times,* Moscow, no. 11, March 11, 1953, p. 28.
[2] *Pravda,* March 10, 1953, p. 3, "The Greatest Friendship," by Mao Tse-tung.

shchev. Stalin, Khrushchev told the assembled Communist leaders in Warsaw in March, 1956, had almost caused a rupture in relations with Communist China. He had insisted, Khrushchev said, that he (Stalin) must have the final word on Chinese affairs, but Mao Tse-tung refused to submit. The tense relations continued up to the time of Stalin's death.[3] This portion of the Stalin heritage was a problem of the first magnitude to his successors.

The Malenkov-Molotov government of the first post-Stalin era did not, however, intend to embark on a radically new course in regard to China. It did not realize either the scope of the problem or the extent of China's new ambitions. Moreover, by appointing a new ambassador to China and granting China economic aid on a limited scale it tried to conserve the type of relations that it had inherited. The trade agreement announced at the end of March, 1953, provided for deliveries of Soviet equipment for a number of China's industries, to be paid for with Chinese metals, food, and raw materials; a more extensive agreement was signed in September, which provided for Soviet aid, over a five-year period, in the construction of fourteen large units of Chinese heavy industry. As before, the Soviet side concentrated its attention and its aid mainly on areas of Manchuria and North China bordering on the Soviet Union—the same areas in which Stalin had had foremost interest. As before, thousands of Soviet advisers, hierarchically organized under the "chief Soviet adviser" in Peking, were active in China's economy, banking, building trades, universities, and military forces. Thousands of Chinese students were studying in Russia.[4] Moscow-to-Peking telephone service was inaugurated in November, 1953. A few months later, direct railway service was begun between the two capitals; however, "symbolically, the Moscow to Peking train arrived two days before the Peking to Moscow train."[5]

Among the most irritating elements of Chinese subordination to the Soviet Union were Stalin's "mixed companies." China's first efforts to do away with these companies had been unavailing. When the economic agreement of September 15, 1953, was signed, *Pravda* hailed it enthusiastically and emphasized the "beneficial cooperation" of the

[3] *The New York Times,* June 4, 1956.
[4] See above, pp. 84 ff.
[5] Richard L. Walker, *China under Communism. The First Five Years,* New Haven, Yale University Press, 1955, p. 278.

two nations; although there was no connection between the new agreement and the "mixed companies," *Pravda*, obviously reflecting a behind-the-scenes controversy, stressed the finality of the Soviet position on the "mixed companies"; "The Soviet-Chinese companies are working successfully on the basis of full equality and mutual interest." [6]

Another annoying remnant of the Stalin days was the unequal status of the two governments in their relationships. Even after the Changchun Railway was turned over to the Peking government, at the end of 1952, Port Arthur remained in Soviet hands as a military base; no less important was the fact that Soviet economic aid was concentrated on Manchuria. In 1953, at a reception given by Molotov on the anniversary of the November Revolution, the press noted the fact that Walter Ulbricht (who for a time after the Berlin uprising had been in disgrace) and the Chinese ambassador were ignored.[7] Again, when Clement Attlee and his Labor Party group stopped in Moscow on their way to China, in the summer of 1954, Molotov begged them: please, do not try to embroil us with the Chinese in Peking.[8] In Peking, on the other hand, at a reception in honor of the "Soviet specialists," Chou En-lai dutifully thanked the Soviet Union for her "high spirit of internationalism"; among those present on this occasion were I. Arkhipov, "chief Soviet adviser," his deputy, I. Zhidkov, and others.[9]

In a book published in Moscow in 1954, Soviet author Y. Arutyunyan stressed the extent of Russian influence in Chinese cultural life; all educational plans and programs, he said, were based on Soviet patterns; Soviet textbooks in Chinese translation were used; at Peking University there were 120 translators at work; a periodical, *The Russian Language*, was being published; 3,356 Soviet books were published in translation; the teaching of Soviet industrialization, collectivization of farming, and building of socialism was made obligatory in all colleges by the Central Committee of the Chinese Communist Party.[10]

The remnants of Stalinism in Soviet-Chinese relations and the wide publicizing of the elements responsible for China's unequal status

[6] *Pravda*, September 18, 1953.
[7] *The New York Times*, January 2, 1954.
[8] D Papers, File K, September 6, 1956.
[9] *Pravda*, October 4, 1953.
[10] Yu. V. Arutyunyan, *Nerushimaya Dryzhba Narodov Sovetskogo Soyuza i Kitaiskoi Narodnoi Respubliki* (The Inviolable Friendship of the Peoples of the Soviet Union and the Chinese People's Republic), Moscow, 1954, pp. 12 and 23.

The Soviet Retreat

were a hurt to a party and a government that believed themselves rapidly approaching the heights of international power and significance. In the Chinese view, the Korean War had been "a great victory" for China. The conflict in Indochina, another area of Chinese influence, could not be settled without China's cooperation. Tibet was already occupied and annexed to China. India, retreating before China, recognized the state of affairs in Tibet by an agreement signed in April, 1954. Foreign missions in Sinkiang were ordered closed because the province was to be ruled from Peking. In 1953 an "autonomous Thai" area was set up in the south, close to Thailand, from where the "Free Thai" movement was appealing to the people of Thailand. These Chinese moves followed the traditional Soviet method of establishing areas of minority nationalities (Finns, Rumanians, Lithuanians) as a channel of influence over neighboring nations.

China's aspirations in regard to her position inside the Communist bloc were also growing. After the end of the Korean War, when the Soviet Union made a grant of a billion rubles for the rehabilitation of North Korea, the Chinese government followed suit and promised a grant of over 300 million dollars.[11] China also wrote off all expenses and costs of supplies for North Korea incurred during the war. These were somewhat unusual steps, since poverty-stricken China was herself obtaining loans from the Soviet Union. Somewhat later the Soviet Union granted North Vietnam 100 million dollars, and in July, 1955, China granted North Vietnam 338 million dollars in a similarly ambitious move imitating the Soviet.[12] China promised to send "technicians" and "specialists" to Korea and to train Koreans in Chinese universities. The Ho Chi-minh regime was obviously dependent for its life and for the rehabilitation of the country on Chinese assistance.

The Communist parties of the Far East were now connected with Peking's Central Committee, where special offices dealt with party affairs in Korea, Japan, and a number of other countries. The new program of the Japanese Communists, adopted in 1952, had been re-edited in Peking.[13] It was reported that during the Korean War Peking

---

[11] Official announcement in Peking, November 23, 1953; the sum was 350 million Chinese dollars.

[12] Official announcement in Peking, July 7, 1955; the sum announced was 800 million Chinese JMP. JMP stands for *Jen min pi* (people's currency); under the official rate 1 JMP equals $1.00.

[13] D Papers, November 5, 1956, vol. 1, pp. 16–20.

had prompted the Japanese Communists to set up guerrilla groups to begin operations as soon as the Chinese troops overran South Korea, and that in accordance with this plan Peking had transferred certain funds to the Japanese Communist Party. When a fight broke out between two Communist factions in Japan, the issue was first submitted to Peking. The dependence of the Japanese Communist Party on Peking was rapidly increasing, although Japanese ties with Moscow were, of course, maintained.[14]

A sudden rise from the depths of humiliation and defeat to unity and influence tends to have the same effect on a nation as on a human being—capabilities are exaggerated, the sense of proportion is lost, ambitions become listless, a feeling of inferiority turns into a *mania grandiosa*. Once the objective conditions have changed and the individual has attained unexpected success, he is prone to overcompensate his former inferiority feelings and act out in an aggressive way his accumulated hostilities. He is ready to convince himself of his tremendous superiority and overwhelming potentiality.

Since the days of the Korean War China had been contending that she was a great power; the very term "great power" seemed to have enormously excited the new leadership. At first, for a short time, Chou En-lai claimed a new status for China in Asia: "We, as one of the greatest powers in Asia. . . ."[15] Soon the limitation to Asia was discarded, and the Peking regime claimed parity with the great powers of the world, conceding only a degree of priority to the Soviet Union.

It was this new outlook that determined China's attitude to the Soviet Union and the course of Sino-Soviet relations in the period ahead. Every other Communist-ruled government understood the subordinate position of a "people's democracy"; under no circumstances could it claim equal rank with Russia. China, however, could and did. The wounds inflicted on China by Stalin had been deep and painful. The contrast between the vista opening for China all over the East and the limitations imposed by Moscow was great. The years 1953–56, the first years after Stalin's death, marked the era, in Sino-Soviet relations, of China's political rehabilitation and her rise to a

---

[14] *Ibid.*, November 6, 1956, vol. 1, p. 34.
[15] *New Times*, Moscow, no. 28, July 10, 1954.

The Soviet Retreat

new, independent status. China achieved this, but not without strenuous efforts and behind-the-scenes fights.

The essentials of "national Communism," meaning independence from Moscow, were conceived by Mao Tse-tung long before Yugoslavia raised the banner of rebellion.[16] Mao's experience with Stalin in 1946–49 and at the Moscow Conference in 1949–50 could only have strengthened him in his attitude. The Chinese leadership introduced the term "great-power chauvinism" as a disguised designation for Stalinism, like the "cult of personality" in Moscow. Great-power chauvinism, meaning encroachment by a great power on China's independence, had to end.

On the issue of relations with the other "socialist countries," profound divergencies were growing in the Soviet Presidium, with Khrushchev and his group deviating from the Stalin patterns. The Khrushchev design of relations was one of reunification of international Communism, reconciliation with the heretics among the satellites, and a determined effort to improve Sino-Soviet relations by granting political and economic concessions.

The celebration of the fifth anniversary of the Communist Chinese regime on October 1, 1954, marked a great advance in Sino-Soviet relations. A huge, spectacular Soviet exposition which opened in Peking during the week of the celebration dominated the Chinese capital and overshadowed Peking's famous imperial palace; the grounds covered 160,000 square yards; 50,000 shrubs and 6,000 trees were planted; thousands of workers, hundreds of craftsmen, and Soviet experts were employed on the job.[17]

The Soviet "government delegation" which came to Peking for the celebration was headed by Khrushchev. This was a departure from usual procedure. The fact that neither Premier Malenkov nor Foreign Minister Molotov accompanied the group was due to the growing

[16] As early as 1940, Mao wrote in his *New Democracy*: ". . . in applying Marxism to China, Chinese Communists must fully and properly unite the universal truth of Marxism with the specific practice of the Chinese revolution; that is to say, the truth of Marxism must be integrated with the characteristics of the nation and given a definite national form before it can be useful; it must not be applied subjectively as a mere formula. Formula-Marxists are only fooling with Marxism and the Chinese revolution, and there is no place for them in the ranks of the Chinese revolution. China's culture should have its own form, namely, a national form. National in form, new-democratic in content—such is our new culture today." (Mao Tse-tung, *Selected Works*, London, Lawrence & Wishart, Ltd., 1954, vol. 3, p. 154.)

[17] *The Times*, London, October 4, 1954.

disagreements in Moscow on the issue of China and the Soviet attitude in general toward members of the "bloc." The Soviet delegation, however, included members of Khrushchev's faction, ministers, and editors; among them were Anastas Mikoyan and V. P. Stepanov, chief of the Chinese Department of the Central Committee. In the triumphal speeches, the theme of China as a great power dominated. Chou En-lai declared that "China is already a great power in the international arena." Khrushchev emphasized that "China has entered the international field as a great power"; in their message of congratulation, the Soviet government and the Central Committee stressed the same idea in similar terms.

In the course of the conversations between the Soviet and Chinese leaders that took place during the visit, five issues were paramount: Soviet military forces in Port Arthur, Soviet economic control through the "mixed companies," pro-Soviet secessionist trends in Manchuria and Sinkiang, China's access to Mongolia, and the Chinese Communist Party's sphere in the Far East.

On the question of Soviet forces in Port Arthur the parties agreed that the withdrawal of these forces, meaning the turning over of the military base to China, would be concluded by May, 1955; this would mean the final evacuation of Soviet armed forces from China. The agreement was a significant concession to Chinese aspirations.

An agreement on the four Sino-Soviet "mixed companies" was a concession of equal significance: the Soviet shares in the companies were to be turned over to China by January 1, 1955. A source of great irritation to the Chinese leadership, a symbol, in the satellite world, of aggressive and exploiting Stalinism, "mixed companies" (see pages 192 ff.) were coming to an end. The Chinese leaders, more independent than their comrades in Europe, were probably the first to achieve the goal of terminating them. It was announced, in the standard way, that the "mixed companies," having fulfilled their purpose, were no longer necessary. China was to reimburse the Soviet Union by deliveries of goods, the items and value of which were not announced.

The two governments agreed to the construction of a railroad through Sinkiang and the extension of the Trans-Mongolian Railroad to connect China and the Soviet Union. In both cases the gain for China was greater than for Russia: while the Soviet Union had already been closely connected with and influential in both Sinkiang and

The Soviet Retreat

Mongolia, Peking was now taking first steps toward firmer control in Sinkiang and penetration of Outer Mongolia.

These Sino-Soviet decisions were made public *in extenso;* other agreements were indicated, but details of these were not revealed. The text of the five-year agreement on "scientific-technical collaboration," which also settled, at least for a time, the sore issue of Soviet "advisers" in China and their salaries, living conditions, and place in Chinese affairs, was not published. The Yugoslav press reported that under this agreement each Soviet adviser was to have an individual contract with the Chinese government; his duties and period of work in China were fixed, and he was obliged, after completion of his term of work, to turn his job over to a previously trained Chinese citizen.[18]

A new agreement on economic assistance was signed which provided for an additional loan of 520 million rubles, Soviet aid in the construction of 15 industrial units, and an increase of Soviet supplies for the equipment of 141 other units built with Soviet assistance.

What China was to deliver in exchange for the far-reaching Soviet concessions was not announced. It was reported, however, that China's new commitments were related to the political situation in Europe at that time, namely the Soviet decision to bring about a military alliance with the "people's democracies" (the "Warsaw Pact") as a counterbalance to the Paris agreements and NATO. Chinese assistance would consist primarily of supplies of manpower. This invitation to China to become directly interested and active in European affairs was novel. Before long representatives of Peking appeared at the Moscow and Warsaw conferences and promised China's help to the Soviet bloc.[19] In his letter to the *People's Daily* of January 1, 1955, Soviet President Voroshilov thanked the Chinese:

> The Peoples of the Soviet Union and of the European People's Democratic countries were pleased and gratified to receive the Chinese representative's declaration that the Chinese people support with all their strength the European people's struggle for the defense of European peace and security.

Although the forthcoming Berlin Conference of foreign ministers was to deal, in the main, with the German question, Moscow proposed that Communist China be invited. Chou En-lai stressed China's interest

[18] *Politika,* Belgrade. Quoted in *Novoye Russkoye Slovo,* New York, September 15, 1955.
[19] See pp. 162–63.

in European affairs before the Soviet delegation left Peking: "I am instructed," he said, "by the People's Government to express full support to the proposition to convene the conference."

Among the subjects discussed and resolved at the October conferences in Peking was the final and complete integration of Manchuria with China. All vestiges of the initial pro-Soviet "autonomy" in the province, its separate agreements with and loans from the Soviet Union, had been terminated. Kao Kang, the former Communist leader of Manchuria, the man responsible for the Manchurian agreements with Moscow, having been demoted in March, 1954, was now discredited and purged; on March 31, 1955, he committed suicide. The purge embraced also the secretary of the party's "East China Bureau," Jao Shu-shin, and nine other ranking leaders. Whether Kang's former ties with the Soviet government were among his crimes is not certain, however, although the official statement mentioned Kao Kang's attempts to "make the Northeast area the independent kingdom of Kao Kang." If pro-Soviet orientation was part of the accusation, this could not have been stated openly, if only because unnecessary friction with Moscow had to be avoided.[20]

On the issue of Mongolia the Soviet government made certain concessions to Chinese Communism so that the country, a Soviet colony, could perhaps develop in time into a buffer between Communist China and the Soviet Union. In 1955 China won the right to send more than 10,000 Chinese technicians and workers to Mongolia to stay there for five years and then, if they wanted, to settle there indefinitely. By two agreements with Ulan Bator, Peking undertook to build in Mongolia a textile factory, a glass factory, a paper mill, roads, bridges, a stadium, and other public works. China gave Mongolia a grant of 160 million tugriks (approximately 160 million rubles), almost equal to the Soviet subsidy of 200 million rubles for the period

[20] Writers and authorities on Chinese Communism have disagreed on whether the purging of Kao Kang had any connection with the general course of Sino-Soviet relations. Peter S. H. Tang, in his *Communist China Today* (New York, Frederick A. Praeger, 1957), disputes the view that Kao Kang maintained special ties with Moscow and enjoyed special favors from the Soviet leaders, as does Léon Trivière (*Monthly Information Bulletin of the International Commission against Concentration Camp Practices*, Brussels, no. 2, March–April, 1955, pp. 33–59). Others, for example Franz Borkenau (*Commentary*, New York, December, 1954), consider Kao Kang a pro-Soviet man in the Chinese Communist Party. A Chinese source says, however, that for a long time Peking would not have dared to downgrade or punish him without the consent of Moscow. Kao Kang's hour struck as soon as the wind from the Soviet began to change (D Papers, December 4, 1956, vol. 2, pp. 147–53).

1958–60. "Mixed companies," already outdated elsewhere, were still active in Mongolia at that time and were not dissolved until 1957.

The situation appeared as a kind of economic competition between China and the Soviet Union on Mongolian soil. Although China had no chance to win in this competition, the very fact of her activities served to stress her political ambition and the Soviet retreat. With the modicum of autonomy granted her, Mongolia has been able since late 1955 to win diplomatic recognition not only from the satellites and Yugoslavia but from non-Communist countries like India, Indonesia, and Burma.[21]

The almost miraculous ability of the Chinese to gain colonies and populate them with Chinese is a phenomenon which has never been overlooked by Russian governments before or after the revolution. Just as Inner Mongolia today has a massive Chinese minority, Outer Mongolia may follow suit as a consequence of the penetration and immigration from east and south, greatly facilitated by the newly emerging modern methods of communication and transportation.

The subordination of the huge, one time Soviet-dominated Sinkiang province was another success for Peking in its silent but relentless drive. From a purely theoretical Communist viewpoint it was a moot question whether Stalin had not been right in his systematic efforts to merge the nationalities of Sinkiang with their Moslem coreligionists across the Soviet borders—the Kazakhs, the Kirghiz, the Uighurs, and others. There was no logical reason why members of the same or similar tribes or nationalities, living beyond an archaic border, should not be united in state formations. Stalin almost succeeded in accomplishing such a merger when, in 1938, the ruler of Sinkiang, Sheng Shih-ts'ai, with the knowledge of Mao Tse-tung, became a member of the Soviet Communist Party.[22] The unfavorable turn of world events, however, kept Stalin from making a new acquisition.

The Chinese Communists, too, had an argument in their favor: the tribes of Central Asia must of course be organized into autonomous state units, but there was no reason why these units should join

[21] A distinction, however, between the two types of relationship was emphasized: the Mongolia-India relations were described dryly as "friendly cooperation of peace-loving nations"; relations of Mongolia with East Germany were "brotherly friendship." (*Jenmin Jihpao* as quoted in *China News Analysis*, Hong Kong, no. 116, January 20, 1956.)

[22] Allan S. Whiting and General Sheng Shin-ts'ai, *Sinkiang: Pawn or Pivot?* East Lansing, Michigan, Michigan State University Press, 1956.

the Soviet Union rather than China. The fact that the Soviet Union was a more advanced country was no longer a valid argument, since equality was now the fundamental principle in the relations between the two largest socialist nations.

Having won this contest, Peking proceeded to consolidate its rule in Sinkiang. It directed its attention to the north, where Soviet separatist moves had always been felt. The army of the former "East Turkestan Republic" was integrated into the Chinese military organization, and some of its non-Chinese leaders were removed or "liquidated." [23] The Lanchow-Urumchi railway, which was built after the October, 1954, agreement, opened practically the whole of Sinkiang to Peking's rule. To strengthen Communist Chinese control over the non-Chinese (non-"Han") majority of the population, thousands of employees were sent to Sinkiang from the east in 1955–56; others followed subsequently.[24] The Communist press now maintained that for a thousand years Sinkiang had prospered only when it was under Chinese rule.

On September 13, 1955, the province of Sinkiang was transformed into an "autonomous region"; its ties with Peking, however, were now closer than ever. Actual power lay in the hands of the Buro of the "regional committee" of the Communist Party of the "Sinkiang-Uighur Autonomous Region," which was headed by Chinese and not Uighurs; this was similar to the system established by the Soviet Union in many Central Asian areas.

Since becoming an autonomous region Sinkiang has served as an important experiment: it has combined Chinese political rule with almost exclusively Soviet economic guidance. Moscow has probably been better informed on developments in Sinkiang than on developments in its European satellites. Whether this situation will produce conflicts and how such conflicts will be resolved, and whether this type of relationship carries within it the seeds of future conflicts, are open questions.

2. CHINA'S GROWING ASPIRATIONS

For a time after the conferences of October, 1954, Sino-Soviet relations were in a phase of improved and closer collaboration. Both

[23] D Papers, July 24, 1958, File K.
[24] *China News Analysis*, Hong Kong, October 7, December 9 and 16, 1955.

China's Growing Aspirations

parties stressed their equal status as the greatest powers of Eurasia and as great world powers in general. The Khrushchev-Bulganin group, which took over in February, 1955, was more inclined to make concessions to Peking's "national Communism." The Soviet-Tito *rapprochement* seemed another step in the direction of improved Sino-Soviet relations.

China took part as an "observer" in the conferences of the purely European Warsaw Pact nations. At the Bandung Conference in April, 1955, in which the Soviet Union did not participate, Chou En-lai appeared as the successful, great leader of the East. In January, 1955, the Soviet government offered some of its allies, among them Communist China, extensive scientific and technical aid in the peaceful utilization of atomic energy; it undertook to build an experimental 6,000-kilowatt atomic pile, with the understanding that the quantity might be increased to 10,000 kilowatts.

The situation in the Far East during the winter of 1954–55 was especially tense. The Soviet government supported China's drive against Formosa and the Pescadores and its drive against the United States. The Chinese leadership was confident that after the successes in Korea and Indonesia it would be possible to solve the Formosan problem, with or without military operations. On October 10, while Khrushchev was in Peking, the Chinese Communist government dispatched a violent message to the United Nations accusing the United States of "aggression." A few weeks later the United States and the Nationalist Chinese government concluded a mutual assistance pact. When Chou En-lai reacted by making a bellicose declaration, the Soviet government announced its complete solidarity with China. On January 28, 1955, the British ambassador to the Soviet Union tried to persuade Molotov to agree—and to induce Peking to agree—to a comprehensive truce in the Formosa Strait; if the Peking government should try to use force, he said, "it would be a mistake to assume that the United States would not assist its allies." Molotov would not agree. The Peking government refused to take part in a session of the Security Council unless certain of its conditions were first met.[25] The Soviet government and press again supported the Chinese Communists.

At the end of February, when a few small islands off China's coast

[25] *International Affairs*, Moscow, no. 4, April, 1955, pp. 91–99, "Britain Abets American Interference in China's Domestic Affairs," by V. Rogov.

fell to the Communist forces, the West expected a general Chinese Communist offensive; Peking's rejection of a proposed cease-fire appeared to confirm these expectations. Since the Peking government could not have made a decision of such importance without the consent and support of Moscow, the danger of a conflagration in Asia and Europe appeared serious. The tension abated, however, during the next few months as preparations began for the Summit Conference. It is likely that Moscow, having at first supported the anti-Formosa drive, succeeded in restraining China from taking further action.[26]

The Soviet press wrote abundantly at the time about the favorable state of Sino-Soviet relations, supporting the course of Communist China.[27] "The efforts to undermine Sino-Soviet friendship," wrote Chinese Ambassador Liu Hsia in *Pravda*,[28] "are tantamount to efforts to make the sun rise in the West." At a football match between Soviet and Chinese teams in the Peking stadium, Mao Tse-tung, Chu Teh, Chou En-lai, and the Soviet ambassador, Pavel Yudin, were present. Symbolically, the match ended in a 2–2 score. After the game Mao descended to the field and thanked both teams.[29] In October, 1957, a "Soviet-Chinese Friendship Association" was founded in Moscow; a "Sino-Soviet Association" in China had existed since 1949.[30] The old ranking Soviet Communist A. A. Andreev was chosen to head the "Soviet-Chinese Friendship Association." At its first meeting the Chinese ambassador eulogized the friendly relations between China and Russia: "Friendship between the Chinese and Soviet peoples is higher than the sky, deeper than the sea, it is like a pine in the forest, always fresh, never drooping." [31]

Collaboration between Moscow and Peking in foreign affairs, in which limitation of China's independence or her relations with pro-Western governments were implied, was part of the alliance. The collaboration related in the first place to China's course toward such countries as Formosa, Japan, South Korea, and members of SEATO—allies of the United States. For the Soviet government the gravity of the situation in the Far East and the threat of a great war made it too dangerous to leave everything to the discretion of the young impetuous

[26] D Papers, September 6, 1956, File K.
[27] *Pravda*, September 4 and October 19 and 20, 1955.
[28] October 1, 1955.
[29] *Pravda*, October 31, 1955.
[30] *Large Soviet Encyclopedia*, vol. 21, p. 256.
[31] *Pravda*, October 30, 1957.

China's Growing Aspirations

ally. China accepted these limitations because they were the reverse side of her need of rapid economic and industrial growth.

Industrialization was the basis of all China's hopes in both the economic and the political fields; a revamping of all phases of social life was part of the transition to Communism, and close ties with Moscow meant the difference between rapid economic growth and stagnation. The price of progress was self-limitation and support of the Soviet Union on crucial issues. In fact, China's economic dependence on Russia was very great in those years.

In 1953–56 the Soviet share in China's foreign trade was between 47 and 56 per cent,[32] and her share in the supply of industrial equipment and complete industrial units was even larger. No data are available concerning Soviet arms supplied to China, but there is no doubt that Russia was the source of nearly all of China's modern armament.

Chinese payments to Russia have never been detailed, but they were very large; they covered not only Soviet imports but also earlier loans and credits and installment payments for the Soviet shares in the "mixed companies." The agricultural products, metals, and raw materials exported to the Soviet Union by China involved a heavy burden for China but were an asset for the Soviet economy. The value of Chinese food products exported to Russia amounted to 1,057 million rubles in 1954, 1,127 million rubles in 1955, and 1,237 million rubles in 1956.[33] Soviet commitments to China between 1950 and 1956 included also complete equipment of 211 industrial units.[34]

The most significant Soviet-Chinese economic development of this period was the agreement signed on April 7, 1956, during the visit of Anastas Mikoyan to Peking, which provided for the construction of 55 industrial units in addition to 156 already in construction, at a cost of 2.5 billion rubles. Although the text of the agreement has remained secret, it was announced that China would make payments by future deliveries of Chinese goods to Russia.

In August, 1956, it was announced that oil prospecting operations in Sinkiang had been very successful and had led to the discovery

---

[32] *Die wirtschaftliche Verflechtung der Volksrepublik China mit der Sowjetunion* (The Economic Involvement of the Chinese People's Republic with the Soviet Union), prepared by the Institut für Asienkunde (Institute of Asian Studies), Hamburg, vol. 3 of *Schriften* (Documents) of the Institut für Asienkunde, Frankfurt-am-Main/Berlin, Alfred Mezner Verlag, 1959, p. 28.

[33] *Ibid.*, p. 22.

[34] *Ibid.*, p. 54.

of new wells.³⁵ In August, 1956, also, the two governments agreed on an ambitious plan for the joint development of the industrial and power potential of the Amur River.

As if in recompense for her economic dependence on Russia, and to stress her own greatness, China provided "technical help" to Burma, Cambodia, Mongolia, and other countries. A special office was set up in Peking to supervise and direct Chinese advisers in underdeveloped countries. The list of countries which were receiving aid from China in 1953–57 reveals the scope of China's economic and political activity and the great effort she had to make in order to fulfill her role:

Foreign Aid Granted by Communist China ³⁶

Country	Date	Period of Maturity	Amount
North Korea	Nov. 23, 1953	4 years (1954–57)	800 million Chinese JMP
Albania	Dec. 3, 1954	Unknown	Unknown
North Vietnam	July 7, 1955	Unknown	800 million Chinese JMP
Cambodia	June 21, 1956	4 years	800 million rials
Mongolia	Aug. 19, 1956	2 years	160 million rubles
Nepal	Oct. 7, 1956	3 years	60 million Indian rupees
Egypt	Dec., 1956	Unknown	200 million Swiss francs
Hungary	May 3, 1957	Unknown	100 million rubles
Ceylon	Sept. 19, 1957	5 years	75 million Ceylonese rupees
Burma	Dec., 1957	Unknown	20 million kyats
Yemen	Jan. 12, 1958	10 years	70 million Swiss francs

Total grants in 1953–57 amounted to about 2 billion JMP.

Li Hsien-nien, Chinese Minister of Finance, stated on June 29, 1957, that China had received from Russia loans totaling 5,294 million JMP, of which 2,174 million had been granted up to 1952, and 3,120 million during the first Five-year Plan. Only two Soviet loans, of 300 million dollars and 520 million rubles respectively, were announced; the discrepancy of more than 5 billion JMP was striking. Probably

---
³⁵ *Pravda*, August 3, 1956.
³⁶ Figures from *Far Eastern Economic Review*, Hong Kong, vol. 24, no. 19, May 8, 1958, p. 580.

Mao and Khrushchev

"Soviet assets" turned over to China and similar sums were involved:[37]

It is noteworthy that China has, as a rule, granted her foreign aid as a free gift, whereas she herself has in general to repay the aid received from the Soviet Union. Only in the case of loans placed at the disposal of Hungary in 1957 and of Yemen in 1958 have repayments been expressly agreed upon. It is not known what arrangement the agreements with Albania and Mongolia contain, nor are any details available so far in regard to the agreement with Burma. But on the other hand it is known that economic assistance to N. Korea and N. Vietnam, which together amounts to 80% of Chinese foreign aid, as well as aid to Egypt, Ceylon, Cambodia, and Nepal, has been given as a free gift.[38]

3. PEKING SUPPORT OF MOSCOW AGAINST THE SATELLITE REBELS

During the storm that shook the Communist parties in 1956–57, China remained loyal to Moscow. The hope entertained in the satellites that Mao, having himself experienced sharp conflicts with Stalin, would support "national Communism" was a vain one. Actually China helped Khrushchev to restore equilibrium and Soviet predominance.

Mao was being loyal when he dispatched Vice-President Chu Teh to the Twentieth Congress of the Soviet Communist Party. Unaware, as were the other foreign Communist leaders (except Tito), of the impending degradation of Stalin, Mao said, in his message read by Chu at the opening session of the Congress, that the great successes of the Soviet Union were due to the invincibility of the Communist Party "created by Lenin and nurtured by Stalin and his closest co-warriors."

As soon, however, as the text of Khrushchev's secret report on Stalin reached Peking, the Chinese Politburo convened an "enlarged session" to discuss it. The official Chinese position was then brought into line with Moscow's. The official *People's Daily* stated—and *Pravda* translated the statement—that Stalin had made a number of mistakes; in particular, "he made a wrong decision on the Yugoslav question." Peking's attitude, however, was a shade different from Khrushchev's; the Chinese did not conceal their higher evaluation of the defunct

[37] *Ibid.*
[38] *Ibid.*

dictator; to them, Stalin's terrorism was not as repulsive as it was to Western and many Russian Communists. The *People's Daily* stated: "Some consider that J. V. Stalin was entirely wrong. This is a serious error. J. V. Stalin was an outstanding Marxist-Leninist, but a Marxist-Leninist who did commit serious mistakes and did not perceive them. . . ."[39] A few weeks later, at the May Day parade, a huge portrait of Stalin adorned the main square in Peking.

On the whole, Communist China approved Khrushchev's attack on the "cult of personality," and it approved also the resumption of friendly relations with Tito; Sino-Yugoslav ties were likewise resumed. The Poles counted on China's moral support in their mounting drive for emancipation. It even seemed, in 1956, that China was on the way to assuming co-leadership in the anti-Soviet movement.

In fact, by her ambiguous position, Communist China gave reason for these expectations. On the one hand her leadership sympathized with the growing trends toward emancipation; independence had been its own immediate goal since 1953. On the other hand, abolition of Stalinism meant also equality between Communist governments, and on this issue China was adamant. Great China of course could be equal to Soviet Russia; but North Vietnam, North Korea, and all future "people's republics"—Nepal, Laos, Burma—could not claim equality with China. "A movement needs a leader," Mao contended. China must lead the "people's democracies" of her sphere. The ideas which were becoming known as "national Communism" were contrary to China's imperial ambitions.

Turbulent 1956, therefore, was for Chinese Communism a period of vacillation between the two trends; in every situation, however, Peking tried to march along with Moscow, the more so since Khrushchev appeared to understand China's desire for independence and China's conception of her role in the East.

When Moscow agreed to Gomulka's far-reaching demands for Poland, Peking approved; when Hungary revolted against Gerö, China went along with Moscow in favor of Nagy; when Moscow released (October 30, 1956) its statement on relations between socialist countries, China, in a lengthy statement, said, "this declaration is correct," and condemned those members of its party who "ignore the principle

[39] *Pravda*, April 7, 1956.

Mao and Khrushchev 439

of equal status."[40] When the Soviet army intervened against Nagy, however, Peking again approved, because "in Hungary counter-revolutionaries have got the upper hand and the Nagy Government announced its withdrawal from the Warsaw treaty." When the Poles, still in a difficult position in relation to Moscow, appealed for support, the Chinese turned their back on them.

China was not untouched by the spreading anti-Russian feeling, and it was not an easy matter to maintain loyalty to Moscow amid the almost universal disillusionment. The abatement of terrorism, Mao's "Let a Hundred Flowers Blossom and a Hundred Schools of Thought Contend," and his "Long-term Coexistence and Mutual Supervision" were the expression of a kind of Chinese "thaw," a concession to the antidictatorial movement. Open and sometimes violent anti-Russian statements were being made publicly. The "Away from Russia!" sentiment was spreading in China as it was in Eastern Europe.

"Soviet imperialism" was criticized, and "imitation of the Soviet system" was widely condemned; use of Soviet textbooks and inventions was questioned. Minister Chang Po-chung (of the Democratic League) said that "the Soviet Union has a heavy industry but no old culture."[41] General Lung Yun, a ranking leader, attacked the Soviet government for its request that the loans granted China in connection with the Korean War be repaid, with interest; the United States, he pointed out, had simply canceled the debts of its allies. A well-known young Chinese writer said that there was no democracy and no freedom in Soviet Russia and that living standards were low. There was widespread criticism of Soviet science, Soviet technology, and Soviet pedagogy.[42] The *People's Daily* reported that Tai Huang, a correspondent of the official New China News Agency, "was against the Soviet Union's sending troops to help Hungary suppress the counter-revolutionary rebellion. He mixed up right and wrong by saying: 'If Soviet Russia's sending troops is correct, then United States aid to Chiang Kai-shek is also correct.'"[43]

The blessings of freedom did not last long; the leadership clamped down on the "rightist opposition." *Pravda* was greatly pleased with the

[40] *Ibid.*, November 2, 1956.
[41] *Osteuropa*, Stuttgart, no. 11, November, 1957, pp. 804–06.
[42] *China News Analysis*, no. 205, November, 1957, pp. 3–4.
[43] *People's Daily*, August 8, 1957. Quoted in *Union Research Service*, Union Research Institute, Hong Kong, August 30, 1957, vol. 8, no. 18, p. 333.

suppression of anti-Soviet trends in China.[44] Chou En-lai came out with a violent attack in an attempt to put an end to the open anti-Sovietism:

> Some object to the study of the Soviet Union's experience and even think that the shortcomings and mistakes in building our country are the result of this study. These are very harmful opinions. We consider that to learn from the Soviet Union is absolutely necessary; the question is only how we do the studying.[45]

At the end of December, 1956, at the height of the post-Hungary confusion, when Tito was again rebelling and vacillation was evident everywhere, an "enlarged meeting" of the Chinese Politburo took place. In a lengthy statement, *People's Daily* reported its criticism of Stalin's "great-power chauvinism," his conceit, his mistakes, and his treatment of other socialist nations. In this respect, the newspaper's position was no longer new; but it then proceeded to criticize Tito and his colleagues for their suggestion that political power in Hungary should be turned over to the worker-elected Hungarian Soviets—a suggestion which, had it been adopted, would have probably meant the removal of the Communist Party from the government. It then emphasized the need to strengthen the solidarity of the international proletariat *"with its center in the Soviet Union."* [46]

A few days after this meeting of the Chinese Politburo Chou En-lai left for an important European tour; his obvious purpose was to assist Khrushchev in the fight against "national Communism," help reconstruct a kind of international organization under Soviet leadership, and persuade the European satellites that there was no alternative to Soviet dominance in their sphere. China's own position vis-à-vis Russia was not the main issue at this moment; Chou assumed the clever, traditionally Chinese, posture of extreme humility, outward inferiority, and submission. This was the only way in which Chinese Communism could retain for itself freedom of action in its Asian domain.

Between January 7 and 19, 1957, Chou visited Moscow, Warsaw, and Budapest. In Moscow, on the occasion of his receiving an honorary degree from the old university, Chou, in a humble speech before the professors, said: "My knowledge and ability are insufficient. They are

[44] *Pravda,* July 15, 1957.
[45] *Ibid.,* June 28, 1957.
[46] *Jenmin Jihpao,* December 29, 1956. Quoted in *Pravda,* December 30, 1956.

not commensurate with the degree which I am accepting. I will study and work with still greater zeal in the fight for peace, in the fight for our Communist cause."[47]

A three-sided meeting took place on January 10 in Moscow: the Chinese guests conferred with Janos Kadar, who had come from Budapest, as well as with Khrushchev, Mikoyan, and Malenkov. After the meeting Chou and his group left for Warsaw and Budapest. In the course of his trip Chou made it unmistakably clear that China favored the Soviet Union as the "center" of world Communism, and that on this issue he disagreed with the Poles. The final Chinese-Polish statement supporting the new Hungarian regime omitted any mention of the special position of the Soviet Union; there was no way to persuade the Poles to retreat from their stand. Gomulka said, " 'The coexistence of nations should not be like the coexistence of various kinds of fish living in one big pond or lake, the bigger fish devouring the smaller ones.' "[48]

On his way back to China Chou stopped in Moscow again, and again with extreme modesty told a "meeting of friendship":

> The Chinese people will continue modestly and seriously to learn from the Soviet Union, to study your advanced experience, advanced science and technology. . . . The Chinese people are fully aware of the fact that our achievements are inseparable from the support and assistance of the Soviet government and the Soviet people. . . . The unity and strengthening of the camp of Socialism, with the great Soviet Union at its head, represents the most important bulwark for the cause of peace in the world and for the progress of humanity.[49]

Khrushchev, in turn, softened in his anti-Stalinism and appropriated the Chinese image of the deceased leader; the notion of a "Stalinist" as well as of Stalin himself, he said, is inseparable from the notion of the high status of a Communist. "When the cause of the revolution was at stake, the defense of the class interests of the proletariat and the revolutionary struggle against our class enemies, Stalin courageously and relentlessly defended the cause of Marxism-Leninism. . . . On these cardinal and main issues, God grant, as they say, that every Communist may fight as Stalin did."[50]

[47] *Izvestia*, January 10, 1957.
[48] *The New York Times* (international edition), January 15, 1957.
[49] *Izvestia*, January 18, 1957.
[50] *Ibid.*, January 19, 1957.

PART FIVE

Khrushchev in Command

CHAPTER 1

THE YEAR OF TROUBLES

1. HEAVY GOING

November, 1956, marked the beginning of a year of trouble for Soviet foreign policy. The twelve-month period between the 1956 and 1957 anniversaries of the Soviet revolution began with a dangerous decline in Soviet prestige, which continued until developments permitted Nikita Khrushchev to grasp the reins more tightly and resume his drive.

The first stage was a period of weakness that was only slightly concealed behind words and gestures. The power of a dynamic government depends not only on its weapons, the size of its army and navy, and its programs and goals, but also on the solidarity, single-mindedness, and self-confidence of its highest leaders. It was precisely the latter that Moscow lacked at that time.

The developments in Hungary had a disturbing effect also on Soviet internal affairs. There were political protests among students in Moscow; in an effort to discover the source of these protests, Khrushchev spent several days at Moscow University. In Leningrad students organized a street demonstration. Hungarian students in Moscow spoke defiantly at Komsomol meetings.[1] Trying to maintain his nonterroristic course, Khrushchev refrained from taking measures which a few years earlier would have put a rapid and tragic end to the mutiny; the fact, however, that the most sensitive segment of the nation—the Soviet youth, among them the sons and daughters of the elite—was protesting and making demands was a disturbing development.

---

[1] See, among other sources, *Hearing before the Subcommittee to Investigate the Administration of the Internal Security Act and Other Internal Security Laws* of the Committee of the Judiciary, United States Senate, Eighty-sixth Congress, First Session. Testimony of Alexander Yurievich Kasnakheyev (in our text given as Kaznacheev) (hereafter referred to as *Kaznacheev Testimony*), December 14, 1959, p. 4.

As a result of the Hungarian crisis also, the fight between the factions in the Presidium, which had subsided for a time, flared with new force. On every new issue the Malenkov-Molotov group had its own proposals. The initial discord among the members of the future "anti-Party group" began to give way to a degree of unity and the idea of a coup to remove Khrushchev from leadership; the contours of a new Presidium, with Molotov as first secretary of the Party and Malenkov as premier, emerged. The December 20–25, 1956, Plenum of the Central Committee, the first since Budapest and Suez, was not entirely devoted to discussion of industrial problems and the economic administration system; although Moscow succeeded in keeping the proceedings secret, it was evident that foreign affairs had been the main subject of discussion and dispute.

The crisis in international Communism, too, deepened in the winter and spring of 1956–57. The Yugoslavs, having been almost won over by concessions and compromises, recoiled; vociferous groups and leaders in almost every country protested against the system of Soviet guidance of Communist countries in world affairs; the Poles, having supposedly settled their disputes with Moscow by new agreements, were in no way reconciled and continued openly to voice their opposition. Numerous leaders, groups of party members, and thousands of sympathizers were turning their backs on a government whose prestige had suffered badly from the revelations about Stalin in February, 1956, and the Hungarian operation in November, 1956.

At a conference in Belgrade late in December, 1956, Yugoslav and Polish Communist leaders announced their common, obviously anti-Moscow, program of noninterference of one Communist country in the affairs of the other.[2] Meantime Moscow tried desperately to mend the rent in international Communism. Conferences one after another with the satellites yielded little consolation: on December 3, Rumanian leaders in Moscow issued a pro-Khrushchev communiqué; early in January, 1957, a conference of the Communist parties of the Soviet Union, Hungary, Rumania, Bulgaria, and Czechoslovakia (Poland and Yugoslavia were absent) took place in Budapest; a few days later the East Germans came to Moscow for a conference; Chou En-lai conferred with the Hungarians and the Poles. In January, 1957, also there were discussions with the Italians and Czechs in Moscow. There

[2] Reuters, December 29, 1956.

were other conferences in which the Soviet Communist Party did not directly participate. The Czech and French parties, the most orthodox supporters of the Soviet course, were especially active.

The most important in this feverish series of conferences were Khrushchev's meetings with Chou En-lai. As indicated in the preceding chapter, China endorsed the Soviet claims of supremacy which, *mutatis mutandis,* could be applied to the Far East. Chou was unable to persuade Gomulka to accept Soviet guidance for Poland, but, on behalf of China, he signed in Moscow a "declaration" approving Soviet armed intervention in Hungary and emphasized that "the highest international obligation of the Soviet Union and China is the strengthening and consolidating of the unity of socialist countries on the basis of the above mentioned principles," [3] meaning, in the first place, Soviet leadership.

The fight against "national Communism"—which was a fight for the survival of the Soviet empire—was absorbing all the attention of the Soviet leadership. While the idea of "national roads to socialism" was not abrogated, the overriding principle of the "community of socialist nations" was more and more stressed. "National Communism" was now vigorously criticized in the Soviet and pro-Soviet press as "revisionism," a term not only of condemnation but expressive of an emotional aversion reminiscent of the "betrayal" of orthodox Marxism by Edward Bernstein and the "revisionists" in Germany early in the century and Lenin's attacks on them. The Yugoslavs were now held guilty of a similar crime. "Revisionism" was rapidly becoming the neuralgic point of the international Communist organism.

Outside the Communist realm, in the Western hemisphere, and especially in Western Europe, the moral standing of Moscow suffered greatly. Even those who had protested against the Suez operations of Britain and France turned against Moscow. One rebuff followed another. On November 7, a few days after the Soviet attack in Budapest, Premier Tage Erlander of Sweden withdrew the invitation extended to Khrushchev and Bulganin to visit Stockholm; in the next few days Denmark and Norway withdrew their invitations. In December, Iceland, which had almost been persuaded to join the neutral camp and which had been on the verge of breaking with NATO, made an about-face and reached an agreement with the United States on the issue of

[3] *Izvestia,* January 19, 1957.

American forces stationed on the island. Among the most violent critics were parties which at various times had been courted by Khrushchev—the British Labor Party and the German Social-Democrats. Even Nehru, the neutralist, expressed disapproval publicly of the Soviet actions in Hungary.

Only a government in full control of the country and facing no open opposition could have reacted to such a series of blows in the way that Khrushchev did during those crucial months. He behaved as though he had unlimited power and tremendous strength; in order to impress doubters and opponents, he exaggerated both the power and the strength. By excessive aggressiveness, he and his regime tried to conceal the existing confusion.

At two diplomatic receptions, on November 17 and 18 respectively, Khrushchev referred to the West in such abusive terms that the Western diplomats at one of the receptions walked out of the Kremlin hall in a body. It was on this occasion that Khrushchev told his guests—"we will bury you." He spoke of "piratical attacks" by France and Britain and of these powers "cutting the throats" of the Egyptians; he spoke of "fascist bands" who attacked Communists in France, Italy, and other countries. The dean of the foreign diplomatic corps, Swedish Ambassador Rolf Solman, lodged a protest with the Soviet Foreign Ministry; the following day, at another reception, Khrushchev told the assembled diplomats that if they did not like his speeches, they could stay at home.[4]

Several times the Soviet leader referred to the situation in the satellites in the most menacing terms: addressing himself to the "imperialists," he stated that the Hungarian events must have taught them a lesson; any new attempt, he said, "will meet with proper rebuff," and the Soviet bloc "is strong enough to curb the aggressor."[5] In another banquet speech he warned the West: "'Don't try to test us as you did in Hungary—with the putsch. You think of doing it not only in Hungary but also in East Germany. Be careful. We are not saints and if necessary we can rap your knuckles.'"[6]

[4] *The New York Times*, November 18, 19, and 20, 1956. The Khrushchev speeches were censored and toned down for publication in the Soviet press.
[5] Khrushchev's answers to questions submitted by V. Koutsky, Editor in Chief of *Rude Pravo* (*Izvestia*, January 1, 1957).
[6] *The New York Times*, April 20, 1957.

Heavy Going

The rehabilitation of Stalin which started late in 1956 was part of this exhibition of extreme belligerence. Khrushchev had no thought of resorting to Stalin's methods in home affairs, but as a "fighter against imperialism" the late leader was once more hailed. "When it comes to fighting imperialism, we are all Stalinists," Khrushchev said at a New Year's reception in Moscow,[7] and the other members of the Presidium agreed. It was obvious that this was the new line approved by the Central Committee a few days before. From then on, renewed, though reserved, praise of Stalin became almost standard. When a highly official Hungarian delegation headed by Istvan Doby and Janos Kadar arrived in Moscow in March, it placed a wreath bearing a respectful inscription on Stalin's sarcophagus.

Stalinism was now not only to be respected but at times even imitated. In foreign affairs this line had two implications:

First, it meant an increased press and radio offensive against the "imperialists," among whom the United States stood first. Only a short time before, Moscow had proposed to Washington concerted action against Britain and France on the Suez Canal issue; now the Soviet government aggressively resumed its old course, and the Soviet press attacked not only Britain and France, but the United States as well, maintaining that there was no difference between them and even that the United States was the main culprit.

Second, in the framework of international Communism, the new attitude toward Stalinism was a renewal of the emphasis on the Russian-led "monolith" and a battlecry against the "revisionists." It was a challenge to Yugoslavia, and it made closer the ties to China, whose Communist Party was gradually becoming the most orthodox, bellicose, and anti-American of all the parties. Now all foreign efforts to reduce the ties between the Communist parties to a mere ideological affinity met with vigorous protests; the military term "camp," Khrushchev insisted, was the accurate designation. All of this had the flavor of a return to the old "general staff of the world revolution."

> Certain leaders [Khrushchev said] are in disagreement about the notion of the "Socialist camp" and want to substitute for it the term "collaboration" or a similar term. I think there can be no more exact definition than the term "Socialist camp," which expresses most clearly the essence of the relationship between the Socialist countries in a

[7] *Ibid.* (international edition), January 2, 1957.

period when there exist the two systems—the Socialist and the capitalist.[8]

During this period there occurred the acrimonious debate on the "Eisenhower doctrine." While the Suez conflict was gradually being settled, and the British, French, and Israeli troops had been withdrawn, Syria remained a danger spot in the Middle East. Abundant arms from the Eastern bloc were stocked in Syria; part of Egypt's aviation had been flown, during the war, to Syrian bases. Syria had maintained the closest ties with Moscow of any of the Arab countries. The possibility of Syria's developing into a Soviet satellite was seriously discussed in Western capitals, which had no confidence in her "positive neutrality." Anxiety mounted, especially in Turkey and Lebanon.

Early in January the United States Congress authorized the President to use military force to "protect the Middle East from the menace of international Communism." The sum of 200 million dollars was envisaged as an aid fund for the countries of this region. James P. Richards was dispatched to the Middle East to initiate the aid program. The Soviet press, which was more antagonistic to Secretary Dulles than to any other Western leader, called the American course the "Eisenhower-Dulles program," and attacked it with violent threats. The program, *Pravda* said, was a plan to "grab riches" and "enslave the peoples" of the Middle East. In his speech before the Supreme Soviet on February 12, Foreign Minister Shepilov emphasized the "solidarity" of the United States, Britain, and France in their anti-Arab policies and the American program of unilateral dominance in the Middle East. In his violent attack, Shepilov exclaimed:

> It is time, it is really time to put an end to the myth that the United States is not a colonial power. It is well known that the American monopolists have for quite a long time been conducting colonial exploitation of the countries of Latin America as well as of the Philippines. . . . the "Eisenhower Doctrine" serves as a good illustration that it is the United States which is now assuming the role of the *main bulwark of the system of colonial oppression.*[9]

[8] *Pravda*, April 17, 1957. In his report to the Twenty-first Congress, however, Khrushchev said: "Yet everyone knows that the socialist camp, embracing the socialist countries of Europe and Asia, is not a military camp, but a community of equal peoples in the struggle for peace and for a better life for the working people, for socialism and communism" (*Pravda*, January 28, 1959).

[9] *Ibid.*, February 13, 1957.

The New Ascent

To America's preparations for a new aggression, Shepilov juxtaposed the Soviet program, which called not only for a collective commitment not to supply arms to the nations of the Middle East, but for "liquidation of foreign bases."

Three days later Shepilov was forced to quit the Foreign Ministry. Although his dismissal was not explained, and "continuity" was stressed when Gromyko took over, it is possible that, in the new wave of anti-Americanism, and with China acquiring new influence in the Communist movement, Shepilov's abortive offer of collaboration with the United States against Britain and France was viewed as an unforgivable deviation.

2. THE NEW ASCENT

The meaning behind this verbal and literary saber-rattling, the deliberate exaggeration of American aggressiveness, and the Soviet attempt to restore its own vigor was not as obvious in the West as it was in the ranking circles of Moscow and in the "people's democracies." The disorientation and confusion were artfully concealed. Feverish activity, a score of conferences, and numerous visits of the highest Soviet leaders to the capitals of the "camp" served to combat the centrifugal forces and provide an antidote to the poison of national independence.

In the end Khrushchev and his group brought the situation under control and came out winners in the ominous contest. The circumstances that made the victory possible deserve particular attention because they throw light on the course of Soviet foreign policy.

The ferment in Eastern Europe continued during the first half of 1957. Poland, outwardly reconciled, was still seething; in Hungary tension was great; Yugoslavia was a fountainhead of anticentralist programs and ideas. Moreover, it was expected in Moscow that trouble would also break out in East Germany, and that then practically all of Eastern Europe, except for Czechoslovakia, would be ready to secede. In a speech in April, Khrushchev admitted that such rumors were widespread in "the foreign press," and warned against "putsches": "He who comes to us with a sword will perish by the sword." [10]

Khrushchev's warnings were not in vain: there was no govern-

[10] *Ibid.*, April 21, 1957.

ment willing to risk a war by helping a rebellious small nation in its fight for independence. The United States, removed by distance, was less affected by the developments than the European nations, and Britain was in a similar position. France and Germany, the two continental powers, were unable to act, although Eastern Europe was a most important component of their security, and although Soviet armies on the Elbe were a constant threat.

West Germany was almost completely inactive in Europe. France, under other circumstances, might have displayed power. Her historical role in Europe, her loyal protection of Poland in the past, her role in the resurrection of Poland after the end of World War I, and her recent ties with Bucharest and Budapest made her, it would appear, the first choice among possible allies of seething Eastern Europe. But with the bulk of her forces engaged in Algeria, and divided emotionally between anti-Germanism and anti-Sovietism, France was unable to intervene; she limited herself to "moral support"—a term that had acquired ironic overtones in those times.

In pursuing its policies in Eastern Europe, the Soviet government discounted France; Khrushchev took over Stalin's dim view of the "beautiful but irresolute" country. "The French are people who cannot make up their mind," he told a French correspondent; expanding Khrushchev's remarks, TASS stated: "France was a wonderful country but unfortunately she did not at present occupy the position that belongs to her by her right as a great power owing to wavering and indecision of her policy on questions of securing peace." [11]

Impotence and futility lay over the national emancipation movements in Europe; the emancipation forces were ridiculously inadequate to face the Russians, and help from outside was lacking; the movements had no prospects, at least at that moment.

None of the rebelling Communist leaders, parties, or individuals saw any reason to retreat, and none had become reconverted to the theory and practice of the "Soviet Union as the leader." But the gust of protesting winds lulled, the storm petered out, and resignation slowly set in. Stalin, the evil one, was dead, but Soviet tanks crushing national movements were a reality and had to be reckoned with.

Khrushchev was winning out.

[11] *The New York Times*, November 16, 1955.

The New Ascent

A series of events between July and November, 1957, helped Khrushchev to overcome the crisis and reconsolidate both the Soviet empire and his own rule.

The first of these events was the attempt of the Communist opposition in the Soviet Presidium, which apparently had a majority in that body, to overthrow Khrushchev and take over the party and the government. The opposition was defeated, however, at the session of the Central Committee held during the last week of June. The Central Committee condemned the "anti-Party group" of Malenkov, Molotov, and Kaganovich, as well as Shepilov (who apparently had joined the opposition in the last stage of the fight), and expelled them from the Central Committee. The group were charged with opposing the "Leninist principle of coexistence," relaxation of international tension, and the program of "catching up with the United States in per capita production of meat, milk and butter." They were not permitted, however, to state their case in their own words.[12]

The expulsion of the well-known veteran leaders practically put an end to Soviet "collective leadership" and opened the road to new "cults of personality." Khrushchev's powers extended to the field of international relations; Andrei Gromyko, the new foreign minister, was the humble executor of the leader's orders. "'Gromyko only says,'" Khrushchev told Averell Harriman, in Gromyko's presence, "'what we tell him to. . . . If he doesn't we'll fire him and get someone who does.'"[13]

On October 26 Marshal Georgi Zhukov, Minister for Defense, was dismissed from his post as well as from the Party's Central Committee. Finally, Premier Nikolai Bulganin was forced to quit. On March 31, 1958, Nikita Khrushchev became premier.

The second event that helped to restore the prestige of the Soviet Union was the launching of the first earth satellite on October 4, 1957. With this exploit the Soviet Union took its place, in the eyes of the world, among the advanced nations in science and technology. Although a part of Soviet programs of production and perfection of arms, the flight of the "red moon" increased Soviet influence and Soviet claims in many other fields. The launching of the artificial satellite,

---
[12] See Part Three, Chap. 1.
[13] *Life*, July 13, 1959, p. 33.

Moscow declared, was proof of the superiority of Soviet socialism over capitalism.

> The sputniks [Khrushchev told two Brazilian journalists] serve as it were to sum up the competition between the socialist and capitalist countries. And socialism has won in this competition.... And that is just another vivid proof that the economy, science and culture and the people's creative genius in all spheres of life develop better and faster under socialism.[14]

The argument was similar to Stalin's claim that victory over Germany had proved the superiority of the Soviet system over capitalism. The "red moon" thesis, which made little impression on the West, was addressed mainly to the ruling parties of the satellites and Eastern allies; in the heated debates of those days it became another reason for Moscow's claim to the role of guide.

The third event in the contest between centrifugal and centripetal forces in the Soviet realm was the negotiations and preparations for the fortieth anniversary of the November Revolution. The main issue was whether a new international Communist organization should emerge out of the occasion.

Since the latter part of 1956 Khrushchev had cautiously been sounding out the other parties on this question. On Moscow's initiative the East Germans and Austrians sent out some feelers;[15] the Soviet *International Affairs* discreetly indicated approval of the idea.[16] Something more comprehensive and more impressive than the Cominform of nine parties that had been dissolved in April was wanted. A "perfect" political and technical network reminiscent of the defunct Comintern's happy days was being discussed: the new organization would appoint its own envoys to the Communist parties in various countries and in this way create the "apparatus" for international action. The plan, if carried out, would certainly increase Moscow's power, particularly in its European and Asian orbits. *Österreichische Volksstimme*,[17] however, admitted that "there exists a divergence of opinions among

---

[14] *International Affairs*, Moscow, no. 12, December, 1957, p. 9.

[15] Günther Nollau, *Die Internationale: Wurzeln und Erscheinungsformen des proletarischen Internationalismus*, Köln, Verlag für Politik und Wirtschaft, 1959, p. 231; *Österreichische Volksstimme*, Vienna, November 28, 1956, quoted in *Ost-Probleme*, Bad Godesberg, no. 50, December 14, 1956, p. 1752.

[16] *International Affairs*, Moscow, no. 11, November, 1956, pp. 20–30.

[17] November 28, 1956.

The New Ascent

our brotherly parties." Resistance to the idea of a new International was considerable, since the Comintern was well remembered as a lever of Soviet dominance over the other parties. Stalin's Cominform had been different, but no better. A new international Communist organization would require a leading organ that would be controlled by the Russians, and a new president or secretary, probably a Russian.

In the feverish climate of 1957 the plan for a new International, which found supporters among the orthodox, "dogmatist" parties and leaders, was opposed by the Polish-Yugoslav wing and the Italians, and also by China, which now usually sided with Moscow. Whether cloaked in terms of "national Communism," "revisionism," "dogmatism," "equality," or "independence," the overriding issue was the same —shall or shall not the Soviet empire exist in its newly expanded area?

Another attempt at Soviet-Yugoslav reconciliation was made when Khrushchev and Tito met briefly (August 1–2) in Bucharest. The parley was apparently a successful one. Khrushchev confirmed that "following the well-known Soviet-Yugoslav meeting in Bucharest, the situation was again restored to normal." [18] "On that occasion," Tito reported to the Congress in Lubliana, "we cleared up some misunderstandings and there remained very little of what could impede our full cooperation and friendly relations." The "very little," however, related, as Tito said later, to the idea of a "socialist camp" and the issue of independence.[19] Soon the "very little" impediment became an abyss.

The Polish and Yugoslav Communist parties, the potential nucleus of a non-Soviet Communist orbit, held a conference of their own in September, 1957, when a delegation from Warsaw, headed by Wladyslaw Gomulka, came to Belgrade; this conference was expected to "far exceed the scope of good relations between Yugoslavia and Poland and become an important event in the relationship of Socialist countries and Communist workers' parties all over the world." [20]

On their arrival in Belgrade the Polish leaders were enthusiastically welcomed by a crowd estimated at over 100,000. In their public speeches and resolutions, Tito and Gomulka stressed their own notion of Communist collaboration based on "equal rights, friendship, and

---

[18] Nikita S. Khrushchev, *For Victory in Peaceful Competition with Capitalism*, New York, E. P. Dutton & Co., Inc., 1960, p. 562.
[19] Tito's speech, September 15, 1957.
[20] *Trybuna Ludu*, Warsaw, September 9, 1957.

non-interference in internal affairs." Although cautiously rejecting the label of "national Communism," and approving much of Soviet foreign policy (for example, the "two Germanys," the Oder-Neisse line, etc.), they looked forward, they stated, to close collaboration of Poland and Yugoslavia in the future. The joint Tito-Gomulka statement concluded:

> . . . both delegations express the conviction that the development of all-around cooperation between the two countries can serve to bring about further rapprochement and brotherhood of the people of Yugoslavia and Poland and the building of Socialism in their countries as well as strengthening the cooperation of the Socialist countries and progressive forces in the world.[21]

Tito publicly stated during the visit that "imitation of the Soviet experience is impossible." With an eye on Moscow, Tito and Gomulka took pains to deny any intention of organizing a separate "faction inside the Socialist movement"; the denials were so frequent that they could only produce a contrary impression, especially in suspicious Moscow.

What the critics of the idea of a new International juxtaposed with it was a loose series of bilateral or multilateral meetings of Communist parties without hard-and-fast statutes, discipline, or superior organs and direction, and even without a leading press organ; regional ties and combinations, it was argued, might have more importance than an over-all organization. The idea proved popular, and it was accepted by the majority of the parties.

During the last phase of his preparations for the November celebrations, which were actually to assume the dimensions and importance of a world-wide Congress of Communist parties—the first since 1935—Khrushchev had obviously arrived at the conclusion that it would be wiser to drop the idea of a formal new International, while maintaining its essence—Soviet leadership. Bilateral and multilateral meetings would serve the purpose: a press organ would be established; the Foreign Departments of the Central Committees would help to strengthen mutual ties.

The November meetings in Moscow marked the end of a year

[21] *Pravda*, September 18, 1957.

The New Ascent

of crisis and a great step forward for the Soviet government. Sixty-four Communist parties sent their highest leaders to Moscow; even Mao Tse-tung, a rare guest abroad, took an active part in the meetings. Only Tito did not attend; he was represented by a number of ranking aides. A group of twelve Communist parties—those which ruled in their countries, except the Yugoslavs—held a separate conference on November 14–16. A full session of the sixty-four parties, including the Yugoslav, was held on November 16–19. The latter conference issued the standard-type "Manifesto" directed against war, rearmament, and atomic weapons, and in favor of "collective security" and peaceful coexistence.

Far more important, however, was the Declaration of the twelve parties, which had to solve the problem of Moscow's leadership. The Chinese and Poles, who often opposed one another, tried hard to insert into the document a statement of their particular theories. Mao went far in frankly advocating Soviet leadership over the Communist parties. The Communist world, he said, must have a leader, and the Soviet Union and its Communist Party was the central body among the Communist parties of the world. In typically Chinese manner, Mao humbly stated that the Chinese party was not worthy of taking over the leadership. (Gomulka claimed later, in his speech of November 19, 1957, that his "Polish style" was recognizable in the Moscow Declaration.) Mikhail Suslov was the spokesman for the Soviet Party. The Declaration stressed the leading role of the Soviet Union, stating that "the cause of peace is upheld by the powerful forces of our era: the invincible camp of Socialist countries headed by the Soviet Union." [22] Recognizing the national peculiarities of individual countries and condemning "dogmatism," the Declaration appealed to the Communist parties to wage a fight against "revisionism" as the most dangerous deviation of the time.

Although Soviet supremacy was not expounded at length in the Declaration, Khrushchev and his party were highly satisfied, and the Central Committee Plenum viewed the conference as a "great success of the world-wide Communist movement." The Communist Party of the Soviet Union, the Central Committee's resolution declared, will comply with its obligation "to strengthen the ties of friendship and

[22] *Ibid.*, November 22, 1957.

proletarian solidarity with the toilers and democratic forces of the world." [23]

Stalin's "monolith" having been reinstated, and Moscow's predominance having been recognized, large slices of old ideology also crept back into their former places. The theory that capitalism cannot live without colonies and the philosophy of the decay of capitalism— old tenets which, under attack from inside the Communist movements, seemed to have been under revision—were now revived. In the Stalinist style, *Pravda* wrote:

> *Imperialism cannot exist without colonial slavery, without violence and suppression of the national rights of peoples, without dividing the whole world into an overwhelming majority of oppressed and an insignificant minority of oppressors. This is why the success of the national-liberating fight of the colonial slaves, the development of sovereign national states which emerge to replace the oppressed colonies and half colonies, are symptoms of a deadly illness and of the inevitable destruction of imperialism.* [24]

The rear-guard battles of the "revisionists" on the issue of a leading periodical for the international Communist movement continued after the Moscow sessions ended. The Poles, the Italians, and, even more emphatically, the Yugoslavs, opposed the project of a periodical because it would in the first place serve as a medium to fight their own "deviations." At a conference held in Prague on March 7–8, 1958, which the Yugoslavs did not attend, it was decided to establish the periodical as a "theoretical and information monthly"; the limitation was intended to be a concession to the dissidents. The first issue of the new monthly, *World Marxist Review,* appeared, in sixteen languages, in September, 1958. The editorial office was located in superorthodox pro-Soviet Prague. The editor in chief came, naturally, from Moscow; he was Alexei Rumyantsev, member of the Central Committee of the Soviet Party, up to then editor of the Moscow *Kommunist,* and subordinated, of course, to Mikhail Suslov of the Soviet Presidium.[25] The first issue contained an announcement that the journal would consider the fight against "revisionism" its main task. The names of the editors were not made public, if only in order not to stress the leading role of

[23] *Ibid.,* December 19, 1957.
[24] *Ibid.,* December 26, 1957. The emphasis is *Pravda's.*
[25] *Est & Ouest,* Paris, no. 197, June 16–30, 1958, p. 18; Günther Nollau, *Die Internationale. Wurzeln und Erscheinungsformen des Proletarischen Internationalismus,* Köln, Verlag für Politik und Wirtschaft, 1959, p. 297.

The New Setup

the Russian editor in chief. Much later, his name was mentioned in the journal, but only as a spokesman for the Editorial Board of *World Marxist Review*.[26]

All this was a triumph for Khrushchev. Tito was isolated, the Italians were retreating, and the Poles were trying to find a place for themselves within the Soviet framework.

3. THE NEW SETUP

The plan of regional associations and sporadic meetings of the Communist parties, which had been suggested by the Italians in 1956–57, was accepted. The plan produced a phenomenon—the emergence of Communist spheres of influence, nuclei of larger configurations, the beginning of a new partition of the world.

Although no written agreements are available and although, for obvious reasons, the Communist press never mentions the new setup, there are a number of incontestable facts that point to such a setup, at least as to three large regions of global Communism.

The first of these is the Soviet sphere, which embraces the satellites of Eastern Europe and the Asian countries of Mongolia and North Korea. In addition, among the "capitalist countries," the Communist Party of West Germany at least, with its leading agencies situated in East Berlin, would also appear to belong to the Soviet sphere; thus, the two Communist parties of Germany constitute a component part of Khrushchev's party machinery. India, Afghanistan, Pakistan, and Iran likewise would appear to belong to the Soviet sphere. This configuration of the Soviet sphere is confirmed by various facts and developments.

The second large region of global Communism is the sphere of the Chinese Communist Party, which probably includes one satellite, North Vietnam; in the non-Communist areas of Asia, certainly Burma, Cambodia, Thailand, Malaya, Laos, South Vietnam, and Singapore are in the Chinese sphere.

Among other facts that have thrown light on the Chinese sphere, the testimony, before a United States Senate subcommittee, of Alex-

---

[26] *World Marxist Review: Problems of Peace and Socialism: Theoretical and Information Journal of Communist and Workers' Parties,* Canadian edition of the monthly journal published in Prague, vol. 2, no. 10, October, 1959, p. 66.

ander Kaznacheev, who was a member of the Soviet Embassy in Burma and defected, obtaining asylum in the United States, has been an important source of information. Kaznacheev has revealed that when, for example, the Soviet Embassy in Rangoon wanted the Burmese Communist Party to make certain changes in its strategy, it did not try to accomplish this by exerting influence on the Party directly, although ties, of course, existed between the Embassy and the Party; the procedure was rather as follows: the Soviet Embassy in Rangoon referred the matter to Moscow, Moscow consulted Peking, and Peking, if it agreed to the changes, instructed Burma accordingly. In its (unpublished) annual report of 1958 the Soviet Embassy said: "We propose that the Soviet Government through our Chinese friends advise the Burmese Communists to speed up their surrender and establish themselves as a legal Communist Party." [27]

In his testimony, Kaznacheev, admitting that no official documents delineating the Chinese sphere are known to exist, stated that the sphere was "well recognized," and he had "met it many times." ". . . I have many facts I gathered during my work that say there is a recognized division of spheres of influence in southeast Asia between China and Soviet Union." [28]

The formation of spheres and the delimitation of the Soviet and Chinese orbits are illustrated in the case of North Korea, whose place between China and Russia deserves attention. During its first five or six years of existence North Korea—government as well as Communist Party—was a regular Soviet satellite. Since the Korean War, however, China's influence there has been on the rise, and China's substantial appropriations for North Korea's rehabilitation have been indicative of China's special interest in the country. It appears that a compromise has been arrived at between Moscow and Peking in regard to North Korea, with the pro-Moscow faction maintaining supreme leadership and the pro-Peking faction constituting a substantial part of the Party Presidium (the "standing committee") as well as of the regime. Of the three rival Communist factions in North Korea, which have been in contention since 1945, the strongest has been the pro-Soviet faction led by Premier Kim Il-sung, the second the pro-Chinese faction composed of former Korean Communists in China,

[27] *Kaznacheev Testimony, op. cit.*, p. 10.
[28] *Ibid.*, p. 8.

The New Setup

and the third the "domestic and independent" group consisting of those who never left the country and had lived in neither the Soviet Union nor China during the Japanese occupation. The trial and execution of thirteen Communist leaders in North Korea in 1953 represented, according to reliable reports,[29] the liquidation of this third, independent, Titoist-inclined faction.

The situation of North Korea, between the Soviet and Chinese "spheres," has been described as follows: the convention of the North Korean Labor (Communist) Party in April, 1956, elected a Central Committee of seventy-one members; on the basis of an agreement between various groups, 65 per cent of these members belong to the pro-Soviet faction, 21 per cent to the pro-Chinese faction, and the rest—"internal" Koreans without affiliation—to neither the pro-Soviet nor the pro-Chinese faction. The chairman of the Central Committee (and first secretary) is the pro-Soviet Kim Il-sung; of the five deputy chairmen, three are pro-Soviet and two pro-Chinese. The Standing Committee (Presidium) of eleven consists of eight pro-Soviet and three pro-Chinese members.[30]

It would appear natural and logical that the Communist Party of South Korea, being illegal and guided from the north, should be in the Soviet orbit.

The third Communist sphere is encompassed in the tutelage exercised by the Italian Communist Party over the Communist movements of North Africa, including Egypt, Morocco, Tunisia, Algeria, and Libya, and also over the Greek and Portuguese parties. The transfer of these parties, which had previously been centered around the French party, to Italian tutelage was due to the difficult position of French Communism on the Algerian issue, and perhaps also to the decline of its influence.[31]

How the other parties have been grouped since November, 1957, is not known.

[29] D Papers, November 22, 1956, vol. 2, pp. 82 and 87–89.
[30] Ibid.
[31] Est & Ouest, Paris, no. 202, October 16–31, 1958, p. 14; no. 205, December 1–15, 1958, p. 8; no. 223, October 16–31, 1959, pp. 4–5. In particular, President Nasser's intelligence service has apparently arrived at the same conclusion, at least as far as Egypt is concerned (see Nasser's article, "Where I Stand and Why," Life, July 20, 1959). In a speech in Damascus in March, 1959, Nasser again confirmed that the Communist Party of Egypt had been under instructions from the Italian Communist Party since 1953 (The New York Times, March 14, 1959).

The Foreign Department of the Soviet Central Committee proved itself able to carry out its complex work as the world center of Communism, the fountainhead of ideas and strategy, and the successful organizer of large congresses, small conferences, and "bilateral and multilateral" parleys and receptions. Official statements on these congresses, conferences, and parleys provide some insight into the workings of this important agency.

The Soviet Party's Foreign Department is headed by two members of the Presidium, Mikhail Suslov and Otto Kuusinen. Suslov, the younger and more energetic of the two, often acts as the Party's representative at Communist congresses abroad, and as official spokesman of the Party at important events in Russia. He has been viewed as a strictly orthodox Leninist, with a touch of Stalinism, though entirely loyal to Khrushchev. The seventy-nine-year-old Finnish leader, Kuusinen, embodies the history of international Communism: he was among Lenin's collaborators in the first Comintern, and served as Stalin's right-hand man in the field of international Communism throughout the latter's rule. In the Party hierarchy Suslov and Kuusinen are subordinated directly to the first secretary of the Central Committee—Nikita Khrushchev.

Among the sizable staff of the Foreign Department, Boris N. Ponomariov, a member of the Central Committee, has an important role; the sections supervised by him embrace the Communist parties of the "capitalist countries." Ponomariov often interprets, via the Soviet press, the attitudes of Soviet Communism toward Titoists, Social-Democrats, and other groups. A number of experienced officers have been taken over by the Party's Foreign Department from the Ministry of Foreign Affairs; among them, for example, is Yuri Andropov, who was Soviet ambassador to Hungary during the uprising of 1956. Bobodjan Gafurov, a member of the Central Committee, a Tadzhik from Central Asia, has a roving assignment as envoy to the Communist parties of Moslem and some other countries. Yan Dzerzhinsky, son of the first president of the Cheka, worked in the Polish division until his death in October, 1960.

The official Minindel (Ministry of Foreign Affairs), under Andrei Gromyko, which is a part of the government structure, is, of course, subordinated to the premier—up to the time of his dismissal in March, 1958, Bulganin, and from then on, in fact and legally, Khrushchev.

The New Setup

The Minindel is more concerned with the non-Communist world, in particular, Soviet policy toward the West. The Foreign Department of the Party, in regard to the "capitalist countries," conducts activities which may be considered routine, as, for example, issuing of circulars, relations with the press, collective appeals of Communist parties, etc.; its intervention in such events as an upheaval in Iraq or the advent of a Castro regime in Cuba is an exception.

On the other hand, the Foreign Department of the Party is more important than the official Ministry of Foreign Affairs in matters of policy within the bloc. The intricate questions of relations between members of the bloc and the fight over recognition or nonrecognition of Moscow's supremacy—issues that have aroused great excitement in international Communism in the last years—are under the jurisdiction of the Foreign Department of the Party. Gromyko's Ministry of Foreign Affairs, in its relations with these countries, performs only routine tasks.

The ultimate coordination and integration of the activities of the two agencies is the prime task of the man who heads both structures and who rules the Soviet Union and its sphere.

CHAPTER 2

THE CRISIS OF NEUTRALISM

Having recovered vigor and dynamism since 1958, the Khrushchev government nevertheless tried to maintain the innovations in Soviet foreign policy that had been introduced since 1954 as modifications of Stalinism. But by now it had digested some bitter experiences and had matured sufficiently to realize the limits set in practice to general principles in international affairs. The specific elements of Khrushchevism—ties with and guidance of the "neutrals," and the belief in a great "peace front" and in the "monolithic unity" of the "socialist" nations—had lost much of their color; on the other hand, a new emphasis was placed on the "invincible" military might of the Soviet state. Soviet foreign policy after 1958, while remaining bold, was based on fewer illusions and fewer vain expectations.

1. THE ARAB NATIONS

The Bandung Conference of 1955 had generated great hopes and produced the notion of a general movement of the "underdeveloped" countries toward alliance with the Soviet Union against "Western imperialism." To the Soviet Union and her allies, Bandung symbolized, as we have seen, the cooperation of the Soviet bloc with the neutral nations and the beginnings of close ties with some of the most populated countries of the globe. Pancha Shilla, the tablet of commandments of "peaceful coexistence" formulated by China and India (Communism and neutralism), was repeatedly quoted and brought into connection with Bandung. While the West rarely discussed the Bandung Conference, the Soviet press and the press of its allies continued to emphasize its influence. In 1956–57 Moscow expected that a second "Bandung Conference" would take place soon. In the Soviet capital the ambassadors of the Bandung governments assembled from time to

The Arab Nations

time—for example, to greet a prominent leader from one of the Bandung countries; if the visitor was a member of royalty, Khrushchev himself sometimes appeared at the receptions.[1]

As time went on, however, and despite all Soviet efforts, the glitter of Bandung dimmed. Although the governments that had proclaimed themselves neutralist did not announce any change in their course, another parley under the leadership of Nehru and Chou, and directed against the West, was not wanted. There were several reasons for this change of heart, including Communist China's too-aggressive course and the fact that Chinese co-leadership was not wished for; nor could the events in Hungary be expected to cement a Communist-neutralist accord.

Moscow made a careful distinction between "positive neutralism" and neutralism plain. What had been taking place since 1957 was a trend from the highly "progressive" brand of neutralism to simple neutralism.

The "Asian-African People's Solidarity Conference" in Cairo in December, 1957, was thus an anticlimax to the original Bandung Conference. In attendance were some 500 representatives from forty-five countries (compared with twenty-nine at Bandung), with the difference, however, that except for the Communist governments most of the governments of the two continents declined to participate. The bitter pill was sweetened by applying a new title—"People's Bandung" —to distinguish the conference from the original, official Bandung. The composition of the Cairo conference was similar to that of the peace congresses—the delegates represented private, sometimes small, leftist and pro-Soviet groups. There was now no reason for the Soviet government to abstain from being represented at an Asian-African conference, and in Cairo its speakers claimed to be carrying on and developing "further" the program of Bandung. The Soviet Union was represented by delegates from its Asian Moslem republics—to prove that it belonged to the bloc of Asian-African nations. Sharaf Rashidov, the Uzbek, headed the Soviet delegation. Soviet delegate A. A. Arzumanyan told a committee of the conference: "We are ready to help you as brother helps brother. Tell us what you need and we will help you and send, to the best of our abilities, money in the form of loans

[1] For example, when the King of Nepal visited the Soviet Union in June, 1958.

or aid."[2] The Soviet and Chinese speakers dominated the conference; the role of the neutrals was reduced to a minimum, and a tiny opposition was silenced.

Although President Nasser did not appear at the conference, he permitted the organization of a permanent headquarters (of the "Council"), with a ten-man secretariat, in Cairo, and promised about 30,000 dollars a year toward its expenses. This was the main gain for Moscow. The headquarters, among the secretaries of which were one Russian and one Chinese, were to serve as a base for activity in Africa —a continent that was then attracting increasing attention. The conference appealed "to all countries of Asia and Africa to create national committees of solidarity" where such did not already exist.[3]

Further conferences on the same pattern which followed in 1958 and 1959 yielded diminishing results. In October, 1958, a "Conference of Writers of Asia and Africa" took place in Soviet Tashkent, thus negating the claim of real neutrality. Fifty countries were represented at the writers' conference. Again a permanent committee was set up to foster liaison. After the close of the conference a large group of delegates went to Moscow, where they were received by Khrushchev.[4] An "economic conference" in Cairo was held in December, 1958, and a large "Youth Conference" in February, 1959; at the latter, however, President Nasser received more plaudits than anyone else.[5]

The opening of the gates to the Middle East by the Soviet Union in 1955–56 had been a major achievement of Khrushchev's new course toward the "uncommitted."

Moscow tried to obtain recognition by the West of its status as a Middle Eastern power; it proposed to the Western powers a joint proclamation of "principles on peace and security in the Near and Middle East." In notes dispatched on February 12, 1957, the Soviet government outlined a six-point program, the most important item of which was an agreement "not to deliver arms to the countries of the Middle East." More important to the Soviet government, however,

[2] *The New York Times*, December 28, 1957.
[3] *Pravda*, December 28, 1957, and January 3 and 4, 1958; *The New York Times*, December 29, 1957, and January 2, 3, and 4, 1958; *New Times*, Moscow, no. 52, December 26, 1957, no. 1, January 1, 1958, and no. 2, January 9, 1958.
[4] *Pravda*, June 15, September 28, October 6, 9, 10, 11, 13, 15, and 23, 1958.
[5] *Ibid.*, February 10, 1959; New York *Herald Tribune*, February 16, 1959; *The New York Times*, February 3 and 4, 1959.

The Arab Nations

than such an agreement would be the fact of being recognized as a Middle Eastern power and being received into a new four-power Middle East pact.

Britain, France, and the United States rejected the Soviet proposal (March 11); the Western governments were able to counter the Soviet suggestions by hints about the massive arms supplies furnished to the Middle East by the Soviet bloc, the developments in Hungary, etc. The exchange of notes and personal letters, which proceeded over a period of several months, bore no fruit.[6]

The Soviet Union had made gains among the Arab nations. Another pledge of Soviet economic and technical assistance to Egypt was made in November, 1957; at a time when Egypt was badly in need of grain, 100,000 tons of wheat were promised; trade agreements and agreements on cultural cooperation between Egypt and the Soviet satellites and Yugoslavia were signed.

In the West, and particularly in Britain, Egypt was seen as gradually drifting into the Soviet orbit. It was feared that, on Soviet orders, Suez Canal arrangements would be manipulated with the object of wrecking Western economy, and that in general the Soviet Union would pull the strings, since isolated Egypt would have to lean more and more on the East. More than half of Egypt's trade was already with the Soviet bloc, and the bulk of new credits would be expected to come from that side. From the exuberance with which the press of the Soviet bloc greeted the initial developments in Egypt, it would appear that similar expectations were held in Moscow: that "positive neutralism" would gradually develop into outright hostility to the West and close ties with the Soviet bloc, and that this would be a first stage of a definite Soviet move into the Arab world. What Stalin had tried and failed to achieve by his crude methods was to be made possible by a more subtle approach on the part of Khrushchev's government: loans, arms, industrialization, and technical help rather than violent upheavals and a distinct Communist political victory would bring about the gradual evolution of the "neutralist" country into a "real democracy."

Soviet hopes in regard to Egypt did not materialize, and by the

[6] The new Soviet notes were dated April 12; the Western replies, June 12. In addition, Bulganin exchanged personal letters with the prime ministers of Britain and France; the latter were repetitions of the formal diplomatic correspondence.

end of 1957, in the newly stabilized situation, Egypt seemed to be moving away.

For a time Syria appeared the most "progressive" and promising Arab nation, and there was hope that Damascus would replace Cairo as the center of pro-Soviet trends in the Middle East. This hope, too, was soon frustrated.

In neither Egypt nor Syria did developments take the desired and expected course. Khrushchev's thesis that extensive Soviet aid could supplement, and to a degree be a substitute for, the local Communist party as a lever of progress proved wrong, and the issue of the relationship between Communism and the "underdeveloped" countries, which had been chased out the door, returned through the window as if to aggravate the situation.

As seen from Moscow, Syria had begun, in 1957, to play a new role. The stores of arms supplied by the Soviet bloc to Syria were intact, and new shipments were arriving; political groups sympathetic to Moscow were more numerous and influential in Syria than in Egypt. The Syrian Communist Party, though illegal, operated in the open, and its leader, Khaled Bagdash, was a member of the Parliament. A group of young leftist Syrian officers were gaining influence; unlike the officers involved in the Naguib-Nasser plot in Cairo a few years before, they were openly and actively pro-Soviet because, in their view, of all the governments, only Moscow had proved its ability to help the Arab nations.

Beginning in the middle of August, developments in Syria occurred rapidly. On August 13 it was announced that an "American plot" had been discovered; three days later a purge of the army began, in the course of which the leftist officers took over the leading posts, while another group of officers were arrested for "plotting" against the government.

The distinct trend to the left was viewed with sympathy by the Soviet press; *New Times* now spoke of a "democratic Syria"—a distinction that Egypt had not earned. In September, Soviet warships arrived for a visit at the Syrian port of Latakia. Tension was rising, and Syria's neighbors were alarmed. On August 23, after the Syrian government had expelled three members of the United States Embassy, the United States State Department dispatched Loy Henderson, a Deputy Under-Secretary, on a tour of Turkey, Lebanon, Jordan, and Iraq. When Henderson returned, early in September, the State Department reported that concern about developments in Syria was prevalent among Syria's neighbors and that Syria might succumb to "international Communism"; it was believed possible that Syria, in one way or another, might become a Soviet satellite. On September 19 Secretary Dulles told the United Nations General Assembly that in Syria "political power is being increasingly taken over by those who depend on Moscow." Additional American arms were airlifted to the countries of the Middle East, and Turkey massed an armed force on the Syrian border.

It was a moot question whether and to what extent Moscow was the initiator in the Syrian developments of those months. Students of Arab affairs and authorities on the Middle East have disagreed on this issue. Walter Z. Laquer, for example, maintains that it was "doubtful whether Moscow had anything to do with this crisis, or whether it knew about it beforehand. As far as the Soviet Union was concerned, the crisis was entirely unnecessary and perhaps harmful."[7] In Mr. Laquer's view, Russia's aims in Syria were only "to make Syria an ally (or client state) rather than a satellite."[8]

However, exact information in the possession of Western foreign offices left no doubt that Moscow really expected to acquire Syria as a satellite; Moscow's active role was great. The London *Times* reported, concerning Communist leadership in Syria (which certainly acted in accordance with Moscow plans), that it was striving toward power and that Khaled Bagdash was "a leading, though little publicized actor; he is the most dominating personality in Syrian politics in spite of lack of office."[9] Syria, President Nasser stated later, was receiving "inspiration and money from abroad."[10]

Soviet total support, including diplomatic protection and military moves, was promised and given the leftist groups in Damascus. The Soviet-Syrian version of the developments was that the Americans, specifically John Foster Dulles, were the authors of an anti-Syrian plot. In an interview with James Reston of *The New York Times*,[11] Khru-

[7] Walter Z. Laquer, *The Soviet Union and the Middle East*, New York, Frederick A. Praeger, 1959, p. 256.
[8] *Ibid.*, p. 254.
[9] *The Times*, London, August 21, 1957.
[10] *The New York Times*, March 14, 1959.
[11] *Ibid.*, October 10, 1957.

shchev said: "The instructions Henderson was carrying out are known. He tried to organize an attack by Arab countries against Syria." Later, pressed by W. R. Hearst, Jr., for a clearer answer concerning the "instruction" to Henderson, Khrushchev said only, "We have received this information through third or fourth persons," and recommended that Hearst make inquiries in Washington.[12] The State Department denied the existence of such an "instruction."

Moscow maintained that Turkey had been incited to start a war on Syria; that Turkey had agreed to certain conditions, namely that the war be limited in scope;[13] and that a new government for Syria, which was to assume office after the victory, had been organized in Ankara. Moscow pretended to be in possession of a secret order of the Turkish General Staff to begin the offensive on a certain day in October. This "Turkish order," however, was never made public by Moscow.

Khrushchev sent messages to seven West European socialist parties stating that the Soviet Union would not "stand idle" in case of a Turkish-Syrian war; in these messages the United States was pointed to as the main culprit in the affair. "Turkey would not last a day," Khrushchev told James Reston.[14] In an interview with British Laborite Aneurin Bevan, Khrushchev explained the Soviet version: "There are gentlemen from Syria in Istanbul under the protection of the Turkish Government who are to manoeuver themselves into office in Syria. Once they are in office something will happen and if it does not happen it will be made to happen. . . . It will be pretended that Syrian independence is in danger and that then this Syrian Government will invite the Turks to enter."[15] (It appears likely that Marshal Zhukov's military intelligence, misled by an informant in Ankara or Damascus, had come into possession of false "documents.")

On October 19, TASS issued a further statement giving numerous but incorrect details of Loy Henderson's negotiations in the Middle Eastern countries; among his contacts, as listed by TASS, were "refugees from Syria who had participated in the recently-discovered conspiracy"; TASS maintained that Henderson had discussed preparations for a possible internal upheaval in Syria, without foreign intervention,

[12] *Pravda,* November 29, 1957.
[13] *New Times,* Moscow, no. 37, September 12, 1957, pp. 1–2.
[14] *The New York Times,* October 11, 1957.
[15] *The Tribune,* London, October 18, 1957.

The Arab Nations

aimed at the removal of pro-Soviet military and civilian leaders. The Soviet Union, TASS concluded, "will take all the necessary steps to come to the aid of the victims of an aggression." The next day Turkey said the Soviet accusations were "absurd" and "nonsensical lies."

The conflict entered the acute stage in the middle of October. Border incidents involving Turkey and Syria increased the tension; border guards started shooting. In a letter to Sir Leslie Munro, President of the United Nations General Assembly, Andrei Gromyko stated that the attack on Syria "is to take place after the Turkish elections on October 27." A photocopy of the "document" proving Turkey's aggressive intentions mentioned the date of October 28 for the start of the attack. Although the United States State Department declared the document a "forgery," and the Arab delegates to whom Gromyko had shown it called it a "hoax," [16] Moscow remained firm. On October 23 the Tiflis radio announced that Marshal Konstantin Rokossovsky, Deputy Defense Minister, was taking command of the Transcaucasian Military District (which borders on Turkey). In Damascus the government decided to distribute arms to the civilian "Popular Resistance Movement" and to cancel all officers' leaves. Hysteria reigned in Syria. The Soviet press sounded a note of great alarm: "Put an end to the provocations against Syria," *Pravda* demanded on October 20. "The imperialist plot against Syria must be thwarted" (October 22). The imperialists intend to grab the riches of Syria, it said the next day. On October 24, an entire page of four-page *Pravda* was devoted to the "menace to Syria and peace."

The war scare—the threatening declarations, the shipments of arms, the dispatch of armies and navies—stopped suddenly a few days after these attacks in the Soviet press. It was hinted that the dismissal of Marshal Zhukov from all his party and governmental posts was the consequence of his blunders in the Syrian affair. On October 29 Khrushchev appeared at a reception at the Turkish Embassy in Moscow—a sensational gesture in view of the severely strained Soviet-Turkish relations that had prevailed for many years. Khrushchev, asked to explain his appearance and to say whether it was a peace gesture, said, "Yes, this is a gesture toward peace." At the same reception he made the announcement of the dismissal of Marshal Zhukov. It is possible that Zhukov was the scapegoat in the inglorious affair.

[16] *The New York Times*, November 1, 1957.

The days of Syria's pro-Soviet orientation, however, were numbered. What Turkey and the United States could not achieve—an end to Syria's drift into the Soviet fold—was to be achieved with the help of another Arab nation. The most active groups behind the merger of Syria and Egypt were the anti-Communist elements in Syria. While Syria's Communists placed their reliance on Russia, their adversaries expected to get help from Egypt, whose troops had landed in Syria on October 13, when the tension was at its height. On February 1, 1958, President Nasser announced the merger of the two countries into the United Arab Republic. Although stressing friendly relations with Moscow, Nasser, by this action, had carried out one of the most distinctly anti-Soviet operations in the Middle East. Soviet hopes of Syria as a base, as an ally, and eventually as a member of the Soviet bloc had to be given up. Communist activity in Syria would now be impossible; outright pro-Soviet moves in the army would be suppressed, and the Egyptian one-party political system would be extended to Syria. Nasser's spectacular move was one of extreme defiance of the Soviet Union and an assertion of his independence. A year later Nasser stated that before the merger with Egypt, Syrian Communists had planned a coup.[17]

These developments posed a difficult dilemma for Moscow. To continue help to and "friendly relations" with Nasser entailed the sacrifice, not only of hopes and expectations, but of the best friends the Soviet government had in the middle East. Breaking off ties with Egypt would appear as an acknowledgment of Khrushchev's blunders, and of the unreality of his designs. Khrushchev could not afford to show his weak points; he continued to pretend that nothing serious had happened in Syria. For a few days after the merger the Soviet press remained silent, but then it resumed the "friendly attitude." The Soviet government was one of the first to recognize the United Arab Republic.

Three months after the merger, President Nasser visited Moscow and was abundantly feted; Syria was not mentioned publicly. Khrushchev stressed Soviet aid to the Arab countries fighting for independence from imperialism; independence from Moscow, the underlying theme of the Syrian issue, was passed over in silence. Moreover, the

[17] Speech in Bombay, April 16, 1959 (*The New York Times*, April 17, 1959).

Soviet government soon agreed to an initial loan of about 100 million dollars to finance the construction of the Aswan Dam in Egypt; other projects, too, were included in the program.

In the meantime Khaled Bagdash had gone into exile and found asylum in Czechoslovakia. The Communist Party became illegal in Syria, and about two hundred Syrian Communists were arrested in December, 1958.[18]

Syria presented the first instance involving the issue of Arab nationalism to face the Soviet Union in its most acute form—that of a merger of Arab states. In this case Moscow suppressed its doubts and stressed its understanding of and sympathy for the Arab movement. The issue of Arab nationalism loomed more importantly when Iraq, the second significant Arab nation, broke off its ties with the West and rejected the old political system.

2. NO STRINGS ATTACHED

The political map of the Middle East was changing rapidly. Only two years before the events just described, Egypt, seemingly on the threshold of becoming a Soviet satellite, had been receiving high praise in Moscow, while Iraq, the Arab anchor of the Baghdad Pact, had been the target of violent attacks on the part of both Moscow and Cairo. The extinction of Syria as a sovereign state in February, 1958, had, it appeared, destroyed Moscow's base in the Arab world.

On July 14, 1958, however, the pro-Western anti-Soviet government of Iraq was overthrown, King Faisal II and Premier Nuri as-Said were killed, and a revolutionary government under Abdul Karim Kassem was set up.

The revolution in Iraq was a cause of rejoicing in the Soviet bloc. In Iraq's internal affairs the upheaval meant liberation for numbers of political prisoners; revival of the Communist movement; press and radio facilities for the leftist groups; and arrests, trials, and executions of leaders and agents of the fallen regime. On the international level the upheaval apparently signified the end of the hated Baghdad Pact. "The Baghdad Pact without Baghdad"—sneered the Soviet press.

The upheaval in Iraq was followed by the landing of British forces in Jordan and United States forces in Lebanon, at the request

[18] *The New York Times*, January 2, 1959.

of the Jordanian and Lebanese governments; there was fear of an imminent Soviet military operation. President Nasser, then on a visit to Yugoslavia, flew to Moscow, and in an eight-hour talk with Khrushchev obtained Khrushchev's promise not to interfere directly in Iraq. Large well-organized anti-American and anti-British demonstrations, however, took place in Moscow on July 18; the slogan was "Hands Off the Arab Lands!" At the United States Embassy windows were smashed and walls smeared with colored ink.

From the Soviet strategic and political viewpoint, Iraq was perhaps the most important of the Arab nations. Situated only about a hundred and fifty miles from the Soviet frontier—a distance covered in twenty minutes by a modern airplane—and separated from Russia by Iranian and Turkish territory, Iraq could serve as a Soviet bridge to Asia Minor and the Arab world in general; she could also serve as the first Soviet satellite in the Middle East, a base of military and economic expansion. Because of her oil resources, her significance in the cold war was certainly not less than that of Suez. After the July upheaval, the small Communist group in Iraq grew rapidly. Of its leading "cadres," about one hundred and fifty were liberated from prisons; a score of emigrants promptly arrived from Iran; others, in growing numbers, began to arrive from Russia.

If Iraq might serve as a Soviet bridge to the Arab countries, the prospective state of "Kurdistan" might, in turn, serve as a bridge from the Soviet Caucasus to Iraq. The Kurd nation, with a population of probably 3 to 4 million, is in an area which belongs to Turkey, Iran, Iraq, and Syria; the Soviet Union maintained that almost 50,000 Kurds lived in adjoining areas within the Soviet Union. A small upper stratum of the Kurdish intelligentsia had been striving for several decades to achieve nationhood and create a Kurdish state. To accomplish this, the opposition and resistance of one or another of the nations involved would have to be overcome, and a "Kurdistan" could emerge only if one of the great powers, in its own interest, raised the flag of Kurd "independence" and gave military help. In 1945–46, during the Soviet occupation of northern Iran, the embryo of a new "Kurd Republic," actually a Soviet satellite, emerged, with Mehabad (in western Iran) as its capital. A Kurd militia, which received arms from the Red Army, allegedly had a strength of 60,000 men. After the withdrawal of Soviet troops from northern Iran, the new "Kurd Republic" collapsed.

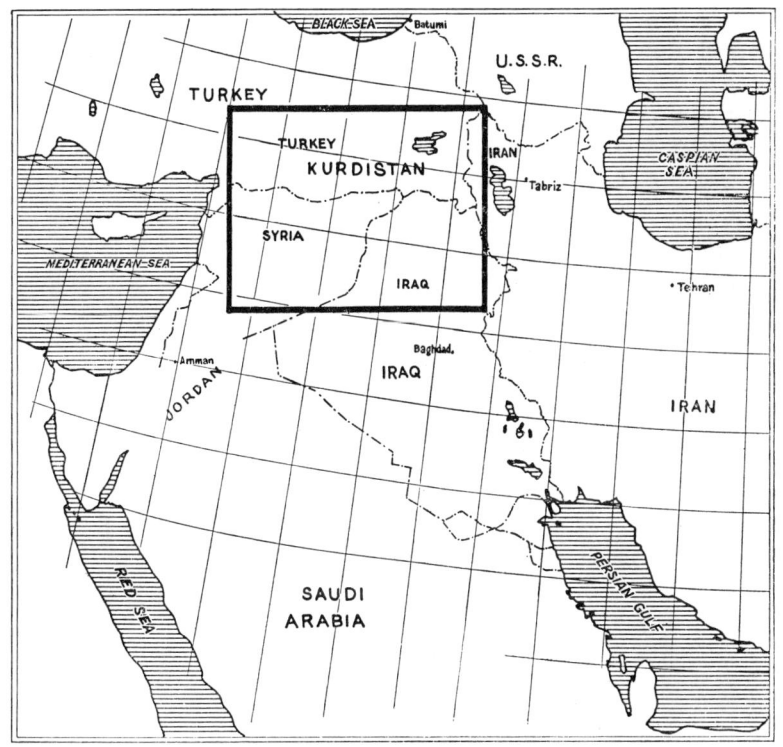

MAP 5. KURDISTAN

(According to the *Large Soviet Encyclopedia*)

At a Middle Eastern Communist conference in Damascus in November, 1947, the program of a "Kurdish State" was again proclaimed. Trying to build up the prestige of the Kurds and their future state, Soviet literature exaggerated not only their importance and the "progressive" character of their national movement, but even their numerical size.[19] With the same intention, Soviet literature emphasized the role of the Soviet Union as one of the "five" nations inhabited by Kurds, although the number of Kurds living on Soviet territory, according to the Soviet census of 1939, was less than 46,000.

[19] The first edition of the *Large Soviet Encyclopedia* (published in 1939, before the Kurd issue had become important for Soviet Middle East policy) gave the total Kurd population as 3.5 to 4 million; the second edition (1953) estimated it at 7 million.

After the upheaval in Iraq, several thousand Kurds, or descendants of Kurdish immigrants, living in Russia were shipped to Iraq. Moscow officially confirmed this fact, but insisted that the transfer was a process of repatriation and that, contrary to Cairo assertions, the "repatriates" were unarmed. (The arms were shipped separately.) At the head of these "repatriated" Kurds stood Mullah Mustafa el Barzani,[20] one of the leaders of the short-lived "Independent Kurdistan Republic" of 1946; he was sentenced to death in Iraq.

Rapprochement of the Soviet bloc with Iraq proceeded rapidly. Soviet and satellite arms and advisers began to arrive in November, 1958; trade missions one after another followed; a treaty between Iraq and China was signed in January, 1959. On the other hand, "Nasserism," tantamount to a pan-Arab movement under Egyptian leadership, was assuming a new meaning for the Soviet; unification of Arab states, which was possible only under Egyptian leadership, was violently rejected; to the Communist bloc, Nasser was an "imperialist" reactionary leader: "Nasserism," stated openly a leader of the Iraqi Communists, "is the ideological tool of the Egyptian big bourgeoisie. Why does he [Nasser] attack us, why did he arrest hundreds of Communists in Egypt and Syria? Nasser is about to fraternize with Imperialism."[21]

Khaled Bagdash, the Syrian Communist leader, toured the capitals of the Soviet bloc, making violent anti-Nasser speeches and juxtaposing with Nasser's United Arab Republic a loose federation of Syria and Egypt, with "autonomy" in internal affairs and freedom granted to the Communist party. Addressing the Twenty-first Congress of the Communist Party in Moscow (February 2, 1959), Bagdash unfolded this program of reconstruction of the United Arab Republic: two separate governments for Egypt and Syria, with far-reaching autonomy in internal affairs, supplemented by a federal government with limited jurisdiction (military affairs, foreign policy). "Democratic freedoms" —meaning legal facilities for leftist parties—were part of the program. The Soviet Party Congress greeted his speech with "stormy approval." Later, President Nasser stated that at that Congress the foundation had been laid for an "All-Arab Communist underground."[22]

[20] *Time*, New York, December 29, 1958.
[21] *Der Tagesspiegel*, Berlin, January 23, 1959.
[22] *The New York Times*, April 17, 1959.

No Strings Attached

Khrushchev himself came out in defense of Arab Communism and against President Nasser:

> Since in the United Arab Republic opinions were recently expressed against the ideas of Communism, and accusations were made against Communists, I, as a Communist, consider it necessary to state, at the Congress of our Communist party, that it is wrong to accuse Communists of supporting efforts toward weakening and disuniting national movements in the fight against imperialism. On the contrary, there exist no more staunch and devoted supporters in the cause of the fight against colonialism than the Communists. . . . It is wrong to accuse Communists of being against the national interests of the Arab peoples. It is well known that Communists, among them also those in Israel, are fighting against Zionism.[23]

The Cairo press rebuked Khrushchev. Nasser wrote a letter to the Soviet premier, who replied in a lengthy message that was not made public. The Moscow-Cairo friendship, which had appeared to be reestablished, broke down a few weeks later, again on the crucial issue of Arab unity.

It had been a consistent principle of Soviet foreign policy to oppose and, if possible, prevent, *rapprochement* or alliance between nearby nations, in particular a merger, and especially in Europe and the Middle East. The possible emergence of a new power where before small, impotent nations had existed, the possible alliance of such

---

[23] Khrushchev's Report at the Twenty-first Extraordinary Party Congress (*Pravda*, January 28, 1959). On Zionism and Israel, however, the Soviet course was not in every respect identical with that of the nationalist Arabs; the latter wanted a more aggressive policy on the part of Moscow, while Moscow did not approve the program of liquidation of the State of Israel. *Pravda* printed in full Mikoyan's answers to queries of an Arab editor at a press conference in Baghdad on April 15, 1960:

"Yuni at-Tai: If the Soviet Union is a friend of the Arabs . . . why does the Soviet Union give support to Israel? If the Soviet Union supports the people of the revolution of July 14, why doesn't it support the slogan of the Arab refugees: 'We shall return'? Why does the Soviet Union support the policy of the imperialists on this issue as it was in Stalin's time and is continued now?

"Mikoyan: I do not understand why you need all these inventions which are distorting the policy of the Soviet Union. The Soviet Union did not create the Palestine issue. The Soviet Union is not responsible for the expulsion of the Arabs from Palestine. You know very well that Israel is influenced by England and the United States, and that the Soviet Union has no influence there at all. We have recognized and are recognizing the legal rights of the Palestine Arabs to return to their land. . . .

"Yuni at-Tai: . . . We are grateful to the Soviet Union for its policy toward the Arab nations, except for its position on the Palestine question.

"Mikoyan: I have already stated my views on that question.

"Yuni at-Tai: Your answer does not satisfy me.

"Mikoyan: I don't have a charm with which I could satisfy all of you." (*Pravda*, April 18, 1960.)

a new power with the West, and its integrated military force—all these were dangers that must be fought before they became too threatening. Moscow had successfully prevented the formation of a strong alliance of the three Baltic states before the war and had fought the "Northern" alliance. The postwar Soviet course had in view, in the first place, non-Soviet nations, for instance the "Common Market," Benelux, the Balkan Federation; but even regarding Communist-ruled states it is doubtful that a merger among any of them would be approved without Moscow's participation. In the highly unlikely case of a Communist upheaval in West Germany, the Soviet government would certainly look askance at any projected merger of the two German states and the emergence of a real Communist power in the heart of Europe.

The same principle was applied to the Arab countries. Separately, each of these countries—Egypt, Syria, Jordan, even Saudi Arabia and Iraq—was welcome as a Soviet ally; but a merger among them, total or partial, could be dangerous. A strong Arab power able to ally itself with Turkey and Iran, and with the West, was not what the Soviet government wanted to create in the Middle East. Moreover, federation or merger of Arab countries might eradicate the influence of pro-Soviet groups and Communist prestige; Egyptian supremacy might lead to the suppression of the relatively stable, though clandestine, Communist groups in the northern Arab states closest to Russia—Syria, Jordan, and, later, Iraq. The decline of the initially pro-British Arab League was satisfying to Moscow; but now Egypt tried consistently to replace the League with a much stronger Cairo-led Pan-Arab combination.

Having tacitly acquiesced in the Egyptian-Syrian merger (and probably having regretted it soon afterwards), Khrushchev definitely opposed Nasser's inclination to unite with Iraq and create a real Arab power almost at the gates of the Soviet Union. "President Nasser," he told a large gathering of diplomats in Moscow on March 16, 1959, "insists on the incorporation of the Iraq Republic into the United Arab Republic . . ."; but Soviet help to national movements, he said, "does not mean that countries which broke the fetters of colonialism must necessarily join some Union of states, submit to one government, or follow the guidance of one leader." [24]

Nasser reacted violently. In a speech from a balcony in Damascus

[24] *Pravda*, March 17, 1959.

No Strings Attached

he attacked the Soviet premier. "We do not accept Khrushchev's defense of the Communist minority in our country because we fought to get rid of foreign protection." The Communists in the United Arab Republic, he said, must be crushed as "agents" of a foreign nation and ideology. He charged that British agents and Communists—a "small dissident group"—had formed an alliance to smash Arab nationalism. "This goal never will be realized." [25]

At about the same time, *Pravda* wrote:

> Events of recent times have justified those Arabs who believe, for instance, that the unification of Iraq with the U.A.R. under present conditions would not increase the strength of the Arab peoples in their struggle for independence, economic development and progress.[26]

Pravda then supplied the ideological foundation for the Soviet rejection of a united Arab state:

> ... one thing is clear: Unification will benefit the peoples only if the necessary economic and political conditions become ripe for it. The existence not only of similarities but also of quite profound differences in economic, political and intellectual development among the Arab countries requires statesmen to take special account of all circumstances that are important for the success of any form of state unification, whether it be confederation, federation or any other form of unification of two or more states. In the final analysis, premature unification does not strengthen but undermines the unity of peoples. It would benefit only enemies of the freedom of peoples, only the imperialists.[27]

Officially, relations between the Soviet Union and Egypt remained normal, even good; new economic and financial agreements were concluded. The breach, however, was deep. Egypt had served as a pillar of "positive neutralism"; along with India's her policy had been praised as a model of a new course in world affairs. Even more than India, Egypt furnished patterns for united neutralist-Communist action against the "imperialists."

The Soviet press continued to stress the abundant Soviet economic

---

[25] *The New York Times*, March 21, 1959. The coolness in relations was also seen in the fact that the Afro-Asian Organization for Economic Cooperation in Cairo on May 2, 1959, barred the Soviet Union from membership on the grounds that she had not taken part in the Bandung Conference of 1955.
[26] *Pravda*, March 30, 1959.
[27] *Ibid.*

help to the underdeveloped countries,[28] and Khrushchev never renounced either his course toward the neutrals or his emphasis on economic aid. For him and for his press, "Aswan" (in Egypt) and "Bhilai" (in India) continued to be popular slogans. At the Twenty-first Congress, in a reference to the metallurgical plant in India, Khrushchev exclaimed:

> Let the first cast iron of this plant be the symbol of the strengthening friendship of the peoples of the Soviet Union and India! [Stormy applause].
> Let all the machinations of the imperialists who are striving to prevent the growth of Soviet-Indian friendship, of our common fight for peace, of the triumph of the principles of peaceful coexistence, perish in the fire of this blast furnace. [Prolonged applause].[29]

The slogans, however, had lost much of their effectiveness. Now India was actually putting distance between herself and the Soviet Union, and Egypt was becoming unreliable; Iraq was no substitute for either India or Egypt. Had it been right, then, to place such reliance on supplies of weapons and loans in billions of rubles? Was it right to ally Communism so closely with heterogeneous, non-Communist movements of underdeveloped nations?

Another important inference from the history of Khrushchevism in action related to the widely announced claim of "no strings attached" in connection with Soviet loans, credits, trade agreements, and other forms of economic aid. In a formal sense, the claim proved correct: no political conditions were set in regard to any Soviet economic agreements with either the non-Communist underdeveloped countries or members of the Soviet bloc; nor were political conditions prescribed, as far as is known, in the negotiations for such agreements. In reality,

---

[28] *International Affairs*, no. 9, September, 1959, pp. 24–25, reviewed the operations of the period 1955–59: the Soviet Union had given credits to:

	Millions of Rubles
India	1,000
Egypt	1,100
Afghanistan	480
Indonesia	427
Ceylon	120
Argentina	400
Iraq	550
Ethiopia	400

[29] Khrushchev's concluding speech at the Twenty-first Extraordinary Party Congress (*Pravda*, February 6, 1959).

The Imperfect Monolith 481

however, there were three kinds of political "strings," one or two of which were usually attached, in practice, to Soviet aid.

First, the receiving government, if it was "neutralist," was expected not to adhere to any pro-Western bloc and not to move from Group 3 to Group 4 of the world's nations.[30] In certain cases the connection between Soviet aid and loyalty to "neutralism" was made obvious: when, along with the agreement on aid, the receiving government pledged neutrality in a special statement (as, for example, the statements given by the king of Afghanistan and his mission in Moscow in July, 1957).

Second, if the receiving government was a "socialist" government, or was expected to join the Soviet bloc, a turn to neutralism (from Group 2 to Group 3) would result in the withdrawal of the promised aid even if an agreement had been concluded (for example, the cancellation of the one-billion-ruble loan to Yugoslavia in 1958, after the Belgrade government refused to sign the Declaration of adherence to the Soviet bloc).

Third, receiving governments in areas close to the Soviet Union must not merge or federate (for example, Egypt and Iraq).

3. THE IMPERFECT MONOLITH

Restoration of a firm and dynamic international Communist organization under Soviet leadership—another of Khrushchev's guiding ideas in the first post-Stalin years—did not materialize either. Khrushchev's assumption that Stalin's personal shortcomings had barred the road to real international solidarity and that he, Khrushchev, would be able to prove the superiority of his methods over those of the late dictator proved wrong. After five years of strenuous efforts, after the sacrifice of much of Stalin's prestige, after modifications in the field of ideology, the bridge carefully built for the return of the heretics to the fold collapsed.

The fight for international Communist unity was waged not only for ideological reasons and the purity of Marxism-Leninism; there were more realistic issues at stake. Recognition of the Soviet Union as the head of the "socialist camp" was understood by all Communist parties as an oath of allegiance by the satellites to the command of

[30] See p. 330.

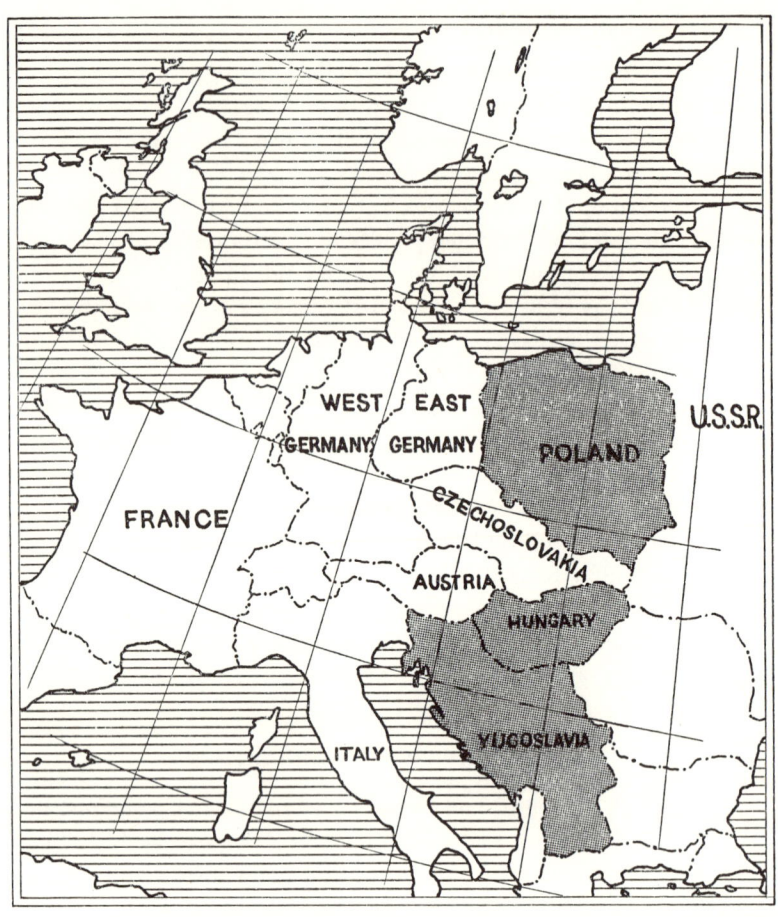

MAP 6. THE GEOPOLITICAL SIGNIFICANCE
OF NATIONAL COMMUNISM

Poland–Hungary–Yugoslavia; From the Baltic to the Adriatic Sea

Moscow. Yugoslavia had refused, as we have seen, to sign such an oath; to Tito, this would have meant, in the first place, subordination of his military forces to the Soviet command, dependence of his foreign policy on the Soviet course, breaking off of most of his ties with the West, and, last but not least, consultation with Moscow in the selection of suitable candidates for leadership. Tito saw no reason to accept this program; independence meant more to him than "monolithic unity."

The Imperfect Monolith

Tito's new defection evoked a storm in the Soviet Party and among the Communist parties loyal to Moscow. The December Plenum of the Central Committee of the Soviet Party (December 16–17, 1957), as we have seen, approved the Declaration signed by all the Communist parties (except Yugoslavia); it stressed again the "unshakable authority of the Soviet Union," and attacked "revisionism" as "the main danger." The Plenum's resolution approving the Declaration was the first shot in a new anti-Yugoslav campaign of the Communist parties loyal to Moscow.

The preparation of a new program for Yugoslav Communism, a draft of which was submitted to the "brotherly parties" for comment, set off a high-level theoretical fight. The draft program did not accept the traditional division of the world into two "camps"; while opposing the Western "blocs," it assumed a similarly negative attitude toward the Warsaw Pact. It emphasized equality between socialist nations; it condemned bureaucracy; it insisted on the necessity of a rapid "withering away" of the state. The press of the loyal Communist parties indulged in detailed criticism of the Yugoslav ideas. *Kommunist* of Moscow, which devoted much space to an examination of the draft program, rejected its main theses as contrary to Marxism-Leninism.[31] The full text of the draft was not published in Russia, however, and the critics concentrated their attention on revisionist ideas or terms picked at random. Tito took into consideration the criticisms of the draft program voiced by the orthodox Communist parties, but the main ideas of "Titoism" were retained in the final text. Consequently, the Soviet bloc abstained from sending greetings and speakers to the Yugoslav Congress in April, 1958, and only ambassadors of the "bloc" appeared, as observers, at the rally. When Yugoslav Vice-President Rankovich proceeded to make a sharp attack on the Soviet leaders, all of the envoys except the Poles walked out, actually slamming the door behind them.

The fury of the attack on Yugoslavia mounted with every passing week; the violence of the accusations was reminiscent of the Stalin era. The satellite press abounded in bitter antirevisionist statements, some of which the Soviet press reprinted in order to prove the unity inside its own camp. A Plenum of the Central Committee in Moscow early

---

[31] *Kommunist*, Moscow, no. 6, April, 1958, pp. 16–29.

in May, ostensibly convened to discuss the development of the chemical industry, devoted some time to a discussion of the Yugoslav deviation. It was decided to send Tito a strong message warning him of the consequences of his course and urging him to submit. The message, handed to Tito by the Soviet ambassador on May 10, was actually an ultimatum. It was rejected by Belgrade, which, in its reply, proposed conferences and discussions.

On May 11, a few hours before President Klimenti Voroshilov was scheduled to arrive in Belgrade, it was announced that the visit had been "postponed." A barrage of invective, condemnation, and demands for excommunication from all sides followed. Tito was the "Trojan horse of the imperialists," Khrushchev told a meeting in Berlin. "Renegades of the working class," wrote the Chinese *Red Flag*, and asked, "Is it not an impudence that they call themselves Communists?" [32]

The international Communist family was consumed by hatred. The hot international discussion revolved around theoretical problems, tenets of Marxism-Leninism, class struggle, and social revolution. But Tito was right when he openly stated that the issue behind the heavy smoke screen of theoretical disputes was his refusal to vow allegiance to the Soviet Union as the supreme leader. "The Yugoslav party program," Tito said on June 15, 1958, "was not the cause of the controversy but a pretext"; the real cause was Yugoslavia's refusal to sign the Declaration adopted in Moscow in November, 1957.

On May 27 the Soviet government dispatched a note to Yugoslavia in which it proposed to postpone for five years the two loans covered in the agreements of January 12, 1956, and August 1, 1956, totaling about 285 million dollars. The Yugoslav government would not agree to the postponement; in its reply of June 3, it maintained that the Soviet proposal amounted to a breach of agreements:

> The government of the Federal People's Republic of Yugoslavia should also call attention to the responsibility which will rest on the U.S.S.R. Government for the damage inflicted on the Yugoslav economy should the Soviet Government adhere to its position. In such case the F.P.R.Y. Government reserves the right to demand just compensation.[33]

[32] *Pravda*, June 30, 1958.
[33] *Ibid.*, July 1, 1958.

The Imperfect Monolith 485

Moscow's reply of June 28 to the Yugoslav note insisted on the thesis that the "Soviet Union strictly complies with its international obligations"; although it proposed to "discuss" the question in a conference, the reply was a definite refusal to reconsider the position on the loans. In fact, the large loans to Yugoslavia, which would be a burden for the Soviet treasury, would serve to increase Yugoslavia's military and industrial potential, and in the changed circumstances this appeared contrary to Soviet interests; the inevitable damage to the reputation of the Soviet resulting from a nonfulfillment of an obligation would have to be taken in stride.

Following Moscow, China began reprisals of her own against Yugoslavia. Peking ceased chartering Yugoslav ships and using Yugoslav ports. To punish the defecting "revisionists," it turned to "capitalist" Greece and Italy, paying them higher shipping rates.

At the height of the controversy with Yugoslavia, Imre Nagy, General Paul Maleter, and two other leaders of the Hungarian uprising of 1956 were executed. The official announcement from Budapest (June 16, 1958) stated that at a trial in Hungary nine persons had been found guilty of conspiracy and setting up a secret organization "with the aim of seizing power by force and overthrowing the Hungarian People's Democracy." Neither the date of the secret trial nor the place where it was held were made known. There were rumors that the trial was held in the Soviet Union. (In March of the same year Janos Kadar had given "a solemn word" to Tito that Nagy would not be brought to trial. On April 4 he told foreign newsmen that trying Nagy was "neither urgent nor important.") [34]

That Nagy's execution was a reprisal against his defender in Belgrade is beyond doubt. Even if the trial had taken place in Hungary, the execution could not have been carried out without Khrushchev's approval. Among Khrushchev's motives must have been his aim of breaking the newly formed ties between Yugoslavia and Hungary and isolating Tito from the other "people's democracies." In a vigorous note (June 23), the Yugoslav government protested against the Nagy trial and execution. The indictment, it said, had been a fraud, and the execution a second violation of Hungary's pledge of safe conduct to the Nagy group. The Nagy affair was reminiscent of the case of Laszlo

[34] *The New York Times*, June 18, 1958.

Rajk, another prominent Hungarian Communist leader, who was executed for the crime of "Titoism" nine years before.

In his fight against the emancipation movement within his orbit, Khrushchev had reverted to the methods of Stalinism.

The embryo of a Polish-Yugoslav alliance which, though losing vigor, continued to exist after the Moscow Declaration of November, 1957, was a danger that recalled the years 1945–47. In the framework of the two-nation association, each member had its particular place, and it was hard to say whose "deviation" was a greater threat to Soviet leadership. An estrangement of Poland from the Soviet Union would perhaps be more ominous than the estrangement of Yugoslavia. Yugoslavia was bold, aggressive, defiant, a bacillus of a contagious disease; Poland, which lay on the great East-West highway, was a bridge to East Germany and West Germany, and on her loyalty to Moscow the imperial structure hinged.

Reluctant to comply with all of Khrushchev's wishes, Gomulka continued for a time to stress Poland's independence and maintain friendly relations with Tito. Poland tried to interpret the November thesis of Soviet guidance in a restricted sense: yes, Russia was historically the first to enter the path of socialism, but this was not tantamount to her right to control the socialist camp in the present. This interpretation was not in accord with the wishes of Moscow and its allies. Significantly, a book reviewing the foreign policies of the members of the "camp," published in Moscow in 1958, omitted discussion of Poland except for an analysis of the Rapacki plan.[35]

In February, 1958, Poland signed another credit agreement with the United States; about the same time it signed an economic cooperation agreement with Yugoslavia. A visit of Yugoslavia's highest leaders to Warsaw was scheduled for May. When the Yugoslav draft of a Communist program was circulated in the capitals of the bloc, the Poles printed it in their monthly theoretical magazine; although critical comments had been made, the issue of the magazine was withdrawn from sale.

New clouds had meantime been gathering over Yugoslavia, and Gomulka's position was becoming difficult; at the Yugoslav Congress

---

[35] *Voprosy vneshnei politiki stran sotsialisticheckogo lagerya (Sbornik statei)* (Issues of Foreign Policies of the Countries of the Socialist Camp), Moscow, 1958.

The Imperfect Monolith 487

his representatives had been almost isolated when they tried to soften the conflict. Poland's mildness no longer suited the Soviet designs; Tito had to cancel his visit to Warsaw.

Having embarked on a vigorous course against Yugoslavia, Khrushchev now took a similar line toward Poland. It was intolerable that on the Nagy issue Poland was standing aside, refusing to approve the execution, and it was intolerable that Warsaw's attitude toward Yugoslav revisionism and toward the West were different from those of Moscow, Peking, and the other members of the bloc. The modicum of independence won by Poland in October, 1956, was too much. At the end of June, 1958, Moscow indicated that it was no longer prepared to tolerate Warsaw's aloofness. Gomulka faced the demand: he must march in step with the rest of the bloc.

Isolated, impotent against the giant neighbor, without a strong ally on the rest of the continent, Poland had to bow and accept Khrushchev's demands. To Moscow this was a *revanche* for the abject defeat in the crucial fall of 1956; to Gomulka it meant realignment and synchronization with the Soviet Union—the end of a chapter in the biography of a hero. In a long speech in Gdansk, Gomulka, accepting Khrushchev's terms, said:

> By its erroneous revisionist theories the Communist League of Yugoslavia isolates, divides Yugoslavia from the community of Socialist countries and thus inflicts damage to the united forces of the Socialist countries and to the entire international workers' movement. . . . Nothing, absolutely nothing justifies their [the Yugoslav comrades'] stand in the present conflict, which is different from the conflict of 1948–50. Today the blame is on Yugoslavia.[36]

On the Nagy issue, Gomulka said:

> Under the pressure of the growing wave of counterrevolution and hostility toward the people's rule, Imre Nagy, a revisionist, was moving step by step towards a surrender to the counterrevolution. He carried out its designs by killing the Socialist order in Hungary. He announced the secession of Hungary from the Warsaw Treaty and appealed for help to the imperialist countries. . . . Only naïve people can be fooled by the reactionary propaganda which has been spun around the Nagy affair. . . . Therefore we have always strengthened and shall strengthen the solidarity and fraternal collaboration with our

[36] *Pravda*, June 30, 1958.

mighty neighbor—the Soviet Union—and with all Socialist countries on the basis of internationalism, friendship and equality.[37]

From then on Gomulka remained true to his new course.

Although the government, under the powerful pressure from the East, had to revise its concessions to the church, restrict freedom of association, rebuild a secret police, and prohibit criticism of the Soviet Union, Poland, in her internal political system, remained the most liberal country in the Soviet orbit. In foreign affairs, however, including relationships within the "socialist camp," she no longer deviated from the Moscow line. The "German danger"—the German claims to Poland's western, formerly German, territories—was stressed as the official basis of the Soviet-Polish alliance. Actually, *raison d'état*—meaning realistic appraisal of Poland's situation, the strength of the contending powers, and prospects in case of a new conflict with Moscow—was the justification of the unpopular alliance with the East. Negation of things Russian, including the Russian language and Russian literature, and emotional attachment to the West, combined with hopelessness and despair, marked the state of mind of the Polish nation. Gomulka lost much of his colorful personality, and some of his stature. Poland was firmly integrated into the bloc, but under her soil were volcanic forces, ever ready to erupt.

[37] *Ibid.*

CHAPTER 3

NEW IMPETUS IN CHINA

Having isolated the "revisionists" and eliminated all consistent opposition, the Soviet bloc was able to resume its moves and drives in world affairs. Communist China and East Germany—the easternmost and westernmost members—had emerged as the two most dynamic and aggressive forces of the "socialist camp." Their political courses, and in particular their places in the framework of Soviet foreign policy, were, however, different.

The Chinese Communist Party, as related above, like its Soviet counterpart had had its own period of weakness and vacillation. In the end it managed to suppress the "one hundred flowers" and to overcome, by methods which had become conventional in the East, the "contradictions among the people." At least since early 1958, Peking had felt free to resume the multilateral drives which soon made the Chinese party the most extreme and, in every sense the most "leftist," among the Communist parties and governments. The vast area which was opening up in Asia, and the easy successes of the Peking government in its own orbit, greatly increased Chinese aspirations.

Peking had never been entirely satisfied with the amendments made by Khrushchev to Stalinism; de-Stalinization in Russia had gone too far for the tastes of Mao's party. Khrushchev's belief in nonviolent revolution as a path to socialism did not go down too well either, and his belief—contrary to the teachings of Lenin—that wars are not inevitable did not convince the Chinese Communists; and his appeal to the "neutrals" was considered at best a stratagem. Even deeper lay the latent disagreement between Moscow and Peking about "peaceful coexistence" with imperialism. In the years of stress and crises—1954 through 1957—Chinese Communism had tried to ignore its own doubts and to maintain a united front; it had usually followed the Soviet lead, and it had appealed to the other "brotherly parties" to go along with Moscow. But the situation was changing.

Experiencing a new buoyancy and enjoying almost unlimited latitude for its activities since 1957–58, Chinese Communism embarked upon a series of drives, both in home and foreign affairs, which were not in complete accord with Soviet theory and practice. A kind of rivalry with Moscow began to develop; China's inferiority, as compared with Russia, was a temporary phenomenon which should not take more than fifteen years to overcome. As to the United States, it was a "paper tiger"; the imperialists were a negligible force:

> Compared to great China and the Socialist camp, with the Soviet Union at its head, the United States, Britain and the whole imperialist camp are nothing but a dwarf. . . . It is China, a backward country in the economic and cultural sense, that has exceeded all the economically and culturally developed capitalist countries of Europe and America in respect to the pace and scope of the popular revolutions.[1]

In October, 1958, China's leading press organ reprinted a number of Mao Tse-tung's statements on the "paper tigers" of the West. In its comments, it stated: ". . . 'Imperialism and its lackeys in various countries are setting like the sun in the West, while Socialism and the national revolutionary movement, which Socialism supports, are ascending like the sun in the East.' "[2]

In the economic field, Peking claimed, just as the Soviet Union would catch up with the United States in the 1970's, China would catch up with Britain, Imperialist Number Two, about the same time, and then, of course, outstrip her. The fantastic idea that China would be on a par with Britain in fifteen years became a tenet. After November, 1957, the claim was regularly stressed in the Chinese press;[3] probably less than fifteen years, the delegates to the Eighth Congress of the Chinese Communist Party were told, would be needed to achieve that goal.

An implied claim of superiority even over the Soviet Union was seen in China's attempt to establish a better social system than existed in Russia. The new Chinese system of wages was to be based on the principle of equal pay rather than piecework (the experiment

---

[1] A leading article in *Jenmin Jihpao* (reprinted in *Pravda,* June 2, 1958).
[2] In *International Affairs,* Moscow, no. 12, December, 1958, p. 93.
[3] *Jenmin Jihpao,* November 25, 1957 (*Pravda,* November 26, 1957). This was later reiterated by Liu Shao-tchi at the Eighth Congress in May, 1958 (report on the Congress by the Chinese News Agency in *Pravda,* May 26, 1958).

New Impetus in China

with equal pay had been relinquished in Russia during Lenin's days); the new Chinese system of "communes" was juxtaposed, as the most virtuous and equitable of institutions, with the Soviet "collective farms." Established at an extremely rapid pace in rural China beginning in the summer of 1958, the communes presented a total but primitive and naïve effort to solve social problems and industrialize China in a way that Lenin had termed indicative of "infantile diseases of Communism."

The Soviet leadership and the Soviet press were obviously embarrassed: they could not openly accuse the "Chinese way to socialism"; on the other hand, they could not accept what amounted to a challenge. For a long time they avoided the issue; the press dutifully, but not too frequently, reported Chinese statements and official resolutions on communes, the "leap forward," etc., but without comment. Privately, the Soviet leadership did not conceal its critical attitude: for example, Khrushchev, in his talks with the Polish leaders during his visit to Poland in the summer of 1959, and his remarks to an American visitor (Senator Hubert Humphrey) that the Chinese communes were "old-fashioned" and "reactionary": "We tried that right after the revolution. It just doesn't work." [4]

In the end, however, Moscow spoke up, because another issue was coming to the fore, namely the transition to perfect, integrated Communism. The Soviet contention, which was accepted by the other parties, was that "we are building Communism," and the "people's democracies" are "building socialism." The Soviet claim of superiority—an emotion the importance of which in Eastern politics cannot be exaggerated—was stressed again and again; it served as the justification for the authorization to Moscow to lead the "camp." We have seen [5] how Tito was greeted in Moscow by the display of huge posters: Here, Communism; there (in Yugoslavia), socialism. On a visit to Poland, Khrushchev said, at the airport in Rzeszow: "Poland is building Socialism, the Soviet Union—Communism." [6] The inference was that when the Soviet Union finally established Communism at home— and perhaps also in its sphere in Europe—other countries (including, in the first place, the countries of the Orient) would lag behind and

[4] *Life*, New York, January 12, 1959.
[5] See p. 351.
[6] *Pravda*, July 21, 1959.

remain for a time longer under the imperfect socialist system. Summing up this generally accepted thesis, the authoritative Soviet *Problems of Philosophy* wrote, in October, 1958:

> It must be assumed that the European Socialist countries united into one Economic Council of Mutual Assistance, will build a special economic zone and will be the first to enter Communism. The Socialist countries of Asia, which have much in common in their economic and cultural development, will constitute another regional zone and will also jointly enter Communism.[7]

Since 1958 Chinese Communism had disagreed with this thesis: its growth, it claimed, had exceeded that of the Soviet Union, and the moral level of its new system was higher than that in the socialist countries of Europe. Why should China stay behind?

> In about three years [said Peng Te-huai in October, 1958] our people will live a happy life, disposing of an abundance of food and clothing. Backwardness and poverty, the result of a thousand years of reactionary dominance, will belong to the past. This is a great victory of the Communist Party of China, these are the great results of the tenacious work of the entire people.[8]

"It appears," said the Chinese Central Committee in its resolution of August 29, 1958, "that the realization of Communism in our country is not something distant." [9]

> China is moving forward [said *Jenmin Jihpao* [10]] with lightning speed. Recently, fifty-year-old peasants were worried whether they would live to see the wonderful age of Communism. Now even eighty- and ninety-year-olds are sure that they will still be able to enjoy the good fortune of Communism.

Discussion of these questions went on for several months; it ended, on the Soviet side, in a compromise: the Russian collective farms and piecework (this "imperfect" Soviet system) was, of course, maintained; as to the future, however, Moscow conceded to China the prospect of a simultaneous achievement of Communism. At the Twenty-first Party Congress in January, 1959, Khrushchev, without at first naming his target, attacked the Chinese theses:

[7] *Voprosy Filosofii* (Problems of Philosophy), Moscow, no. 10, October, 1958, p. 34.
[8] *Pravda*, October 2, 1958.
[9] *Hsinhua*, September 9, 1958 (in *Pravda*, September 11, 1958).
[10] August 6, 1958, quoted in *Politische Studien*, Munich, 1959, p. 807.

The history of the development of our country included a period of "war communism," when we were temporarily obliged to depart from the principle of distribution according to work and adopt equalitarian distribution according to the number of mouths. This was not due to abundance, but to an acute shortage of food and consumer goods. By the most stringent discipline in food distribution, the state was able to avert mass famine and supply the fighters of the Red Army and the urban population with regular, if meager, rations, at times only an eighth of a pound of bread a day. . . .

. . . V. I. Lenin most directly stated then that, without a material stake for all personnel in the results of their work, the country's productive capacity could not be raised, a Socialist economy could not be built and the millions of people would not be led toward Socialism.

With the change to peaceful construction, monetary pay for workers and employees was introduced. . . .[11]

Proceeding to criticize anonymous "social scientists," Khrushchev continued:

In articles and lectures, some social scientists voice the view that distribution according to work signifies application of the bourgeois system to a Socialist society. They ask whether the time has not come to shift from this principle to the equalitarian distribution of the social product among all personnel. One cannot agree with this view.

A partial victory for China, however, was conceded by Khrushchev in his outline of the prospects for the future:

How will the further development of the Socialist countries toward Communism proceed? Can one imagine one of the Socialist countries attaining Communism and introducing the Communist principles of production and distribution, while other countries are left trailing somewhere behind in the early stages of building Socialist society?

This prospect is highly improbable if one takes into account the laws governing the economic development of the Socialist system. From the theoretical standpoint it would be more correct to assume that by successfully employing the potentialities inherent in Socialism, the Socialist countries will enter the higher phases of Communist society more or less simultaneously. We base ourselves on the fact that new laws of development, laws unknown to human society in the past, operate in the Socialist economic system. . . .

There is no doubt that, with the further growth and strengthening of the world Socialist system, all the Socialist countries will develop with increasing success. The conditions necessary for the transition

[11] *Pravda*, January 28, 1959.

from the first phase of Communism to its second phase will be established at an increasingly faster pace in these countries.[12]

The traditional Communist theory of a gradual rather than a simultaneous transition to Communism was, following Khrushchev's speech, attacked in *Pravda* (February 9, 1959) by the ranking Soviet theoretician P. Fedoseyev.

Transition to Communism was, however, in the future; at present China trailed behind, and she was obliged, like any other member of the "camp," to acknowledge Soviet superiority. To Moscow this was the main issue. The alignment of the members of the "camp" according to rank—an extremely important matter in relation to the issue of Moscow's supreme leadership—was made annually on the eve of May Day, when the Central Committee announced the slogans for the celebration: for example, "6. Brotherly greetings to all peoples fighting for national independence, peace, democracy and Socialism! . . . 12. Long live the world system of Socialism—the indestructible bulwark of peace and security of peoples!" etc.

In the long list of slogans for 1958, the Soviet Union was, of course, "building Communism," while China, the European "people's democracies," Korea, and Mongolia were "building socialism"; only North Vietnam still lagged behind—she was "building a new life." Yugoslavia was included in the cohort of ranking nations "building socialism."

In the slogans of 1959, China, still behind the Soviet Union, was "building socialism"; Vietnam had advanced and was now, like Korea, Mongolia, and the European members of the "camp," "building socialism." Yugoslavia, on the other hand, had been demoted: only "brotherly greetings were sent to the toilers of Yugoslavia"; Tito's country was not recognized as building socialism.

In 1960 China was still "building socialism"; all other members of the "camp" maintained their previous rank. Yugoslavia, however, had not been pardoned and again received only cool "brotherly greetings." The Soviet Union, of course, was far in the lead: it was "building Communism."

These problems, seemingly removed from the area of direct international politics, constituted the background for an evolving new type of alliance. Her new high rank signified greater claims and more inde-

[12] *Ibid.*

New Impetus in China

pendence for China, at least in Asia. If the Soviet Union had a free hand in her dealings with Italy, France, and the satellites, China needed no Soviet consent for her actions in regard to India, Thailand, or Indonesia. Summit conferences of the four powers, if discussion of Far Eastern affairs was on the agenda, were contrary to China's designs unless Peking was represented. Close alliance, consultation with Moscow, and common action were called for only in regard to such issues as Formosa, Japan, or Korea, in which the United States was directly involved; otherwise China felt strong enough to go her own way.

The summit conference that Moscow had been calling for since December, 1957, was to discuss, among other issues, the Middle East situation. Jordan, Lebanon, and Iraq were high on the list of East-West controversies. On July 19, 1958, Khrushchev proposed to the West that, in addition to the "Big Four," India be invited to the conference. About twenty-five messages relating to the conference were exchanged between the heads of government of the powers. The Western suggestion that the conference be held within the framework of the United Nations was considered; Khrushchev accepted the suggestion on July 23. The fact, however, that Moscow had proposed an invitation to India and not one to China aggravated the situation. A visit to China by Khrushchev became necessary.

Khrushchev spent four days in Peking (July 31 to August 3, 1958). Greater secrecy than usual was maintained about his discussions with the Chinese leaders. The day after his return to Moscow, however, Moscow withdrew its request for a summit conference within the framework of the United Nations and proposed a more conventional form of discussion without the participation of the heads of government.

In a way this was a victory for China; by implication it was also a setback for India. In this development was contained the embryo of the future Sino-Indian conflict.

Khrushchev's visit to China was followed by a renewal of the Chinese drive against Formosa, a drive again fully supported by Moscow. Beginning on August 23, the island of Quemoy was bombarded daily by the Communist Chinese forces; hundreds of casualties were counted. A quick surrender by Quemoy was expected, when, finally, air-borne supplies began to arrive at the battered island. An exchange of letters between Moscow and Washington stressed the seriousness of the situation; Khrushchev stated that his military forces would, if necessary, go to the aid of Communist China. When, as a result of these exchanges, new talks between the ambassadors of the United States and China, which had been going on for some time, were scheduled to resume in Warsaw, tension abated, and the bombardment of Quemoy eased.

At the same time impetuous Peking was continuing its drives and starting new ones, crossing borders by armed force, creating *faits accomplis,* and proposing "peaceful negotiations" which, if they took place, often led nowhere. Bhutan was invaded; the plan of a Chinese-oriented "Himalayan Federation" to embrace Bhutan, Sikkim, and Nepal, was emerging in Peking.[13] The uprising in Tibet in March, 1959, followed by the flight of the Dalai Lama to India, was another feature of the changing image of China. In July–August, 1959, Chinese troops crossed the Indian border on the east and west, claiming an area of over 50,000 square miles, and creating a *fait accompli.* The North Vietnam drive in Laos made progress; China's old border conflict with Burma could not be definitely settled.

These developments posed new problems for the Soviet government. China was in the main using the same methods of expansion that had served Stalin in Eastern Europe after the war: local Communist groups in Southeast Asia were supported and armed by Peking just as their counterparts in Europe had been by the Soviet. But now the Soviet Union insisted on "peaceful coexistence"—meaning less violence and less Communist underground activity—and, in the first place, close cooperation with neutralist India. The Soviet press frequently restricted its reports on the Chinese offensive to a minimum, often reporting only official Chinese announcements. In connection with China's conflict with India it went farther: it printed the official statements of both sides. For the first time in decades the Soviet government was refusing to take sides in favor of a Communist ally. Its attitude was officially stated as follows:

> It is impossible not to express regret about the incident that occurred at the Chinese-Indian border. The Soviet Union maintains

[13] *The New Leader,* New York, September 7 and November 9, 1959.

New Impetus in China

friendly relations with the Chinese People's Republic as well as with India. . . .

The "leading Soviet circles," TASS concluded, "are confident that both governments will resolve the misunderstandings, taking into consideration mutual interests, in the spirit of the traditional friendship between the peoples of China and India." [14]

The statements implied that Moscow would support India against China, although not militarily. (For military support India would have to turn to the violently rejected SEATO.) A few weeks later Khrushchev arrived in Peking to take part in the celebration of the tenth anniversary of Communist China. Chou En-lai greeted the Soviet guest with a challenge in the form of praise of the Chinese communes. Without going into the matter of the communes Khrushchev lectured the Chinese on "peaceful coexistence of socialist and capitalist states." (Relations between "capitalist India" and "socialist China" were obviously part of the problem of socialist-capitalist coexistence.) We should not probe by force "the stability of the capitalist system," Khrushchev said. "Marxists have recognized and do recognize only liberating, just wars, and have always condemned and do condemn predatory, imperialistic wars."

Khrushchev tried to dampen the extreme belligerency of the Peking leaders: "The socialist countries, taking up a position against wars, are in favor of peaceful coexistence not because capitalism is still strong. No. In general we don't need wars. It is impossible to impose by force of arms, against the will of a people, even such a noble and progressive social order as socialism. Therefore the socialist countries, conducting a consistent policy of peace, are concentrating their efforts on peaceful construction and by building socialism they inspire the people and lead them forward." [15]

A sense of proportion is necessary, however, if we are to assess correctly the state of Sino-Soviet relations; it would be wrong to exaggerate the significance of the disagreements and the behind-the-scenes fights; it would be a blunder to expect a definite breaking off of the alliance. Simultaneously with the political developments reviewed in this chapter the economic collaboration of Moscow and Peking was making progress. In August, 1958, both governments

[14] *Pravda,* September 10, 1959.
[15] *Ibid.,* October 1, 1959.

signed an agreement on additional Soviet "technical help" including the building of forty-seven new industrial units in China. Even more significant was the agreement of February 7, 1959, which provided for Soviet assistance during the years 1959–67 in the building of seventy-eight units. The value of Soviet imports and technical advice for this purpose was said to be 5 billion rubles.

Soviet activities in Burma in the late 1950's were to a degree typical for the entire area of Southeast Asia. In Burma the Chinese Embassy cooperated closely with the Burmese Communist underground. The Chinese Embassy was much larger than the Soviet Embassy, and had a well-selected staff. The Soviet Embassy, reflecting the Moscow spirit, looked askance at the Burmese Communist underground and its subversive course:

> . . . up to now the Soviet Government has succeeded in pressing Peking not to interfere in Burmese affairs too openly. But the fact is, and that fact is published in Burmese press and revealed by Burmese Government, that Red Chinese supply Communist insurgents, and Communist insurgents can exist only because of the support.[16]

Moscow tried to maintain its reputation among the Burmese Communists. To counteract suspicion and accusations (probably spread by the Chinese), Bobodjan Gafurov, a ranking Soviet leader, was dispatched to Asia by the Foreign Department of the Central Committee. In Burma he met secretly with local underground Communist leaders, and he assured them of Soviet understanding and sympathy. He visited Burma more than once in the course of his travels in Asia. His activities among the Moslems of Africa and Asia (he himself was a native of Tadzhikistan) were of course pro-Soviet, which sometimes meant anti-Chinese.

In its report to the Foreign Ministry early in 1959, the Soviet Embassy in Rangoon criticized the Chinese attitude toward Burma's border conflict with China. China's actions in Tibet during and after the uprising there were disapproved by the leading personalities in the Soviet Embassy. In general China was considered bellicose, aggressive, against "coexistence," and skeptical about peace with the imperialists.

Burma, like several other countries of the Far and Middle East,

[16] *Kaznacheev Testimony, op. cit.,* p. 12. The details on Burma given below are based on the author's interview with Mr. Kaznacheev.

New Impetus in China

was gradually moving from "friendly ('positive') neutralism" to plain "neutralism"; the distinction, stressed in Moscow, was an important one.

The initial hope placed by Khrushchev in the "neutralists" suffered greatly from these developments. In the years that had passed since the Bandung Conference neutralist Egypt had evolved into a vigorous anti-Communist nation, India had been attacked by a Communist power, and Communist China, which along with India had tried to organize an alliance of Asia and Africa against the "imperialists," appeared the most aggressive and expansionist power, a threat to the independence of her neighbors and the "uncommitted."

China also initiated a new course toward Japan. Since this phase of her policies directly involved the United States, it could be carried out only with Moscow's support. The ambitious Chinese program for Japan involved the dissolution of the Japanese-American alliance and removal of United States forces from Japan as a precondition to normal relations between Japan and China. Sino-Japanese relations had been deteriorating since May, 1958. Existing trade agreements had been broken, China's industrial contracts had been cancelled, and the fisheries agreement had not been renewed.

In 1955–56 the Soviet government had tried, despite the Japanese-American alliance and the presence of American forces in Japan, to establish a modicum of normal relations with Japan. The only results achieved at that time were the cessation of the state of war, repatriation of additional Japanese prisoners of war, and an agreement on fishing rights. In 1958, however, as China assumed a more aggressive policy, Moscow's attitude toward Japan also began to stiffen.

In September and November, 1958, the Soviet government dispatched strongly worded notes protesting Japan's alliance with the "aggressor," the United States. Early in 1960 Khrushchev withdrew certain promises previously made to the Japanese government. Moscow was following, it appears, a line that had originated in Peking. On January 27, 1960, it informed Tokyo that the Soviet government was withdrawing its promise (of 1956) to restore the islands of Shikotan and Habomai to Japan when a peace treaty was signed by the two governments:

... the Soviet Government considers it necessary to state that only under the condition of a withdrawal of all foreign troops from the territory of Japan and after the signing of a peace treaty between the U.S.S.R. and Japan will the islands of Habomai and Shikotan be turned over to Japan. . . .[17]

A "Pacific peace zone," which would embrace the nations of the Far East and include the United States, was again suggested by Khrushchev.[18] The zone was to emerge only after the withdrawal of American forces from Japan and Taiwan; the core of the zone was to consist of three nations—the Soviet Union, Communist China, and Japan. This was a concession to China's new aggressive spirit and a program of Soviet-Chinese Communist domination in the Pacific, or at least in its western part; it was symptomatic of China's growing significance in the Far East.

[17] *Pravda,* January 29, 1960.
[18] *International Affairs,* Moscow, no. 5, May, 1959, pp. 3–5.

CHAPTER 4

GERMANY

1. UNSTABLE STABILITY

On the surface there had been only few changes on the German question since Stalin's death. What the Soviet government had inherited from the late dictator was still there: partition of the country, Soviet armies in the eastern part, loyal satellite leaders in power, and nonrecognition by the West of what was emerging as economically the most advanced "people's democracy." Khrushchev's methods—new relations with Bonn and a modicum of trade with West Germany—were not entirely successful. For Moscow, Germany was, as she had been twenty and thirty years before, both a desirable ally and a dreaded enemy, both a promise and a threat.

The East German government, under Walter Ulbricht and Otto Grotewohl, was the Western counterpart of the Eastern stormy petrel, Peking. Although less independent of Moscow than the Chinese Communist government and less important in Soviet eyes, it was bellicose, orthodox, and dynamic; it considered itself an unfinished business, an illogical embryo of a logical future all-German government. The official Soviet contention that the "German Democratic Republic" (DDR) was a "historical reality" was considered everywhere as only a diplomatic phrase and a cliché; the DDR must either expand or be reduced to a cipher. By its very nature the DDR was expansionist and aggressive; although contained by Moscow, it was meant to serve as the "shock troops" of the "socialist camp" in Europe. In 1959 the military and paramilitary organizations of East Germany comprised about one million men; in addition about 400,000 Soviet troops were stationed in East Germany.

The slogan of "confederation of the two Germanys" was still adhered to, with the important limitation, however, that the confederation should not set up a government for the whole of Germany; only a "council" with consultative power was to be established. Actually the program of a "democratic unification" with West Germany has been relinquished, at least for a time. Less cunning and more outspoken than Stalin, Khrushchev was frankly stating that Communist rule in West Germany was a precondition of unification. Stalin's pretended adherence to "self-determination" for the Germans was giving way to a program of Communism for the whole of Germany as a prerequisite of unification. In his speech in Leipzig on March 7, 1959, Khrushchev said:

> What does the reunification of Germany mean under present conditions of the existence of two German states? On what basis could it be accomplished? The advocates of working-class interests cannot even think of making the workers and peasants of the German Democratic Republic, who have set up a workers' and peasants' state and are successfully building Socialism, lose all their gains through reunification and agree to live as before in capitalist bondage.[1]

The Soviet ambassador in Bonn, Andrei Smirnov, told a group of German political leaders that among the Soviet conditions for reunification were the following: "Big industry would have to be nationalized . . . the power of 'monopoly capital' would have to be broken and the working class [meaning the Communist party] would have to assume political dominance." [2] This would mean Communist rule over the whole of the country.

The prospect of a new, real pro-Western great power emerging in the center of Europe remained, in Khrushchev's eyes, a great danger. Prevention or suppression of West Germany's rearmament had, since Stalin's days, been one of the outstanding objectives of Soviet policy. But the growth, although at a moderate pace, of Germany's power continued. Moscow appealed to the socialist parties of the West; it threatened Bonn with A-bombs and missiles; it called for summit conferences; Communist sympathizers conducted drives against her all over the world. The campaigns, however, yielded diminishing results, and Khrushchev's government, strong and always self-assured, looked with misgivings at the rising ghost.

[1] *Pravda*, March 27, 1959.
[2] *The New York Times*, March 14, 1960.

2. NEUTRALITY AND DISENGAGEMENT

"Neutralization" had been among the plans for Germany favored by Moscow. Successor to the demilitarization prescribed at Potsdam in 1945, neutralization would provide for a permanent ban on any substantial rearming of Germany. The idea of neutralization, an emotional residue of the first postwar era, was gladly accepted and supported by parties and governments which, in the 1950's, still viewed Germany and her possible "militarism" as a serious danger. In many instances this attitude was generated by the highest motives; neutralization of Germany, however, if accepted by the Western powers, would remove for Moscow a significant barrier on the road leading to the West. "Disengagement," a widely discussed plan supported by the Soviet Union in the middle 1950's, was one of the forms of neutralization.

By 1957 Moscow was supporting the plan of a neutral belt of lands stretching from the far north of Europe through the heart of the continent to the Mediterranean and embracing West Germany (see Map 7). The uninterrupted belt was to serve as a buffer between the East, under Soviet tutelage, and the West. It was to become a no man's land which, like any other demilitarized area, would eventually fall under the authority of its strongest neighbor. The neutralization plan had a number of component parts:

First: In the north, the Baltic Sea was to become a "Sea of Peace." In September, 1957, Premier Gomulka of Poland called upon the nations of the Baltic and Scandinavia to ban nuclear weapons and missiles from their area; he had in view, in the first place, the two NATO nations, Norway and Denmark, the latter of which was taking steps toward collaboration between its navy and that of West Germany. Another part of Gomulka's program involved closing of the "Sea of Peace" to the navies of the non-Baltic nations and forbidding the entry of military ships from the West. The navies of the other Baltic nations, including the new navy of West Germany, were greatly inferior to the Soviet navy. Thus the Baltic would become a mare clausum of the Soviet Union.[3]

The blueprint for the neutralization of the Baltic was not ac-

[3] *Osteuropa*, Stuttgart, no. 2, February, 1958, pp. 106–11.

ceptable to the Western nations. Khrushchev nevertheless continued to insist upon it, and in June, 1959, on the occasion of a visit of Walter Ulbricht and Otto Grotewohl to Moscow, proposed it again. There was no positive response to the renewed suggestion.

Second: About the time that Gomulka announced his plan for the Baltic, Adam Rapacki, Poland's foreign minister, made public a plan of neutralization of Central Europe that called for a zone free from production and stockpiling of atomic weapons and to embrace Poland, Czechoslovakia, and East and West Germany; the other powers would commit themselves not to use atomic arms against the areas of these nations. The Soviet government and the Consultative Committee of the Warsaw Pact announced their support of the Rapacki plan; Moscow proposed a summit conference of the big powers to discuss it.

In the West the Rapacki plan at first evoked both interest and criticism; to counter some objections and doubts, Rapacki submitted a more detailed blueprint on February 15, 1958. On November 4, 1958, he modified his plan, presenting it as a first stage of a far-reaching program of disarmament in Central Europe. The Rapacki plan was rejected by the West as an effort to consolidate Soviet predominance in Central and Eastern Europe.

Third: Moving southward, Austria was already pledged to neutrality by the treaties of 1955.

Fourth: A "Balkan pact" in one form or another was to round out the neutral zone in the south. In September, 1957, Rumanian Premier Chivu Stoica addressed messages to Bulgaria, Albania, Turkey, Greece, and Yugoslavia inviting them to take part in a conference with the purpose of arriving at "regional cooperation for peace."

The well-publicized proposals of Moscow and the satellites produced no results; not even preliminary discussions were held. Denmark, Norway, and Greece declined to participate; Turkey did not respond. The attraction of "neutralism," so strong several years before, was gone.

3. BERLIN, THE ABORTIVE SUMMIT, AND NEW MILITANCY

A component part of "neutralization" and the "peace zones," the idea of *status quo* for a time served Khrushchev as a slogan.

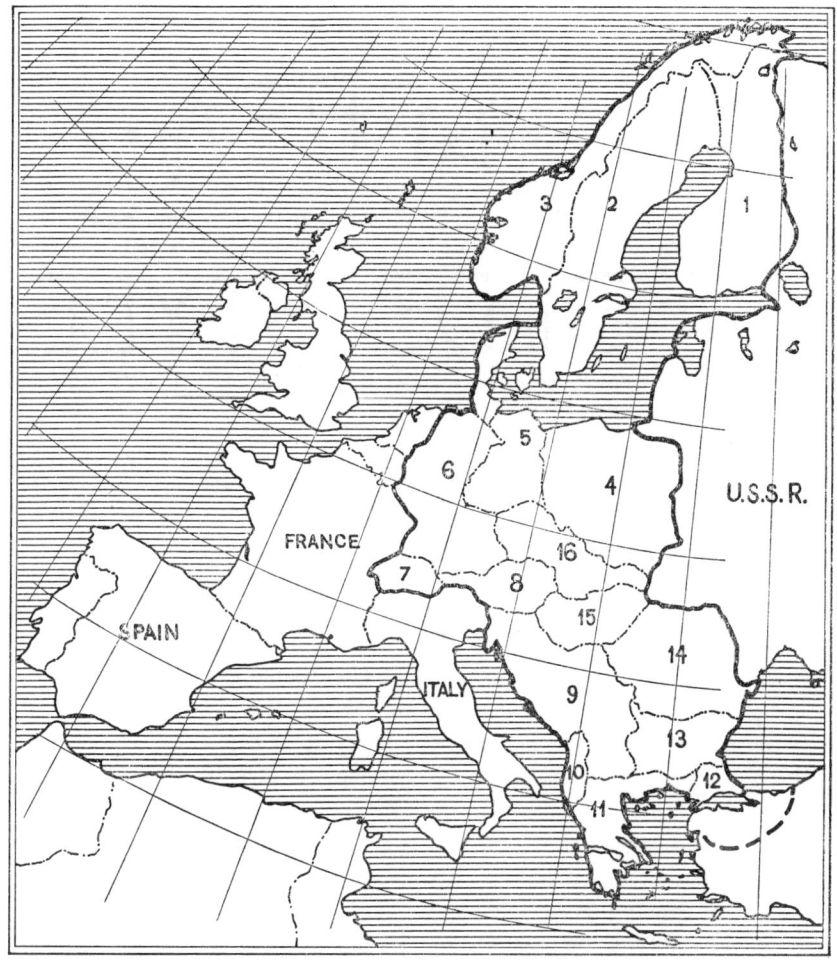

MAP 7. DISENGAGEMENT

The Belt of Neutral Nations in Europe as Proposed by
the Soviet Bloc in 1957–58

1. Finland
2. Sweden
3. Norway
4. Poland
5. The German Democratic Republic
6. The German Federated Republic
7. Switzerland
8. Austria
9. Yugoslavia
10. Albania
11. Greece
12. Turkey
13. Bulgaria
14. Rumania
15. Hungary
16. Czechoslovakia

"*Status quo*" combined "peaceful coexistence" with "hands off" Eastern Europe, and implied stable frontiers and recognition of East Germany. In a press interview Khrushchev stated:

> ... to recognize the status quo in the German question means to proceed from the existence of two Germanys: the German Democratic Republic—a state which follows the road of Socialist development—and the Federative Republic of Germany—a state with a capitalistic order. On the basis of the status quo conditions could be created for the solution of the German problem.[4]

Addressing a public meeting in Bitterfeld (East Germany) on July 9, 1958, Khrushchev said:

> State frontiers have scarcely ever been changed without war.... We say: It is necessary, as the diplomats put it, to recognize the *status quo,* to establish good relations between states, to recognize the necessity for peaceful coexistence of states, with everything that entails, to end the cold war, to create conditions for all-round contacts and trade among all countries.[5]

However, a *status quo* implied more stability than was desirable for certain other "socialist nations" (to Communist China, for example, it would mean peace with the Nationalist Government); it was also contrary to the belief in the progress of the social revolution in our time. Khrushchev had some difficulty in reconciling revolution with the *status quo.* In conversations with Western visitors he tried to interpret *status quo* in a particular way: world-wide revolutionary transformation, he said, is part of our era, and the West, by agreeing to the *status quo* accepts by implication the necessity, legality, and inevitability of the great change. In an interview with Adlai E. Stevenson, Khrushchev said:

> ... a process is taking place in which the peoples want to live under a new system of society, and it is necessary that one agree and reconcile himself with this fact. The process should take place without interference. If this principle [of noninterference] were accepted it would improve the international climate and we would welcome it.[6]

The essence of Khrushchev's notion of the *status quo* was, as Mr. Stevenson formulated it, "... the non-Communist world must stand

---

[4] *Pravda,* December 24, 1957.
[5] Nikita S. Khrushchev, *For Victory in Peaceful Competition with Capitalism,* New York, E. P. Dutton & Co., Inc., 1960, p. 538.
[6] *U. S. News and World Report,* Washington, D.C., September 5, 1958, p. 71.

Berlin and the Abortive Summit

aside while his 'new system of society' exploits the nationalist awakening and social unrest in the world, and spreads from country to country."

Khrushchev eventually relinquished the *status quo* slogan.

Another move, contrary to the *status quo,* and a step toward a gradual solution of the German problem was the Soviet drive toward West Berlin.

The Berlin problem was now to become a major issue in world affairs and the basis of a protracted conflict between Moscow and the West. The Soviet government was not unaware, when it embarked on its new drive in November, 1958, that it would meet with profound disagreements and political fights. But Berlin was worth it. Whether speedy or slow, total or partial, a victory on Berlin would mean added power and prestige for the entire "socialist camp"; the Western powers would again have to move over and accept the German-Soviet satellite as a nation equal to all other nations; this would mean degradation of the Bonn regime and, by implication, of NATO. To the Communist bloc, a success on the Berlin issue would prove (to the "dogmatists" in the first place) the possibilities inherent in "peaceful coexistence," and how right Khrushchev was in his new attitude toward war and progress toward Communism without military operations.

On November 10, 1958, Khrushchev came out with his proposal that West Berlin be made a "free city," meaning that all foreign troops would be withdrawn. The implication was that since the German police of the Western sectors would not be equal to the Eastern forces, "popular movements" staged by Ulbricht-Grotewohl in the "free" city would soon lead to a merger of the two parts of the old capital.

At first the chances that the Soviet Union would emerge the winner in the controversy, without a military conflict, appeared good. Khrushchev's government, like its predecessor, had never believed in the real solidarity of the Western powers. Moscow attentively studied the "contradictions" between them, which it often exaggerated, and it had more than a simple hope that under determined Soviet pressure one or another of those powers would relax in its determination and that the others would then have to follow suit. Initial developments seemed to confirm that these expectations were not entirely unfounded.

Khrushchev's idea was not rejected outright by John Foster Dulles. By his "agents' theory," as the Germans termed it, Dulles indicated that if the border police of the DDR which guarded the roads from the West to Berlin would act and be viewed as agents of the Soviet government, a solution could be found. A few weeks later Dulles publicly stated that "general elections might not be the only method" of unifying Germany; to Moscow this seemed like another hint of possible *de facto* recognition of the DDR. While the United States Secretary of State was not prepared to accept more than a tiny part of Khrushchev's plans, the attitude of the British government aroused more optimism in Moscow. Dissatisfied with the slow progress of "relaxation of tensions" under American guidance, and attributing this to specific trends in Washington, both political parties in Britain were convinced that a fresh and vigorous British approach might help, especially during Dulles's illness. In their view, the trends prevailing in the Soviet Union were toward prosperity, internal stability, and a kind of half-bourgeois social setup under Communist labels; Khrushchev, they argued, was determined to look for peaceful solutions of outstanding issues, and in this he deserved understanding.

On February 21, 1959, Prime Minister Macmillan arrived in Moscow for a ten-day visit to the Soviet Union. The negotiations did not go smoothly, and at one point the British guest almost cancelled a scheduled trip to the Ukraine; the final communiqué included the statement that on various questions "no agreement could be reached." On one of the most important issues, however, that of Germany's rearmament and "disengagement," there were hints in the discussion of concessions and possible compromises. The British and Soviet delegations, the communiqué said, ". . . agreed that further study could usefully be made of the possibilities of increasing security by some method of limitation of forces and weapons, both conventional and nuclear, in an agreed area of Europe, coupled with an appropriate system of inspection."

This British course was not in accord with the policy of either Bonn or Washington. It produced tension between London and Bonn that lasted for a year and served to arouse suspicions that Prime Minister Macmillan was prepared, in a final settlement with Moscow, to accede, at least partially, to the Soviet-proposed schemes for the DDR. To Moscow, the split in the Western coalition was confirmation that the Western front could be broken by Soviet firmness and insistence.

A conference of foreign ministers of the four powers and the ministers of both the Bundesrepublik and the DDR was convened in Geneva to discuss the Berlin problem. The sessions, with one substantial interruption, lasted from May 11 to August 5, 1959. The Western powers proposed to conclude a limited agreement for a specified period, reduce somewhat the military contingents in Berlin, and deal with DDR guards in connection with transit through the DDR to Berlin. Moscow rejected the Western proposals, insisting on more far-reaching ones; these, in turn, were unacceptable to the West. The conference ended with no agreement reached; it was assumed that the summit meeting, which was expected to take place before the end of the year, would deal with and resolve the question of Berlin.

Khrushchev's visit to the United States in the latter part of September, 1959, was the next stage in the discussions of the Berlin issue. The visit occurred after the death of Secretary Dulles, who had been hated but highly respected in the Kremlin. The new Secretary of State, Christian A. Herter, had not yet attained full authority. As to the President and the United States, Khrushchev had formed his views beforehand, and what he observed on his visit seemed to strengthen him in his impressions: that the magic terms "peace," "conciliation," and "friendship" would work miracles in the country; that a skillful diplomat could obtain concessions from the United States, especially since Britain had become more conciliatory. Khrushchev's speeches during his travels in the United States and the reports from America of editors of Soviet newspapers reflected the wishful thinking of the supreme Soviet leadership that in these twelve days Khrushchev "shook America." The anxiety in Bonn and Paris about Khrushchev's negotiations with President Eisenhower, about a possible "deal" between the "super-powers," about possible far-reaching concessions by Eisenhower, could only have increased Moscow's optimism.

Before leaving the United States the Soviet leader told correspondents: "On all subjects that we touched upon, we had a great deal in common both as regards our evaluation of the situation and the need to improve relations between our countries. . . . I have no doubt whatsoever that the President is sincere in his desire to improve relations between our countries."[7]

Khrushchev, who had for a number of years been attacking American "leading circles" for their "preparation of a war" and their "militarism," surprised his home audience when he returned to Moscow on September 28, 1959:

> I would like to tell you, dear comrades, that I have no doubt that the President is prepared to exert his efforts and his will to bring about agreement between our countries to create friendly relations between our peoples and settle pressing problems in the interests of a durable peace.[8]

On October 6, 1959, in Vladivostok, close to the borders of China, where the United States President was being denounced as the worst type of imperialist, aggressor, warmonger, and pirate, Khrushchev told a mass meeting:

> I must say that I liked speaking to him [President Eisenhower]—an intelligent man who appreciates the gravity of the international situation. . . . "I'm a military man [Eisenhower said to Khrushchev] and, speaking frankly, I greatly fear war." "Yes [Khrushchev replied], you have put it very well; only an impudent man can have no fear of war in our time."[9]

Although no specific promises on the Berlin question were given Khrushchev in Washington, and the official statements were noncommittal, Moscow viewed the prospects as good. After numerous diplomatic exchanges and postponements, it was decided to hold the Summit Conference in May, 1960. Khrushchev, the first mover in and the indefatigable partisan of the parley, had reason to expect a favorable result, especially on the Berlin issue. The Soviet's main adversary in this case, Chancellor Adenauer, was not invited to the conference (he preferred not to participate officially in order to preclude an invitation to the DDR); the only other possible adversary was French President de Gaulle.

At the end of March Khrushchev made a prolonged visit to France, where he talked at length with the President and appeared at numerous meetings and conferences and before various societies. He used

---

[7] *Face to Face with America. The Story of N. S. Khrushchev's Visit to the U.S.A., September 15–27, 1959,* Moscow, Foreign Languages Publishing House, 1960, p. 386.
[8] *Ibid.,* p. 471.
[9] *Ibid.,* p. 397.

Berlin and the Abortive Summit

the argument which, in the Soviet view, must be utterly convincing to France, namely, the threat of war to a country that had three times in the course of seventy years been ravaged by Germany. Untiringly and forcefully, Khrushchev stressed this point again and again. On March 23 he said in Paris: "I believe that the German revenge-seekers are a bigger threat to France than to any other country.... Now that militarism is being revived in Western Germany one must prevent a repetition of the errors of the past." [10] The next day, at a luncheon given for him by French Premier Michel Debré, Khrushchev said: "We possess all the prerequisites for administering a proper rebuff to any attempt to launch new aggression against us or against other peaceloving nations which are our friends." [11] On the same day, at a reception, he said: "If we expose German militarism we do so because it may, under certain circumstances, embark on adventures...." [12] The following day, addressing a parliamentary group, he said that France could have prevented the Second World War had it heeded Soviet advice: "... but some western statesmen were not wise enough to curb the aggressor and avert the Second World War." Therefore, he said: "Let us not be shortsighted and let us prevent the German militarists from repeating what Hitler did during the Second World War." [13]

On his tour of France, in Bordeaux, Nîmes, Marseilles, Dijon, Rheims, Lille, Rouen, and other places, Khrushchev spoke in the same vein. He relentlessly referred to the devastation and atrocities perpetrated by the invaders in most of these cities; he drew analogies between them and Russian sufferings at the hands of the Germans, to reach the conclusion that the German menace must cement Soviet-French collaboration against the Adenauer government.

But Khrushchev failed to win the French President over to his program; firm and uncompromising, de Gaulle insisted on the traditional Western demand of free elections in Germany as a prerequisite for a solution of the German problem. For Berlin, de Gaulle demanded of Khrushchev "absolute respect for the *status quo*" as a precondition for "relaxation of tensions." [14] Khrushchev was not discouraged, however; he was sure that public opinion in France was on his side. Back

---

[10] *N. S. Khrushchev in France March 23–April 3, 1960. Speeches, Interviews, T.V. Addresses, Report to Moscow Meeting*, London, Soviet Booklet No. 71, May, 1960, p. 13.
[11] *Ibid.*, p. 15.
[12] *Ibid.*, p. 19.
[13] *Ibid.*, pp. 40 and 41.
[14] *Le Monde*, Paris, April 5, 1960.

in Moscow, he still expected that the Western powers "will sooner or later arrive at the same conclusions as ours." [15]

Preparations for the forthcoming Summit Conference made it imperative for the Western powers to work out a common policy on the Berlin issue. De Gaulle's firmness, along with Adenauer's influence and Washington's general disinclination to yield the Western position on Berlin, determined the prospective policy: no substantial concessions to the Khrushchev program. Secretary of State Herter and Undersecretary of State C. Douglas Dillon announced the American position in unmistakable terms.

Since the Berlin issue was the most important item on the proposed agenda of the Summit Conference (nobody seriously expected important decisions in the fruitless disarmament talks), the conference was doomed. Pessimism prevailed in the foreign offices of the Western powers; the Western press predicted an abortive parley. Failure of the parley, which would be painful to all parties, would be a particularly hard blow to Nikita Khrushchev. Khrushchev had not only initiated the idea of the conference, but had staked much of his and his party's prestige on its outcome; he believed that a solution of the Berlin question arrived at by the conference would prove that his political course was superior to any other Communist course and was the best way of dealing with the "imperialists," especially the United States.

Instead of calling off the obviously doomed conference, Khrushchev took advantage of a comparatively unimportant American intelligence incident to attack the United States government and accuse it of "sabotaging" the conference. This incident was the flight of a U-2 plane from American bases in Turkey and Pakistan over Russia. According to the Soviet version, the plane was to land in Norway; spotted over Soviet territory, Khrushchev ordered the U-2 shot down: it came down in the region of the Urals. The pilot, Francis Gary Powers, who parachuted to the ground, was arrested. Khrushchev appeared before the Supreme Soviet to accuse the United States of illicit, "aggressive" operations. He then left for Paris to demand, as a precondition of his attendance at the Summit Conference, that President Eisenhower apologize and promise to punish the perpetrators of "the crime." This, he insisted, was necessary in order to prove Washington's

---

[15] *N. S. Khrushchev in France March 23–April 3, 1960, op. cit.*, p. 99.

Berlin and the Abortive Summit

sincerity, since by staging the "aggressive operation" of the U-2 on the very eve of the Summit Conference, the United States government had proved its belligerence and indifference to its outcome. Macmillan and de Gaulle were expected to press President Eisenhower to accept Khrushchev's demands. Thus, even if the Berlin question were not resolved in Khrushchev's favor, the fact that the head of the "socialist camp" had brought the American President to his knees would more than compensate for the postponement of the solution of the Berlin problem.

The French and British leaders refused, however, to help Khrushchev against the United States President. They were aware of something of which the public and even the press were ignorant—that the secret reconnaissance operations which all the powers had been conducting for a long time and on a large scale could not be temporarily halted for the duration of the Summit Conference. The magnitude of international tensions of the past decade had made secret gathering of information in peacetime as much a fact of life as the production of arms. Khrushchev, however, called the flight of the unarmed U-2 an "act of aggression," and the Soviet press accused the Pentagon of an "attack" upon the Soviet Union.

Khrushchev would least of all have been prepared to experiment with a temporary halting of Soviet espionage activities. Numerous agents of Soviet intelligence were doing their jobs abroad, and large sums had been invested in reconnaissance operations that were yielding a rich harvest. Soviet agents operating at or near military installations reported on their observations; others reported from within military units or research establishments in various countries. Military attachés had built up efficient intelligence networks with the help of local "friends." While espionage cases that become known usually constitute only a small fraction of the total, the size and regularity of Soviet reconnaissance activity could have been deduced from reports, most of them official, made during and after the Paris Conference: in the summer of 1960 two secretaries of the Soviet Embassy in Washington were expelled for espionage; a member of the Soviet delegation to the United Nations was expelled for the same kind of activity during Khrushchev's visit to the United States; two Soviet Embassy officials were expelled from Switzerland in May, 1960, when the U-2 affair was becoming known; a Polish Embassy official was expelled from Norway in July, 1960. Prime Minister Macmillan told the House of Commons on July 21, 1960, that 18 satellite agents had been expelled in the last two years from Britain, in addition to "a number of other spies posing as students, etc." In West Germany, over a period of eight years, 468 spies working directly for the Soviet Union (in addition to those working for the satellites) were arrested. Soviet naval units, equipped for espionage, were reported near American, British, and German shores.[16] There is no basic difference between espionage in the air, on the sea, or on land; espionage such as that conducted by the Soviet Union in Canada and Britain, which made it possible for Moscow to acquire the secrets of the atomic bomb, was at least as important as the American U-2 reconnaissance flights.

The abortive Paris Conference was the starting point of a series of new tactics in Soviet foreign policy; at first, the change was one of style rather than substance. Khrushchev did not proceed to solve the Berlin question unilaterally, nor did he drop his ideas of "peaceful coexistence" and the "not-inevitable war." What changed radically were the terminology and techniques of his policy, which created the impression of a real war being planned. In foreign affairs, however, style and technique play a substantial role; in the case of the Soviet post-Paris course of 1960 they produced results some of which were hardly desired even by their initiators.

Not only did the number of diplomatic *démarches*, accompanied by protests and accusations, increase substantially, but the tone and language became so bellicose that they were sometimes reminiscent of the Vyshinsky days. Attacks on the United States became violent; Soviet demands were regularly coupled with threats of retaliation by military means, especially missiles; short-term ultimatums were issued.

President Eisenhower, yesterday Khrushchev's "friend" and "man of peace," became a *bête noire;* attacks on a purely personal level were intended to degrade him in the eyes of the world.

> I think that when the President is no longer President, and if he would want to work for us, we could assign him a job as head of a kindergarten (I am sure he would not harm children). But it is danger-

[16] *The New York Times* (international edition), July 23 and August 15, 1960; *New York Herald Tribune* (European edition), July 23, 1960; *Neue Zürcher Zeitung,* May 11, 1960; *La Libre Belgique,* May 19, 1960; United States Information Service (USIS) press release, Washington, D.C., May 18 and 19, 1960.

ous to let such a man govern a nation, because he could do things that it would be hard to undo.[17]

On June 27 the Soviet Union and its allies walked out of the East-West disarmament conference in defiance. An American plane, an RB-47, was shot down by the Soviet air force on July 15. Moscow claimed that the plane had violated Soviet air space; four American fliers lost their lives. United States protests that the plane had not flown over Soviet territory, and repeated suggestions that the incident be investigated by a neutral international body, were rejected. A number of American tourists in Russia were accused of "espionage" and ordered to leave; "vigilance" against American spies again became a slogan of the day.

Khrushchev announced in the Supreme Soviet that Soviet forces would attack and destroy the foreign bases from which reconnaissance flights over the Soviet Union originated. Diplomatic notes to Turkey, Pakistan, and Norway (the countries involved in the U-2 affair) repeated this threat in specific terms. Marshal Rodion Malinovsky went even further, saying, in an Order, that not only would such bases be attacked, but also the powers "which have built these bases and control them," meaning the United States.

On a visit to Austria, Khrushchev gave a new and dangerous definition to that country's neutrality: Austrian neutrality, he said, would be violated if rockets shot from American bases in Italy overflew Austria on their way to the Soviet Union or the "people's democracies." "Neutrality," he said, "is not a mountain range which can isolate one from the outside world."[18] This new definition of neutrality was a threat also to the other neutral nations of Europe and Asia.

As had Khrushchev in Austria, Anastas Mikoyan, on the occasion of a visit of friendship to Norway, attacked Norway's allies—the United States, France, and Britain. For this he was rebuked by the Norwegian foreign minister, Halvar Lange.

The belligerent language, the rattling of sabres, and the threat of missiles were a puzzle to the governments that had expressed confidence in Khrushchev's peaceful intentions. In the abundant diplomatic and personal correspondence of those months, Prime Minister Macmillan's message addressed to Khrushchev was the most eloquent:

[17] *Pravda*, June 4, 1960.
[18] New York *Herald Tribune* (European edition), July 7, 1960.

I write to you now so plainly because I have the memory of our frank discussions with you in mind. I simply do not understand what your purpose is today. [Macmillan warned the Soviet Premier] If the present trend of events in the world continues we may all of us one day, either by miscalculation or by mischance, find ourselves caught in a situation from which we cannot escape.[19]

The new Soviet techniques found expression also in the developments in Latin America and Africa that were attracting world attention in the summer of 1960.

In Cuba, the revolutionary system, after a year of gradual evolution, was assuming a radical, leftist trend. The most spectacular of Cuba's "anti-imperialist" acts—acts always warmly greeted by Moscow—occurred in the spring of 1960, when American industrial units were seized by the Cuban government and Cuban–United States tension almost developed into an economic war. In itself, little Cuba was of no significance to the Soviet government; there were three reasons, however, why the issue of Cuba was of formidable importance to Moscow.

First, Cuba was the Soviet gate to Latin America, and the Cuban revolution was expected to set off popular movements and unheavals on a continent that had remained a reliable support of the United States. Systematically the Soviet press now registered, sometimes exaggerating them, pro-Cuban trends and movements in Mexico, Venezuela, Peru, Brazil, Argentina, Chile, Uruguay, Colombia, Ecuador; it quoted the Latin-American press to prove the sympathy of the continent to the "Yankee—no" movements. This, Moscow thought, was the way to isolate, weaken, and render impotent the anti-Communist giant.

Second, according to the Soviet conception, the fact that Cuba had so rapidly become a political and economic dictatorship without having passed through an intermediary stage of a "noncommitted" nation or a "neutral," represented a peculiar type of development. The old scheme that had applied to India, Egypt, and other countries was not applicable to the Western Hemisphere because of geographical proximity to and economic dependence on the United States. Moscow conjectured that Cuba might soon present a new form of "national road to socialism," if economic difficulties, after the ties with the United States were broken, did not pave the way for a countermove-

[19] *The New York Times* (international edition), July 21, 1960.

Berlin and the Abortive Summit

ment. It was therefore deemed important for every member of the Soviet bloc to give Cuba all the aid she needed—military, economic, diplomatic, and propagandistic; help to Cuba seemed now more important than help to the countries of Asia and Africa, and perhaps even than to the already existing "socialist nations."

Third, an element of personal ambition is present in almost every significant political venture, and Cuba was an issue for Khrushchev personally. Six years before, Guatemala, after an internal upheaval, had tried to obtain arms from the Soviet bloc; the movement had been stopped and the new regime overthrown under the direct impact of Washington. But this had occurred soon after Stalin's death, when Georgi Malenkov and Vyacheslav Molotov were in power. Now the superiority of Khrushchev's methods over those of Stalin and the Stalinists had to be demonstrated in Cuba, just as they had to prove successful in Berlin.

In February, 1960, Anastas Mikoyan visited Cuba, signed a trade agreement with her and granted her a loan of 100 million dollars. In June (about the time that Japan withdrew the invitation to President Eisenhower) Khrushchev accepted an invitation to visit Cuba. An agreement providing for the delivery of Soviet oil to Cuba and the sale of Cuban sugar to Russia was signed in Moscow that month. On July 18 Khrushchev received Raul Castro, brother of Premier Fidel Castro, in a five-hour audience and promised him all possible help. Five days later, Mao Tse-tung received a Cuban trade-union delegation. The next day, in a move of assistance to Cuba that implied rivalry with the Soviet Union, a Sino-Cuban trade agreement was signed. Khrushchev said on July 9:

> Figuratively speaking, Soviet artillerists can, in case of necessity, support the Cuban people by rocket fire if the aggressive forces of the Pentagon should dare to start an intervention against Cuba.[20]

The following day, President Eisenhower stated that "the United States will not be deterred by the threat Mr. Khrushchev is making" and "will not permit the establishment of a regime dominated by international Communism in the Western Hemisphere." Khrushchev promised that the Soviet Union would buy the 700,000 tons of Cuban sugar that the United States had refused to buy.

[20] *Pravda*, July 10, 1960.

In Moscow there developed heated antagonism to the Monroe Doctrine, which, according to the Soviet press and leadership, was dead: "What will the United States of America not permit?" Khrushchev asked. "Who gave it such a right? What are they—a prosecutor? What right is given to the United States of America to decide the fate of other countries and other nations?" Back in Cuba, Raul Castro, referring to his visit with Khrushchev, told a public meeting:

> If there is aggression [meaning a United States attack on Cuba], there will be rockets, and plenty of them. There are two kinds of rockets, rockets of peace and rockets of war. We have chosen disinterestedly the aid of the rockets of peace.[21]

Meantime the Communist party in Cuba was gaining importance and influence, and a large new military force was being built up. In his two trips to Eastern Europe, Raul Castro had acquired substantial arms to equip a new Cuban military force. President Dorticos stated at a trade-union meeting on August 10 that Moscow had offered Cuba, among other things, atomic weapons. Cuba was growing into an important Soviet-Chinese fortress in America, the guns of which were aimed to the north.

The same fighting spirit dominated Soviet policy in regard to the former Belgian colony of the Congo, after the country attained independence on July 1, 1960. About a decade behind the dominions and colonies of Asia in gaining formal sovereignty, the African nations at first had trod a similar path. They, too, were initially inclined to the Bandung type of government and policy—meaning a coalition of nationalism and Communism—that had been popular in Asia several years before. Bandung emotions, however, tend to fade as the new nations become more discerning of colors and shades and develop their own alliances.

In Africa the Bandung trends were still alive. Although these trends could not compensate for the deterioration in Asia of the Bandung scheme favored by Khrushchev, the Soviet leader tried to apply in Africa the methods that, in the initial stage, had been so successful in Asia and the Arab countries. He accepted invitations to visit Guinea and Ghana; Soviet delegations visited various African countries; Soviet economic help was envisaged. When the Congo con-

[21] New York *Herald Tribune* (European edition), August 5, 1960.

Berlin and the Abortive Summit

flict broke out, the Soviet Union rushed forward as the most unselfish defender of the Congo's independence from Belgium and the West as a whole.

The conflict in the Congo grew to dangerous proportions. The language of official Soviet statements and of the Soviet press became aggressive in the extreme: demands for unmasking the "provocations" of the imperialists and their "monstrous schemes" were intermingled with offers of Soviet military help; the Belgians were not the only culprits—the United States, and even West Germany, were among the accused. Many of the Soviet diplomatic *démarches* ended with a threat: "the Soviet government warns. . . ." A false rumor that a group of American soldiers had arrived in the Congo served as the subject of a bellicose Soviet note and of speeches in the United Nations: "impermissible," said the Soviet protest; "unless the group is withdrawn, the Soviet government will have to draw the conclusions for its action."[22]

Close cooperation and collaboration bound the Soviet representatives in the Congo to Premier Patrice Lumumba; their actions—against Belgium, the West, and the United Nations and its secretary general, Dag Hammarskjöld—were coordinated; both parties often spoke in the same terms. Moscow repeated its offer of troops to replace United Nations forces. On August 5 Moscow announced that

> should the troops sent to the Congo in accordance with the decision of the Security Council be unable to secure effectively the removal of the interventionist [Belgian] troops, then troops of those countries which will be prepared to take part in carrying out that just action should be sent to the Congo.[23]

The post-Summit trends of Soviet foreign policy produced various effects, not all of them in accord with Moscow's plans and desires. The "popular movements" in Europe and Asia that were expected to support the emphatic new anti-American trends did not materialize anywhere. The expected rallying of the Communist parties around Moscow and the liquidation of centrifugal trends did not occur; on the contrary, the violent attacks in the official Soviet and satellite press on the "dogmatists" and "leftist sectarians," and the behind-the-scenes

[22] Soviet note of July 19, 1960.
[23] New York *Herald Tribune* (European edition), August 6–7, 1960.

disputes on the issue of the "not-inevitable war," revealed the growing bitterness in the "camp" and the danger of secessions.

On the other hand, the new tactics successfully demonstrated the formidable Soviet force and the power of Soviet intimidation in regard to the nonbellicose nations of the West. Moscow counted on Western pacifism and disunion: some of the small nations, threatened and intimidated, were reconsidering their ties with the West; Britain initiated new conversations on the subject of American bases; Cuba and the Congo proceeded on their anti-Western course, relying on promised Soviet military help.

Developments revealed again the essential content of the Khrushchev era of Soviet history. Khrushchev had not been responsible for the internal social revolution in Russia—the transformation of old Russia into another type of social organization had been completed by his predecessors; he did not rehabilitate the Soviet economy after the war—this had been almost achieved when he came to power; he did not succeed in accomplishing the outbreak of new pro-Soviet "popular movements" in capitalist countries. He did, however, succeed, beyond any expectations, in enhancing the prestige of Russia as a military power. By missiles and bombers rather than by ideas and ideals, he was successful in attracting the weak and small countries; by a torrent of terrible threats, well-founded in and supported by unprecedented military strength, he impressed the world. Military greatness, with all that it implied in terms of potential crises, was the foundation of Khrushchev's foreign-political course at the start of the decade of the 1960's.

Conclusion

At the beginning of the 1960's, Stalin's formidable empire in Europe was being maintained without aggrandizement and without losses. The reforms and innovations, however, which had become imperative during Stalin's last years, and which were introduced after his death to reinforce and widen the structure, were less than wholly successful.

The first element of Khrushchevism in foreign affairs, as we have seen, was the hope placed in the "neutrals" as allies of Communism in common opposition to the West. In preceding chapters it was shown how great these hopes were and how inspiring were the early successes. The developments in the late 1950's proved that the grandiose hopes could not materialize. Although the process of decolonization continued and the number of independent nations was growing, and although "neutralism" was often preferred by the new governments, all Soviet efforts to assume the role of guide and create a real alliance between the Soviet bloc and the "neutralists" and thus, in an evolutionary way, enlarge the number of "socialist states" were in vain. The great hopes placed in Egypt, Syria, and India did not materialize; Iraq was a question mark; the nations of South Asia were becoming antagonistic toward their Communist neighbor. The value of financial assistance as a political lever had been greatly overestimated by Moscow. In Europe, as we have seen, the Soviet effort to build up a belt of neutrals was rejected by all concerned except the "people's democracies." Facts had proved that a nation could be won over to the "socialist camp" either by a strong Communist party or by an invading army, and by nothing else.

Khrushchev's initial attempt to reunite all Communist parties under one—the Soviet—roof was not successful. The Soviet leader had spent probably half of all his working time and half of his enormous energy on efforts to reconcile the dissidents. For a moment in 1956 it seemed that he was reaching his goal, but once again the edifice began to disintegrate. The Soviet empire continued to exist as it had existed under Stalin—without Yugoslavia and with heretics in all parts.

Only now, with terrorism reduced and with slits having appeared in the iron curtain, the world had been able to observe the fermentation in Eastern Europe, the points of possible eruptions, and the beginnings of new interstate formations.

Moreover, a situation that Stalin had refused to recognize was developing in the Far East: the effort of a Communist ally to attain the stature of a great power. China was not a great power; she would need decades and decades to acquire the prerequisites of greatness in politics. But the prospect of a second Communist empire was as abhorrent to Khrushchev as it had been to Stalin. Moscow accepted everything about China—her own "roads to socialism," her childish communes, her belief that she would overtake England in fifteen years "or before that," her experiments with "a hundred flowers," and her recurring bouts of terrorism—but one thing was out of the question: acquiescence in her great-power behavior on an equal footing with the Soviet Union. It did not seem likely that in the early 1960's the danger would become acute, but the first stages of an ominous development were already discernible.

For these total and partial failures Khrushchev was able to compensate by unparalleled Soviet military achievements, especially since the Soviet launching of the first satellite into space. The progress in this area was spectacular. Soviet claims of success grew to claims of superiority; threats of the use of Soviet military power were becoming a regular feature of Soviet diplomatic exchanges. The tenor of the new course was indicated by Khrushchev at the time when Soviet missile production was going into high gear:

> We are convinced that very soon the peoples of those countries in which American military bases have been set up many thousands of kilometers from America herself will come to realize more fully what a terrible danger these bases constitute for their countries, and will resolutely demand the immediate abolition of foreign bases on their territory.[1]

In a talk with President Nasser of Egypt on July 25, 1958, Khrushchev said that the Soviet Union had weapons which "could easily

---

[1] *International Affairs,* Moscow, no. 11, November, 1957, p. 15. Khrushchev's replies to questions submitted by P. Dampson of the Toronto (Canada) *Telegram.*

Conclusion 525

turn the United States Sixth Fleet into coffins of molten steel." [2]

In a letter to Chancellor Konrad Adenauer of West Germany, Khrushchev wrote, on August 18, 1958: "The Soviet Union possesses a missile technique in quantities and of a quality which no other country has." [3] About the same time he told Averell Harriman in Moscow: "In five or seven years we will be stronger than you." [4]

In less than one year, Moscow was claiming universal superiority in arms. In its editorial of March 7, 1960, *Pravda* said: "The Soviet Union has become the strongest power in the world." Finally, speaking in Baghdad on April 10, 1960, Anastas Mikoyan claimed "military superiority of the Soviet Union," which, he said, is even "recognized by American generals." [5]

It was not Khrushchev's fault that the strength of Communism as a set of ideas and ideals was declining while Soviet military power was increasing; he certainly wanted success in both areas. Whatever his intentions, the effectiveness of his two tools was undergoing change.

The development most disturbing to the Soviet government since the middle of the 1950's was the re-emergence of real European powers on the soil of the old continent. This process of re-emergence brought to an end the extraordinary situation in Europe that had existed since 1945 and that had made possible Stalin's stupendous successes in world affairs.

After the destruction of France at the start, and of Germany and Italy at the end, of the war there remained an impotent, decimated Western Europe, an aggregate of lands which appeared minuscule beside the approaching giant from the East, a mere appendage of Eurasia, a group of nations unable to defend themselves and dependent for their defense on assistance from beyond the seas.

This one-power structure of Europe was the source of constant tension. "Relaxation" was impossible, exhortations were in vain, Soviet promises served no purpose, peace slogans remained unconvincing, "peace congresses" were unimpressive. Even at the price of a compromise with Moscow, there would have been no peace for the West-

[2] Associated Press from Cairo, July 25, 1958.
[3] *Pravda*, August 27, 1959.
[4] *The New York Times*, July 5, 1959.
[5] *Pravda*, April 11, 1960.

ern nations. The fundamental fact of Europe's political structure doomed all efforts toward relaxation and conciliation.

These well-known facts were decisive in the international relations of the entire postwar era; their impact reached far beyond the shores of Europe. The security or insecurity of the United States has derived from the insecurity of Western Europe. If Western Europe were overrun, America would face, across the sea, a unified armed power which had integrated the military potential of at least three great countries. The United States is part of the political "West" not only because of ideological reasons, or its preference for this or that economic system, or its adherence to the ideals of liberty; it belongs to the West for reasons of independence and survival.

Multiplicity in the political structure of Europe, which is identical with the independence of European nations, is an element and a precondition of American and British security. With the principle of multiplicity and independence violated to the extent that it has been since 1944, no efforts can produce a lasting *détente*.

Moreover, real disarmament remains impossible so long as these fundamental facts dominate international relations. Contrary to the well-known contention, it is not armament that provokes conflicts; nor would disarmament guarantee peace. The adage that "guns go off by themselves" if accumulated in large quantities is not true; guns go off only when a regime, in pursuit of its own aims, orders missiles put into the muzzles. Partial or even total disarmament will not eliminate wars if fundamental political abnormalities continue.

For the Soviet Union NATO is both too little and too much: as a huge alliance of fifteen nations it appears large; but anchored in the main overseas, thousands of miles away, it appears less impressive. Russia feels herself definitely a continent-bound power, with all that such a position implies in terms of world affairs. Russia is a more perfect type of continental power than any of the other great nations. Her thinking and her perception of the world have been traditionally the thinking and perception of a continental power. Her notion of national (or Communist) growth is continental; her wars have, with few exceptions, been continental wars; her empires have been land empires; the dangers to her security and her main enemies in the past have been Sweden, Poland, Turkey, Germany, France, and the attacks from both sides in the relations with these countries were at-

Conclusion

tacks over land frontiers. The most recent Soviet ventures into Africa and the Caribbean area cannot alter the essentially continental nature of Soviet empire-building, just as Russia's moves into the Western Hemisphere in the nineteenth century did not alter the Eurasian essence of her empire.

This is not to say that Russia has not had or has no naval forces; nor does it at all mean that the Soviet Union does not care about military aviation, atomic arms, etc. Nor does it mean that ideological issues have not influenced her course in foreign affairs. Of course, Moscow says,

> The future war, if unleashed, will be marked by a mass application of aerial military forces, various rocket arms and different means of mass destruction; atomic, nuclear, chemical and bacteriological weapons.
>
> However, the Soviet Union always proceeds from the assumption that the most modern, latest arms, among them also the means of mass destruction, do not lessen the decisive significance of land forces, navy and aviation.[6]

For Soviet foreign policy the rebirth of France and Germany as powers in Europe has been the overriding development of the current era. In France, for a longer period than in the other nations, the anti-German trend coupled with pro-Russian sentiment competed, after the war, with the Western apprehension about Soviet expansion; the impact of this trend on France's course paralyzed the nation. Immersed in military operations in Indochina and Africa, France has been less active in Europe than she might otherwise have been.

Beginning in mid-1958 France began to return to Europe as the main field of her interests. The new policy implies, along with greater activity in Europe, an attempt to resume a guiding role in Western European affairs. Charles de Gaulle's notion of the greatness of his country implies opposition to any "pretensions to hegemony of the two rivals [the United States and the Soviet Union]"; it is to France, he says, that "it falls to take, in this essential domain, the necessary initiative." In de Gaulle's view, it was President Roosevelt who made possible, by his neglect of France and Western Europe, the formidable expansion of the Soviet Union; the process must now be reversed. When, twice in this century, Europe was menaced by Germany, alli-

---

[6] *Large Soviet Encyclopedia*, Moscow, 2d ed., vol. 41 (1956), p. 73.

ance with Russia was necessary; now, however, the menace has disappeared, and *rapprochement* with Western Germany has become imperative.

This course has led logically to a growing opposition to the Soviet course. Moscow has reacted to this deviation of France from its previous course with criticism and objections. It has, however, tended to underestimate France as a great power. Since the 1930's it has minimized France's potentialities; in its own way it has shared the Nazi theory of the "decay of France." Because France, having undergone terrible suffering in World War I, did not, during the 1930's, display her old vigor and determination, the notion spread in Russia also that France was done with permanently, or at least until a socialist revolution should take place. The facts that vigor does not evaporate in a few years, that France had served for long periods as the master of Europe, and that she might be expected to carry brilliant performances still in her knapsack, were overlooked.

What has worried Moscow more and what she has attached greater attention to is the re-emergence of Germany as a real power on the continent; the implications of such a re-emergence Moscow sees clearly.

Just as the evaluation of France is lower in the Soviet Union than elsewhere, the evaluation of Germany's power potential and influence is greater than elsewhere. As we have seen, this has been the case since the 1920's. In the 1950's the appraisal of Germany rose again. At present, "the evaluation of West Germany in the Soviet Union is obviously so high that one could define it as an overrating"—this was the impression of the Adenauer group when it visited Moscow in 1955.

Since the end of the last century ideological ties have bound Russian Bolsheviks to German Marxism. In a way Lenin himself was the protagonist of all the eventual pro-German trends of his party. His "defeatism" in 1914–17 implied the expectation of an imminent social revolution in Germany—in Germany before any other country. During the first years of the Communist International, German was the semiofficial language of the organization, and the Russian leaders—Lenin, Zinoviev, Bukharin—addressed its meetings in German. Lenin expected that Russian leadership in the Comintern would be of short duration, that it would have to be turned over to the Germans, whose history

Conclusion

had made them more suitable, in his view, for assuming this role.

These views on Germany were, to a large extent, taken over by Stalin.

Developments in Europe after the Versailles Treaty—the rise of defeated Germany to new power in the 1930's, German dynamism, German industrial capabilities, and German wars—greatly impressed Moscow. In April, 1958, Anastas Mikoyan stated: "Were it not for two devastating wars Germany, I think, would be richer than America." [7]

The fact that the positions of the four Western powers in NATO are formally equal does not mean that their political courses are identical. To Moscow, the degree of opposition of each of them to Soviet policy is important: the range is from lukewarm "coexistence" to chilly *status quo* or "containment," and from "containment" to a more aggressive policy of "liberation." The Soviet government bases its course on the fact that, because of its geographical situation and its great strength, the United States takes a middle position in this scale of policies: when, for example, North Korea violated the *status quo* and attacked the south, the United States rushed into war, but she was satisfied with restoration of the *status quo;* when Stalin stretched out his hand to grasp West Berlin, she built up the airlift, but she was satisfied with restoration of the unstable *status quo ante;* in 1953 she could send only food to the East Berlin strikers, and in November, 1956, she could not send armed help to Hungary, but she would have gone to war if a Soviet operation had jeopardized the *status quo* in Iran, Yugoslavia, or West Germany. United States appropriations for defense remained stable, while the Soviet Union introduced new and dangerous weapons. Despite her recognition of the unhealthy shape of the European system and of the danger and conflicts inherent in it, the United States could not be pushed onto other paths.

Another task was, however, being performed by the United States which was at least as important as "containment" and the guarding of the *status quo:* the United States has served as the great protector of two continental nations—France and Germany—during their rehabilitation and their resumption of the functions of big powers. The United States has been the shield behind which France and Germany have proceeded to regain their vigor. The United States was barring the

[7] *Pravda,* April 29, 1958.

road to that Eastern power which was interested in keeping France and Germany impotent. It was as if the American eagle, standing in the middle of Europe, had spread its wings to the north and south to shield the moves and actions which otherwise would have been impossible.

The re-emergence of continental powers in Europe and the increased ability of Europe to defend herself will eventually enable the United States to reduce or withdraw her military forces stationed there. This, too, cannot occur until power relationships change substantially, and until the Soviet Union faces a strong opponent on her own continent.

Thus the rehabilitation of Western Europe and the re-emergence of powers in the West are giving a new impetus to emancipation trends in the Eastern bloc. They imply the contraction of Stalin's empire on the old continent. Disintegration of the empire in Asia proceeds in a different way—through the growth of the imperial designs of another Communist government.

The West, and in the first place the United States, will support, diplomatically as well as economically, every step toward the emancipation of the "people's democracies" in East and West, in whatever form the process should develop: the effort of a single satellite to gain independence, a passing alliance of two or several satellites, a loose cooperation, or a firm federation of some of the satellites in defense of their independence against encroachments from whatever other power. On the other hand, the United States will never acquiesce in the present state of affairs in Central Europe or the Far East; one-power predominance is contrary to her security.

In the course of time Russia will have to return to her own shores —only this can create an adequate condition for the "relaxation of tensions." Empires of the magnitude of Stalin's Russia are passing phenomena in world history; they are bound to fall. The wars which have historically marked the road of their decay may take place or be avoided. It will depend on the wisdom and far-sightedness of Moscow's leadership whether the transition to a peaceful era will be strewn with millions of corpses and smoldering ruins, or will proceed in a way that accords better with the scientific, cultural, and humanitarian standards of our times.

INDEX

A

Adenauer, Konrad, 53, 141, 243 n, 262, 510, 512, 525
Afghanistan, 287, 310-318
  American influence, 311
  Khrushchev's visit, 316
    economic agreement, 316, 317
  Pushtunistan, 312, 313
  Soviet-Afghan border disputes, 312
  Soviet trade agreement, 313
Alexandrov, A., 122
Allen, George, 32, 396
Andreev, A. A., 434
Andropov, Yuri, 369, 375, 462
Anti-NATO alignment, 160-165
  Conference of European Countries on Safeguarding European Peace and Security, 160
  position of Poland, Czechoslovakia, and DDR, 164
  Pact of Mutual Assistance and Unified Command, 163
  (See also Warsaw Pact)
  Prague Conference, 164, 165
  Warsaw Conference, 163
Antonov, A. I., 163
Apostol, Gheorghe, 180
Arzumanyan, A. A., 465
Asian-African People's Solidarity Conference (1957), 465
  composition, 465
  headquarters, 465
Aus der Internationalen Arbeiterbewegung (From the International Labor Movement), 43
Austria, 110, 145, 195, 228, 230, 287, 504, 515
  Austrian State Treaty, 248-261
    Austrian-Soviet conference in Moscow (1955), 256, 257
    dissolution of Allied Control Council, 260
    foreign ministers' conference in Vienna, 259

    Khokhlov incident, 253
    political situation, 250
    Russian concessions, 250
    mixed companies, 195
Azizov, C., 79

B

Bacteriological war, 65
Baghdad Pact, 201, 388, 399, 403
  joining of Iran, 216
  Turkish-Iraqi alliance, 203
Balkan Pact (1953), 33
  (See also Yugoslavia)
Bandung Conference, 157, 279, 296-302, 391, 433, 464
  Pancha Shilla (Five Principles), 464
  participants, 298, 299
  subjects under discussion, 300, 301
  Ten Principles adopted, 301
Bao Dai, 152
Bata, Istvan, 39
Belgrade Conference (1956), 446
  anti-Moscow program, 446
Ben-Gurion, David, 112, 416
Beria, Lavrenti, 3, 40, 121, 172, 183
Berlin Conference (1954), 141-146, 251, 262, 429
  Austrian question, 145, 146
  (See also Four-power Conference)
  collective security in Europe, 144
  Soviet delegation, 141
  two plans for Germany, 142-144
Berman, Jakub, 336, 358
Bernstein, Edward, 447
Bevan, Aneurin, 415, 470
Bevin, Ernest, 107
Bhutan, 496
Bidault, Georges, 150
Bierut, Boleslaw, 42, 168, 180, 185, 189
  death, 338
Blank, Theodor, 54
Boffa, Giuseppe, 365

531

Bolshevik, 31, 32
Borba, 349, 355, 379, 381
Borkenau, Franz, 430 n
Britain, 234-239, 408, 412, 418, 508
  alliance with Israel, 408, 412
  attitude of, toward the German problem, 508
  Khrushchev's visit to London, 234-239
    subjects of discussion, 236, 237
  war in Egypt, 412
    cease-fire, 418
    Labor Party demonstrations, 415
Bukharin, Nikolai, 528
Bulganin, Nikolai, 101, 160, 162, 221, 230, 264, 277, 278, 280, 281, 307, 320, 339, 340, 345, 357, 410, 415, 416, 453
  visit to London, 234-239
Bulgaria, 186
  mixed companies, 193, 195
Burma, 86, 287, 289, 293, 298
  Khrushchev's visit, 310
  Mikoyan's visit, 318
  Soviet activities, 498
  Soviet-Burmese trade agreement, 306
  U Nu's visit to Russia, 306
Byrnes, James F., 5, 106
  Byrnes Treaty, 50

C

Cambodia, 154
Castro, Fidel, 517
Castro, Raul, 517
CEMA (*see* Council for Economic Mutual Assistance)
Chang Po-chung, 439
Chervenkov, Vulko, 42, 168, 180, 186, 349
Chiang Kai-shek, 71
China, 67-76, 79-83, 90, 195, 424-430, 485, 489-496
  acknowledgment of Soviet superiority, 494
  Chinese aspirations, 425, 489, 490
  Chinese Communist Party, 489
    program, 76, 91
  Chinese drive against Formosa, 495
  Chinese penetration, 81
  Chinese thaw, 439
  commune system, 491
  conflict with India, 496
  drive for liberation of Asian nations, 78, 85, 86
  drive toward autonomy, 72
  fifth anniversary of Communist Chinese regime, 427
    subjects under discussion, 428-430
  foreign aid granted by China, 456
  military and economic dependence on Russia, 79
  mixed companies, 195
  Moscow Conference (1949), 79-83
  Outer Mongolia, 75, 80
  Pancha Shilla, 464
  participation in Korean War, 88, 90
  program for Japan, 499
  Russian influence in Chinese cultural life, 428
  Russian penetration, 75
  Sinkiang, 73, 74, 80, 431, 432
  Sino-Indian agreement, 297
  Sino-Mongol agreement, 93
  Sino-Soviet relations, 426
  Soviet advisers, 83, 84 n, 85
  Soviet-Chinese economic agreement, 435
  Stalin's attitude toward, 71, 72
  Trade Union Conference, 70
    emphasis on Soviet superiority, 71, 77
    purpose, 70-71
Chou En-lai, 64, 69, 92, 93, 147, 154, 157, 297, 299, 393, 428, 429, 433, 440, 441, 447, 497
Chuikov, General, 127, 172, 173
Churchill, Winston, 48, 49, 128, 275, 277
  German issue, 48
  Quebec decision, 49
  speech on Soviet Union, 130
Clark, Mark, 65
Cominform (*see* Communist Information Bureau)
Comintern (*see* Communist International)
Commin, Pierre, 239
Communist Information Bureau, dissolution, 349
Communist International, 24-27
  characteristics, 25
  disbandment, 26
  Executive Committee of the Communist International, 25
  monolithic structure, 24
  Second Congress of the International, 24
    achievements, 24
  statutes, 25
Conant, James B., 178

Index 533

Confederation, Stalin's interpretation, 22
Conference of European Countries on Safeguarding European Peace and Security, 160-163
  aim, 161
  pledge of Chinese military help, 162
Conference of Writers of Asia and Africa (1958), 466
Congo, 518, 519
  United Nations forces, 519
Council for Economic Mutual Assistance (CEMA), 37
  secretariat, 38
CPSU (*see* Communist Party of the Soviet Union)
CPY (*see* Communist Party of Yugoslavia)
Cuba, 516-518
  Cuban Communist Party, 518
  Mikoyan's visit, 517
  seizure of American industrial units, 516
  trade agreements with China and the Soviet Union, 517
Cyrankiewicz, Joseph, 180, 301
Czechoslovakia, 170, 171
  police actions, 184, 185

D

Dalai Lama, 496
Daud, Mohammed, 313
David, Vaclav, 126
DDR (German Democratic Republic) (*see* East Germany)
Debré, Michel, 511
Dedjer, Vladimir, 5
Department of International Liaison (*Otdel Mezhdunarodnykh Svyazei*, OMS), 43
Derevyanko, Kuzma, 62
Deutsche Bauernpartei (German Peasant Party), 36 *n*
Dibrova, P. T., 175
Dillon, C. Douglas, 512
Dimitrov, Georgi, 29, 70
Doby, Istvan, 449
Dulles, John Foster, 13, 96, 107, 129, 130, 153, 158, 259, 285, 318, 395, 406, 469, 508
Dzerzhinsky, Yan, 462

E

East Germany, 50-53, 171-179, 501
  conference in Moscow, 179

German Democratic Republic (DDR), 35 *n*, 139
  formation of, 52
  military force, 53
  mixed companies, 196
  policy, 53
  political and economic changes, 173
  reunification with West Germany, 51, 502
  Soviet High Commissioner, 172
  uprising in Berlin, 174, 175
    implications, 178, 179
    role of Volkspolizei, 174
    Soviet army intervention, 175, 176
EDC (*see* European Defense Community)
Eden, Anthony, 127, 142, 146, 236, 281, 403, 410, 415
Egypt, 288, 289, 293, 389-396, 406-421, 467
  Arab-Israeli tension, 391, 400
  Aswan High Dam, 404, 405
  attitude toward Communism, 390
  breach in Soviet-Egyptian relations, 479
  consolidation of Arab nations, 396
  merger with Syria into the United Arab Republic, 472
  recognition of Communist China, 404
  Soviet-Egyptian negotiations, 393
  statistics on arms deal, 395 *n*
  Suez crisis, 406-421
    nationalization of Suez Canal, 406, 408
    war wih Israel, 412, 418
Ehrenburg, Ilya, 64
Eisenhower, Dwight D., 128, 129, 277, 281, 413, 416, 512
Erlander, Tage, 147
European Defense Community (EDC), 54, 56
  anti-EDC trends, 59
  French opposition to, 153, 155
  signing of treaty, 58
  Soviet drive against, 275
  Soviet reaction, 58

F

Faisal II, 473
Fatemi, Hussein, 204, 212, 213
Faure, Edgar, 281
Federation, Lenin's interpretation, 21 *n*
Fedoseyev, P., 494

Figl, Leopold, 145
Finland, 19, 269-274, 287
   importance to Soviet Union, 269
   joining the Nordic Council, 273
   Porkkala question, 272
   position in the Russian empire, 19, 20
   territorial questions, 274
   Treaty of Friendship, Cooperation, and Mutual Assistance, 270
For a Socialist Yugoslavia, 30
For Freedom, 31
For Lasting Peace, For a People's Democracy, 123
For Victory, 30
Foreign Department of the Central Committee of the Communist Party, 4, 43, 462
   bulletin, 43
   communication with satellites, 44
   daily work, 43
   functions, 462
   staff, 462
   structure, 4
Foreign Ministers' Conference in Geneva (1959), 509
Foreign Ministers' Conference in Paris (1946), 106
   Soviet program, 106, 107
   British opposition, 107
Fortieth anniversary of the November Revolution, 454, 457, 458
   Declaration of the twelve parties, 457
   Stalin's monolith theory reinstated, 458
   discussion of a new international Communist organization, 454
Forward, 31
Four-power Conference, 131, 141-146
   exchange of diplomatic notes on, 131, 132
   German problem, 141-143
   (*See also* Berlin Conference)
   problem of Korean unification, 134
France, 241, 408, 510, 511
   alliance with Israel, 408, 412
   French Communist Party, 241, 242
   Khrushchev's visit, 510, 511
   Socialist and government delegations visit Moscow, 239-244
   war in Egypt, 412
      cease-fire, 418

G

Gafurov, Bobodjan, 462, 498
Gaitskell, Hugh, 238, 415
Gandhi, Mohandas, 292, 295
De Gaulle, Charles, 59, 510, 511, 513, 528
General-gubernator, 19
Geneva Conference (1954), 134, 147-155
   attitude of the United States, 155
   Far Eastern issues, 146
      Indochina, 148-150
      Korea, 150-154
   triumph for Communist China, 147, 154
German Democratic Republic (DDR) (*see* East Germany)
Germany, 45-49, 142, 282
   admission to NATO, 159
   Berlin Blockade, 53
   Eden's program for, 142
   General-Vertrag of the Western powers, 54
   German partition, 47-50
      (*See also* East Germany *and* West Germany)
   Molotov's program for, 139, 142
   neutralization of, 51
   rejection of German rearmament, 52
   Soviet-German relations, history, 45
   Stalin's attitude toward, 46, 47
   suggested free elections, 56
   Summit Conference in Geneva (1955), 277-285
      German issue, 282
   territorial changes, 49
Gerö, Erno, 356, 357, 368, 370
Gheorghiu-Dej, Gheorghe, 42, 180
Global Communism, 459
   Chinese sphere, 459
   Italian Communist Party sphere, 461
   Soviet sphere, 459
Glubb Pasha, John, 400
Gomulka, Wladyslaw, 40, 185, 336, 359, 374, 441, 455, 457, 486-488, 503
Gottwald, Klement, 42
Grebennik, K., 369
Grechko, Andrei A., 173
Gromyko, Andrei, 107, 122, 125, 127, 141, 281, 307, 345, 420, 451, 453, 462, 471
Gross, Archbishop, 336

Index

Grotewohl, Otto, 37, 53, 162, 172, 174, 180, 182, 501
Gruber, Karl, 251
Guber, Alexander, 295
Gubernator (governor), 19
Gubernia (province), 19

H

Hammarskjöld, Dag, 127, 519
Hassen Fahmi Ragab, 391
Hegedüs, Andreas, 192, 369
Henderson, Loy, 468
  negotiations in the Middle East, 470
Herter, Christian A., 509, 512
Himalayan Federation, 496
Ho Chi-minh, 77, 86, 150-152
Hopkins, Harry, 49
Hull, Cordell, 49
Hungary, 184, 368-382
  Hungarian uprising, 368-382
    Declaration of neutrality, 376
    Hungarian Communist Party, position in, 371
    Kadar forms new government, 376, 377
    Nagy's government, 371
    statistics, 381
    withdrawal from Warsaw Pact, 375
  mixed companies, 193, 195
  police actions, 184

I

Iceland, 447
  agreement with United States, 447
Ilyichev, Ivan I., 253, 259
India, 287, 292, 303-305, 307-310
  conflict with China, 496
  Khrushchev's visit, 307-310
  Kashmir problem, 309
  Sino-Indian agreement, 297
    Pancha Shilla (Five Principles), 297, 464
  Soviet relations with India, 303-305
    industrial aid, 303
    Nehru's visit to Russia, 305
Indochina, 86, 150-154
  French prestige, 152
  French loss of Dien Bien Phu, 151
  Soviet program for Indochina, 150
  truce agreements, 154
    International Commission, 154
Indonesia, 287, 289, 298, 318-320
  Soviet-Indonesian trade agreements, 319

Soviet loans, 320
International Affairs, 304, 306, 398, 454
International Communist organization (*see* Communist International)
International Socialist Congress, 279
Iran, 109, 110, 203-215, 293, 294
  anti-Shah uprising, 210, 211
  attitude toward the United States, 206, 211
  Azerbaijan Democratic Party, 109
  British oil concession, 207
  changes in Soviet-Iranian treaty of 1921, 215
  Communist leaders, 209
  joining of the Baghdad Pact, 216
  Kurdistan, 110
  return of the Shah, 213
  Soviet fishing concession, 207
  Tudeh Party, 204, 208, 213
Iraq, 473, 474
  creation of a Kurdish state, 474
  revolution in Iraq, 473
  significance to Soviet Union, 474
Israel, 111-113, 412
  alliance with France and Britain, 408, 412
  occupation of the Sinai peninsula and the Ghaza strip, 412
Izvestia, 113

J

Jamali, Fadhil, 300
Japan, 94-100
  Allied Council for Japan, 99
  American-Japanese alliance, 95
  Japanese Communist Party, 95
  peace treaty, 96-98
  violation of Japanese air space, 99
Joliot-Curie, Frederic, 64
Jordan, 400, 473

K

Kadar, Janos, 370, 371, 376, 441, 449, 485
Kaganovich, Lazar, 230, 240, 331, 360, 453
Kao Kang, 73, 79, 80, 430
Kardelj, Edward, 23, 33, 71, 343
Kazakhs, 431
Kaznacheev, Alexander, 460
Kekkonen, Urho, 272
Khaled Bagdash, 400, 468, 469, 473, 476
Khokhlov, Nikolai, 253

Khrushchev, Nikita, 4, 101, 119, 121, 168, 180, 227, 242, 245, 263, 281, 283, 307-310, 322, 343, 345, 355, 357, 360, 362, 366, 378, 399, 403, 409, 423, 427, 438, 441, 445, 448, 453, 455, 462, 470, 471, 477, 478, 481, 491, 493, 499, 502, 506, 507, 514, 515, 517, 524
   attacks on Eisenhower, 514
   attacks on the United States, 514
   background, 218
   defending Arab Communism, 477
   foreign policy, 222, 228
   new theses, 322-331
     anti-American trends, 328, 329
     denunciation of Stalin, 326
     nonviolent transformation possible, 324, 325
     proposed Socialist united front, 327
     war no longer inevitable, 322-324
   personal qualities, 218
   political rise, 219
   visit to Afghanistan, 316
   visit to Burma, 310
   Soviet technical assistance, 310
   visit to France, 510, 511
   visit to India, 307-310
     Kashmir problem, 309
   visit to London, 234-239
     contacts with the Labor Party, 237, 238
     negotiations with Eden, 236
     subjects of discussion, 236, 237
   visit to Peking, 495, 497
   visit to the United States, 509
   reaction to the United States, 509
Kim Il-sung, 61, 133, 152, 460
Kim Pa, 62
Kirghiz, 431
Kiselev, Yevgeni, 369
Kislenko, Andrei, 96, 99
Komar, Waclaw, 360
Kommunist, 187, 191, 233, 295, 325, 328, 348, 458, 483
Kommunistische Partei Deutschlands (KPD), West German Communist Party, 42
Konev, Ivan, 164
Koplenig, Johann, 249
Korean War, 60-69, 86-88, 90, 129, 148-150
   armistice, 133
   Chinese role, 60, 87, 88
   Communist proposals for reunification, 148, 149
     Western refusal, 150
   North Korean army and equipment, 62
   Russian role, 61, 86
   Stalin's role, 60
   truce conference, 66, 126
     Indian compromise, 69
     prisoner-of-war issue, 66-69, 126, 133
Kostov, Traicho, 42
Kotelawala, John, 300
Kovacz, Istvan, 189, 356
Kozhedub, Ivan, 62
Kozhevinikov, F., 122
Kozyrev, S., 122
KPD (*see Kommunistische Partei Deutschlands*)
Kraskevich, Major General, 253
Kumykin, P. N., 307
Kurdistan (*see* Iraq)
Kuusinen, Otto, 462
Kuznetsov, Vasily V., 148, 299

L

Lange, Halvar, 515
Laos, 154
Laquer, Walter Z., 469
Lavrentiev, Anatoli, 23
Lebanon, 104, 400, 405 n, 469, 473, 474
Lebedev, Viktor, 37, 231
Lee Sang Jo, 61
Lenin, 21, 528
   Federation, meaning, 21 n
   "Theses on the National and Colonial Question," 21
Lenin Peak, 7
Libya, 105
Li Fu-chun, 79
Li Hsien-nien, 436
Li Li-san, 70
Litvinov, Maxim, 4
Liu Hsia, 434
Liu Shao-chi, 70, 78
Lodge, Henry Cabot, 417
Luca, Vasile, 186
Ludwig, Emil, 46
Lumumba, Patrice, 519
Lung Yun, 439

M

Macmillan, Harold, 259, 277, 285, 508, 513, 516

Index

Malenkov, Georgi, 3, 4, 43, 121, 125, 168, 172, 180, 187, 211, 331, 453, 517
  foreign policy, 138
  importance of German question, 138
  resignation, 191, 221
Maleter, Pal, 376, 485
Malik, Jacob, 96, 99, 100, 141
Malinovsky, Rodion, 62, 515
Manuilsky, Dimitri, 329
Mao Tse-tung, 70, 73, 75, 79, 87, 89, 195, 231, 365, 422, 427, 431, 437, 457, 490, 517
Marshall, George, 50
Mendès-France, Pierre, 153, 276
Menon, Krishna, 69, 118, 251, 299
Meretskov, Marshal Kiril, 85
Middle East (*see specific countries and under* Soviet Foreign Policy)
Mikoyan, Anastas, 117, 121, 168, 197, 227, 230, 257, 318, 323, 343, 345, 356, 360, 369, 370, 374, 378 n, 428, 435, 441, 477 n, 515, 517, 525, 529
  tour of Asia, 318
  visit to Cuba, 517
  visit to Norway, 515
Minc, Hilary, 358
Mindszenty, Cardinal, Joseph, 336
Minindel (*see* Ministry of Foreign Affairs)
Ministry of Foreign Affairs, 4, 462
Moch, Jules, 52
Mohammed Ali, 202, 300
Mollet, Guy, 239, 242, 410, 416
Molotov, Vyacheslav, 3, 5-8, 51, 104, 106, 108, 117, 121, 128, 135, 141, 147, 159, 168, 172, 222, 227, 229, 230, 233, 259, 271, 275, 281, 284, 323, 331, 343, 360, 406, 433, 453, 517
  attitude toward Yugoslavia, 122 n
  collective security in Europe, 144
  decline in prestige, 7, 233
  experience, 6
  program for Germany, 139
  type of statesman, 5
Molotov, Mme. Polina Zhemchuzhina, 7, 232 n
Molotov Peak, 7
Morgenthau Plan, 49
  Washington opposition, 49
Moscow Conference (1949), 79-83
  basic treaty, 81-83
  Soviet-Chinese companies, 83
  Soviet-Chinese Military Commission, 82
  Soviet loan, 83
  Outer Mongolia, 80, 81
  Sinkiang, 80
Mossadegh, Mohammed, 204, 211, 212
Mustafa el Barzani, 476

N

Naguib, Mohammed, 111
Nagy, Imre, 41, 42, 180, 181, 188, 189, 191, 356, 369, 370, 374, 375, 378, 381, 485, 487
Nam Il, 61, 67, 148
Nashkovski, Marian, 370
Nasser, Gamal Abdel, 111, 390, 391, 396, 404, 407, 466, 472, 478, 524
National Communism, significance for the Soviet Union, 180, 364-367
National Demokratische Partei Deutschlands (NDPD), 36 n
NATO (*see* North Atlantic Treaty Organization)
Nehru, Jawaharlal, 69, 86, 157, 251, 279, 288, 292, 296, 297, 301
Nepal, 86, 496
Nenni, Pietro, 245
New Struggle, 30
New Times, 32, 58, 111, 118, 150, 156, 283, 391, 411, 468
Nguyen (*see* Ho Chi-minh)
Nineteenth Congress of the Communist Party, 92, 93
  Chinese-Mongolian railway, 93
  Port Arthur, 93
Nordic Council, 273
North Atlantic Treaty Organization, 54, 144, 157, 160, 254, 277, 278, 447, 526, 529
  German rearmament, 54
  West Germany admitted, 159
North Korea, 460
  (*See also* Korean War)
North Vietnam, 154
Norway, 515
  Mikoyan's visit, 515
Nova Borba, 356
Nova Mysl, 190
Novikov, K., 122
Novotny, Antonin, 180, 190
Novo Vreme, 187
Nuri as-Said, 473

O

Ochab, Edward, 338, 358
October Revolution (*see* Poland)
OMS (*Otdel Mezhdunarodnykh Svyazei*) (*see* Department of International Liaison)
Österreichische Volksstimme, 32, 248, 454

P

Paasikivi, Juho K., 272
Pact of Mutual Assistance and Unified Command, 163
  Political Consultative Committee, 163
  Russian commander of unified military forces, 164
Pak Heung Yung, 64
Pak Sang Hyon, 62
Pakistan, 202, 313, 314, 320, 321
  Afghan-Pakistani controversy, 314
  agreement between Turkey and Pakistan, 202
  member of the Baghdad Pact, 321
  Mikoyan's visit, 318
  trade agreement with the Soviet Union, 321
Pancha Shilla (*see under* Bandung Conference *and* India)
Patrascanu, Lucretius, 186
Pauker, Ana, 29
Pavlov, A., 122
Peng Teh-huai, 163, 492
People's Commissariat for Foreign Affairs, 9
People's Daily, 429, 437, 439
People's Democracies, 34-44, 335-337
  armies, strength, 39
  Hungary, 368-382
  party-to-party relations, 41
  Poland, 338, 339, 358-363
  police agencies, 40
  prerogatives of Soviet ambassador, 37
  program of industrialization, 38, 39
  purpose, 38
  Soviet alliances, 34 *n*
  standing of Soviet ambassador, 36
  urge toward emancipation, 335
    contributing factors, 335-337
People's Front (*see* Socialist Alliance of the Working People of Yugoslavia)
Pham Van Dong, 148, 300
Philip, André, 241
Philippines, 292

Pieck, Wilhelm, 53, 141
Pineau, Christian, 242, 418
Pishevari, Jaafar, 110
Plenum, 227 *ff*.
Poland, 166, 230, 358-363, 486-488
  anti-Moscow program, 446
  Bezpieka, 183
    leaders, 183
  credit agreement with the United States, 486
  Gomulka's visit to Belgrade, 455
  police actions, 185
  Polish rebellion (October Revolution), 358-363
    Gomulka's program, 361, 362
    Polish delegation in Moscow, 363
    Soviet negotiations in Warsaw, 360
  possibility of a Polish-Yugoslav alliance, 486
  reaction to Hungarian uprising, 363
  Soviet pressure, 487
Ponomariov, Boris N., 462
Popov, Georgi M., 37, 231
Popovič, Koča, 5, 201
Potsdam Conference, 11
  program of Soviet growth, 104, 105
  Balkans, 105
  North Africa, 105
Powers, Francis Gary, 512
Prague Conference (1954), 164, 165
Pravda, 44, 64, 69, 109, 113, 121, 129, 176, 177, 187, 190, 212, 258, 344, 355, 373, 380, 381, 398, 412, 450, 458, 471, 479, 525
Pritt, Denis N., 64
Problems of Philosophy, 492
Prodanovich, Iovan, 355
Pukar, 357
Pushkin, Georgi, 37, 141

R

Raab, Julius, 255, 260
Radkiewicz, Stanislaw, 185, 336
Raikovich, Miliutin, 355
Rajk, Laszlo, 42, 486
Rakoszi, Mathias, 42, 168, 180, 181, 191, 348, 349, 352, 356
Rankovich, Alexander, 33, 357, 483
Rapacki, Adam, 504
  Rapacki plan, 504
Rashidov, Sharaf, 318, 465
Rastvorov, Yuri, 62, 88
Rhee, Syngman, 133
Richards, James P., 450

Index

Rokossovsky, Marshal Konstantin, 39, 338, 359, 361, 362, 471
Romulo, Carlos, 300
Roosevelt, Franklin D., 49
Roshchin, Nikolai, 85
Rostovsky (delegate to Peking conference, 1950), 70
Rumania, 186
   mixed companies, 193, 195
Rumyantsev, Alexei, 458
Russia (see Soviet Union)

S

Saiffudin Kitchlu, 118
San Francisco Conference (1951), 96
   Soviet peace program for Japan, 97
Sanzo Nozaka, 95
Sastroamidjojo, Ali, 296
Schuman, Robert, 52, 59
Schwarzkopf, Norman, 207
SEATO, 154, 155
Second Congress of the Polish Workers Party, 220
SED (see Sozialistische Einheitspartei Deutschlands)
Semionov, Vladimir, 37, 141, 172, 173, 178
Serov, Ivan, 235, 307, 377
Sharett, Moshe, 412
Sheng Shih-ts'ai, 73, 431
Shepilov, Dimitri, 190, 230, 279, 323, 345, 394, 399, 404, 407, 410, 414, 417, 420, 450, 453
Shock brigade (udarnaya brigada), 12
Shukry-al-Kuwatly, 400
Sikkim, 496
Sino-Soviet Friendship Association, 89
Siroky, Villiam, 162, 180, 190
Sixth Congress of the Communist International, 291
Slansky, Rudolf, 42
Smirnov, Andrei, 502
Sobolev, A., 122
Socialist Alliance of the Working People of Yugoslavia, 33
Socialist International, 24, 245
Sokolovsky, Marshal Vasily, 117
Soloviev (delegate to Peking conference, 1950), 70
South Vietnam, 154
Southeast Asia Treaty Organization, 154, 155
Soviet foreign policy, 3, 10-17, 30-32, 51, 56, 80, 94, 110-113, 129-132, 203-215, 230, 240, 255-257, 262-266, 270, 277-279, 284-287, 303-306, 340-347, 370-373, 385-389, 416, 423, 428, 435, 487, 502-504, 523, 524
   abstention from moves leading to war, 12
   Adenauer's visit to Moscow, 262-266
   release of German prisoners-of-war, 267
   aid to underdeveloped countries, 480 n
   annulment of British and French alliances with the Soviet Union, 159
   antagonism to the Monroe Doctrine, 518
   Austria, 110, 129, 228, 230
   Austrian State Treaty, 248-261
   Austrian-Soviet conference in Moscow (1955), 256, 257
   change in Soviet policy, 255
   foreign ministers' conference in Vienna, 259
   signing of treaty, 260
   Burma, 306, 498
   China, 73-75, 428-430, 524
   attitude to, 524
   effort to resurrect Manchuria, 73
   Formosa question, 433
   Manchuria, 430
   mixed companies in, 423, 428
   Mongolia, 430
   Outer Mongolia, 75, 80
   Sinkiang, 73, 74, 80
   Soviet aid to, 423, 429, 435
   Stalin's attitude toward Chinese Communism, 430
   withdrawal of Soviet forces in Port Arthur, 428
   conservation of Soviet power, 12-16
   antagonism between capitalist powers, reasons for, 16
   inevitability of war, 14
   war, balance-of-power tactics in, 16
   cooperation with the Congo, 519
   Cuba, interest in, 516-518
   diplomatic relations with West Germany, establishment of, 261-269
   Egypt, 467, 472
   aid to, 467
   breach in relations with, 479
   financing the Aswan Dam, 473
   negotiations with, 393
   specialists to, 397

Soviet foreign policy—*Continued*
  extension of the socialist realm, 11
  Finland, 269, 274
    joining the Nordic Council, 273
    Porkkala question, 272
    territorial questions, 274
    Treaty of Friendship, Cooperation, and Mutual Assistance, 270
  French Socialist and government delegations visit Moscow, 239-244
    subjects of discussion, 240, 242
  Germany, 51, 55, 56
    Berlin blockade, 53
    Berlin problem, 507
    draft for peace treaty with, 56, 57
    neutralization of, 51, 503
    program for, 142
    reunification of, 51, 55, 502
  Hungarian uprising, 368-382
    attitude of Soviet press, 372, 373
    centers of Soviet control, 369
    kidnaping of Nagy group, 381
    Soviet intervention, 370, 373
  India, 303-305, 496
  Indochina, program for, 150
  Iran, dealings with, 109, 110, 203-215
  Iraq, significance, 474
  Israel, 111-113
    anti-Israel trend, 402
    attitude to, 477 n
  Japan, importance of, 94, 95
    peace program for, 97
    withdrawal of promises to, 499, 500
  Korea, program for, 148
  Korean War, 129, 132
    aid to North Korea, 133
    alliance with North Korea, 86 n
  lessening of tension according to Molotov, 139, 142
  Malenkov-Molotov course, 127
    program, 129, 138
  Middle East, 385-389
    Khrushchev's policy, 387
    Stalinist tradition, 386
    Suez crisis, attitude during, 409, 414, 416, 418
  mixed companies, 230
  Moscow Conference, 79-83
  neutral belt in Europe, 503, 504
  neutral countries, different groups of, 286, 287
  neutralism, definition, 465
    conclusions, 523
  Pakistan, trade agreement with, 321
  Poland, 230, 487
    negotiations in Warsaw, 360
    pressure on, 487
  proposal for collective security in Europe, 144, 156
  re-emergence of France and Germany, 527
    implications, 528
  relaxation of tensions, 247
  Soviet espionage activities, 513, 514
  Soviet-Chinese Friendship Association, 434
  Soviet-Indonesian trade agreements, 319
  Summit Conference in Geneva, 277-285
    foreign ministers' conference, 284, 285
    German issue, 278, 279, 282
    opposition to united Germany, 284
    Soviet motivations, 277
  transition of capitalism to socialism, 10
  Turkey, 101, 107, 109, 470
    Eastern Turkey, 108, 109
    Montreux Convention, 104, 107
    relations with, 101, 108
  United States, 56, 518
    antagonism to Monroe Doctrine, 518
    hate-America campaign, 56, 63
    offensive against, 243
  West German rearmament, prevention of, 502
  Yugoslavia, 30-32, 229, 485
    anti-Tito propaganda, 31, 32
    attacks on, 483
    attempt at reconciliation with, 455
    breaking trade agreements with, 231
    fight against, 30-32
    Khrushchev's visit to, 345, 346
    settlement of conflict with, 340-354
    Soviet-Yugoslav trade agreements, 347
    trials of Titoists, 30
Soviet regime, 167, 168
  post-Stalin innovations, 167
  economic policy, 167
  government, 168
  police system, 167

Index

Soviet-satellite crises, 169, 179, 187-197
  policies, 187-192
    raising living standards, 187
    slowing down of heavy industry, 187
    popular movements, 169
    Czechoslovakia, 170, 171
    East Germany, 171-179
    (*See also* Hungary, Poland, and Yugoslavia)
  reasons, 168, 169
Soviet sphere, Asian, 60
  Eastern European, 18, 104, 105
  statistics, 18, 18 n, 60
Soviet Union, 135-139, 188-197, 445-449, 453-458
  abolition of mixed companies, 192-197
  Beria crisis, 183, 184
  cancellation of satellite debts, 197
  collectivization of farming, 188, 189
  decline in Soviet prestige, 445
  elimination of restrictions, 135
  fight against national Communism, 447
  first satellite launching, 453
  Fortieth Anniversary of the November Revolution, 454, 457, 458
  hydrogen bomb, 138
  Khrushchev premier, 453
  military achievements, 524
  New Economic Policy (NEP), 189
  opposition to Khrushchev, 453
  reaction to Hungarian crisis, 446
  rehabilitation of Stalin, 449
    implications, 449
  rejection of Stalinist theories, 136, 137
  relaxation, 123
  Weltanschauung, 137
Sozialistische Einheitspartei Deutschlands (SED), Socialist Unity Party of Germany, 37, 43, 53, 171
Sputnik, 454
Spychalski, Marion, 336
Stalin, 3, 43, 89, 118, 329
  attitude toward Germany, 46, 47
  brink-of-war policy, 13, 14
    Berlin operation of 1948–1949, 13
    Greek uprising of 1944–1948, 14
    Korean War, 14
  death, 118
  funeral, 119
  empire building, methods, 19, 20
  feelings toward Chinese, 5, 71, 89, 93 n
  feelings toward Jews, 5, 111
  main ideas on foreign policy, 10-17
  report to the Fifteenth Congress, 15
  Teheran conference, 48
  Yalta conference, 49
Stalin-Hitler pact, 9
Stalin Peak, 7
Stepanov, V. P., 428
Stettinius, Edward, 106
Stimson, Henry L., 49
Stoica, Chivu, 504
Sukarno, 289, 292, 319, 415
Summit Conference in Geneva (1955), 275-285
  Eisenhower's "open skies" plan, 282
  foreign ministers' conference, 284, 285
  German issue, 278, 279, 282
  motivations, 277, 278
Summit Conference in Paris (1960), 510
  common policy of the Western powers, 512
  U-2 incident, 512
    Khrushchev's use of, 512, 513
Suslov, Mikhail, 230, 369, 370, 378 n, 457, 458, 462
Syria, 397, 400, 450, 472
  border incidents, 471
  merger with Egypt into the United Arab Republic, 472
  role, 468
  Soviet aid, 469
  Syrian Communist Party, 468

T

Tägliche Rundschau, 172
Tang, Peter S. H., 430 n
T'ao Shih-yeath, 74
Teheran Conference, 48
Tibet, 85, 86, 496
  uprising, 496
Tildy, Zoltan, 374
Tito, Marshal, 28, 161, 167, 194, 200, 229, 279, 305, 343, 350, 357, 379, 455, 482, 483, 484
  anti-Western ideas, 28
  controversy with Molotov, 344
  visit to Moscow, 350-354
    Soviet concessions, 353
Togliatti, Palmiro, 350
Tozanski, Jacek, 336

Tribüne, 174
Trivière, Léon, 430 n
Trotsky, Leon, 329
Truman Doctrine, 108
Turkey, 101, 104, 198-200, 470
  agreement with Pakistan, 202
  alliance with Iraq, 203
  bilateral Soviet-Turkish agreement, 199
  Eastern Turkey, 108, 109
  member of the Balkan Pact, 200
  Montreux Convention, 104, 107
  Soviet-Turkish relations, 101
Twentieth Party Congress (1956), 233, 322
  Khrushchev's new theses, 322-331
  opposition to Khrushchev, 331-333

U

Uighur Seyfuddin, 80
Uighurs, 431
Ulbricht, Walter, 37, 42, 51, 53, 168, 171, 174, 180, 182, 191, 501
Under the Banner of Internationalism, 31
Union of Soviet Socialist Republics (USSR) (*see* Soviet Union)
Union Republics, 21
United Arab Republic (*see under* Egypt *and* Syria)
United Nations, 62, 65, 68, 125, 134, 413, 469
  admission of Japan, 99
  Korean War prisoners, 134
  Suez crisis, 413, 414
    military forces dispatched to area, 418
  election of Dag Hammarskjöld, 127
  Hungarian appeals, 375
  military forces to the Congo, 519
  Syria, 469, 471
United States, 96-98, 416, 420, 450, 529
  American-Japanese alliance, 95
  arms deal with Egypt, 393
  Aswan Dam question, 405
  attitude during Suez crisis, 408, 416, 420
  attitude toward the German problem, 508
  conditions for summit conference, 130
  Eisenhower doctrine, 450
  food to Berlin, 177
  Khrushchev's visit, 509

Pakistani-American negotiations, 202
peace treaty with Japan, 96-98
political position, 529
position in Korean War, 66
protector of France and Germany, 529
suggested demilitarization of Germany, 50
Truman doctrine, 108
U Nu, 279, 289, 292, 297, 305-306

V

V-Ch network, 44
Vietnam, 154
Voroshilov, Klimenti, 117, 160, 257, 299, 357, 375, 400, 415, 429, 484
Voznesensky, Nikolai, 3, 119
Vulkov, Ivan, 186
Vyshinsky, Andrei, 4, 8-10, 56, 68, 92, 117, 121, 125, 134
  antagonism to Molotov, 9
  comparison with Joseph Fouché, 10
  Menshevik past, 8

W

Warsaw Pact, 163, 164
  reasons for, 164
West Germany, 261-269
  diplomatic relations with Russia, establishment of, 261-269
  Adenauer's visit to Moscow, 263-266
  Western reaction, 268
  (*See also* Germany)
White, Harry Dexter, 49
World Council of Churches, 279
World Marxist Review, 458
Wyszinsky, Stefan, 185

Y

Yakovlev (delegate to Peking conference, 1950), 70
Yalta Conference, 49
Yudin, Pavel, 172, 173
Yugoslavia, 27-34, 229, 287, 340-357, 446, 482, 484, 485, 486
  agreements with Rumania, 354
  anti-Moscow program, 446
  Belgrade Conference, 347
    national roads to Communism, 346
    Soviet-Yugoslav trade agreements, 347
  Chinese reprisals, 485

Index

Yugoslavia—*Continued*
 Communist Party of, 23
 elimination of restrictions, 135
 independence, 482
 negotiations with Hungary, 348
 Polish visit, 455
 possibility of Polish-Yugoslav alliance, 486
 reaction to Hungarian uprising, 379, 380
 Soviet delegation's visit, 345, 346
 Yalta debates, 357
 Yugoslav rebellion, 27-34
  achievements, 34
  Balkan Federation, 29
  Balkan Pact (1953), 33, 200
  CPY expulsion from Cominform, 30
  Fourth Congress of the People's Front, 33
  rapprochement with the West, 32
  South Slav Federation, 29
  Titoist movement, 29
 Yu Tsedenbal, 92, 93

Z

Zapotocky, Antonin, 189, 190, 349
Zahedi, Fazlollah, 211, 213
Zhdanov, Andrei, 3, 4, 43
Zhivkov, Todor, 180, 186
Zhukov, Marshal Georgi K., 62, 281, 354, 453, 471
Zhukov, Yevgeni, 92, 295
Zinoniev, Gregori, 15 n, 25, 75, 528
Zorin, Valerian, 126